CORNELL STUDIES IN CIVIL LIBERTY

Bill of Rights READER

LEADING CONSTITUTIONAL CASES

Bill of Rights
READER

Leading Constitutional Cases

MILTON R. KONVITZ

★

Cornell University Press

ITHACA, NEW YORK

PRINTED IN THE UNITED STATES OF AMERICA BY THE

VAIL-BALLOU PRESS, INC., BINGHAMTON, NEW YORK

For Josef my son

Let a man learn to look for the permanent
in the mutable and fleeting;

let him learn to bear the disappearance of things
he was wont to reverence
without losing his reverence.—*Emerson*

Preface

IN THE seventeenth century it appeared to John Milton that "none can love freedom heartily, but good men; the rest love not freedom, but licence." To us, three centuries later, it appears that "the rest" love not freedom, but restraint. The contest before our eyes, at home and abroad, is not between freedom and anarchy, but between freedom and tyranny. In this contest the Constitution of the United States, the constitutions of the states, and the traditions, ideals, and aspirations of the American people are on the side of freedom. In the opposing camp, within the United States, is—again to quote from John Milton—an "inquisitorious and tyrannical duncery." Such men have always played a role in the American drama. To their contemporaries they have a satanic character; they are seen as grand inquisitors and as men with an overweening ambition to win power sufficient to control the destinies of millions of human beings—push-button tyrants. But to the next generation, or once they are defeated, they appear as pathetic dunces. One recalls their names—in the North, in the South, as leaders of the Know-Nothing movement shortly before the Civil War or as heads of the American nativism that is periodically resurgent—with a wry smile and sees that their role was really a minor one.

A man cannot, however, order his life and thoughts as if he were the historian of his own generation. For in his own time a man is an actor; he sees events take place before his very eyes, and in some way or other he participates in them. Only years later will it be possible for him to recollect his emotions, and the events that generated them, in tranquillity. In his own day he is challenged continually to make existential commitments, and among them—if he belongs with Milton's "good men" who love freedom—will be an engagement in the fight to prevent the men, whom history will judge to have been dunces, from becoming in fact inquisitors and tyrants. One must engage in this fight, yet the fight is precisely the stage on which the characters of the "duncery" play their parts. If there were no fight, these men would be lost in the anonymous masses; but they have it in their power to start a fight—they know how to use "fighting words" and how to libel individuals and groups, they can tell big lies, and they can tell the truth, but with malice—and so the engagement against them is unavoidable.

In this engagement the Constitution of the United States is both a sword and a shield—for all combatants, on either side. Without freedom of speech and the press, there would be no forum from which our freedoms could be threatened; but without freedom of speech and the press, how could we protect ourselves and our liberties? And our liberties include much besides freedom of speech and the press: freedom of religion, for instance, and the many rights that give us a sense of personal security.

It has been responsibly asserted that our basic freedoms are being threatened. In these days it is sometimes declared that if the Bill of Rights were pending in Congress today, it could not be passed. On the other hand, we are told that the threats to our freedoms are highly exaggerated and that there is no witch hunting and no hysteria.

We can take our choice which side to believe. Even in the Supreme Court sides are being taken: Justices Black and Douglas, as will be seen from their dissenting opinions in this volume, have repeatedly cried out against what they consider a whittling down process to which the Bill of Rights has been subjected; and Justice Jackson has noted a constriction of freedom as congenial to the temper of the times.

But to use the Constitution, as a sword or as a shield, one must know what it contains—and what it lacks. There is much evidence that only a small fraction of American citizens have any knowledge of the Bill of Rights—what our constitutional freedoms are, why we have them, why they are important to us. More often than not, our minds are filled with slogans and with ragtags of fact and sentiment.

As a contribution to the education of that mythical character, the average, educated American who is interested in the great issues and the great debates of his day, this book of leading constitutional cases on the Bill of Rights has been prepared.

The reader will find in this book close to four score cases, all but several decided by the Supreme Court. They deal with different aspects of the Bill of Rights (by which we mean not only the first eight or ten amendments, but also the Civil War Amendments and some of the provisions of the original Constitution, like those prohibiting bills of attainder and test oaths—in brief, all provisions incorporating civil and political liberties wherever they may appear in the Constitution).

After the book was completed, I realized, with some emotion, that not a single opinion by Justice Holmes or Justice Brandeis had been included. Ten years ago this would have been unthinkable; at that time it seemed to many of us that Holmes and Brandeis had written for the ages. Yet today we find that it is not their opinions so much as those of Justices Murphy, Rutledge, Black, and Douglas that speak with a special urgency and relevance. With this experience before us, we may anticipate that the next generation will select the opinions of Justices not yet named to the Court. Yet there is continuity; but it is the continuity of the living: men stand upon the shoulders of their forefathers, and see further; and if not further, at least differently—but being men, stand upon the shoulders of their forefathers they must.

I have included many concurring and dissenting opinions, for it is necessary to see some decisions in their context of dispute and conflict; and some points often stand out clearly only after we have overheard the Justices in their debate. If freedom is fundamentally spiritual and not merely a reflection of material forces, we cannot dispense with the dialogue between man and man. As long as the dialogue continues and there is no resort to brute force, hope remains that our Bill of Rights will survive and will ever be a candle that gives light to all that are in the house; that its light will shine forth before men that we may have and that they may see our good works. If it is true that, as Jefferson said, "The natural progress of things is for liberty to yield and government to gain ground," then it is equally true, as Woodrow Wilson added, that "the history of liberty is a history of resistance." Often that resistance is directed against the Supreme Court itself by one of its own members when he thinks that a majority of the Court do not sufficiently stand up against "the natural progress of things." Thus it is that a dissenting opinion often is, if not the candle itself, at least a match that may yet light the candle.

This book was made possible by a fellowship granted by the John Simon Guggenheim Memorial Foundation. It represents, however, the independent work of the author, who is alone responsible for it.

M. R. K.

New York State School of Industrial and Labor Relations
Cornell University
June 18, 1954

Contents

Table of Cases

Bill of Rights READER

LEADING CONSTITUTIONAL CASES

★ I ★

Bill of Rights

in the United States Constitution

First Ten Amendments

AMENDMENT I

Congress shall make no law respecting an establishment of religion, or prohibiting the free exercise thereof; or abridging the freedom of speech, or of the press; or the right of the people peaceably to assemble and to petition the Government for a redress of grievances. *write up complaints send to the gov.*

AMENDMENT II

A well regulated Militia, being necessary to the security of a free State, the right of the people to keep and bear Arms, shall not be infringed.

AMENDMENT III

No Soldier shall, in time of peace be quartered in any house, without the consent of the Owner, nor in time of war, but in a manner to be prescribed by law.

AMENDMENT IV

The right of the people to be secure in their persons, houses, papers, and effects, against unreasonable searches and seizures, shall not be violated, and no Warrants shall issue, but upon prob-

1

able cause, supported by Oath or affirmation, and particularly describing the place to be searched, and the persons or things to be seized.

AMENDMENT V

No person shall be held to answer for a capital, or otherwise infamous crime, unless on a presentment or indictment of a Grand Jury, except in cases arising in the land or naval forces, or in the Militia, when in actual service in time of War or public danger; nor shall any person be subject for the same offence to be twice put in jeopardy of life or limb; nor shall be compelled in any criminal case to be a witness against himself, nor be deprived of life, liberty, or property, without due process of law; nor shall private property be taken for public use, without just compensation.

AMENDMENT VI

In all criminal prosecutions, the accused shall enjoy the right to a speedy and public trial, by an impartial jury of the State and district wherein the crime shall have been committed, which district shall have been previously ascertained by law, and to be informed of the nature and cause of the accusation; to be confronted with the witnesses against him; to have compulsory process for obtaining witnesses in his favor, and to have the Assistance of Counsel for his defence.

AMENDMENT VII

In suits at common law, where the value in controversy shall exceed twenty dollars, the right of trial by jury shall be preserved, and no fact tried by a jury, shall be otherwise re-examined in any Court of the United States, than according to the rules of the common law.

AMENDMENT VIII

Excessive bail shall not be required, nor excessive fines imposed, nor cruel and unusual punishments inflicted.

AMENDMENT IX

The enumeration in the Constitution, of certain rights, shall not be construed to deny or disparage others retained by the people.

AMENDMENT X

The powers not delegated to the United States by the Constitution, nor prohibited by it to the States, are reserved to the States respectively, or to the people.

Other Amendments

AMENDMENT XIII

Sec. 1. Neither slavery nor involuntary servitude, except as a punishment for crime whereof the party shall have been duly convicted, shall exist within the United States, or any place subject to their jurisdiction.

Sec. 2. Congress shall have power to enforce this article by appropriate legislation.

AMENDMENT XIV

Sec. 1. All persons born or naturalized in the United States, and subject to the jurisdiction thereof, are citizens of the United States and of the State wherein they reside. No State shall make or enforce any law which shall abridge the privileges or immunities of citizens of the United States; nor shall any State deprive any person of life, liberty, or property, without due process of law; nor deny to any person within its jurisdiction the equal protection of the laws. . . .

Sec. 5. The Congress shall have power to enforce, by appropriate legislation, the provisions of this article.

AMENDMENT XV

Sec. 1. The right of citizens of the United States to vote shall not be denied or abridged by the United States or by any State on account of race, color, or previous condition of servitude.

Sec. 2. The Congress shall have power to enforce this article by appropriate legislation.

AMENDMENT XIX

The right of citizens of the United States to vote shall not be denied or abridged by the United States or by any State on account of sex.

Congress shall have power to enforce this article by appropriate legislation.

Provisions from Original Constitution

ARTICLE I

Sec. 9. . . . The Privilege of the Writ of Habeas Corpus shall not be suspended, unless when in Cases of Rebellion or Invasion the public Safety may require it.

No Bill of Attainder or ex post facto Law shall be passed.

Sec. 10. No State shall . . . pass any Bill of Attainder, ex post facto Law, or Law impairing the Obligation of Contracts. . . .

ARTICLE III

Sec. 2. . . . The trial of all Crimes, except in cases of Impeachment, shall be by Jury. . . .

ARTICLE IV

Sec. 2. The Citizens of each State shall be entitled to all Privileges and Immunities of Citizens in the several States.

ARTICLE VI

. . . No religious Test shall ever be required as a Qualification to any Office or public Trust under the United States.

★ II ★

The Rule of Law

1. *The Executive Is under Law Made by Congress*

YOUNGSTOWN SHEET & TUBE CO. *v.* SAWYER

343 US 579 (1952)

[This is the *Steel Seizure Case* of 1952. Government officials tried to settle the labor dispute between the steel industry and its employees. When these efforts failed, President Truman issued an order directing the Secretary of Commerce to seize the steel mills and to operate them. The order was not based upon any statutory authority but on a claim that seizure was necessary to avoid a national catastrophe, for American armed forces were then fighting in Korea. The steel companies procured from the United States District Court an injunction restraining the Secretary of Commerce from acting under the authority of the executive order. The Supreme Court in a 6-to-3 decision upheld the injunction on the ground that the President's order was not within his constitutional powers. In the Court's opinion by Justice Black emphasis is on the theory that the President is without constitutional power to seize private property even when an emergency exists. Justice Douglas in a concurring opinion also emphasized this point. Justices Frankfurter, Jackson, Clark, and Burton, however, in concurring opinions placed emphasis on the fact that Congress had placed on the books statutory provisions (as in the Labor Management Relations Act of 1947) designed to meet emergency situations. Chief Justice Vinson and Justices Reed and Minton dissented on the ground that the statutes of Congress did not prohibit the seizure and that the President had the

5

constitutional duty to execute and preserve the congressional defense program.

[The essential difference between the majority and minority members of the Court was over the question whether the President had attempted to *make* law or had used his judgment as to how best to *execute* the laws made by Congress. The minority position was that the President had only attempted to execute the laws of Congress relating to the defense program of the United States, while the majority view was that he had attempted to by-pass the laws that provide procedures in case of labor disputes that create national emergencies and to impose his own law.

[In a case in which seven separate opinions have been written it is hazardous to state that there was any one significant proposition on which all Justices agreed; still it would appear that all of them did agree that the Constitution rejects the notion that the President is a lawmaker. Laws are made by Congress and executed by the President. The Government of the United States is one with "distributed authority." This scheme may retard action at times, until Congress should decide what measures to enact, but the doctrine of the separation of powers was adopted "not to promote efficiency but to preclude the exercise of arbitrary power . . . , to save the people from autocracy."

[This is an essential meaning of "the rule of law," of the theory of "a government of laws and not of men."

[From among the opinions in the case we have selected the Court's opinion by Justice Black and the concurring opinion of Justice Jackson.]

Mr. Justice Black delivered the opinion of the Court:

We are asked to decide whether the President was acting within his constitutional power when he issued an order directing the Secretary of Commerce to take possession of and operate most of the Nation's steel mills. The mill owners argue that the President's order amounts to lawmaking, a legislative function which the Constitution has expressly confided to the Congress and not to the President. The Government's position is that the order was made on findings of the President that his action was necessary to avert a national catastrophe which would inevitably result from a stoppage of steel production, and that in meeting this grave emergency the President was acting within the aggregate of his constitutional powers as the Nation's Chief Executive and the Commander in Chief of the Armed Forces of the United States. The issue emerges here from the following series of events:

In the latter part of 1951, a dispute arose between the steel companies and their employees over terms and conditions that should be included in new collective bargaining agreements. Long-continued conferences failed to resolve the dispute. On December 18, 1951, the employees' representative, United Steelworkers of America, C.I.O., gave notice of an intention to strike when the existing bargaining agreements expired on December 31. Thereupon the Federal Mediation and Conciliation Service intervened in an effort to get labor and management to agree. This failing, the President on December 22, 1951, referred the dispute to the Federal Wage Stabilization Board to investigate and make recommendations for fair and equitable terms of settlement. This Board's report resulted in no settlement. On April 4, 1952, the Union gave notice of a nation-wide strike called to begin at 12:01 A.M. April 9. The indispensability of steel as a component of substantially all weapons and other war materials led the President to believe that the proposed work stoppage would immediately jeopardize our national defense and that governmental seizure of the steel mills was necessary in order to assure the continued availability of steel. Reciting these considerations for his action, the President, a few hours before the strike was to begin, issued Executive Order 10340. . . . The order directed the Secretary of Commerce to take possession of and operate most of the steel mills throughout the country. The Secretary immediately issued his own possessory orders, calling upon the presidents of the various seized companies to serve as operating managers for the United States. They were directed to carry on their activities in accordance with regulations and directions of the Secretary. The next morning the President sent a message to Congress reporting his action. . . . Twelve days later he sent a second message. . . . Congress has taken no action.

Obeying the Secretary's orders under protest, the companies brought proceedings against him in the District Court. Their complaints charged that the seizure was not authorized by an act of Congress or by any constitutional provisions. The District Court was asked to declare the orders of the President and the Secretary invalid and to issue preliminary and permanent injunctions restraining their enforcement. Opposing the motion for preliminary injunction, the United States asserted that a strike disrupting steel production for even a brief period would so endanger the well-being and safety of the Nation that the President had "inherent power" to do what he had done—power "supported by the Constitution, by historical precedent, and by court decisions." The Government also contended that in any event no preliminary injunction should be issued because the companies had made no showing that their available legal remedies were inadequate or that their injuries from seizure would be irreparable. Holding against the Government on all points, the District Court on April 30 issued a preliminary injunction restraining the Secretary from "continuing the seizure and possession of the plant . . . and from acting under the purported authority of Executive Order No. 10340." . . . On the same day the Court of Appeals stayed the District Court's injunction. . . . Deeming it best that the issues raised be promptly decided by this Court, we granted certiorari on May 3 and set the cause for argument on May 12. . . .

The President's power, if any, to issue the order must stem either from an act of Congress or from the Constitution itself. There is no statute that expressly authorizes the President to take possession of property as he did here. Nor is there any act of Congress to which our attention has been directed from which such a power can fairly be implied. Indeed, we do not understand the Government to rely on statutory authorization for this seizure. There are two statutes which do authorize the President to take both personal and real property under certain conditions. However, the Government admits that these conditions were not met and that the President's order was not rooted in either of them. The Government refers to the seizure provisions of one of these statutes ($ 201 (b) of the Defense Production Act) as "much too cumbersome, involved, and time-consuming for the crisis which was at hand."

Moreover, the use of the seizure technique to solve labor disputes in order to prevent work stoppages was not only unauthorized by any congressional enactment; prior to this controversy, Congress had refused to adopt that method of settling labor disputes. When the Taft-Hartley Act was under consideration in 1947, Congress rejected an amendment which would have authorized such governmental seizures in cases of emergency. Apparently it was thought that the technique of seizure, like that of compulsory arbitration, would interfere with the process of collective bargaining. Consequently, the plan Congress adopted in that Act did not provide for seizure under any circumstances. Instead, the plan sought to bring about settlements by use of the customary devices of mediation, conciliation, investigation by boards of inquiry, and public reports. In some instances temporary injunctions were authorized to provide cooling-off periods. All this failing, the unions were left free to strike if the majority of the employees, by secret ballot, expressed a desire to do so.

It is clear that if the President had authority to issue the order he did, it must be found in some provision of the Constitution. And it is not claimed that express constitutional language grants this power to the President. The contention is that presidential power should be implied from the aggregate of his powers under Article II of the Constitution. Particular reliance is placed on the provisions which say that "the executive Power shall be vested in a President . . ."; that "he shall take Care that the Laws be faithfully executed"; and that he "shall be Commander in Chief of the Army and Navy of the United States."

The order cannot properly be sustained as an exercise of the President's military power as Commander in Chief of the Armed Forces. The Government attempts to do so by citing a number of cases upholding broad powers in military commanders engaged in day-to-day fighting in a theater of war. Such cases need not concern us here. Even though "theater of war" be an expanding concept, we cannot with faithfulness to our constitutional system hold that the Commander in Chief of the Armed Forces has the ultimate power as such to take possession of private property in order to keep labor disputes from stopping production. This is a job for the Nation's lawmakers, not for its military authorities.

Nor can the seizure order be sustained because of the several constitutional provisions that grant executive power to the President. In the framework of our Constitution, the President's power to see that the laws are faithfully executed refutes the idea that he is to be a lawmaker. The Constitution limits his functions in the lawmaking process to the recommending of laws he thinks wise and the vetoing of laws he thinks bad. And the Constitution is neither silent nor equivocal about who shall make laws which the President is to execute. The first section of the first article says that "All legislative Powers herein granted shall be vested in a Congress of the United States. . . ." After granting many powers to the Congress, Article I goes on to provide that Congress may "make all Laws which shall be necessary and proper for carrying into Execution the foregoing Powers and all other Powers vested by this Constitution in the Government of the United States, or in any Department or Officer thereof."

The President's order does not direct that a congressional policy be executed in a manner prescribed by Congress—it directs that a presidential policy be executed in a manner prescribed by the President. The preamble of the order itself, like that of many statutes, sets out reasons why the President believes certain policies should be adopted, proclaims these policies as rules of conduct to be followed, and again, like a statute, authorizes a government official to promulgate additional rules and regulations consistent with the policy proclaimed and needed to carry that policy into execution. The power of Congress to adopt such public policies as those proclaimed by the order is beyond question. It can authorize the taking of private property for public use. It can make laws regulating the relationships between employers and employees, prescribing rules designed to settle labor disputes, and fixing wages and working conditions in certain fields of our economy. The Constitution did not subject this lawmaking power of Congress to presidential or military supervision or control.

It is said that other Presidents without congressional authority have taken possession of private business enterprises in order to settle labor disputes. But even if this be true, Congress has not thereby lost its exclusive constitutional authority to make laws necessary and proper to carry out the powers vested by the Constitution "in the Government of the United States, or any Department or Officer thereof."

The Founders of this Nation entrusted the lawmaking power to the Congress alone in both good and bad times. It would do no good to recall the historical events, the fears of power and the hopes for freedom that lay behind their choice. Such a review would but confirm our holding that this seizure order cannot stand.

The judgment of the District Court is affirmed.

Mr. Justice Jackson, concurring in the judgment and opinion of the Court:

. . . The Solicitor General seeks the power of seizure in three clauses of the Executive Article, the first reading, "The executive Power shall be vested in a President of the United States of America." Lest I be thought to exaggerate, I quote the interpretation which his brief puts upon it: "In our view, this clause constitutes a grant of all the executive powers of which the Government is capable." If that be true, it is difficult to see why the forefathers bothered to add several specific items, including some trifling ones.

The example of such unlimited executive power that must have most impressed the forefathers was the prerogative exercised by George III, and the description of its evils in the Declaration of Independence leads me to doubt that they were creating their new Executive in his image. Continental European examples were no more appealing. And if we seek instruction from our own times, we can match it only from the executive powers in those governments we disparagingly describe as totalitarian. I cannot accept the view that this clause is a grant in bulk of all conceivable executive power but regard it as an allocation to the presidential office of the generic powers thereafter stated.

The clause on which the Government next relies is that "The President shall be Commander in Chief of the Army and Navy of the United States. . . ." These cryptic words have given rise to some of the most persistent controversies in our constitutional history. Of course, they imply something more than an empty title. But just what authority goes with the name has plagued presidential advisers who would not waive or narrow it by nonassertion yet cannot say where it begins or ends. It undoubtedly puts the Nation's armed forces under presidential command. Hence, this loose appellation is sometimes advanced as support for any presidential action, internal or external, involving use of force, the idea being that it vests power to do anything, anywhere, that can be done with an army or navy.

That seems to be the logic of an argument tendered at our bar—that the President having, on his own responsibility, sent American troops abroad derives from that act "affirmative power" to seize the means of producing a supply of steel for them. To quote, "Perhaps the most forceful illustrations of the scope of Presidential power in this connection is the fact that American troops in Korea, whose safety and effectiveness are so directly involved here, were sent to the field by an exercise of the President's constitutional powers." Thus, it is said he has invested himself with "war powers."

I cannot foresee all that it might entail if the Court should indorse this argument. Nothing in our Constitution is plainer than that declaration of a war is entrusted only to Congress. Of course, a state of war may in fact exist without a formal declaration. But no doctrine that the Court could promulgate would seem to me more sinister and alarming than that a President whose conduct of foreign affairs is so largely uncontrolled, and often even is unknown, can vastly enlarge his mastery over the internal affairs of the country by his own commitment of the Nation's armed forces to some foreign venture. I do not, however, find it necessary or appropriate to consider the legal status of the Korean enterprise to discountenance argument based on it.

Assuming that we are in a war *de facto*, whether it is or is not a war *de jure*, does that empower the Commander-in-Chief to seize industries he thinks necessary to supply our army? The Constitution expressly places in Congress power "to raise and *support* Armies" and "to *provide* and *maintain* a Navy." (Emphasis supplied.) This certainly lays upon Congress primary responsibility for supplying the armed forces. Congress alone controls the raising of revenues and their appropriation and may determine in what manner and by what means they shall be spent for military and naval procurement. I suppose no one would doubt that Congress can take over war supply as a Government enterprise. On the other hand, if Congress sees fit to rely on free private enterprise collectively bargaining with free labor for support and maintenance of our armed forces can the Executive because of lawful disagreements incidental to that process, seize the facility for operation upon Government-imposed terms?

There are indications that the Constitution did not contemplate that the title Commander-in-Chief *of the Army and Navy* will constitute him also Commander-in-Chief of the country, its industries and its inhabitants. He has no monopoly of "war powers," whatever they are. While Congress cannot deprive the President of the command of the army and navy, only Congress can provide him an army or navy to command. It is also empowered to make rules for the "Government and Regulation of land and naval forces," by which it may to some unknown extent impinge upon even command functions.

That military powers of the Commander-in-Chief were not to supersede representative government of internal affairs seems obvious from the Constitution and from elementary American history. Time out of mind, and even now in many parts of the world, a military commander can seize private housing to shelter his troops. Not so, however, in the United States, for the Third Amendment says, "No Soldier shall, in time of peace be quartered in any house, without the consent of the Owner, nor in time of war, but in a manner to be prescribed by law." Thus, even in war time, his seizure of needed military housing must be authorized by Congress. It also was expressly left to Congress to "provide for calling forth the Militia to execute the Laws of the Union, suppress Insurrections and repel Invasions. . . ." Such a limitation on the command power, written at a time when the militia rather than a standing army was contemplated as the military weapon of the Republic, underscores the Constitution's policy that Congress, not the Executive, should control utilization of the war power as an instrument of domestic policy. Congress, fulfilling that function, has authorized the President to use the army to enforce certain civil rights. On the other hand, Congress has forbidden him to use the army for the purpose of executing general laws except when *expressly* authorized by the Constitution or by Act of Congress. . . .

We should not use this occasion to circumscribe, much less to contract, the lawful role of the President as Commander-in-Chief. I should indulge the widest latitude of interpretation to sustain his exclusive function to command the instruments of national force, at least when turned against the outside world for the security of our society. But, when it is turned inward, not because of rebellion but because of a lawful economic struggle between industry and labor, it should have no such indulgence. His command power is not such an absolute as might be implied from that office in a militaristic system but is subject to limitations consistent with a constitutional Republic whose law and policy-making branch is a representative Congress. The purpose of lodging dual titles in one man was to insure that the civilian would control the military, not to enable the military to subordinate the presidential office. No penance would ever expiate the sin against free government of holding that a President can escape control of executive powers by law through assuming his military role. What the power of command may include I do not try to envision, but I think it is not a military prerogative, without support of law, to seize persons or property because they are important or even essential for the military and naval establishment.

The third clause in which the Solicitor General finds seizure powers is that "he shall take Care that the Laws be faithfully executed. . . ." That authority must be matched against words of the Fifth Amendment that "No person shall be . . . deprived of life, liberty or property, without due process of law. . . ." One gives a governmental authority that reaches so far as there is law, the other gives a private right that authority shall go no farther. These signify about all there is of the principle that ours is a government of laws, not of men, and that we submit ourselves to rulers only if under rules. . . .

The Solicitor General, acknowledging that Congress has never authorized the seizure here, says practice of prior Presidents has authorized it. He seeks color of legality from claimed executive precedents, chief of which is President Roosevelt's seizure on June 9, 1941, of the California plant of the North American Aviation Company. Its superficial similarities with the present case, upon analysis, yield to distinctions so decisive that it cannot be regarded as even a precedent, much less an authority for the present seizure.

The appeal, however, that we declare the existence of inherent powers *ex necessitate* to meet an emergency asks us to do what many think would be wise, although it is something the forefathers omitted. They knew what emergencies were, knew the pressures they engender for authoritative action, knew, too, how they afford a ready pretext for usurpation. We may also suspect that they suspected that emergency powers would tend to kindle emergencies. Aside from suspension of the privilege of the writ of habeas corpus in time of rebellion or invasion, when the public safety may require it, they made no express provision for exercise of extraordinary authority because of a crisis. I do not think we rightfully may so amend their work, and, if we could, I am not convinced it would be wise to do so, although many modern nations have forthrightly recognized that war and economic crises may upset the normal balance between liberty and authority. Their experience with emergency powers may not be irrelevant to the argument here that we should say that the Executive, of his own volition, can invest himself with undefined emergency powers.

Germany, after the First World War, framed the Weimar Constitution, designed to secure her liberties in the Western tradition. However, the President of the Republic, without concurrence of the Reichstag, was empowered temporarily to suspend any or all individual rights if public safety and order were seriously disturbed or endangered. This proved a temptation to every government, whatever its shade of opinion, and in 13 years suspension of rights was invoked on more than 250 occasions. Finally, Hitler persuaded President Von Hindenberg to suspend all such rights, and they were never restored.

The French Republic provided for a very different kind of emergency government known as the "state of siege." It differed from the German emergency dictatorship, particularly in that emergency powers could not be assumed at will by the Executive but could only be granted as a parliamentary measure. And it did not, as in Germany, result in a suspension or abrogation of law but was a legal institution governed by special legal rules and terminable by parliamentary authority.

Great Britain also has fought both World Wars under a sort of temporary dictatorship created by legislation. As Parliament is not bound by written constitutional limitations, it established a crisis government simply by delegation to its Ministers of a larger measure than usual of its own unlimited power, which is exercised under its supervision by Ministers whom it may dismiss. This has been called the "highwater mark in the voluntary surrender of liberty," but, as Churchill put it, "Parliament stands custodian of these surrendered liberties, and its most sacred duty will be to restore them in their fullness when victory has crowned our exertions and our perseverance." Thus, parliamentary control made emergency powers compatible with freedom.

This contemporary foreign experience may be inconclusive as to the wisdom of lodging emergency powers somewhere in a modern government. But it suggests that emergency powers are consistent with free government only when their control is lodged elsewhere than in the Executive who exercises them. That is the safeguard that would be nullified by our adoption of the "inherent powers" formula. Nothing in my experience convinces me that such risks are warranted by any real necessity, although such powers would, of course, be an executive convenience. . . .

In view of the ease, expedition and safety with which Congress can grant and has granted large emergency powers, certainly ample to embrace this crisis, I am quite unimpressed with the argument that we should affirm possession of them without statute. Such power either has no beginning or it has no end. If it exists, it need submit to no legal restraint. I am not alarmed that it would plunge us straightway into dictatorship, but it is at least a step in that wrong direction. . . .

The essence of our free Government is "leave to live by no man's leave, underneath the law"—to be governed by those impersonal forces which we call law. Our Government is fashioned to fulfill this concept so far as humanly possible. The Executive, except for recommendation and veto, has no legislative power. The executive action we have here originates in the individual will of the President and represents an exercise of authority without law. No one, perhaps not even the President, knows the limits of the power he may seek to exert in this instance and the parties affected cannot learn the limit of their rights. We do not know today what powers over labor or property would be claimed to flow from Government possession if we should legalize it, what rights to compensation would be claimed or recognized, or on what contingency it would end. With all its defects, delays and inconveniences, men have discovered no technique for long preserving free government except that the Executive be under the law, and that the law be made by parliamentary deliberations.

Such institutions may be destined to pass away. But it is the duty of the Court to be last, not first, to give them up.

2. The Rule of Law versus Martial Rule

DUNCAN v. KAHANAMOKU

327 US 304 (1946)

[Immediately following the attack by the Japanese on Pearl Harbor, the Governor of Hawaii placed the Territory under martial rule and suspended the privilege of the writ of habeas corpus, the effect of which was to supplant civil with military authority and to substitute military justice for the civil courts. The Governer acted under the provisions of the Hawaiian Arganic Act, adopted by Congress in 1900. A section of the act, however, provided that the Constitution of the United States shall have the same force and effect in the Territory as elsewhere in the United States. Duncan and White, civilians, were tried and convicted by military tribunals in Hawaii. They applied for writs of habeas corpus in the District Court of Hawaii. The military authorities maintained that the writ had been legally suspended and that, therefore, the District Court had no jurisdiction to issue the writ. The District Court issued the writs after finding that if the civil courts had not been closed by order, they could have functioned, and so there was no justification for the trial of Duncan and White by military, rather than regular, tribunals.

[The Supreme Court, by a 6-to-2 vote, upheld this view of the District Court. There was no justification for the subordination of civilians to complete military rule and for subjecting them to military trials that lack many of the safeguards that we associate with normal court procedures. Martial rule could have been imposed without supplanting the courts by military tribunals for the trial of loyal civilians and without substituting military orders for criminal laws.

[The case is an excellent illustration of another phase of the rule of law, the superiority of civil over military authority: "The established principle of every free people is, that the law shall alone govern; and to it the military must always yield."

[The Court's opinion was written by Justice Black. We present that opinion, together with Justice Murphy's concurring opinion, which spells out some significant implications. The concurring opinion by Chief Justice Stone and the dissenting opinion by Justice Burton, in which Justice Frankfurter concurred, are omitted. Justice Jackson did not participate.]

Mr. Justice Black delivered the opinion of the Court:

The petitioners in these cases were sentenced to prison by military tribunals in Hawaii. Both are civilians. The question before us is whether the military tribunals had power to do this. The United States District Court for Hawaii in habeas corpus proceedings held that the military tribunals had no such power and ordered that they be set free. The Circuit Court of Appeals reversed, and ordered that the petitioners be returned to prison. Both cases thus involve the rights of individuals charged with crime and not connected with the armed forces to have their guilt or innocence determined in courts of law which provide established procedural safeguards, rather than by military tribunals which fail to afford many of these safeguards. Since these judicial safe-guards are prized privileges of our system of government we granted certiorari.

The following events led to the military tribunals' exercise of jurisdiction over the petitioners. On December 7, 1941, immediately following the surprise air attack by the Japanese on Pearl Harbor, the Governor of Hawaii by proclamation undertook to suspend the privilege of the writ of habeas corpus and to place the Territory under "martial law." Section 67 of the Hawaiian Organic Act authorizes the Territorial Governor to take this action "in case of rebellion or invasion, or imminent danger thereof, when the public safety requires it." His action was to remain in effect only "until communication can be had with the President and his decision thereon made known." The President approved the Governor's action on December 9th. The Governor's proclamation also authorized and requested the Commanding General, "during the . . . emergency and until danger of invasion is removed, to exercise all the powers normally exercised" by the Governor and by the "judicial officers and employees of this Territory."

Pursuant to this authorization the commanding general immediately proclaimed himself Military Governor and undertook the defense of the Territory and the maintenance of order. On December 8th, both civil and criminal courts were forbidden to summon jurors and witnesses and to try cases. The commanding general established military tribunals to take the place of the courts. These were to try civilians charged with violating the laws of the United States and of the Territory, and rules, regulations, orders or policies of the Military Government. Rules of evidence and procedure of courts of law were not to control the military trials. In imposing penalties the military tribunals were to be "guided by, but not limited to the penalties authorized by the courts martial manual, the laws of the United States, the Territory of Hawaii, the District of Columbia, and the customs of war in like cases." The rule announced was simply that punishment was to be "commensurate with the offense committed" and the the the death penalty might be imposed "in appropriate cases." Thus the military authorities took over the government of Hawaii. They could and did, by simply promulgating orders, govern the day to day activities of civilians who lived, worked, or were merely passing through there. The military tribunals interpreted the very orders promulgated by the military authorities and proceeded to punish violators. The sentences imposed were not subject to direct appellate court review, since it has long been established that military tribunals are not part of our judicial system. . . . The military undoubtedly assumed that its rule was not subject to any judicial control whatever, for by orders issued on August 25,

1943, it prohibited even accepting of a petition for writ of habeas corpus by a judge or judicial employee or the filing of such a petition by a prisoner or his attorney. Military tribunals could punish violators of these orders by fine, imprisonment or death.

White, the petitioner in No. 15, was a stockbroker in Honolulu. Neither he nor his business was connected with the armed forces. On August 20, 1942, more than eight months after the Pearl Harbor attack, the military police arrested him. The charge against him was embezzling stock belonging to another civilian in violation of chapter 183 of the Revised Laws of Hawaii. Though by the time of White's arrest the courts were permitted "as agents of the Military Governor" to dispose of some non-jury civil cases, they were still forbidden to summon jurors and to exercise criminal jurisdiction. On August 22d, White was brought before a military tribunal designated as a "Provost Court." The "Court" orally informed him of the charge. He objected to the tribunal's jurisdiction but the objection was overruled. He demanded to be tried by a jury. This request was denied. His attorney asked for additional time to prepare the case. This was refused. On August 25th he was tried and convicted. The tribunal sentenced him to five years imprisonment. Later the sentence was reduced to four years.

Duncan, the petitioner in No. 14, was a civilian shipfitter employed in the Navy Yard at Honolulu. On February 24th, 1944, more than two years and two months after the Pearl Harbor attack, he engaged in a brawl with two armed Marine sentries at the yard. He was arrested by the military authorities. By the time of his arrest the military had to some extent eased the stringency of military rule. Schools, bars and motion picture theatres had been reopened. Courts had been authorized to "exercise their normal jurisdiction." They were once more summoning jurors and witnesses and conducting criminal trials. There were important exceptions, however. One of these was that only military tribunals were to try "Criminal Prosecutions for violations of military orders." As the record shows, these military orders still covered a wide range of day to day civilian conduct. Duncan was charged with violating one of these orders, . . . which prohibited assault on military or naval personnel with intent to resist or hinder them in the discharge of their duty. He was, therefore, tried by a military tribunal rather than the Territorial Court, although the general laws of Hawaii made assault a crime. . . . A conviction followed and Duncan was sentenced to six months imprisonment.

Both White and Duncan challenged the power of the military tribunals to try them by petitions for writs of habeas corpus filed in the District Court for Hawaii on March 14 and April 14, 1944, respectively. Their petitions urged both statutory and Constitutional grounds. The court issued orders to show cause. Returns to these orders contended that Hawaii had become part of an active theatre of war constantly threatened by invasion from without; that the writ of habeas corpus had therefore properly been suspended and martial law had validly been established in accordance with the provisions of the Organic Act; that consequently the District Court did not have jurisdiction to issue the writ; and that the trials of petitioners by military tribunals pursuant to orders by the Military Governor issued because of military necessity were valid. Each petitioner filed a traverse to the returns, which traverse challenged among other things the suspension of habeas corpus, the establishment of martial law and the validity of the Military Governor's orders, asserting that such action could not be taken except when required by military necessity due to actual or threatened invasion, which even if it did exist on December 7, 1941, did not exist when the petitioners were tried; and that, whatever the necessity for martial law, there was no justification for trying them in military tribunals rather than the regular courts of law. The District Court, after separate trials found in each case, among other things, that the courts had always been able to function but for the military orders closing them, and that consequently there was no military necessity for the trial of petitioners by military tribunals rather than regular courts. It accordingly held the trials void and ordered the release of the petitioners. . . .

Did the Organic Act during the period of martial law give the armed forces power to supplant all civilian laws and to substitute military for judicial trials under the conditions that existed in Hawaii at the time these petitioners were tried? The relevant conditions, for our purposes, were the same when both petitioners were tried. The answer to the question depends on a correct interpretation of the Act. But we need not construe the Act, insofar as the power of the military might be used to meet other and different conditions and situations. The boundaries of the situation with reference to which we do interpret the scope of the Act can be more sharply defined by stating at this point some different conditions which either would or might conceivably have affected to a greater or lesser extent the scope of the authorized military power. We note first that at the time the alleged offenses were committed the dangers apprehended by the military were not sufficiently imminent to cause them to require civilians to evacuate the area or even to evacuate any of the buildings necessary to carry on the business of the courts. In fact, the buildings had long been open and actually in use for certain kinds of trials. Our question does not involve the well-established power of the military to exercise jurisdiction over members of the armed forces, those directly connected with such forces, or enemy belligerents, prisoners of war, or others charged with violating the laws of war. We are not concerned with the recognized power of the military to try civilians in tribunals established as a part of a temporary military government over occupied enemy territory or territory regained from an enemy where civilian government cannot and does not function. For Hawaii since annexation has been held by and loyal to the United States. Nor need we here consider the power of the military simply to arrest and detain civilians interfering with a necessary military function at a time of turbulence and danger from insurrection or war. And finally, there was no specialized effort of the military here to enforce orders which related only to military functions, such as, for illustration, curfew rules or blackouts. For these petitioners were tried before tribunals set up under a military program which took over all government and superseded all civil laws and courts. If the Organic Act, properly interpreted, did not give the armed forces this awesome power, both petitioners are entitled to their freedom.

In interpreting the Act we must first look to its language. Section 67 makes it plain that Congress did intend the Governor of Hawaii, with the approval of the President, to invoke military aid under certain circumstances. But Congress did not specifically state to what extent the army could be used or what power it could exercise. It certainly did not explicitly declare that the Governor in conjunction with the military could for days, months or years close all the courts and supplant them with military tribunals. . . . If a power thus to obliterate the judicial system of Hawaii can be found at all in the Organic Act, it must be inferred from § 67's provision for placing the Territory under "martial law." But the term "martial law" carries no precise meaning. The Constitution does not refer to "martial law" at all and no Act of Congress has defined the term. It has been employed in various ways by different people at different times. By some it has been identified as "military law" limited to members of, and those connected with, the armed forces. Others have said that the term does not imply a system of established rules but denotes simply some kind of day to day expression of a General's will dictated by what he considers the imperious necessity of the moment. . . .

Since the Act's language does not provide a satisfactory answer, we look to the legislative history for possible further aid in interpreting the term "martial law" as used in the statute. The government contends that the legislative history shows that Congress intended to give the armed forces extraordinarily broad powers to try civilians before military tribunals. Its argument is as follows: That portion of the language of § 67 which proscribes the prerequisites to declaring martial law is identical with a part of the language of the original Constitution of Hawaii. Before Congress enacted the Organic Act the Supreme Court of Hawaii had construed that language as giving the Hawaiian President power to authorize military tribunals to try civilians charged with crime whenever the public safety required it. . . . When Congress passed the Organic Act it simply enacted the applicable language of the Hawaiian Constitution and with it the interpretation of that language by the Hawaiian Supreme Court. . . .

As we shall indicate later, military trials of civilians charged with crime, especially when not made subject to judicial review, are so obviously contrary to our political traditions and our institution of jury trials in courts of law, that the tenuous circumstance offered by the government can hardly suffice to persuade us that Congress was willing to enact a Hawaiian Supreme Court decision permitting such a radical departure from our steadfast beliefs.

Partly in order to meet this objection the government further contends that Congress . . . not only authorized military trials of civilians in Hawaii, but also could and intended to provide that "martial law" in Hawaii should not be limited by the United States Constitution or by established Constitutional practice. But when the Organic Act is read as a whole and in the light of its legislative history it becomes clear that Congress did not intend the Constitution to have a limited application to Hawaii. Along with § 67 Congress enacted § 5 of the Organic Act which provides "that the Constitution . . . shall have the same force and effect within the said Territory as elsewhere in the United States." . . .

It follows that civilians in Hawaii are entitled to the Constitutional guarantee of a fair trial to the same extent as those who live in any other part of our country. We are aware that conditions peculiar to Hawaii might imperatively demand extraordinarily speedy and effective measures in the event of actual or threatened invasion. But this also holds true for other parts of the United States. Extraordinary measures in Hawaii, however necessary, are not supportable on the mistaken premise that Hawaiian inhabitants are less entitled to Constitutional protection than others. For here Congress did not in the Organic Act exercise whatever power it might have had to limit the application of the Constitution. . . . The people of Hawaii are therefore entitled to Constitutional protection to the same extent as the inhabitants of the 48 States. And Congress did not . . . authorize the military trials of petitioners. Whatever power the Organic Act gave the Hawaiian military authorities, such power must therefore be construed in the same way as a grant of power to troops stationed in any one of the states.

Since both the language of the Organic Act and its legislative history fail to indicate that the scope of "martial law" in Hawaii includes the supplanting of courts by military tribunals we must look to other sources in order to interpret that term. We think the answer may be found in the birth, development and growth of our governmental institutions up to the time Congress passed the Organic Act. Have the principles and practices developed during the birth and growth of our political institutions been such as to persuade us that Congress intended that loyal civilians in loyal territory should have their daily conduct governed by military orders substituted for criminal laws, and that such civilians should be tried and punished by military tribunals? Let us examine what those principles and practices have been, with respect to the position of civilian government and the courts and compare that with the standing of military tribunals throughout our history.

People of many ages and countries have feared and unflinchingly opposed the kind of subordination of executive, legislative and judicial authorities to complete military rule which according to the government Congress has authorized here. In this country that fear has become part of our cultural and political institutions. The story of that development is well known and we see no need to retell it all. But we might mention a few pertinent incidents. As early as the 17th Century our British ancestors took political action against aggressive military rule. When James I and Charles I authorized martial law for purposes of speedily punishing all types of crimes committed by civilians the protest led to the historic Petition of Right which in uncompromising terms objected to this arbitrary procedure and prayed that it be stopped and never repeated. When later the American colonies declared their independence one of the grievances listed by Jefferson was that the King had endeavored to render the military superior to the civil power. The executive and military officials who later found it necessary to utilize the armed forces to keep order in a young and turbulent nation, did not lose sight of the philosophy embodied in the Petition of Right and the Declaration of Independence, that existing civilian government and especially the courts were not to be interfered with by the exercise of military power. In 1787, the year in which the Constitution was formulated, the Governor of Massachusetts colony used the militia to cope with Shay's rebellion. In his instructions to the Commander of the troops the Governor listed the "great objects" of the mission. The troops were to "protect the judicial courts . . . ," "to assist the civil magistrates in executing the laws . . . ," and to "aid them in apprehending the disturbers of the public peace. . . ." The Commander was to consider himself "constantly as under the direction of the civil officer, saving where any armed force shall appear and oppose . . . his . . . marching to execute these orders." President Washington's instructions to the Commander of the troops sent into Pennsylvania to suppress the

Whiskey Rebellion of 1794 were to the same effect. The troops were to see to it that the laws were enforced and were to deliver the leaders of armed insurgents to the regular courts for trial. The President admonished the Commanding General "that the judge can not be controlled in his functions." In the many instances of the use of troops to control the activities of civilians that followed, the troops were generally again employed merely to aid and not to supplant the civilian authorities. The last noteworthy incident before the enactment of the Organic Act was the rioting that occurred in the Spring of 1899 at the Coeur-d'Alene mines of Shoshone County, Idaho. The President ordered the regular troops to report to the Governor for instructions and to support the civil authorities in preserving the peace. Later the State Auditor as agent of the Governor, and not the Commanding General, ordered the troops to detain citizens without trial and to aid the Auditor in doing all he thought necessary to stop the riot. Once more, the military authorities did not undertake to supplant the courts and to establish military tribunals to try and punish ordinary civilian offenders.

Courts and their procedural safeguards are indispensable to our system of government. They were set up by our founders to protect the liberties they valued. . . . Our system of government clearly is the antithesis of total military rule and the founders of this country are not likely to have contemplated complete military dominance within the limits of a Territory made part of this country and not recently taken from an enemy. They were opposed to governments that placed in the hands of one man the power to make, interpret and enforce the laws. Their philosophy has been the people's throughout our history. For that reason we have maintained legislatures chosen by citizens or their representatives and courts and juries to try those who violate legislative enactments. We have always been especially concerned about the potential evils of summary criminal trials and have guarded against them by provisions embodied in the Constitution itself. . . . Legislatures and courts are not merely cherished American institutions; they are indispensable to our government.

Military tribunals have no such standing. For as this Court has said before: ". . . the military should always be kept in subjection to the laws of the country to which it belongs, and that he is no friend to the Republic who advocates the contrary. The established principle of every free people is, that the law shall alone govern; and to it the military must always yield." *Dow* v. *Johnson*, 100 US 158. Congress prior to the time of the enactment of the Organic Act had only once authorized the supplanting of the courts by military tribunals. Legislation to that effect was enacted immediately after the South's unsuccessful attempt to secede from the Union. Insofar as that legislation applied to the

Southern States after the war was at an end it was challenged by a series of Presidential vetos as vigorous as any in the country's history. And in order to prevent this Court from passing on the constitutionality of this legislation Congress found it necessary to curtail our appellate jurisdiction. Indeed, prior to the Organic Act, the only time this Court had ever discussed the supplanting of courts by military tribunals in a situation other than that involving the establishment of a military government over recently occupied enemy territory, it had emphatically declared that "civil liberty and this kind of martial law cannot endure together; the antagonism is irreconcilable; and, in the conflict, one or the other must perish." *Ex parte Milligan,* 4 Wall. (US) 2.

We believe that when Congress passed the Hawaiian Organic Act and authorized the establishment of "martial law" it had in mind and did not wish to exceed the boundaries between military and civilian power, in which our people have always believed, which responsible military and executive officers had heeded, and which had become part of our political philosophy and institutions prior to the time Congress passed the Organic Act. The phrase "martial law" as employed in that Act, therefore, while intended to authorize the military to act vigorously for the maintenance of an orderly civil government and for the defense of the Islands against actual or threatened rebellion or invasion, was not intended to authorize the supplanting of courts by military tribunals, yet the government seeks to justify the punishment of both White and Duncan on the ground of such supposed Congressional authorization. We hold that both petitioners are now entitled to be released from custody.

Reversed.

Mr. Justice Murphy, concurring:

The Court's opinion, in which I join, makes clear that the military trials in these cases were unjustified by the martial law provisions of the Hawaiian Organic Act. Equally obvious, as I see it, is the fact that these trials were forbidden by the Bill of Rights of the Constitution of the United States, which applies in both spirit and letter to Hawaii. Indeed, the unconstitutionality of the usurpation of civil power by the military is so great in this instance as to warrant this Court's complete and outright repudiation of the action.

Abhorrence of military rule is ingrained in our form of government. Those who founded this nation knew full well that the arbitrary power of conviction and punishment for pretended offenses is the hallmark of despotism. . . . History had demonstrated that fact to them time and again. They shed their blood to win independence from a ruler who they alleged was attempting to render the "military independent of and superior to the civil power" and who was "depriving us of the benefits of trial by jury." In the earliest state constitutions they inserted definite provisions placing the military under "strict subordination" to the civil power at all times and in all cases. And in framing the Bill of Rights of the Federal Constitution they were careful to make sure that the power to punish would rest primarily with the civil authorities at all times. They believed that a trial by an established court, with an impartial jury, was the only certain way to protect an individual against oppression. The Bill of Rights translated that belief into reality by guaranteeing the observance of jury trials and other basic procedural rights foreign to military proceedings. This supremacy of the civil over the military is one of our great heritages. It has made possible the attainment of a high degree of liberty regulated by law rather than by caprice. Our duty is to give effect to that heritage at all times, that it may be handed down untarnished to future generations.

Such considerations led this Court in *Ex parte Milligan* to lay down the rule that the military lacks any constitutional power in war or in peace to substitute its tribunals for civil courts that are open and operating in the proper and unobstructed exercise of their jurisdiction. Only when a foreign invasion or civil war actually closes the courts and renders it impossible for them to administer criminal justice can martial law validly be invoked to suspend their functions. Even the suspension of power under those conditions is of a most temporary character. "As necessity creates the rule, so it limits its duration; for if this government is continued after the courts are reinstated, it is a gross usurpation of power." . . .

Tested by the *Milligan* rule, the military proceedings in issue plainly lack constitutional sanction. . . .

There can be no question but that when petitioners White and Duncan were subjected to military trials on August 25, 1942, and March 2, 1944, respectively, the territorial courts of Hawaii were perfectly capable of exercising their normal criminal jurisdiction had the military allowed them to do so. . . . In short, the Bill of Rights disappeared by military fiat rather than by military necessity.

Moreover, there is no question here as to the loyalty of the Hawaiian judiciary or as to the desire and ability of the judges to co-operate fully with military requirements. There is no evidence of disorder in the community which might have prevented the courts from conducting jury trials. . . .

The so-called "open court" rule of the *Milligan Case*, to be sure, has been the subject of severe criticism, especially by military commentators. That criticism is repeated by the Government in these cases. It is said that the fact that courts are open is but one of many factors relevant to determining the necessity and hence the constitutionality of military trials of civilians. The argument is made that however adequate the "open court" rule may have been in 1628 or 1864 it is distinctly unsuited to modern warfare conditions where all of the territories of a warring nation may be in combat zones or imminently threatened with long-range attack even while civil courts are operating. Hence if a military commander, on the basis of his conception of military necessity, requires all civilians accused of crime to be tried summarily before martial law tribunals, the Bill of Rights must bow humbly to his judgment despite the unquestioned ability of the civil courts to exercise their criminal jurisdiction.

The argument thus advanced is as untenable today as it was when cast in the language of Plantagenets, the Tudors and the Stuarts. It is a rank appeal to abandon the fate of all our liberties to the reasonableness of the judgment of those who are trained primarily for war. It seeks to justify military usurpation of civilian authority to punish crime without regard to the potency of the Bill of Rights. It deserves repudiation. . . .

From time immemorial despots have used real or imagined threats to the public welfare as an excuse for needlessly abrogating human rights. That excuse is no less unworthy of our traditions when used in this day of atomic warfare or at a future time when some other type of warfare may be devised. The right to jury trial and the other constitutional rights of an accused individual are too fundamental to be sacrificed merely through a reasonable fear of military assault. There must be some overpowering factor that makes a recognition of those rights incompatible with the public safety before we should consent to their temporary suspension. If those rights may safely be respected in the face of a threatened invasion no valid reason exists for disregarding them. In other words, the civil courts must be utterly incapable of trying criminals or of dispensing justice in their usual manner before the Bill of Rights may be temporarily suspended. "Martial law in relation to closing the courts cannot arise from a *threatened* invasion. The necessity must be actual and present; the invasion real, such as effectually closes the courts and deposes the civil administration." *Ex parte Milligan.* . . .

Delays in the civil courts and slowness in their procedure are also cited as an excuse for shearing away their criminal jurisdiction, although lack of knowledge of any undue delays in the Hawaiian courts is admitted. It is said that the military "cannot brook a delay" and that "the punishment must be swift; there is an element of time in it, and we cannot afford to let the trial linger and be protracted." This military attitude toward constitutional processes is not novel. Civil liberties and military expediency are often irreconcilable. It does take time to secure a grand jury indictment, to allow the accused to procure and confer with counsel to permit the preparation of a defense, to form a petit jury, to respect the elementary rules of procedure and evidence and to judge guilt or innocence according to accepted rules of law. But experience has demonstrated that such time is well spent. It is the only method we have of insuring the protection of constitutional rights and of guarding against oppression. The swift trial and punishment which the military desires is precisely what the Bill of Rights outlaws. We would be false to our trust if we allowed the time it takes to give effect to constitutional rights to be used as the very reason for taking away those rights. It is our duty, as well as that of the military, to make sure that such rights are respected whenever possible, even though time may be consumed. . . .

It is further said that the issuance of military orders relating to civilians required that the military have at its disposal some sort of tribunal to enforce those regulations. Any failure of civil courts to convict violators of such regulations would diminish the authority and ability to discharge military responsibilities. This is the ultimate and most vicious of the arguments used to justify military trials. It assumes without proof that civil courts are incompetent and are prone to free those who are plainly guilty. . . .

The final reason advanced relates to the testimony of military leaders that Hawaii is said to have a "heterogeneous population with all sorts of affinities and loyalties which are alien in many cases to the philosophy of life of the American Government," one-third of the civilian population being of Japanese descent. . . .

The implication apparently is that persons of Japanese descent, including those of American background and training, are of such doubtful loyalty as a group as to constitute a menace justifying the denial of the procedural rights of all accused persons in Hawaii. It is also implied that persons of Japanese descent are unfit for jury duty in Hawaii and that the problems arising when they serve on juries are so great as to warrant dispensing with the entire jury system in Hawaii if the military so desires. The lack of any factual or logical basis for such implications is clear. It is a known fact that there have been no recorded acts of sabotage, espionage or fifth column activities by persons of Japanese descent in Hawaii either on or subsequent to December 7, 1941. There was thus no security reason for excluding them from juries, even making the false assumption that it was impossible to separate the loyal from the disloyal. And if there were problems arising from the use of racially mixed juries, elimination of all jury trials was hardly a reasonable or sensible answer to those problems. Especially deplorable, however, is this use of the iniquitous doctrine of racism to justify the imposition of military trials. Racism has no place whatever in our civilization. The Constitution as well as the conscience of mankind disclaims its use for any purpose, military or otherwise. It can only result, as it does in this instance, in striking down individual rights and in aggravating rather than solving the problems toward which it is directed. It renders impotent the ideal of the dignity of the human personality, destroying something of what is noble in our way of life. We must therefore reject it completely whenever it arises in the course of a legal proceeding.

The reasons here advanced for abandoning the "open court" rule of the *Milligan Case* are without substance. To retreat from that rule is to open the door to rampant militarism and the glorification of war, which have destroyed so many nations in history. There is a very necessary part in our national life for the military; it has defended this country well in its darkest hours of trial. But militarism is not our way of life. It is to be used only in the most extreme circumstances. Moreover, we must be on constant guard against an excessive use of any power, military or otherwise, that results in the needless destruction of our rights and liberties. There must be a careful balancing of interests. And we must ever keep in mind that "The Constitution of the United States is a law for rulers and people, equally in war and in peace, and covers with the shield of its protection all classes of men, at all times, and under all circumstances." *Ex parte Milligan.*

3. The Reach of Habeas Corpus

YAMASHITA v. STYER

327 US 1 (1946)

[General Yamashita, of the Japanese Army in the Philippine Islands, surrendered to and became a prisoner of the United States Army. Soon after this event he was charged with violation of the law of war for permitting Japanese soldiers to commit brutal atrocities against the civilian population of the Philippine Islands and prisoners of war. He was tried by American Army officers, was found guilty, and was sentenced to death by hanging.

[In this case, a habeas corpus proceeding, the Supreme Court unanimously held that the Court had the right to examine into the question of whether or not the military tribunal had legal authority to try Yamashita as an enemy combatant for violation of the law of war. This was in effect a reaffirmation of the decision in the case of the eight Nazi saboteurs. *Ex parte Quirin,* 317 US 1 (1942). The decision, even as thus limited in scope, gives considerable reach to the writ of habeas corpus: a military tribunal that tries an enemy war criminal must submit the question of its jurisdiction to the regular civil courts of the United States.

[Justices Murphy and Rutledge would go even further and maintain that the Court should subject to scrutiny the procedure and rules of evidence used by the military tribunal and test them by the demands of the Due Process Clause of the Fifth Amendment.

[The decision, which in effect affirmed the sentence, was 6 to 2; Justice Jackson did not participate.]

Mr. Chief Justice Stone delivered the opinion of the Court:

. . . From the petitions and supporting papers it appears that prior to September 3, 1945, petitioner was the Commanding General of the Fourteenth Army Group of the Imperial Japanese Army in the Philippine Islands. On that date he surrendered to and became a prisoner of war of the United States Army Forces in Baguio, Philippine Islands. On September 25th, by order of respondent, Lieutenant General Wilhelm D. Styer, Commanding General of the United States Army Forces, Western Pacific, which command embraces the Philippine Islands, petitioner was served with a charge prepared by the Judge Advocate General's Department of the Army, purporting to charge petitioner with a violation of the law of war. On October 8, 1945, petitioner, after pleading not guilty to the charge, was held for trial before a military commission of five Army officers appointed by order of General Styer. The order appointed six Army officers, all lawyers, as defense counsel. Throughout the proceedings which followed, including those before this Court, defense counsel have demonstrated their professional skill and resourcefulness and their proper zeal for the defense with which they were charged.

On the same date a bill of particulars was filed by the prosecution, and the commission heard a motion made in petitioner's behalf to dismiss the charge on the ground that it failed to state a violation of the law of war. On October 29th the commission was reconvened, a supplemental bill of particulars was filed, and the motion to dismiss was denied. The trial then proceeded until its conclusion on December 7, 1945, the commission hearing two hundred and eighty-six witnesses, who gave over three thousand pages of testimony. On that date petitioner was found guilty of the offense as charged and sentenced to death by hanging.

The petitions for habeas corpus set up that the detention of petitioner for the purpose of the trial was unlawful for reasons which are now urged as showing that the military commission was without lawful authority or jurisdiction to place petitioner on trial, as follows:

(a) That the military commission which tried and convicted petitioner was not lawfully created, and that no military commission to try petitioner for violations of the law of war could lawfully be convened after the cessation of hostilities between the armed forces of the United States and Japan;

(b) that the charge preferred against petitioner fails to charge him with a violation of the law of war;

(c) that the commission was without authority and jurisdiction to try and convict petitioner because the order governing the procedure of the commission permitted the admission in evidence of depositions, affidavits, and hearsay and opinion evidence, and because the commission's rulings admitting such evidence were in violation of the 25th and 38th Articles of War and the Geneva Convention, and deprived petitioner of a fair trial in violation of the due process clause of the Fifth Amendment;

(d) that the commission was without authority and jurisdiction in the premises because of the failure to give advance notice of petitioner's trial to the neutral power representing the interests of Japan as a belligerent as required by Article 60 of the Geneva Convention.

On the same grounds the petitions for writs of prohibition set up that the commission is without authority to proceed with the trial.

The Supreme Court of the Philippine Islands, after hearing argument, denied the petition for habeas corpus presented to it, on the ground, among others, that its jurisdiction was limited to an inquiry as to the jurisdiction of the commission to place petitioner on trial for the offense charged, and that the commission, being validly constituted by the order of General Styer, had jurisdiction over the person of petitioner and over the trial for the offense charged.

In *Ex parte Quirin,* 317 US 1, we had occasion to consider at length the sources and nature of the authority to create military commissions for the trial of enemy combatants for offenses against the law of war. We there pointed out that Congress, in the exercise of the power conferred upon it by Article 1, § 8, cl. 10 of the Constitution to "define and punish . . . Offenses against the Law of Nations . . ." of which the law of war is a part, had by the Articles of War recognized the "military commission" appointed by military command, as it had previously existed in United States Army practice, as an appropriate tribunal for the trial and punishment of offenses against the law of war. . . . Article 2 includes among those persons subject to the Articles of War the personnel of our own military establishment. But this, as Article 12 indicates, does not exclude from the class of persons subject to trial by military commissions "any other person who by the law of war is subject to trial by military tribunals," and who, under Article 12, may be tried by court martial, or under Article 15 by military commission.

We further pointed out that Congress, by sanctioning trial of enemy combatants for violations of the law of war by military commission, had not attempted to codify the law of war or to mark its precise boundaries. Instead, by Article 15 it had incorporated, by reference, as within the preexisting jurisdiction of military commissions created by appropriate military command, all offenses which are defined as such by the law of war, and which may constitutionally be included within that jurisdiction. It thus adopted the system of military common law applied by military tribunals so far as it should be recognized and deemed applicable by the courts, and as further defined and supplemented by the Hague Convention, to which the United States and the Axis powers were parties.

We also emphasized in *Ex parte Quirin,* as we do here, that on application for habeas corpus we are not concerned with the guilt or innocence of the petitioners. We consider here only the lawful power of the commission to try the petitioner for the offense charged. In the present cases it must be recognized throughout that the military tribunals which Congress has sanctioned by the Articles of War are not courts whose rulings and judgments are made subject to review by this Court. . . . They are tribunals whose determinations are reviewable by the military authorities either as provided in the military orders constituting such tribunals or as provided by the Articles of War. Congress conferred on the courts no power to review their determinations save only as it has granted judicial power "to grant writs of habeas corpus for the purpose of an inquiry into the cause of restraint of liberty." . . . The courts may inquire whether the detention complained of is within the authority of those detaining the petitioner. If the military tribunals have lawful authority to hear, decide and condemn, their action is not subject to judicial review merely because they have made a wrong decision on disputed facts. Correction of their errors of decision is not for the courts but for the military authorities which are alone authorized to review their decisions. . . .

Finally, we held in *Ex parte Quirin*, as we hold now, that Congress by sanctioning trials of enemy aliens by military commission for offenses against the law of war had recognized the right of the accused to make a defense. . . . It has not foreclosed their right to contend that the Constitution or laws of the United States withhold authority to proceed with the trial. It has not withdrawn, and the Executive branch of the government could not, unless there was suspension of the writ, withdraw from the courts the duty and power to make such inquiry into the authority of the commission as may be made by habeas corpus.

With these governing principles in mind we turn to the consideration of the several contentions urged to establish want of authority in the commission. We are not here concerned with the power of military commissions to try civilians. See *Ex parte Milligan*, 4 Wall. (US) 2, 132; *Sterling* v. *Constantin*, 287 US 378; *Ex parte Quirin*. The Government's contention is that General Styer's order creating the commission conferred authority on it only to try the purported charge of violation of the law of war committed by petitioner, an enemy belligerent, while in command of a hostile army occupying United States territory during time of war. Our first inquiry must therefore be whether the present commission was created by lawful military command and, if so, whether authority could thus be conferred on the commission to place petitioner on trial after the cessation of hostilities between the armed forces of the United States and Japan.

The authority to create the Commission. General Styer's order for the appointment of the commission was made by him as Commander of the United States Army Forces, Western Pacific. His command includes, as part of a vastly greater area, the Philippine Islands, where the alleged offenses were committed, where petitioner surrendered as a prisoner of war, and where, at the time of the order convening the commission, he was detained as a prisoner in custody of the United States Army. The Congressional recognition of military commissions and its sanction of their use in trying offenses against the law of war to which we have referred, sanctioned their creation by military command in conformity to long established American precedents. Such a commission may be appointed by any field commander, or by any commander competent to appoint a general court martial, as was General Styer, who had been vested with that power by order of the President. . . .

It thus appears that the order creating the commission for the trial of petitioner was authorized by military command, and was in complete conformity to the Act of Congress sanctioning the creation of such tribunals for the trial of offenses against the law of war committed by enemy combatants. And we turn to the question whether the authority to create the commission and direct the trial by military order continued after the cessation of hostilities. . . .

We cannot say that there is no authority to convene a commission after hostilities have ended to try violations of the law of war committed before their cessation, at least until peace has been officially recognized by treaty or proclamation of the political branch of the Government. In fact, in most instances the practical administration of the system of military justice under the law of war would fail if such authority were thought to end with the cessation of hostilities. For only after their cessation could the greater number of offenders and the principal ones be apprehended and subjected to trial.

No writer on international law appears to have regarded the power of military tribunals, otherwise competent to try violations of the law of war, as terminating before the formal state of war has ended. . . .

The charge. Neither Congressional action nor the military orders constituting the commission authorized it to place petitioner on trial unless the charge preferred against him is of a violation of the law of war. The charge, so far as now relevant, is that petitioner, between October 9, 1944 and September 2, 1945, in the Philippine Islands,

while commander of armed forces of Japan at war with the United States of America and its allies, unlawfully disregarded and failed to discharge his duty as commander to control the operations of the members of his command, permitting them to commit brutal atrocities and other high crimes against people of the United States and of its allies and dependencies, particularly the Philippines; and he . . . thereby violated the laws of war.

Bills of particulars, filed by the prosecution by order of the commission, allege a series of acts, one hundred and twenty-three in number, committed by members of the forces under petitioner's command during the period mentioned. The first item specifies the execution of

a deliberate plan and purpose to massacre and exterminate a large part of the civilian population of Batangas Province, and to devastate and destroy public, private and religious property therein, as a result of which more than 25,000 men, women and children, all unarmed noncombatant civilians,

were brutally mistreated and killed, without cause or trial, and entire settlements were devastated and destroyed wantonly and without military necessity.

Other items specify acts of violence, cruelty and homicide inflicted
upon the civilian population and prisoners of war, acts of wholesale
pillage and the wanton destruction of religious monuments.

It is not denied that such acts directed against the civilian population of an occupied country and against prisoners of war are recognized
in international law as violations of the law of war. . . . But it is urged
that the charge does not allege that petitioner has either committed or
directed the commission of such acts, and consequently that no violation is charged as against him. But this overlooks the fact that the gist of
the charge is an unlawful breach of duty by petitioner as an army commander to control the operations of the members of his command by
"permitting them to commit" the extensive and widespread atrocities
specified. The question then is whether the law of war imposes on an
army commander a duty to take such appropriate measures as are
within his power to control the troops under his command for the
prevention of the specified acts which are violations of the law of war
and which are likely to attend the occupation of hostile territory by an
uncontrolled soldiery, and whether he may be charged with personal
responsibility for his failure to take such measures when violations result. That this was the precise issue to be tried was made clear by the
statement of the prosecution at the opening of the trial.

It is evident that the conduct of military operations by troops whose
excesses are unrestrained by the orders or efforts of their commander
would almost certainly result in violations which it is the purpose of
the law of war to prevent. Its purpose to protect civilian populations and
prisoners of war from brutality would largely be defeated if the commander of an invading army could with impunity neglect to take reasonable measures for their protection. Hence the law of war presupposes that its violation is to be avoided through the control of the
operations of war by commanders who are to some extent responsible
for their subordinates. . . .

We do not make the laws of war but we respect them so far as they
do not conflict with the commands of Congress or the Constitution.
There is no contention that the present charge, thus read, is without
the support of evidence, or that the commission held petitioner responsible for failing to take measures which were beyond his control
or inappropriate for a commanding officer to take in the circumstances.
We do not here appraise the evidence on which petitioner was convicted. We do not consider what measures, if any, petitioner took to
prevent the commission, by the troops under his command, of the plain

violations of the law of war detailed in the bill of particulars, or whether such measures as he may have taken were appropriate and sufficient to discharge the duty imposed upon him. These are questions within the peculiar competence of the military officers composing the commission and were for it to decide. . . . It is plain that the charge on which petitioner was tried charged him with a breach of his duty to control the operations of the members of his command, by permitting them to commit the specified atrocities. This was enough to require the commission to hear evidence tending to establish the culpable failure of petitioner to perform the duty imposed on him by the law of war and to pass upon its sufficiency to establish guilt. . . .

The Proceedings before the Commission. The regulations prescribed by General MacArthur governing the procedure for the trial of petitioner by the commission directed that the commission should admit such evidence "as in its opinion would be of assistance in proving or disproving the charge, or such as in the commission's opinion would have probative value in the mind of a reasonable man," and that in particular it might admit affidavits, depositions or other statements taken by officers detailed for that purpose by military authority. The petitions in this case charged that in the course of the trial the commission received, over objection by petitioner's counsel, the deposition of a witness taken pursuant to military authority by a United States Army captain. It also, over like objection, admitted hearsay and opinion evidence tendered by the prosecution. Petitioner argues as ground for the writ of habeas corpus, that Article 25 of the Articles of War prohibited the reception in evidence by the commission of depositions on behalf of the prosecution in a capital case, and that Article 38 prohibited the reception of hearsay and of opinion evidence.

We think that neither Article 25 nor Article 38 is applicable to the trial of an enemy combatant by a military commission for violations of the law of war. . . .

By thus recognizing military commissions in order to preserve their traditional jurisdiction over enemy combatants unimpaired by the Articles, Congress gave sanction, as we held in *Ex parte Quirin,* to any use of the military commission contemplated by the common law of war. But it did not thereby make subject to the Articles of War persons other than those defined by Article 2 as being subject to the Articles, nor did it confer the benefits of the Articles upon such persons. The Articles recognized but one kind of military commission, not two. But they sanctioned the use of that one for the trial of two classes of persons, to one of which the Articles do, and to the other of which they do not apply in such trials. Being of this latter class, petitioner cannot claim the benefits of the Articles, which are applicable only to the members of the other class. Petitioner, an enemy combatant, is therefore not a person made subject to the Articles of War by Article 2, and the military commission before which he was tried, though sanctioned, and its jurisdiction saved, by Article 15, was not convened by virtue of the Articles of War, but pursuant to the common law of war. It follows that the Articles of War, including Articles 25 and 38, were not applicable to petitioner's trial and imposed no restrictions upon the procedure to be followed. The Articles left the control over the procedure in such a case where it had previously been, with the military command. . . .

We cannot say that the commission, in admitting evidence to which objection is now made, violated any act of Congress, treaty or military command defining the commission's authority. For reasons already stated we hold that the commission's rulings on evidence and on the mode of conducting these proceedings against petitioner are not reviewable by the courts, but only by the reviewing military authorities. From this viewpoint it is unnecessary to consider what, in other situations, the Fifth Amendment might require, and as to that no intimation one way or the other is to be implied. Nothing we have said is to be taken as indicating any opinion on the question of the wisdom of considering such evidence, or whether the action of a military tribunal in admitting evidence, which Congress or controlling military command has directed to be excluded, may be drawn in question by petition for habeas corpus or prohibition. . . .

It thus appears that the order convening the commission was a lawful order, that the Commission was lawfully constituted, that petitioner was charged with violation of the law of war, and that the commission had authority to proceed with the trial, and in doing so did not violate any military, statutory or constitutional command. . . . We therefore conclude that the detention of petitioner for trial and his detention upon his conviction, subject to the prescribed review by the military authorities, were lawful, and that the petition for certiorari, and leave to file in this Court petitions for writs of habeas corpus and prohibition should be, and they are denied.

Mr. Justice Murphy, dissenting:

The significance of the issue facing the Court today cannot be overemphasized. An American military commission has been established to try a fallen military commander of a conquered nation for an alleged war crime. The authority for such action grows out of the exercise of the power conferred upon Congress by Article 1, § 8, cl. 10 of the Constitution to "define and punish . . . Offenses against the Law of Nations. . . ." The grave issue raised by this case is whether a military commission so established and so authorized may disregard the procedural rights of an accused person as guaranteed by the Constitution, especially by the due process clause of the Fifth Amendment.

The answer is plain. The Fifth Amendment guarantee of due process of law applies to "any person" who is accused of a crime by the Federal Government or any of its agencies. No exception is made as to those who are accused of war crimes or as to those who possess the status of an enemy belligerent. Indeed, such an exception would be contrary to the whole philosophy of human rights which makes the Constitution the great living document that it is. The immutable rights of the individual, including those secured by the due process clause of the Fifth Amendment, belong not alone to the members of those nations that excel on the battlefield or that subscribe to the democratic ideology. They belong to every person in the world, victor or vanquished, whatever may be his race, color or beliefs. They rise above any status of belligerency or out-lawry. They survive any popular passion or frenzy of the moment. No court or legislature or executive, not even the mightiest army in the world, can ever destroy them. Such is the universal and indestructible nature of the rights which the due process clause of the Fifth Amendment recognizes and protects when life or liberty is threatened by virtue of the authority of the United States.

The existence of these rights, unfortunately, is not always respected. They are often trampled under by those who are motivated by hatred, aggression or fear. But in this nation individual rights are recognized and protected, at least in regard to governmental action. They cannot be ignored by any branch of the Government, even the military, except under the most extreme and urgent circumstances.

The failure of the military commission to obey the dictates of the due process requirements of the Fifth Amendment is apparent in this case. The petitioner was the commander of an army totally destroyed by the superior power of this nation. While under heavy and destructive attack by our forces, his troops committed many brutal atrocities and other high crimes. Hostilities ceased and he voluntarily surrendered. At that point he was entitled, as an individual protected by the due process clause of the Fifth Amendment, to be treated fairly and justly according to the accepted rules of law and procedure. He was also entitled to a fair trial as to any alleged crimes and to be free from charges of legally unrecognized crimes that would serve only to permit his accusers to satisfy their desires for revenge.

A military commission was appointed to try the petitioner for an alleged war crime. The trial was ordered to be held in territory over which the United States has complete sovereignty. No military necessity or other emergency demanded the suspension of the safeguards of due process. Yet petitioner was rushed to trial under an improper charge, given insufficient time to prepare an adequate defense, deprived of the benefits of some of the most elementary rules of evidence and summarily sentenced to be hanged. In all this needless and unseemly haste there was no serious attempt to charge or to prove that he committed a recognized violation of the laws of war. He was not charged with personally participating in the acts of atrocity or with ordering or condoning their commission. Not even knowledge of these crimes was attributed to him. It was simply alleged that he unlawfully disregarded and failed to discharge his duty as commander to control the operations of the members of his command, permitting them to commit the acts of atrocity. The recorded annals of warfare and the established principles of international law afford not the slightest precedent for such a charge. This indictment in effect permitted the military commission to make the crime whatever it willed, dependent upon its biased view as to petitioner's duties and his disregard thereof, a practice reminiscent of that pursued in certain less respected nations in recent years.

In my opinion, such a procedure is unworthy of the traditions of our people or of the immense sacrifices that they have made to advance the common ideals of mankind. The high feelings of the moment doubtless will be satisfied. But in the sober after glow will come the realization of the boundless and dangerous implications of the procedure sanctioned today. No one in a position of command in an army, from sergeant to general, can escape those implications. Indeed, the fate of some future President of the United States and his chiefs of staff and military advisers may well have been sealed by this decision. But even more significant will be the hatred and ill-will growing out of the application of this unprecedented procedure. That has been the inevitable effect of every method of punishment disregarding the element of personal culpability. The effect in this instance, unfortunately, will be magnified infinitely for here we are dealing with the rights of man on an international level. To subject an enemy belligerent to an unfair trial, to charge him with an unrecognized crime, or to vent on him our retributive emotions only antagonizes the enemy nation and hinders the reconciliation necessary to a peaceful world.

That there were brutal atrocities inflicted upon the helpless Filipino people, to whom tyranny is no stranger, by Japanese armed forces under the petitioner's command is undeniable. Starvation, execution or massacre without trial, torture, rape, murder and wanton destruction of property were foremost among the outright violations of the laws of war and of the conscience of a civilized world. That just punishment should be meted out to all those responsible for criminal acts of this nature is also beyond dispute. But these factors do not answer the problem in this case. They do not justify the abandonment of our devotion to justice in dealing with a fallen enemy commander. To conclude otherwise is to admit that the enemy has lost the battle but has destroyed our ideals.

War breeds atrocities. From the earliest conflicts of recorded history to the global struggles of modern times inhumanities, lust and pillage have been the inevitable by-products of man's resort to force and arms. Unfortunately, such despicable acts have a dangerous tendency to call forth primitive impulses of vengeance and retaliation among the victimized peoples. The satisfaction of such impulses in turn breeds resentment and fresh tension. Thus does the spiral of cruelty and hatred grow.

If we are ever to develop an orderly international community based upon a recognition of human dignity it is of the utmost importance that the necessary punishment of those guilty of atrocities be as free as possible from the ugly stigma of revenge and vindictiveness. Justice must be tempered by compassion rather than by vengeance. In this, the first case involving this momentous problem ever to reach this Court, our responsibility is both lofty and difficult. We must insist, within the confines of our proper jurisdiction, that the highest standards of justice be applied in this trial of an enemy commander conducted under the authority of the United States. Otherwise stark retribution will be free to masquerade in a cloak of false legalism. And the hatred and cynicism engendered by that retribution will supplant the great ideals to which this nation is dedicated.

This Court fortunately has taken the first and most important step toward insuring the supremacy of law and justice in the treatment of an enemy belligerent accused of violating the laws of war. Jurisdiction properly has been asserted to inquire "into the cause of restraint of liberty" of such a person. . . . Thus the obnoxious doctrine asserted by the Government in this case, to the effect that restraints of liberty resulting from military trials of war criminals are political matters completely outside the arena of judicial review, has been rejected fully and unquestionably. This does not mean, of course, that the foreign affairs and policies of the nation are proper subjects of judicial inquiry. But when the liberty of any person is restrained by reason of the authority of the United States the writ of habeas corpus is available to test the legality of that restraint, even though direct court review of the restraint is prohibited. The conclusive presumption must be made, in this country at least, that illegal restraints are unauthorized and unjustified by any foreign policy of the Government and that commonly accepted juridical standards are to be recognized and enforced. On that basis judicial inquiry into these matters may proceed within its proper sphere.

The determination of the extent of review of war trials calls for judicial statesmanship of the highest order. The ultimate nature and scope of the writ of habeas corpus are within the discretion of the judiciary unless validly circumscribed by Congress. Here we are confronted with a use of the writ under circumstances novel in the history of the Court. For my own part, I do not feel that we should be confined by the traditional lines of review drawn in connection with the use of the writ by ordinary criminals who have direct access to the judiciary in the first instance. Those held by the military lack any such access; consequently the judicial review available by habeas corpus must be wider than usual in order that proper standards of justice may be enforceable.

But for the purposes of this case I accept the scope of review recognized by the Court at this time. As I understand it, the following issues in connection with war criminal trials are reviewable through the use of the writ of habeas corpus: (1) whether the military commission was lawfully created and had authority to try and to convict the accused of a war crime; (2) whether the charge against the accused stated a violation of the laws of war; (3) whether the commission, in admitting certain evidence, violated any law or military command defining the commission's authority in that respect; and (4) whether the commission lacked jurisdiction because of a failure to give advance notice to the protecting power as required by treaty or convention.

The Court, in my judgment, demonstrates conclusively that the military commission was lawfully created in this instance and that petitioner could not object to its power to try him for a recognized war crime. Without pausing here to discuss the third and fourth issues, however, I find it impossible to agree that the charge against the petitioner stated a recognized violation of the laws of war. . . .

Nothing in all history or in international law, at least as far as I am aware, justifies such a charge against a fallen commander of a defeated force. To use the very inefficiency and disorganization created by the victorious forces as the primary basis for condemning officers of the defeated armies bears no resemblance to justice or to military reality.

International law makes no attempt to define the duties of a commander of an army under constant and overwhelming assault; nor does it impose liability under such circumstances for failure to meet the ordinary responsibilities of command. The omission is understandable. . . .

The only conclusion I can draw is that the charge made against the petitioner is clearly without precedent in international law or in the annals of recorded military history. This is not to say that enemy commanders may escape punishment for clear and unlawful failures to prevent atrocities. But that punishment should be based upon charges fairly drawn in light of established rules of international law and recognized concepts of justice.

But the charge in this case, as previously noted, was speedily drawn and filed but three weeks after the petitioner surrendered. The trial proceeded with great dispatch without allowing the defense time to prepare an adequate case. Petitioner's rights under the due process clause of the Fifth Amendment were grossly and openly violated without any justification. All of this was done without any thorough investigation and prosecution of those immediately responsible for the atrocities, out of which might have come some proof or indication of personal culpability on petitioner's part. Instead the loose charge was made that great numbers of atrocities had been committed and that petitioner was the commanding officer; hence he must have been guilty of disregard of duty. Under that charge the commission was free to establish whatever standard of duty on petitioner's part that it desired. By this flexible method a victorious nation may convict and execute any or all leaders of a vanquished foe, depending upon the prevailing degree of vengeance and the absence of any objective judicial review.

At a time like this when emotions are understandably high it is difficult to adopt a dispassionate attitude toward a case of this nature. Yet now is precisely the time when that attitude is most essential. While peoples in other lands may not share our beliefs as to due process and the dignity of the individual, we are not free to give effect to our emotions in reckless disregard of the rights of others. We live under the Constitution, which is the embodiment of all the high hopes and aspirations of the new world. And it is applicable in both war and peace. We must act accordingly. Indeed, an uncurbed spirit of revenge and retribution, masked in formal legal procedure for purposes of dealing with a fallen enemy commander, can do more lasting harm than all of the atrocities giving rise to that spirit. The people's faith in the fairness and objectiveness of the law can be seriously undercut by that spirit. The fires of nationalism can be further kindled. And the hearts of all mankind can be embittered and filled with hatred, leaving forlorn and impoverished the noble ideal of malice toward none and charity to all. These are the reasons that lead me to dissent in these terms.

Mr. Justice Rutledge, dissenting:

Not with ease does one find his views at odds with the Court's in a matter of this character and gravity. Only the most deeply felt convictions could force one to differ. That reason alone leads me to do so now, against strong considerations for withholding dissent.

More is at stake than General Yamashita's fate. There could be no possible sympathy for him if he is guilty of the atrocities for which his death is sought. But there can be and should be justice administered according to law. In this stage of war's aftermath it is too early for Lincoln's great spirit, best lighted in the Second Inaugural, to have wide hold for the treatment of foes. It is not too early, it is never too early, for the nation steadfastly to follow its great constitutional traditions, none older or more universally protective against unbridled power than due process of law in the trial and punishment of men, that is, of all men, whether citizens, aliens, alien enemies or enemy belligerents. It can become too late.

This long-held attachment marks the great divide between our enemies and ourselves. Theirs was a philsophy of universal force. Ours is one of universal law, albeit imperfectly made flesh of our system and so dwelling among us. Every departure weakens the tradition, whether it touches the high or the low, the powerful or the weak, the triumphant or the conquered. If we need not or cannot be magnanimous, we can keep our own law on the plane from which it has not descended hitherto and to which the defeated foes' never rose.

With all deference to the opposing views of my brethren, whose attachment to that tradition needless to say is no less than my own, I cannot believe in the face of this record that the petitioner has had the fair trial our Constitution and laws command. Because I cannot reconcile what has occurred with their measure, I am forced to speak. At bottom my concern is that we shall not forsake in any case, whether Yamashita's or another's, the basic standards of trial which, among other guaranties, the nation fought to keep; that our system of military justice shall not alone among all our forms of judging be above or beyond the fundamental law or the control of Congress within its orbit of authority; and that this Court shall not fail in its part under the Constitution to see that these things do not happen.

This trial is unprecedented in our history. Never before have we tried and convicted an enemy general for action taken during hostilities or otherwise in the course of military operations or duty. Much less have we condemned one for failing to take action. The novelty is not lessened by the trial's having taken place after hostilities ended and the enemy, including the accused, had surrendered. Moreover, so far as the time permitted for our consideration has given opportunity I have not been able to find precedent for the proceeding in the system of any nation founded in the basic principles of our constitutional democracy, in the laws of war or in other internationally binding authority or usage. . . .

It is not in our tradition for anyone to be charged with crime which is defined after his conduct, alleged to be criminal, has taken place; or in language not sufficient to inform him of the nature of the offense or to enable him to make defense. Mass guilt we do not impute to individuals, perhaps in any case but certainly in none where the person is not charged or shown actively to have participated in or knowingly to have failed in taking action to prevent the wrongs done by others, having both the duty and the power to do so.

It is outside our basic scheme to condemn men without giving reasonable opportunity for preparing defense; in capital or other serious crimes to convict on "official documents . . . ; affidavits; . . . documents or translations thereof; diaries . . . , photographs, motion picture films, and . . . newspapers" or on hearsay, once, twice or thrice removed, more particularly when the documentary evidence or some of it is prepared *ex parte* by the prosecuting authority and includes not only opinion but conclusions of guilt. Nor in such cases do we deny the rights of confrontation of witnesses and cross-examination.

Our tradition does not allow conviction by tribunals both authorized and bound by the instrument of their creation to receive and consider evidence which is expressly excluded by Act of Congress or by treaty obligation; nor is it in accord with our basic concepts to make the tribunal, specially constituted for the particular trial, regardless of those prohibitions the sole and exclusive judge of the credibility, probative value and admissibility of whatever may be tendered as evidence.

The matter is not one merely of the character and admissibility of evidence. It goes to the very competency of the tribunal to try and punish consistently with the Constitution, the laws of the United States made in pursuance thereof, and treaties made under the nation's authority.

All these deviations from the fundamental law, and others, occurred in the course of constituting the commission, the preparation for trial and defense, the trial itself, and therefore, in effect, in the sentence imposed. Whether taken singly in some instances as departures from specific constitutional mandates or in totality as in violation of the Fifth Amendment's command that *no* person shall be deprived of life, liberty or property without due process of law, a trial so vitiated cannot withstand constitutional scrutiny.

One basic protection of our system and one only, petitioner has had. He has been represented by able counsel, officers of the army he fought. Their difficult assignment has been done with extraordinary fidelity, not only to the accused but to their high conception of military justice, always to be administered in subordination to the Constitution and consistent Acts of Congress and treaties. But, as will appear, even this conceded shield was taken away in much of its value, by denial of reasonable opportunity for them to perform their function. . . .

My brother Murphy has discussed the charge with respect to the substance of the crime. With his conclusions in this respect I agree. My own primary concern will be with the constitution of the commission and other matters taking place in the course of the proceedings, relating chiefly to the denial of reasonable opportunity to prepare petitioner's defense and the sufficiency of the evidence, together with serious questions of admissibility, to prove an offense, all going as I think to the commission's jurisdiction.

Necessarily only a short sketch can be given concerning each matter. And it may be stated at the start that, although it was ruled in *Ex parte Quirin, supra,* that this Court had no function to review the evidence, it was not there or elsewhere determined that it could not ascertain whether conviction is founded upon evidence expressly excluded by Congress or treaty; nor does the Court purport to do so now.

Wholly apart from the violation of the Articles of War and of the Geneva Convention, I am completely unable to accept or to understand the Court's ruling concerning the applicability of the due process clause of the Fifth Amendment to this case. Not heretofore has it been held that any human being is beyond its universally protecting spread in the guaranty of a fair trial in the most fundamental sense. That door is dangerous to open. I will have no part in opening it. For once it is ajar, even for enemy belligerents, it can be pushed back wider for others, perhaps ultimately for all.

The Court does not declare expressly that petitioner as an enemy belligerent has no constitutional rights, a ruling I could understand but not accept. Neither does it affirm that he has some, if but little, constitutional protection. Nor does the Court defend what was done. I think the effect of what it does is in substance to deny him all such safeguards. And this is the great issue in the cause.

For it is exactly here we enter wholly untrodden ground. The safe signposts to the rear are not in the sum of protections surrounding jury trials or any other proceeding known to our law. Nor is the essence of the Fifth Amendment's elementary protection comprehended in any single one of our time-honored specific constitutional safeguards in trial, though there are some without which the words "fair trial" and all they connote become a mockery.

Apart from a tribunal concerned that the law as applied shall be an instrument of justice, albeit stern in measure to the guilt established, the heart of the security lies in two things. One is that conviction shall not rest in any essential part upon unchecked rumor, report, or the results of the prosecution's *ex parte* investigations, but shall stand on proven fact; the other, correlative, lies in a fair chance to defend. This embraces at the least the rights to know with reasonable clarity in advance of the trial the exact nature of the offense with which one is to be charged; to have reasonable time for preparing to meet the charge and to have the aid of counsel in doing so, as also in the trial itself; and if, during its course, one is taken by surprise, through the injection of new charges or reversal of rulings which brings forth new masses of evidence, then to have further reasonable time for meeting the unexpected shift.

So far as I know, it has not yet been held that any tribunal in our system, of whatever character, is free to receive such evidence "as *in its opinion* would be *of assistance* in proving or disproving the charge" or, again as in its opinion, "would have probative value in the mind of a reasonable man"; and, having received what in its unlimited discretion it regards as sufficient, is also free to determine what weight may be given to the evidence received without restraint.

When to this fatal defect in the directive, however innocently made, are added the broad departures from the fundamentals of fair play in the proof and in the right to defend which occurred throughout the proceeding, there can be no accommodation with the due process of law which the Fifth Amendment demands.

All this the Court puts to one side with the short assertion that no question of due process under the Fifth Amendment or jurisdiction reviewable here is presented. I do not think this meets the issue, standing alone or in conjunction with the suggestion which follows that the Court gives no intimation one way or the other concerning what Fifth Amendment due process might require in other situations. . . .

It is not necessary to recapitulate. The difference between the Court's view of this proceeding and my own comes down in the end to the view, on the one hand, that there is no law restrictive upon these proceedings other than whatever rules and regulations may be prescribed for their government by the executive authority or the military and, on the other hand, that the provisions of the Articles of War, of the Geneva Convention and the Fifth Amendment apply.

I cannot accept the view that anywhere in our system resides or lurks a power so unrestrained to deal with any human being through any process of trial. What military agencies or authorities may do with our enemies in battle or invasion, apart from proceedings in the nature of trial and some semblance of judicial action, is beside the point. Nor has any human being heretofore been held to be wholly beyond elementary procedural protection by the Fifth Amendment. I cannot consent to even implied departure from that great absolute.

It was a great patriot who said: "He that would make his own liberty secure must guard even his enemy from oppression; for if he violates this duty he establishes a precedent that will reach himself." [Thomas Paine.]

4. Fair Notice of What Acts the Law Will Punish

WINTERS v. NEW YORK

333 US 507 (1948)

[There can hardly be "the rule of law" if a person may be held to have violated "a statute which either forbids or requires the doing

of an act in terms so vague that men of common intelligence must
necessarily guess at its meaning and differ as to its application. . . ."
Such a statute, the Supreme Court has said, "violates the first essential
of due process of law." *Connelly* v. *General Construction Co.*, 269 US
385 (1925). "The Constitution requires that a statute must not be too
vague to allow the citizen to ascertain what course of conduct he must
follow to put himself safely within the bounds of the law." The certainty required is not tested from the would-be violator's standpoint;
"the test is rather whether adequate guidance is given to those who
would be law-abiding." *United States* v. *Five Gambling Devices*, 346
US 441 (1953), dissenting opinion of Justice Clark.

[The *Winters Case* is an illustration of this important principle of
constitutional law. It is also an illustration of the difficulty judges en-
counter as they attempt to apply it to a specific statute; for while six
Justices concluded that the statute in question failed to satisfy the
principle, three Justices dissented.

[The case could also be read in connection with cases involving
the publication of indecent or obscene literature, like the *Ulysses* and
Gordon cases, which appear later in this volume.]

Mr. Justice Reed delivered the opinion of the Court:

Appellant is a New York City bookdealer, convicted . . . of a misdemeanor for having in his possession with intent to sell certain magazines charged to violate subsection 2 of § 1141 of the New York Penal
Law. It reads as follows:

§ 1141. Obscene prints and articles
1. A person . . . who,
2. Prints, utters, publishes, sells, lends, gives away, distributes or shows,
or has in his possession with intent to sell, lend, give away, distribute or show,
or otherwise offers for sale, loan, gift or distribution, any book, pamphlet,
magazine, newspaper or other printed paper devoted to the publication,
and principally made up of criminal news, police reports, or accounts of
criminal deeds, or pictures, or stories of deeds of bloodshed, lust or
crime. . . .
Is guilty of a misdemeanor. . . .

The validity of the statute was drawn in question in the state courts
as repugnant to the Fourteenth Amendment to the Constitution of the
United States in that it denied the accused the right of freedom of
speech and press, protected against state interference by the Fourteenth Amendment. . . . The principle of a free press covers distribution as well as publication. . . .

The appellant contends that the subsection violates the right of free
speech and press because it is vague and indefinite. It is settled that a

statute so vague and indefinite, in form and as interpreted, as to permit within the scope of its language the punishment of incidents fairly within the protection of the guarantee of free speech is void, on its face, as contrary to the Fourteenth Amendment. . . . A failure of a statute limiting freedom of expression to give fair notice of what acts will be punished and such a statute's inclusion of prohibitions against expressions, protected by the principles of the First Amendment, violates an accused's rights under procedural due process and freedom of speech or press. Where the alleged vagueness of a state statute has been cured by an opinion of the state court, confining a statute punishing the circulation of publications "having a tendency to encourage or incite the commission of any crime" to "encouraging an actual breach of law," this Court affirmed a conviction under the stated limitation of meaning. The accused publication was read as advocating the commission of the crime of indecent exposure. *Fox* v. *Washington,* 236 US 273.

We recognize the importance of the exercise of a state's police power to minimize all incentives to crime, particularly in the field of sanguinary or salacious publications with their stimulation of juvenile delinquency. Although we are dealing with an aspect of a free press in its relation to public morals, the principles of unrestricted distribution of publications admonish us of the particular importance of a maintenance of standards of certainty in the field of criminal prosecution for violation of statutory prohibitions against distribution. We do not accede to appellee's suggestion that the constitutional protection for a free press applies only to the exposition of ideas. The line between the informing and the entertaining is too elusive for the protection of that basic right. Everyone is familiar with instances of propaganda through fiction. What is one man's amusement, teaches another's doctrine. Though we can see nothing of any possible value to society in these magazines, they are as much entitled to the protection of free speech as the best of literature. . . . They are equally subject to control if they are lewd, indecent, obscene or profane. . . .

On its face, the subsection here involved violates the rule of the *Stromberg Case,* 283 US 359, and *Herndon Case,* 301 US 242, that statutes which include prohibitions of acts fairly within the protection of a free press are void. It covers detective stories, treatises on crime, reports of battle carnage, et cetera. In recognition of this obvious defect, the New York Court of Appeals limited the scope by construction. Its only interpretation of the meaning of the pertinent subsection is that given in this case. After pointing out that New York statutes against indecent or obscene publications have generally been construed to refer to sexual impurity, it interpreted the section here in question to forbid these publications as "indecent or obscene" in a different manner. The Court held that collections of criminal deeds of bloodshed or lust "can be so massed as to become vehicles for inciting violent and depraved crimes against the person and in that case such publications are indecent or obscene in an admissible sense. . . ." "This idea," its opinion goes on to say, "was the principal reason for the enactment of the statute." . . .

The Court of Appeals by this authoritative interpretation made the subsection applicable to publications that, besides meeting the other particulars of the statute, so massed their collection of pictures and stories of bloodshed and of lust "as to become vehicles for inciting violent and depraved crimes against the person." Thus, the statute forbids the massing of stories of bloodshed and lust in such a way as to incite to crime against the person. This construction fixes the meaning of the statute for this case. The interpretation by the Court of Appeals puts these words in the statute as definitely as if it had been so amended by the legislature. . . . As lewdness in publications is punishable under § 1141 (1) and the usual run of stories of bloodshed, such as detective stories, are excluded, it is the massing as an incitation to crime that becomes the important element.

Acts of gross and open indecency or obscenity, injurious to public morals, are indictable at common law, as violative of the public policy that requires from the offender retribution for acts that flaunt accepted standards of conduct. . . . When a legislative body concludes that the mores of the community call for an extension of the impermissible limits, an enactment aimed at the evil is plainly within its power, if it does not transgress the boundaries fixed by the Constitution for freedom of expression. The standards of certainty in statutes punishing for offenses is higher than in those depending primarily upon civil sanction for enforcement. The crime "must be defined with appropriate definiteness." . . . There must be ascertainable standards of guilt. Men of common intelligence cannot be required to guess at the meaning of the enactment. The vagueness may be from uncertainty in regard to persons within the scope of the act, . . . or in regard to the applicable tests to ascertain guilt. . . .

This Court goes far to uphold state statutes that deal with offenses, difficult to define, when they are not entwined with limitations on free expression. We have the same attitude toward federal statutes. Only a definite conviction by a majority of this Court that the conviction violates the Fourteenth Amendment justifies reversal of the court primarily charged with responsibility to protect persons from conviction under a vague state statute.

The impossibility of defining the precise line between permissible uncertainty in statutes caused by describing crimes by words well understood through long use in the criminal law—obscene, lewd, lascivious, filthy, indecent or disgusting—and the unconstitutional vagueness that leaves a person uncertain as to the kind of prohibited conduct—massing stories to incite crime—has resulted in three arguments of this case in this Court. The legislative bodies in draftsmanship obviously have the same difficulty as do the judicial in interpretation. Nevertheless despite the difficulties, courts must do their best to determine whether or not the vagueness is of such a character "that men of common intelligence must necessarily guess at its meaning." . . . The entire text of the statute or the subjects dealt with may furnish an adequate standard. The present case as to a vague statute abridging free speech involves the circulation of only vulgar magazines. The next may call for decision as to free expression of political views in the light of a statute intended to punish subversive activities.

The subsection of the New York Penal Law, as now interpreted by the Court of Appeals, prohibits distribution of a magazine principally made up of criminal news or stories of deeds of bloodshed, or lust, so massed as to become vehicles for inciting violent and depraved crimes against the person. But even considering the gloss put upon the literal meaning by the Court of Appeals' restriction of the statute to collections of stories "so massed as to become vehicles for inciting violent and depraved crimes against the person . . . not necessarily . . . sexual passion," we find the specification of publications, prohibited from distribution, too uncertain and indefinite to justify the conviction of this petitioner. Even though all detective tales and treatises on criminology are not forbidden, and though publications made up of criminal deeds not characterized by bloodshed or lust are omitted from the interpretation of the Court of Appeals, we think fair use of collections of pictures and stories would be interdicted because of the utter impossibility of the actor or the trier to know where this new standard of guilt would draw the line between the allowable and the forbidden publications. No intent or purpose is required—no indecency or obscenity in any sense heretofore known to the law. "So massed as to incite to crime" can become meaningful only by concrete instances. This one example is not enough. The clause proposes to punish the printing and circulation of publications that courts or juries may think influence generally persons to commit crimes of violence against the person. No conspiracy to commit a crime is required. . . . It is not an effective notice of new crime. The clause has no technical or common law meaning. Nor can light as to the meaning be gained from the section as a whole or the Article of the Penal Law under which it appears. . . .

The statute as construed by the Court of Appeals does not limit punishment to the indecent and obscene, as formerly understood. When stories of deeds of bloodshed, such as many in the accused magazines, are massed so as to incite to violent crimes, the statute is violated. It does not seem to us that an honest distributor of publications could know when he might be held to have ignored such a prohibition. Collections of tales of war horrors, otherwise unexceptionable, might well be found to be "massed" so as to become "vehicles for inciting violent and depraved crimes." Where a statute is so vague as to make criminal an innocent act, a conviction under it cannot be sustained. . . .

To say that a state may not punish by such a vague statute carries no implication that it may not punish circulation of objectionable printed matter, assuming that it is not protected by the principles of the First Amendment, by the use of apt words to describe the prohibited publications. . . . Neither the states nor Congress are prevented by the requirement of specificity from carrying out their duty of eliminating evils to which, in their judgment, such publications give rise.

Reversed.

Mr. Justice Frankfurter, joined by Mr. Justice Jackson and Mr. Justice Burton, dissenting:

By today's decision the Court strikes down an enactment that has been part of the laws of New York for more than sixty years, and New York is but one of twenty States having such legislation. . . .

This body of laws represents but one of the many attempts by legislatures to solve what is perhaps the most persistent, intractable, elusive, and demanding of all problems of society—the problem of crime, and, more particularly, of its prevention. By this decision the Court invalidates such legislation of almost half the States of the Union. The destructiveness of the decision is even more far-reaching. This is not one of those situations where power is denied to the States because it belongs to the Nation. These enactments are invalidated on the ground that they fall within the prohibition of the "vague contours" of the Due Process Clause. The decision thus operates equally as a limitation upon Congressional authority to deal with crime, and, more especially, with juvenile delinquency. These far-reaching consequences result from the Court's belief that what New York, among a score of States, has prohibited, is so empty of meaning that no one desirous of obeying the law could fairly be aware that he was doing that which was prohibited. . . .

The action of this Court today in invalidating legislation having the support of almost half the States of the Union rests essentially on abstract notions about "indefiniteness." The Court's opinion could have been written by one who had never read the issues of "Headquarters Detective" which are the basis of the prosecution before us, who had never deemed their contents as relevant to the form in which the New York legislation was cast, had never considered the bearing of such "literature" on juvenile delinquency, in the allowable judgment of the legislature. Such abstractions disregard the considerations that may well have moved and justified the State in not being more explicit than these State enactments are. Only such abstract notions would reject the judgment of the States that they have outlawed what they have a right to outlaw, in the effort to curb crimes of lust and violence, and that they have not done it so recklessly as to occasion real hazard that other publications will thereby be inhibited, or also be subjected to prosecution.

This brings our immediate problem into focus. No one would deny, I assume, that New York may punish crimes of lust and violence. Presumably also, it may take appropriate measures to lower the crime rate. But he must be a bold man indeed who is confident that he knows what causes crime. Those whose lives are devoted to an understanding of the problem are certain only that they are uncertain regarding the role of the various alleged "causes" of crime. . . . Is it to be seriously questioned, however, that the State of New York, or the Congress of the United States, may make incitement of crime itself an offense? He too would indeed be a bold man who denied that incitement may be caused by the written word no less than by the spoken. . . .

Not to make the magazines with which this case is concerned part of the Court's opinion is to play "Hamlet" without Hamlet. But the Court sufficiently summarizes one aspect of what the State of New York here condemned when it says "we can see nothing of any possible value to society in these magazines." From which it jumps to the conclusion that, nevertheless, "they are as much entitled to the protection of free speech as the best of literature." Wholly neutral futilities, of course, come under the protection of free speech as fully as do Keats' poems or Donne's sermons. But to say that these magazines have "nothing of any possible value to society" is only half the truth. This merely denies them goodness. It disregards their mischief. As a result of appropriate judicial determination, these magazines were found to come within the prohibition of the law against inciting "violent and depraved crimes against the person," and the defendant was convicted because he exposed for sale such materials. The essence of the Court's decision is that it gives publications which have "nothing of any possible value to society" constitutional protection but denies to the States the power to prevent the grave evils to which, in their rational judgment, such publications give rise. The legislatures of New York and the other States were concerned with these evils and not with neutral abstractions of harmlessness. . . .

A recent murder case before the High Court of Australia sheds light on the considerations which may well have induced legislation such as that now before us, and on the basis of which the New York Court of Appeals sustained its validity. The murder was committed by a lad who had just turned seventeen years of age, and the victim was the driver of a taxicab. I quote the following from the opinion of Mr. Justice Dixon:

In his evidence . . . Graham [a friend of the defendant and apparently a very reliable witness] said that he knew Boyd Sinclair [the murderer] and his moods very well and that he just left him; that Boyd had on a number of occasions outlined plans for embarking on a life of crime, plans based mainly on magazine thrillers which he was reading at the time. They included the obtaining of a motor car and an automatic gun. . . .

"Magazine thrillers" hardly characterizes what New York has outlawed. New York does not lay hold of publications merely because they are "devoted to and principally made up of criminal news or police reports or accounts of criminal deeds, regardless of the manner of treatment." . . . The aim of the publication must be incitation to "violent and depraved crimes against the person" by so massing "pictures and stories of criminal deeds of bloodshed or lust" as to encourage like deeds in others. It would be sheer dogmatism in a field not within the professional competence of judges to deny to the New York legislature the right to believe that the intent of the type of publications which it has proscribed is to cater to morbid and immature minds— whether chronologically or permanently immature. It would be sheer dogmatism to deny that in some instances, as in the case of young Boyd Sinclair, deeply embedded, unconscious impulses may be discharged into destructive and often fatal action. . . .

Since Congress and the States may take measures against "violent and depraved crimes," can it be claimed that "due process of law" bars measures against incitement to such crimes? But if they have power to deal with incitement, Congress and the States must be allowed the effective means for translating their policy into law. No doubt such a law presents difficulties in draftsmanship where publications are the instruments of incitement. The problem is to avoid condemnation so unbounded that neither the text of the statute nor its subject matter affords "a standard of some sort." . . . Legislation must put people on notice as to the kind of conduct from which to refrain. Legislation must also avoid so tight a phrasing as to leave the area for evasion ampler than that which is condemned. How to escape, on the one hand, having a law rendered futile because no standard is afforded by which conduct is to be judged, and, on the other, a law so particularized as to defeat itself through the opportunities it affords for evasion, involves an exercise of judgment which is at the heart of the legislative process. It calls for the accommodation of delicate factors. But this accommodation is for the legislature to make and for us to respect, when it concerns a subject so clearly within the scope of the police power as the control of crime. Here we are asked to declare void the law which expresses the balance so struck by the legislature, on the ground that the legislature has not expressed its policy clearly enough. That is what it gets down to. . . .

What is there in the condemned law that leaves men in the dark as to what is meant by publications that exploit "criminal deeds of bloodshed or lust" thereby "inciting violent and depraved crimes"? What real risk do the Conan

Doyles, the Edgar Allan Poes, the William Rougheads, the ordinary tribe of detective story writers, their publishers, or their booksellers run? . . .

The Court has been led into error, if I may respectfully suggest, by confusing want of certainty as to the outcome of different prosecutions for similar conduct, with want of definiteness in what the law prohibits. But diversity in result for similar conduct in different trials under the same statute is an unavoidable feature of criminal justice. So long as these diversities are not designed consequences but due merely to human fallibility, they do not deprive persons of due process of law. . . .

And so I conclude that New York, in the legislation before us, has not exceeded its constitutional power to control crime. The Court strikes down laws that forbid publications inciting to crime, and as such not within the constitutional immunity of free speech, because in effect it does not trust State tribunals, nor ultimately this Court, to safeguard inoffensive publications from condemnation under this legislation. Every legislative limitation upon utterance, however valid, may in a particular case serve as an inroad upon the freedom of speech which the Constitution protects. . . .

★ III ★

Freedom of Religion

1. Freedom to Believe and Freedom to Act

REYNOLDS v. UNITED STATES

98 US 145 (1878)

[The Constitution permits unlimited freedom of religious belief. There may be few absolutes in constitutional law, but freedom of religious belief is such an absolute.

[When it comes, however, to acting out one's belief, religious belief will not always exempt one from the provisions of the criminal law. The state may punish a person who handles a live copperhead snake even if he does this in the course of a religious or church service. *Bunn* v. *North Carolina,* 336 US 942 (1949), dismissing appeal of *State* v. *Massey,* 229 NC 734.

[For Mormons, polygamous marriages were at one time a religious duty. When Utah was a Territory, Congress enacted a statute making polygamy a criminal offense. This led to the *Reynolds Case* in the Supreme Court, which at once became a leading case. The opinion of Chief Justice Waite has often been cited and quoted. His opinion is notable also for his quotation from Jefferson's famous wall-of-separation letter, which was used effectively by the Court some seventy years later in the *Everson Case,* which is given later in this chapter.]

Mr. Chief Justice Waite delivered the opinion of the Court:

This is an indictment for bigamy under Section 5352, Revised Statutes, which, omitting its exceptions, is as follows: "Every person having a husband or wife living, who marries another, whether married or single, in a Territory, or other place over which the United States have exclusive jurisdiction, is guilty of bigamy, and shall be punished by a fine of not more than $500, and by imprisonment for a term of not more than five years." . . .

On the trial, the plaintiff in error, the accused, proved that at the time of his alleged second marriage he was, and for many years before had been, a member of the Church of Jesus Christ of Latter-Day Saints, commonly called the Mormon Church, and a believer in its doctrines; that it was an accepted doctrine of that church "That it was the duty of male members of said Church, circumstances permitting, to practice polygamy: . . . that this duty was enjoined by different books which the members of said Church believed to be of divine origin, and among others the Holy Bible, and also that the members of the Church believed that the practice of polygamy was directly enjoined upon the male members thereof by the Almighty God, in a revelation to Joseph Smith, the founder and prophet of said Church; that the failing or refusing to practice polygamy by such male members of said Church, when circumstances would admit, would be punished, and that the penalty for such failure and refusal would be damnation in the life to come." He also proved "That he had received permission from the recognized authorities in said Church to enter into polygamous marriage; . . . that Daniel H. Wells, one having authority in said Church to perform the marriage ceremony, married the said defendant on or about the time the crime is alleged to have been committed, to some woman by the name of Schofield, and that such marriage ceremony was performed under and pursuant to the doctrines of said Church."

Upon this proof he asked the court to instruct the jury that if they found from the evidence that he "was married as charged (if he was married) in pursuance of and in conformity with what he believed at the time to be religious duty, that the verdict must be 'not guilty.'" This request was refused, and the court did charge "That there must have been a criminal intent, but that if the defendant, under the influence of a religious belief that it was right—under an inspiration, if you please, that it was right—deliberately married a second time, having a first wife living, the want of consciousness of evil intent, the want of understanding on his part that he was committing a crime, did not excuse him; but the law inexorably in such case implies the criminal intent."

Upon this charge and refusal to charge the question is raised, whether religious belief can be accepted as a justification of an overt act made criminal by the law of the land. The inquiry is not as to the power of Congress to prescribe criminal laws for the Territories, but as to the guilt of one who knowingly violates a law which has been properly enacted, if he entertains a religious belief that the law is wrong.

Congress cannot pass a law for the government of the Territories which shall prohibit the free exercise of religion. The first amendment to the Constitution expressly forbids such legislation. Religious freedom is guarantied everywhere throughout the United States, so far as congressional interference is concerned. The question to be determined is, whether the law now under consideration comes within this prohibition.

The word "religion" is not defined in the Constitution. We must go elsewhere, therefore, to ascertain its meaning, and nowhere more appropriately, we think, than to the history of the times in the midst of which the provision was adopted. The precise point of the inquiry is, what is the religious freedom which has been guarantied?

Before the adoption of the Constitution, attempts were made in some of the Colonies and States to legislate not only in respect to the establishment of religion, but in respect to its doctrines and precepts as well. The people were taxed, against their will, for the support of religion, and sometimes for the support of particular sects to whose tenets they could not and did not subscribe. Punishments were prescribed for a failure to attend upon public worship, and sometimes for entertaining heretical opinions. The controversy upon this general subject was animated in many of the States, but seemed at last to culminate in Virginia. In 1784, the House of Delegates of that State having under consideration "A bill establishing provision for teachers of the Christian religion," postponed it until the next session, and directed that the bill should be published and distributed, and that the People be requested "to signify their opinion respecting the adoption of such a bill at the next session of Assembly."

This brought out a determined opposition. Amongst others, Mr. Madison prepared a "Memorial and Remonstrance," which was widely circulated and signed, and in which he demonstrated "that religion, or the duty we owe the Creator," was not within the cognizance of civil government. At the next session the proposed bill was not only defeated, but another, "for establishing religious freedom," drafted by Mr. Jefferson, was passed. In the preamble of this Act religious freedom is defined; and after a recital "That to suffer the civil magistrate to intrude his powers into the field of opinion, and to restrain the profession or propagation of principles on supposition of their ill tendency, is a dangerous fallacy which at once destroys all religious liberty," it is declared "that it is time enough for the rightful purposes of civil government for its officers to interfere when principles break out into overt acts against peace and good order." In these two sentences is found the true distinction between what properly belongs to the Church and what to the State.

In a little more than a year after the passage of this statute the convention met which prepared the Constitution of the United States. Of this convention Mr. Jefferson was not a member, he being then absent as minister to France. As soon as he saw the draft of the Constitution proposed for adoption, he, in a letter to a friend, expressed his disappointment at the absence of an express declaration insuring the freedom of religion, but was willing to accept it as it was, trusting that the good sense and honest intentions of the people would bring about the necessary alterations. Five of the States, while adopting the Constitution, proposed amendments. Three, New Hampshire, New York and Virginia, included in one form or another a declaration of religious freedom in the changes they desired to have made, as did also North Carolina, where the convention at first declined to ratify the Constitution until the proposed amendments were acted upon. Accordingly, at the first session of the first Congress the amendment now under consideration was proposed with others by Mr. Madison. It met the views of the advocates of religious freedom, and was adopted. Mr. Jefferson afterwards, in reply to an address to him by a committee of the Danbury Baptist Association, took occasion to say: "Believing with you that religion is a matter which lies solely between man and his God; that he owes account to none other for his faith or his worship; that the legislative powers of the Government reach actions only, and not opinions, I contemplate with sovereign reverence that act of the whole American people which declared that their Legislature should 'make no law respecting an establishment of religion or prohibiting the free exercise thereof,' thus building a wall of separation between Church and State. Adhering to this expression of the Supreme will of the Nation in behalf of the rights of conscience, I shall see, with sincere satisfaction, the progress of those sentiments which tend to restore man to all his natural rights, convinced he has no natural right in opposition to his social duties." Coming as this does from an acknowledged leader of the advocates of the measure, it may be accepted almost as an authoritative declaration of the scope and effect of the amendment thus secured. Congress was deprived of all legislative power over mere opinion, but was left free to reach actions which were in violation of social duties or subversive of good order.

Polygamy has always been odious among the Northern and Western Nations of Europe and, until the establishment of the Mormon Church, was almost exclusively a feature of the life of Asiatic and African people. At common law, the second marriage was always void, and from the earliest history of England polygamy has been treated as an offense against society. After the establishment of the ecclesiastical courts, and until the time of James I., it was punished through the instrumentality of those tribunals, not merely because ecclesiastical rights had been violated, but because upon the separation of the ecclesiastical courts from the civil, the ecclesiastical were supposed to be the most appropriate for the trial of matrimonial causes and offenses against the rights of marriage; just as they were for testamentary causes and the settlement of the estates of deceased persons.

By the Statute of 1 James I., ch. 11, the offense, if committed in England or Wales, was made punishable in the civil courts, and the penalty was death. As this statute was limited in its operation to England and Wales, it was at a very early period re-enacted, generally with some modifications, in all the Colonies. In connection with the case we are now considering, it is a significant fact that on the 8th of December, 1788, after the passage of the Act establishing religious freedom, and after the convention of Virginia had recommended as an amendment to the Constitution of the United States the declaration in a Bill of Rights that "All men have an equal, natural and unalienable right to the free exercise of religion, according to the dictates of conscience," the Legislature of that State substantially enacted the Statute of James I., death penalty included, because as recited in the preamble, "It hath been doubted whether bigamy or polygamy be punishable by the laws of this Commonwealth." From that day to this we think it may safely be said there never has been a time in any State of the Union when polygamy has not been an offense against society, cognizable by the civil courts and punishable with more or less severity. In the face of all this evidence, it is impossible to believe that the constitutional guaranty of religious freedom was intended to prohibit legislation in respect to this most important feature of social life. Marriage, while from its very nature a sacred obligation, is, nevertheless, in most civilized nations, a civil contract, and usually regulated by law. . . . There cannot be a doubt that, unless restricted by some form of constitution, it is within the legitimate scope of the power of every civil government to determine whether polygamy or monogamy shall be the law of social life under its dominion.

In our opinion the statute immediately under consideration is within the legislative power of Congress. It is constitutional and valid as prescribing a rule of action for all those residing in the Territories, and in places over which the United States have exclusive control. This being so, the only question which remains is, whether those who make polygamy a part of their religion are excepted from the operation of the statute. If they are, then those who do not make polygamy a part of their religious belief may be found guilty and punished, while those who do must be acquitted and go free. This would be introducing a new element into criminal law. Laws are made for the government of actions, and while they cannot interfere with mere religious belief and opinions, they may with practices. Suppose one believed that human sacrifices were a necessary part of religious worship, would it be seriously contended that the civil government under which he lived could not interfere to prevent a sacrifice? Or if a wife religiously believed it was her duty to burn herself upon the funeral pile of her dead husband, would it be beyond the power of the civil government to prevent her carrying her belief into practice?

So here, as a law of the organization of society under the exclusive dominion of the United States, it is provided that plural marriages shall not be allowed. Can a man excuse his practices to the contrary because of his religious belief? To permit this would be to make the professed doctrines of religious belief superior to the law of the land, and in effect to permit every citizen to become a law unto himself. Government could exist only in name under such circumstances.

A criminal intent is generally an element of crime, but every man is presumed to intend the necessary and legitimate consequences of what he knowingly does. Here the accused knew he had been once married, and that his first wife was living. He also knew that his second marriage was forbidden by law. When, therefore, he married the second time, he is presumed to have intended to break the law. And the breaking of the law is the crime. Every act necessary to constitute the crime was knowingly done, and the crime was, therefore, knowingly committed. Ignorance of a fact may sometimes be taken as evidence of a want of criminal intent, but not ignorance of the law. The only defense of the accused in this case is his belief that the law ought not to have been enacted. It matters not that his belief was a part of his professed religion; it was still belief, and belief only.

In *Regina* v. *Wagstaffe*, 10 Cox, Cr. Cas., 531, the parents of a sick child, who omitted to call in medical attendance because of their religious belief that what they did for its cure would be effective, were held not to be guilty of manslaughter, while it was said the contrary would have been the result if the child had actually been starved to death by the parents, under the notion that it was their religious duty to abstain from giving it food. But when the offense consists of a positive act which is knowingly done, it would be dangerous to hold that the offender might escape punishment because he religiously believed the law which he had broken ought never to have been made. No case, we believe, can be found that has gone so far. . . .

[Judgment of conviction affirmed.]

2. Wall of Separation between Church and State

a. Bus Fares for Parochial School Pupils

EVERSON v. BOARD OF EDUCATION OF TOWNSHIP OF EWING

330 US 1 (1947)

[In the preceding case, *Reynolds* v. *United States,* the Supreme Court quoted from Jefferson's wall-of-separation letter, but this was done only in passing. In the *Everson Case,* however, the Supreme Court for the first time spelled out the doctrine of the separation of church and state and held that the First Amendment clause against an establishment of religion was intended to erect, in Jefferson's words, "a wall of separation between Church and State." The Court also held that this meaning and intention of the First Amendment apply to both the Federal Government and the states.

[With respect to these issues there was unanimity in the Court; four Justices, however—Jackson, Frankfurter, Rutledge, and Burton—held that the majority of the Court were in error when they decided that the wall of separation had not been breached when tax money was used to reimburse parents for the transportation by bus of their children to and from Roman Catholic parochial schools. Such use of public money, said the dissenting Justices, is a violation by the state of the provision of the First Amendment that no law shall be made "respecting an establishment of religion."

[This decision was sharply attacked by the Roman Catholic bishops of the United States in a public statement published on November 21, 1948. The statement argued that Jefferson's "metaphor" specifies only that there shall be no "established Church," no state religion; that the First Amendment means only that the Federal Government may not prefer one religion over another; that this amendment is no limitation on the powers of the states; that the decision pointed up the "impending danger of a judicial 'establishment of secularism' that would ban God from public life."

[Much use has been made of the decision of the Court and of the attacks on the decision in the controversy over congressional bills to use federal funds to aid elementary and secondary education—a controversy that has often agitated and divided the American people.]

Mr. Justice Black delivered the opinion of the Court:

A New Jersey statute authorizes its local school districts to make rules and contracts for the transportation of children to and from schools. The appellee, a township board of education, acting pursuant to this statute, authorized reimbursement to parents of money expended by them for the bus transportation of their children on regular busses operated by the public transportation system. Part of this money was for the payment of transportation of some children in the community to Catholic parochial schools. These church schools give their students, in addition to secular education, regular religious instruction conforming to the religious tenets and modes of worship of the Catholic faith. The superintendent of these schools is a Catholic priest.

The appellant, in his capacity as a district taxpayer, filed suit in a State court challenging the right of the Board to reimburse parents of parochial school students. . . .

The only contention here is that the State statute and the resolution, insofar as they authorized reimbursement to parents of children attending parochial schools, violate the Federal Constitution. . . .

The New Jersey statute is challenged as a "law respecting the establishment of religion." The First Amendment, as made applicable to the states by the Fourteenth, . . . commands that a state "shall make no law respecting an establishment of religion, or prohibiting the free exercise thereof." . . . These words of the First Amendment reflected in the minds of early Americans a vivid mental picture of conditions and practices which they fervently wished to stamp out in order to preserve liberty for themselves and for their posterity. Doubtless their goal has not been entirely reached; but so far has the Nation moved toward it that the expression, "law respecting the establishment of religion," probably does not so vividly remind present-day Americans of the evils, fears, and political problems that caused that expression to be written into our Bill of Rights. Whether this New Jersey law is one respecting an "establishment of religion" requires an understanding of the meaning of that language, particularly with respect to the imposition of taxes. Once again, therefore, it is not inappropriate briefly to review the background and environment of the period in which that constitutional language was fashioned and adopted.

A large proportion of the early settlers of this country came here from Europe to escape the bondage of laws which compelled them to support and attend government favored churches. The centuries immediately before and contemporaneous with the colonization of America had been filled with turmoil, civil strife, and persecutions, generated in large part by established sects determined to maintain their absolute political and religious supremacy. With the power of government supporting them, at various times and places, Catholics had persecuted Protestants, Protestants had persecuted Catholics, Protestant sects had persecuted other Protestant sects, Catholics of one shade of belief had persecuted Catholics of another shade of belief, and all of these had from time to time persecuted Jews. In efforts to force loyalty to whatever religious group happened to be on top and in league with the government of a particular time and place, men and women had been fined, cast in jail, cruelly tortured, and killed. Among the offenses for which these punishments had been inflicted were such things as speaking disrespectfully of the views of ministers of government-established churches, non-attendance at those churches, expressions of non-belief in their doctrine, and failure to pay taxes and tithes to support them.

These practices of the old world were transplanted to and began to thrive in the soil of the new America. The very charters granted by the English Crown to the individuals and companies designated to make the laws which would control the destinies of the colonials authorized these individuals and companies to erect religious establishments which all, whether believers or nonbelievers, would be required to support and attend. An exercise of this authority was accompanied by a repetition of many of the old-world practices and persecutions. Catholics found themselves hounded and proscribed because of their faith; Quakers who followed their conscience went to jail; Baptists were peculiarly obnoxious to certain dominant Protestant sects; men and women of varied faiths who happened to be in a minority in a particular locality were persecuted because they steadfastly persisted in worshipping God only as their own consciences dictated. And all of these dissenters were compelled to pay tithes and taxes to support government-sponsored churches whose ministers preached inflammatory sermons designed to strengthen and consolidate the established faith by generating a burning hatred against dissenters.

These practices became so commonplace as to shock the freedom-loving colonials into a feeling of abhorrence. The imposition of taxes to pay ministers' salaries and to build and maintain churches and church property aroused their indignation. It was these feelings which found expression in the First Amendment. No one locality and no one group throughout the Colonies can rightly be given entire credit for having aroused the sentiment that culminated in adoption of the Bill of Rights' provisions embracing religious liberty. But Virginia, where the established church had achieved a dominant influence in political affairs and where many excesses attracted wide public attention, provided a great stimulus and able leadership for the movement. The people there, as elsewhere, reached the conviction that individual religious liberty could be achieved best under a government which was stripped of all power to tax, to support, or otherwise to assist any or all religions, or to interfere with the beliefs of any religious individual or group.

The movement toward this end reached its dramatic climax in Virginia in 1785–86 when the Virginia legislative body was about to renew Virginia's tax levy for the support of the established church. Thomas Jefferson and James Madison led the fight against this tax. Madison wrote his great Memorial and Remonstrance against the law. In it, he eloquently argued that a true religion did not need the support of law; that no person, either believer or non-believer, should be taxed to support a religious institution of any kind; that the best interest of a society required that the minds of men always be wholly free; and that cruel persecutions were the inevitable result of government-established religions. Madison's Remonstrance received strong support throughout Virginia, and the Assembly postponed consideration of the proposed tax measure until its next session. When the proposal came up for consideration at that session, it not only died in committee, but the Assembly enacted the famous "Virginia Bill for Religious Liberty" originally written by Thomas Jefferson. The preamble to that Bill stated among other things that

Almighty God hath created the mind free; that all attempts to influence it by temporal punishments or burthens, or by civil incapacitations, tend only to beget habits of hypocrisy and meanness, and are a departure from the plan of the Holy author of our religion, who being Lord both of body and mind, yet chose not to propagate it by coercions on either . . . ; that to compel a man to furnish contributions of money for the propagation of opinions which he disbelieves, is sinful and tyrannical; that even the forcing him to support this or that teacher of his own religious persuasion, is depriving him of the comfortable liberty of giving his contributions to the particular pastor, whose morals he would make his pattern. . . .

And the statute itself enacted

That no man shall be compelled to frequent or support any religious worship, place, or ministry whatsoever, nor shall be enforced, restrained, molested, or burthened in his body or goods, nor shall otherwise suffer on account of his religious opinions or belief. . . .

This Court has previously recognized that the provisions of the First Amendment, in the drafting and adoption of which Madison and Jefferson played such leading roles, had the same objective and were intended to provide the same protection against governmental intrusion on religious liberty as the Virginia statute. . . . Prior to the adoption of the Fourteenth Amendment, the First Amendment did not apply as a restraint against the states. Most of them did soon provide similar constitutional protections for religious liberty. But some states persisted for about half a century in imposing restraints upon the free exercise of religion and in discriminating against particular religious group[s]. In recent years, so far as the provision against the establishment of a religion is concerned, the question has most frequently arisen in connection with proposed state aid to church schools and efforts to carry on religious teachings in the public schools in accordance with the tenets of a particular sect. Some churches have either sought or accepted state financial support for their schools. Here again the efforts to obtain state aid or acceptance of it have not been limited to any one particular faith. The state courts, in the main, have remained faithful to the language of their own constitutional provisions designed to protect religious freedom and to separate religions and governments. Their decisions, however, show the difficulty in drawing the line between tax legislation which provides funds for the welfare of the general public and that which is designed to support institutions which teach religion.

The meaning and scope of the First Amendment, preventing establishment of religion or prohibiting the free exercise thereof, in the light of its history and the evils it was designed forever to suppress, have been several times elaborated by the decisions of this Court prior to the application of the First Amendment to the states by the Fourteenth. The broad meaning given the Amendment by these earlier cases has been accepted by this Court in its decisions concerning an individual's religious fredom rendered since the Fourteenth Amendment was interpreted to make the prohibitions of the First applicable to state action abridging religious freedom. There is every reason to give the same application and broad interpretation to the "establishment of religion" clause. . . .

The "establishment of religion" clause of the First Amendment means at least this: Neither a state nor the Federal Government can set up a church. Neither can pass laws which aid one religion, aid all religions, or prefer one religion over another. Neither can force nor influence a person to go to or to remain away from church against his will or force him to profess a belief or disbelief in any religion. No person can be punished for entertaining or professing religious beliefs or disbeliefs, for church attendance or non-attendance. No tax in any amount, large or small, can be levied to support any religious activities or institutions, whatever they may be called, or whatever form they may adopt to teach or practice religion. Neither a state nor the Federal Government can, openly or secretly, participate in the affairs of any religious organizations or groups and vice versa. In the words of Jefferson, the clause against establishment of religion by law was intended to erect "a wall of separation between Church and State." . . .

We must consider the New Jersey statute in accordance with the foregoing limitations imposed by the First Amendment. But we must not strike that state statute down if it is within the State's constitutional power even though it approaches the verge of that power. . . . New Jersey cannot consistently with the "establishment of religion" clause of the First Amendment contribute tax-raised funds to the support of an institution which teaches the tenets and faith of any church. On the other hand, other language of the amendment commands that New Jersey cannot hamper its citizens in the free exercise of their own religion. Consequently, it cannot exclude individual Catholics, Lutherans, Mohammedans, Baptists, Jews, Methodists, Non-believers, Presbyterians, or the members of any other faith, *because of their faith, or lack of it,* from receiving the benefits of public welfare legislation. While we do not mean to intimate that a state could not provide transportation only to children attending public schools, we must be careful, in protecting the citizens of New Jersey against state-established churches, to be sure that we do not inadvertently prohibit New Jersey from extending its general state law benefits to all its citizens without regard to their religious belief.

Measured by these standards, we cannot say that the First Amendment prohibits New Jersey from spending tax-raised funds to pay the bus fares of parochial school pupils as a part of a general program under which it pays the fares of pupils attending public and other schools. It is undoubtedly true that children are helped to get to church schools. There is even a possibility that some of the children might not be sent to the church schools if the parents were compelled to pay [for] their children going to and from church [schools out of their own] pockets when transportation to a public school would have been paid for by the State. The same possibility exists where the state requires a local transit company to provide reduced fares to school children including those attending parochial schools, or where a municipally owned transportation system undertakes to carry all school children free of charge. Moreover, state-paid policemen, detailed to protect children going to and from church schools from the very real hazards of traffic, would serve much the same purpose and accomplish much the same result as state provisions intended to guarantee free transportation of a kind which the state deems to be best for the school children's welfare. And parents might refuse to risk their children to the serious danger of traffic accidents going to and from parochial schools, the approaches to which were not protected by policemen.

Similarly, parents might be reluctant to permit their children to attend schools which the state had cut off from such general government services as ordinary police and fire protection, connections for sewage disposal, public highways and sidewalks. Of course, cutting off church schools from these services, so separate and so indisputably marked off from the religious function, would make it far more difficult for the schools to operate. But such is obviously not the purpose of the First Amendment. That Amendment requires the state to be a neutral in its relations with groups of religious believers and non-believers; it does not require the state to be their adversary. State power is no more to be used so as to handicap religions than it is to favor them.

This Court has said that parents may, in the discharge of their duty under state compulsory education laws, send their children to a religious rather than a public school if the school meets the secular educational requirements which the state has power to impose. . . . It appears that these parochial schools meet New Jersey's requirements. The State contributes no money to the schools. It does not support them. Its legislation, as applied, does no more than provide a general program to help parents get their children, regardless of their religion, safely and expeditiously to and from accredited schools.

The First Amendment has erected a wall between church and state. That wall must be kept high and impregnable. We could not approve the slightest breach. New Jersey has not breached it here.

Affirmed.

Mr. Justice Jackson, dissenting:

I find myself, contrary to first impressions, unable to join in this decision. I have a sympathy, though it is not ideological, with Catholic citizens who are compelled by law to pay taxes for public schools, and also feel constrained by conscience and discipline to support other schools for their own children. Such relief to them as this case involves is not in itself a serious burden to taxpayers and I had assumed it to be as little serious in principle. Study of this case convinces me otherwise. The Court's opinion marshals every argument in favor of state aid and puts the case in its most favorable light, but much of its reasoning confirms my conclusions that there are no good grounds upon which to support the present legislation. In fact, the undertones of the opinion, advocating complete and uncompromising separation of Church from State, seem utterly discordant with its conclusion yielding support to their commingling in educational matters. The case which irresistibly comes to mind as the most fitting precedent is that of Julia who, according to Byron's reports, "whispering 'I will ne'er consent,'—consented."

The Township of Ewing is not furnishing transportation to the children in any form; it is not operating school busses itself or contracting for their operation; and it is not performing any public service of any kind with this taxpayer's money. All school children are left to ride as ordinary paying passengers on the regular busses operated by the public transportation system. What the Township does, and what the taxpayer complains of, is at stated intervals to reimburse parents for the fares paid, provided the children attend either public schools or Catholic Church schools. This expenditure of tax funds has no possible effect on the child's safety or expedition in transit. As passengers on the public busses they travel as fast and no faster, and are as safe and no safer, since their parents are reimbursed as before. . . .

Whether the taxpayer constitutionally can be made to contribute aid to parents of students because of their attendance at parochial schools depends upon the nature of those schools and their relation to the Church. The Constitution says nothing of education. It lays no obligation on the states to provide schools and does not undertake to regulate state systems of education if they see fit to maintain them. But they cannot, through school policy any more than through other means, invade rights secured to citizens by the Constitution of the United States. . . . One of our basic rights is to be free of taxation to support a transgression of the constitutional command that the authorities "shall make no law respecting an establishment of religion, or prohibiting the free exercise thereof." . . .

The function of the Church school is a subject on which this record is meager. It shows only that the schools are under superintendence of a priest and that "religion is taught as part of the curriculum." But we know that such schools are parochial only in name—they, in fact, represent a world-wide and age-old policy of the Roman Catholic Church. Under the rubric "Catholic Schools," the Canon Law of the Church, by which all Catholics are bound, provides:

> 1215. Catholic children are to be educated in schools where not only nothing contrary to Catholic faith and morals is taught, but rather in schools where religious and moral training occupy the first place. . . .
>
> 1216. In every elementary school the children must, according to their age, be instructed in Christian doctrine.
>
> The young people who attend the higher schools are to receive a deeper religious knowledge, and the bishops shall appoint priests qualified for such work by their learning and piety.
>
> 1217. Catholic children shall not attend non-Catholic, indifferent, schools that are mixed, that is to say, schools open to Catholics and non-Catholics alike. The bishop of the diocese only has the right, in harmony with the instructions of the Holy See, to decide under what circumstances, and with what safeguards to prevent loss of faith, it may be tolerated that Catholic children go to such schools.
>
> 1224. The religious teaching of youth in any school is subject to the authority and inspection of the Church.
>
> The local Ordinaries have the right and duty to watch that nothing is taught contrary to faith or good morals, in any of the schools of their territory.
>
> They, moreover, have the right to approve the books of Christian

doctrine and the teachers of religion, and to demand, for the sake of safeguarding religion and morals, the removal of teachers and books. . . .

It is no exaggeration to say that the whole historic conflict in temporal policy between the Catholic Church and non-Catholics comes to a focus in their respective school policies. The Roman Catholic Church, counseled by experience in many ages and many lands and with all sorts and conditions of men, takes what, from the viewpoint of its own progress and the success of its mission, is a wise estimate of the importance of education to religion. It does not leave the individual to pick up religion by chance. It relies on early and indelible indoctrination in the faith and order of the Church by the word and example of persons consecrated to the task.

Our public school, if not a product of Protestantism, at least is more consistent with it than with the Catholic culture and scheme of values. It is a relatively recent development dating from about 1840. It is organized on the premises that secular education can be isolated from all religious teaching so that the school can inculcate all needed temporal knowledge and also maintain a strict and lofty neutrality as to religion. The assumption is that after the individual has been instructed in worldly wisdom he will be better fitted to choose his religion. Whether such a disjunction is possible, and if possible whether it is wise, are questions I need not try to answer.

I should be surprised if any Catholic would deny that the parochial school is a vital, if not the most vital, part of the Roman Catholic Church. If put to the choice, that venerable institution, I should expect, would forego its whole service for mature persons before it would give up education of the young, and it would be a wise choice. Its growth and cohesion, discipline and loyalty, spring from its schools. Catholic education is the rock on which the whole structure rests, and to render tax aid to its Church school is indistinguishable to me from rendering the same aid to the Church itself.

It is of no importance in this situation whether the beneficiary of this expenditure of tax-raised funds is primarily the parochial school and incidentally the pupil, or whether the aid is directly bestowed on the pupil with indirect benefits to the school. The state cannot maintain a Church and it can no more tax its citizens to furnish free carriage to those who attend a Church. The prohibition against establishment of religion cannot be circumvented by a subsidy, bonus or reimbursement of expense to individuals for receiving religious instruction and indoctrination.

The Court, however, compares this to other subsidies and loans to individuals and says, "Nor does it follow that a law has a private rather than a public purpose because it provides that tax-raised funds will be paid to reimburse individuals on account of money spent by them in a way which furthers a public program. . . ." Of course, the state may pay out tax-raised funds to relieve pauperism, but it may not under our Constitution do so to induce or reward piety. It may spend funds to secure old age against want, but it may not spend funds to secure religion against skepticism. It may compensate individuals for loss of employment, but it cannot compensate them for adherence to a creed.

It seems to me that the basic fallacy in the Court's reasoning, which accounts for its failure to apply the principles it avows, is in ignoring the essentially religious test by which beneficiaries of this expenditure are selected. A policeman protects a Catholic, of course—but not because he is a Catholic; it is because he is a man and a member of our society. The fireman protects the Church school—but not because it is a Church school; it is because it is property, part of the assets of our society. Neither the fireman nor the policeman has to ask before he renders aid "Is this man or building identified with the Catholic Church?" But before these school authorities draw a check to reimburse for a student's fare they must ask just that question, and if the school is a Catholic one they may render aid because it is such, while if it is of any other faith or is run for profit, the help must be withheld. To consider the converse of the Court's reasoning will best disclose its fallacy. That there is no parallel between police and fire protection and this plan of reimbursement is apparent from the incongruity of the limitation of this Act if applied to police and fire service. Could we sustain an Act that said the police shall protect pupils on the way to or from public schools and Catholic schools but not while going to and coming from other schools, and firemen shall extinguish a blaze in public or Catholic school buildings but shall not put out a blaze in Protestant Church schools or private schools operated for profit? That is the true analogy to the case we have before us and I should think it pretty plain that such a scheme would not be valid. . . .

There is no answer to the proposition, more fully expounded by Mr. Justice Rutledge, that the effect of the religious freedom Amendment to our Constitution was to take every form of propagation of religion out of the realm of things which could directly or indirectly be made public business and thereby be supported in whole or in part at taxpayers' expense. That is a difference which the Constitution sets up between religion and almost every other subject matter of legislation, a difference which goes to the very root of religious freedom and which the Court is overlooking today. This freedom was first in the Bill of Rights because it was first in the forefathers' minds; it was set forth in absolute terms, and its strength is its rigidity. It was intended not only to keep the states' hands out of religion, but to keep religion's hands off the state, and, above all, to keep bitter religious controversy out of public life by denying to every denomination any advantage from getting control of public policy or the public purse. Those great ends I cannot but think are immeasurably compromised by today's decision.

This policy of our Federal Constitution has never been wholly pleasing to most religious groups. They all are quick to invoke its protections; they all are irked when they feel its restraints. . . .

I cannot read the history of the struggle to separate political from ecclesiastical affairs, well summarized in the opinion of Mr. Justice Rutledge in which I generally concur, without a conviction that the Court today is unconsciously giving the clock's hands a backward turn.

Mr. Justice Frankfurter joins in this opinion.

Mr. Justice Rutledge, with whom Mr. Justice Frankfurter, Mr. Justice Jackson and Mr. Justice Burton agree, dissenting:

Congress shall make no law respecting an establishment of religion, or prohibiting the free exercise thereof. . . ." US Const, Am Art 1.

Well aware that Almighty God hath created the mind free; . . . that to compel a man to furnish contributions of money for the propagation of opinions which he disbelieves, is sinful and tyrannical . . .

We, the General Assembly, do enact, That no man shall be compelled to frequent or support any religious worship, place, or ministry whatsoever, nor shall be enforced, restrained, molested, or burthened in his body or goods, nor shall otherwise suffer, on account of his religious opinions or belief. . . .

I cannot believe that the great author of those words [Jefferson], or the men who made them law, could have joined in this decision. Neither so high nor so impregnable today as yesterday is the wall raised between church and state by Virginia's great statute of religious freedom and the First Amendment, now made applicable to all the states by the Fourteenth. New Jersey's statute sustained is the first, if indeed it is not the second breach to be made by this Court's action. That a third, and a fourth, and still others will be attempted, we may be sure. . . .

This case forces us to determine squarely for the first time what was "an establishment of religion" in the First Amendment's conception; and by that measure to decide whether New Jersey's action violates its command. . . .

I.

Not simply an established church, but any law respecting an establishment of religion is forbidden. The Amendment was broadly but not loosely phrased. It is the compact and exact summation of its author's views formed during his long struggle for religious freedom. In Madison's own words characterizing Jefferson's Bill for Establishing Religious Freedom, the guaranty he put in our national charter, like the bill he piloted through the Virginia Assembly, was "a Model of technical precision, and perspicuous brevity." Madison could not have confused "church" and "religion," or "an established church" and "an establishment of religion."

The Amendment's purpose was not to strike merely at the official establishment of a single sect, creed or religion, outlawing only a formal relation such as had prevailed in England and some of the colonies. Necessarily it was to uproot all such relationships. But the object was broader than separating church and state in this narrow sense. It was to create a complete and permanent separation of the spheres of religious activity and civil authority by comprehensively forbidding every form of public aid or support for religion. In proof the Amendment's wording and history unite with this Court's consistent utterances whenever attention has been fixed directly upon the question.

"Religion" appears only once in the Amendment. But the word governs two prohibitions and governs them alike. It does not have two meanings, one narrow to forbid "an establishment" and another, much broader, for securing "the free exercise thereof." "Thereof" brings down "religion" with its entire and exact content, no more and no less, from the first into the second guaranty, so that Congress and now the states are as broadly restricted concerning the one as they are regarding the other.

No one would claim today that the Amendment is constricted, in "prohibiting the free exercise" of religion, to securing the free exercise of some formal or creedal observance, of one sect or of many. It secures all forms of religious expression, creedal, sectarian or nonsectarian, wherever and however taking place, except conduct which trenches upon the like freedoms of others or clearly and presently endangers the community's good order and security. For the protective purposes of this phase of the basic freedom, street preaching, oral or by distribution of literature, has been given "the same high estate under the First Amendment as . . . worship in the churches and preaching from the pulpits." And on this basis parents have been held entitled to send their children to private, religious schools. . . . Accordingly, daily religious education commingled with secular is "religion" within the guaranty's comprehensive scope. So are religious training and teaching in whatever form. The word connotes the broadest content, determined not by the form or formality of the teaching or where it occurs, but by its essential nature regardless of those details.

"Religion" has the same broad significance in the twin prohibition concerning "an establishment." The Amendment was not duplicitous. "Religion" and "establishment" were not used in any formal or technical sense. The prohibition broadly forbids state support, financial or other, of religion in any guise, form or degree. It outlaws all use of public funds for religious purposes.

II.

No provision of the Constitution is more closely tied to or given content by its generating history than the religious clause of the First Amendment. It is at once the refined product and the terse summation of that history. The history includes not only Madison's authorship and the proceedings before the First Congress, but also the long and intensive struggle for religious freedom in America, more especially in Virginia, of which the Amendment was the direct culmination. In the documents of the times, particularly of Madison, who was leader in the Virginia struggle before he became the Amendment's sponsor, but also in the writings of Jefferson and others and in the issues which engendered them is to be found irrefutable confirmation of the Amendment's sweeping content.

For Madison, as also for Jefferson, religious freedom was the crux of the struggle for freedom in general. . . . Madison was coauthor with George Mason of the religious clause in Virginia's great Declaration of Rights of 1776. He is credited with changing it from a mere statement of the principle of tolerance to the first official legislative pronouncement that freedom of conscience and religion are inherent rights of the individual. He sought also to have the Declaration expressly condemn the existing Virginia establishment. But the forces supporting it were then too strong.

Accordingly Madison yielded on this phase but not for long. At once he resumed the fight, continuing it before succeeding legislative sessions. As a member of the General Assembly in 1779 he threw his full weight behind Jefferson's historic Bill for Establishing Religious Freedom. That bill was a prime phase of Jefferson's broad program of democratic reform undertaken on his return from the Continental Congress in 1776 and submitted for the General Assembly's consideration in 1779 as his proposed revised Virginia code. With Jefferson's departure for Europe in 1784, Madison became the Bill's prime sponsor. Enactment failed in successive legislatures from its introduction in June, 1779, until its adoption in January, 1786. But during all this time the fight for religious freedom moved forward in Virginia on various fronts with growing intensity. Madison led throughout, against Patrick Henry's powerful opposing leadership until Henry was elected governor in November, 1784.

The climax came in the legislative struggle of 1784–1785 over the Assessment Bill. . . . This was nothing more nor less than a taxing measure for the support of religion, designed to revive the payment of tithes suspended since 1777. So long as it singled out a particular sect for preference it incurred the active and general hostility of dissentient groups. It was broadened to include them, with the result that some subsided temporarily in their opposition. As altered, the bill gave to each taxpayer the privilege of designating which church should receive his share of the tax. In default of designation the legislature applied it to pious uses. But what is of the utmost significance here, "in its final form the bill left the taxpayer the option of giving his tax to education."

Madison was unyielding at all times, opposing with all his vigor the general and nondiscriminatory as he had the earlier particular and discriminatory assessments proposed. The modified Assessment Bill passed second reading in December, 1784, and was all but enacted. Madison and his followers, however, maneuvered deferment of final consideration until November, 1785. And before the Assembly reconvened in the fall he issued his historic Memorial and Remonstrance.

This is Madison's complete, though not his only, interpretation of religious liberty. It is a broadside attack upon all forms of "establishment" of religion, both general and particular, nondiscriminatory or selective. Reflecting not only the many legislative conflicts over the Assessment Bill and the Bill for Establishing Religious Freedom but also, for example, the struggles for religious incorporations and the continued maintenance of the glebes, the Remonstrance is at once the most concise and the most accurate statement of the views of the First Amendment's author concerning what is "an establishment of religion." . . .

The Remonstrance, stirring up a storm of popular protest, killed the Assessment Bill. It collapsed in committee shortly before Christmas, 1785. With this, the way was cleared at last for enactment of Jefferson's bill for Establishing Religious Freedom. Madison promptly drove it through in January of 1786, seven years from the time it was first introduced. This dual victory substantially ended the fight over establishments, settling the issue against them. . . .

The next year Madison became a member of the Constitutional Convention. Its work done, he fought valiantly to secure the ratification of its great product in Virginia as elsewhere, and nowhere else more effectively. Madison was certain in his own mind that under the Constitution "there is not a shadow of right in the general government to intermeddle with religion" and that "this subject is, for the honor of America, perfectly free and unshackled. The government has no jurisdiction over it. . . ." Nevertheless he pledged that he would work for a Bill of Rights, including a specific guaranty of religious freedom, and Virginia, with other states, ratified the Constitution on this assurance.

Ratification thus accomplished, Madison was sent to the first Congress. There he went at once about performing his pledge to establish freedom for the nation as he had done in Virginia. Within a little more than three years from his lgislative victory at home he had proposed and secured the submission and ratification of the First Amendment as the first article of our Bill of Rights.

All the great instruments of the Virginia struggle for religious liberty thus became warp and woof of our constitutional tradition, not simply by the course of history, but by the common unifying force of Madison's life, thought and sponsorship. He epitomized the whole of that tradition in the Amendment's compact, but nonetheless comprehensive, phrasing.

As the Remonstrance discloses throughout, Madison opposed every form and degree of official relation between religion and civil authority. For him religion was a wholly private matter beyond the scope of civil power either to restrain or to support. Denial or abridgment of religious freedom was a violation of rights both of conscience and of natural equality. State aid was no less obnoxious or destructive to freedom and to religion itself than other forms of state interference. "Establishment" and "free exercise" were correlative and coextensive ideas, representing only different facets of the single great and fundamental freedom. The Remonstrance, following the Virginia statute's example, referred to the history of religious conflict and the effects of all sorts of establishments, current and historical, to suppress religion's free exercise. With Jefferson, Madison believed that to tolerate any fragment of establishment would be by so much to perpetuate restraint upon that freedom. Hence he sought to tear out the institution not partially but root and branch, and to bar its return forever.

In no phase was he more unrelentingly absolute than in opposing state support or aid by taxation. Not even "three pence" contribution was thus to be exacted from any citizen for such a purpose. Remonstrance, ¶ 3. Tithes had been the lifeblood of establishment before and after other compulsions disappeared. Madison and his coworkers made no exceptions or abridgments to the complete separation they created. Their objection was not to small tithes. It was to any tithes whatsoever. "If it were lawful to impose a small

tax for religion, the admission would pave the way for oppressive levies."
Not the amount but "the principle of assessment was wrong." And the principle was as much to prevent "the interference of law in religion" as to restrain
religious intervention in political matters. In this field the authors of our
freedom would not tolerate "the first experiment on our liberties" or "wait
till usurped power had strengthened itself by exercise, and entangled the
question in precedents." Remonstrance, ¶ 3. Nor should we.

In view of this history no further proof is needed that the Amendment
forbids any appropriation, large or small, from public funds to aid or support
any and all religious exercises. But if more were called for, the debates in
the First Congress and this Court's consistent expressions, whenever it has
touched on the matter directly, supply it.

By contrast with the Virginia history, the congressional debates on consideration of the Amendment reveal only sparse discussion, reflecting the
fact that the essential issues had been settled. Indeed the matter had become
so well understood as to have been taken for granted in all but formal phrasing. Hence, the only enlightening reference shows concern, not to preserve
any power to use public funds in aid of religion, but to prevent the Amendment from outlawing private gifts inadvertently by virtue of the breadth of
its wording. . . .

III.

Compulsory attendance upon religious exercises went out early in the
process of separating church and state, together with forced observance of
religious forms and ceremonies. Test oaths and religious qualification for
office followed later. These things none devoted to our great tradition of
religious liberty would think of bringing back. Hence today, apart from
efforts to inject religious training or exercises and sectarian issues into the
public schools, the only serious surviving threat to maintaining that complete
and permanent separation of religion and civil power which the First Amendment commands is through use of the taxing power to support religion, religious establishments, or establishments having a religious foundation whatever their form or special religious function.

Does New Jersey's action furnish support for religion by use of the taxing
power? Certainly it does, if the test remains undiluted as Jefferson and Madison made it, that money taken by taxation from one is not to be used or given
to support another's religious training or belief, or indeed one's own. Today
as then the furnishing of "contributions of money for the propagation of
opinions which he disbelieves" is the forbidden exaction; and the prohibition is absolute for whatever measure brings that consequence and whatever
amount may be sought or given to that end.

The funds used here were raised by taxation. The Court does not dispute,
nor could it, that their use does in fact give aid and encouragement to religious instruction. It only concludes that this aid is not "support" in law. But
Madison and Jefferson were concerned with aid and support in fact, not
as a legal conclusion "entangled in precedents." . . . Here parents pay
money to send their children to parochial schools and funds raised by taxa-

tion are used to reimburse them. This not only helps the children to get to school and the parents to send them. It aids them in a substantial way to get the very thing which they are sent to the particular school to secure, namely, religious training and teaching.

Believers of all faiths, and others who do not express their feeling toward ultimate issues of existence in any creedal form, pay the New Jersey tax. When the money so raised is used to pay for transportation to religious schools, the Catholic taxpayer to the extent of his proportionate share pays for the transportation of Lutheran, Jewish and otherwise religiously affiliated children to receive their non-Catholic religious instruction. Their parents likewise pay proportionately for the transportation of Catholic children to receive Catholic instruction. Each thus contributes to "the propagation of opinions which he disbelieves" in so far as their religions differ, as do others who accept no creed without regard to those differences. Each thus pays taxes also to support the teaching of his own religion, an exaction equally forbidden since it denies "the comfortable liberty" of giving one's contribution to the particular agency of instruction he approves.

New Jersey's action therefore exactly fits the type of exaction and the kind of evil at which Madison and Jefferson struck. Under the test they framed it cannot be said that the cost of transportation is no part of the cost of education or of the religious instruction given. That it is a substantial and a necessary element is shown most plainly by the continuing and increasing demand for the state to assume it. Nor is there pretense that it relates only to the secular instruction given in religious schools or that any attempt is or could be made toward allocating proportional shares as between the secular and the religious instruction. It is precisely because the instruction is religious and relates to a particular faith, whether one or another, that parents send their children to religious schools. . . . And the very purpose of the state's contribution is to defray the cost of conveying the pupil to the place where he will receive not simply secular, but also and primarily religious, teaching and guidance.

Indeed the view is sincerely avowed by many of various faiths, that the basic purpose of all education is or should be religious, that the secular cannot be and should not be separated from the religious phase and emphasis. Hence, the inadequacy of public or secular education and the necessity for sending the child to a school where religion is taught. But whatever may be the philosophy or its justification, there is undeniably an admixture of religious with secular teaching in all such institutions. That is the very reason for their being. Certainly for purposes of constitutionality we cannot contradict the whole basis of the ethical and educational convictions of people who believe in religious schooling.

Yet this very admixture is what was disestablished when the First Amendment forbade "an establishment of religion." Commingling the religious with the secular teaching does not divest the whole of its religious permeation and emphasis or make them of minor part, if proportion were material. Indeed, on any other view, the constitutional prohibition always could be brought to naught by adding a modicum of the secular.

An appropriation from the public treasury to pay the cost of transportation to Sunday school, to weekday special classes at the church or parish house, or to the meetings of various young people's religious societies, such as the Y.M.C.A., the Y.W.C.A., the Y.M.H.A., the Epworth League, could not withstand the constitutional attack. This would be true, whether or not secular activities were mixed with the religious. If such an appropriation could not stand, then it is hard to see how one becomes valid for the same thing upon the more extended scale of daily instruction. Surely constitutionality does not turn on where or how often the mixed teaching occurs.

Finally, transportation, where it is needed, is as essential to education as any other element. Its cost is as much a part of the total expense, except at times in amount, as the cost of textbooks, of school lunches, of athletic equipment, of writing and other materials; indeed of all other items composing the total burden. Now as always the core of the educational process is the teacher-pupil relationship. Without this the richest equipment and facilities would go for naught. . . . Without buildings, without equipment, without library, textbooks and other materials, and without transportation to bring teacher and pupil together in such an effective teaching environment, there can be not even the skeleton of what our times require. Hardly can it be maintained that transportation is the least essential of these items, or that it does not in fact aid, encourage, sustain and support, just as they do, the very process which is its purpose to accomplish. No less essential is it, or the payment of its cost, than the very teaching in the classroom or payment of the teacher's sustenance. Many types of equipment, now considered essential, better could be done without.

For me, therefore, the feat is impossible to select so indispensable an item from the composite of total costs, and characterize it as not aiding, contributing to, promoting or sustaining the propagation of beliefs which it is the very end of all to bring about. Unless this can be maintained, and the Court does not maintain it, the aid thus given is outlawed. Payment of transportation is no more, nor is it any the less essential to education, whether religious or secular, than payment for tuitions, for teachers' salaries, for buildings, equipment and necessary materials. Nor is it any the less directly related, in a school giving religious instruction, to the primary religious objective all those essential items of cost are intended to achieve. No rational line can be drawn between payment for such larger, but not more necessary, items and payment for transportation. The only line that can be so drawn is one between more dollars and less. Certainly in this realm such a line can be no valid constitutional measure. . . . Now, as in Madison's time, not the amount but the principle of assessment is wrong. . . .

IV.

. . . To say that New Jersey's appropriation and her use of the power of taxation for raising the funds appropriated are not for public purposes but are for private ends, is to say that they are for the support of religion and religious teaching. Conversely, to say that they are for public purposes is to say that they are not for religious ones.

This is precisely for the reason that education which includes religious training and teaching, and its support, have been made matters of private right and function, not public, by the very terms of the First Amendment. That is the effect not only in its guaranty of religion's free exercise, but also in the prohibition of establishments. It was on this basis of the private character of the function of religious education that this Court held parents entitled to send their children to private, religious schools. . . . Now it declares in effect that the appropriation of public funds to defray part of the cost of attending those schools is for a public purpose. If so, I do not understand why the state cannot go farther or why this case approaches the verge of its power.

In truth this view contradicts the whole purpose and effect of the First Amendment as heretofore conceived. The "public function"—"public welfare"—"social legislation" argument seeks, in Madison's words, to "employ Religion [that is, here, religious education] as an engine of Civil policy." Remonstrance, ¶ 5. It is of one piece with the Assessment Bill's preamble, although with the vital difference that it wholly ignores what that preamble explicitly states.

Our constitutional policy is exactly the opposite. It does not deny the value or the necessity for religious training, teaching or observance. Rather it secures their free exercise. But to that end it does deny that the state can undertake or sustain them in any form or degree. For this reason the sphere of religious activity, as distinguished from the secular intellectual liberties, has been given the twofold protection and, as the state cannot forbid, neither can it perform or aid in performing the religious function. The dual prohibition makes that function altogether private. It cannot be made a public one by legislative act. This was the very heart of Madison's Remonstrance, as it is of the Amendment itself.

It is not because religious teaching does not promote the public or the individual's welfare, but because neither is furthered when the state promotes religious education, that the Constitution forbids it to do so. Both legislatures and courts are bound by that distinction. In failure to observe it lies the fallacy of the "public function"—"social legislation" argument, a fallacy facilitated by easy transference of the argument's basing from due process unrelated to any religious aspect to the First Amendment.

By no declaration that a gift of public money to religious uses will promote the general or individual welfare, or the cause of education generally, can legislative bodies overcome the Amendment's bar. Nor may the courts sustain their attempts to do so by finding such consequences for appropriations which in fact give aid to or promote religious uses. . . . Legislatures are free to make, and courts to sustain, appropriations only when it can be found that in fact they do not aid, promote, encourage or sustain religious teaching or observances, be the amount large or small. No such finding has been or could be made in this case. The Amendment has removed this form of promoting the public welfare from legislative and judicial competence to make a public function. It is exclusively a private affair.

The reasons underlying the Amendment's policy have not vanished with time or diminished in force. Now as when it was adopted the price of religious freedom is double. It is that the church and religion shall live both within and upon that freedom. There cannot be freedom of religion, safeguarded by the state, and intervention by the church or its agencies in the state's domain or dependency on its largesse. . . . The great condition of religious liberty is that it be maintained free from sustenance, as also from other interferences, by the state. For when it comes to rest upon that secular foundation it vanishes with the resting. . . . Public money devoted to payment of religious costs, educational or other, brings the quest for more. It brings too the struggle of sect against sect for the larger share or for any. Here one by numbers alone will benefit most, there another. That is precisely the history of societies which have had an established religion and dissident groups. . . . It is the very thing Jefferson and Madison experienced and sought to guard against, whether in its blunt or in its more screened forms. The end of such strife cannot be other than to destroy the cherished liberty. The dominating group will achieve the dominant benefit; or all will embroil the state in their dissensions. . . .

Exactly such conflicts have centered of late around providing transportation to religious schools from public funds. The issue and the dissension work typically, in Madison's phrase, to "destroy that moderation and harmony which the forbearance of our laws to intermeddle with Religion, has produced amongst its several sects." . . . This occurs, as he well knew, over measures at the very threshold of departure from the principle. . . .

In these conflicts wherever success has been obtained it has been upon the contention that by providing the transportation the general cause of education, the general welfare, and the welfare of the individual will be forwarded; hence that the matter lies within the realm of public function, for legislative determination. State courts have divided upon the issue, some taking the view that only the individual, others that the institution receives the benefit. A few have recognized that this dichotomy is false, that both in fact are aided.

The majority here does not accept in terms any of those views. But neither does it deny that the individual or the school, or indeed both, are benefited directly and substantially. To do so would cut the ground from under the public function—social legislation thesis. On the contrary, the opinion concedes that the children are aided by being helped to get to the religious schooling. By converse necessary implication as well as by the absence of express denial, it must be taken to concede also that the school is helped to reach the child with its religious teaching. The religious enterprise is common to both, as is the interest in having transportation for its religious purposes provided.

Notwithstanding the recognition that this two-way aid is given and the absence of any denial that religious teaching is thus furthered, the Court concludes that the aid so given is not "support" of religion. It is rather only support of education as such, without reference to its religious content, and thus becomes public welfare legislation. To this elision of the religious element from the case is added gloss in two respects, one that the aid extended partakes of the nature of a safety measure, the other that failure to provide it would make the state unneutral in religious matters, discriminating against or hampering such children concerning public benefits all others receive.

As will be noted, the one gloss is contradicted by the facts of record and the other is of whole cloth with the "public function" argument's excision of the religious factor. But most important is that this approach, if valid, supplies a ready method for nullifying the Amendment's guaranty, not only for this case and others involving small grants in aid for religious education, but equally for larger ones. The only thing needed will be for the Court again to transplant the "public welfare—public function" view from its proper nonreligious due process bearing to First Amendment application, holding that religious education is not "supported" though it may be aided by the appropriation, and that the cause of education generally is furthered by helping the pupil to secure that type of training.

This is not therefore just a little case over bus fares. In paraphrase of Madison, distant as it may be in its present form from a complete establishment of religion, it differs from it only in degree; and is the first step in that direction. . . . Today as in his time "the same authority which can force a citizen to contribute three pence only . . . for the support of any one [religious] establishment, may force him" to pay more; or "to conform to any other establishment in all cases whatsoever." And now, as then, "either . . . we must say, that the will of the Legislature is the only measure of their authority; and that in the plentitude of this authority, they may sweep away all our fundamental rights; or, that they are bound to leave this particular right untouched and sacred." Remonstrance, ¶ 15.

The realm of religious training and belief remains, as the Amendment made it, the kingdom of the individual man and his God. It should be kept inviolately private, not "entangled . . . in precedents" or confounded with what legislatures legitimately may take over into the public domain.

V.

No one conscious of religious values can be unsympathetic toward the burden which our constitutional separation puts on parents who desire religious instruction mixed with secular for their children. They pay taxes for others' children's education, at the same time the added cost of instruction for their own. Nor can one happily see benefits denied to children which others receive, because in conscience they or their parents for them desire a different kind of training others do not demand.

But if those feelings should prevail, there would be an end to our historic constitutional policy and command. No more unjust or discriminatory in fact is it to deny attendants at religious schools the cost of their transportation than it is to deny them tuitions, sustenance for their teachers, or any other educational expense which others receive at public cost. Hardship in fact there is which none can blink. But, for assuring to those who undergo it the greater, the most comprehensive freedom, it is one written by design and firm intent into our basic law.

Of course discrimination in the legal sense does not exist. The child attending the religious school has the same right as any other to attend the public school. But he foregoes exercising it because the same guaranty which assures this freedom forbids the public school or any agency of the state to give or aid him in securing the religious instruction he seeks.

Were he to accept the common school, he would be the first to protest the teaching there of any creed or faith not his own. And it is precisely for the reason that their atmosphere is wholly secular that children are not sent to public schools. . . . But that is a constitutional necessity, because we have staked the very existence of our country on the faith that complete separation between the state and religion is best for the state and best for religion. Remonstrance, ¶¶ 8, 12.

That policy necessarily entails hardship upon persons who forego the right to educational advantages the state can supply in order to secure others it is precluded from giving. Indeed this may hamper the parent and the child forced by conscience to that choice. But it does not make the state unneutral to withhold what the Constitution forbids it to give. On the contrary it is only by observing the prohibition rigidly that the state can maintain its neutrality and avoid partisanship in the dissensions inevitable when sect opposes sect over demands for public moneys to further religious education, teaching or training in any form or degree, directly or indirectly. Like St. Paul's freedom, religious liberty with a great price must be bought. And for those who exercise it most fully, by insisting upon religious education for their children mixed with secular, by the terms of our Constitution the price is greater than for others.

The problem then cannot be cast in terms of legal discrimination or its absence. This would be true, even though the state in giving aid should treat all religious instruction alike. Thus, if the present statute and its application were shown to apply equally to all religious schools of whatever faith, yet in the light of our tradition it could not stand. For then the adherent of one creed still would pay for the support of another, the childless taxpayer with others more fortunate. Then too there would seem to be no bar to making appropriations for transportation and other expenses of children attending public or other secular schools, after hours in separate places and classes for their exclusively religious instruction. The person who embraces no creed also would be forced to pay for teaching what he does not believe. Again, it was the furnishing of "contributions of money for the propagation of opinions which he disbelieves" that the fathers outlawed. That consequence and effect are not removed by multiplying to all-inclusiveness the sects for which support is exacted. The Constitution requires, not comprehensive identification of state with religion, but complete separation. . . .

Two great drives are constantly in motion to abridge, in the name of education, the complete division of religion and civil authority which our forefathers made. One is to introduce religious education and observances into the public schools. The other, to obtain public funds for the aid and support of various private religious schools. . . . In my opinion both avenues were closed by the Constitution. Neither should be opened by this

Court. The matter is not one of quantity, to be measured by the amount of money expended. Now as in Madison's day it is one of principle, to keep separate the separate spheres as the First Amendment drew them; to prevent the first experiment upon our liberties; and to keep the question from becoming entangled in corrosive precedents. We should not be less strict to keep strong and untarnished the one side of the shield of religious freedom than we have been of the other.

The judgment should be reversed.

b. Released Time

McCOLLUM v. BOARD OF EDUCATION

333 US 203 (1948)

[The question considered in this case was whether there was a breach in the wall of separation between church and state when, under a "released time" arrangement, religious instruction classes were conducted during regular school time within a public school building by denominational teachers. Eight Justices held that this arrangement violated the First Amendment as made applicable to the states by the Fourteenth Amendment. They reaffirmed the broad principles that were formulated the previous year in the *Everson Case*, only this time they found that the constitutional guaranty had been violated.

[Justice Reed alone dissented—not, however, with respect to the broad principles involved, but with respect to their application to the facts in the case. He dissented on the ground that the "released time" arrangements constituted no violation of the provisions of the First Amendment.]

Mr. Justice Black delivered the opinion of the Court:

This case relates to the power of a state to utilize its tax-supported public school system in aid of religious instruction insofar as that power may be restricted by the First and Fourteenth Amendments to the Federal Constitution.

The appellant, Vashti McCollum, began this action for mandamus against the Champaign Board of Education in the Circuit Court of Champaign County, Illinois. Her asserted interest was that of a resident and taxpayer of Champaign and of a parent whose child was then enrolled in the Champaign public schools. Illinois has a compulsory education law which, with exceptions, requires parents to send their children, aged seven to sixteen, to its tax-supported public schools where the children are to remain in attendance during the hours when the schools are regularly in session. Parents who violate this law commit a misdemeanor punishable by fine unless the children attend private or parochial schools which meet educational standards fixed by the State. District boards of education are given general supervisory powers over the use of the public school buildings within the school district. . . .

Appellant's petition for mandamus alleged that religious teachers, employed by private religious groups, were permitted to come weekly into the school buildings during the regular hours set apart for secular teaching, and then and there for a period of thirty minutes substitute their religious teaching for the secular education provided under the compulsory education law. The petitioner charged that this joint public-school religious-group program violated the First and Fourteenth Amendments to the United States Constitution. The prayer of her petition was that the Board of Education be ordered to "adopt and enforce rules and regulations prohibiting all instruction in and teaching of religious education in all public schools in Champaign School District Number 71, . . . and in all public school houses and buildings in said district when occupied by public schools." . . .

Although there are disputes between the parties as to various inferences that may or may not properly be drawn from the evidence concerning the religious program, the following facts are shown by the record without dispute. In 1940 interested members of the Jewish, Roman Catholic, and a few of the Protestant faiths formed a voluntary association called the Champaign Council on Religious Education. They obtained permission from the Board of Education to offer classes in religious instruction to public school pupils in grades four to nine inclusive. Classes were made up of pupils whose parents signed printed cards requesting that their children be permitted to attend; they were held weekly, thirty minutes for the lower grades, forty-five minutes for the higher. The council employed the religious teachers at no expense to the school authorities, but the instructors were subject to the approval and supervision of the superintendent of schools. The classes were taught in three separate religious groups by Protestant teachers, Catholic priests, and a Jewish Rabbi, although for the past several years there have apparently been no classes instructed in the Jewish religion. Classes were conducted in the regular classrooms of the school building. Students who did not choose to take the religious instruction were not released from public school duties; they were required to leave their classrooms and go to some other place in the school building for pursuit of their secular studies. On the other hand, students who were released from secular study for the religious instructions were required to be present at the religious classes. Reports of their presence or absence were to be made to their secular teachers.

The foregoing facts, without reference to others that appear in the record, show the use of tax-supported property for religious instruction and the close cooperation between the school authorities and the religious council in promoting religious education. The operation of the state's compulsory education system thus assists and is integrated with the program of religious instruction carried on by separate religious sects. Pupils compelled by law to go to school for secular education are released in part from their legal duty upon the condition that they attend the religious classes. This is beyond all question a utilization of the tax-established and tax-supported public school system to aid religious groups to spread their faith. And it falls squarely under the ban of the First Amendment (made applicable to the States by the Fourteenth) as we interpreted it in *Everson v. Board of Education.* . . . The majority in the *Everson Case,* and the minority . . . , agreed that the First Amendment's language, properly interpreted, had erected a wall of separation between Church and State. They disagreed as to the facts shown by the record and as to the proper application of the First Amendment's language to those facts.

Recognizing that the Illinois program is barred by the First and Fourteenth Amendments if we adhere to the views expressed both by the majority and the minority in the *Everson Case,* counsel for the respondents challenge those views as *dicta* and urge that we reconsider and repudiate them. They argue that historically the First Amendment was intended to forbid only government preference of one religion over another, not an impartial governmental assistance of all religions. In addition they ask that we distinguish or overrule our holding in the *Everson Case* that the Fourteenth Amendment made the "establishment of religion" clause of the First Amendment applicable as a prohibition against the States. After giving full consideration to the arguments presented we are unable to accept either of these contentions.

To hold that a state cannot consistently with the First and Fourteenth Amendments utilize its public school system to aid any or all religious faiths or sects in the dissemination of their doctrines and ideals does not, as counsel urge, manifest a governmental hostility to religion or religious teachings. A manifestation of such hostility would be at war with our national tradition as embodied in the First Amendment's guaranty of the free exercise of religion. For the First Amendment rests upon the premise that both religion and government can best work to achieve their lofty aims if each is left free from the other within its respective sphere. Or, as we said in the *Everson Case,* the First Amendment has erected a wall between Church and State which must be kept high and impregnable.

Here not only are the state's tax-supported public school buildings

used for the dissemination of religious doctrines. The State also affords
sectarian groups an invaluable aid in that it helps to provide pupils for
their religious classes through use of the state's compulsory public
school machinery. This is not separation of Church and State. . . .
Reversed. . . .

*Mr. Justice Frankfurter delivered the following opinion, in which Mr.
Justice Jackson, Mr. Justice Rutledge and Mr. Justice Burton join:*

We dissented in *Everson* v. *Board of Education,* . . . because in our view
the Constitutional principle requiring separation of Church and State compelled invalidation of the ordinance sustained by the majority. Illinois has
here authorized the commingling of sectarian with secular instruction in the
public schools. The Constitution of the United States forbids this.

This case, in the light of the *Everson* decision, demonstrates anew that
the mere formulation of a relevant Constitutional principle is the beginning
of the solution of a problem, not its answer. This is so because the meaning
of a spacious conception like that of the separation of Church from State is
unfolded as appeal is made to the principle from case to case. We are all
agreed that the First and the Fourteenth Amendments have a secular reach
far more penetrating in the conduct of Government than merely to forbid
an "established church." But agreement, in the abstract, that the First
Amendment was designed to erect a "wall of separation between Church and
State," does not preclude a clash of views as to what the wall separates.
Involved is not only the Constitutional principle but the implications of
judicial review in its enforcement. Accommodation of legislative freedom
and Constitutional limitations upon that freedom cannot be achieved by a
mere phrase. We cannot illuminatingly apply the "wall-of-separation" metaphor until we have considered the relevant history of religious education in
America, the place of the "released time" movement in that history, and its
precise manifestation in the case before us.

To understand the particular program now before us as a conscientious
attempt to accommodate the allowable functions of Government and the
special concerns of the Church within the framework of our Constitution and
with due regard to the kind of society for which it was designed, we must put
this Champaign program of 1940 in its historic setting. Traditionally, organized education in the Western world was Church education. It could hardly
be otherwise when the education of children was primarily study of the Word
and the ways of God. Even in the Protestant countries, where there was a
less close identification of Church and State, the basis of education was largely
the Bible, and its chief purpose inculcation of piety. To the extent that the
State intervened, it used its authority to further aims of the Church.

The emigrants who came to these shores brought this view of education
with them. Colonial schools certainly started with a religious orientation.
When the common problems of the early settlers of the Massachusetts Bay

Colony revealed the need for common schools, the object was the defeat of "one chief project of that old deluder Satan, to keep men from the knowledge of the Scriptures." . . .

The evolution of colonial education, largely in the service of religion, into the public school system of today is the story of changing conceptions regarding the American democratic society, of the functions of State-maintained education in such a society and of the role therein of the free exercise of religion by the people. The modern public school derived from a philosophy of freedom reflected in the First Amendment. It is appropriate to recall that the Remonstrance of James Madison, an event basic in the history of religious liberty, was called forth by a proposal which involved support to religious education. . . . As the momentum for popular education increased and in turn evoked strong claims for State support of religious education, contests not unlike that which in Virginia had produced Madison's Remonstrance appeared in various forms in other States. New York and Massachusetts provide famous chapters in the history that established dissociation of religious teaching from State-maintained schools. In New York, the rise of the common schools led, despite fierce sectarian opposition, to the barring of tax funds to church schools, and later to any school in which sectarian doctrine was taught. In Massachusetts, largely through the efforts of Horace Mann, all sectarian teachings were barred from the common school to save it from being rent by denominational conflict. The upshot of these controversies, often long and fierce, is fairly summarized by saying that long before the Fourteenth Amendment subjected the States to new limitations, the prohibition of furtherance by the State of religious instruction became the guiding principle, in law and feeling, of the American people. In sustaining Stephen Girard's will, this Court referred to the inevitable conflicts engendered by matters "connected with religious polity" and particularly "in a country composed of such a variety of religious sects as our country." . . . That was more than one hundred years ago.

Separation in the field of education, then, was not imposed upon unwilling States by force of superior law. In this respect the Fourteenth Amendment merely reflected a principle then dominant in our national life. To the extent that the Constitution thus made it binding upon the States, the basis of the restriction is the whole experience of our people. Zealous watchfulness against fusion of secular and religious activities by Government itself, through any of its instruments but especially through its educational agencies, was the democratic response of the American community to the particular needs of a young and growing nation, unique in the composition of its people. A totally different situation elsewhere, as illustrated for instance by the English provisions for religious education in State-maintained schools, only serves to illustrate that free societies are not cast in one mould. . . . Different institutions evolve from different historic circumstances.

It is pertinent to remind that the establishment of this principle of Separation in the field of education was not due to any decline in the religious beliefs of the people. Horace Mann was a devout Christian, and the deep religious feeling of James Madison is stamped upon the Remonstrance. The secular public school did not imply indifference to the basic role of religion in the life of the people, nor rejection of religious education as a means of fostering it. The claims of religion were not minimized by refusing to make the public schools agencies for their assertion. The non-sectarian or secular public school was the means of reconciling freedom in general with religious freedom. The sharp confinement of the public schools to secular education was a recognition of the need of a democratic society to educate its children, insofar as the State undertook to do so, in an atmosphere free from pressures in a realm in which pressures are most resisted and where conflicts are most easily and most bitterly engendered. Designed to serve as perhaps the most powerful agency for promoting cohesion among a heterogeneous democratic people, the public school must keep scrupulously free from entanglement in the strife of sects. The preservation of the community from divisive conflicts, of Government from irreconcilable pressures by religious groups, of religion from censorship and coercion however subtly exercised, requires strict confinement of the State to instruction other than religious, leaving to the individual's church and home, indoctrination in the faith of his choice. This development of the public school as a symbol of our secular unity was not a sudden achievement nor attained without violent conflict. While in small communities of comparatively homogeneous religious beliefs, the need for absolute separation presented no urgencies, elsewhere the growth of the secular school encountered the resistance of feeling strongly engaged against it. But the inevitability of such attempts is the very reason for Constitutional provisions primarily concerned with the protection of minority groups. And such sects are shifting groups, varying from time to time, and place to place, thus representing in their totality the common interest of the nation.

Enough has been said to indicate that we are dealing not with a full-blown principle, nor one having the definiteness of a surveyor's metes and bounds. But by 1875 the separation of public education from Church entanglements, of the State from the teaching of religion, was firmly established in the consciousness of the nation. In that year President Grant made his famous remarks to the Convention of the Army of the Tennessee:

> Encourage free schools and resolve that not one dollar appropriated for their support shall be appropriated to the support of any sectarian schools. Resolve that neither the state nor nation, nor both combined, shall support institutions of learning other than those sufficient to afford every child growing up in the land the opportunity of a good common school education, unmixed with sectarian, pagan, or atheistical dogmas. Leave the matter of religion to the family altar, the church and the private school, supported entirely by private contributions. Keep the church and the state forever separate. . . .

So strong was this conviction, that rather than rest on the comprehensive prohibitions of the First and Fourteenth Amendments, President Grant urged that there be written into the United States Constitution particular elaborations, including a specific prohibition against the use of public funds for sectarian education, such as had been written into many State constitutions.

By 1894, in urging the adoption of such a provision in the New York Constitution, Elihu Root was able to summarize a century of the nation's history: "It is not a question of religion, or of creed, or of party; it is a question of declaring and maintaining the great American principle of eternal separation between Church and State." . . . The extent to which this principle was deemed a presupposition of our Constitutional system is strikingly illustrated by the fact that every State admitted into the Union since 1876 was compelled by Congress to write into its constitution a requirement that it maintain a school system "free from sectarian control."

Prohibition of the commingling of sectarian and secular instruction in the public school is of course only half the story. A religious people was naturally concerned about the part of the child's education entrusted "to the family altar, the church, and the private school." The promotion of religious education took many forms. Laboring under financial difficulties and exercising only persuasive authority, various denominations felt handicapped in their task of religious education. Abortive attempts were therefore frequently made to obtain public funds for religious schools. But the major efforts of religious inculcation were a recognition of the principle of Separation by the establishment of church schools privately supported. Parochial schools were maintained by various denominations. These, however, were often beset by serious handicaps, financial and otherwise, so that the religious aims which they represented found other directions. There were experiments with vacation schools, with Saturday as well as Sunday schools. They all fell short of their purpose. It was urged that by appearing to make religion a one-day-a-week matter, the Sunday school, which acquired national acceptance, tended to relegate the child's religious education, and thereby his religion, to a minor role not unlike the enforced piano lesson.

Out of these inadequate efforts evolved the week-day church school, held on one or more afternoons a week after the close of the public school. But children continued to be children; they wanted to play when school was out, particularly when other children were free to do so. Church leaders decided that if the week-day church school was to succeed, a way had to be found to give the child his religious education during what the child conceived to be his "business hours."

The initiation of the movement may fairly be attributed to Dr. George U. Wenner. The underlying assumption of his proposal, made at the Interfaith Conference on Federation held in New York City in 1905, was that the public school unduly monopolized the child's time and that the churches were entitled to their share of it. This, the schools should "release." Accordingly, the Federation, citing the example of the Third Republic of France, urged that upon the request of their parents children be excused from public school on Wednesday afternoon, so that the churches could provide "Sunday school on Wednesday." This was to be carried out on church premises under church authority. Those not desiring to attend church schools would continue their normal classes. Lest these public school classes unfairly compete with the church education, it was requested that the school authorities refrain from scheduling courses or activities of compelling interest or importance.

The proposal aroused considerable opposition and it took another decade for a "released time" scheme to become part of a public school system. Gary, Indiana, inaugurated the movement. At a time when industrial expansion strained the communal facilities of the city, Superintendent of Schools Wirt suggested a fuller use of the school buildings. Building on theories which had become more or less current, he also urged that education was more than instruction in a classroom. The school was only one of several educational agencies. The library, the playground, the home, the church, all have their function in the child's proper unfolding. Accordingly, Wirt's plan sought to rotate the schedules of the children during the school-day so that some were in class, others were in the library, still others in the playground. And some, he suggested to the leading ministers of the City, might be released to attend religious classes if the churches of the City cooperated and provided them. They did, in 1914, and thus was "released time" begun. The religious teaching was held on church premises and the public schools had no hand in the conduct of these church schools. They did not supervise the choice of instructors or the subject matter taught. Nor did they assume responsibility for the attendance, conduct or achievement of the child in a church school; and he received no credit for it. The period of attendance in the religious schools would otherwise have been a play period for the child, with the result that the arrangement did not cut into public school instruction or truly affect the activities or feelings of the children who did not attend the church schools.

From such a beginning "released time" has attained substantial proportions. In 1914–15, under the Gary program, 619 pupils left the public schools for the church schools during one period a week. According to responsible figures almost 2,000,000 in some 2,200 communities participated in "released time" programs during 1947. A movement of such scope indicates the importance of the problem to which the "released time" programs are directed. But to the extent that aspects of these programs are open to Constitutional objection, the more extensively the movement operates, the more ominous the breaches in the wall of separation.

Of course, "released time" as a generalized conception, undefined by differentiating particularities, is not an issue for Constitutional adjudication. Local programs differ from each other in many and crucial respects. Some "released time" classes are under separate denominational auspices, others are conducted jointly by several denominations, often embracing all the religious affiliations of a community. Some classes in religion teach a limited sectarianism; others emphasize democracy, unity and spiritual values not anchored in a particular creed. Insofar as these are manifestations merely of the free exercise of religion, they are quite outside the scope of judicial concern, except insofar as the Court may be called upon to protect the right of religious freedom. It is only when challenge is made to the share that the public schools have in the execution of a particular "released time" program that close judicial scrutiny is demanded of the exact relation between the religious instruction and the public educational system in the specific situation before the Court.

The substantial differences among arrangements lumped together as "released time" emphasize the importance of detailed analysis of the facts to which the Constitutional test of Separation is to be applied. How does "released time" operate in Champaign? Public school teachers distribute to their pupils cards supplied by church groups, so that the parents may indicate whether they desire religious instruction for their children. For those desiring it, religious classes are conducted in the regular classrooms of the public schools by teachers of religion paid by the churches and appointed by them, but, as the State court found, "subject to the approval and supervision of the Superintendent." The courses do not profess to give secular instruction in subjects concerning religion. Their candid purpose is sectarian teaching. While a child can go to any of the religious classes offered, a particular sect wishing a teacher for its devotees requires the permission of the school superintendent "who in turn will determine whether or not it is practical for said group to teach in said school system." If no provision is made for religious instruction in the particular faith of a child, or if for other reasons the child is not enrolled in any of the offered classes, he is required to attend a regular school class, or a study period during which he is often left to his own devices. Reports of attendance in the religious classes are submitted by the religious instructor to the school authorities, and the child who fails to attend is presumably deemed a truant.

Religious education so conducted on school time and property is patently woven into the working scheme of the school. The Champaign arrangement thus presents powerful elements of inherent pressure by the school system in the interest of religious sects. The fact that this power has not been used to discriminate is beside the point. Separation is a requirement to abstain from fusing functions of Government and of religious sects, not merely to treat them all equally. That a child is offered an alternative may reduce the constraint; it does not eliminate the operation of influence by the school in matters sacred to conscience and outside the school's domain. The law of imitation operates, and non-conformity is not an outstanding characteristic of children. The result is an obvious pressure upon children to attend. Again, while the Champaign school population represents only a fraction of the more than two hundred and fifty sects of the nation, not even all the practicing sects in Champaign are willing or able to provide religious instruction. The children belonging to these non-participating sects will thus have inculcated in them a feeling of separatism when the school should be the training ground for habits of community, or they will have religious instruction in a faith which is not that of their parents. As a result, the public school system of Champaign actively furthers inculcation in the religious tenets of some faiths, and in the process sharpens the consciousness of religious differences at least among some of the children committed to its care. These are consequences not amenable to statistics. But they are precisely the consequences against which the Constitution was directed when it prohibited the Government common to all from becoming embroiled, however innocently, in the destructive religious conflicts of which the history of even this country records some dark pages.

Mention should not be omitted that the integration of religious instruction within the school system as practiced in Champaign is supported by arguments drawn from educational theories as diverse as those derived from Catholic conceptions and from the writings of John Dewey. Movements like "released time" are seldom single in origin or aim. Nor can the intrusion of religious instruction into the public school system of Champaign be minimized by saying that it absorbs less than an hour a week; in fact, that affords evidence of a design constitutionally objectionable. If it were merely a question of enabling a child to obtain religious instruction with a receptive mind the thirty or forty-five minutes could readily be found on Saturday or Sunday. If that were all, Champaign might have drawn upon the French system, known in its American manifestation as "dismissed time," whereby one school day is shortened to allow all children to go where they please, leaving those who so desire to go to a religious school. The momentum of the whole school atmosphere and school planning is presumably put behind religious instruction, as given in Champaign, precisely in order to secure for the religious instruction such momentum and planning. To speak of "released time" as being only half or three quarters of an hour is to draw a thread from a fabric.

We do not consider, as indeed we could not, school programs not before us which, though colloquially characterized as "released time," present situations differing in aspects that may well be constitutionally crucial. Different forms which "released time" has taken during more than thirty years of growth include programs which, like that before us, could not withstand the test of the Constitution; others may be found unexceptionable. We do not now attempt to weigh in the Constitutional scale every separate detail or various combination of factors which may establish a valid "released time" program. We find that the basic Constitutional principle of absolute Separation was violated when the State of Illinois, speaking through its Supreme Court, sustained the school authorities of Champaign in sponsoring and effectively furthering religious beliefs by its educational arrangement.

Separation means separation, not something less. Jefferson's metaphor in describing the relation between Church and State speaks of a "wall of separation," not of a fine line easily overstepped. The public school is at once the symbol of our democracy and the most pervasive means for promoting our common destiny. In no activity of the State is it more vital to keep out divisive forces than in its schools, to avoid confusing, not to say fusing, what the Constitution sought to keep strictly apart. "The great American principle of eternal separation"—Elihu Root's phrase bears repetition—is one of the vital reliances of our Constitutional system for assuring unities among our people stronger than our diversities. It is the Court's duty to enforce this principle in its full integrity.

We renew our conviction that "we have staked the very existence of our country on the faith that complete separation between the state and religion is best for the state and best for religion." *Everson* v. *Board of Education.*

If nowhere else, in the relation between Church and State, "good fences make good neighbors."

Mr. Justice Jackson, concurring:

I join the opinion of Mr. Justice Frankfurter, and concur in the result reached by the Court, but with these reservations: I think . . . that we should place some bounds on the demands for interference with local schools that we are empowered or willing to entertain. I make these reservations a matter of record in view of the number of litigations likely to be started as a result of this decision. . . .

To me, the sweep and detail of these complaints is a danger signal which warns of the kind of local controversy we will be required to arbitrate if we do not place appropriate limitation on our decision and exact strict compliance with jurisdictional requirements. Authorities list 256 separate and substantial religious bodies to exist in the continental United States. Each of them, through the suit of some discontented but unpenalized and untaxed representative, has as good a right as this plaintiff to demand that the courts compel the schools to sift out of their teaching everything inconsistent with its doctrines. If we are to eliminate everything that is objectionable to any of these warring sects or inconsistent with any of their doctrines, we will leave public education in shreds. Nothing but educational confusion and a discrediting of the public school system can result from subjecting it to constant law suits.

While we may and should end such formal and explicit instruction as the Champaign plan and can at all times prohibit teaching of creed and catechism and ceremonial and can forbid forthright proselyting in the schools, I think it remains to be demonstrated whether it is possible, even if desirable, to comply with such demands as plaintiff's completely to isolate and cast out of secular education all that some people may reasonably regard as religious instruction. Perhaps subjects such as mathematics, physics or chemistry are, or can be, completely secularized. But it would not seem practical to teach either practice or appreciation of the arts if we are to forbid exposure of youth to any religious influences. Music without sacred music, architecture minus the cathedral, or painting without the scriptural themes would be eccentric and incomplete, even from a secular point of view. Yet the inspirational appeal of religion in these guises is often stronger than in forthright sermon. Even such a "science" as biology raises the issue between evolution and creation as an explanation of our presence on this planet. Certainly a course in English literature that omitted the Bible and other powerful uses of our mother tongue for religious ends would be pretty barren. And I should suppose it is a proper, if not an indispensable, part of preparation for a worldly life to know the roles that religion and religions have played in the tragic story of mankind. The fact is that, for good or for ill, nearly everything in our culture worth transmitting, everything which gives meaning to life, is saturated with religious influences, derived from paganism, Judaism, Christianity—both Catholic and Protestant—and other faiths accepted by a large part of the world's peoples. One can hardly respect a system of education that would leave the student wholly ignorant of the currents of religious thought that move the world society for a part in which he is being prepared.

But how one can teach, with satisfaction or even with justice to all faiths, such subjects as the story of the Reformation, the Inquisition, or even the New England effort to found "a Church without a Bishop and a State without a King," is more than I know. It is too much to expect that mortals will teach subjects about which their contemporaries have passionate controversies with the detachment they may summon to teaching about remote subjects such as Confucius or Mohammed. When instruction turns to proselyting and imparting knowledge becomes evangelism is, except in the crudest cases, a subtle inquiry.

The opinions in this case show that public educational authorities have evolved a considerable variety of practices in dealing with the religious problem. Neighborhoods differ in racial, religious and cultural compositions. It must be expected that they will adopt different customs which will give emphasis to different values and will induce different experiments. And it must be expected that, no matter what practice prevails, there will be many discontented and possibly belligerent minorities. We must leave some flexibility to meet local conditions, some chance to progress by trial and error. While I agree that the religious classes involved here go beyond permissible limits, I also think the complaint demands more than plaintiff is entitled to have granted. So far as I can see this Court does not tell the State court where it may stop, nor does it set up any standards by which the State court may determine that question for itself.

The task of separating the secular from the religious in education is one of magnitude, intricacy and delicacy. To lay down a sweeping constitutional doctrine as demanded by complainant and apparently approved by the Court, applicable alike to all school boards of the nation, "to immediately adopt and enforce rules and regulations prohibiting all instruction in and teaching of religious education in all public schools," is to decree a uniform, rigid and, if we are consistent, an unchanging standard for countless school boards representing and serving highly localized groups which not only differ from each other but which themselves from time to time change attitudes. It seems to me that to do so is to allow zeal for our own ideas of what is good in public instruction to induce us to accept the role of a super board of education for every school district in the nation.

It is idle to pretend that this task is one for which we can find in the Constitution one word to help us as judges to decide where the secular ends and the sectarian begins in education. Nor can we find guidance in any other legal source. It is a matter on which we can find no law but our own prepossessions. If with no surer legal guidance we are to take up and decide every variation of this controversy, raised by persons not subject to penalty or tax but who are dissatisfied with the way schools are dealing with the problem, we are likely to have much business of the sort. And, more importantly, we are likely to make the legal "wall of separation between church and state" as winding as the famous serpentine wall designed by Mr. Jefferson for the University he founded.

Mr. Justice Reed, dissenting: . . .

The phrase "an establishment of religion" may have been intended by Congress to be aimed only at a state church. When the First Amendment was pending in Congress in substantially its present form, "Mr. Madison said, he apprehended the meaning of the words to be, that Congress should not establish a religion, and enforce the legal observation of it by law, nor compel men to worship God in any manner contrary to their conscience." Passing years, however, have brought about the acceptance of a broader meaning, although never until today, I believe, has this Court widened its interpretation to any such degree as holding that recognition of the interest of our nation in religion, through the granting, to qualified representatives of the principal faiths, of opportunity to present religion as an optional, extracurricular subject during released school time in public school buildings, was equivalent to an establishment of religion. A reading of the general statements of eminent statesmen of former days, referred to in the opinions in this case and in *Everson* v. *Board of Education,* will show that circumstances such as those in this case were far from the minds of the authors. The words and spirit of those statements may be wholeheartedly accepted without in the least impugning the judgment of the State of Illinois.

Mr. Jefferson, as one of the founders of the University of Virginia, a school which from its establishment in 1819 has been wholly governed, managed and controlled by the State of Virginia, was faced with the same problem that is before this Court today: the question of the constitutional limitation upon religious education in public schools. In his annual report as Rector, to the President and Directors of the Literary Fund, dated October 7, 1822, approved by the Visitors of the University of whom Mr. Madison was one, Mr. Jefferson set forth his views at some length. These suggestions of Mr. Jefferson were adopted and . . . the Regulations of the University of October 4, 1824, provided that:

> Should the religious sects of this State, or any of them, according to the invitation held out to them, establish within, or adjacent to, the precincts of the University, schools for instruction in the religion of their sect, the students of the University will be free, and expected to attend religious worship at the establishment of their respective sects, in the morning, and in time to meet their school in the University at its stated hour.

Thus, the "wall of separation between church and state" that Mr. Jefferson built at the University which he founded did not exclude religious education from that school. The difference between the generality of his statements on the separation of church and state and the specificity of his conclusions on education are considerable. A rule of law should not be drawn from a figure of speech.

Mr. Madison's Memorial and Remonstrance against Religious Assessments relied upon by the dissenting Justices in *Everson* is not applicable here. . . . Throughout the Remonstrance, Mr. Madison speaks of the "establishment" sought to be effected by the act. It is clear from its historical setting and its language that the Remonstrance was a protest against an effort by Virginia to support Christian sects by taxation. Issues similar to those raised by the instant case were not discussed. Thus, Mr. Madison's approval of Mr. Jefferson's report as Rector gives, in my opinion, a clearer indication of his views on the constitutionality of religious education in public schools than his general statements on a different subject.

This Court summarized the amendment's accepted reach into the religious field, as I understood its scope, in *Everson* v. *Board of Education*. . . . I agree . . . that none of our governmental entities can "set up a church." I agree that they cannot "aid" all or any religions or prefer one "over another." But "aid" must be understood as a purposeful assistance directly to the church itself or to some religious group or organization doing religious work of such a character that it may fairly be said to be performing ecclesiastical functions. "Prefer" must give an advantage to one "over another." I agree that pupils cannot "be released in part from their legal duty" of school attendance upon condition that they attend religious classes. But as Illinois has held that it is within the discretion of the School Board to permit absence from school for religious instruction no legal duty of school attendance is violated. . . . If the sentence in the Court's opinion, concerning the pupils' release from legal duty, is intended to mean that the Constitution forbids a school to excuse a pupil from secular control during school hours to attend voluntarily a class in religious education, whether in or out of school buildings, I disagree. Of course, no tax can be levied to support organizations intended "to teach or practice religion." I agree too that the state cannot influence one toward religion against his will or punish him for his beliefs. Champaign's religious education course does none of these things.

It seems clear to me that the "aid" referred to by the Court in the *Everson Case* could not have been those incidental advantages that religious bodies, with other groups similarly situated, obtain as a by-product of organized society. This explains the well-known fact that all churches receive "aid" from government in the form of freedom from taxation. The *Everson* decision itself justified the transportation of children to church schools by New Jersey for safety reasons. It accords with *Cochran* v. *Louisiana State Bd. of Edu.*, 281 US 370, where this Court upheld a free textbook statute of Louisiana against a charge that it aided private schools on the ground that the books were for the education of the children, not to aid religious schools. Likewise the National School Lunch Act aids all school children attending tax exempt schools. In *Bradfield* v. *Roberts*, 175 US 291, this Court held proper the payment of money by the Federal Government to build an addition to a hospital, chartered by individuals who were members of a Roman Catholic sisterhood, and operated under the auspices of the Roman Catholic Church. This was done over the objection that it aided the establishment of religion. While obviously in these instances the respective churches, in a certain sense, were aided, this Court has never held that such "aid" was in violation of the First or Fourteenth Amendment.

Well-recognized and long-established practices support the validity of the Illinois statute here in question. That statute, as construed in this case, is comparable to those in many states. All differ to some extent. New York may be taken as a fair example. In many states the program is under the supervision of a religious council composed of delegates who are themselves communicants of various faiths. As is shown by *Bradfield* v. *Roberts*, the fact that the members of the council have religious affiliations is not significant. In some, instruction is given outside of the school buildings; in others, within these buildings. Metropolitan centers like New York usually would have available quarters convenient to schools. Unless smaller cities and rural communities use the school buildings at times that do not interfere with recitations, they may be compelled to give up religious education. I understand that pupils not taking religious education usually are given other work of a secular nature within the schools. Since all these states use the facilities of the schools to aid the religious education to some extent, their desire to permit religious education to school children is thwarted by this Court's judgment. Under it, as I understand its language, children cannot be released or dismissed from school to attend classes in religion while other children must remain to pursue secular education. Teachers cannot keep the records as to which pupils are to be dismissed and which retained. To do so is said to be an "aid" in establishing religion; the use of public money for religion.

Cases running into the scores have been in the state courts of last resort that involved religion and the schools. Except where the exercises with religious significance partook of the ceremonial practice of sects or groups, their constitutionality has been generally upheld. Illinois itself promptly struck down as violative of its own constitution required exercises partaking of a religious ceremony. *Ring* v. *Board of Education,* 245 Ill. 334. In that case compulsory religious exercises—a reading from the King James Bible, the Lord's Prayer and the singing of hymns—were forbidden as "worship services." In this case, the Supreme Court of Illinois pointed out that in the *Ring Case,* the activities in the school were ceremonial and compulsory; in this, voluntary and educational. . . .

The practices of the federal government offer many examples of this kind of "aid" by the state to religion. The Congress of the United States has a chaplain for each House who daily invokes divine blessings and guidance for the proceedings. The armed forces have commissioned chaplains from early days. They conduct the public services in accordance with the liturgical requirements of their respective faiths, ashore and afloat, employing for the purpose property belonging to the United States and dedicated to the services of religion. Under the Servicemen's Readjustment Act of 1944, eligible veterans may receive training at government expense for the ministry in denominational schools. The schools of the District of Columbia have opening exercises which "include a reading from the Bible without note or comment, and the Lord's prayer."

In the United States Naval Academy and the United States Military Academy, schools wholly supported and completely controlled by the federal government, there are a number of religious activities. Chaplains are attached to both schools. Attendance at church services on Sunday is compulsory at both the Military and Naval Academies. At West Point the Protestant services are held in the Cadet Chapel, the Catholic in the Catholic Chapel, and the Jewish in the Old Cadet Chapel; at Annapolis only Protestant services are held on the reservation, midshipmen of other religious persuasions attend the churches of the city of Annapolis. These facts indicate that both schools since their earliest beginnings have maintained and enforced a pattern of participation in formal worship.

With the general statements in the opinions concerning the constitutional requirement that the nation and the states, by virtue of the First and Fourteenth Amendments, may "make no law respecting an establishment of religion," I am in agreement. But, in the light of the meaning given to those words by the precedents, customs, and practices which I have detailed above, I cannot agree with the Court's conclusion that when pupils compelled by law to go to school for secular education are released from school so as to attend the religious classes, churches are unconstitutionally aided. Whatever may be the wisdom of the arrangement as to the use of the school buildings made with The Champaign Council of Religious Education, it is clear to me that past practice shows such cooperation between the schools and a non-ecclesiastical body is not forbidden by the First Amendment. When actual church services have always been permitted on government property, the mere use of the school buildings by a non-sectarian group for religious education ought not to be condemned as an establishment of religion. For a non-sectarian organization to give the type of instruction here offered cannot be said to violate our rule as to the establishment of religion by the state. The prohibition of enactments respecting the establishment of religion do not bar every friendly gesture between church and state. It is not an absolute prohibition against every conceivable situation where the two may work together, any more than the other provisions of the First Amendment—free speech, free press—are absolutes. If abuses occur such as the use of the instruction hour for sectarian purposes, I have no doubt, in view of the *Ring Case*, that Illinois will promptly correct them. If they are of a kind that tend to the establishment of a church or interfere with the free exercise of religion, this Court is open for a review of an erroneous decision. This Court cannot be too cautious in upsetting practices embedded in our society by many years of experience. A state is entitled to have great leeway in its legislation when dealing with the important social problems of its population. A definite violation of legislative limits must be established. . . . Devotion to the great principle of religious liberty should not lead us into a rigid interpretation of the constitutional guarantee that conflicts with accepted habits of our people. This is an instance where, for me, the history of past practices is determinative of the meaning of a constitutional clause. . . .

c. The McCollum Case Limited

ZORACH v. CLAUSON

343 US 306 (1952)

[In the *McCollum Case* religious instruction was given *within* the public school building. The New York City "released time" program called for the religious courses to be operated *outside* the public school building. The pupils who did not choose to attend the religious courses of their respective denominations were required to remain in their public school classrooms. Six Justices found this system sufficiently different from that presented in the *McCollum Case* to conclude that it violated no constitutional provision.

[Justices Black and Jackson dissented, maintaining that there was no essential difference between this case and the previous one. Justice Frankfurter's dissent emphasized that the state courts had not permitted proof that the New York City program involved coercion of pupils to join the sectarian classes. He also sharply differentiated a "dismissed time" from a "released time" system. Under the former *all* students are dismissed and are free to do with their "dismissed time" as they or their parents may see fit; some of them may go to their church schools, others may go home. This system would involve no coercion. The "released time" system may, however, involve coercion of the reluctant. If it is coercive, it should be declared unconstitutional.

[Again all Justices avowed belief in the principle of separation of church and state. The dissenters, however, maintained that the principle was, in this case, honored in the breach rather than in the observance.]

Mr. Justice Douglas delivered the opinion of the Court:

New York City has a program which permits its public schools to release students during the school day so that they may leave the school buildings and school grounds and go to religious centers for religious instruction or devotional exercises. A student is released on written request of his parents. Those not released stay in the classrooms. The churches make weekly reports to the schools, sending a list of children who have been released from public school but who have not reported for religious instruction.

This "released time" program involves neither religious instruction in public school classrooms nor the expenditure of public funds. All costs, including the application blanks, are paid by the religious organizations. The case is therefore unlike *McCollum* v. *Board of Education,* 333 U.S. 203, which involved a "released time" program from

Illinois. In that case the classrooms were turned over to religious instructors. We accordingly held that the program violated the First Amendment which (by reason of the Fourteenth Amendment) prohibits the states from establishing religion or prohibiting its free exercise.

Appellants, who are taxpayers and residents of New York City and whose children attend its public schools, challenge the present law, contending it is in essence not different from the one involved in the *McCollum Case*. Their argument, stated elaborately in various ways, reduces itself to this: the weight and influence of the school is put behind a program for religious instruction; public school teachers police it, keeping tab on students who are released; the classroom activities come to a halt while the students who are released for religious instruction are on leave; the school is a crutch on which the churches are leaning for support in their religious training; without the cooperation of the schools this "released time" program, like the one in the *McCollum Case*, would be futile and ineffective. . . .

The briefs and arguments are replete with data bearing on the merits of this type of "released time" program. Views *pro* and *con* are expressed, based on practical experience with these programs and with their implications. We do not stop to summarize these materials nor to burden the opinion with an anlysis of them. For they involve considerations not germane to the narrow constitutional issue presented. They largely concern the wisdom of the system, its efficiency from an educational point of view, and the political considerations which have motivated its adoption or rejection in some communities. Those matters are of no concern here, since our problem reduces itself to whether New York by this system has either prohibited the "free exercise" of religion or has made a law "respecting an establishment of religion" within the meaning of the First Amendment.

It takes obtuse reasoning to inject any issue of the "free exercise" of religion into the present case. No one is forced to go to the religious classroom and no religious exercise or instruction is brought to the classrooms of the public schools. A student need not take religious instruction. He is left to his own desires as to the manner or time of his religious devotions, if any.

There is a suggestion that the system involves the use of coercion to get public school students into religious classrooms. There is no evidence in the record before us that supports that conclusion. The present record indeed tells us that the school authorities are neutral in this regard and do no more than release students whose parents so request. If in fact coercion were used, if it were established that any one or more teachers were using their office to persuade or force students to take the religious instruction, a wholly different case would be presented. Hence we put aside that claim of coercion both as respects the "free exercise" of religion and "an establishment of religion" within the meaning of the First Amendment.

Moreover, apart from that claim of coercion, we do not see how New York by this type of "released time" program has made a law respecting an establishment of religion within the meaning of the First Amendment. There is much talk of the separation of Church and State in the history of the Bill of Rights and in the decisions clustering around the First Amendment. . . . There cannot be the slightest doubt that the First Amendment reflects the philosophy that Church and State should be separated. And so far as interference with the "free exercise" of religion and an "establishment" of religion are concerned, the separation must be complete and unequivocal. The First Amendment within the scope of its coverage permits no exception; the prohibition is absolute. The First Amendment, however, does not say that in every and all respects there shall be a separation of Church and State. Rather, it studiously defines the manner, the specific ways, in which there shall be no concert or union or dependency one on the other. That is the common sense of the matter. Otherwise the state and religion would be aliens to each other—hostile, suspicious, and even unfriendly. Churches could not be required to pay even property taxes. Municipalities would not be permitted to render police or fire protection to religious groups. Policemen who helped parishioners into their places of worship would violate the Constitution. Prayers in our legislative halls; the appeals to the Almighty in the messages of the Chief Executive; the proclamations making Thanksgiving Day a holiday; "so help me God" in our courtroom oaths—these and all other references to the Almighty that run through our laws, our public rituals, our ceremonies would be flouting the First Amendment. A fastidious atheist or agnostic could even object to the supplication with which the Court opens each session: "God save the United States and this Honorable Court."

We would have to press the concept of separation of Church and State to these extremes to condemn the present law on constitutional grounds. The nullification of this law would have wide and profound effects. A Catholic student applies to his teacher for permission to leave the school during hours on a Holy Day of Obligation to attend a mass. A Jewish student asks his teacher for permission to be excused for Yom Kippur. A Protestant wants the afternoon off for a family baptismal ceremony. In each case the teacher requires parental consent in writing. In each case the teacher, in order to make sure the student is not a truant, goes further and requires a report from the priest, the rabbi, or the minister. The teacher in other words cooperates in a religious program to the extent of making it possible for her students to participate in it. Whether she does it occasionally for a few students, regularly for one, or pursuant to a systematized program designed to further the religious needs of all the students does not alter the character of the act.

We are a religious people whose institutions presuppose a Supreme Being. We guarantee the freedom to worship as one chooses. We make room for as wide a variety of beliefs and creeds as the spiritual needs of man deem necessary. We sponsor an attitude on the part of government that shows no partiality to any one group and that lets each flourish according to the zeal of its adherents and the appeal of its dogma. When the state encourages religious instruction or cooperates with religious authorities by adjusting the schedule of public events to sectarian needs, it follows the best of our traditions. For it then respects the religious nature of our people and accommodates the public service to their spiritual needs. To hold that it may not would be to find in the Constitution a requirement that the government show a callous indifference to religious groups. That would be preferring those who believe in no religion over those who do believe. Government may not finance religious groups nor undertake religious instruction nor blend secular and sectarian education nor use secular institutions to force one or some religion on any person. But we find no constitutional requirement which makes it necessary for government to be hostile to religion and to throw its weight against efforts to widen the effective scope of religious influence. The government must be neutral when it comes to competition between sects. It may not thrust any sect on any person. It may not make a religious observance compulsory. It may not coerce anyone to attend church, to observe a religious holiday, or to take religious instruction. But it can close its doors or suspend its operations as to those who want to repair to their religious sanctuary for worship or instruction. No more than that is undertaken here.

This program may be unwise and improvident from an educational or a community viewpoint. That appeal is made to us on a theory, previously advanced, that each case must be decided on the basis of "our own prepossessions." . . . Our individual preferences, however, are not the constitutional standard. The constitutional standard is the separation of Church and State. The problem, like many problems in constitutional law, is one of degree. . . .

In the *McCollum Case* the classrooms were used for religious instruction and the force of the public school was used to promote that instruction. Here, as we have said, the public schools do no more than accommodate their schedules to a program of outside religious instruction. We follow the *McCollum Case*. But we cannot expand it to cover the present released time program unless separation of Church and State means that public institutions can make no adjustments of their schedules to accommodate the religious needs of the people. We cannot read into the Bill of Rights such a philosophy of hostility to religion. Affirmed [constitutionality sustained].

Mr. Justice Black, dissenting:

. . . I see no significant difference between the invalid Illinois system and that of New York here sustained. Except for the use of the school buildings in Illinois, there is no difference between the systems which I consider even worthy of mention. In the New York program, as in that of Illinois, the school authorities release some of the children on the condition that they attend the religious classes, get reports on whether they attend, and hold the other children in the school building until the religious hour is over. As we attempted to make categorically clear, the *McCollum* decision would have been the same if the religious classes had not been held in the school buildings. We said:

> Here *not only* are the state's tax-supported public school buildings used for the dissemination of religious doctrines. The State *also* affords sectarian groups an invaluable aid in that it helps to provide pupils for their religious classes through use of the state's compulsory public school machinery. *This* is not separation of Church and State. (Emphasis supplied.)

McCollum thus held that Illinois could not constitutionally manipulate the compelled classroom hours of its compulsory school machinery so as to channel children into sectarian classes. Yet that is exactly what the Court holds New York can do.

I am aware that our *McCollum* decision on separation of church and state has been subjected to a most searching examination throughout the country. Probably few opinions from this Court in recent years have attracted more attention or stirred wider debate. Our insistence on "a wall between Church and State which must be kept high and inpregnable" has seemed to some a correct exposition of the philosophy and a true interpretation of the language of the First Amendment to which we should strictly adhere. With equal conviction and sincerity, others have thought the *McCollum* decision fundamentally wrong and have pledged continuous warfare against it. The opinions in the court below and the briefs here reflect these diverse viewpoints. In dissenting today, I mean to do more than give routine approval to our *McCollum* decision. I mean also to reaffirm my faith in the fundamental philosophy expressed in *McCollum* and *Everson v. Board of Education.* . . .

Difficulty of decision in the hypothetical situations mentioned by the Court, but not now before us, should not confuse the issues in this case. Here the sole question is whether New York can use its compulsory education laws to help religious sects get attendants presumably too unenthusiastic to go unless moved to do so by the pressure of this state machinery. That this is the plan, purpose, design and consequence of the New York program cannot be denied. The state thus makes religious sects beneficiaries of its power to compel children to attend secular schools. Any use of such coercive power by the state to help or hinder some religious sects or to prefer all religious sects over nonbelievers or vice versa is just what I think the First Amendment forbids. In considering whether a state has entered this forbidden field the question is not whether it has entered too far but whether it has entered at all. New York is manipulating its compulsory education laws to help religious sects get pupils. This is not separation but combination of Church and State.

The Court's validation of the New York system rests in part on its statement that Americans are "a religious people whose institutions presuppose a Supreme Being." This was at least as true when the First Amendment was adopted; and it was just as true when eight justices of this Court invalidated the released time system in *McCollum* on the premise that a state can no more "aid all religions" than it can aid one. It was precisely because Eighteenth Century Americans were a religious people divided into many fighting sects that we were given the constitutional mandate to keep Church and State completely separate. Colonial history had already shown that, here as elsewhere, zealous sectarians entrusted with governmental power to further their causes, would sometimes torture, maim and kill those they branded "heretics," "atheists" or "agnostics." The First Amendment was therefore to insure that no one powerful sect or combination of sects could use political or governmental power to punish dissenters whom they could not convert to their faith. Now as then, it is only by wholly isolating the state from the religious sphere and compelling it to be completely neutral, that the freedom of each and every denomination and of all nonbelievers can be maintained. It is this neutrality the Court abandons today when it treats New York's coercive system as a program which *merely* "encourages religious instruction or cooperates with religious authorities." The abandonment is all the more dangerous to liberty because of the Court's legal exaltation of the orthodox and its derogation of unbelievers.

Under our system of religious freedom, people have gone to their religious sanctuaries not because they feared the law but because they loved their God. The choice of all has been as free as the choice of those who answered the call to worship moved only by the music of the old Sunday morning church bells. The spiritual mind of man has thus been free to believe, disbelieve, or doubt, without repression, great or small, by the heavy hand of government. Statutes authorizing such repression have been stricken. Before today, our judicial opinions have refrained from drawing invidious distinctions between those who believe in no religion and those who do believe. The First Amendment has lost much if the religious follower and the atheist are no longer to be judicially regarded as entitled to equal justice under law.

State help to religion injects political and party prejudices into a holy field. It too often substitutes force for prayer, hate for love, and persecution for persuasion. Government should not be allowed, under cover of the soft euphemism of "co-operation," to steal into the sacred area of religious choice.

Mr. Justice Frankfurter, dissenting:

By way of emphasizing my agreement with Mr. Justice Jackson's dissent, I add a few words.

The Court tells us that in the maintenance of its public schools, "[The State government] can close its doors or suspend its operations" so that its citizens may be free for religious devotions or instruction. If that were the issue, it would not rise to the dignity of a constitutional controversy. Of course a State may provide that the classes in its schools shall be dismissed, for any reason, or no reason, on fixed days, or for special occasions. The essence of this case is that the school system did not "close its doors" and did not "suspend its operations." There is all the difference in the world between letting the children out of school and letting some of them out of school into religious classes. If every one is free to make what use he will of time wholly unconnected from schooling required by law—those who wish sectarian instruction devoting it to that purpose, those who have ethical instruction at home, to that, those who study music, to that—then of course there is no conflict with the Fourteenth Amendment.

The pith of the case is that formalized religious instruction is substituted for other school activity which those who do not participate in the released-time program are compelled to attend. The school system is very much in operation during this kind of released time. If its doors are closed, they are closed upon those students who do not attend the religious instruction in order to keep them within the school. That is the very thing which raises the constitutional issue. It is not met by disregarding it. Failure to discuss this issue does not take it out of the case.

Again, the Court relies upon the absence from the record of evidence of coercion in the operation of the system. "If in fact coercion were used," according to the Court, "if it were established that any one or more teachers were using their office to persuade or force students to take the religious instruction, a wholly different case would be presented." Thus, "coercion" in the abstract is acknowledged to be fatal. But the Court disregards the fact that as the case comes to us, there could be no proof of coercion, for the petitioners were not allowed to make proof of it. Petitioners alleged that "The operation of the released time program has resulted and inevitably results in the exercise of pressure and coercion upon parents and children to secure attendance by the children for religious instruction." This allegation—that coercion was in fact present and is inherent in the system, no matter what disavowals might be made in the operating regulations—was denied by respondents. Thus were drawn issues of fact which cannot be determined, on any conceivable view of judicial notice, by judges out of their own knowledge or experience. Petitioners sought an opportunity to adduce evidence in support of these allegations at an appropriate trial. And though the courts below cited the concurring opinion in *McCollum* v. *Board of Education* to "emphasize the importance of detailed analysis of the facts to which the Constitutional test of Separation is to be applied," they denied that opportunity on the ground that such proof was irrelevant to the issue of constitutionality. . . .

The result in the *McCollum Case* . . . was based on principles that received unanimous acceptance by this Court, barring only a single vote. I agree with Mr. Justice Black that those principles are disregarded in reaching the result in this case. Happily they are not disavowed by the Court. From this I draw the hope that in future variations of the problem which are bound to come here, these principles may again be honored in the observance.

The deeply divisive controversy aroused by the attempts to secure public school pupils for sectarian instruction would promptly end if the advocates of such instruction were content to have the school "close its doors or suspend operations"—that is, dismiss classes in their entirety, without discrimination—instead of seeking to use the public schools as the instrument for security of attendance at denominational classes. The unwillingness of the promoters of this movement to dispense with such use of the public schools betrays a surprising want of confidence in the inherent power of the various faiths to draw children to outside sectarian classes—an attitude that hardly reflects the faith of the greatest religious spirits.

Mr. Justice Jackson, dissenting:

This released time program is founded upon a use of the State's power of coercion, which, for me, determines its unconstitutionality. Stripped to its essentials, the plan has two stages, first, that the State compels each student to yield a large part of his time for public secular education and, second, that some of it be "released" to him on condition that he devote it to sectarian religious purposes.

No one suggests that the Constitution would permit the State directly to require this "released" time to be spent "under the control of a duly constituted religious body." This program accomplishes that forbidden result by indirection. If public education were taking so much of the pupils' time as to injure the public or the students' welfare by encroaching upon their religious opportunity, simply shortening everyone's school day would facilitate voluntary and optional attendance at Church classes. But that suggestion is rejected upon the ground that if they are made free many students will not go to the Church. Hence, they must be deprived of freedom for this period, with Church attendance put to them as one of the two permissible ways of using it.

The greater effectiveness of this system over voluntary attendance after school hours is due to the truant officer who, if the youngster fails to go to the Church school, dogs him back to the public schoolroom. Here schooling is more or less suspended during the "released time" so the nonreligious attendants will not forge ahead of the churchgoing absentees. But it serves as a temporary jail for a pupil who will not go to Church. It takes more subtlety of mind than I possess to deny that this is governmental constraint in support of religion. It is as unconstitutional, in my view, when exerted by indirection as when exercised forthrightly.

As one whose children, as a matter of free choice, have been sent to privately supported Church schools, I may challenge the Court's suggestion that opposition to this plan can only be antireligious, atheistic, or agnostic. My evangelistic brethren confuse an objection to compulsion with an objection to religion. It is possible to hold a faith with enough confidence to believe that what should be rendered to God does not need to be decided and collected by Caesar.

The day that this country ceases to be free for irreligion it will cease to be free for religion—except for the sect that can win political power. The same epithetical jurisprudence used by the Court today to beat down those who oppose pressuring children into some religion can devise as good epithets tomorrow against those who object to pressuring them into a favored religion. And, after all, if we concede to the State power and wisdom to single out "duly constituted religious" bodies as exclusive alternatives for compulsory secular instruction, it would be logical to also uphold the power and wisdom to choose the true faith among those "duly constituted." We start down a rough road when we begin to mix compulsory public education with compulsory godliness. . . .

The distinction attempted between that case [McCollum] and this is trivial, almost to the point of cynicism, magnifying its nonessential details and disparaging compulsion which was the underlying reason for invalidity. A reading of the Court's opinion in that case along with its opinion in this case will show such difference of overtones and undertones as to make clear that the McCollum Case has passed like a storm in a teacup. The wall which the Court was professing to erect between Church and State has become even more warped and twisted than I expected. Today's judgment will be more interesting to students of psychology and of the judicial processes than to students of constitutional law.

d. Bible Reading in Public Schools

DOREMUS v. BOARD OF EDUCATION

5 NJ 435 (1950)

[Some states prohibit "sectarian" instruction in the public schools. Many states permit or require the teacher to read passages from the Bible or from the Old Testament, but prohibit the teacher from making any comment on what he has read. Practices with respect to this matter differ sharply. Most of the statutes permitting or requiring Bible reading have been adopted in the twentieth century. In the Doremus Case the Supreme Court of New Jersey unanimously held that the Old Testament and the Lord's Prayer are not "sectarian" and that their use in the public schools of that state is not prohibited by the Federal or by the State Constitution.

[An appeal to the United States Supreme Court was dismissed. 342 US 429 (1952). Six Justices, in an opinion by Justice Jackson, held that "no case or controversy" had been presented to the Court because neither appellant had standing to raise the constitutional question before the Supreme Court. The opinion of the Court did not reach the merits of the controversy. Justices Douglas, Reed, and Burton dissented on the ground that a taxpayer or parent has an adequate interest in the conduct of the public schools to maintain a suit such as that presented before the Court in this case.]

Justice Case:

. . . . The action was originated under the Declaratory Judgment Act . . . to test the constitutionality of R.S. 18:14–77 and 78. Those statutory provisions are:

[18:14–77.] At least five verses taken from that portion of the Holy Bible known as the Old Testament shall be read, or caused to be read, without comment, in each public school classroom, in the presence of the pupils therein assembled, by the teacher in charge, at the opening of school upon every school day, unless there is a general assemblage of the classes at the opening of the school on any school day, in which event the reading shall be done, or caused to be done, by the principal or teacher in charge of the assemblage and in the presence of the classes so assembled.

[18:14–78.] No religious service or exercise, except the reading of the Bible and the repeating of the Lord's Prayer, shall be held in any school receiving any portion of the moneys appropriated for the support of public schools. . . .

Considered with the statute was the directive issued by the defendant Board of Education of the Borough of Hawthorne that "any student may be excused during the reading of the Bible upon request." There was no request that a student be excused. . . .

Appellants present this line of reasoning: The principle of the separation of the church and state is established in the constitution of the United States, namely, the first and fourteenth amendments which prohibit the intermingling of religious and secular education in the public schools; the reading of the Bible and the reciting of the Lord's Prayer in the public schools are religious services, religious exercises and religious instruction; they are of themselves in aid of one or more religions and in preference of one religion over another; and therefore those acts are contrary to the named constitutional provisions. The gist of the argument is that compliance with the statute necessarily involves sectarian worship and sectarian instruction and therefore violates the Federal Constitution. . . .

Was it the intent of the First Amendment that the existence of a Supreme Being should be negated and that the governmental recognition of God should be suppressed? Not that, surely. The temper of the times during which the agitation for and the accomplishment of the amendment was had, the events which led to the adoption of the amendment, the contemporaneous and subsequent interpretation by way of statute and public practice, the very wording of the amendment, all forcefully support that answer.

Instances could be multiplied going to the undeniable result that the Constitution itself assumes as an unquestioned fact the existence and authority of God and that preceding, contemporaneously with and after the adoption of the constitutional amendment all branches of the government followed a course of official conduct which openly accepts the existence of God as Creator and Ruler of the Universe; a course of conduct that has been accepted as not in conflict with the constitutional mandate.

The United States Constitution in Article I, section 7 provides that the President shall have ten days (Sundays excepted) within which to determine whether he will affirm or veto a bill. The essential idea of an oath seems to be that it is a recognition of God's authority and an undertaking by the affiant to accomplish the transaction to which it refers as required by His laws. . . . The Constitution recognized that divine authority by directing that in the alternative an oath or an affirmance be taken in certain instances. With particularity it framed the oath, or affirmance, to be taken by the President. The origin of the privilege, in the alternative, to affirm rather than to take an oath is not to be understood, necessarily, as a concession to disbelief in God. The privilege was accorded, or at least made more generous, in New Jersey, in 1727 because the Quakers, although a God-fearing group, were conscientiously scrupulous against taking an oath. . . .

The first ten amendments, called the Bill of Rights, were offered and adopted speedily after the adoption of the Constitution and were a product of the motives and conditions which culminated in the parent instrument. The confederated colonies and, later, the states organized as a constitutional nation, acknowledged the existence of and bowed before the Supreme Being. The Declaration of Independence, phrased in the political ideology of Thomas Jefferson, frankly grounded its position in the unalienable rights endowed by God, the Creator, made appeal to Him, the Supreme Judge of the world, for the rectitude of that position and expressed trust in the Divine Providence for protection in the fulfillment thereof. The Articles of Confederation recited the beneficent intervention of the Great Governor of the world.

Contemporary construction of a constitutional provision which has been followed since the founding of our government is entitled to the greatest respect. . . . Specifically, acts by the First Congress, which proposed the first ten amendments, have been judicially considered as of the highest authority in providing a contemporaneous exposition of constitutional provisions. . . . On September 24, 1789, the day the first Congress adopted the resolution submitting the First Amendment to the states, it adopted a resolution requesting the President to recommend to the people "a day of public thanksgiving and prayer, to be observed by acknowledging, with grateful hearts, the many signal favors of Almighty God, especially by affording them an opportunity to establish a Constitution of government for their safety and happiness." . . . That Congress also adopted a resolution providing for a chaplain for each house . . . ; and every session of congress, from that time forward, has been convened with prayer.

Courts have functioned normally since before our national history began upon the assumption of the sanctity of an oath. Public officers uniformly qualify by being sworn. The statute upon the taking of an oath by the justices and judges of the United States courts is illustrative:—"Each justice or judge of the United States shall take the following oath or affirmation before performing the duties of his office: 'I, ———, do solemnly swear (or affirm) that I will administer justice without respect to persons, and do equal right to the poor and to the rich, and that I will faithfully and impartially discharge and perform all the duties incumbent upon me as ——— according to the best of my abilities and understanding, agreeably to the Constitution and laws of the United States. *So help me God.*'"

The Thanksgiving Proclamation issued annually by the President, founded originally in resolution and continued through the years by tradition, gives, by its continuity and content, a striking reflection of the acceptance by our nation, and specifically by our government, of the idea and the existence of God. Our coined dollar for years beyond memory has carried the inscription "In God We Trust." It seems, *McCollum* v. *Board of Education*, 333 U.S. 203 . . . (dissenting opinion of Mr. Justice Reed) that not only does Congress still have in each house a chaplain who daily invokes divine blessings and guidance for the proceedings but that the armed forces have had commissioned chaplains from early days and that these chaplains, so commissioned, conduct public services in accordance with the liturgical requirements of their several faiths; and that chaplains are attached to each of the schools, governmentally supported and controlled, for the training of military and naval cadets. The United States Congress has enacted that "Whoever utters any . . . profane language by means of radio communication shall be fined not more than $10,000 or imprisoned not more than two years, or both." In our national anthem we reverently sing:

> . . . May the heav'n rescued land
> Praise the Power that hath made and preserved us a nation,
> Then conquer we must, when our cause it is just
> And this be our motto—"In God is our trust."

What has been said of the Federal Government could almost be repeated, *mutatis mutandis,* with reference to our State. For illustration: with respect to blasphemy, our own statute . . . provides that any person who shall willfully blaspheme the name of God shall be guilty of a misdemeanor. An early statute, III Anne, 1704, punished, *inter alia,* "cursing" and "swearing." But the Crimes Act of March 18, 1796, . . . provided in section 20 the statutory cast that has come down through the various revisions without great change. . . . Property used for religious purposes has long been and is largely exempt from taxation. . . . Beyond that it may suffice for the purpose of showing our governmental attitude to refer to a persistent and specific recognition of "Almighty God" in the several constitutions of our state. The first constitution, adopted July 2nd, 1776, provided . . . that "no person shall ever within this colony be deprived of the inestimable privilege of worshiping Almighty God in a manner agreeable to the dictates of his own conscience; nor under any pretense whatsoever, compelled to attend any place of worship, contrary to his own faith and judgment." The second constitution, . . . 1844, contained this preamble: "We, the people of the state of New Jersey, grateful to Almighty God for the civil and religious liberty which He hath so long permitted us to enjoy, and looking to Him for a blessing upon our endeavors to secure and transmit the same unimpaired to succeeding generations, do ordain and establish this constitution:". It also repeated, in Art. I, par. 3, the language quoted *supra* (except the words "ever within this colony") from the first constitution. In both respects our present constitution, adopted in 1947, follows the 1844 instrument.

The United States Supreme Court, speaking through Mr. Justice Brewer in *Church of the Holy Trinity* v. *United States,* 143 U.S. 457 (1892), found no dissonance in the provisions of the first amendment and various official declarations placing God at the apex of all things and said: "There is a universal language pervading them all, having one meaning; they affirm and reaffirm that this is a religious nation. These are not individual sayings, declarations of private persons; they are organic utterances; they speak the voice of the entire people."

Appellants rely mainly on the decisions in the United States Supreme

Court in *Everson* v. *Board of Education* and *McCollum* v. *Board of Education*. . . .

Appellants contend that the statutory direction provides for religious instruction and religious worship and is in aid of one or more religions and in preference of one religion over another; and it is upon that argument that they seek support in the *Everson* and *McCollum* decisions. No charge is made that, in the reading, passages were selected with the purpose or the result of giving a sectarian bias; the Bible itself is indicated as sectarian. We are of the opinion that the characterizations of the statute and of the Book are not sound, that the holdings in the cited cases involve essential elements wholly lacking in the instant case, and that consequently the decisions are not in point and are not binding. Further, we think that the reasoning followed in reaching those decisions was not intended to, and does not, reach the facts of the present case.

Appellants concede that there are twelve states which prescribe the reading of the Bible in public school classes: Alabama, Arkansas, Delaware, Florida, Georgia, Idaho, Kentucky, Maine, Massachusetts, Pennsylvania, Tennessee and New Jersey; and that the statutes of five other states make its use permissive: Indiana, Iowa, Kansas, North Dakota and Oklahoma; and also that the cases on the subject which sustain the reading of the Bible (among them decisions by the courts of Texas, Colorado, Michigan, Minnesota and New York) outnumber the cases in which Bible reading was interdicted. It could be added that a bylaw of the Board of Education requires the reading of the Bible and the Lord's Prayer in the public schools of the District of Columbia; that a Mississippi statute . . . requires a course in the Principles of Morality and Good Manners, the same to include "the Mosaic Ten Commandments"; and that the Bible is read in a large number of schools in many states where the statutes are silent on the subject.

Appellants further state that the reading of the Bible in the public schools has been struck down in Illinois, Louisiana, Wisconsin and Ohio; and that while decisions upholding the reading of the Bible are more numerous, the better reasoning, "considered in the light of the United States Supreme Court decisions in the *Everson* and *McCollum* Cases," leads inevitably to the conclusion of unconstitutionality. We have given our reasons for believing that the last-named Supreme Court decisions do not lead to or lean toward that conclusion; and we are not impressed by the alleged pertinency of the state decisions cited by appellants. . . .

We consider that the Old Testament, because of its antiquity, its content, and its wide acceptance, is not a sectarian book when read without comment. . . . It is accepted by three great religions, the Jewish, the Roman Catholic and the Protestant, and, at least in part, by others. There are different versions, but the statute makes no distinction. The adherents of those religions constitute the great bulk of our population. There are religious groups other than the Jewish, the Roman Catholic and the Protestant, but in this country they are numerically small and, in point of impact upon our national life, negligible. This is not a criticism, simply the statement of a fact from which it is to be gathered that the tenets of these minor groups had no vital part in the formation of our national character. And it is not to say that because a religious group is small, it thereby loses its constitutional rights or that it is not entitled to the protection of those rights. The application is that some of our national incidents are developments from the almost universal belief in God which so strongly shaped and nurtured our people during the colonial period and the formative years of our constitutional government, with the result that we accept as a commendable part of our public life certain conditions and practices which in a country of different origins would be rejected; just as some acts would be offensive here, which, as Cooley . . . says, "in a Mahometan or Pagan country might be passed by without notice, or even be regarded as meritorious." Again, take the instance of an atheist:— he has all the protection of the Constitution; he may not be held to any religious function or to the support, financial or otherwise, of a religious establishment; he may entertain his belief or the lack of belief as he will; but he lives in a country where theism is in the warp and woof of the social and the governmental fabric and he has no authority to eradicate from governmental activities every vestige of the existence of God. He could not, we hypothesize, prevent, on constitutional grounds, the houses of Congress from opening their sessions with prayer to the Almighty for guidance in their deliberations, even though he were a member of Congress, or from maintaining chaplains for service with the armed forces, even though he were a member of those forces. . . . A situation so supposed would be more exposed than our own to a charge of sectarianism because the argument might point to the sectarian affiliations of the clergyman or the chaplain. We are speaking in terms of the Constitution upon the situations which that document was intended to reach, specifically upon whether or not the inhibition against the making of a law respecting an establishment of religion or prohibiting the free exercise thereof is violated by the reading, without comment, of a few verses, daily, in our public schools, from the Old Testament, and upon whether a statute which requires that to be done sets up religious instruction, or religious worship, which, within the meaning of our cases, is in aid of one or more religions, or prefers one religion above another. The reading does not, obviously effect or tend to effect the setting up, or the establishment, of a religion and, just as obviously, it does not prohibit the free exercise of any religion. We have noted the absence of allegation or proof that the plaintiffs or either of them are harmed by the statute of which they complain and we have withheld from considering a disposal of the case upon that technical ground; but we should, and do, recall that no burden of participation is put upon a pupil by the statute, and that by the regulation of the school board under whose jurisdiction the issue arose a pupil would, upon request, be excused from the class room during the brief exercises. The contention that one religion is preferred above another is vague and intangible; no religious group is a party to the cause; no person or sect is charging that his or its beliefs are prejudiced. The incidents which were condemned in the *McCollum Case* as being contrary to the separation of church and state appear to be entirely absent.

As to the permissive repeating of the Lord's Prayer: That short supplication to the Divinity was given its name because it was enjoined by Christ as an appropriate form of prayer. It is used by Roman Catholics and Protestants with slight variations. But nothing therein is called to our attention as not proper to come from the lips of any believer in God, His fatherhood, and His supreme power. Christ was a Jew and He was speaking to Jews; and it is said, on excellent Jewish authority, (Dr. Philip Bernstein, Rabbi of the Temple B'rith Kodesh, Rochester, N.Y., "What the Jews Believe," *Life Magazine*, September 11, 1950, p. 161), that the prayer was based upon the ancient Jewish prayer called "the Kaddish"—"Exalted and hallowed be the name of God throughout the world . . . May His Kingdom come, His will be done." *We find nothing in the Lord's Prayer that is controversial, ritualistic or dogmatic.* It is a prayer to "God, our Father." It does not contain Christ's name and makes no reference to Him. It is, in our opinion, in the same position as is the Bible reading and needs no special comment beyond what has just been said. . . .

While it is necessary that there be a separation between church and state, it is not necessary that the state should be stripped of religious sentiment. It may be a tragic experience for this country and for its conception of life, liberty and the pursuit of happiness if our people lose their religious feeling and are left to live their lives without faith. Who can say that those attributes which Thomas Jefferson in his notable document called "unalienable rights" endowed by the Creator may survive a loss of belief in the Creator? The American people are and always have been theistic. . . . The influence which that force contributed to our origins and the direction which it has given to our progress are beyond calculation. It may be of the highest importance to the nation that the people remain theistic, not that one or another sect or denomination may survive, but that belief in God shall abide. It was, we are led to believe, to that end that the statute was enacted; so that at the beginning of the day the children should pause to hear a few words from the wisdom of the ages and to bow the head in humility before the Supreme Power. No rites, no ceremony, no doctrinal teaching; just a brief moment with eternity. *Great results follow from elements which to human perception are small.* It may be that the true perspective engendered by that recurring short communion with the eternal forces will be effective to keep our people from permitting government to become a man-made robot which will crush even the Constitution itself. Our way of life is on challenge. Organized atheistic society is making a determined drive for supremacy by conquest as well as by infiltration. Recent history has demonstrated that when such a totalitarian power comes into control it exercises a ruthless supremacy over men and ideas, and over such remnants of religious worship as it permits to exist. We are at a crucial hour in which it may behoove our people to conserve all of the elements which have made our land what it is. Faced with this threat to the continuance of elements deeply imbedded in our national life the adoption of a public policy with respect thereto is a reasonable function to be performed by those on whom responsibility lies. Subject to constitutional limitations, the legislature has exclusive jurisdiction over matters of public policy, . . . and the courts should be very sure of their ground before they restrict that legislative field.

The statute under attack has been on the statute books for 47 years, and the substance of it, that is, the permission to read the Bible and to repeat the Lord's Prayer, for more than eighty years. It is common knowledge that the schools have conducted those exercises throughout such periods. This has been without question until now. As was said in *Legg* v. *Passaic County,* 122 N.J.L. 100 (1939), ". . . One of the fundamental policies of our jurisprudence is not to declare unconstitutional a statute which has been in force without any substantial challenge for many years unless its unconstitutionality is obvious." . . .

Manifestly, as we have indicated, the disputed statutes do not impinge upon the strict wording of the First Amendment. They do not go to the establishment of religion or against the free exercise thereof. How far the intendment of the amendment goes beyond the literal phrasing thereof has never been determined. But it is clear, we think, that the sense of the amendment does not serve to prohibit government from recognizing the existence and sovereignty of God and that the motives which inspired the amendment and the interpretation given by the several departments of the Federal Government concurrently with and subsequent to the submission and adoption of the amendment are inconsistent with any other conclusion. It is a cardinal rule in the construction of constitutional and statutory enactments that the provision made by way of remedy shall be studied in the light of the evil against which the remedy was erected. . . . The fact is that the First Amendment does not say, and so far as we are able to determine was not intended to say, that God shall not be acknowledged by our government as God. Our view is that a prohibition which is not in the language of the amendment and which is contrary to the intention of those who framed and adopted the instrument should not now be read into it. We consider that the Old Testament and the Lord's Prayer, pronounced without comment, are not sectarian, and that the short exercise provided by the statute does not constitute sectarian instruction or sectarian worship but is a simple recognition of the Supreme Ruler of the Universe and a deference to His Majesty; that since the exercise is not sectarian, no justiciable sectarian advantage or disadvantage flows therefrom; and that, in any event, the presence of a scholar at, and his participation in, that exercise is, under the directive of the Board of Education, voluntary.

We conclude that the statutes are not in violation of the Federal Constitution and that the judgment below should be affirmed. . . .

e. Bible Distribution in Public Schools

TUDOR v. BOARD OF EDUCATION OF RUTHERFORD
14 NJ 31 (1953)

[A Protestant organization, the Gideons International, attempts "to win men and women for the Lord Jesus Christ" by the distribution of the Bible in hotels, hospitals, and, more recently, public schools. For public schools the "Gideons Bible" consists of the New Testament, the Book of Psalms, and the Book of Proverbs. Pupils are given an opportunity to get free copies to take home. Objections to distribution of the "Gideons Bible" to public school pupils have been voiced by both Roman Catholics and Jews. In the *Rutherford Case* the Supreme Court of New Jersey unanimously held that the local board of education violated the Federal and State Constitutions when it gave permission for the distribution of the "Gideons Bible," a sectarian book, to public school pupils. The opinion of Chief Justice Vanderbilt is notable as being the first judicial opinion by a high court on the issue and also for using expert testimony on the harm done to children by the action of the Gideons in the public schools.]

The opinion of the Court was delivered by Chief Justice Vanderbilt:

I

The Gideons International is a nonprofit corporation organized under the laws of the State of Illinois, whose object is "to win men and women for the Lord Jesus Christ, through . . . (c) placing the Bible—God's Holy Words—or portions thereof in hotels, hospitals, schools, institutions, and also through the distribution of same for personal use." In recent years it began a campaign to make available to pupils in the public schools of this country the so-called "Gideon Bible," which was characterized by the International in its pleadings as "a book containing all of the New Testament, all of the Book of Psalms from the Old Testament, all of the Book of Proverbs from the Old Testament; all without note or comment, conformable to the edition of 1611, commonly known as the Authorized, or King James version of the Holy Bible." In furtherance of this campaign it applied by letter to the Board of Education of the Borough of Rutherford for permission to distribute its Bible to the public schools of that municipality: . . .

Gentlemen:

The Gideons of Passaic and Bergen County, consisting of local business men, hereby offer to furnish, without charge, a volume containing the book of Psalms, Proverbs and the New Testament to each of the children in the schools of Rutherford from the fifth grade up through the eighth grade, and High School.

This offer is part of a national campaign conducted by the Gideons International to furnish the Word of God free to the young people of our country from the fifth grade through the high school. If God's word is heard and heeded, if it is read and believed, we believe that this is the answer to the problem of juvenile delinquency.

If your board approves this distribution, we will be glad to have our committee work out the details with the principals of the schools.

Yours very truly,

PASSAIC COUNTY CAMP OF GIDEONS . . .

The proposal was considered at a meeting of the Board of Education on November 5, 1951, at which time there was voiced some opposition to the proposal by a Catholic priest and a Jewish rabbi on the grounds that the Gideons' New Testament was sectarian and forbidden to Catholic and Jewish children under the laws of their respective religions. The proposal, however, was passed by the board with one dissenting vote, the resolution adopted providing that "the Gideons International be allowed to furnish copies of the New Testament, Psalms and Proverbs to those pupils who request them." Under date of November 21, 1951, the following request form for signature of the parents was prepared by the Board of Education and distributed to the pupils of the public schools of Rutherford:

Rutherford Public Schools,
Rutherford, N.J.
November 21, 1951

To all Parents:

At the regular meeting of the Board of Education on November 5, 1951, The Gideon Bible Society presented a request that the New Testament, Psalms and Proverbs be made available, without cost, to all children who wish a copy. The Board approved this request provided the distribution be voluntary. *If you wish a copy of this Bible, will you please sign the slip below and return it with your child to the school he attends by Friday, December 21.*

_____

School

_____   _____
                                                              Date
Please request The Gideon Bible Society to provide my child _____
_____, with a copy of the New Testament, Psalms and Proverbs. This request involves no obligation on my part or on the part of the Board of Education.

Signed_____
Parent or Guardian

On January 14, 1952, the Board of Education was advised by its counsel that the proposed distribution was in his opinion legal. At a principal's meeting on February 6, 1952, the following instructions were issued:

(a) Only names of pupils whose parents had previously signed for the Bibles should be used in any announcement.

(b) Pupils whose parents had signed for Bibles are to report to the home room at the close of the session and no other pupils are to be in the room when the Bibles are distributed.

(c) Any announcement of names for the purpose of reporting after school should not include a reference as to the purpose of reporting.

Prior to the distribution of the books the present action was commenced demanding judgment as to the validity of the distribution under the Federal and New Jersey Constitutions and seeking an injunction against it. . . .

The plaintiff Bernard Tudor is an adherent of the Jewish religion, while plaintiff Ralph Lecoque is a member of the Catholic faith, each being a New Jersey citizen and taxpayer of Rutherford and a parent of a pupil in a Rutherford public school. Each contends that the Gideon Bible is "a sectarian work of peculiar religious value and significance to members of the Protestant faith," Mr. Tudor claiming that "its distribution to children of the Jewish faith violates the teachings, tenets and principles of Judaism," while Mr. Lecoque states that "its distribution to children of Catholic faith violates the teachings, tenets and principles of Catholicism." After this action was commenced, the child of plaintiff Ralph Lecoque transferred from the public school to a Catholic parochial school and to the extent that the complaint was based upon his status as a parent, the issue became moot. The State of New Jersey was originally named as a party defendant but the action as to it has been dismissed. The Synagogue Council of America and the National Community Relations Advisory Council have submitted a brief amici curiae.

II

The American doctrine of the separation of Church and State cannot be understood apart from its history for it is the epitome of centuries of struggle and conflict. In 311 A.D. Christians were still being persecuted; but shortly thereafter the Fourth Century witnessed the toleration of Christianity in the Roman World. In 313 A.D. Constantine, the ruler of the West, and Licinius, the emperor of the East, met in Italy and proclaimed the Edict of Milan, which made the toleration of the Christian religion "a part of a universal toleration of all religions, and it establishes absolute freedom of worship," Innes, *Church and State*, p. 23. In 410 A.D. Rome was sacked by Alaric. Italy, as well as Spain and Africa, fell to the Teutonic barbarians, but these conquests did not spell defeat for Christianity. The attitude of the invaders is illustrated by the words of Theodoric, speaking shortly after the fall of Rome:

> That to pretend to a dominion over the conscience is to usurp the prerogative of God; that by the nature of things the power of sovereigns is confined to external government; that they have no right of punishment, but over those who disturb the public peace, of which they are the guardians; and that the most dangerous heresy is that of a sovereign who separates himself from a part of his subjects, because they believe not according to his belief. Innes, *Church and State*, p. 51.

After the collapse of the Roman Empire the Church remained as the one stable, permanent element in society. Gradually it came to claim not merely equality with the State, but actual superiority. Thomas Aquinas summed up the Church's attitude:

The highest aim of mankind is eternal happiness. To this chief aim of mankind all earthly aims must be subordinated. This chief aim cannot be realized through human direction alone but must obtain divine assistance which is only to be obtained through the Church. Therefore the State, through which earthly aims are obtained, must be subordinated to the Church. Church and State are as two swords which God has given to Christendom for protection; both of these, however, are given by him to the Pope and the temporal sword by him handed to the rulers of the State. Bates, *Religious Liberty: An Inquiry* (1945), p. 140.

The Church's claim of supremacy did not go unchallenged. Charlemagne, who had been crowned by the Pope, deliberately crowned his own son as successor without consulting the Pope. The struggle for supremacy was on between Church and State, and the history of the Middle Ages in Europe is largely a history of this continuing conflict. The struggles between Pope Gregory VII and Emperor Henry IV in the Eleventh Century, and between the English kings Henry II and John and Celestine III and Innocent III a century later were but phases of the conflict. The Church reached the height of its supremacy over the State in the Thirteenth Century, under Innocent III, who informed the Patriarch of Constantinople that "the Lord left to Peter (the Pope) the government not of the Church only but of the whole world," and advised Philip Augustus of France that "single rulers have single provinces and single kings have single kingdoms, but Peter, as in the plentitude, so in the extent of his power, is preëminent over all since he is the vicar of Him Whose is the earth and fullness thereof, the whole world and all that dwell therein." Bates, *Religious Liberty: An Inquiry*, pp. 140–141. During his rule Innocent was not only a spiritual leader but he was also the supreme temporal chief of the Italian State, the Spanish Peninsula, the Scandinavian States, Hungary, Bohemia, Poland, Servia, Bosnia, Bulgaria, and the Christian state of Syria. 17 *Encyclopedia Britannica*, (14th ed.) "Papacy," p. 203.

The fourteenth century witnessed the growth of new ideas. In 1324 Marsilius of Padua in his *Defensor Pacis* denied the right of the Church to interfere in any matters which were not spiritual. He expounded the very ideas that centuries later were credited to Locke, Montesquieu, Rousseau and Jefferson. Marsilius was far ahead of his age when he claimed that "no man may be punished for his religion." Acton, "History of Freedom in Christianity," in *Essays on Freedom and Power*, p. 65.

But the doctrine of religious liberty and the separation of Church and State were not established in Europe even with the advent of the Reformation. The Reformation brought forth the more prevalent Erastian doctrine of state supremacy and the use of religion to help carry out state policy. The peace of Augsburg in 1555 was a compromise between Lutherans and Catholics, based on the theory that the religion of a province was to be determined by the religion of its ruler (*cuius regio, eius religio*). To the same effect was the peace of Westphalia in 1648 ending a thirty year religious war which swept Central Europe. . . . In England under Queen Elizabeth the Thirty-nine Articles of the Church of England were adopted and the supremacy of the Crown over the Church was clearly established. Bloody struggles between Anglicans, Catholics and Dissenters continued. By the Seventeenth Century Catholics were regarded with disfavor and in 1647 the Constitution established by Cromwell granted religious freedom to all except Catholics. In the Glorious Revolution of 1689 the Act of Toleration under William and Mary established religious toleration in England, but again Catholics were excepted.

By 1787 in Europe no nation had established complete freedom of worship or the mutual independence of religion and civil government. There had been steps in that direction and there were those who strongly advocated the separation of Church and State but the Erastian doctrine still prevailed. In almost every country there was a state-supported or at least a state-favored religion while the other faiths were treated with varying degrees of toleration. In Spain the Inquisition was still in existence in 1787 while at the other extreme Holland represented the utmost in religious toleration and freedom for all faiths. In 1784 James Madison summed up the centuries of bloody religious battles in Europe: "Torrents of blood have been spilt in the world in vain attempts of the secular arm to extinguish religious discord, by proscribing all differences in religious opinions." Blau, *Cornerstones of Religious Freedom in America* (1949), p. 85. While America has been free from religious wars, our history has had its dark pages of religious persecution.

III

Religion was a strong motivating force in the American colonies. People of all faiths flocked to the New World, many with the hope that here for the first time they could enjoy religious freedom. Unfortunately to America these earlier settlers also brought the Old World idea of a state established and state dominated religion. Many of the original charters granted by the Crown required the settlers to establish a religion that was to be supported by all, believers and nonbelievers alike. Thus in early Virginia all ministers were required to conform to the canons of the Church of England. Quakers were banished and Catholics were disqualified from public office, while priests were not permitted in the colony. In New York Peter Stuyvesant established the Dutch Reformed Church, which all settlers were required to support. Baptists who attempted to hold services in their homes were subject to fines, whipping and banishment. Quakers were unwelcome and subject to persecution. . . . In New England generally the Calvinist Congregational Church was the established religion.

Religious freedom in the colonies was far from an established fact. In the Massachusetts Bay Colony Anne Hutchinson in 1638 was tried and convicted as a blasphemer and seducer of the faithful and as a teacher of erroneous doctrines, because she held meetings in her home where she advocated the direct intuition of God's grace and love instead of obedience to the laws of the Church and the State. Roger Williams was banished because "he broached and divulged divers new and dangerous opinions, against the authority of the magistrates." Stokes, *Church and State in the United States* (1950), Vol. I, p. 195. Catholics were persecuted and in 1647 the General Court ordered that:

> No Jesuit or spiritual or ecclesiastical person ordained by the pope or see of Rome shall henceforth come into Massachusetts. Any person not freeing himself of suspicion shall be jailed, then banished. If taken a second time he shall be put to death. Pfeffer, *Church, State and Freedom* (1953), p. 68.

Despite these instances of intolerance and persecution there were successful examples of religious freedom. In 1649, largely due to the efforts of Cecil Calvert, the second Lord Baltimore, Maryland granted toleration to all Trinitarian Christians. In Rhode Island through the efforts of John Clarke, a follower of Roger Williams, Charles II granted a charter in 1663 which provided for complete religious freedom. In 1683 Pennsylvania received from William Penn its "Frame of Government" which stated that all who believed in "One Almighty God" should be protected and all who believed in "Jesus Christ the Savior of the World" could hold civil office.

The history of religious freedom in the province of New Jersey was not fundamentally different from that in the other colonies, although Stokes states that we "had a better colonial record in the matter of toleration than most of the colonies." *Church and State in the United States, supra,* Vol. 1, p. 435. The grantees of the Concessions of 1665, Lord Berkeley and Sir George Carteret, offered liberty of worship as an inducement to settlers. This was continued under the Quakers by a Law of 1681 in West Jersey and in East Jersey by a Law of 1683. Nevertheless, despite what appeared to be the establishment of religious freedom in the Province of New Jersey, . . . there was strong anti-Catholic feeling in the colony, and holders of civil office were required to take an oath against the Pope. . . . By the king's instructions to Lord Cornbury . . . in 1702 he was to permit a liberty of conscience to all persons except Papists. Our Constitution of 1776 provides:

XVIII. Free Exercise of Religion. That no person shall ever within this colony be deprived of the inestimable privilege of worshipping Almighty God in a manner agreeable to the dictates of his own conscience; nor under any pretense whatsoever, compelled to attend any place of worship, contrary to his own faith and judgment; nor shall any person within this colony, ever be obliged to pay tithes, taxes or any other rates, for the purpose of building or repairing any church or churches, place or places of worship, or for the maintenance of any minister or ministry, contrary to what he believes to be right, or has deliberately or voluntarily engaged himself to perform.

But the very next article of this same Constitution, after providing that there shall be "no establishment of any one religious sect in this province in preference to another," goes on to guarantee civil rights and the right to hold civil office to all who are of the "protestant sect." The exclusion of Catholics from this guarantee of civil rights and from holding civil office was not eliminated until the Constitution of 1844.

Generally speaking it can then be said that religious toleration varied from one province to another with very few approaching a system of full religious freedom. Pfeffer reviews the religious atmosphere in the colonies:

Summarizing the colonial period, we may note that the proprietary regimes permitted a considerable degree of toleration, at least in comparison with the other colonies. This difference may be explained partly by the idealism of the proprietors and partly by the economic necessity of attracting large numbers of settlers in order to preserve and make profitable the proprietor's substantial investment.

Even in the proprietary colonies, however, the death of the idealistic founder, Calvert, Williams, or Penn, resulted in considerable backsliding, and the imposition of restrictions on civil and religious rights, particularly of non-Protestants. The limited tolerance which did exist did not include Catholics, Jews, Unitarians, or Deists. The variety and degree of discrimination against them varied. Primarily, the discrimination was political—the non-Protestants could not vote or hold office. But the restrictions were not always limited to political disabilities. Public performance of Catholic worship was prohibited almost everywhere, and as late as 1756 the colony which had been founded by the Catholic Calverts enacted a law subjecting Catholics to double taxation.

Perhaps the incident that most ironically illustrates the turnabout after the death of the idealistic founder is the action of a Rhode Island court which in 1762 denied the petition of two Jews for naturalization on the ground that to grant the petition would be "inconsistent with the first principles on which the colony was founded." *Church, State and Freedom*, p. 79.

It was left to Virginia to lead the struggle for religious freedom and the separation of church and state. In 1784 there was proposed in its House of Delegates a "bill establishing provision for teachers of the Christian religions." Action thereon was postponed until the next session in order that the bill could be publicized and distributed to the people who could then make known their views. The issue was fought on a very high plane of principle with Thomas Jefferson, James Madison and George Mason aligned with the opposition. It was then that James Madison wrote his famous *A Memorial and Remonstrance* in which he presented his views that religion was not a matter within the scope of civil government. For complete historical background and full text reference is made to Mr. Justice Rutledge's dissenting opinion in *Everson* v. *Board of Education,* 330 U.S. 1. At the next session the proposed bill was defeated and in its place an Act "for establishing religious freedom" drafted by Thomas Jefferson was passed, the preamble of which stated: "that to suffer the civil magistrate to intrude his powers into the field of opinion, and to restrain the profession or propagation of principles on supposition of their ill tendency, is a dangerous fallacy which at once destroys all religious liberty." The bill further provided "that it is time enough for the rightful purposes of civil government for its officers to interfere when principles break out into overt acts against peace and good order." In his opinion for the court in *Reynolds* v. *United States,* 98 U.S. 145, Mr. Chief Justice Waite states that "in these two sentences is found the true distinction between what properly belongs to the Church and what to the State."

It was a little over a year later that the Convention met in Philadelphia to draft the Constitution of the United States. The Convention failed to include in the proposed Constitution any Bill of Rights or any provision concerning freedom of religion. Although adopting the Constitution, several states did so only on the understanding that a Bill of Rights would be added including a provision for a declaration of religious liberty. At the very first session of Congress the first ten amendments, or Bill of Rights, were proposed and largely through the efforts of James Madison were adopted, the First Amendment providing that "Congress shall make no law respecting an establishment of religion, or prohibiting the free exercise thereof." It took us over fourteen centuries and an incalculable amount of persecution to gain the religious tolerance and freedom expounded in 313 A.D. by the rulers of the Roman world.

The First Amendment, of course, applied only to the federal government, but it has been held that upon the adoption of the Fourteenth Amendment the prohibitions of the First Amendment were applicable to state action abridging religious freedom, *Cantwell* v. *Connecticut,* 310 U.S. 296.

IV

The charge here is sectarianism. The defendant Board of Education is accused of showing a preference by permitting the distribution of the King James version of the New Testament, which is unacceptable to those of the Jewish faith and, in fact, in conflict with their tenets. This violates the mandate of the First Amendment, as incorporated into the Fourteenth Amendment, prohibiting the making of any law "respecting an establishment of religion" and the requirement of Article I, paragraph 4 of the New Jersey Constitution that "there shall be no establishment of one religious sect in preference to another." By its very terms the New Jersey constitutional provision prohibits any such religious preference, while the First Amendment to the Federal Constitution has been judicially interpreted as so providing. As stated by Mr. Justice Black in his opinion for the majority of the Court in *Everson* v. *Board of Education:*

The "establishment of religion" clause of the First Amendment means at least this: Neither a state nor the Federal Government can set up a church. Neither can pass laws which aid one religion, aid all religions, or prefer one religion over another. . . .

That amendment [First] requires the state to be a neutral in its relations with groups of religious believers and non-believers.

In *Zorach* v. *Clausen,* 343 U.S. 306, Mr. Justice Douglas in his opinion for the majority of the court stated: "The government must be neutral when it comes to competition between sects." . . .

We are well aware of the ever continuing debates that have been taking place in this country for many years as to the meaning which should be given to the First Amendment. There are those who contend that our forefathers never intended to erect a "wall of separation" between Church and State. On the other hand, there are those who insist upon this absolute separation between Church and State. The plaudits and the criticisms of the various majority, concurring, and dissenting opinions rendered by the United States Supreme Court in *Everson* v. *Board of Education, McCollum* v. *Board of Education,* and *Zorach* v. *Clausen,* still continue.

But regardless of what our views on this fundamental question may be, our decision in this case must be based upon the undoubted doctrine of both the Federal Constitution and our New Jersey Constitution, that the state or any instrumentality thereof cannot under any circumstances show a preference for one religion over another. Such favoritism cannot be tolerated and must be disapproved as a clear violation of the Bill of Rights of our Constitutions.

This brings us to the heart of our problem here—namely, whether the resolution of the Board of Education displays that favoritism that is repugnant to our constitution. By permitting the distribution of the Gideon Bible, has the Board of Education established one religious sect in preference to another? Although as to the Catholic plaintiff this action has become moot due to the withdrawal of his child from the public schools of Rutherford, some testimony was presented at the trial as to his claim of sectarianism so we will at times refer to such testimony in our opinion. Our decision, however, is based upon the claim of the Jewish plaintiff that the resolution of the Rutherford Board of Education constitutes a preference of one religion over the Hebrew faith.

A review of the testimony at the trial convinces us that the King James version or Gideon Bible is unacceptable to those of the Jewish faith. In this regard Rabbi Joachim Prinz testified:

The New Testament is in profound conflict with the basic principles of Judaism. It is not accepted by the Jewish people as a sacred book. The Bible of the Jewish people is the Old Testament. The New Testament is not recognized as part of the Bible. The teachings of the New Testament are in complete and profound conflict with what Judaism teaches. It presupposes the concept of Jesus of Nazareth as a divinity, a concept which we do not accept.

They are in complete and utter conflict with what we teach, for we teach the oneness of God, which to our—and in accordance with our belief, excludes the existence of a Son of God. We accept Jesus of Nazareth as one of the figures of Jewish history, a Jew born, a Jew, died as a Jew, but we do not accept Jesus of Nazareth as the Christ. . . .

No, it is certainly not a nonsectarian book. It is a book that is—expresses the view of one denomination among the many religious denominations of the world.

Dr. Bernard J. Bamberger, rabbi of the West End Synagogue in New York City and former president of the Synagogue Council of America, stated:

Well, the New Testament, of course, is itself a complex document which contains a great many different writings, and so forth. Some of the passages and some of those writings are in themselves not necessarily in conflict with Judaism, but a very great many of them are in conflict with Judaism, first, because they teach certain doctrines which are contradictory to doctrines taught by Judaism, and also because in certain passages the New Testament writers directly attack certain Jewish beliefs which are very sacred to Jews.

He concluded that the King James Version was "completely not a non-sectarian book." Rabbi Irving Schnipper, in answer to a question whether the teachings of the New Testament are in conflict with his teaching of the children of the plaintiff Bernard Tudor, testified: "Definitely, the New Testament itself is in direct opposition to the teachings of Judaism." Nor is there any doubt that the King James version of the Bible is as unacceptable to Catholics as the Douay version is to Protestants. According to the testimony in this case the canon law of the Catholic Church provides that "Editions of the original text of the sacred scriptures published by non-Catholics are forbidden *ipso jure*."

The defendant refers us to various statements by legal scholars and others to show that the Bible is not sectarian, but rather is the universal book of the Christian world, but in many of these statements the question of the New Testament was not discussed. In *Doremus v. Board of Education of the Borough of Hawthorne*, 5 N.J. 435, relied on by the defendant, the issue was whether R.S. 18:14–77 and 78, providing for compulsory reading in the public schools of five verses of the Old Testament and permissive reading of the Lord's Prayer violated the Federal Constitution. In upholding the constitutionality of the statutes we specifically stated . . . : "We consider that the Old Testament and the Lord's Prayer, pronounced without comment, are not sectarian, and that the short exercise provided by the statute does not constitute sectarian instruction or sectarian worship. . . ." We adhere to the *Doremus Case*, but its holding does not apply here, where clearly the issue of sectarianism is present. Here the issue is the distribution of the New Testament. The uncontradicted evidence presented by the plaintiff reveals that as far as the Jewish faith is concerned, the Gideon Bible is a sectarian book, the teachings of which are in conflict with the doctrines of his religion as well as that of his child, who is a pupil in the Rutherford public school. The full force of the violation of both the state and federal constitutions is revealed when we perceive what might happen if a single school board were besieged by three separate applications for the distribution of Bibles—one from Protestants as here, another from Catholics for the distribution of the Douay Bible and a third from Jews for the same privilege for their Bible.

We find from the evidence presented in this case that the Gideon Bible is a sectarian book, and that the resolution of the defendant Board of Education to permit its distribution through the public school system of the Borough of Rutherford was in violation of the First Amendment of the United States Constitution, as incorporated into the Fourteenth Amendment, and of Article I, paragraph 4, of the New Jersey Constitution. It therefore must be set aside.

V

The defendant contends that the distribution of the Gideon Bible in no way injects any issue of the "free exercise" of religion, that "no one is forced to take a New Testament and no religious exercise or instrument is brought to the classrooms of the public schools." In other words, it asserts the arguments of *Zorach* v. *Clausen,* that the "accommodation" of religion is permissible. This argument, however, ignores the realities of life. . . . Prof. Isidore Chein, Supervisor of Psychology and Acting Director of the Research Center for Mental Health at New York University, testified on behalf of the plaintiff:

. . . I would expect that a slip of this kind, distributed under the authority of the school, would create a subtle pressure on the child which would leave him with a sense that he is not quite as free as the statement on that slip says; in other words, that he will be something of an outcast and a pariah if he does not go along with this procedure.

. . . I think that they would be in a situation where they have to play along with this or else feel themselves to be putting themselves in a public position where they are different, where they are not the same as other people, and the whole pressure would exist on them to conform.

Dr. Dan Dodson, professor in the School of Education of New York University and director of curriculum and research in the Center for Human Relations Studies, when questioned as to the divisive effect of the distribution of the Gideon Bible stated:

I would say that any instance of this kind in which the—a document that has the importance that this has to certain religious groups, including my own, would be distributed or used as a means of propaganda or indoctrination by official channels, such as the school system, would create tensions among the religious groups; there would be a controversial problem.

I would say that it would raise questions among the children as to who is and who isn't, in terms of receiving the Bible. It would also create problems as to why some accepted it and others didn't. That would be divisive.

See also *People ex rel. Ring* v. *Board of Education,* 245 Ill. 334, were the court maintained that the fact that pupils could request to be excused from religious exercise did not make the requirement of sectarian Bible reading constitutional, and *Miller* v. *Cooper,* 52 N.M. 355, where the plaintiffs brought an action seeking, among other things, an injunction against the dissemination of allegedly sectarian literature among the public school pupils in violation of the provisions of the Federal and State Constitutions. The court there granted this relief, saying:

The charge that the defendants were using the school as a medium for the dissemination of religious pamphlets published by the Presbyterian Church presents a different situation. It is true that the teachers did not hand them to the pupils or instruct that they be taken or read. The pamphlets were, however, kept in plain sight in a school room and were available to pupils and the supply was evidently replenished from time to time. We condemned such practice . . . and condemn it here and hold that the trial court was in error when it failed to enjoin such acts. . . .

We cannot accept the argument that here, as in the *Zorach Case*, the State is merely "accommodating" religion. It matters little whether the teachers themselves will distribute the Bibles or whether that will be done by members of the Gideons International. The same vice exists, that of preference of one religion over another. This is all the more obvious when we realize the motive of the Gideons. Its purpose is "to win men and women for the Lord Jesus Christ, through . . . (c) placing the Bible—God's Holy Word . . . or portions thereof in hotels, hospitals, schools, institutions, and also through distribution of some for personal use." The society is engaged in missionary work, accomplished in part by placing the King James version of the Bible in the hands of public school children throughout the United States. To achieve this end it employs the public school system as the medium of distribution. It is at the school that the pupil receives the request slip to take to his parents for signature. It is at the school that the pupil actually receives his Gideon Bible. In other words, the public school machinery is used to bring about the distribution of these Bibles to the children of Rutherford. In the eyes of the pupils and their parents the Board of Education has placed its stamp of approval upon this distribution and, in fact, upon the Gideon Bible itself. Dr. Dodson further testified:

I would say it would leave a lefthanded implication that the school thought this was preferential in terms of what is the divine word, and that the backing of the State would inevitably be interpreted as being behind it.

Dr. William Heard Kilpatrick stated:

The Protestants would feel that the school is getting behind this thing; the Catholics would feel that the school is getting behind a Protestant affair; the Jews would feel that the school is getting behind the Protestant religion as opposed to their religion; and the people who don't accept any religion would feel that the school is actually trying to teach the religion through this means.

This is more than mere "accommodation" of religion permitted in the *Zorach Case*. The school's part in this distribution is an active one and cannot be sustained on the basis of a mere assistance to religion.

We are here concerned with a vital question involving the very foundation of our civilization. Centuries ago our forefathers fought and died for the principles now contained in the Bill of Rights of the Federal and New Jersey Constitutions. It is our solemn duty to preserve these rights and to prohibit any encroachment upon them. To permit the distribution of the King James version of the Bible in the public schools of this state would be to cast aside all the progress made in the United States and throughout New Jersey in the field of religious toleration and freedom. We would be renewing the ancient struggles among the various religious faiths to the detriment of all. This we must decline to do.

The . . . resolution of the Board of Education of the Borough of Rutherford under review is stricken [and order of injunction issued].

3. Constitutional Status of Private Schools

a. Liberty of the Teacher

MEYER v. NEBRASKA

262 US 390 (1923)

[During and immediately after World War I some state legislatures and local school boards sought to prohibit the teaching of the German language. In some instances the prohibition had a special impact on the Lutheran parochial schools, which used German extensively in their teaching program. The supreme courts of Iowa, Ohio, and Nebraska upheld such prohibiting acts as constitutional on the broad ground that the legislature alone could decide what the common welfare demanded. These laws and decisions were challenged before the Supreme Court of the United States in the *Meyer Case*. The Court reversed all the state decisions by declaring the Nebraska statute unconstitutional as violative of the teacher's right to teach and of the parents' right to engage him. "Mere knowledge of the German language," said the Court, "cannot reasonably be regarded as harmful." The teacher of German engages, therefore, in a legal profession—a calling which cannot be outlawed by mere legislative fiat. The act also interfered wrongfully "with the opportunities of pupils to acquire knowledge, and with the power of parents to control the education of their own."

[A state may make reasonable regulations for all schools and may require that instruction be in English. But it may not prohibit the teaching of subjects in addition to those in the curriculum required by the state, when the teaching of such subjects will not be injurious to the health or morals of the child.

[Justices Holmes and Sutherland dissented. Holmes contended that reasonable minds might differ as to the wisdom of the Nebraska law, and therefore he was "unable to say that the Constitution of the United States prevents the experiment being tried." His dissent appears in *Bartels* v. *Iowa*, 262 US 404 (1923), a companion case to the *Meyer Case*.]

Mr. Justice McReynolds delivered the opinion of the Court:

Plaintiff in error was tried and convicted in the district court for Hamilton county, Nebraska, under an information which charged that on May 25, 1920, while an instructor in Zion Parochial School, he unlawfully taught the subject of reading in the German language to Raymond Parpart, a child of ten years, who had not attained and successfully passed the eighth grade. The information is based upon "An Act Relating to the Teaching of Foreign Languages in the State of Nebraska," approved April 9, 1919, which follows:

Section 1. No person, individually or as a teacher, shall, in any private, denominational, parochial or public school, teach any subject to any person in any language other than the English language.
Sec. 2. Languages, other than the English language, may be taught as languages only after a pupil shall have attained and successfully passed the eighth grade as evidenced by a certificate of graduation issued by the county superintendent of the county in which the child resides.
Sec. 3. Any person who violates any of the provisions of this act shall be deemed guilty of a misdemeanor and upon conviction, shall be subject to a fine of not less than twenty-five ($25) dollars, nor more than one hundred ($100) dollars or be confined in the county jail for any period not exceeding thirty days for each offense.
Sec. 4. Whereas, an emergency exists, this act shall be in force from and after its passage and approval.

The supreme court of the state affirmed the judgment of conviction. It declared the offense charged and established was "the direct and intentional teaching of the German language as a distinct subject to a child who had not passed the eighth grade," in the parochial school maintained by Zion Evangelical Lutheran Congregation, a collection of Biblical stories being used therefor. And it held that the statute forbidding this did not conflict with the 14th Amendment, but was a valid exercise of the police power. . . .

The problem for our determination is whether the statute, as construed and applied, unreasonably infringes the liberty guaranteed to the plaintiff in error by the 14th Amendment. "No state . . . shall deprive any person of life, liberty, or property without due process of law."

While this court has not attempted to define with exactness the liberty thus guaranteed, the term has received much consideration, and some of the included things have been definitely stated. Without doubt, it denotes not merely freedom from bodily restraint, but also the right of the individual to contract, to engage in any of the common occupations of life, to acquire useful knowledge, to marry, establish a home and bring up children, to worship God according to the dictates of his own conscience, and, generally, to enjoy those privileges long recognized at common law as essential to the orderly pursuit of happiness by free men. . . . The established doctrine is that this liberty may not be interfered with, under the guise of protecting the public interest, by legislative action which is arbitrary or without reasonable relation to some purpose within the competency of the state to effect. Determination by the legislature of what constitutes proper exercise of police power is not final or conclusive, but is subject to supervision by the courts. . . .

The American people have always regarded education and acquisition of knowledge as matters of supreme importance, which should be diligently promoted. The Ordinance of 1787 declares: "Religion, morality and knowledge being necessary to good government and the happiness of mankind, schools and the means of education shall forever be encouraged." Corresponding to the right of control, it is the natural duty of the parent to give his children education suitable to their station in life; and nearly all the states, including Nebraska, enforce this obligation by compulsory laws.

Practically, education of the young is only possible in schools conducted by especially qualified persons who devote themselves thereto. The calling always has been regarded as useful and honorable,—essential, indeed, to the public welfare. Mere knowledge of the German language cannot reasonably be regarded as harmful. Heretofore it has been commonly looked upon as helpful and desirable. Plaintiff in error taught this language in school as part of his occupation. His right thus to teach and the right of parents to engage him so to instruct their children, we think, are within the liberty of the Amendment.

The challenged statute forbids the teaching in school of any subject except in English; also the teaching of any other language until the pupil has attained and successfully passed the eighth grade, which is not usually accomplished before the age of twelve. The supreme court of the state has held that "the so-called ancient or dead languages" are not "within the spirit or the purpose of the act." . . . Latin, Greek, Hebrew are not proscribed; but German, French, Spanish, Italian, and every other alien speech are within the ban. Evidently the legislature has attempted materially to interfere with the calling of modern language teachers, with the opportunities of pupils to acquire knowledge, and with the power of parents to control the education of their own.

It is said the purpose of the legislation was to promote civic development by inhibiting training and education of the immature in foreign tongues and ideals before they could learn English and acquire American ideals; and "that the English language should be and become the mother tongue of all children reared in this state." It is also affirmed that the foreign-born population is very large, that certain communities commonly use foreign words, follow foreign leaders, move in a foreign atmosphere, and that the children are thereby hindered from becoming citizens of the most useful type, and the public safety is imperiled.

That the state may do much, go very far, indeed, in order to improve the quality of its citizens, physically, mentally, and morally, is clear; but the individual has certain fundamental rights which must be respected. The protection of the Constitution extends to all,—to those who speak other languages as well as to those born with English on the tongue. Perhaps it would be highly advantageous if all had ready understanding of our ordinary speech, but this cannot be coerced by methods which conflict with the Constitution,—a desirable end cannot be promoted by prohibited means.

For the welfare of his Ideal Commonwealth, Plato suggested a law which should provide

that the wives of our guardians are to be common, and their children are to be common, and no parent is to know his own child nor any child his parent. . . . The proper officers will take the offspring of the good parents to the pen or fold, and there they will deposit them with certain nurses who dwell in a separate quarter; but the offspring of the inferior, or of the better when they chance to be deformed, will be put away in some mysterious, unknown place, as they should be.

In order to submerge the individual and develop ideal citizens, Sparta assembled the males at seven into barracks and intrusted their subsequent education and training to official guardians. Although such measures have been deliberately approved by men of great genius, their ideas touching the relation between individual and state were wholly different from those upon which our institutions rest; and it hardly will be affirmed that any legislature could impose such restrictions upon the people of a state without doing violence to both letter and spirit of the Constitution.

The desire of the legislature to foster a homogeneous people with American ideals, prepared readily to understand current discussions of civic matters, is easy to appreciate. Unfortunate experiences during the late war, and aversion toward every characteristic of truculent adversaries, were certainly enough to quicken that aspiration. But the means adopted, we think, exceed the limitations upon the power of the state, and conflict with rights assured to plaintiff in error. The interference is plain enough, and no adequate reason therefor in time of peace and domestic tranquillity has been shown.

The power of the state to compel attendance at some school and to make reasonable regulations for all schools, including a requirement that they shall give instructions in English, is not questioned. Nor has challenge been made of the state's power to prescribe a curriculum for institutions which it supports. Those matters are not within the present controversy. . . . No emergency has arisen which renders knowledge by a child of some language other than English so clearly harmful as to justify its inhibition, with the consequent infringement of rights long freely enjoyed. We are constrained to conclude that the statute as applied is arbitrary, and without reasonable relation to any end within the competency of the state.

As the statute undertakes to interfere only with teaching which involves a modern language, leaving complete freedom as to other matters, there seems no adequate foundation for the suggestion that the purpose was to protect the child's health by limiting his mental activities. It is well known that proficiency in a foreign language seldom comes to one not instructed at an early age, and experience shows that this is not injurious to the health, morals, or understanding of the ordinary child. . . .

Reversed.

b. Liberty of the Parents

PIERCE v. SOCIETY OF THE SISTERS OF THE HOLY NAMES

268 US 510 (1925)

[Oregon by statute attempted to prohibit parochial and private schools for children between eight and sixteen by requiring their attendance at public schools only. The Supreme Court unanimously held the statute unconstitutional; children, said the Court, are not mere creatures of the state. A state may not attempt to standardize its children by forcing them to accept public school instruction only.

[Occasionally the courts face the problem of adjusting conflicting claims of the state and the parents. Members of the Old Order Amish Church have claimed that their children, when they reach the age of fourteen years, should be exempt from compulsory school attendance laws, which, in Pennsylvania, require attendance up to the age of seventeen years. The court held that the school law was paramount to the claim of religious conscience. *Commonwealth* v. *Beiler,* 168 Pa. Super. 462, 79 A. 2d 134 (1951).]

Mr. Justice McReynolds delivered the opinion of the Court:

The challenged act, effective September 1, 1926, requires every parent, guardian, or other person having control or charge or custody of a child between eight and sixteen years to send him "to a public school for the period of time a public school shall be held during the current year" in the district where the child resides; and failure so to do is declared a misdemeanor. There are exemptions—not specially important here—for children who are not normal, or who have completed the eighth grade, or whose parents or private teachers reside at considerable distances from any public school, or who hold special permits from the county superintendent. The manifest purpose is to compel general attendance at public schools by normal children, between eight and sixteen, who have not completed the eighth grade. And without doubt enforcement of the statute would seriously impair, perhaps destroy, the profitable features of appellees' business, and greatly diminish the value of their property.

Appellee the Society of Sisters is an Oregon corporation, organized in 1880, with power to care for orphans, educate and instruct the youth, establish and maintain academies or schools, and acquire necessary real and personal property. It has long devoted its property and effort to the secular and religious education and care of children, and has acquired the valuable good will of many parents and guardians. It conducts interdependent primary and high schools and junior colleges, and maintains orphanages for the custody and control of children between eight and sixteen. In its primary schools many children between those ages are taught the subjects usually pursued in Oregon public schools during the first eight years. Systematic religious instruction and moral training according to the tenets of the Roman Catholic Church are also regularly provided. All courses of study, both temporal and religious, contemplate continuity of training under appellee's charge; the primary schools are essential to the system and the most profitable. It owns valuable buildings, especially constructed and equipped for school purposes. The business is remunerative,—the annual income from primary schools exceeds $30,000,—and the successful conduct of this requires long-time contracts with teachers and parents. The Compulsory Education Act of 1922 has already caused the withdrawal from its schools of children who would otherwise continue, and their income has steadily declined. The appellants, public officers, have proclaimed their purpose strictly to enforce the statute.

After setting out the above facts, the Society's bill alleges that the enactment conflicts with the right of parents to choose schools where their children will receive appropriate mental and religious training, the right of the child to influence the parents' choice of a school, the right of schools and teachers therein to engage in a useful business or profession, and is accordingly repugnant to the Constitution and void. And, further, that unless enforcement of the measure is enjoined, the corporation's business and property will suffer irreparable injury.

Appellee Hill Military Academy is a private corporation organized in 1908 under the laws of Oregon, engaged in owning, operating, and conducting for profit an elementary, college preparatory, and military training school for boys between the ages of five and twenty-one years. The average attendance is one hundred, and the annual fees received for each student amount to some $800. The elementary department is divided into eight grades, as in the public schools; the college preparatory department has four grades, similar to those of the public high schools; the courses of study conform to the requirements of the state board of education. Military instruction and training are also given, under the supervision of an Army officer. It owns considerable real and personal property, some useful only for school purposes. The business and incident good will are very valuable. In order to conduct its affairs long-time contracts must be made for supplies, equipment, teachers, and pupils. Appellants, law officers of the state and county, have publicly announced that the Act of November 7, 1922, is valid, and have declared their intention to enforce it. By reason of the statute and threat of enforcement, appellee's business is being destroyed and its property depreciated; parents and guardians are refusing to make contracts for the future instruction of their sons, and some are being withdrawn. . . .

No question is raised concerning the power of the state reasonably to regulate all schools, to inspect, supervise, and examine them, their teachers and pupils; to require that all children of proper age attend some school, that teachers shall be of good moral character and patriotic disposition, that certain studies plainly essential to good citizenship must be taught, and that nothing be taught which is manifestly inimical to the public welfare.

The inevitable practical result of enforcing the act under consideration would be destruction of appellees' primary schools, and perhaps all other private primary schools for normal children within the state of Oregon. Appellees are engaged in a kind of undertaking not inherently harmful, but long regarded as useful and meritorious. Certainly there is nothing in the present records to indicate that they have failed to discharge their obligations to patrons, students, or the state. And there are no peculiar circumstances or present emergencies which demand extraordinary measures relative to primary education.

. . . The fundamental theory of liberty upon which all governments in this Union repose excludes any general power of the state to standardize its children by forcing them to accept instruction from public teachers only. The child is not the mere creature of the state; those who nurture him and direct his destiny have the right, coupled with the high duty, to recognize and prepare him for additional obligations.

Appellees are corporations, and therefore, it is said, they cannot claim for themselves the liberty which the 14th Amendment guarantees. Accepted in the proper sense, this is true. . . . But they have business and property for which they claim protection. These are threatened with destruction through the unwarranted compulsion which appellants are exercising over present and prospective patrons of their schools. And this court has gone very far to protect against loss threatened by such action. . . .

[Decrees enjoining enforcement of the statute affirmed.]

4. Freedom to Engage in Missionary Work

TUCKER v. TEXAS

326 US 517 (1945)

[In many parts of the world there is freedom of religious worship but no freedom to make converts, to evangelize, or to follow the calling of a religious missionary. This freedom has been tested in many cases brought before the Supreme Court by Jehovah's Witnesses, who claimed local or state interference with their efforts to distribute their religious literature on the streets of municipalities, or from door to door, or their playing of phonograph records on streets to willing auditors. The Court has been reluctant to sustain police restrictions against such activities, whether imposed by a municipality (e.g., *Lovell* v. *Griffin*, 303 US 444, 1938), or a company-owned town (*Marsh* v. *Alabama*, 326 US 501, 1946), or, as in the present case, by a defense housing development.

[Restrictions in the interests of public peace and order are considered below, under "Freedom of Speech and Press."

[In the present case Chief Justice Stone and Justices Reed and Burton dissented, on the ground that there was no showing that the property, owned by the United States, had been dedicated to general use by the public.]

Mr. Justice Black delivered the opinion of the Court:

The appellant was charged in the Justice Court of Medina County, Texas, with violating . . . the Texas Penal Code which makes it an offense for any "peddler or hawker of goods or merchandise" wilfully to refuse to leave premises after having been notified to do so by the owner or possessor thereof. The appellant urged in his defense that he was not a peddler or hawker of merchandise, but a minister of the gospel engaged in the distribution of religious literature to willing recipients. He contended that to construe the Texas statute as applicable to his activities would, to that extent, bring it into conflict with the Constitutional guarantees of freedom of press and religion. Const. Amend. 1. His contention was rejected and he was convicted. . . .

The facts shown by the record need be but briefly stated. Appellant is an ordained minister of the group known as Jehovah's Witnesses. In accordance with the practices of this group he calls on people from door to door, presents his religious views to those willing to listen, and distributes religious literature to those willing to receive it. In the course of his work, he went to the Hondo Navigation Village located in Medina County, Texas. The village is owned by the United States under a Congressional program which was designed to provide housing for persons engaged in National Defense activities. According to all indications the village was freely accessible and open to the public and had the characteristics of a typical American town. The Federal Public Housing Authority had placed the buildings in charge of a manager whose duty it was to rent the houses, collect the rents, and generally to supervise operations, subject to over-all control by the Authority. He ordered appellant to discontinue all religious activities in the village. Appellant refused. Later the manager ordered appellant to leave the village. Insisting that the manager had no right to suppress religious activities, appellant declined to leave, and his arrest followed. At the trial the manager testified that the controlling Federal agency had given him full authority to regulate the conduct of those living in the village, and that he did not allow preaching by ministers of any denomination without a permit issued by him in his discretion. He thought this broad authority was entrusted to him, at least in part, by a regulation, which the Authority's Washington office had allegedly promulgated. He testified that this regulation provided that no peddlers or hawkers could come into or remain in the village without getting permission from the manager. . . .

The foregoing statement of facts shows their close similarity to the facts which led us this day to decide in *Marsh* v. *Alabama,* 326 US

501, that managers of a company-owned town could not bar all distribution of religious literature within the town, or condition distribution upon a permit issued at the discretion of its management.

The only difference between this case and *Marsh* v. *Alabama* is that here instead of a private corporation, the Federal Government owns and operates the village. This difference does not affect the result. Certainly neither Congress nor Federal agencies acting pursuant to Congressional authorization may abridge the freedom of press and religion safeguarded by the First Amendment. True, under certain circumstances it might be proper for security reasons to isolate the inhabitants of a settlement, such as Hondo Village, which houses workers engaged in producing war materials. But no such necessity and no such intention on the part of Congress or the Public Housing Authority are shown here.

It follows from what we have said that to the extent that the Texas statute was held to authorize appellant's punishment for refusing to refrain from religious activities in Hondo Village it is an invalid abridgement of the freedom of press and religion. . . .

5. Ecclesiastical Self-Government— The Liberty of Churches

WATSON v. JONES
13 Wall (US) 679 (1872)

[It is estimated that the number of churches in the United States is over 325,000, with a total membership of more than 80,000,000 persons, belonging to at least 230 denominations. Many of these churches and denominations had their origin in schisms. Factional disputes have often involved the question of the ultimate disposition or control of the church funds or property. American courts could have used property law issues in such a way as to make the courts arbiters of religious doctrines and practices. They have scrupulously avoided doing this. Rather they have held that when a church belongs to a denomination which is governed by a hierarchy, the members must abide by the decision of their own ecclesiastical authorities. This was the decision of the Supreme Court in *Watson* v. *Jones,* in which the factional dispute grew out of difference over slavery.

[This case was followed by the Court in 1952 when a similar issue was presented to it involving a split in the Russian Orthodox Church in North America. After the Bolshevik Revolution in 1917 a separatist movement developed within the Russian Orthodox Church in the United States. The schismatics declared themselves independent of the mother church and the Patriarch in Moscow, and they sought to win control of the church property and ecclesiastical positions. The New York Legislature passed statutes in 1945 and 1948 to aid the schismatics in their efforts to gain autonomy and thus free the church of atheistic and subversive influences. With this legislative aid separatists tried to eject from the Cathedral in New York those who occupied it by authority of the church authorities in Moscow. The Supreme Court, by an 8-to-1 vote, held that the New York legislation was unconstitutional as a violation of the guaranty of freedom of religion.

[Separatists, schismatics, dissenters may leave a church and organize their own congregation. They have a constitutional right to do this. But if the church was subject to an ecclesiastical authority—e.g., the Patriarch in Moscow—then the church property cannot be taken over by the separatists; it remains with those who are loyal to the church. *Kedroff* v. *Saint Nicholas Cathedral*, 344 US 94 (1952).

[This decision is in the interests of religious freedom. It reaffirms the decision of the *Watson Case:* the state is not to be an arbiter of religious beliefs and practices. If clergymen are guilty of subversive activities, they may be punished in the same way as the law may punish others; but neither the legislature nor the courts may take church property and positions away from one faction and turn them over to another faction on the ground that the action would free the church from subversive influences.]

Mr. Justice Miller delivered the opinion of the Court:

. . . This is a case of a division or schism in a church. It is a question as to which of two bodies shall be recognized as the Third or Walnut Street Presbyterian Church [Louisville, Ky.] . . . The issue here is no longer a mere question of eldership, but it is a separation of the original church members and officers into two distinct bodies, with distinct members and officers, each claiming to be the true Walnut Street Presbyterian Church, and denying the right of the other to any such claim. . . .

From the commencement of the late war of insurrection to its close, the General Assembly of the Presbyterian Church at its annual meetings expressed, in declaratory statements or resolutions, its sense of the obligation of all good citizens to support the Federal Government in that struggle; and when, by the Proclamation of President Lincoln, emancipation of the slaves of the States in insurrection was announced, that body also expressed views favorable to emancipation, and adverse to the institution of slavery. At its meeting in Pittsburg, in May, 1865, instructions were given to the Presbyteries, the Board of Missions, and to the sessions of the Churches, that when any persons from the Southern States should make application for employment as missionaries, or for admission as members or ministers of churches, inquiry should be made as to their sentiments in regard to loyalty to the government, and on the subject of slavery; and if it was found that they had been guilty of voluntarily aiding the war of the rebellion, or held the doctrine announced by the large body of the churches in the insurrectionary States, which had organized a new General Assembly, that "the system of Negro slavery in the South is a divine institution, and that it is the peculiar mission of the Southern Church to conserve that institution" they should be required to repent and forsake these sins before they could be received.

In the month of September, thereafter, the Presbytery of Louisville, under whose immediate jurisdiction was the Walnut Street Church, adopted and published in pamphlet form, what is called "a declaration and testimony against the erroneous and heretical doctrines and practices which have obtained and been propagated in the Presbyterian Church of the United States during the last five years." This declaration denounced, in the severest terms, the action of the General Assembly in the matters we have just mentioned, declared their intention to refuse to be governed by that action, and invited the co-operation of all the members of the Presbyterian Church who shared these sentiments of the declaration, in a concerted resistance to what they called the usurpation of authority by the Assembly. . . .

The General Assembly of 1866 denounced the declaration and testimony, and declared that every Presbytery which refused to obey its order should be *ipso facto* dissolved and called to answer before the next General Assembly, giving the Louisville Presbytery an opportunity for repentance and conformity. The Louisville Presbytery divided, and the adherents of the declaration and testimony sought and obtained admission in 1868, into "The Presbyterian Church of the Confederate States." . . .

In January, 1866, the congregation of the Walnut Street Church become divided in the manner stated above, each claiming to constitute the Church. . . .

On the 19th June, 1866, the Synod of Kentucky became divided, the opposing parties in each claiming to constitute respectively the true Presbytery and the true Synod; each meanwhile recognizing and claiming to adhere to the same General Assembly. Of these contesting bodies, the appellants adhered to one; the appellees to another.

On the 1st of June, 1867, the Presbytery and Synod recognized by the appellants, were declared by the General Assembly to be "in no sense the true and lawful Synod and Presbytery in connection with and under the care and authority of the General Assembly of the Presbyterian

Church in the United States of America"; and were permanently excluded from connection with or representation in the Assembly; by the same resolution the Synod and Presbytery adhered to by appellees were declared to be the true and lawful Presbytery of Louisville, and Synod of Kentucky.

The Synod of Kentucky thus excluded by a resolution adopted the 28th June, 1867, declared "That, in its future action, it will be governed by this recognized sundering of all its relation to the aforesaid revolutionary body (the General Assembly) by the acts of that body itself." The Presbytery took substantially the same action. . . .

The division and separation finally extended to the Presbytery of Louisville and the Synod of Kentucky. It is now complete and apparently irreconcilable, and we are called upon to declare the beneficial uses of the church property in this condition of total separation between the members of what was once a united and harmonious congregation of the Presbyterian Church.

The questions which have come before the civil courts concerning the rights to property held by ecclesiastical bodies, may, so far as we have been able to examine them, be profitably classified under three general heads, which of course do not include cases governed by considerations applicable to a church established and supported by law as the religion of the State.

1. The first of these is when the property which is the subject of controversy has been, by the deed or will of the donor, or other instrument by which the property is held, by the express terms of the instrument devoted to the teaching, support or spread of some specific form of religious doctrine or belief.

2. The second is when the property is held by a religious congregation which, by the nature of its organization, is strictly independent of other ecclesiastical associations, and so far as church government is concerned, owes no fealty or obligation to any higher authority.

3. The third is where the religious congregation or ecclesiastical body holding the property is but a subordinate member of some general church organization in which there are superior ecclesiastical tribunals with a general and ultimate power of control more or less complete in some supreme judicatory over the whole membership of that general organization.

In regard to the first of these classes it seems hardly to admit of a rational doubt that an individual or an association of individuals may dedicate property by way of trust to the purpose of sustaining, supporting and propagating definite religious doctrines or principles, providing that in doing so they violate no law of morality, and give to the instrument by which their purpose is evidenced, the formalities which the laws require. And it would seem also to be the obvious duty of the court, in a case properly made, to see that the property so dedicated is not diverted from the trust which is thus attached to its use. So long as there are persons qualified within the meaning of the original dedication, and who are also willing to teach the doctrines or principles prescribed in the act of dedication, and so long as there is any one so interested in the execution of the trust as to have a standing in court, it must be that they can prevent the diversion of the property or fund to other and different uses. This is the general doctrine of courts of equity as to charities, and it seems equally applicable to ecclesiastical matters.

In such case, if the trust is confided to a religious congregation of the independent or congregational form of church government, it is not in the power of the majority of that congregation, however preponderant, by reason of a change of views on religious subjects, to carry the property so confided to them to the support of new and conflicting doctrine. A pious man building and dedicating a house of worship to the sole and exclusive use of those who believe in the doctrine of the Holy Trinity, and placing it under the control of a congregation which at the time holds the same belief, has a right to expect that the law will prevent that property from being used as a means of support and dissemination of the Unitarian doctrine, and as a place of Unitarian worship. Nor is the principle varied when the organization to which the trust is confided is of the second or associated form of church government. The protection which the law throws around the trust is the same. And though the task may be a delicate one and a difficult one, it will be the duty of the court in such cases, when the doctrine to be taught or the form of worship to be used is definitely and clearly laid down, to inquire whether the party accused of violating the trust is holding or teaching a different doctrine, or using a form of worship which is so far variant as to defeat the declared objects of the trust. . . .

The second class of cases which we have described has reference to the case of a church of a strictly congregational or independent organization, governed solely within itself, either by a majority of its members or by such other local organism as it may have instituted for the purpose of ecclesiastical government; and to property held by such a church, either by way of purchase or donation, with no other specific trust attached to it in the hands of the church than that it is for the use of that congregation as a religious society.

In such cases, where there is a schism which leads to a separation into distinct and conflicting bodies, the rights of such bodies to the use of the property must be determined by the ordinary principles which govern voluntary associations. If the principle of government in such cases is that the majority rules, then the numerical majority of members must control the right to the use of the property. If there be within the congregation officers in whom are vested the powers of such control, then those who adhere to the acknowledged organism by which the body is governed are entitled to the use of the property. The minority in choosing to separate themselves into a distinct body, and refusing to recognize the authority of the governing body, can claim no rights in the property from the fact that they had once been members of the Church or congregation. This ruling admits of no inquiry into the existing religious opinions of those who comprise the legal or regular organization; for, if such was permitted, a very small minority, without any officers of the church among them, might be found to be the only faithful supporters of the religious dogmas of the founders of the Church. There being no such trust imposed upon the property when purchased or given, the court will not imply one for the purpose of expelling from its use those who by regular succession and order constitute the Church, because they may have changed in some respect their views of religious truth. . . .

But the third of these classes of cases is the one which is oftenest found in the courts, and which, with reference to the number and difficulty of the questions involved, and to other considerations, is every way the most important.

It is the case of property acquired in any of the usual modes for the general use of a religious congregation which is itself part of a large and general organization of some religious denomination, with which it is more or less intimately connected by religious views and ecclesiastical government.

The case before us is one of this class, growing out of a schism which has divided the congregation and its officers, and the presbytery and synod, and which appeals to the courts to determine the right to the use of the property so acquired. Here is no case of property devoted forever by the instrument which conveyed it, or by any specific declaration of its owner, to the support of any special religious dogmas, or any peculiar form of worship, but of property purchased for the use of a religious congregation, and so long as any existing religious congregation can be ascertained to be that congregation, or its regular and legitimate successor, it is entitled to the use of the property. In the case of an independent congregation we have pointed out how this identity, or succession, is to be ascertained, but in cases of this character we are bound to look at the fact that the local congregation is itself but a member of a much larger and more important religious organization, and is under its government and control, and is bound by its orders and judgments. There are in the Presbyterian system of ecclesiastical government, in regular succession, the Presbytery over the session or local church, the Synod over the Presbytery, and the General Assembly over all. These are called, in the language of the church organs, "judicatories," and they entertain appeals from the decisions of those below, and prescribe corrective measures in other cases.

In this class of cases we think the rule of action which should govern the civil courts, founded in a broad and sound view of the relations of church and state under our system of laws, and supported by a preponderating weight of judicial authority is, that, whenever the questions of discipline or of faith, or ecclesiastical rule, custom or law have been decided by the highest of these church judicatories to which the matter has been carried, the legal tribunals must accept such decisions as final, and as binding on them, in their application to the case before them. . . .

In this country the full and free right to entertain any religious belief, to practice any religious principle, and to teach any religious doctrine which does not violate the laws of morality and property, and which does not infringe personal rights, is conceded to all. The law knows no heresy, and is committed to the support of no dogma, the establishment of no sect. The right to organize voluntary religious associations to assist in the expression and dissemination of any religious doctrine, and to create tribunals for the decision of controverted questions of faith within the association, and for the ecclesiastical government of all the individual members, congregations and officers within the general association, is unquestioned. All who unite themselves to such a body do so with an implied consent to this government, and are bound to submit to it. But it would be a vain consent and would lead to the total subversion of such religious bodies, if any one aggrieved by one of their decisions could appeal to the secular courts and have them reversed. It is of the essence of these religious unions, and of their right to establish tribunals for the decision of questions arising among themselves, that those decisions should be binding in all cases of ecclesiastical cognizance, subject only to such appeals as the organism itself provides for. . . .

But it is a very different thing where a subject matter of dispute, strictly and purely ecclesiastical in its character—a matter over which the civil courts exercise no jurisdiction—a matter which concerns theological controversy, church discipline, ecclesiastical government, or the conformity of the members of the church to the standard of morals required of them—becomes the subject of its action. It may be said here, also, that no jurisdiction has been conferred on the tribunal to try the particular case before it, or that, in its judgment, it exceeds the powers conferred upon it, or that the laws of the church do not authorize the particular form of proceeding adopted; and, in a sense often used in the courts, all of those may be said to be questions of jurisdiction. But it is easy to see that if the civil courts are to inquire into all these matters, the whole subject of the doctrinal theology, the usages and customs, the written laws, and fundamental organization of every religious denomination may, and must, be examined into with minuteness and care, for they would become, in almost every case, the *criteria* by which the validity of the ecclesiastical decree would be determined in the civil court. This principle would deprive these bodies of the right of construing their own church laws, would open the way to all the evils which we have depicted . . . and would in effect transfer to the civil courts where property rights were concerned the decision of all ecclesiastical questions. . . .

But we need pursue this subject no further. Whatever may have been the case before the Kentucky court, the appellants in the case presented to us have separated themselves wholly from the church organization to which they belonged when this controversy commenced. They now deny its authority, denounce its action and refuse to abide by its judgments. They have first erected themselves into a new organization, and have since joined themselves to another totally different, if not hostile, to the one to which they belonged when the difficulty first began. Under any of the decisions which we have examined, the appellants, in their present position, have no right to the property, or to the use of it, which is the subject of this suit. . . .

★ IV ★

Freedom of Assembly and Petition

DE JONGE v. OREGON

299 US 353 (1937)

[The First Amendment provides that Congress shall make no law "abridging . . . the right of the people peaceably to assemble, and to petition the Government for a redress of grievances." Not until 1876 was the Supreme Court called upon to construe this provision. In *United States* v. *Cruikshank*, 92 US 542 (1876) the Court gave this provision a restricted meaning, holding that the First Amendment guarantees to citizens the freedom to assemble in order that they may petition Congress for a redress of grievances. Apparently, only a peaceful assembly called for this purpose was constitutionally protected. Freedom of assembly was thus dependent upon the right of petition, which had its origin in Magna Carta, reaffirmed in the Bill of Rights of 1689.

[In the *De Jonge Case*, however, freedom of assembly was liberated from dependence upon the right of petition and was held to be as fundamental as are freedom of speech and freedom of the press. In this case the meeting was called under the auspices of the Communist Party, but the Court held that it is a matter of constitutional indifference under whose auspices a meeting is called, or who the speakers are; the only question is whether "their utterances transcend the bounds of the freedom of speech which the Constitution protects."

[In this significant unanimous decision the Court also held that freedom of speech and of the press and the right of peaceable assembly are safeguarded against infringement by state action: these freedoms are assimilated into the Due Process Clause of the Fourteenth Amendment.]

Mr. Chief Justice Hughes delivered the opinion of the Court:

Appellant, Dirk De Jonge, was indicted in Multnomah County, Oregon, for violation of the Criminal Syndicalism Law of that State. The act . . . defines "criminal syndicalism" as "the doctrine which advocates crime, physical violence, sabotage, or any unlawful acts or methods as a means of accomplishing or effecting industrial or political change or revolution." With this preliminary definition the Act proceeds to describe a number of offenses, embracing the teaching of criminal syndicalism, the printing or distribution of books, pamphlets, etc., advocating that doctrine, the organization of a society or assemblage which advocates it, and presiding at or assisting in conducting a meeting of such an organization, society or group. The prohibited acts are made felonies, punishable by imprisonment for not less than one year nor more than ten years, or by a fine of not more than $1,000, or by both.

We are concerned with but one of the described offenses and with the validity of the statute in this particular application. The charge is that appellant assisted in the conduct of a meeting which was called under the auspices of the Communist Party, an organization advocating criminal syndicalism. The defense was that the meeting was public and orderly and was held for a lawful purpose; that, while it was held under the auspices of the Communist Party, neither criminal syndicalism nor any unlawful conduct was taught or advocated at the meeting either by appellant or by others. Appellant moved for a direction of acquittal, contending that the statute as applied to him, for merely assisting at a meeting called by the Communist Party at which nothing unlawful was done or advocated, violated the due process clause of the Fourteenth Amendment of the Constitution of the United States.

This contention was overruled. Appellant was found guilty as charged and was sentenced to imprisonment for seven years. The judgment was affirmed by the Supreme Court of the State. . . . The case comes here on appeal.

The record does not present the evidence adduced at the trial. The parties have substituted a stipulation of facts. . . .

The stipulation, after setting forth the charging part of the indictment, recites in substance the following: That on July 27, 1934, there was held in Portland a meeting which had been advertised by handbills issued by the Portland section of the Communist Party; that the number of persons in attendance was variously estimated at from 150 to 300;

that some of those present, who were members of the Communist Party, estimated that not to exceed 10 to 15 per cent of those in attendance were such members; that the meeting was open to the public without charge and no questions were asked of those entering, with respect to their relation to the Communist Party; that the notice of the meeting advertised it as a protest against illegal raids on workers' halls and homes and against the shooting of striking longshoremen by Portland police; that the chairman stated that it was a meeting held by the Communist Party; that the first speaker dwelt on the activities of the Young Communist League; that the defendant De Jonge, the second speaker, was a member of the Communist Party and went to the meeting to speak in its name; that in his talk he protested against conditions in the county jail, the action of city police in relation to the maritime strike then in progress in Portland and numerous other matters; that he discussed the reason for the raids on the Communist headquarters and workers' halls and offices; that he told the workers that these attacks were due to efforts on the part of the steamship companies and stevedoring companies to break the maritime longshoremen's and seamen's strike; that they hoped to break the strike by pitting the longshoremen and seamen against the Communist movement; that there was also testimony to the effect that defendant asked those present to do more work in obtaining members for the Communist Party and requested all to be at the meeting of the party to be held in Portland on the following evening and to bring their friends to show their defiance to local police authority and to assist them in their revolutionary tactics; that there was also testimony that defendant urged the purchase of certain communist literature which was sold at the meeting; that while the meeting was still in progress it was raided by the police; that the meeting was conducted in an orderly manner; that defendant and several others who were actively conducting the meeting were arrested by the police; and that on searching the hall the police found a quantity of communist literature.

The stipulation then set forth various extracts from the literature of the Communist Party to show its advocacy of criminal syndicalism. The stipulation does not disclose any activity by the defendant as a basis for his prosecution other than his participation in the meeting in question. Nor does the stipulation show that the communist literature distributed at the meeting contained any advocacy of criminal syndicalism or of any unlawful conduct. It was admitted by the Attorney General of the State in his argument at the bar of this Court that the literature distributed in the meeting was not of that sort and that the extracts contained in the stipulation were taken from communist literature found elsewhere. Its introduction in evidence was for the purpose of showing that the Communist Party as such did advocate the doctrine of criminal syndicalism, a fact which is not disputed on this appeal.

The indictment charged as follows:

The said Dirk De Jonge, Don Cluster, Edward R. Denny and Earl Stewart on the 27th day of July, A.D. 1934, in the county of Multnomah and state of Oregon, then and there being, did then and there unlawfully and feloniously preside at, conduct and assist in conducting an assemblage of persons, organization, society and group, to wit: The Communist Party, a more particular description of which said assemblage of persons, organization, society and group is to this grand jury unknown, which said assemblage of persons, organization, society and group did then and there unlawfully and feloniously teach and advocate the doctrine of criminal syndicalism and sabotage, contrary to the statutes in such cases made and provided, and against the peace and dignity of the state of Oregon.

On the theory that this was a charge that criminal syndicalism and sabotage were advocated at the meeting in question, defendant moved for acquittal, insisting that the evidence was insufficient to warrant his conviction. The trial court denied his motion, and error in this respect was assigned on appeal. The Supreme Court of the State put aside that contention by ruling that the indictment did not charge that criminal syndicalism or sabotage was advocated at the meeting described in the evidence, either by defendant or by anyone else. The words of the indictment that "said assemblage of persons, organization, society, and group did then and there unlawfully and feloniously teach and advocate the doctrine of criminal syndicalism and sabotage," referred not to the meeting in question, or to anything then and there said or done by defendant or others, but to the advocacy of criminal syndicalism and sabotage by the Communist Party in Multnomah County. The ruling of the State court upon this point was precise. . . .

In this view, lack of sufficient evidence as to illegal advocacy or action at the meeting became immaterial. Having limited the charge to defendant's participation in a meeting called by the Communist Party, the state court sustained the conviction upon that basis regardless of what was said or done at the meeting.

We must take the indictment as thus construed. Conviction upon a charge not made would be sheer denial of due process. It thus appears that, while defendant was a member of the Communist Party, he was not indicted for participating in its organization, or for joining it, or for soliciting members or for distributing its literature. He was not charged with teaching or advocating criminal syndicalism or sabotage or any unlawful acts, either at the meeting or elsewhere. He was accordingly deprived of the benefit of evidence as to the orderly and unlawful conduct of the meeting and that it was not called or used for the advocacy of criminal syndicalism or sabotage or any unlawful action. His sole offense as charged, and for which he was convicted and sentenced to imprisonment for seven years, was that he had assisted in the conduct of a public meeting, albeit otherwise lawful, which was held under the auspices of the Communist Party.

The broad reach of the statute as thus applied is plain. While defendant was a member of the Communist Party, that membership was not necessary to conviction on such a charge. A like fate might have attended any speaker, although not a member, who "assisted in the conduct" of the meeting. However innocuous the object of the meeting, however lawful the subjects and tenor of the addresses, however reasonable and timely the discussion, all those assisting in the conduct of the meeting would be subject to imprisonment as felons if the meeting were held by the Communist Party. . . . Thus, if the Communist Party had called a public meeting in Portland to discuss the tariff, or the foreign policy of the Government, or taxation, or relief, or candidacies for the offices of President, members of Congress, Governor, or state legislators, every speaker who assisted in the conduct of the meeting would be equally guilty with the defendant in this case, upon the charge as here defined and sustained. The list of illustrations might be indefinitely extended to every variety of meetings under the auspices of the Communist Party although held for the discussion of political issues or to adopt protests and pass resolutions of an entirely innocent and proper character.

While the States are entitled to protect themselves from the abuse of the privileges of our institutions through an attempted substitution of force and violence in the place of peaceful political action in order to effect revolutionary changes in government, none of our decisions go to the length of sustaining such a curtailment of the right of free speech and assembly as the Oregon statute demands in its present application. . . . The right of peaceable assembly is a right cognate to those of free speech and free press and is equally fundamental. As this Court said in *United States* v. *Cruikshank*, 92 U.S. 542: "The very idea of a government, republican in form, implies a right on the part of its citizens to meet peaceably for consultation in respect to public affairs and to petition for a redress of grievances." The First Amendment of the Federal Constitution expressly guarantees that right against abridgment by Congress. But explicit mention there does not argue exclusion elsewhere. For the right is one that cannot be denied without violating those fundamental principles of liberty and justice which lie at the base of all civil and political institutions—principles which the Fourteenth Amendment embodies in the general terms of its due process clause. . . .

These rights may be abused by using speech or press or assembly in order to incite to violence and crime. The people through their legislatures may protect themselves against that abuse. But the legislative intervention can find constitutional justification only by dealing with the abuse. The rights themselves must not be curtailed. The greater the importance of safeguarding the community from incitements to the overthrow of our institutions by force and violence, the more imperative is the need to preserve inviolate the constitutional rights of free speech, free press and free assembly in order to maintain the opportunity for free political discussion, to the end that government may be responsive to the will of the people and that changes, if desired, may be obtained by peaceful means. Therein lies the security of the Republic, the very foundation of constitutional government.

It follows from these considerations that, consistently with the Federal Constitution, peaceable assembly for lawful discussion cannot be made a crime. The holding of meetings for peaceable political action cannot be proscribed. Those who assist in the conduct of such meetings cannot be branded as criminals on that score. The question, if the rights of free speech and peaceable assembly are to be preserved, is not as to the auspices under which the meeting is held but as to its purpose; not as to the relations of the speakers, but whether their utterances transcend the bounds of the freedom of speech which the Constitution protects. If the persons assembling have committed crimes elsewhere, if they have formed or are engaged in a conspiracy against the public peace and order, they may be prosecuted for their conspiracy or other violation of valid laws. But it is a different matter when the State, instead of prosecuting them for such offenses, seizes upon mere participation in a peaceable assembly and a lawful public discussion as the basis for a criminal charge.

We are not called upon to review the findings of the state court as to the objectives of the Communist Party. Notwithstanding those objectives, the defendant still enjoyed his personal right of free speech and to take part in a peaceable assembly having a lawful purpose, although called by that party. The defendant was none the less entitled to discuss the public issues of the day and thus in a lawful manner, without incitement to violence or crime, to seek redress of alleged grievances. That was of the essence of his guaranteed personal liberty.

We hold that the Oregon statute as applied to the particular charge as defined by the state court is repugnant to the due process clause of the Fourteenth Amendment. The judgment of conviction is reversed. . . .

HAGUE v. COMMITTEE FOR INDUSTRIAL ORGANIZATION

307 US 496 (1939)

[An ordinance of Jersey City, New Jersey, prohibited public assembly on the streets or in the public buildings or parks of the city without a permit from the director of public safety, and this public official was authorized to refuse to issue a permit "for the purpose of preventing riots, disturbances or disorderly assemblage." Alleging that the individuals requesting permits were Communists, the police denied numerous persons the right to hold public assemblies called for the purpose of organizing workers into unions, the right to distribute pamphlets, and the right to rent a hall for a public meeting. The police stopped persons as they entered the city, seized literature in their possession, and arrested or "deported" them. The persons against whom these actions were taken denied that they were Communists and contended that their sole purpose was to explain to workers their rights under the National Labor Relations Act and why they should join the C.I.O.

[The Court in a 5-to-2 decision (Justices McReynolds and Butler dissented) held the ordinance unconstitutional. There were opinions by Justices Roberts and Stone and Chief Justice Hughes. All the five Justices seem to have agreed on the fundamental issue of the controversy, namely, that the ordinance could be used as an "instrument of arbitrary suppression of free expression of views on national affairs for the prohibition of all speaking will undoubtedly 'prevent' such eventualities," that is, "riots, disturbances or disorderly assemblage."

[Justices Roberts and Black were of the opinion that the ordinance violated the right of citizens of the United States to assemble to discuss their rights and privileges under the National Labor Relations Act. This privilege belongs to citizens of the United States and is protected against infringement by the state under the Fourteenth Amendment.

[Justices Stone and Reed would put the decision on the broader principle that "freedom of speech and of assembly for any lawful purpose are rights of personal liberty secured to all persons, without regard to citizenship, by the due process clause of the Fourteenth Amendment." These freedoms are not privileges or immunities peculiar to national citizenship; they are protected against infringement by the state whether their exercise is attempted by citizens or aliens. Nor was it material to Stone and Reed that the purpose of the meetings was to discuss the National Labor Relations Act; it was enough that the meetings were called for any "lawful purpose."

[On the scope of the Privileges and Immunities Clause of the Fourteenth Amendment, see Milton R. Konvitz, *The Constitution and Civil Rights* (New York: Columbia University Press, 1947), ch. ii.]

Mr. Justice Roberts . . . :

The question now presented is whether freedom to disseminate information concerning the provisions of the National Labor Relations Act, to assemble peaceably for discussion of the Act, and of the opportunities and advantages offered by it, is a privilege or immunity of a citizen of the United States secured against State abridgment by sec. 1 of the Fourteenth Amendment; and whether Rev. Stat. § 1979 and § 24 (14) of the Judicial Code, 28 U.S.C.A. § 41 (14) afford redress in a federal court for such abridgment. This is the narrow question presented by the record, and we confine our decision to it, without consideration of broader issues which the parties urge. . . . The bill alleges, and the findings sustain the allegation, that the respondents [labor organizers] had no other purpose than to inform citizens of Jersey City by speech, and by the written word, respecting matters growing out of national legislation, the constitutionality of which this court has sustained.

Although it has been held that the Fourteenth Amendment created no rights in citizens of the United States, but merely secured existing rights against state abridgment, it is clear that the right peaceably to assemble and to discuss these topics, and to communicate respecting them, whether orally or in writing, is a privilege inherent in citizenship of the United States which the Amendment protects.

In the *Slaughter-House Cases* it was said, 16 Wall. 79, 21 L. ed. 409: "The right to peaceably assemble and petition for redress of grievances, the privilege of the writ of habeas corpus, are rights of the citizen guaranteed by the Federal Constitution."

In *United States* v. *Cruikshank*, 92 U.S. 542, the court said:

The right of the people peaceably to assemble for the purpose of petitioning Congress for a redress of grievances, or for any thing else connected with the powers or the duties of the national government, is an attribute of national citizenship, and, as such, under the protection of, and guaranteed by, the United States. The very idea of a government, republican in form, implies a right on the part of its citizens to meet peaceably for consultation in respect to public affairs and to petition for a redress of grievances. . . .

No expression of a contrary view has ever been voiced by this court.

The National Labor Relations Act declares the policy of the United States to be to remove obstructions to commerce by encouraging collective bargaining, protecting full freedom of association and self-organization of workers, and, through their representatives, negotiating as to conditions of employment.

Citizenship of the United States would be little better than a name if it did not carry with it the right to discuss national legislation and the benefits, advantages, and opportunities to accrue to citizens there-from. All of the respondents' proscribed activities had this single end and aim. The District Court had jurisdiction under sec. 24 (14).

Natural persons, and they alone, are entitled to the privileges and immunities which sec. 1 of the Fourteenth Amendment secures for "citizens of the United States." Only the individual respondents may, therefore, maintain this suit.

What has been said demonstrates that, in the light of the facts found, privileges and immunities of the individual respondents as citizens of the United States, were infringed by the petitioners [Mayor Frank Hague and other officials of Jersey City], by virtue of their official positions, under color of ordinances of Jersey City, unless, as petitioners contend, the city's ownership of streets and parks is as absolute as one's ownership of his home, with consequent power altogether to exclude citizens from the use thereof, or unless, though the city holds the streets in trust for public use, the absolute denial of their use to the respondents is a valid exercise of the police power.

The findings of fact negative the latter assumption. In support of the former the petitioners rely upon *Davis* v. *Massachusetts*, 167 U.S. 43. There it appeared that, pursuant to enabling legislation, the city of Boston adopted an ordinance prohibiting anyone from speaking, dis-charging fire arms, selling goods, or maintaining any booth for public amusement on any of the public grounds of the city except under a permit from the Mayor. Davis spoke on Boston Common without a permit and without applying to the Mayor for one. He was charged with a violation of the ordinance and moved to quash the complaint, inter alia, on the ground that the ordinance abridged his privileges and immunities as a citizen of the United States and denied him due process of law because it was arbitrary and unreasonable. His contentions were overruled and he was convicted. The judgment was affirmed by the Supreme Court of Massachusetts and by this court.

The decision seems to be grounded on the holding of the State court that the Common "was absolutely under the control of the legislature," and that it was thus "conclusively determined there was no right in the plaintiff in error to use the common except in such mode and subject to such regulations as the legislature in its wisdom may have deemed proper to prescribe." The Court added that the Fourteenth Amendment did not destroy the power of the states to enact police regulations as to a subject within their control or enable citizens to use public property in defiance of the constitution and laws of the State.

The ordinance there in question apparently had a different purpose from that of the one here challenged, for it was not directed solely at the exercise of the right of speech and assembly, but was addressed as well to other activities, not in the nature of civil rights, which doubtless might be regulated or prohibited as respects their enjoyment in parks. In the instant case the ordinance deals only with the exercise of the right of assembly for the purpose of communicating views entertained by speakers, and is not a general measure to promote the public convenience in the use of the streets or parks.

We have no occasion to determine whether, on the facts disclosed, the *Davis Case* was rightly decided, but we cannot agree that it rules the instant case. Wherever the title of streets and parks may rest, they have immemorially been held in trust for the use of the public and, time out of mind, have been used for purposes of assembly, communicating thoughts between citizens, and discussing public questions. Such use of the streets and public places has, from ancient times, been a part of the privileges, immunities, rights, and liberties of citizens. The privilege of a citizen of the United States to use the streets and parks for communication of views on national questions may be regulated in the interest of all; it is not absolute, but relative, and must be exercised in subordination to the general comfort and convenience, and in consonance with peace and good order; but it must not, in the guise of regulation, be abridged or denied.

We think the court below was right in holding the ordinance void on its face. It does not make comfort or convenience in the use of streets or parks the standard of official action. It enables the Director of Safety to refuse a permit on his mere opinion that such refusal will prevent "riots, disturbances or disorderly assemblage." It can thus, as the record discloses, be made the instrument of arbitrary suppression of free expression of views on national affairs for the prohibition of all speaking will undoubtedly "prevent" such eventualities. But uncontrolled official suppression of the privilege cannot be made a substitute for the duty to maintain order in connection with the exercise of the right. . . .

★ V ★

Freedom of Speech and Press:

Some Basic Principles

1. The Freedom Not to Speak

WEST VIRGINIA STATE BOARD OF EDUCATION v. BARNETTE

319 US 624 (1943)

[In 1940 there came before the Supreme Court *Minersville School District* v. *Gobitis*, 310 US 586, in which the Court upheld the requirement of participation by pupils in public schools in the ceremony of saluting the national flag. The Court held that a pupil belonging to Jehovah's Witnesses could not constitutionally claim exemption from this requirement on the ground that the flag salute would violate her religious beliefs and scruples. Justice Stone was the only dissenter.

[This decision was widely attacked. Three years later, in the *Barnette Case,* the Court dramatically reversed itself and expressly overruled the *Gobitis* decision. Justices Roberts, Reed, and Frankfurter dissented. In the *Barnette Case* the majority decision was put on the broad ground that the compulsory flag salute was an invasion of the sphere of intellect and spirit—a sphere protected from official control by the First and Fourteenth Amendments. National unity may be fostered by persuasion and example, but there may be no coerced uniformity. The Constitution guarantees the freedom to differ even "as to things that touch the heart of the existing order." Citizens may not be forced "to confess by word or act" their faith in any "orthodox" politics, nationalism, religion, or other matters of opinion.

[Justice Frankfurter, dissenting, said that the remedy for the unwise legislation involved in this case was to be found in the legislature and not in the courts. Much legislation affecting freedom of thought and speech, he said, "should offend a free-spirited society" and is yet constitutional. "Reliance for the most precious interests of civilization, therefore, must be found outside of their vindication in courts of law. Only a persistent positive translation of the faith of a free society into the convictions and habits of a community is the ultimate reliance against unabated temptations to fetter the human spirit."]

Mr. Justice Jackson delivered the opinion of the Court:

Following the decision by this Court on June 3, 1940, in *Minersville School Dist.* v. *Gobitis*, 310 US 586, the West Virginia legislature amended its statutes to require all schools therein to conduct courses of instruction in history, civics, and in the Constitutions of the United States and of the State "for the purpose of teaching, fostering and perpetuating the ideals, principles and spirit of Americanism, and increasing the knowledge of the organization and machinery of the government." Appellant Board of Education was directed, with advice of the State Superintendent of Schools, to "prescribe the courses of study covering these subjects" for public schools. The Act made it the duty of private, parochial and denominational schools to prescribe courses of study "similar to those required for the public schools."

The Board of Education on January 9, 1942, adopted a resolution containing recitals taken largely from the Court's *Gobitis* opinion and ordering that the salute to the flag become "a regular part of the program of activities in the public schools," that all teachers and pupils "shall be required to participate in the salute honoring the Nation represented by the Flag; provided, however, that refusal to salute the Flag be regarded as an Act of insubordination, and shall be dealt with accordingly."

The resolution originally required the "commonly accepted salute to the Flag" which it defined. Objections to the salute as "being too much like Hitler's" were raised by the Parent and Teachers Association, the Boy and Girl Scouts, the Red Cross, and the Federation of Women's Clubs. Some modification appears to have been made in deference to these objections, but no concession was made to Jehovah's Witnesses. What is now required is the "stiff-arm" salute, the saluter to keep the right hand raised with palm turned up while the following is repeated: "I pledge allegiance to the Flag of the United States of America and to the Republic for which it stands; one Nation, indivisible, with liberty and justice for all."

Failure to conform is "insubordination" dealt with by expulsion. Readmission is denied by statute until compliance. Meanwhile the expelled child is "unlawfully absent" and may be proceeded against as a delinquent. His parents or guardians are liable to prosecution, and if convicted are subject to fine not exceeding $50 and jail term not exceeding thirty days.

Appellees, citizens of the United States and of West Virginia, brought suit in the United States District Court for themselves and others similarly situated asking its injunction to restrain enforcement of these laws and regulations against Jehovah's Witnesses. The Witnesses are an unincorporated body teaching that the obligation imposed by law of God is superior to that of laws enacted by temporal government. Their religious beliefs include a literal version of Exodus, Chapter 20, verses 4 and 5, which says: "Thou shalt not make unto thee any graven image, or any likeness of anything that is in heaven above, or that is in the earth beneath, or that is in the water under the earth; thou shalt not bow down thyself to them, nor serve them." They consider that the flag is an "image" within this command. For this reason they refuse to salute it.

Children of this faith have been expelled from school and are threatened with exclusion for no other cause. Officials threaten to send them to reformatories maintained for criminally inclined juveniles. Parents of such children have been prosecuted and are threatened with prosecutions for causing delinquency. . . .

This case calls upon us to reconsider a precedent decision, as the Court throughout its history often has been required to do. Before turning to the *Gobitis Case,* however, it is desirable to notice certain characteristics by which this controversy is distinguished.

The freedom asserted by these appellees does not bring them into collision with rights asserted by any other individuals. It is such conflicts which most frequently require intervention of the State to determine where the rights of one end and those of another begin. But the refusal of these persons to participate in the ceremony does not interfere with or deny rights of others to do so. Nor is there any question in this case that their behavior is peaceable and orderly. The sole conflict is between authority and rights of the individual. The State asserts power to condition access to public education on making a prescribed sign and profession and at the same time to coerce attendance by punishing both parent and child. The latter stand on a right of self-determination in matters that touch individual opinion and personal attitude.

As the present Chief Justice [Stone] said in dissent in the *Gobitis Case,* the State may "require teaching . . . in our history and in the structure and organization of our government, including the guaranties of civil liberty, which tend to inspire patriotism and love of country."

Here, however, we are dealing with a compulsion of students to declare a belief. They are not merely made acquainted with the flag salute so that they may be informed as to what it is or even what it means. The issue here is whether this slow and easily neglected route to aroused loyalties constitutionally may be short-cut by substituting a compulsory salute and slogan. This issue is not prejudiced by the Court's previous holding that where a State, without compelling attendance, extends college facilities to pupils who voluntarily enroll, it may prescribe military training as part of the course without offense to the Constitution. It was held that those who take advantage of its opportunities may not on ground of conscience refuse compliance with such conditions. *Hamilton* v. *University of California*, 293 US 245. In the present case attendance is not optional. That case is also to be distinguished from the present one because, independently of college privileges or requirements, the State has power to raise militia and impose the duties of service therein upon its citizens.

There is no doubt that, in connection with the pledges, the flag salute is a form of utterance. Symbolism is a primitive but effective way of communicating ideas. The use of an emblem or flag to symbolize some system, idea, institution, or personality, is a short cut from mind to mind. Causes and nations, political parties, lodges and ecclesiastical groups seek to knit the loyalty of their followings to a flag or banner, a color or design. The State announces rank, function, and authority through crowns and maces, uniforms and black robes; the church speaks through the Cross, the Crucifix, the altar and shrine, and clerical raiment. Symbols of State often convey political ideas just as religious symbols come to convey theological ones. Associated with many of these symbols are appropriate gestures of acceptance or respect: a salute, a bowed or bared head, a bended knee. A person gets from a symbol the meaning he puts into it, and what is one man's comfort and inspiration is another's jest and scorn.

Over a decade ago Chief Justice Hughes led this Court in holding that the display of a red flag as a symbol of opposition by peaceful and legal means to organized government was protected by the free speech guaranties of the Constitution. *Stromberg* v. *California*, 283 US 359. Here it is the State that employs a flag as a symbol of adherence to government as presently organized. It requires the individual to communicate by word and sign his acceptance of the political ideas it thus bespeaks. Objection to this form of communication when coerced is an old one, well known to the framers of the Bill of Rights.

It is also to be noted that the compulsory flag salute and pledge requires affirmation of a belief and an attitude of mind. It is not clear whether the regulation contemplates that pupils forego any contrary convictions of their own and become unwilling converts to the prescribed ceremony or whether it will be acceptable if they simulate assent by words without belief and by a gesture barren of meaning. It is now a commonplace that censorship or suppression of expression of opinion is tolerated by our Constitution only when the expression presents a clear and present danger of action of a kind the State is empowered to prevent and punish. It would seem that involuntary affirmation could be commanded only on even more immediate and urgent grounds than silence. But here the power of compulsion is invoked without any allegation that remaining passive during a flag salute ritual creates a clear and present danger that would justify an effort even to muffle expression. To sustain the compulsory flag salute we are required to say that a Bill of Rights which guards the individual's right to speak his own mind, left it open to public authorities to compel him to utter what is not in his mind.

Whether the First Amendment to the Constitution will permit officials to order observance of ritual of this nature does not depend upon whether as a voluntary exercise we would think it to be good, bad or merely innocuous. Any credo of nationalism is likely to include what some disapprove or to omit what others think essential, and to give off different overtones as it takes on different accents or interpretations. If official power exists to coerce acceptance of any patriotic creed, what it shall contain cannot be decided by courts, but must be largely discretionary with the ordaining authority, whose power to prescribe would no doubt include power to amend. Hence validity of the asserted power to force an American citizen publicly to profess any statement of belief or to engage in any ceremony of assent to one, presents questions of power that must be considered independently of any idea we may have as to the utility of the ceremony in question.

Nor does the issue as we see it turn on one's possession of particular religious views or the sincerity with which they are held. While religion supplies appellees' motive for enduring the discomforts of making the issue in this case, many citizens who do not share these religious views hold such a compulsory rite to infringe constitutional liberty of the individual. It is not necessary to inquire whether non-conformist beliefs will exempt from the duty to salute unless we first find power to make the salute a legal duty.

The *Gobitis* decision, however, *assumed,* as did the argument in that case and in this, that power exists in the State to impose the flag salute discipline upon school children in general. The Court only examined and rejected a claim based on religious beliefs of immunity from an unquestioned general rule. The question which underlies the flag salute controversy is whether such a ceremony so touching matters of opinion and political attitude may be imposed upon the individual by official authority under powers committed to any political organization under our Constitution. We examine rather than assume existence of this power and, against this broader definition of issues in this case, re-examine specific grounds assigned for the *Gobitis* decision.

1. It was said that the flag-salute controversy confronted the Court with "the problem which Lincoln cast in memorable dilemma: 'Must a government of necessity be too *strong* for the liberties of its people, or too *weak* to maintain its own existence?' " and that the answer must be in favor of strength. *Minersville School Dist.* v. *Gobitis.*

We think these issues may be examined free of pressure or restraint growing out of such considerations.

It may be doubted whether Mr. Lincoln would have thought that the strength of government to maintain itself would be impressively vindicated by our confirming power of the state to expel a handful of children from school. Such oversimplification, so handy in political debate, often lacks the precision necessary to postulates of judicial reasoning. If validly applied to this problem, the utterance cited would resolve every issue of power in favor of those in authority and would require us to override every liberty thought to weaken or delay execution of their policies.

Government of limited power need not be anemic government. Assurance that rights are secure tends to diminish fear and jealousy of strong government, and by making us feel safe to live under it makes for its better support. Without promise of a limiting Bill of Rights it is doubtful if our Constitution could have mustered enough strength to enable its ratification. To enforce those rights today is not to choose weak government over strong government. It is only to adhere as a means of strength to individual freedom of mind in preference to officially disciplined uniformity for which history indicates a disappointing and disastrous end.

The subject now before us exemplifies this principle. Free public education, if faithful to the ideal of secular instruction and political neutrality, will not be partisan or enemy of any class, creed, party, or faction. If it is to impose any ideological discipline, however, each party or denomination must seek to control, or failing that, to weaken the influence of the educational system. Observance of the limitations of the Constitution will not weaken government in the field appropriate for its exercise.

2. It was also considered in the *Gobitis Case* that functions of educational officers in states, counties and school districts were such that to interfere with their authority "would in effect make us the school board for the country."

The Fourteenth Amendment, as now applied to the States, protects the citizen against the State itself and all of its creatures—Boards of Education not excepted. These have, of course, important, delicate, and highly discretionary functions, but none that they may not perform within the limits of the Bill of Rights. That they are educating the young for citizenship is reason for scrupulous protection of Constitutional freedoms of the individual, if we are not to strangle the free mind at its source and teach youth to discount important principles of our government as mere platitudes.

Such Boards are numerous and their territorial jurisdiction often small. But small and local authority may feel less sense of responsibility to the Constitution, and agencies of publicity may be less vigilant in calling it to account. The action of Congress in making flag observance voluntary and respecting the conscience of the objector in a matter so vital as raising the Army contrasts sharply with these local regulations in matters relatively trivial to the welfare of the nation. There are village tyrants as well as village Hampdens, but none who acts under color of law is beyond reach of the Constitution.

3. The *Gobitis* opinion reasoned that this is a field "where courts possess no marked and certainly no controlling competence," that it is committed to the legislatures as well as the courts to guard cherished liberties and that it is constitutionally appropriate to "fight out the wise use of legislative authority in the forum of public opinion and before legislative assemblies rather than to transfer such a contest to the judicial arena," since all the "effective means of inducing political changes are left free."

The very purpose of a Bill of Rights was to withdraw certain subjects from the vicissitudes of political controversy, to place them beyond the reach of majorities and officials and to establish them as legal principles to be applied by the courts. One's right to life, liberty, and property, to free speech, a free press, freedom of worship and assembly, and other fundamental rights may not be submitted to vote; they depend on the outcome of no elections.

In weighing arguments of the parties it is important to distinguish between the due process clause of the Fourteenth Amendment as an instrument for transmitting the principles of the First Amendment and those cases in which it is applied for its own sake. The test of legislation which collides with the Fourteenth Amendment, because it also collides with the principles of the First, is much more definite than the test when only the Fourteenth is involved. Much of the vagueness of the due process clause disappears when the specific prohibitions of the First become its standard. The right of a State to regulate, for example, a public utility may well include, so far as the due process test is concerned, power to impose all of the restrictions which a legislature may have a "rational basis" for adopting. But freedoms of speech and of press, of assembly, and of worship may not be infringed on such slender grounds. They are susceptible of restriction only to prevent grave and immediate danger to interests which the state may lawfully protect. It is important to note that while it is the Fourteenth Amendment which bears directly upon the State it is the more specific limiting principles of the First Amendment that finally govern this case.

Nor does our duty to apply the Bill of Rights to assertions of official authority depend upon our possession of marked competence in the field where the invasion of rights occurs. True, the task of translating the majestic generalities of the Bill of Rights, conceived as part of the pattern of liberal government in the eighteenth century, into concrete restraints on officials dealing with the problems of the twentieth century, is one to disturb self-confidence. These principles grew in soil which also produced a philosophy that the individual was the center of society, that his liberty was attainable through mere absence of governmental restraints, and that government should be entrusted with few controls and only the mildest supervision over men's affairs. We must transplant these rights to a soil in which the laissez-faire concept or principle of non-interference has withered at least as to economic affairs, and social advancements are increasingly sought through closer integration of society and through expanded and strengthened governmental controls. These changed conditions often deprive precedents of reliability and cast us more than we would choose upon our judgment. But we act in these matters not by authority of our competence but by force of our commissions. We cannot, because of modest estimates of our competence in such specialties as public education, withhold the judgment that history authenticates as the function of this Court when liberty is infringed.

4. Lastly, and this is the very heart of the *Gobitis* opinion, it reasons that "national unity is the basis of national security," that the authorities have "the right to select appropriate means for its attainment," and hence reaches the conclusion that such compulsory measures toward "national unity" are constitutional. Upon the verity of this assumption depends our answer in this case.

National unity as an end which officials may foster by persuasion and example is not in question. The problem is whether under our Constitution compulsion as here employed is a permissible means for its achievement.

Struggles to coerce uniformity of sentiment in support of some end thought essential to their time and country have been waged by many good as well as by evil men. Nationalism is a relatively recent phenomenon but at other times and places the ends have been racial or territorial security, support of a dynasty or regime, and particular plans for saving souls. As first and moderate methods to attain unity have failed, those bent on its accomplishment must resort to an ever increasing severity. As governmental pressure toward unity becomes greater, so strife becomes more bitter as to whose unity it shall be. Probably no deeper division of our people could proceed from any provocation than from finding it necessary to choose what doctrine and whose program public educational officials shall compel youth to unite in embracing. Ultimate futility of such attempts to compel coherence is the lesson of every such effort from the Roman drive to stamp out Christianity as a disturber of its pagan unity, the Inquisition, as a means to religious and dynastic unity, the Siberian exiles as a means to Russian unity, down to the fast failing efforts of our present totalitarian enemies. Those who begin coercive elimination of dissent soon find themselves exterminating dissenters. Compulsory unification of opinion achieves only the unanimity of the graveyard.

It seems trite but necessary to say that the First Amendment to our Constitution was designed to avoid these ends by avoiding these beginnings. There is no mysticism in the American concept of the State or of the nature or origin of its authority. We set up government by consent of the governed, and the Bill of Rights denies those in power any legal opportunity to coerce that consent. Authority here is to be controlled by public opinion, not public opinion by authority.

The case is made difficult not because the principles of its decision are obscure but because the flag involved is our own. Nevertheless, we apply the limitations of the Constitution with no fear that freedom to be intellectually and spiritually diverse or even contrary will disintegrate the social organization. To believe that patriotism will not flourish if patriotic ceremonies are voluntary and spontaneous instead of a compulsory routine is to make an unflattering estimate of the appeal of our institutions to free minds. We can have intellectual individualism and the rich cultural diversities that we owe to exceptional minds only at the price of occasional eccentricity and abnormal attitudes. When they are so harmless to others or to the State as those we deal with here, the price is not too great. But freedom to differ is not limited to things that do not matter much. That would be a mere shadow of freedom. The test of its substance is the right to differ as to things that touch the heart of the existing order.

If there is any fixed star in our constitutional constellation, it is that no official, high or petty, can prescribe what shall be orthodox in politics, nationalism, religion, or other matters of opinion or force citizens to confess by word or act their faith therein. If there are any circumstances which permit an exception, they do not now occur to us.

We think the action of the local authorities in compelling the flag salute and pledge transcends constitutional limitations on their power and invades the sphere of intellect and spirit which it is the purpose of the First Amendment to our Constitution to reserve from all official control.

The decision of this Court in *Minersville School Dist.* v. *Gobitis* and the holdings of those few *per curiam* decisions which preceded and foreshadowed it are overruled, and the judgment enjoining enforcement of the West Virginia Regulation is affirmed.

2. The Freedom Not to Listen

PUBLIC UTILITIES COMMISSION v. POLLAK

343 US 451 (1952)

[In this "captive audience" case it appears that the Public Utilities Commission of the District of Columbia issued an order permitting the Capital Transit Company to broadcast on its buses and street cars radio programs consisting of 90 percent music and 10 percent announcements and commercial advertising.

[The Supreme Court held that these facts did not show a violation of any constitutional guaranty. Justice Black concurred, agreeing that the musical programs did not violate the First Amendment but making it clear that the broadcasting of news, speeches, commentators' views, or propaganda of any kind would, in his opinion, violate the Constitution. Justice Douglas dissented. He agreed with the views of Judge Edgerton of the United States Court of Appeals, who said that forcing a "captive audience" to listen is a violation of the "freedom of attention," which is destroyed by forced listening. "If Transit obliged its passengers to read what it liked," said Judge Edgerton, "or get off the car, invasion of their freedom would be obvious." Freedom of speech is guaranteed to every citizen so that he may reach the minds of willing, not coerced, listeners.

[Justice Frankfurter did not participate on the ground that, "as a victim of the practice," his feelings were "so strongly engaged" that he feared that his unconscious feelings may "operate in the ultimate judgment" or create the impression that they have so operated.]

Mr. Justice Burton delivered the opinion of the Court:

The principal question here is whether, in the District of Columbia, the Constitution of the United States precludes a street railway company from receiving and amplifying radio programs through loud speakers in its passenger vehicles under the circumstances of this case. The service and equipment of the company are subject to regulation by the Public Utilities Commission of the District of Columbia. The Commission, after an investigation and public hearings disclosing substantial grounds for doing so, has concluded that the radio service is not inconsistent with public convenience, comfort and safety and "tends to improve the conditions under which the public ride." The Commission, accordingly, has permitted the radio service to continue despite vigorous protests from some passengers that to do so violates their constitutional rights. For the reasons hereafter stated, we hold that neither the operation of the service nor the action of the Commission permitting its operation is precluded by the Constitution.

The Capital Transit Company, here called Capital Transit, is a privately owned public utility corporation, owning an extensive street railway and bus system which it operates in the District of Columbia under a franchise from Congress. Washington Transit Radio, Inc., here called Radio, also is a privately owned corporation doing business in the District of Columbia.

In March, 1948, Capital Transit experimented with "music as you ride" radio programs received and amplified through loud speakers in a streetcar and in a bus. Those vehicles were operated on various lines at various hours. A poll of passengers who heard the programs showed that 92% favored their continuance. Experience in other cities was studied. Capital Transit granted Radio the exclusive right to install, maintain, repair and use radio reception equipment in Capital Transit's streetcars, busses, terminal facilities, waiting rooms and division headquarters. Radio, in return, agreed to contract with a broadcasting station for programs to be received during a minimum of eight hours every day, except Sundays. To that end Radio secured the services of Station WWDC-FM. Its programs were to meet the specifications stated in Capital Transit's contract. Radio agreed to pay Capital Transit, after a 90-day trial, $6 per month per radio installation, plus additional compensation dependent upon the station's receipts from sources such as commercial advertising on the programs. In February, 1949, when more than 20 installations had been made, the service went into regular operation. At the time of the Commission's hearings, October 27–November 1, 1949, there were 212. On that basis the minimum annual payment to Capital Transit came to $15,264. The potential minimum would be $108,000 based upon 1,500 installations. The contract covered five years, with an automatic five-year renewal in the absence of notice to the contrary from either party.

This proceeding began in July, 1949, when the Commission, on its own motion, ordered an investigation. . . .

The Commission concluded "that the installation and use of radios in streetcars and busses of the Capital Transit Company is not inconsistent with public convenience, comfort, and safety" and dismissed its investigation. . . .

In this proceeding the courts are expressly restricted to the facts found by the Commission, insofar as those findings do not appear to be unreasonable, arbitrary or capricious.

After reciting that it had given careful consideration to the testimony bearing on public convenience, comfort and safety, the Commission said that—

From the testimony of record, the conclusion is inescapable that radio reception in streetcars and busses is not an obstacle to safety of operation.

Further, it is evident that public comfort and convenience is not impaired and that, in fact, through the creation of better will among passengers, it tends to improve the conditions under which the public ride. . . .

In view of the findings and conclusions of the Commission, there can be little doubt that, apart from the constitutional questions here raised, there is no basis for setting aside the Commission's decision. It is within the statutory authority of the Commission to prohibit or to permit and regulate the receipt and amplification of radio programs under such conditions that the total utility service shall not be unsafe, uncomfortable or inconvenient. . . .

Applicability of the First and Fifth Amendments.—It was held by the court below that the action of Capital Transit in installing and operating the radio receivers, coupled with the action of the Public Utilities Commission in dismissing its own investigation of the practice, sufficiently involved the Federal Government in responsibility for the radio programs to make the First and Fifth Amendments to the Constitution of the United States applicable to this radio service. These Amendments concededly apply to and restrict only the Federal Government and not private persons. . . .

We find in the reasoning of the court below a sufficiently close relation between the Federal Government and the radio service to make it necessary for us to consider those Amendments. In finding this relation we do not rely on the mere fact that Capital Transit operates a public utility on the streets of the District of Columbia under authority of Congress. Nor do we rely upon the fact that, by reason of such federal authorization, Capital Transit now enjoys a substantial monopoly of street railway and bus transportation in the District of Columbia. We do, however, recognize that Capital Transit operates its service under the regulatory supervision of the Public Utilities Commission of the District of Columbia which is an agency authorized by Congress. We rely particularly upon the fact that that agency, pursuant to protests against the radio program, ordered an investigation of it and, after formal public hearings, ordered its investigation dismissed on the ground that the public safety, comfort and convenience were not impaired thereby. . . .

No violation of the First Amendment.—Pollak and Martin contend that the radio programs interfere with their freedom of conversation and that of other passengers by making it necessary for them to compete against the programs in order to be heard. The Commission, however, did not find, and the testimony does not compel a finding, that the programs interfered substantially with the conversation of passengers or with rights of communication constitutionally protected in public places. It is suggested also that the First Amendment guarantees a freedom to listen only to such points of view as the listener wishes to hear. There is no substantial claim that the programs have been used for objectionable propaganda. There is no issue of that kind before us. The inclusion in the program of a few announcements explanatory and commendatory of Capital Transit's own services does not sustain such an objection.

No violation of the Fifth Amendment.—The court below has emphasized the claim that the radio programs are an invasion of constitutional rights of privacy of the passengers. This claim is that no matter how much Capital Transit may wish to use radio in its vehicles as part of its service to its passengers and as a source of income, no matter how much the great majority of its passengers may desire radio in those vehicles, and however positively the Commission, on substantial evidence, may conclude that such use of radio does not interfere with the convenience, comfort and safety of the service but tends to improve it, yet if one passenger objects to the programs as an invasion of his constitutional right of privacy, the use of radio on the vehicles must be discontinued. This position wrongly assumes that the Fifth Amendment secures to each passenger on a public vehicle regulated by the Federal Government a right of privacy substantially equal to the privacy to which he is entitled in his own home. However complete his right of privacy may be at home, it is substantially limited by the rights of others when its possessor travels on a public thoroughfare or rides in a public conveyance. Streetcars and busses are subject to the immediate control of their owner and operator and, by virtue of their dedication to public service, they are for the common use of all of their passengers. The Federal Government in its regulation of them is not only entitled, but is required, to take into consideration the interests of all concerned.

In a public vehicle there are mutual limitations upon the conduct of everyone, including the vehicle owner. These conflicting demands limit policies on such matters as operating schedules and the location of car or bus stops, as well as policies relating to the desirability or nature of radio programs in the vehicles. Legislation prohibiting the making of artificially amplified raucous sounds in public places has been upheld. *Kovacs* v. *Cooper,* 336 U.S. 77. . . . Conversely, where a regulatory body has jurisdiction, it will be sustained in its protection of activities in public places when those activities do not interfere with the general public convenience, comfort and safety. The supervision of such practices by a Public Utilities Commission in the manner prescribed in the District of Columbia meets the requirements both of substantive and procedural due process when it is not arbitrarily and capriciously exercised.

The contention of Pollak and Martin would permit an objector, with a status no different from that of other passengers, to override not only the preference of the majority of the passengers but also the considered judgment of the federally authorized Public Utilities Commission, after notice, investigation and public hearings, and upon a record reasonably justifying its conclusion that the policy of the owner and operator did not interfere with public convenience, comfort and safety but tended, in general, to improve the utility service.

We do not agree with that contention. The protection afforded to the liberty of the individual by the Fifth Amendment against the action of the Federal Government does not go that far. The liberty of each individual in a public vehicle or public place is subject to reasonable limitations in relation to the rights of others.

This Court expresses no opinion as to the desirability of radio programs in public vehicles. In this case that is a matter for decision between Capital Transit, the public and the Public Utilities Commission. The situation is not unlike that which arises when a utility makes a change in its running schedules or in the locations of its shops in the interest of the majority of the passengers but against the vigorous protests of the few who are inconvenienced by the change.

While the court below expressly refrained from stating its view of the constitutionality of the receipt and amplification in public vehicles of musical programs containing no commercial advertising and other announcements, it is clear that if programs containing commercial advertising and other announcements are permissible, then programs limited to the type of music here contracted for would not be less so. . . .

Reversed.

Separate opinion of Mr. Justice Black:

I concur in the Court's holding that this record shows no violation of the Due Process Clause of the Fifth Amendment. I also agree that Capital Transit's musical programs have not violated the First Amendment. I am of the opinion, however, that subjecting Capital Transit's passengers to the broadcasting of news, public speeches, views, or propaganda of any kind and by any means would violate the First Amendment. To the extent, if any, that the Court holds the contrary, I dissent.

Mr. Justice Douglas, dissenting:

This is a case of first impression. There are no precedents to construe; no principles previously expounded to apply. We write on a clean slate.

The case comes down to the meaning of "liberty" as used in the Fifth Amendment. Liberty in the constitutional sense must mean more than freedom from unlawful governmental restraint; it must include privacy as well, if it is to be a repository of freedom. The right to be let alone is indeed the beginning of all freedom. Part of our claim to privacy is in the prohibition of the Fourth Amendment against unreasonable searches and seizures. It gives the guarantee that a man's home is his castle beyond invasion either by inquisitive or by officious people. A man loses that privacy of course when he goes upon the streets or enters public places. But even in his activities outside the home he has immunities from controls bearing on privacy. He may not be compelled against his will to attend a religious service; he may not be forced to make an affirmation or observe a ritual that violates his scruples; he may not be made to accept one religious, political, or philosophical creed as against another. Freedom of religion and freedom of speech guaranteed by the First Amendment give more than the privilege to worship, to write, to speak as one chooses; they give freedom not to do nor to act as the government chooses. The First Amendment in its respect for the conscience of the individual honors the sanctity of thought and belief. To think as one chooses, to believe what one wishes are important aspects of the constitutional right to be let alone.

If we remembered this lesson taught by the First Amendment, I do not believe we would construe "liberty" within the meaning of the Fifth Amendment as narrowly as the Court does. The present case involves a form of coercion to make people listen. The listeners are of course in a public place; they are on streetcars traveling to and from home. In one sense it can be said that those who ride the streetcars do so voluntarily. Yet in a practical sense they are forced to ride, since this mode of transportation is today essential for many thousands. Compulsion which comes from circumstances can be as real as compulsion which comes from a command.

The streetcar audience is a captive audience. It is there as a matter of necessity, not of choice. One who is in a public vehicle may not of course complain of the noise of the crowd and the babble of tongues. One who enters any public place sacrifices some of his privacy. My protest is against the invasion of his privacy over and beyond the risks of travel.

The government may use the radio (or television) on public vehicles for many purposes. Today it may use it for a cultural end. Tomorrow it may use it for political purposes. So far as the right of privacy is concerned the purpose makes no difference. The music selected by one bureaucrat may be as offensive to some as it is soothing to others. The news commentator chosen to report on the events of the day may give overtones to the news that please the bureau head but which rile the streetcar captive audience. The political philosophy which one radio speaker exudes may be thought by the official who makes up the streetcar programs to be best for the welfare of the people. But the man who listens to it on his way to work in the morning and on his way home at night may think it marks the destruction of the Republic.

One who tunes in on an offensive program at home can turn it off or tune in another station, as he wishes. One who hears disquieting or unpleasant programs in public places, such as restaurants, can get up and leave. But the man on the streetcar has no choice but to sit and listen, or perhaps to sit and to try *not* to listen.

When we force people to listen to another's ideas, we give the propagandist a powerful weapon. Today it is a business enterprise working out a radio program under the auspices of government. Tomorrow it may be a dominant political or religious group. Today the purpose is benign; there is no invidious cast to the programs. But the vice is inherent in the system. Once privacy is invaded, privacy is gone. Once a man is forced to submit to one type of radio program, he can be forced to submit to another. It may be but a short step from a cultural program to a political program.

If liberty is to flourish, government should never be allowed to force people to listen to any radio program. The right of privacy should include the right to pick and choose from competing entertainments, competing propaganda, competing political philosophies. If people are let alone in those choices, the right of privacy will pay dividends in character and integrity. The strength of our system is in the dignity, the resourcefulness, and the independence of our people. Our confidence is in their ability as individuals to make the wisest choice. That system cannot flourish if regimentation takes hold. The right of privacy, today violated, is a powerful deterrent to any one who would control men's minds.

3. The Police Power and Freedom of Speech and Press

a. Protecting the Privacy of Home

BREARD v. CITY OF ALEXANDRIA

341 US 622 (1951)

[In an earlier case, *Martin v. Struthers*, 319 US 141 (1943), the Court held that a municipality lacks the power constitutionally to prohibit a person from going from door to door ringing the doorbell for the purpose of distributing to the householder a handbill announcing a religious meeting. In effect the decision said that while it is admittedly an inconvenience to be summoned to one's door to receive a handbill or pamphlet, this is a small price to pay for the sustenance of a free press and freedom of speech. The occupant could, however, post a notice on his door that he did not wish to be disturbed by uninvited peddlers or distributors.

[A majority of the Court distinguished the *Martin Case* from the *Breard Case* because the latter involved the ringing of doorbells by persons who solicited subscriptions for nationally-known magazines. Door-to-door solicitation for this commercial purpose could be prohibited by municipal ordinance.

[Justices Black and Douglas dissented on the ground that the ordinance infringed the constitutional guaranty of liberty of the press. Chief Justice Vinson also dissented on the ground that the ordinance discriminated against interstate commerce in favor of local vendors.]

Mr. Justice Reed delivered the opinion of the Court:

The appellant here, Jack H. Breard, a regional representative of Keystone Readers Service, Inc., a Pennsylvania corporation, was arrested while going from door to door in the City of Alexandria, Louisiana, soliciting subscriptions for nationally known magazines. The arrest was solely on the ground that he had violated an ordinance because he had not obtained the prior consent of the owners of the residences solicited. Breard, a resident of Texas, was in charge of a crew of solicitors who go from house to house in the various cities and towns in the area under Breard's management and solicit subscriptions for nationally known magazines and periodicals including among others the *Saturday Evening Post, Ladies Home Journal, Country Gentleman, Holiday, Newsweek, American Home, Cosmopolitan, Esquire, Pic, Parents, Today's Woman* and *True*. These solicitors spend only a few days in each city depending upon its size. Keystone sends a card from its home office to the new subscribers acknowledging receipt of the subscription and thereafter the periodical is forwarded to the subscriber by the publisher in interstate commerce through the mails.

The ordinance under which the arrest was made, so far as is here pertinent, reads as follows:

Section 1. Be it ordained by the council of the city of Alexandria, Louisiana, in legal session convened that the practice of going in and upon private residences in the City of Alexandria, Louisiana by solicitors, peddlers, hawkers, itinerant merchants or transient vendors of merchandise not having been requested or invited so to do by the owner or owners, occupant or occupants of said private residences for the purpose of soliciting orders for the sale of goods, wares and merchandise and/or disposing of and/or peddling or hawking the same is declared to be a nuisance and punishable as such nuisance as a misdemeanor.

It, or one of similar import, has been on the statute books of Alexandria for many years. It is stipulated that:

Such ordinance was enacted by the City Council, among other reasons, because some householders complained to those in authority that in some instances, for one reason or another, solicitors were undesirable or discourteous, and some householders complained that, whether a solicitor was courteous or not, they did not desire any uninvited intrusion into the privacy of their home. . . .

At appellant's trial for violation of the ordinance there was a motion to quash on the ground that the ordinance violates the Due Process Clause of the Fourteenth Amendment to the Federal Constitution; that it violates the Federal Commerce Clause, art. 1, § 8, cl. 3; and that it violates the guarantees of the First Amendment of freedom of speech and of the press, made applicable to the states by the Fourteenth Amendment to the Constitution of the United States. Appellant's motion to quash was overruled by the trial court and he was found guilty and sentenced to pay a $25 fine or serve 30 days in jail. The Supreme Court of Louisiana affirmed appellant's conviction and expressly rejected the federal constitutional objections. . . .

All declare for liberty and proceed to disagree among themselves as to its true meaning. There is equal unanimity that opportunists, for private gain, cannot be permitted to arm themselves with an acceptable principle, such as that of a right to work, a privilege to engage in interstate commerce, or a free press, and proceed to use it as an iron standard to smooth their path by crushing the living rights of others to privacy and repose. This case calls for an adjustment of constitutional rights in the light of the particular living conditions of the time and place. Everyone cannot have his own way and each must yield something to the reasonable satisfaction of the needs of all.

It is true that the knocker on the front door is treated as an invitation or license to attempt an entry, justifying ingress to the home by solicitors, hawkers and peddlers for all kinds of salable articles. When such visitors are barred from premises by notice or order, however, subsequent trespasses have been punished. Door-to-door canvassing has flourished increasingly in recent years with the ready market furnished by the rapid concentration of housing. The infrequent and still welcome solicitor to the rural home became to some a recurring nuisance in towns when the visits were multiplied. Unwanted knocks on the door by day or night are a nuisance or worse to peace and quiet. The local retail merchant, too, has not been unmindful of the effective competition furnished by house-to-house selling in many lines. As a matter of business fairness, it may be thought not really sporting to corner the quarry in his home and through his open door put pressure on the prospect to purchase. As the exigencies of trade are not ordinarily expected to have a higher rating constitutionally than the tranquillity of the fireside, responsible municipal officers have sought a way to curb the annoyances while preserving complete freedom for desirable visitors to the homes. The idea of barring classified salesmen from homes by means of notices posted by individual householders was rejected early as less practical than an ordinance regulating solicitors. . . .

First Amendment.— . . . We come to a point not heretofore urged. . . . This is that such an ordinance is an abridgment of freedom of speech and the press. Only the press or oral advocates of ideas could urge this point. It was not open to the solicitors for gadgets or brushes. The point is not that the press is free of the ordinary restraints and regulations of the modern state, such as taxation or labor regulation, . . . but, as stated in appellant's brief, "because the ordinance places an arbitrary, unreasonable and undue burden upon a well established and essential method of distribution and circulation of lawful magazines and periodicals and, in effect, is tantamount to a prohibition of the utilization of such method." Regulation necessarily has elements of prohibition. Thus the argument is not that the money-making activities of the solicitor entitles him to go "in or upon private residences" at will, but that the distribution of periodicals through door-to-door canvassing is entitled to First Amendment protection. This kind of distribution is said to be protected because the mere fact that money is made out of the distribution does not bar the publications from First Amendment protection. We agree that the fact that periodicals are sold does not put them beyond the protection of the First Amendment. The selling, however, brings into the transaction a commercial feature.

The First and Fourteenth Amendments have never been treated as absolute. Freedom of speech or press does not mean that one can talk or distribute where, when and how one chooses. Rights other than those of the advocates are involved. By adjustment of rights, we can have both full liberty of expression and an orderly life.

The case that comes nearest to supporting appellant's contention is *Martin* v. *Struthers*, 319 U.S. 141. . . . There a municipal ordinance forbidding anyone summoning the occupants of a residence to the door to receive advertisements was held invalid as applied to the free distribution of dodgers "advertising a religious meeting." Attention was directed in note 1 of that case to the fact that the ordinance was not aimed "solely at commercial advertising." It was said: "The ordinance does not control anything but the distribution of literature, and in that respect it substitutes the judgment of the community for the judgment of the individual householder."

The decision to release the distributor was because: "Freedom to distribute information to every citizen wherever he desires to receive it is so clearly vital to the preservation of a free society that, putting aside reasonable police and health regulations of time and manner of distribution, it must be fully preserved."

There was dissent even to this carefully phrased application of the principles of the First Amendment. As no element of the commercial entered into this free solicitation and the opinion was narrowly limited to the precise fact of the free distribution of an invitation to religious services, we feel that it is not necessarily inconsistent with the conclusion reached in this case. . . .

This makes the constitutionality of Alexandria's ordinance turn upon a balancing of the conveniences between some householders' desire for privacy and the publisher's right to distribute publications in the precise way that those soliciting for him think brings the best results. The issue brings into collision the rights of the hospitable housewife, peering on Monday morning around her chained door with those of Mr. Breard's courteous, well-trained but possibly persistent solicitor, offering a bargain on culture and information through a joint subscription to *Satevepost, Pic* and *Today's Woman*. Behind the housewife are many housewives and homeowners in the towns where . . . ordinances offer their aid. Behind Mr. Breard are "Keystone" with an annual business of $5,000,000 in subscriptions and the periodicals with their use of house-to-house canvassing to secure subscribers for their valuable publications, together with other housewives who desire solicitors to offer them the opportunity and remind and help them, at their doors, to subscribe for publications.

Subscriptions may be made by anyone interested in receiving the magazines without the annoyances of house-to-house canvassing. We think those communities that have found these methods of sale obnoxious may control them by ordinance. It would be, it seems to us, a misuse of the great guarantees of free speech and free press to use that guarantee to force a community to admit the solicitors of publications to the home premises of its residents. We see no abridgement of the principles of the First Amendment in this ordinance.

Affirmed.

Mr. Justice Black, with whom Mr. Justice Douglas joins, dissenting:

On May 3, 1943, this Court held that cities and states could not enforce laws which impose flat taxes on the privilege of door-to-door sales of religious literature, *Jones* v. *Opelika*, 319 U.S. 103; *Murdock* v. *Pennsylvania*, 319 U.S. 105; or which make it unlawful for persons to go from home to home knocking on doors and ringing doorbells to invite occupants to religious, political or other kinds of public meetings. *Martin* v. *Struthers*, 319 U.S. 141. Over strong dissents, these laws were held to invade liberty of speech, press and religion in violation of the First and Fourteenth Amendments. Today a new majority adopts the position of the former dissenters and sustains a city ordinance forbidding door-to-door solicitation of subscriptions to the *Saturday Evening Post*, *Newsweek* and other magazines. Since this decision cannot be reconciled with the *Jones*, *Murdock* and *Martin* v. *Struthers* cases, it seems to me that good judicial practice calls for their forthright overruling. But whether this is done or not, it should be plain that my disagreement with the majority of the Court as now constituted stems basically from a different concept of the reach of the constitutional liberty of the press rather than from any difference of opinion as to what former cases have held.

Today's decision marks a revitalization of the judicial views which prevailed before this Court embraced the philosophy that the First Amendment gives a preferred status to the liberties it protects. I adhere to that preferred position philosophy. It is my belief that the freedom of the people of this Nation cannot survive even a little governmental hobbling of religious or political ideas, whether they be communicated orally or through the press.

The constitutional sanctuary for the press must necessarily include liberty to publish and circulate. In view of our economic system, it must also include freedom to solicit paying subscribers. Of course homeowners can if they wish forbid newsboys, reporters or magazine solicitors to ring their doorbells. But when the homeowner himself has not done this, I believe that the First Amendment, interpreted with due regard for the freedoms it guarantees, bars laws like the present ordinance which punish persons who peacefully go from door to door as agents of the press.

b. Protecting the Repose and Quiet of Streets and Neighborhoods

KOVACS v. COOPER

336 US 77 (1949)

[In 1897 the Supreme Court held that a city may absolutely or conditionally prohibit public speaking in a public street or park. *Davis* v. *Massachusetts*, 167 US 43 (1897). In the *Hague Case*, above, the Court, except for Justice Butler, held that the *Davis Case* did not govern the Jersey City case. Justice Roberts in the *Hague Case* said that the streets and parks have from ancient times been used for the communication of thoughts and views and the discussion of public issues. While this use may be regulated, it may not be abridged or denied.

[In 1948 the Court had before it an ordinance which prohibited the use of loud-speaker devices in public places without police permission. The police had denied a permit for the use of a sound truck to deliver a religious lecture in a public park. The Court held the ordinance unconstitutional. Justices Frankfurter, Reed, Burton, and Jackson dissented. *Saia* v. *New York*, 334 US 558 (1948). In the following year the Court considered *Kovacs* v. *Cooper*. This time eight Justices agreed that sound amplification in public places is subject to reasonable regulation, but Justices Frankfurter and Jackson went further and said that the use of sound trucks on public streets may be prohibited altogether. Justices Murphy, Black, Douglas, and Rutledge dissented—Murphy absolutely, the others on a construction of the facts in the case.]

Mr. Justice Reed announced the judgment of the Court . . . :

This appeal involves the validity of a provision of Ordinance No. 430 of the City of Trenton, New Jersey. It reads as follows:

4. That it shall be unlawful for any person, firm or corporation, either as principal, agent or employee, to play, use or operate for advertising purposes, or for any other purpose whatsoever, on or upon the public streets, alleys or thoroughfares in the City of Trenton, any device known as a sound truck, loud speaker or sound amplifier, or radio or phonograph with a loud speaker or sound amplifier, or any other instrument known as a calliope or any instrument of any kind or character which emits therefrom loud and raucous noises and is attached to and upon any vehicle operated or standing upon said streets or public places aforementioned.

The appellant was found guilty of violating this ordinance by the appellee, a police judge of the City of Trenton. . . .

We took jurisdiction to consider the challenge made to the constitu-

tionality of the section on its face and as applied on the ground that
§ 1 of the Fourteenth Amendment of the United States Constitution
was violated because the section and the conviction are in contravention of rights of freedom of speech, freedom of assemblage and freedom
to communicate information and opinions to others. The ordinance is
also challenged as violative of the Due Process Clause of the Fourteenth Amendment on the ground that it is so obscure, vague, and indefinite as to be impossible of reasonably accurate interpretation. . . .

At the trial in the Trenton police court, a city patrolman testified that
while on his post he heard a sound truck broadcasting music. Upon
going in the direction of said sound, he located the truck on a public
street near the municipal building. As he approached the truck, the
music stopped and he heard a man's voice broadcasting from the truck.
The appellant admitted that he operated the mechanism for the music
and spoke into the amplifier. The record from the police court does not
show the purpose of the broadcasting but the opinion in the Supreme
Court suggests that the appellant was using the sound apparatus to
comment on a labor dispute then in progress in Trenton.

The contention that the section is so vague, obscure and indefinite
as to be unenforceable merits only a passing reference. This objection
centers around the use of the words "loud and raucous." While these
are abstract words, they have through daily use acquired a content
that conveys to any interested person a sufficiently accurate concept of
what is forbidden. . . .

We think the words of § 4 of this Trenton ordinance comply with
the requirements of definiteness and clarity, set out above.

The scope of the protection afforded by the Fourteenth Amendment,
for the right of a citizen to play music and express his views on matters
which he considers to be of interest to himself and others on a public
street through sound amplification devices mounted on vehicles, must
be considered. Freedom of speech, freedom of assembly and freedom
to communicate information and opinion to others are all comprehended on this appeal in the claimed right of free speech. They will
be so treated in this opinion.

The use of sound trucks and other peripatetic or stationary broadcasting devices for advertising, for religious exercises and for discussion
of issues or controversies has brought forth numerous municipal
ordinances. The avowed and obvious purpose of these ordinances is
to prohibit or minimize such sounds on or near the streets since some
citizens find the noise objectionable and to some degree an interference
with the business or social activities in which they are engaged or the
quiet that they would like to enjoy. A satisfactory adjustment of the
conflicting interests is difficult as those who desire to broadcast can

hardly acquiesce in a requirement to modulate their sounds to a pitch that would not rise above other street noises nor would they deem a restriction to sparsely used localities or to hours after work and before sleep—say 6 to 9 P.M.—sufficient for the exercise of their claimed privilege. Municipalities are seeking actively a solution. . . . Unrestrained use throughout a municipality of all sound amplifying devices would be intolerable. Absolute prohibition within municipal limits of all sound amplification, even though reasonably regulated in place, time and volume, is undesirable and probably unconstitutional as an unreasonable interference with normal activities. . . .

This ordinance . . . is an exercise of the authority granted to the city by New Jersey "to prevent disturbing noises," . . . nuisances well within the municipality's power to control. The police power of a state extends beyond health, morals and safety, and comprehends the duty, within constitutional limitations, to protect the well-being and tranquility of a community. A state or city may prohibit acts or things reasonably thought to bring evil or harm to its people. . . .

We accept the determination of New Jersey that § 4 applies only to vehicles with sound amplifiers emitting loud and raucous noises. Courts are inclined to adopt that reasonable interpretation of a statute which removes it farthest from possible constitutional infirmity. . . . We need not determine whether this ordinance so construed is regulatory or prohibitory. All regulatory enactments are prohibitory so far as their restrictions are concerned, and the prohibition of this ordinance as to a use of streets is merely regulatory. Sound trucks may be utilized in places such as parks or other open spaces off the streets. The constitutionality of the challenged ordinance as violative of appellant's right of free speech does not depend upon so narrow an issue as to whether its provisions are cast in the words of prohibition or regulation. The question is whether or not there is a real abridgment of the rights of free speech.

Of course, even the fundamental rights of the Bill of Rights are not absolute. . . .

Hecklers may be expelled from assemblies and religious worship may not be disturbed by those anxious to preach a doctrine of atheism. The right to speak one's mind would often be an empty privilege in a place and at a time beyond the protecting hand of the guardians of public order. . . .

City streets are recognized as a normal place for the exchange of ideas by speech or paper. But this does not mean the freedom is beyond all control. We think it is a permissible exercise of legislative discretion to bar sound trucks with broadcasts of public interest, amplified to a loud and raucous volume, from the public ways of municipalities. On the business streets of cities like Trenton, with its more than 125,000 people, such distractions would be dangerous to traffic at all hours useful for the dissemination of information, and in the residential thoroughfares the quiet and tranquility so desirable for city dwellers would likewise be at the mercy of advocates of particular religious, social or political persuasions. We cannot believe that rights of free speech compel a municipality to allow such mechanical voice amplification on any of its streets.

The right of free speech is guaranteed every citizen that he may reach the minds of willing listeners and to do so there must be opportunity to win their attention. This is the phase of freedom of speech that is involved here. We do not think the Trenton ordinance abridges that freedom. It is an extravagant extension of due process to say that because of it a city cannot forbid talking on the streets through a loud speaker in a loud and raucous tone. Surely such an ordinance does not violate our people's "concept of ordered liberty" so as to require federal intervention to protect a citizen from the action of his own local government. . . . Opportunity to gain the public's ears by objectionably amplified sound on the streets is no more assured by the right of free speech than is the unlimited opportunity to address gatherings on the streets. The preferred position of freedom of speech in a society that cherishes liberty for all does not require legislators to be insensible to claims by citizens to comfort and convenience. To enforce freedom of speech in disregard of the rights of others would be harsh and arbitrary in itself. That more people may be more easily and cheaply reached by sound trucks, perhaps borrowed without cost from some zealous supporter, is not enough to call forth constitutional protection for what those charged with public welfare reasonably think is a nuisance when easy means of publicity are open. Section 4 of the ordinance bars sound trucks from broadcasting in a loud and raucous manner on the streets. There is no restriction upon the communication of ideas or discussion of issues by the human voice, by newspapers, by pamphlets, by dodgers. We think that the need for reasonable protection in the homes or business houses from the distracting noises of vehicles equipped with such sound amplifying devices justifies the ordinance.

Affirmed.

Mr. Justice Black, with whom Mr. Justice Douglas, and Mr. Justice Rutledge, concur, dissenting:

. . . The appellant was charged and convicted by interpreting the ordinance as an absolute prohibition against the use of sound amplifying devices. . . .

Nevertheless, in this Court the requisite majority for affirmance of appellant's conviction is composed in part of Justices who give the New Jersey ordinance a construction different from that given it by the state courts. That is not all. Affirmance here means that the appellant will be punished for an offense with which he was not charged, to prove which no evidence was offered, and of which he was not convicted. . . .

The New Jersey ordinance is on its face, and as construed and applied in this case by that state's courts, an absolute and unqualified prohibition of amplifying devices on any of Trenton's streets at any time, at any place, for any purpose, and without regard to how noisy they may be. . . .

There are many people who have ideas that they wish to disseminate but who do not have enough money to own or control publishing plants, newspapers, radios, moving picture studios, or chains of show places. Yet everybody knows the vast reaches of these powerful channels of communication which from the very nature of our economic system must be under the control and guidance of comparatively few people. On the other hand, public speaking is done by many men of divergent minds with no centralized control over the ideas they entertain so as to limit the causes they espouse. It is no reflection on the value of preserving freedom for dissemination of the ideas of publishers of newspapers, magazines, and other literature, to believe that transmission of ideas through public speaking is also essential to the sound thinking of a fully informed citizenry.

It is of particular importance in a government where people elect their officials that the fullest opportunity be afforded candidates to express and voters to hear their views. It is of equal importance that criticism of governmental action not be limited to criticisms by press, radio, and moving pictures. In no other way except public speaking can the desirable objective of widespread public discussion be assured. For the press, the radio, and the moving picture owners have their favorites, and it assumes the impossible to suppose that these agencies will at all times be equally fair as between the candidates and officials they favor and those whom they vigorously oppose. And it is an obvious fact that public speaking today without the sound amplifiers is a wholly inadequate way to reach the people on a large scale. Consequently, to tip the scales against transmission of ideas through public speaking, as the Court does today, is to deprive the people of a large part of the basic advantages of the receipt of ideas that the First Amendment was designed to protect.

There is no more reason that I can see for wholly prohibiting one useful instrument of communication than another. If Trenton can completely bar the streets to the advantageous use of loud speakers, all cities can do the same. In that event preference in the dissemination of ideas is given those who can obtain the support of newspapers, etc., or those who have money enough to buy advertising from newspapers, radios, or moving pictures. This Court should no more permit this invidious prohibition against the dissemination of ideas by speaking than it would permit a complete blackout of the press, the radio, or moving pictures. It is wise for all who cherish freedom of expression to reflect upon the plain fact that a holding that the audiences of public speakers can be constitutionally prohibited is not unrelated to a like prohibition in other fields. And the right to freedom of expression should be protected from absolute censorship for persons without, as for persons with, wealth and power. At least, such is the theory of our society.

I am aware that the "blare" of this new method of carrying ideas is susceptible of abuse and may under certain circumstances constitute an intolerable nuisance. But ordinances can be drawn which adequately protect a community from unreasonable use of public speaking devices without absolutely denying to the community's citizens all information that may be disseminated or received through this new avenue for trade in ideas. I would agree without reservation to the sentiment that "unrestrained use throughout a municipality of all sound amplifying devices would be intolerable." And of course cities may restrict or absolutely ban the use of amplifiers on busy streets in the business area. A city ordinance that reasonably restricts the volume of sound, or the hours during which an amplifier may be used, does not, in my mind, infringe the constitutionally protected area of free speech. It is because this ordinance does none of these things, but is instead an absolute prohibition of all uses of an amplifier on any of the streets of Trenton at any time that I must dissent.

I would reverse the judgment.

c. Speech That Is a Violation of Public Peace and Order

FEINER v. NEW YORK

340 US 315 (1951)

[A university student, using a loud speaker, addressed a crowd, which included some Negroes, from a box on the sidewalk in Syracuse, New York. He called then-President Truman "a bum" and said that Negroes "should rise up in arms and fight for their rights." Policemen asked him to stop speaking; as he ignored their requests, they arrested him. He was convicted for disorderly conduct. By a 6-to-3 decision the Supreme Court upheld the conviction on the ground that the speaker had created a clear danger of disorder on the public streets of the city. The dissenting Justices (Black, Douglas, and Minton) maintained that the speaker was punished for his unpopular views, expressed to an unsympathetic audience; that he was arrested before there was a present danger of a riot; that the police should have protected him in the exercise of his constitutional rights against anyone in the crowd who may have threatened him with violence rather than have thrown their weight against him. The majority, however, were impressed with the fact that the state trial and appeals courts found that the speaker had created danger to public order.

[Justice Frankfurter's concurring opinion is a scholarly, helpful analysis and classification of the different types of free speech cases considered by the Court. It appears as part of another case decided the same day, *Niemotko* v. *Maryland,* which appears later in this volume.]

Mr. Chief Justice Vinson delivered the opinion of the Court:

Petitioner was convicted of the offense of disorderly conduct, a misdemeanor under the New York penal laws, in the Court of Special Sessions of the City of Syracuse and was sentenced to thirty days in the county penitentiary. . . .

On the evening of March 8, 1949, petitioner Irving Feiner was addressing an open-air meeting at the corner of South McBride and Harrison Streets in the City of Syracuse. At approximately 6:30 P.M., the police received a telephone complaint concerning the meeting, and two officers were detailed to investigate. One of these officers went to the scene immediately, the other arriving some twelve minutes later. They found a crowd of about seventy-five or eighty people, both Negro and white, filling the sidewalk and spreading out into the street. Petitioner, standing on a large wooden box on the sidewalk, was addressing the crowd through a loud-speaker system attached to an automobile. Although the purpose of his speech was to urge his listeners to attend a meeting to be held that night in the Syracuse Hotel, in its course he was making derogatory remarks concerning President Truman, the American Legion, the Mayor of Syracuse, and other local political officials.

The police officers made no effort to interfere with petitioner's speech, but were first concerned with the effect of the crowd on both pedestrian and vehicular traffic. They observed the situation from the opposite side of the street, noting that some pedestrians were forced to walk in the street to avoid the crowd. Since traffic was passing at the time, the officers attempted to get the people listening to petitioner back on the sidewalk. The crowd was restless and there was some pushing, shoving and milling around. One of the officers telephoned the police station from a nearby store, and then both policemen crossed the street and mingled with the crowd without any intention of arresting the speaker.

At this time, petitioner was speaking in a "loud, high-pitched voice." He gave the impression that he was endeavoring to arouse the Negro people against the whites, urging that they rise up in arms and fight for equal rights. The statements before such a mixed audience "stirred up a little excitement." Some of the onlookers made remarks to the police about their inability to handle the crowd and at least one threatened violence if the police did not act. There were others who appeared to be favoring petitioner's arguments. Because of the feeling that existed in the crowd both for and against the speaker, the officers finally "stepped in to prevent it from resulting in a fight." One of the officers approached the petitioner, not for the purpose of arresting him, but to get him to break up the crowd. He asked petitioner to get down off the box, but the latter refused to accede to his request and continued talking. The officer waited for a minute and then demanded that he cease talking. Although the officer had thus twice requested petitioner to stop over the course of several minutes, petitioner not only ignored him but continued talking. During all this time, the crowd was pressing closer around petitioner and the officer. Finally, the officer told petitioner he was under arrest and ordered him to get down from the box, reaching up to grab him. Petitioner stepped down, announcing over the microphone that "the law has arrived, and I suppose they will take over now." In all, the officer had asked petitioner to get down off the box three times over a space of four or five minutes. Petitioner had been speaking for over a half hour.

On these facts, petitioner was specifically charged with violation . . . of the Penal Law of New York. . . .

We are not faced here with blind condonation by a state court of arbitrary police action. Petitioner was accorded a full, fair trial. The trial judge heard testimony supporting and contradicting the judgment of the police officers that a clear danger of disorder was threatened. After weighing this contradictory evidence, the trial judge reached the conclusion that the police officers were justified in taking action to prevent a breach of the peace. The exercise of the police officers' proper discretionary power to prevent a breach of the peace was thus approved by the trial court and later by two courts on review. The courts below recognized petitioner's right to hold a street meeting at this locality, to make use of loud-speaking equipment in giving his speech, and to make derogatory remarks concerning public officials and the American Legion. They found that the officers in making the arrest were motivated solely by a proper concern for the preservation of order and protection of the general welfare, and that there was no evidence which could lend color to a claim that the acts of the police were a cover for suppression of petitioner's views and opinions. Petitioner was thus neither arrested nor convicted for the making or the content of his speech. Rather, it was the reaction which it actually engendered.

. . . The findings of the New York courts as to the condition of the crowd and the refusal of petitioner to obey the police requests, supported as they are by the record of this case, are persuasive that the conviction of petitioner for violation of public peace, order and authority does not exceed the bounds of proper state police action. This Court respects, as it must, the interest of the community in maintaining peace and order on its streets. . . . We cannot say that the preservation of that interest here encroaches on the constitutional rights of this petitioner.

We are well aware that the ordinary murmurings and objections of a hostile audience cannot be allowed to silence a speaker, and are also mindful of the possible danger of giving overzealous police officials complete discretion to break up otherwise lawful public meetings. "A State may not unduly suppress free communication of views, religious or other, under the guise of conserving desirable conditions." *Cantwell v. Connecticut.* . . . But we are not faced here with such a situation. It is one thing to say that the police cannot be used as an instrument for the suppression of unpopular views, and another to say that, when as here the speaker passes the bounds of argument or persuasion and undertakes incitement to riot, they are powerless to prevent a breach of the peace. Nor in this case can we condemn the considered judgment of three New York courts approving the means which the police, faced with a crisis, used in the exercise of their power and duty to preserve peace and order. The findings of the state courts as to the existing situation and the imminence of greater disorder coupled with petitioner's deliberate defiance of the police officers convince us that we should not reverse this conviction in the name of free speech.

Affirmed. . . .

Mr. Justice Black, dissenting:

The record before us convinces me that petitioner, a young college student, has been sentenced to the penitentiary for the unpopular views he expressed on matters of public interest while lawfully making a street-corner speech in Syracuse, New York. Today's decision, however, indicates that we must blind ourselves to this fact because the trial judge fully accepted the testimony of the prosecution witnesses on all important points. Many times in the past this Court has said that despite findings below, we will examine the evidence for ourselves to ascertain whether federally protected rights have been denied; otherwise review here would fail of its purpose in safeguarding constitutional guarantees. Even a partial abandonment of this rule marks a dark day for civil liberties in our Nation.

But still more has been lost today. Even accepting every "finding of fact" below, I think this conviction makes a mockery of the free speech guarantees of the First and Fourteenth Amendments. The end result of the affirmance here is to approve a simple and readily available technique by which cities and states can with impunity subject all speeches, political or otherwise, on streets or elsewhere, to the supervision and censorship of the local police. I will have no part or parcel in this holding which I view as a long step toward totalitarian authority.

Considering only the evidence which the state courts appear to have accepted, the pertinent 'facts" are: Syracuse city authorities granted a permit for O. John Rogge, a former assistant attorney general, to speak in a public school building on March 8, 1948, on the subject of racial discrimination and civil liberties. On March 8th, however, the authorities cancelled the permit. The Young Progressives under whose auspices the meeting was scheduled then arranged for Mr. Rogge to speak at the Hotel Syracuse. The gathering on the street where petitioner spoke was held to protest the cancellation and to publicize the meeting at the hotel. In this connection, petitioner used derogatory but not profane language with reference to the city authorities, President Truman and the American Legion. After hearing some of these remarks, a policeman, who had been sent to the meeting by his superiors, reported to Police Headquarters by telephone. To whom he reported or what was said does not appear in the record, but after returning from the call, he and another policeman started through the crowd toward petitioner. Both officers swore they did not intend to make an arrest when they started, and the trial court accepted their statements. They also said, and the court believed, that they heard and saw "angry mutterings," "pushing," "shoving and milling around" and "restlessness." Petitioner spoke in a "loud, high pitched voice." He said that "colored people don't have equal rights and they should rise up in arms and fight for them." One man who heard this told the officers that if they did not take that "S . . . O . . . B . . ." off the box, he would. The officers then approached petitioner for the first time. One of them first "asked" petitioner to get off the box, but petitioner continued urging his audience to attend Rogge's speech. The officer next "told" petitioner to get down, but he did not. The officer finally "demanded" that petitioner get down, telling him he was under arrest. Petitioner then told the crowd that "the law had arrived and would take over" and asked why he was arrested. The officer first replied that the charge was "unlawful assembly" but later changed the ground to "disorderly conduct."

The Court's opinion apparently rests on this reasoning: The policeman, under the circumstances detailed, could reasonably conclude that serious fighting or even riot was imminent; therefore he could stop petitioner's speech to prevent a breach of peace; accordingly, it was "disoderly conduct" for petitioner to continue speaking in disobedience of the officer's request. As to the existence of a dangerous situation on the street corner, it seems farfetched to suggest that the "facts" show any imminent threat of riot or uncontrollable disorder. It is neither unusual nor unexpected that some people at public street meetings mutter, mill about, push, shove, or disagree, even violently, with the speaker. Indeed, it is rare where controversial topics are discussed that an outdoor crowd does not do some or all of these things. Nor does one isolated threat to assault the speaker forebode disorder. Especially should the danger be discounted where, as here, the person threatening was a man whose wife and two small children accompanied him and who, so far as the record shows, was never close enough to petitioner to carry out the threat.

Moreover, assuming that the "facts" did indicate a critical situation, I reject the implication of the Court's opinion that the police had no obligation to protect petitioner's constitutional right to talk. The police of course have power to prevent breaches of the peace. But if, in the name of preserving order, they ever can interfere with a lawful public speaker, they first must make all reasonable efforts to protect him. Here the policeman did not even pretend to try to protect petitioner. According to the officers' testimony, the crowd was restless but there is no showing of any attempt to quiet it; pedestrians were forced to walk into the street, but there was no effort to clear a path on the sidewalk; one person threatened to assault petitioner but the officers did nothing to discourage this when even a word might have sufficed. Their duty was to protect petitioner's right to talk, even to the extent of arresting the man who threatened to interfere. Instead, they shirked that duty and acted only to suppress the right to speak.

Finally, I cannot agree with the Court's statement that petitioner's disregard of the policeman's unexplained request amounted to such "deliberate defiance" as would justify an arrest or conviction for disorderly conduct. On the contrary, I think that the policeman's action was a "deliberate defiance" of ordinary official duty as well as of the constitutional right of free speech. For at least where time allows, courtesy and explanation of commands are basic elements of good official conduct in a democratic society. Here petitioner was "asked" then "told" then "commanded" to stop speaking, but a man making a lawful address is certainly not required to be silent merely because an officer directs it. Petitioner was entitled to know why he should cease doing a lawful act. Not once was he told. I understand that people in authoritarian countries must obey arbitrary orders. I had hoped that there was no such duty in the United States.

In my judgment, today's holding means that as a practical matter, minority speakers can be silenced in any city. Hereafter, despite the First and Fourteenth Amendments, the policeman's club can take heavy toll of a current administration's public critics. Criticism of public officials will be too dangerous for all but the most courageous. . . .

In this case I would reverse the conviction, thereby adhering to the great principles of the First and Fourteenth Amendments as announced for this Court in 1940 by Mr. Justice Roberts:

> In the realm of religious faith and in that of political belief, sharp differences arise. In both fields, the tenets of one man may seem the rankest error to his neighbor. To persuade others to his own point of view, the pleader, as we know, at times resorts to exaggeration, to vilification of men who have been, or are, prominent in church or state, and even to false statement. But the people of this nation have ordained in the light of history, that, in spite of the probability of excesses and abuses, these liberties are, in the long view, essential to enlightened opinion and right conduct on the part of the citizens of a democracy. *Cantwell* v. *Connecticut*, 310 US 296. . . .

Mr. Justice Douglas, with whom Mr. Justice Minton concurs, dissenting:

Feiner, a university student, made a speech on a street corner in Syracuse, New York, on March 8, 1949. The purpose of the speech was to publicize a meeting of the Young Progressives of America to be held that evening. A permit authorizing the meeting to be held in a public school auditorium had been revoked and the meeting shifted to a local hotel.

Feiner delivered his speech in a small shopping area in a predominantly colored residential section of Syracuse. He stood on a large box and spoke over loudspeakers mounted on a car. His audience was composed of about 75 people, colored and white. A few minutes after he started two police officers arrived.

The speech was mainly devoted to publicizing the evening's meeting and protesting the revocation of the permit. It also touched on various public issues. The following are the only excerpts revealed by the record:

> Mayor Costello [of Syracuse] is a champagne-sipping bum; he does not speak for the Negro people.
> The 15th Ward is run by corrupt politicians, and there are horse rooms operating there.
> President Truman is a bum.
> Mayor O'Dwyer is a bum.
> The American Legion is a Nazi Gestapo.
> The Negroes don't have equal rights; they should rise up in arms and fight for their rights.

There was some pushing and shoving in the crowd and some angry muttering. That is the testimony of the police. But there were no fights and no "disorder" even by the standards of the police. There was not even any heckling of the speaker.

But after Feiner had been speaking about 20 minutes a man said to the police officers, "If you don't get that son of a bitch off, I will go over and get him off there myself." It was then that the police ordered Feiner to stop speaking; when he refused, they arrested him.

Public assemblies and public speech occupy an important role in American life. One high function of the police is to protect these lawful gatherings so that the speakers may exercise their constitutional rights. When unpopular causes are sponsored from the public platform there will commonly be mutterings and unrest and heckling from the crowd. When a speaker mounts a platform it is not unusual to find him resorting to exaggeration, to vilification of ideas and men, to the making of false charges. But those extravagances . . . do not justify penalizing the speaker by depriving him of the platform or by punishing him for his conduct.

A speaker may not, of course, incite a riot any more than he may incite a breach of the peace by the use of "fighting words." . . . But this record shows no such extremes. It shows an unsympathetic audience and the threat of one man to haul the speaker from the stage. It is against that kind of threat that speakers need police protection. If they do not receive it and instead the police throw their weight on the side of those who would break up the meetings, the police become the new censors of speech. Police censorship has all the vices of the censorship from city halls which we have repeatedly struck down. . . .

TERMINIELLO v. CHICAGO
337 US 1 (1949)

[In the *Feiner Case,* it will be recalled, the Court found that the speaker had created a clear danger of public disorder; in the face of such danger, he should not have persisted in continuing his outdoor speech. In the *Terminiello Case* the speech was delivered in a hall hired for the occasion. This, it seems, is an important difference; for people who hear parts of a speech through an amplifying device as they walk on the street are members of a "captive audience," while people who attend a speech in a hall do so voluntarily. Another important difference is that Terminiello was convicted, not for creating a clear danger of public disorder, but for causing a breach of peace by delivering a speech which "stirs the public to anger, invites dispute, [or] brings about a condition of unrest." Terminiello, said the Court, could not, under these circumstances, be punished: "A function of free speech . . . is to invite dispute," induce a condition of unrest, create "dissatisfaction with conditions as they are," or even stir people to anger.

[The decision was 5 to 4, with Chief Justice Vinson and Justices Frankfurter, Jackson, and Burton dissenting. Three of these Justices dissented on what amounts to a procedural point, while Jackson dissented on this ground and also because he read the facts as showing that Terminiello had in fact incited the friendly audience in the hall and had provoked the hostile mob outside the hall, and that violence between the two crowds was threatened.]

Mr. Justice Douglas delivered the opinion of the Court:
Petitioner after jury trial was found guilty of disorderly conduct in violation of a city ordinance of Chicago and fined. The case grew out of an address he delivered in an auditorium in Chicago under the auspices of the Christian Veterans of America. The meeting commanded considerable public attention. The auditorium was filled to capacity with over eight hundred persons present. Others were turned away. Outside of the auditorium a crowd of about one thousand persons gathered to protest against the meeting. A cordon of policemen was

assigned to the meeting to maintain order; but they were not able to prevent several disturbances. The crowd outside was angry and turbulent.

Petitioner in his speech condemned the conduct of the crowd outside and vigorously, if not viciously, criticized various political and racial groups whose activities he denounced as inimical to the nation's welfare.

The trial court charged that "breach of the peace" consists of any "misbehavior which violates the public peace and decorum"; and that the "misbehavior may constitute a breach of the peace if it stirs the public to anger, invites dispute, brings about a condition of unrest, or creates a disturbance, or if it molests the inhabitants in the enjoyment of peace and quiet by arousing alarm." Petitioner did not take exception to that instruction. But he maintained at all times that the ordinance as applied to his conduct violated his right of free speech under the Federal Constitution. . . .

The argument here has been focused on the issue of whether the content of petitioner's speech was composed of derisive, fighting words, which carried it outside the scope of the constitutional guarantees. See *Chaplinsky* v. *New Hampshire,* 315 U.S. 568. . . . We do not reach that question, for there is a preliminary question that is dispositive of the case.

As we have noted, the statutory words "breach of the peace" were defined in instructions to the jury to include speech which "stirs the public to anger, invites dispute, brings about a condition of unrest, or creates a disturbance. . . ." That construction of the ordinance is a ruling on a question of state law that is as binding on us as though the precise words had been written into the ordinance. . . .

The vitality of civil and political institutions in our society depends on free discussion. As Chief Justice Hughes wrote in *De Jonge* v. *Oregon,* 299 U.S. 353, . . . it is only through free debate and free exchange of ideas that government remains responsive to the will of the people and peaceful change is effected. The right to speak freely and to promote diversity of ideas and programs is therefore one of the chief distinctions that sets us apart from totalitarian regimes.

Accordingly a function of free speech under our system of government is to invite dispute. It may indeed best serve its high purpose when it induces a condition of unrest, creates dissatisfaction with conditions as they are, or even stirs people to anger. Speech is often provocative and challenging. It may strike at prejudices and preconceptions and have profound unsettling effects as it presses for acceptance of an idea. That is why freedom of speech, though not absolute, . . . is nevertheless protected against censorship or punishment, unless shown likely to produce a clear and present danger of a serious substantive evil that arises far above public inconvenience, annoyance, or unrest. . . . There is no room under our Constitution for a more restrictive view. For the alternative would lead to standardization of ideas either by legislatures, courts, or dominant political or community groups.

The ordinance as construed by the trial court seriously invaded this province. It permitted conviction of petitioner if his speech stirred people to anger, invited public dispute, or brought about a condition of unrest. A conviction resting on any of those grounds may not stand. . . .

But it is said that throughout the appellate proceedings the Illinois courts assumed that the only conduct punishable and punished under the ordinance was conduct constituting "fighting words." . . . Petitioner was not convicted under a statute so narrowly construed. For all anyone knows he was convicted under the parts of the ordinance (as construed) which, for example, make it an offense merely to invite dispute or to bring about a condition of unrest. We cannot avoid that issue by saying that all Illinois did was to measure petitioner's conduct, not the ordinance, against the Constitution. Petitioner raised both points—that his speech was protected by the Constitution; that the inclusion of his speech within the ordinance was a violation of the Constitution. . . .

Reversed.

Mr. Justice Jackson, dissenting:

The Court reverses this conviction by reiterating generalized approbations of freedom of speech with which, in the abstract, no one will disagree. Doubts as to their applicability are lulled by avoidance of more than passing reference to the circumstances of Terminiello's speech and judging it as if he had spoken to persons as dispassionate as empty benches, or like a modern Demosthenes practicing his Philippics on a lonely seashore.

But the local court that tried Terminiello was not indulging in theory. It was dealing with a riot and with a speech that provoked a hostile mob and incited a friendly one, and threatened violence between the two. When the trial judge instructed the jury that it might find Terminiello guilty of inducing a breach of the peace if his behavior stirred the public to anger, invited dispute, brought about unrest, created a disturbance or molested peace and quiet by arousing alarm, he was not speaking of these as harmless or abstract conditions. He was addressing his words to the concrete behavior and specific consequences disclosed by the evidence. He was saying to the jury, in effect, that if this particular speech added fuel to the situation already so inflamed as to threaten to get beyond police control, it could be punished as inducing a breach of peace. When the light of the evidence not recited by the Court is thrown upon the Court's opinion, it discloses that underneath a little issue of Terminiello and his hundred-dollar fine lurk some of the most far-reaching constitutional questions that can confront a people who value both liberty and order. This Court seems to regard these as enemies of each other and to be of the view that we must forego order to achieve liberty. So it fixes its eyes on a conception of freedom of speech so rigid as to tolerate no concession to society's need for public order.

An old proverb warns us to take heed lest we "walk into a well from looking at the stars." To show why I think the Court is in some danger of doing just that, I must bring these deliberations down to earth by a long recital of facts.

Terminiello, advertised as a Catholic Priest, but revealed at the trial to be under suspension by his Bishop, was brought to Chicago from Birmingham, Alabama, to address a gathering that assembled in response to a call signed by Gerald L. K. Smith, which, among other things, said:

> . . . The same people who hate Father Coughlin hate Father Terminiello. They have persecuted him, hounded him, threatened him, but he has remained unaffected by their anti-Christian campaign against him. You will hear all sorts of reports concerning Father Terminiello. But remember that he is a Priest in good standing and a fearless lover of Christ and America.

The jury may have considered that this call attempted to capitalize the hatreds this man had stirred and foreshadowed, if it did not intend to invite the kind of demonstration that followed.

Terminiello's own testimony shows the conditions under which he spoke. So far as material it follows:

> . . . We got there [the meeting place] approximately fifteen or twenty minutes past eight. The car stopped at the front entrance. There was a crowd of three or four hundred congregated there shouting and cursing and picketing. . . .
>
> When we got there the pickets were not marching; they were body to body and covered the sidewalk completely, some on the steps so that we had to form a flying wedge to get through. Police escorted us to the building, and I noticed four or five others there.
>
> They called us "God damned Fascists, Nazis, ought to hang the so and sos." When I entered the building I heard the howls of the people outside. . . . There were four or five plain clothes officers standing at the entrance to the stage and three or four at the entrance to the back door.
>
> The officers threatened that if they broke the door again they would arrest them and every time they opened the door a little to look out something was thrown at the officers, including ice-picks and rocks.
>
> A number of times the door was broken, was partly broken through. There were doors open this way and they partly opened and the officers looked out two or three times and each time ice-picks, stones and

bottles were thrown at the police at the door. I took my place on the stage, before this I was about ten or fifteen minutes in the body of the hall.

I saw a number of windows broken by stones or missiles. I saw the back door being forced open, pushed open.

The front door was broken partly open after the doors were closed. There were about seven people seated on the stage. Smith opened the meeting with prayer, the Pledge of Allegiance to the Flag and singing of America. There were other speakers who spoke before me and before I spoke I heard things happening in the hall and coming from the outside.

I saw rocks being thrown through windows and that continued throughout at least the first half of the meeting, probably longer, and again attempts were made to force the front door, rather the front door was forced partly. The howling continued on the outside, cursing could be heard audibly in the hall at times. Police were rushing in and out of the front door protecting the front door, and there was a general commotion, all kinds of noises and violence—all from the outside.

Between the time the first speaker spoke and I spoke, stones and bricks were thrown in all the time. I started to speak about 35 or 40 minutes after the meeting started, a little later than nine o'clock. . . .

The Court below, in addition to this recital, heard other evidence, that the crowd reached an estimated number of 1,500. Picket lines obstructed and interfered with access to the building. The crowd constituted "a surging, howling mob hurling epithets at those who would enter and tried to tear their clothes off." One young woman's coat was torn off and she had to be assisted into the meeting by policemen. Those inside the hall could hear the loud noises and hear those on the outside yell, "Fascists, Hitlers!" and curse words like "damn Fascists." Bricks were thrown through the windowpanes before and during the speaking. About 28 windows were broken. The street was black with people on both sides for at least a block either way; bottles, stink bombs and brickbats were thrown. Police were unable to control the mob, which kept breaking the windows at the meeting hall, drowning out the speaker's voice at times and breaking in through the back door of the auditorium. About 17 of the group outside were arrested by the police.

Knowing of this environment, Terminiello made a long speech, from the stenographic record of which I omit relatively innocuous passages and add emphasis to what seems especially provocative:

Father Terminiello: Now, I am going to whisper my greetings to you, Fellow Christians. I will interpret it. I said, "Fellow *Christians*," and I suppose there are *some of the scum got in by mistake,* so I want to tell a story about *the scum:*

. . . And nothing I could say tonight could begin to express the contempt I have for the *slimy scum* that got in by mistake.

. . . The subject I want to talk to you tonight about is the attempt *that is going on right outside this hall tonight,* the attempt that is going on to *destroy America by revolution.* . . .

I know I was told one time that my winter quarters were ready for me in Siberia. I was told that. Now, I am talking about the fifty-seven varieties that we have in America and we have fifty-seven varieties of pinks and reds and pastel shades in this country; and all of it can be traced back to the twelve years we spent under the New Deal, because that was the build-up for what is going on in the world today. . . .

Now, we are going to get the threats of the people of Argentine, the people of Spain. We have now declared, according to our officials, to have declared Franco to have taken the place of Hitler. *Franco was the savior of what was left of Europe.*

Now, let me say, I am going to talk about—I almost said, about the Jews. Of course, I would not want to say that. However, I am going to talk about some Jews, I hope that—I am a Christian minister. We must take a Christian attitude. I don't want you to go from this hall with hatred in your heart for any person, for no person. . . .

Now, this danger which we face—let us call them Zionist Jews if you will, let's call them atheistic, communistic Jewish or Zionist Jews, then let us not fear to condemn them. You remember the Apostles when they went into the upper room after the death of the Master, they went in there, after locking the doors; they closed the windows. (At this time there was a very loud noise as if something was being thrown into the building.)

Don't be disturbed. That happened by the way, while Mr. Gerald Smith was saying "Our Father who art in heaven;" (just then a rock went through the window.) *Do you wonder they were persecuted in other countries in the world?* . . .

That is why I say to you, men, don't you do it. Walk out of here dignified. The police will protect you. Put the women on the inside, where there will be no hurt to them. Just walk; don't stop and argue. . . . They want to picket our meetings. They don't want us to picket their meetings. It is the same kind of tolerance, if we said there was a bedbug in bed, "We don't care for you," or if we looked under the bed and found a snake and said, "I am going to be tolerant and leave the snake there." We will not be tolerant of that mob out there. We are not going to be tolerant any longer.

We are strong enough. We are not going to be tolerant of their smears any longer. We are going to *stand up and dare them to smear us.*

So, my friends, since we spent much time tonight trying to quiet the howling mob, I am going to bring my thoughts to a conclusion, and the conclusion is this. We must all be like the Apostles before the coming of the Holy Ghost. We must not lock ourselves in an upper room for fear of the Jews. I speak of the Communistic Zionistic Jew, and those are not American Jews. We don't want them here; we want them to go back where they came from. . . .

Such was the speech. Evidence showed that it stirred the audience not only to cheer and applaud but to expressions of immediate anger, unrest and alarm. One called the speaker a "God damned liar" and was taken out by the police. Another said that "Jews, niggers and Catholics would have to be gotten rid of." One response was, "yes, the Jews are all killers, murderers. If we don't kill them first, they will kill us." The anti-Jewish stories elicited exclamations of "Oh!" and "Isn't that terrible!" and shouts of "Yes, send the Jews back to Russia," "Kill the Jews," "Dirty kikes," and much more of ugly tenor. This is the specific and concrete kind of anger, unrest and alarm, coupled with that of the mob outside, that the trial court charged the jury might find to be a breach of peace induced by Terminiello. It is difficult to believe that this Court is speaking of the same occasion, but it is the only one involved in this litigation.

Terminiello, of course, disclaims being a fascist. Doubtless many of the indoor audience were not consciously such. His speech, however, followed, with fidelity that is more than coincidental, the pattern of European fascist leaders.

The street mob, on the other hand, included some who deny being communists, but Terminiello testified and offered to prove that the demonstration was communist-organized and communist-led. He offered literature of left-wing organizations calling members to meet and "mobilize" for instruction as pickets and exhorting followers: "All out to fight Fascist Smith."

As this case declares a nation-wide rule that disables local and state authorities from punishing conduct which produces conflicts of this kind, it is unrealistic not to take account of the nature, methods and objectives of the forces involved. This was not an isolated, spontaneous and unintended collision of political, racial or ideological adversaries. It was a local manifestation of a world-wide and standing conflict between two organized groups of revolutionary fanatics, each of which has imported to this country the strong-arm technique developed in the struggle by which their kind has devastated Europe. Increasingly, American cities have to cope with it. One faction organizes a mass meeting, the other organizes pickets to harass it; each organizes squads to counteract the other's pickets; parade is met with counterparade. Each of these mass demonstrations has the potentiality, and more than a few the purpose, of disorder and violence. This technique appeals not to reason but to fears and mob spirit; each is a show of force designed to bully adversaries and to overawe the indifferent. We need not resort to speculation as to the purposes for which these tactics are calculated nor as to their consequences. Recent European history demonstrates both.

Hitler summed up the strategy of the mass demonstration as used by both fascism and communism: "We should not work in secret conventicles but in mighty mass demonstrations, and it is not by dagger and poison or pistol that the road can be cleared for the movement but *by the conquest of the streets*. We must teach the Marxists that the future *master of the streets* is National Socialism, just as it will some day be the master of the state." . . .

The present obstacle to mastery of the streets by either radical or reactionary mob movements is not the opposing minority. It is the authority of local governments which represent the free choice of democratic and law-abiding elements, of all shades of opinion but who, whatever their differences, submit them to free elections which register the results of their free discussion. The fascist and communist groups, on the contrary, resort to these terror tactics to confuse, bully and discredit those freely chosen governments. Violent and noisy shows of strength discourage participation of moderates in discussions so fraught with violence and real discussion dries up and disappears. And people lose faith in the democratic process when they see public authority flouted and impotent and begin to think the time has come when they must choose sides in a false and terrible dilemma such as was posed as being at hand by the call for the Terminiello meeting: "Christian Nationalism or World Communism—Which?"

This drive by totalitarian groups to undermine the prestige and effectiveness of local democratic governments is advanced whenever either of them can win from this Court a ruling which paralyzes the power of these officials. This is such a case. The group of which Terminiello is a part claims that his behavior, because it involved a speech, is above the reach of local authorities. If the mild action those authorities have taken is forbidden, it is plain that hereafter there is nothing effective left that they can do. If they can do nothing as to him, they are equally powerless as to rival totalitarian groups. Terminiello's victory today certainly fulfills the most extravagant hopes of both right and left totalitarian groups, who want nothing so much as to paralyze and discredit the only democratic authority that can curb them in their battle for the streets.

I am unable to see that the local authorities have transgressed the Federal Constitution. Illinois imposed no prior censorship or suppression upon Terminiello. On the contrary, its sufferance and protection was all that enabled him to speak. It does not appear that the motive in punishing him is to silence the ideology he expressed as offensive to the State's policy or as untrue, or has any purpose of controlling his thought or its peaceful communication to others. There is no claim that the proceedings against Terminiello are designed to discriminate against him or the faction he represents or the ideas that he bespeaks. There is no indication that the charge against him is a mere pretext to give the semblance of legality to a covert effort to silence him or to prevent his followers or the public from hearing any truth that is in him.

A trial court and jury has found only that in the context of violence and disorder in which it was made, this speech was a provocation to immediate breach of the peace and therefore cannot claim constitutional immunity from punishment. Under the Constitution as it has been understood and applied, at least until most recently, the State was within its powers in taking this action.

Rioting is a substantive evil, which I take it no one will deny that the State and the City have the right and the duty to prevent and punish. Where an offense is induced by speech, the Court has laid down and often reiterated a test of the power of the authorities to deal with the speaking as also an offense. "The question in every case is whether the words *used are used in such circumstances* and are of *such a nature* as to create a *clear and present danger* that they will bring about the substantive evils that Congress [or the State or City] has a right to prevent." (Emphasis supplied.) Mr. Justice Holmes in *Schenck* v. *United States*, 249 U.S. 47. No one ventures to contend that the State on the basis of this test, for whatever it may be worth, was not justified in punishing Terminiello. In this case the evidence proves beyond dispute that danger of rioting and violence in response to the speech was clear, present and immediate. If this Court has not silently abandoned this long standing test and substituted for the purposes of this case an unexpressed but more stringent test, the action of the State would have to be sustained.

Only recently this Court held that a state could punish as a breach of the peace use of epithets such as "damned racketeer" and "damned fascists," addressed to only one person, an official, because likely to provoke the average person to retaliation. But these are mild in comparison to the epithets "slimy scum," "snakes," "bedbugs," and the like, which Terminiello hurled at an already inflamed mob of his adversaries. Mr. Justice Murphy, writing for a unanimous Court in *Chaplinsky* v. *New Hampshire*, 315 U.S. 568, said:

> There are certain well-defined and narrowly limited classes of speech, the prevention and punishment of which have never been thought to raise any Constitutional problem. These include the lewd and obscene, the profane, the libelous and the insulting or 'fighting' words—those which by their very utterance inflict injury or tend to incite an immediate breach of the peace. It has been well observed that such utterances are no essential part of any exposition of ideas, and are of such slight social value as a step to truth that any benefit that may be derived from them is clearly outweighed by the social interest in order and morality. "Resort to epithets or personal abuse is not in any proper sense communication of information or opinion safeguarded by the Constitution, and its punishment as a criminal act would raise no question under that instrument." *Cantwell* v. *Connecticut*, 310 U.S. 296.

. . . How this present decision, denying state power to punish civilly one who precipitated a public riot involving hundreds of fanatic fighters in a most violent melee, can be squared with those unanimous statements of law, is incomprehensible to me. . . .

However, these wholesome principles are abandoned today and in their place is substituted a dogma of absolute freedom for irresponsible and provocative utterance which almost completely sterilizes the power of local authorities to keep the peace as against this kind of tactics. . . .

This case demonstrates also that this Court's service to free speech is essentially negative and can consist only of reviewing actions by local magistrates. But if free speech is to be a practical reality, affirmative and immediate protection is required; and it can come only from nonjudicial sources. It depends on local police, maintained by law-abiding taxpayers, and who, regardless of their own feelings, risk themselves to maintain supremacy of law. Terminiello's theoretical right to speak free from interference would have no reality if Chicago should withdraw its officers to some other section of the city, or if the men assigned to the task should look the other way when the crowd threatens Terminiello. Can society be expected to keep these men at Terminiello's service if it has nothing to say of his behavior which may force them into dangerous action?

No one will disagree that the fundamental, permanent and overriding policy of police and courts should be to permit and encourage utmost freedom of utterance. It is the legal right of any American citizen to advocate peaceful adoption of fascism or communism, socialism or capitalism. He may go far in expressing sentiments whether pro-semitic or anti-semitic, pro-Negro or anti-Negro, pro-Catholic or anti-Catholic. He is legally free to argue for some anti-American system of government to supersede by constitutional methods the one we have. It is our philosophy that the course of government should be controlled by a consensus of the governed. This process of reaching intelligent popular decisions requires free discussion. Hence we should tolerate no law or custom of censorship or suppression.

But we must bear in mind also that no serious outbreak of mob violence, race rioting, lynching or public disorder is likely to get going without help of some speech-making to some mass of people. A street may be filled with men and women and the crowd still not be a mob. Unity of purpose, passion and hatred, which merges the many minds of a crowd into the mindlessness of a mob, almost invariably is supplied by speeches. It is naive, or worse, to teach that oratory with this object or effect is a service to liberty. No mob has ever protected any liberty, even its own, but if not put down it always winds up in an orgy of lawlessness which respects no liberties.

In considering abuse of freedom by provocative utterances it is necessary to observe that the law is more tolerant of discussion than are most individuals or communities. Law is so indifferent to subjects of talk that I think of none that it should close to discussion. Religious, social and political topics that in other times or countries have not been open to lawful debate may be freely discussed here.

Because a subject is legally arguable, however, does not mean that public sentiment will be patient of its advocacy at all times and in all manners. So it happens that, while peaceful advocacy of communism or fascism is tolerated by the law, both of these doctrines arouse passionate reactions. A great number of people do not agree that introduction to America of communism or fascism is even debatable. Hence many speeches, such as that of Terminiello, may be legally permissible but may nevertheless in some surroundings, be a menace to peace and order. When conditions show the speaker that this is the case, as it did here, there certainly comes a point beyond which he cannot indulge in provocations to violence without being answerable to society. . . .

The ways in which mob violence may be worked up are subtle and various. Rarely will a speaker directly urge a crowd to lay hands on a victim or class of victims. An effective and safer way is to incite mob action while pretending to deplore it, after the classic example of Antony, and this was not lost on

Terminiello. And whether one may be the cause of mob violence by his own personification or advocacy of ideas which a crowd already fears and hates, is not solved merely by going through a transcript of the speech to pick out "fighting words." The most insulting words can be neutralized if the speaker will smile when he says them, but a belligerent personality and an aggressive manner may kindle a fight without use of words that in cold type shock us. True judgment will be aided by observation of the individual defendant, as was possible for this jury and trial court but impossible for us. . . .

Invocation of constitutional liberties as part of the strategy for overthrowing them presents a dilemma to a free people which may not be soluble by constitutional logic alone.

But I would not be understood as suggesting that the United States can or should meet this dilemma by suppression of free, open and public speaking on the part of any group or ideology. Suppression has never been a successful permanent policy; any surface serenity that it creates is a false security, while conspirational forces go underground. My confidence in American institutions and in the sound sense of the American people is such that if with a stroke of the pen I could silence every fascist and communist speaker, I would not do it. . . .

This Court has gone far toward accepting the doctrine that civil liberty means the removal of all restraints from these crowds and that all local attempts to maintain order are impairments of the liberty of the citizen. The choice is not between order and liberty. It is between liberty with order and anarchy without either. There is danger that, if the Court does not temper its doctrinaire logic with a little practical wisdom it will convert the constitutional Bill of Rights into a suicide pact.

I would affirm the conviction.

d. Group Libel

BEAUHARNAIS v. ILLINOIS

343 US 250 (1952)

[The guaranty of freedom of the press does not protect a person when he makes statements about another person that are libelous. A libel may be the basis of a civil suit for damages or of a criminal prosecution. While the truth may be a complete defense in a civil libel case, in a criminal libel case some states provide that truth is a defense only when the statement is published with good motives for justifiable ends. Illinois extended this law of criminal libel to punish publications which libel a group by identifying its members by their race, creed, or religion. Beauharnais, a white-supremacy agitator, was convicted under this law. The Supreme Court upheld the group libel statute as constitutional.

[The decision was 5 to 4, with Justices Reed, Jackson, Black, and

Douglas dissenting. Students of free speech are as divided about the constitutionality and wisdom of group libel laws as are members of the Court. For some years a group libel law was under consideration by Congress—to punish use of the mails by publications that libel certain groups—but counsel on the bill was divided and Congress has not enacted the bill. Should groups that agitate race or religious hatred aggravate the dangers to public peace, the debate over group libel statutes will again become a subject of immediate public interest.]

Mr. Justice Frankfurter delivered the opinion of the Court:

The petitioner was convicted upon information in the Municipal Court of Chicago of violating the Illinois Penal Code. He was fined $200. The section provides:

> It shall be unlawful for any person, firm or corporation to manufacture, sell, or offer for sale, advertise or publish, present or exhibit in any public place in this state any lithograph, moving picture, play, drama or sketch, which publication or exhibition portrays depravity, criminality, unchastity, or lack of virtue of a class of citizens, of any race, color, creed or religion which said publication or exhibition exposes the citizens of any race, color, creed or religion to contempt, derision, or obloquy or which is productive of breach of the peace or riots. . . .

Beauharnais challenged the statute as violating the liberty of speech and of the press guaranteed as against the States by the Due Process Clause of the Fourteenth Amendment, and as too vague, under the restrictions implicit in the same Clause, to support conviction for crime. The Illinois courts rejected these contentions and sustained defendant's conviction. . . . We granted certiorari in view of the serious questions raised concerning the limitations imposed by the Fourteenth Amendment on the power of a State to punish utterances promoting friction among racial and religious groups. . . .

The information, cast generally in the terms of the statute, charged that Beauharnais "did unlawfully . . . exhibit in public places lithographs, which publications portray depravity, criminality, unchastity or lack of virtue of citizens of Negro race and color and which exposes [*sic*] citizens of Illinois of the Negro race and color to contempt, derision, or obloquy. . . ." The lithograph complained of was a leaflet setting forth a petition calling on the Mayor and City Council of Chicago "to halt the further encroachment, harassment and invasion of white people, their property, neighborhoods and persons, by the Negro. . . ." Below was a call for "One million self respecting white people in Chicago to unite . . . " with the statement added that "If persuasion and the need to prevent the white race from becoming mongrelized by the negro will not unite us, then the aggression . . . rapes, robberies, knives, guns and marijuana of the negro, surely will." This, with more language, similar if not so violent, concluded with an attached application for membership in the White Circle League of America, Inc.

The testimony at the trial was substantially undisputed. From it the jury could find that Beauharnais was president of the White Circle League; that, at a meeting on January 6, 1950, he passed out bundles of the lithographs in question, together with other literature, to volunteers for distribution on downtown Chicago street corners the following day; that he carefully organized that distribution, giving detailed instructions for it; and that the leaflets were in fact distributed . . . in accordance with his plan and instructions. The court, together with other charges on burden of proof and the like, told the jury "if you find . . . that the defendant, Joseph Beauharnais, did . . . manufacture, sell, or offer for sale, advertise or publish, present or exhibit in any public place the lithograph . . . then you are to find the defendant guilty. . . ." He refused to charge the jury, as requested by the defendant, that in order to convict they must find "that the article complained of was likely to produce a clear and present danger of a serious substantive evil that rises far above public inconvenience, annoyance or unrest." Upon this evidence and these instructions, the jury brought in the conviction here for review.

The statute before us is not a catchall enactment left at large by the State court which applied it. . . . It is a law specifically directed at a defined evil, its language drawing from history and practice in Illinois and in more than a score of other jurisdictions a meaning confirmed by the Supreme Court of that State in upholding this conviction. We do not, therefore, parse the statute as grammarians or treat it as an abstract exercise in lexicography. . . .

The Illinois Supreme Court tells us that § 224a "is a form of criminal libel law." . . . The defendant, the trial court and the Supreme Court consistently treated it as such. The defendant offered evidence tending to prove the truth of parts of the utterance, and the courts below considered and disposed of this offer in terms of ordinary criminal libel precedents. Section 224a does not deal with the defense of truth, but by the Illinois Constitution, . . . "in all trials for libel, both civil and criminal, the truth, when published with good motives and for justifiable ends, shall be a sufficient defense." . . . Similarly, the action of the trial court in deciding as a matter of law the libelous character of the utterance, leaving to the jury only the question of publication, follows the settled rule in prosecutions for libel in Illinois and other States. Moreover, the Supreme Court's characterization of the words pro-

hibited by the statute as those "liable to cause violence and disorder"
paraphrases the traditional justification for punishing libels criminally,
namely their "tendency to cause breach of the peace."

Libel of an individual was a common-law crime, and thus criminal
in the colonies. Indeed, at common law, truth or good motives was no
defense. In the first decades after the adoption of the Constitution, this
was changed by judicial decision, statute or constitution in most States,
but nowhere was there any suggestion that the crime of libel be abolished. Today, every American jurisdiction—the forty-eight States, the
District of Columbia, Alaska, Hawaii and Puerto Rico—punish libels
directed at individuals.

There are certain well-defined and narrowly limited classes of speech, the
prevention and punishment of which has never been thought to raise any
Constitutional problem. These include the lewd and obscene, the profane, the
libelous, and the insulting or 'fighting' words—those which by their very utterance inflict injury or tend to incite an immediate breach of the peace. It has
been well observed that such utterances are no essential part of any exposition
of ideas, and are of such slight social value as a step to truth that any benefit
that may be derived from them is clearly outweighed by the social interest in
order and morality. 'Resort to epithets or personal abuse is not in any proper
sense communication of information or opinion safeguarded by the Constitution, and its punishment as a criminal act would raise no question under that
instrument.' *Cantwell* v. *Connecticut,* 310 U.S. 296. . . .

Such were the views of a unanimous Court in *Chaplinsky* v. *New
Hampshire,* 315 U.S. 571.

No one will gainsay that it is libelous falsely to charge another with
being a rapist, robber, carrier of knives and guns, user of marijuana.
The precise question before us, then, is whether the protection of
"liberty" in the Due Process Clause of the Fourteenth Amendment
prevents a State from punishing such libels—as criminal libel has been
defined, limited and constitutionally recognized time out of mind—
directed at designated collectivities and flagrantly disseminated. There
is even authority, however dubious, that such utterances were also
crimes at common law. It is certainly clear that some American jurisdictions have sanctioned their punishment under ordinary criminal
libel statutes. We cannot say, however, that the question is concluded
by history and practice. But if an utterance directed at an individual
may be the object of criminal sanctions, we cannot deny to a State
power to punish the same utterance directed at a defined group, unless
we can say that this is a wilful and purposeless restriction unrelated to
the peace and well-being of the State.

Illinois did not have to look beyond her own borders or await the
tragic experience of the last three decades to conclude that wilful pur-

veyors of falsehood concerning racial and religious groups promote strife and tend powerfully to obstruct the manifold adjustments required of free, ordered life in a metropolitan, polyglot community. From the murder of the abolitionist Lovejoy in 1837 to the Cicero riots of 1951, Illinois has been the scene of exacerbated tension between races, often flaring into violence and destruction. In many of these outbreaks, utterances of the character here in question, so the Illinois legislature could conclude, played a significant part. The law was passed on June 29, 1917, at a time when the State was struggling to assimilate vast numbers of new inhabitants, as yet concentrated in discrete racial or national or religious groups—foreign-born brought to it by the crest of the great wave of immigration, and Negroes attracted by jobs in war plants and the allurements of northern claims. Nine years earlier, in the very city where the legislature sat, what is said to be the first northern race riot had cost the lives of six people, left hundreds of Negroes homeless and shocked citizens into action far beyond the borders of the State. Less than a month before the bill was enacted, East St. Louis had seen a day's rioting, prelude to an outbreak, only four days after the bill became law, so bloody that it led to Congressional investigation. A series of bombings had begun which was to culminate two years later in the awful race riot which held Chicago in its grip for seven days in the summer of 1919. Nor has tension and violence between the groups defined in the statute been limited in Illinois to clashes between whites and Negroes.

In the face of this history and its frequent obligato of extreme racial and religious propaganda, we would deny experience to say that the Illinois legislature was without reason in seeking ways to curb false or malicious defamation of racial and religious groups, made in public places and by means calculated to have a powerful emotional impact on those to whom it was presented. "There are limits to the exercise of these liberties [of speech and of the press]. The danger in these times from the coercive activities of those who in the delusion of racial or religious conceit would incite violence and breaches of the peace in order to deprive others of their equal right to the exercise of their liberties, is emphasized by events familiar to all. These and other transgressions of those limits the states appropriately may punish." This was the conclusion, again of a unanimous Court, in 1940. *Cantwell v. Connecticut. . . .*

It may be argued, and weightily, that this legislation will not help matters; that tension and on occasion violence between racial and religious groups must be traced to causes more deeply embedded in our society than the rantings of modern Know-nothings. Only those lacking responsible humility will have a confident solution for problems as intractable as the frictions attributable to differences of race, color or religion. This being so, it would be out of bounds for the judiciary to deny the legislature a choice of policy, provided it is not unrelated to the problem and not forbidden by some explicit limitation on the State's power. That the legislative remedy might not in practice mitigate the evil, or might itself raise new problems, would only manifest once more the paradox of reform. It is the price to be paid for the trial-and-error inherent in legislative efforts to deal with obstinate social issues. "The science of government is the most abstruse of all sciences; if, indeed, that can be called a science which has but few fixed principles, and practically consists in little more than the exercise of a sound discretion, applied to the exigencies of the state as they arise. It is the science of experiment." *Anderson* v. *Dunn,* 6 Wheat. 204. Certainly the Due Process Clause does not require the legislature to be in the vanguard of science—especially sciences as young as human ecology and cultural anthropology. . . .

Long ago this Court recognized that the economic rights of an individual may depend for the effectiveness of their enforcement on rights in the group, even though not formally corporate, to which he belongs. . . . Such group-protection on behalf of the individual may, for all we know, be a need not confined to the part that a trade union plays in effectuating rights abstractly recognized as belonging to its members. It is not within our competence to confirm or deny claims of social scientists as to the dependence of the individual on the position of his racial or religious group in the community. It would, however, be arrant dogmatism, quite outside the scope of our authority in passing on the powers of a State, for us to deny that the Illinois Legislature may warrantably believe that a man's job and his educational opportunities and the dignity accorded him may depend as much on the reputation of the racial and religious group to which he willy-nilly belongs, as it does on his own merits. This being so, we are precluded from saying that speech concededly punishable when immediately directed at individuals cannot be outlawed if directed at groups with whose position and esteem in society the affiliated individual may be inextricably involved.

We are warned that the choice open to the Illinois legislature here may be abused, that the law may be discriminatorily enforced; prohibiting libel of a creed or of a racial group, we are told, is but a step from prohibiting libel of a political party.

Every power may be abused, but the possibility of abuse is a poor reason for denying Illinois the power to adopt measures against criminal libels sanctioned by centuries of Anglo-American law. "While this Court sits" it retains and exercises authority to nullify action which encroaches on freedom of utterance under the guise of punishing libel. Of course discussion cannot be denied and the right, as well as the duty, of criticism must not be stifled.

The scope of the statute before us, as construed by the Illinois court, disposes of the contention that the conduct prohibited by the law is so ill-defined that judges and juries in applying the statute and men in acting cannot draw from it adequate standards to guide them. . . .

It is suggested that while it was clearly within the constitutional power of Illinois to punish this utterance if the proceeding were properly safeguarded, in this particular case Illinois denied the defendant rights which the Due Process Clause commands. Specifically, it is argued that the defendant was not permitted to raise at the trial defenses constitutionally guaranteed in a criminal libel prosecution: (1) the defense of truth; (2) justification of the utterance as "fair comment"; and (3) its privilege as a means for redressing grievances.

Neither by proffer of evidence, requests for instructions, motion before or after verdict did the defendant seek to justify his utterance as "fair comment" or as privileged. Nor has the defendant urged as a ground for reversing his conviction in this Court that his opportunity to make those defenses was denied below. And so, whether a prosecution for libel of a racial or religious group is unconstitutionally invalid where the State did deny the defendant such opportunities is not before us. Certainly the State may cast the burden of justifying what is patent defamation upon the defamer. The benefits of hypothetical defenses, never raised below or pressed upon us, are not to be invoked in the abstract.

As to the defense of truth, Illinois in common with many States requires a showing not only that the utterance state the facts, but also that the publication be made "with good motives and for justifiable ends." Ill. Const. Art. II, § 4. Both elements are necessary if the defense is to prevail. What has been called "the common sense of American criminal law," as formulated, with regard to necessary safeguards in criminal libel prosecutions, in the New York constitution of 1821, Art. VII, § 8, has been adopted in terms by Illinois. The teaching of a century and a half of criminal libel prosecutions in this country would go by the board if we were to hold that Illinois was not within her rights in making this combined requirement. Assuming that defendant's offer of proof directed to a part of the defense was adequate, it did not satisfy the entire requirement which Illinois could exact.

Libellous utterances, not being within the area of constitutionally protected speech, it is unnecessary, either for us or for the State courts, to consider the issues behind the phrase "clear and present danger." Certainly no one would contend that obscene speech, for example, may be punished only upon a showing of such circumstances. Libel, as we have seen, is in the same class.

We find no warrant in the Constitution for denying to Illinois the power to pass the law here under attack. But it bears repeating—although it should not—that our finding that the law is not constitutionally objectionable carries no implication of approval of the wisdom of the legislation or of its efficacy. These questions may raise doubts in our minds as well as in others. It is not for us, however, to make the legislative judgment. We are not at liberty to erect those doubts into fundamental law.

Affirmed.

Mr. Justice Black, with whom Mr. Justice Douglas concurs, dissenting:

This case is here because Illinois inflicted criminal punishment on Beauharnais for causing the distribution of leaflets in the city of Chicago. The conviction rests on the leaflet's contents, not on the time, manner or place of distribution. Beauharnais is head of an organization that opposes amalgamation and favors segregation of white and colored people. After discussion, an assembly of his group decided to petition the mayor and council of Chicago to pass laws for segregation. Volunteer members of the group agreed to stand on street corners, solicit signers to petitions addressed to the city authorities, and distribute leaflets giving information about the group, its beliefs and its plans. In carrying out this program a solicitor handed out a leaflet which was the basis of this prosecution. . . .

That Beauharnais and his group were making a genuine effort to petition their elected representatives is not disputed. Even as far back as 1689, the Bill of Rights exacted of William & Mary said: "It is the right of the subjects to petition the King; and all commitments and prosecutions for such petitioning are illegal." And 178 years ago the Declaration of Rights of the Colonial Congress proclaimed to the monarch of that day that his American subjects had "a right peaceably to assemble, consider of their grievances, and petition the King; and that all prosecutions, prohibitory proclamations, and commitments for the same, are illegal." After independence was won, Americans stated as the first unequivocal command of their Bill of Rights: "Congress shall make no law . . . abridging the freedom of speech, or of the press; or the right of the people peaceably to assemble, and to petition the Government for a redress of grievances." Without distortion, this First Amendment could not possibly be read so as to hold that Congress has power to punish Beauharnais and others for petitioning Congress as they have here sought to petition the Chicago authorities. . . . And we have held in a number of prior cases that the Fourteenth Amendment makes the specific prohibitions of the First Amendment equally applicable to the states.

In view of these prior holdings, how does the Court justify its holding today that states can punish people for exercising the vital freedoms intended to be safeguarded from suppression by the First Amendment? The prior holdings are not referred to; the Court simply acts on the bland assumption that the First Amendment is wholly irrelevant. It is not even accorded the respect of a passing mention. This follows logically, I suppose, from recent constitutional doctrine which appears to measure state laws solely by this Court's notions of civilized "canons of decency," reasonableness, etc. . . . Under this "reasonableness" test, state laws abridging First Amendment freedoms are sustained if found to have a "rational basis." . . . Today's case degrades First Amendment freedoms to the "rational basis" level. It is now a certainty that the new "due process" coverall offers far less protection to liberty than would adherence to our former cases compelling states to abide by the unequivocal First Amendment command that its defined freedoms shall not be abridged.

The Court's holding here and the constitutional doctrine behind it leave the right of assembly, petition, speech and press almost completely at the mercy of state legislative, executive, and judicial agencies. I say "almost" because state curtailment of these freedoms may still be invalidated if a majority of this Court conclude that a particular infringement is "without reason," or is "a wilful and purposeless restriction unrelated to the peace and well being of the State." But lest this encouragement should give too much hope as to how and when this Court might protect these basic freedoms from state invasion, we are cautioned that state legislatures must be left free to "experiment" and to make "legislative" judgments. We are told that mistakes may be made during the legislative process of curbing public opinion. In such event the Court fortunately does not leave those mistakenly curbed, or any of us for that matter, unadvised. Consolation can be sought and must be found in the philosophical reflection that state legislative error in stifling speech and press "is the price to be paid for the trial-and-error inherent in legislative efforts to deal with obstinate social issues." My own belief is that no legislature is charged with the duty or vested with the power to decide what public issues Americans can discuss. In a free country that is the individual's choice, not the state's. State experimentation in curbing freedom of expression is startling and frightening doctrine in a country dedicated to self-government by its people. I reject the holding that either state or nation can punish people for having their say in matters of public concern. . . .

Unless I misread history the majority is giving libel a more expansive scope and more respectable status than it was ever accorded even in the Star Chamber. For here it is held to be punishable to give publicity to any picture, moving picture, play, drama or sketch, or any printed matter which a judge may find unduly offensive to any race, color, creed or religion. In other words, in arguing for or against the enactment of laws that may differently affect huge groups, it is now very dangerous indeed to say something critical of one of the groups. And any "person, firm or corporation" can be tried for this crime. "Person, firm or corporation" certainly includes a book publisher, newspaper, radio or television station, candidate or even a preacher.

It is easy enough to say that none of this latter group have been proceeded against under the Illinois Act. And they have not—yet. But emotions bubble and tempers flare in racial and religious controversies, the kind here involved. It would not be easy for any court, in good conscience, to narrow this Act so as to exclude from it any of those I have mentioned. Furthermore, persons tried under the Act could not even get a jury trial except as to the bare fact of publication. Here, the court simply charged the jury that Beauharnais was guilty if he had caused distribution of the leaflet. Such trial by judge rather than by jury was outlawed in England in 1792 by Fox's Libel Law.

This Act sets up a system of state censorship which is at war with the kind of free government envisioned by those who forced adoption of our Bill of Rights. The motives behind the state law may have been to do good. But the same can be said about most laws making opinions punishable as crimes. History indicates that urges to do good have led to the burning of books and even to the burning of "witches."

No rationalization on a purely legal level can conceal the fact that state laws like this one present a constant overhanging threat to freedom of speech, press and religion. Today Beauharnais is punished for publicity expressing strong views in favor of segregation. Ironically enough, Beauharnais, convicted of crime in Chicago, would probably be given a hero's reception in many other localities, if not in some parts of Chicago itself. Moreover, the same kind of state law that makes Beauharnais a criminal for advocating segregation in Illinois can be utilized to send people to jail in other states for advocating equality and nonsegregation. What Beauharnais said in his leaflet is mild compared with usual arguments on both sides of racial controversies.

We are told that freedom of petition and discussion are in no danger "while this Court sits." This case raises considerable doubt. Since those who peacefully petition for changes in the law are not to be protected "while this Court sits," who is? I do not agree that the Constitution leaves freedom of petition, assembly, speech, press or worship at the mercy of a case-by-case, day-by-day majority of this Court. I had supposed that our people could rely for their freedom on the Constitution's commands, rather than on the grace of this Court on an individual case basis. To say that a legislative body can, with this Court's approval, make it a crime to petition for and publicly discuss proposed legislation seems as farfetched to me as it would be to say that a valid law could be enacted to punish a candidate for President for telling the people his views. I think the First Amendment, with the Fourteenth, "absolutely" forbids such laws without any "ifs" or "buts" or "whereases." Whatever the danger, if any, in such public discussions, it is a danger the Founders deemed outweighed by the danger incident to the stifling of thought and speech. The Court does not act on this view of the Founders. It calculates what it deems to be the danger of public discussion, holds the scales are tipped on the side of state suppression, and upholds state censorship. This method of decision offers little protection to First Amendment liberties "while this Court sits."

If there be minority groups who hail this holding as their victory, they might consider the possible relevancy of this ancient remark: "Another such victory and I am undone."

Mr. Justice Douglas, dissenting:

Hitler and his Nazis showed how evil a conspiracy could be which was aimed at destroying a race by exposing it to contempt, derision, and obloquy. I would be willing to concede that such conduct directed at a race or group in this country could be made an indictable offense. For such a project would be more than the exercise of free speech. Like picketing, it would be free speech plus.

I would also be willing to concede that even without the element of conspiracy there might be times and occasions when the legislative or executive branch might call a halt to inflammatory talk, such as the shouting of "fire" in a school or a theatre.

My view is that if in any case other public interests are to override the plain command of the First Amendment, the peril of speech must be clear and present, leaving no room for argument, raising no doubts as to the necessity of curbing speech in order to prevent disaster.

The First Amendment is couched in absolute terms—freedom of speech shall not be abridged. Speech has therefore a preferred position as contrasted to some other civil rights. For example, privacy, equally sacred to some, is protected by the Fourth Amendment only against unreasonable searches and seizures. There is room for regulation of the ways and means of invading privacy. No such leeway is granted the invasion of the right of free speech guaranteed by the First Amendment. Until recent years that had been the course and direction of constitutional law. Yet recently the Court in this and in other cases has engrafted the right of regulation onto the First Amendment by placing in the hands of the legislative branch the right to regulate "within reasonable limits" the right of free speech. This to me is an ominous and alarming trend. The free trade in ideas which the Framers of the Constitution visualized disappears. In its place there is substituted a new orthodoxy—an orthodoxy that changes with the whims of the age or the day, an orthodoxy which the majority by solemn judgment proclaims to be essential to the safety, welfare, security, morality, or health of society. Free speech in the constitutional sense disappears. Limits are drawn—limits dictated by expediency, political opinion, prejudices or some other desideratum of legislative action.

An historic aspect of the issue of judicial supremacy was the extent to which legislative judgment would be supreme in the field of social legislation. The vague contours of the Due Process Clause were used to strike down laws deemed by the Court to be unwise and improvident. That trend has been reversed. In matters relating to business, finance, industrial and labor conditions, health and the public welfare, great leeway is now granted the legislature, for there is no guarantee in the Constitution that the *status quo* will be preserved against regulation by government. Freedom of speech, however, rests on a different constitutional basis. The First Amendment says that freedom of speech, freedom of press, and the free exercise of religion shall not be abridged. That is a negation of power on the part of each and every department of government. Free speech, free press, free exercise of religion are placed separate and apart; they are above and beyond the police power; they are not subject to regulation in the manner of factories, slums, apartment houses, production of oil, and the like.

The Court in this and in other cases places speech under an expanding legislative control. Today a white man stands convicted for protesting in unseemly language against our decisions invalidating restrictive covenants. Tomorrow a Negro will be hailed before a court for denouncing lynch law in heated terms. Farm laborers in the west who compete with field hands drifting up from Mexico; whites who feel the pressure of orientals; a minority which finds employment going to members of the dominant religious group —all of these are caught in the mesh of today's decision. Debate and argument even in the courtroom are not always calm and dispassionate. Emotions sway speakers and audiences alike. Intemperate speech is a distinctive characteristic of man. Hot heads blow off and release destructive energy in the process. They shout and rave, exaggerating weaknesses, magnifying error, viewing with alarm. So it has been from the beginning; and so it will be throughout time. The Framers of the Constitution knew human nature as well as we do. They too had lived in dangerous days; they too knew the suffocating influence of orthodoxy and standardized thought. They weighed the compulsions for restrained speech and thought against the abuses of liberty. They chose liberty. That should be our choice today no matter how distasteful to us the pamphlet of Beauharnais may be. It is true that this is only one decision which may later be distinguished or confined to narrow limits. But it represents a philosophy at war with the First Amendment—a constitutional interpretation which puts free speech under the legislative thumb. It reflects an influence moving ever deeper into our society. It is notice to the legislatures that they have the power to control unpopular blocs. It is a warning to every minority that when the Constitution guarantees free speech it does not mean what it says.

Mr. Justice Jackson, dissenting:

. . . Punishment of printed words, based on their *tendency* either to cause breach of the peace or injury to persons or groups, in my opinion, is justifiable only if the prosecution survives the "clear and present danger" test. It is the most just and workable standard yet evolved for determining criminality of words whose injurious or inciting tendencies are not demonstrated by the event but are ascribed to them on the basis of probabilities.

Its application is important in this case because it takes account of the particular form, time, place, and manner of communication in question. "The moving picture screen, the radio, the newspaper, the handbill, the sound truck and the street corner orator have differing natures, values, abuses and dangers. Each, in my view, is a law unto itself. . . ." *Kovacs* v. *Cooper*, 336 U.S. 77. . . . It would consider whether a leaflet is so emotionally exciting to immediate action as the spoken word, especially the incendiary street or public speech. . . . It will inquire whether this publication was obviously so foul and extreme as to defeat its own ends, whether its appeals for money

—which has a cooling effect on many persons—would not negative its inflammatory effect, whether it would not impress the passer-by as the work of an irresponsible who needed mental examination.

One of the merits of the clear and present danger test is that the triers of fact would take into account the realities of race relations and any smouldering fires to be fanned into holocausts. Such consideration might well warrant a conviction here when it would not in another and different environment.

Group libel statutes represent a commendable desire to reduce sinister abuses of our freedoms of expression—abuses which I have had occasion to learn can tear apart a society, brutalize its dominant elements, and persecute, even to extermination, its minorities. While laws or prosecutions might not alleviate racial or sectarian hatreds and may even invest scoundrels with a specious martyrdom, I should be loath to foreclose the States from a considerable latitude of experimentation in this field. Such efforts, if properly applied, do not justify frenetic forebodings of crushed liberty. But these acts present most difficult policy and technical problems, as thoughtful writers who have canvassed the problem more comprehensively than is appropriate in a judicial opinion have well pointed out.

No group interest in any particular prosecution should forget that the shoe may be on the other foot in some prosecution tomorrow. In these, as in other matters, our guiding spirit should be that each freedom is balanced with a responsibility, and every power of the State must be checked with safeguards. Such is the spirit of our American law of criminal libel, which concedes the power to the State, but only as a power restrained by recognition of individual rights. I cannot escape the conclusion that as the Act has been applied in this case it lost sight of the rights.

4. Previous Restraints or Censorship

NEAR v. MINNESOTA

283 US 697 (1931)

[Historically, censorship of publications was associated with licensing: a book or pamphlet could not be published unless it was first submitted to a censor or licensing official and his approval was procured. Publication without such a license from the censor was a criminal offense. It was against such censorship or previous restraint on publication that John Milton protested in his *Areopagitica* in 1644. In the minds of Englishmen licensing by censors was associated with ecclesiastical supervision, the Inquisition, the Star Chamber, and monopolies. In 1695 the licensing system in England ended forever. Liberty of the press, wrote Blackstone in 1769, "consists in laying no previous restraints upon publication, and not in freedom from censure for criminal matters when published."

[Essentially this is the position of liberty of the press under the

Constitution: freedom from preliminary restraint, Justice Holmes has said, "extends as well to the false as to the true; the subsequent punishment may extend as well to the true as to the false." *Patterson* v. *Colorado*, 205 US 454 (1907).

[Licensing requirements are frowned upon by the courts more than any other restrictive device. Even in the case of moving pictures, as we shall see, the Supreme Court has reached the point where it thinks that censorship is inconsistent with the demands of the Constitution. Licensing in radio broadcasting remains an exception to the rule. *Communications Commission* v. *N.B.C.*, 319 US 239 (1943). Injunctions against picketing in labor disputes are a form of previous restraint by judicial act and fall into a separate category. This matter is considered at a later point.

[In *Near* v. *Minnesota,* which condemns censorship as unconstitutional, the decision was 5 to 4, with Justices Butler, Van Devanter, McReynolds, and Sutherland dissenting. It is doubtful whether any Justice would dissent from the opinion of Chief Justice Hughes today.]

Mr. Chief Justice Hughes delivered the opinion of the Court:

Chapter 285 of the Session Laws of Minnesota for the year 1925 provides for the abatement, as a public nuisance, of a "malicious, scandalous and defamatory newspaper, magazine or other periodical." Section one of the act is as follows:

Section 1: Any person who, as an individual, or as a member or employee of a firm, or association or organization, or as an officer, director, member or employee of a corporation, shall be engaged in the business of regularly or customarily producing, publishing or circulating, having in possession, selling or giving away,

(a) an obscene, lewd and lascivious newspaper, magazine, or other periodical, or

(b) a malicious, scandalous and defamatory newspaper, magazine or other periodical,

is guilty of a nuisance, and all persons guilty of such nuisance may be enjoined, as hereinafter provided.

Participation in such business shall constitute a commission of such nuisance and render the participant liable and subject to the proceedings, orders and judgments provided for in this act. Ownership, in whole or in part, directly or indirectly, of any such periodical, or of any stock or interest in any corporation or organization which owns the same in whole or in part, or which publishes the same, shall constitute such participation.

In actions brought under (b) above, there shall be available the defense that the truth was published with good motives and for justifiable ends and in such actions the plaintiff shall not have the right to report [*sic*] to issues or editions of periodicals taking place more than three months before the commencement of the action.

Section two provides that whenever any such nuisance is committed or exists, the county attorney of any county where any such periodical is published or circulated, or, in case of his failure or refusal to proceed upon written request in good faith of a reputable citizen, the attorney general, or upon like failure or refusal of the latter, any citizen of the county, may maintain an action in the district court of the county in the name of the state to enjoin perpetually the persons committing or maintaining any such nuisance from further committing or maintaining it. Upon such evidence as the court shall deem sufficient, a temporary injunction may be granted. The defendants have the right to plead by demurrer or answer, and the plaintiff may demur or reply as in other cases.

The action, by section three, is to be "governed by the practice and procedure applicable to civil actions for injunctions," and after trial the court may enter judgment permanently enjoining the defendants found guilty of violating the act from continuing the violation and, "in and by such judgment, such nuisance may be wholly abated." The court is empowered, as in other cases of contempt, to punish disobedience to a temporary or permanent injunction by fine of not more than $1,000 or by imprisonment in the county jail for not more than twelve months.

Under this statute, . . . the county attorney of Hennepin county brought this action to enjoin the publication of what was described as a "malicious, scandalous and defamatory newspaper, magazine and periodical," known as *The Saturday Press*, published by the defendants in the city of Minneapolis. The complaint alleged that the defendants, on September 24, 1927, and on eight subsequent dates in October and November, 1927, published and circulated editions of that periodical which were "largely devoted to malicious, scandalous and defamatory articles" concerning Charles G. Davis, Frank W. Brunskill, the *Minneapolis Tribune*, the *Minneapolis Journal*, Melvin C. Passolt, George E. Leach, the Jewish Race, the members of the grand jury of Hennepin county impaneled in November, 1927, and then holding office, and other persons, as more fully appeared in exhibits annexed to the complaint, consisting of copies of the articles described and constituting 327 pages of the record. While the complaint did not so allege, it appears from the briefs of both parties that Charles G. Davis was a special law enforcement officer employed by a civic organization, that George E. Leach was mayor of Minneapolis, that Frank W. Brunskill was its chief of police, and that Floyd B. Olson (the relator in this action) was county attorney.

Without attempting to summarize the contents of the voluminous exhibits attached to the complaint, we deem it sufficient to say that the articles charged in substance that a Jewish gangster was in control of gambling, bootlegging and racketeering in Minneapolis, and that law enforcing officers and agencies were not energetically performing their duties. Most of the charges were directed against the chief of police; he was charged with gross neglect of duty, illicit relations with gangsters, and with participation in graft. The county attorney was charged with knowing the existing conditions and with failure to take adequate measures to remedy them. The mayor was accused of inefficiency and dereliction. One member of the grand jury was stated to be in sympathy with the gangsters. A special grand jury and a special prosecutor were demanded to deal with the situation in general, and, in particular, to investigate an attempt to assassinate one Guilford, one of the original defendants, who, it appears from the articles, was shot by gangsters after the first issue of the periodical had been published. There is no question but that the articles made serious accusations against the public officers named and others in connection with the prevalence of crimes and the failure to expose and punish them. . . .

This statute, for the suppression as a public nuisance of a newspaper or periodical, is unusual, if not unique, and raises questions of grave importance transcending the local interests involved in the particular action. It is no longer open to doubt that the liberty of the press and of speech is within the liberty safeguarded by the due process clause of the 14th Amendment from invasion by state action. It was found impossible to conclude that this essential personal liberty of the citizen was left unprotected by the general guaranty of fundamental rights of person and property. . . . Liberty of speech and of the press is . . . not an absolute right, and the state may punish its abuse. . . . Liberty, in each of its phases, has its history and connotation and, in the present instance, the inquiry is as to the historic conception of the liberty of the press and whether the statute under review violates the essential attributes of that liberty. . . .

The statute is not aimed at the redress of individual or private wrongs. Remedies for libel remain available and unaffected. The statute, said the state court, "is not directed at threatened libel but at an existing business which, generally speaking, involves more than libel." It is aimed at the distribution of scandalous matter as "detrimental to public morals and to the general welfare," tending "to disturb the peace of the community" and "to provoke assaults and the commission of crime." In order to obtain an injunction to suppress the future publication of the newspaper or periodical, it is not necessary to prove the falsity of the charges that have been made in the publication condemned. In the present action there was no allegation that the matter published was not true. It is alleged, and the statute requires the allegation, that the publication was "malicious." But, as in prosecutions for libel, there is no requirement of proof by the state of malice in fact as distinguished from malice inferred from the mere publication of the defamatory matter. The judgment in this case proceeded upon the mere proof of publication. The statute permits the defense, not of the truth alone, but only that the truth was published with good motives and for justifiable ends. It is apparent that under the statute the publication is to be regarded as defamatory if it injures reputation, and that it is scandalous if it circulates charges of reprehensible conduct, whether criminal or otherwise, and the publication is thus deemed to invite public reprobation and to constitute a public scandal. The court sharply defined the purpose of the statute, bringing out the precise point, in these words: "There is no constitutional right to publish a fact merely because it is true. It is a matter of common knowledge that prosecutions under the criminal libel statutes do not result in efficient repression or suppression of the evils of scandal. Men who are the victims of such assaults seldom resort to the courts. This is especially true if their sins are exposed and the only question relates to whether it was done with good motives and for justifiable ends. This law is not for the protection of the person attacked nor to punish the wrongdoer. It is for the protection of the public welfare." . . .

If we cut through mere details of procedure, the operation and effect of the statute in substance is that public authorities may bring the owner or publisher of a newspaper or periodical before a judge upon a charge of conducting a business of publishing scandalous and defamatory matter—in particular that the matter consists of charges against public officers of official dereliction—and unless the owner or publisher is able and disposed to bring competent evidence to satisfy the judge that the charges are true and are published with good motives and for justifiable ends, his newspaper or periodical is suppressed and further publication is made punishable as a contempt. This is of the essence of censorship.

The question is whether a statute authorizing such proceedings in restraint of publication is consistent with the conception of the liberty of the press as historically conceived and guaranteed. In determining the extent of the constitutional protection, it has been generally, if not universally, considered that it is the chief purpose of the guaranty to prevent previous restraints upon publication. The struggle in England, directed against the legislative power of the licenser, resulted in renunciation of the censorship of the press. The liberty deemed to be established was thus described by Blackstone: "The liberty of the press is indeed essential to the nature of a free state; but this consists in laying no *previous* restraints upon publications, and not in freedom from censure for criminal matter when published. Every freeman has an undoubted right to lay what sentiments he pleases before the public; to forbid this, is to destroy the freedom of the press; but if he publishes what is improper, mischievous or illegal, he must take the consequence of his own temerity." . . . The distinction was early pointed out between the extent of the freedom with respect to censorship under our constitutional system and that enjoyed in England. Here, as Madison said, "The great and essential rights of the people are secured against legislative as well as against executive ambition. They are secured, not by laws paramount to prerogative, but by constitutions paramount to laws. This security of the freedom of the press requires that it should be exempt not only from previous restraint by the executive, as in Great Britain, but from legislative restraint also." . . . This court said, in *Patterson* v. *Colorado,* 205 U.S. 454: "In the first place, the main purpose of such constitutional provisions is 'to prevent all such *previous restraints* upon publications as had been practised by other governments,' and they do not prevent the subsequent punishment of such as may be deemed contrary to the public welfare. . . . The preliminary freedom extends as well to the false as to the true; the subsequent punishment may extend as well to the true as to the false. This was the law of criminal libel apart from statute in most cases, if not in all. . . ."

The criticism upon Blackstone's statement has not been because immunity from previous restraint upon publication has not been regarded as deserving of special emphasis, but chiefly because that immunity cannot be deemed to exhaust the conception of the liberty guaranteed by state and Federal constitutions. The point of criticism has been "that the mere exemption from previous restraints cannot be all that is secured by the constitutional provisions"; and that "the liberty of the press might be rendered a mockery and a delusion, and the phrase itself a by-word, if, while every man was at liberty to publish what he pleased, the public authorities might nevertheless punish him for harmless publications." 2 Cooley, *Constitutional Limitations,* 8th ed., p. 885. But it is recognized that punishment for the abuse of the liberty accorded to the press is essential to the protection of the public, and that the common law rules that subject the libeler to responsibility for the public offense, as well as for the private injury, are not abolished by the protection extended in our constitutions. . . . The law of criminal libel rests upon that secure foundation. There is also the conceded authority of courts to punish for contempt when publications directly tend to prevent the proper discharge of judicial functions. . . . In the present case, we have no occasion to inquire as to the permissible scope of subsequent punishment. For whatever wrong the appellant has committed or may commit, by his publications, the state appropriately affords both public and private redress by its libel laws. As has been noted, the statute in question does not deal with punishments; it provides for no punishment, except in case of contempt for violation of the court's order, but for suppression and injunction, that is, for restraint upon publication.

The objection has also been made that the principle as to immunity from previous restraint is stated too broadly, if every such restraint is deemed to be prohibited. That is undoubtedly true; the protection even as to previous restraint is not absolutely unlimited. But the limitation has been recognized only in exceptional cases. "When a nation is at war many things that might be said in time of peace are such a hindrance to its effort that their utterance will not be endured so long as men fight and that no court could regard them as protected by any constitutional right." *Schenck* v. *United States,* 249 U.S. 47. No one would question but that a government might prevent actual obstruction to its recruiting service or the publication of the sailing dates of transports or the number and location of troops. On similar grounds, the primary requirements of decency may be enforced against obscene publications. The security of the community life may be protected against incitements to acts of violence and the overthrow by force of orderly government. The constitutional guaranty of free speech does not "protect a man from an injunction against uttering words that may have all the effect of force. . . ." *Schenck* v. *United States.* These limitations are not applicable here. Nor are we now concerned with questions as to the extent of authority to prevent publications in order to protect private rights according to the principles governing the exercise of the jurisdiction of courts of equity.

The exceptional nature of its limitations places in a strong light the general conception that liberty of the press, historically considered and taken up by the Federal Constitution, has meant, principally, although not exclusively, immunity from previous restraints or censorship. The conception of the liberty of the press in this country had broadened with the exigencies of the colonial period and with the efforts to secure freedom from oppressive administration. That liberty was especially cherished for the immunity it afforded from previous restraint of the publication of censure of public officers and charges of official misconduct. . . .

The fact that for approximately one hundred and fifty years there has been almost an entire absence of attempts to impose previous restraints upon publications relating to the malfeasance of public officers is significant of the deep-seated conviction that such restraints would violate constitutional right. Public officers, whose character and conduct remain open to debate and free discussion in the press, find their remedies for false accusations in actions under libel laws providing for redress and punishment, and not in proceedings to restrain the publication of newspapers and periodicals. The general principle that the constitutional guaranty of the liberty of the press gives immunity from previous restraints has been approved in many decisions under the provision of state constitutions.

The importance of this immunity has not lessened. While reckless assaults upon public men, and efforts to bring obloquy upon those who are endeavoring faithfully to discharge official duties, exert a baleful influence and deserve the severest condemnation in public opinion, it cannot be said that this abuse is greater, and it is believed to be less, than that which characterized the period in which our institutions took shape. Meanwhile, the administration of government has become more complex, the opportunities for malfeasance and corruption have multiplied, crime has grown to most serious proportions, and the danger of its protection by unfaithful officials and of the impairment of the fundamental security of life and property by criminal alliances and official neglect, emphasizes the primary need of a vigilant and courageous press, especially in great cities. The fact that the liberty of the press may be abused by miscreant purveyors of scandal does not make any the less necessary the immunity of the press from previous restraint in dealing with official misconduct. Subsequent punishment for such abuses as may exist is the appropriate remedy, consistent with constitutional privilege. . . .

Judgment reversed.

LOVELL v. GRIFFIN

303 US 444 (1938)

[This case illustrates the scope of the decision in the previous case of *Near* v. *Minnesota*. An ordinance that required official permission to distribute publications was condemned as unconstitutional by a unanimous Court. An ordinance might meet the constitutional test only if it left no discretion to the licensing official but merely attempted to impose reasonable and well-defined restrictions as to time and place in order to maintain public order and prevent disorderly conduct. *Lovell* v. *Griffin* should be compared with *Tucker* v. *Texas* and *Breard* v. *City of Alexandria*, above.

[This case is important also because it expressly assimilates distribution of literature to publication for constitutional protection.]

Mr. Chief Justice Hughes delivered the opinion of the Court:

Appellant, Alma Lovell, was convicted in the recorder's court of the City of Griffin, Ga., of the violation of a city ordinance and was sentenced to imprisonment for fifty days in default of the payment of a fine of $50. . . .

The ordinance in question is as follows:

1. That the practice of distributing, either by hand or otherwise, circulars, handbooks, advertising, or literature of any kind, whether said articles are being delivered free, or whether same are being sold, within the limits of the City of Griffin, without first obtaining written permission from the City Manager of the City of Griffin, such practice shall be deemed a nuisance, and punishable as an offense against the City of Griffin.

2. The Chief of Police of the City of Griffin and the police force of the City of Griffin are hereby required and directed to suppress the same and to abate any nuisance as is described in the first section of this ordinance.

The violation, which is not denied, consisted of the distribution without the required permission of a pamphlet and magazine in the nature of religious tracts, setting forth the gospel of the "Kingdom of Jehovah." Appellant did not apply for a permit, as she regarded herself as sent "by Jehovah to do His work" and that such an application would have been "an act of disobedience to His commandment."

Upon the trial, with permission of the court, appellant demurred to the charge and moved to dismiss it upon a number of grounds, among which was the contention that the ordinance violated the Fourteenth Amendment of the Constitution of the United States in abridging "the freedom of the press" and prohibiting "the free exercise of petitioner's religion." . . .

The ordinance in its broad sweep prohibits the distribution of "circulars, handbooks, advertising, or literature of any kind." It manifestly applies to pamphlets, magazines, and periodicals. The evidence against appellant was that she distributed a certain pamphlet and a magazine called the *Golden Age*. Whether in actual administration the ordinance is applied, as apparently it could be, to newspapers does not appear. The city manager testified that "every one applies to me for a license to dilstribute literature in this City. None of these people (including defendant) secured a permit from me to distribute literature in the City of Griffin." The ordinance is not limited to "literature" that is obscene or offensive to public morals or that advocates unlawful conduct. There is no suggestion that the pamphlet and magazine distributed in the instant case were of that character. The ordinance embraces "literature" in the widest sense.

The ordinance is comprehensive with respect to the method of distribution. It covers every sort of circulation "either by hand or otherwise." There is thus no restriction in its application with respect to time or place. It is not limited to ways which might be regarded as inconsistent with the maintenance of public order, or as involving disorderly conduct, the molestation of the inhabitants, or the misuse or littering of the streets. The ordinance prohibits the distribution of literature of any kind at any time, at any place, and in any manner without a permit from the city manager.

We think that the ordinance is invalid on its face. Whatever the motive which induced its adoption, its character is such that it strikes at the very foundation of the freedom of the press by subjecting it to license and censorship. The struggle for the freedom of the press was primarily directed against the power of the licensor. It was against that power that John Milton directed his assault by his [Areopagitica] "Appeal for the Liberty of Unlicensed Printing." And the liberty of the press became initially a right to publish "without a license what formerly could be published only with one." While this freedom from previous restraint upon publication cannot be regarded as exhausting the guaranty of liberty, the prevention of that restraint was a leading purpose in the adoption of the constitutional provision. . . . Legislation of the type of the ordinance in question would restore the system of license and censorship in its baldest form.

The liberty of the press is not confined to newspapers and periodicals. It necessarily embraces pamphlets and leaflets. These indeed have been historic weapons in the defense of liberty, as the pamphlets of Thomas Paine and others in our own history abundantly attest. The press in its historic connotation comprehends every sort of publication which affords a vehicle of information and opinion. . . .

The ordinance cannot be saved because it relates to distribution and not to publication. "Liberty of circulating is as essential to that freedom as liberty of publishing; indeed, without the circulation, the publication would be of little value." *Ex parte Jackson,* 96 U.S. 727. . . .
Reversed.

NIEMOTKO *v.* MARYLAND

340 US 268 (1951)

[The city of Havre de Grace, Maryland, followed the practice of requiring a license for use of a public park for meetings. There was no narrowly drawn ordinance, with reasonable and definite standards to guide the officials. The Court unanimously condemned the official practice as unconstitutional.

[The concurring opinion of Justice Frankfurter covers this case and also *Feiner* v. *New York,* given above, and *Kunz* v. *New York,* which follows. See the editorial note introducing the *Feiner Case.*]

Mr. Chief Justice Vinson delivered the opinion of the Court:

Appellants are two members of the religious group known as Jehovah's Witnesses. At the invitation of local coreligionists, they scheduled Bible talks in the public park of the city of Havre de Grace, Maryland. Although there is no ordinance prohibiting or regulating the use of this park, it has been the custom for organizations and individuals desiring to use it for meetings and celebrations of various kinds to obtain a permit from the Park Commissioner. In conformity with this practice, the group requested permission of the Park Commissioner for use of the park on four consecutive Sundays in June and July, 1949. This permission was refused.

Having been informed that an Elks' Flag Day ceremony was scheduled for the first Sunday, the applicants did not pursue their request for the use of the park for that particular day, but, instead, filed a written request with the City Council for the following three Sundays. This request was filed at the suggestion of the Mayor, it appearing that under the custom of the municipality there is a right of appeal to the City Council from the action of the Park Commissioner. The Council held a hearing at which the request was considered. At this hearing the applicants and their attorney appeared. The request was denied.

Because they were awaiting the decision of the Council on their application, the applicants took no further steps on the second Sunday, but, after the denial of the request, they proceeded to hold their meeting on the third Sunday. No sooner had appellant Niemotko opened the meeting and commenced delivering his discourse, than the police, who had been ordered to the park by the Mayor, arrested him. At the meeting held in the park on the fourth and following Sunday, appellant Kelley was arrested before he began his lecture.

Appellants were subsequently brought to trial before a jury on a charge of disorderly conduct under the Maryland disorderly conduct statute. . . . They were convicted and each fined $25 and costs. . . .

A brief recital of the facts as they were adduced at this trial will suffice to show why these convictions cannot stand. At the time of the arrest of each of these appellants, there was no evidence of disorder, threats of violence or riot. There was no indication that the appellants conducted themselves in a manner which could be considered as detrimental to the public peace or order. On the contrary, there was positive testimony by the police that each of the appellants had conducted himself in a manner beyond reproach. It is quite apparent that any disorderly conduct which the jury found must have been based on the fact that appellants were using the park without a permit, although as we have indicated above, there is no statute or ordinance prohibiting or regulating the use of the park without a permit.

This Court has many times examined the licensing systems by which local bodies regulate the use of their parks and public places. . . . In those cases this Court condemned statutes and ordinances which required that permits be obtained from local officials as a prerequisite to the use of public places, on the grounds that a license requirement constituted a prior restraint on freedom of speech, press and religion, and, in the absence of narrowly drawn, reasonable and definite standards for the officials to follow, must be invalid. . . . In the instant case we are met with no ordinance or statute regulating or prohibiting the use of the park; all that is here is an amorphous "practice," whereby all authority to grant permits for the use of the parks is in the Park Commission and the City Council. No standards appear anywhere; no narrowly drawn limitations; no circumscribing of this absolute power; no substantial interest of the community to be served. It is clear that all that has been said about the invalidity of such limitless discretion must be equally applicable here.

This case points up with utmost clarity the wisdom of this doctrine. For the very possibility of abuse, which those earlier decisions feared, has occurred here. Indeed, rarely has any case been before this Court which shows so clearly an unwarranted discrimination in a refusal to issue such a license. It is true that the City Council held a hearing at which it considered the application. But we have searched the record in vain to discover any valid basis for the refusal. In fact, the Mayor testified that the permit would probably have been granted if, at the hearing, the applicants had not started to "berate" the Park Commissioner for his refusal to issue the permit. The only question asked of the Witnesses at the hearing pertained to their alleged refusal to salute the flag, their views on the Bible, and other issues irrelevant to unencumbered use of the public parks. The conclusion is inescapable that the use of the park was denied because of the City Council's dislike for or disagreement with the Witnesses or their views. The right to equal protection of the laws, in the exercise of those freedoms of speech and religion protected by the First and Fourteenth Amendments, has a firmer foundation than the whims or personal opinions of a local governing body.

In this Court, it is argued that state and city officials should have the power to exclude religious groups, as such, from the use of the public parks. But that is not this case. For whatever force this contention could possibly have is lost in the light of the testimony of the Mayor at the trial that within his memory permits had always been issued for religious organizations and Sunday-school picnics. We might also point out that the attempt to designate the park as a sanctuary for peace and quiet not only does not defeat these appellants, whose own conduct created no disturbance, but this position is also more than slightly inconsistent, since, on the first Sunday here involved, the park was the situs for the Flag Day ceremony of the Order of Elks.

It thus becomes apparent that the lack of standards in the license-issuing "practice" renders that "practice" a prior restraint in contravention of the Fourteenth Amendment, and that the completely arbitrary and discriminatory refusal to grant the permits was a denial of equal protection. Inasmuch as the basis of the convictions was the lack of the permits, and that lack was, in turn, due to the unconstitutional defects discussed, the convictions must fall.

Reversed. . . .

Mr. Justice Frankfurter concurring in the result:

The issues in these cases concern living law in some of its most delicate aspects. To smother differences of emphasis and nuance will not help its wise development. When the way a result is reached may be important to results hereafter to be reached, law is best respected by individual expression of opinion.

These cases present three variations upon a theme of great importance. Legislatures, local authorities, and the courts have for years grappled with claims of the right to disseminate ideas in public places as against claims of an effective power in government to keep the peace and to protect other interests of a civilized community. These cases are of special interest because they show the attempts of three communities to meet the problem in three different ways. It will, I believe, further analysis to use the three situations as cross-lights on one another.

I.

1. Nos. 17 and 18.—Havre de Grace, Maryland, sought to solve this tangled problem by permitting its park commissioner and city council to act as censors. The city allowed use of its park for public meetings, including those of religious groups, but by custom a permit was required. In this case, the city council questioned the representatives of Jehovah's Witnesses, who had requested a license, about their views on saluting the flag, the Catholic Church, service in the armed forces, and other matters in no way related to public order or public convenience in use of the park. The Mayor testified that he supposed the permit was denied "because of matters that were

brought out at [the] meeting." When Niemotko and Kelley, Jehovah's Witnesses, attempted to speak, they were arrested for disturbing the peace. There was no disturbance of the peace and it is clear that they were arrested only for want of a permit.

2. No. 50.—New York City set up a licensing system to control the use of its streets and parks for public religious services. The New York Court of Appeals construed the city's ordinance so as to sanction the right of the Police Commissioner to revoke or refuse a license for street-preaching if he found the person was likely to "ridicule" or "denounce" religion. In 1946, after hearings before a Fourth Deputy Police Commissioner, Kunz's license was revoked because he had "ridiculed" and "denounced" religion while speaking in one of New York's crowded centers, and it was thought likely that he would continue to do so. In 1947 and 1948 he was refused a license on the sole ground of the determination made in 1946. In September of 1948 he was arrested for speaking at Columbus Circle without a license.

3. No. 93.—Syracuse, New York, did not set up a licensing system but relied on a statute which is in substance an enactment of the commonlaw offense of breach of the peace. Feiner, the defendant, made a speech near the intersection of South McBride and Harrison Streets in Syracuse. He spoke from a box located on the parking between the sidewalk and the street, and made use of sound amplifiers attached to an automobile. A crowd of 75 to 80 persons gathered around him, and several pedestrians had to go into the highway in order to pass by. Two policemen observed the meeting. In the course of his speech, Feiner referred to the Mayor of Syracuse as a "champagne-sipping bum," to the President as a "bum," and to the American Legion as "Nazi Gestapo agents." Feiner also indicated in an excited manner that Negroes did not have equal rights and should rise up in arms. His audience included a number of Negroes.

One man indicated that if the police did not get the speaker off the stand, he would do it himself. The crowd, which consisted of both those who opposed and those who supported the speaker, was restless. There was not yet a disturbance but, in the words of the arresting officer whose story was accepted by the trial judge, he "stepped in to prevent it from resulting in a fight. After all there was angry muttering and pushing." Having ignored two requests to stop speaking, Feiner was arrested.

II.

Adjustment of the inevitable conflict between free speech and other interests is a problem as persistent as it is perplexing. It is important to bear in mind that this Court can only hope to set limits and point the way. It falls to the lot of legislative bodies and administrative officials to find practical solutions within the frame of our decisions. There are now so many of these decisions, arrived at by the *ad hoc* process of adjudication, that it is desirable to make a cruise of the timber.

In treating the precise problem presented by the three situations before us —how to reconcile the interest in allowing free expression of ideas in public places with the protection of the public peace and of the primary uses of streets and parks—we should first set to one side decisions which are apt to mislead rather than assist. Contempt cases and convictions under State and Federal statutes aimed at placing a general limitation upon what may be said or written, bring additional factors into the equation. Cases like *Near* v. *Minnesota*, 283 US 697, . . . and *Grosjean* v. *American Press Co.*, 297 US 233, . . . are rooted in historic experience regarding prior restraints on publication. They give recognition to the role of the press in a democracy, a consideration not immediately pertinent. The picketing cases are logically relevant since they usually involve, in part, dissmination of information in public places. But here also enter economic and social interests outside the situations before us. . . .

The cases more exclusively concerned with restrictions upon expression in its divers forms in public places have answered problems varying greatly in content and difficulty.

1. The easiest cases have been those in which the only interest opposing free communication was that of keeping the streets of the community clean. This could scarcely justify prohibiting the dissemination of information by handbills or censoring their contents. In *Lovell* v. *Griffin*, 303 US 444, . . . an ordinance requiring a permit to distribute pamphlets was held invalid where the licensing standard was "not limited to ways which might be regarded as inconsistent with the maintenance of public order or as involving disorderly conduct, the molestation of the inhabitants, or the misuse or littering of the streets." . . . In *Hague* v. *C.I.O.*, 307 US 496, . . . a portion of the ordinance declared invalid prohibited the distribution of pamphlets. In *Schneider* v. *Irvington*, 308 US 147, . . . three of the four ordinances declared invalid by the Court prohibited the distribution of pamphlets. In *Jamison* v. *Texas*, 318 US 413, . . . the Court again declared invalid a municipal ordinance prohibiting the distribution of all handbills.

2. In a group of related cases, regulation of solicitation has been the issue. Here the opposing interest is more substantial—protection of the public from fraud and from criminals who use solicitation as a device to enter homes. The fourth ordinance considered in *Schneider* v. *Irvington* allowed the chief of police to refuse a permit if he found, in his discretion, that the canvasser was not of good character or was canvassing for a project not free from fraud. The ordinance was found invalid because the officer who could, in his discretion, make the determinations concerning "good character" and "project not free from fraud" in effect held the power of censorship. In *Cantwell* v. *Connecticut*, 310 US 296, . . . conviction was, in part, under a State statute requiring a permit for religious solicitation. The statute was declared invalid because the licensing official could determine what causes were religious, allowing a "censorship of religion." . . . Again, in *Largent* v. *Texas*, 318 US 418, . . . an ordinance requiring a permit from the mayor, who was to issue the permit only if he deemed it "proper or advisable," was declared invalid as creating an administrative censorship. The Court has also denied the right of those in control of a company town or Government housing project to prohibit solicitation by Jehovah's Witnesses. . . . In *Thomas* v. *Collins*, 323 US 516, . . . the solicitation was in the

interest of labor rather than religion. There a State statute requiring registration of labor organizers was found unconstitutional when invoked to enjoin a speech in a public hall. The interest of the State in protecting its citizens through the regulation of vocations was deemed insufficient to support the statute.

3. Whether the sale of religious literature by Jehovah's Witnesses can be subjected to nondiscriminatory taxes on solicitation has introduced another opposing interest—the right of the community to raise funds for the support of the government. In *Jones* v. *Opelika*, 319 US 103, . . . and in *Murdock* v. *Pennsylvania*, 319 US 105, . . . the Court held that imposition of the tax upon itinerants was improper. In *Follett* v. *McCormick*, 321 US 573, . . . the Court went further to hold unconstitutional the imposition of a flat tax on book agents upon a resident who made his living selling religious books.

4. *Martin* v. *Struthers*, 319 US 141, . . . represents another situation. An ordinance of the City of Struthers, Ohio, forbade knocking on the door or ringing the doorbell of a residence in order to deliver a handbill. Prevention of crime and assuring privacy in an industrial community where many worked on night shifts, and had to obtain their sleep during the day, were held insufficient to justify the ordinance in the case of handbills distributed on behalf of Jehovah's Witnesses.

5. In contrast to these decisions, the Court held in *Prince* v. *Massachusetts*, 321 US 158, . . . that the application to Jehovah's Witnesses of a State statute providing that no boy under 12 or girl under 18 should sell periodicals on the street was constitutional. Claims of immunity from regulation of religious activities were subordinated to the interest of the State in protecting its children.

6. Control of speeches made in streets and parks draws on still different considerations—protection of the public peace and of the primary uses of travel and recreation for which streets and parks exist.

(a) The pioneer case concerning speaking in parks and streets is *Davis* v. *Massachusetts*, 167 US 43, . . . in which this Court adopted the reasoning of the opinion below written by Mr. Justice Holmes, while on the Massachusetts Supreme Judicial Court. . . . The Boston ordinance which was upheld required a permit from the mayor for any person to "make any public address, discharge any cannon or firearm, expose for sale any goods, . . ." on public grounds. This Court respected the finding that the ordinance was not directed against free speech but was intended as "a proper regulation of the use of public grounds." . . .

An attempt to derive from dicta in the *Davis Case* the right of a city to exercise any power over its parks, however arbitrary or discriminatory, was rejected in *Hague* v. *C.I.O.* . . . . The ordinance presented in the *Hague Case* required a permit for meetings on public ground, the permit to be refused by the licensing official only "for the purpose of preventing riots, disturbances or disorderly assemblage." The facts of the case, however, left no doubt that the licensing power had been made an "instrument of arbitrary suppression of free expression of views on national affairs." . . . The holding of the *Hague Case* was not that a city could not subject the use of its streets and parks to reasonable regulation. The holding was that the licensing officials could not be given power arbitrarily to suppress free expression, no matter under what cover of law they purported to act.

Cox v. *New Hampshire,* 312 US 569, . . . made it clear that the United States Constitution does not deny localities the power to devise a licensing system if the exercise of discretion by the licensing officials is appropriately confined. A statute requiring a permit and license fee for parades had been narrowly construed by the State courts. The license could be refused only for "considerations of time, place and manner so as to conserve the public convenience," and the license fee was "to meet the expense incident to the maintenance of public order in the matter licensed." . . . The licensing system was sustained even though the tax, ranging from a nominal amount to $300, was determined by the licensing officials on the facts of each case.

(b) Two cases have involved the additional considerations incident to the use of sound trucks. In *Saia* v. *New York,* 334 US 558, . . . the ordinance required a license from the chief of police for use of sound amplification devices in public places. The ordinance was construed not to prescribe standards to be applied in passing upon a license application. In the particular case, a license to use a sound truck in a small city park had been denied because of complaints about the noise which resulted when sound amplifiers had previously been used in the park. There was no indication that the license had been refused because of the content of the speeches. Nevertheless, the Court held the ordinance unconstitutional. In *Kovacs* v. *Cooper,* 336 US 77, . . . part of the Court construed the ordinance as allowing conviction for operation of any sound truck, emitting "loud and raucous" noises, and part construed the ordinance to ban all sound trucks. The limits of the decision of the Court upholding the ordinance are therefore not clear, but the result in any event does not leave the *Saia* decision intact.

(c) On a few occasions the Court has had to pass on a limitation upon speech by a sanction imposed after the event rather than by a licensing statute. In *Cantwell* v. *Connecticut,* 310 US 296, . . . one of the convictions was for common-law breach of the peace. The problem was resolved in favor of the defendant . . . in view of the inquiry whether, on the facts of the case, there was "such clear and present menace to public peace and order as to render him liable to conviction of the common law offense in question." . . .

In *Chaplinsky* v. *New Hampshire,* 315 US 568, . . . a State statute had enacted the common-law doctrine of "fighting words": "No person shall address any offensive, derisive or annoying word to any other person who is lawfully in any street or other public place, nor call him by any offensive or derisive name. . . ." The State courts had previously held the statute applicable only to the use in a public place of words directly tending to cause a breach of the peace by the persons to whom the remark was addressed. The conviction of a street speaker who called a policeman a "damned racketeer" and "damned Fascist" was upheld.

7. One other case should be noted, although it involved a conviction for

breach of peace in a private building rather than in a public place. In *Terminiello* v. *Chicago,* 337 US 1, . . . the holding of the Court was on an abstract proposition of law, unrelated to the facts in the case. A conviction was overturned because the judge had instructed the jury that "breach of the peace" included speech which "stirs the public to anger, invites disputes, brings about a condition of unrest, or creates a disturbance. . . ." The holding apparently was that breach of the peace may not be defined in such broad terms, certainly as to speech in a private hall.

The results in these multifarious cases have been expressed in language looking in two directions. While the Court has emphasized the importance of "free speech," it has recognized that "free speech" is not in itself a touchstone. The Constitution is not unmindful of other important interests, such as public order, if interference with free expression of ideas is not found to be the overbalancing consideration. More important than the phrasing of the opinions are the questions on which the decisions appear to have turned.

(1) What is the interest deemed to require the regulation of speech? The State cannot of course forbid public proselyting or religious argument merely because public officials disapprove the speaker's views. It must act in patent good faith to maintain the public peace, to assure the availability of the streets for their primary purposes of passenger and vehicular traffic, or for equally indispensable ends of modern community life.

(2) What is the method used to achieve such ends as a consequence of which public speech is constrained or barred? A licensing standard which gives an official authority to censor the content of a speech differs *toto coelo* from one limited by its terms, or by nondiscriminatory practice, to considerations of public safety and the like. Again, a sanction applied after the event assures consideration of the particular circumstances of a situation. The net of control must not be cast too broadly.

(3) What mode of speech is regulated? A sound truck may be found to affect the public peace as normal speech does not. A man who is calling names or using the kind of language which would reasonably stir another to violence does not have the same claim to protection as one whose speech is an appeal to reason.

(4) Where does the speaking which is regulated take place? Not only the general classifications—streets, parks, private buildings—are relevant. The location and size of a park; its customary use for the recreational, esthetic and contemplative needs of a community; the facilities, other than a park or street corner, readily available in a community for airing views, are all pertinent considerations in assessing the limitations the Fourteenth Amendment puts on State power in a particular situation.

III.

Due regard for the interests that were adjusted in the decisions just canvassed affords guidance for deciding the cases before us.

1. In the *Niemotko Case,* neither danger to the public peace, nor consideration of time and convenience to the public, appears to have entered into denial of the permit. Rumors that there would be violence by those

opposed to the meeting appeared only after the Council made its decision, and in fact never materialized. The city allowed other religious groups to use the park. To allow expression of religious views by some and deny the same privilege to others merely because they or their views are unpopular, even deeply so, is a denial of equal protection of the law forbidden by the Fourteenth Amendment.

2. The *Kunz Case* presents a very different situation. We must be mindful of the enormous difficulties confronting those charged with the task of enabling the polyglot millions in the City of New York to live in peace and tolerance. Street-preaching in Columbus Circle is done in a milieu quite different from preaching on a New England village green. Again, religious polemic does not touch the merely ratiocinative nature of man, and the ugly facts disclosed by the record of this case show that Kunz was not reluctant to offend the deepest religious feelings of frequenters of Columbus Circle. Especially in such situations, this Court should not substitute its abstract views for the informed judgment of local authorities confirmed by local courts.

I cannot make too explicit my conviction that the City of New York is not restrained by anything in the Constitution of the United States from protecting completely the community's interests in relation to its streets. But if a municipality conditions holding street meetings on the granting of a permit by the police, the basis which guides licensing officials in granting or denying a permit must not give them a free hand, or a hand effectively free when the actualities of police administration are taken into account. It is not for this Court to formulate with particularity the terms of a permit system which would satisfy the Fourteenth Amendment. No doubt, finding a want of such standards presupposes some conception of what is necessity to meet the constitutional requirement we draw from the Fourteenth Amendment. But many a decision of this Court rests on some inarticulate major premise and is none the worse for it. A standard may be found inadequate without the necessity of explicit delineation of the standards that would be adequate, just as doggerel may be felt not to be poetry without the need of writing an essay on what poetry is.

Administrative control over the right to speak must be based on appropriate standards, whether the speaking be done indoors or out-of-doors. The vice to be guarded against is arbitrary action by officials. The fact that in a particular instance an action appears not arbitrary does not save the validity of the authority under which the action was taken.

In the present case, Kunz was not arrested for what he said on the night of arrest, nor because at that time he was disturbing the peace or interfering with traffic. He was arrested because he spoke without a license, and the license was refused because the police commissioner thought it likely on the basis of past performance that Kunz would outrage the religious sensibilities of others. If such had been the supportable finding on the basis of fair standards in safeguarding peace in one of the most populous centers of New York City, this Court would not be justified in upsetting it. It would not be censorship in advance. But here the standards are defined neither by language nor by settled construction to preclude discriminatory or arbitrary action by officials. The ordinance, as judicially construed, provides that anyone who, in the judgment of the licensing officials, would "ridicule" or "denounce" religion creates such a danger of public disturbance that he cannot speak in any park or street in the City of New York. Such a standard, considering the informal procedure under which it is applied, too readily permits censorship of religion by the licensing authorities. . . . The situation here disclosed is not, to reiterate, beyond control on the basis of regulation appropriately directed to the evil.

3. Feiner was convicted under New York Penal Law § 722. . . .

Here, Feiner forced pedestrians to walk in the street by collecting a crowd on the public sidewalk, he attracted additional attention by using sound amplifiers, he indulged in name-calling, he told part of his audience that it should rise up in arms. In the crowd of 75 to 80 persons, there was angry muttering and pushing. Under these circumstances, and in order to prevent a disturbance of the peace, an officer asked Feiner to stop speaking. When he had twice ignored the request, Feiner was arrested. The trial judge concluded that "the officers were fully justified in feeling that a situation was developing which could very, very easily result in a serious disorder." His view was sustained by an intermediate appellate court and by a unanimous decision of the New York Court of Appeals. . . . The estimate of a particular local situation thus comes here with the momentum of the weightiest judicial authority of New York.

This Court has often emphasized that in the exercise of our authority over state court decisions the Due Process Clause must not be construed in an abstract and doctrinaire way by disregarding local conditions. In considering the degree of respect to be given findings by the highest court of a State in cases involving the Due Process Clause, the course of decisions by that court should be taken into account. Particularly within the area of due process colloquially called "civil liberties," it is important whether such a course of decisions reflects a cavalier attitude toward civil liberties or real regard for them. Only unfamiliarity with its decisions and the outlook of its judges could generate a notion that the Court of Appeals of New York is inhospitable to claims of civil liberties or is wanting in respect for this Court's decisions in support of them. It is pertinent, therefore, to note that all members of the New York Court accepted the finding that Feiner was stopped not because the listeners or police officers disagreed with his views but because these officers were honestly concerned with preventing a breach of the peace. This unanimity is all the more persuasive since three members of the Court had dissented, only three months earlier, in favor of Kunz, a man whose vituperative utterances must have been highly offensive to them.

. . . Where conduct is within the allowable limits of free speech, the police are peace officers for the speaker as well as for his hearers. But the power effectively to preserve order cannot be displaced by giving a speaker complete immunity. Here, there were two police officers present for 20 minutes. They interfered only when they apprehended imminence of violence. It is not a constitutional principle that, in acting to preserve order, the police must proceed against the crowd, whatever its size and temper, and not against the speaker.

It is true that breach-of-peace statutes, like most tools of government, may be misused. Enforcement of these statutes calls for public tolerance and intelligent police administration. These, in the long run, must give substance to whatever this Court may say about free speech. But the possibility of misuse is not alone a sufficient reason to deny New York the power here asserted or so limit it by constitutional construction as to deny its practical exercise.

KUNZ v. NEW YORK
340 US 290 (1951)

[An ordinance of the City of New York required a permit for public meetings on streets. It failed to define the circumstances under which officials might refuse to issue permits. The officials construed the ordinance as authorizing them to refuse a permit, in their discretion, if the applicant *in the past* had ridiculed or denounced some religious belief. Kunz had engaged in attacks on Catholics and Jews; when he applied for a permit to speak, he was denied one for this reason; he spoke at Columbus Circle without a permit and was arrested. The Court held that the ordinance was unconstitutional as a previous restraint on rights guaranteed by the First Amendment. Only Justice Jackson dissented. For Justice Frankfurter's concurring opinion, see the preceding case.]

Mr. Chief Justice Vinson delivered the opinion of the Court:

New York City has adopted an ordinance which makes it unlawful to hold public worship meetings on the streets without first obtaining a permit from the city police commissioner. Appellant, Carl Jacob Kunz, was convicted and fined $10 for violating this ordinance by holding a religious meeting without a permit. . . .

Appellant is an ordained Baptist minister who speaks under the auspices of the "Outdoor Gospel Work," of which he is the director. He has been preaching for about six years, and states that it is his conviction and duty to "go out on the highways and byways and preach the word of God." In 1946, he applied for and received a permit under the ordinance in question, there being no question that appellant comes within the classes of persons entitled to receive permits under the ordinance. This permit, like all others, was good only for the calendar year in which issued. In November, 1946, his permit was revoked after a hearing by the police commissioner. The revocation was based on evidence that he had ridiculed and denounced other religious beliefs in his meetings.

Although the penalties of the ordinance apply to anyone who "ridicules and denounces other religious beliefs," the ordinance does not specify this as a ground for permit revocation. Indeed, there is no mention in the ordinance of any power of revocation. However, appellant did not seek judicial or administrative review of the revocation proceedings, and any question as to the propriety of the revocation is not before us in this case. In any event, the revocation affected appellant's rights to speak in 1946 only. Appellant applied for another permit in 1947, and again in 1948, but was notified each time that his application was "disapproved," with no reason for the disapproval being given. On September 11, 1948, appellant was arrested for speaking at Columbus Circle in New York City without a permit. It is from the conviction which resulted that this appeal has been taken.

Appellant's conviction was thus based upon his failure to possess a permit for 1948. We are here concerned only with the propriety of the action of the police commissioner in refusing to issue that permit. Disapproval of the 1948 permit application by the police commissioner was justified by the New York courts on the ground that a permit had previously been revoked "for good reasons." It is noteworthy that there is no mention in the ordinance of reasons for which such a permit application can be refused. This interpretation allows the police commissioner, an administrative official, to exercise discretion in denying subsequent permit applications on the basis of his interpretation, at that time, of what is deemed to be conduct condemned by the ordinance. We have here, then, an ordinance which gives an administrative official discretionary power to control in advance the right of citizens to speak on religious matters on the streets of New York. As such, the ordinance is clearly invalid as a prior restraint on the exercise of First Amendment rights.

In considering the right of a municipality to control the use of public streets for the expression of religious views, we start with the words of Mr. Justice Roberts that "Wherever the title of streets and parks may rest, they have immemorially been held in trust for the use of the public and, time out of mind, have been used for purposes of assembly, communicating thoughts between citizens, and discussing public questions." *Hague* v. *C.I.O.*, 307 US 496. . . .

The court below has mistakenly derived support for its conclusion from the evidence produced at the trial that appellant's religious meetings had, in the past, caused some disorder. There are appropriate public remedies to protect the peace and order of the community if appellant's speeches should result in disorder or violence. "In the present case, we have no occasion to inquire as to the permissible scope of subsequent punishment." *Near* v. *Minnesota*, 283 US 697. We do not express any opinion on the propriety of punitive remedies which the New York authorities may utilize. We are here concerned with suppression—not punishment. It is sufficient to say that New York cannot vest restraining control over the right to speak on religious subjects in an administrative official where there are no appropriate standards to guide his action.

Reversed. . . .

Mr. Justice Jackson, dissenting:

Essential freedoms are today threatened from without and within. It may become difficult to preserve here what a large part of the world has lost—the right to speak, even temperately, on matters vital to spirit and body. In such a setting, to blanket hateful and hate-stirring attacks on races and faiths under the protections for freedom of speech may be a noble innovation. On the other hand, it may be a quixotic tilt at windmills which belittles great principles of liberty. Only time can tell. But I incline to the latter view and cannot assent to the decision. . . .

This Court today initiates the doctrine that language such as this, in the environment of the street meeting, is immune from prior municipal control. We would have a very different question if New York had presumed to say that Kunz could not speak his piece in his own pulpit or hall. But it has undertaken to restrain him only if he chooses to speak at street meetings. There is a world of difference. The street preacher takes advantage of people's presence on the streets to impose his message upon what, in a sense, is a captive audience. A meeting on private property is made up of an audience that has volunteered to listen. The question, therefore, is not whether New York could, if it tried, silence Kunz, but whether it must place its streets at his service to hurl insults at the passerby.

What Mr. Justice Holmes said for a unanimous Court in *Schenck* v. *United States*, 249 US 47, . . . has become an axiom: "The most stringent protection of free speech would not protect a man in falsely shouting fire in a theatre and causing a panic." This concept was applied in one of its few unanimous decisions in recent years, when, through Mr. Justice Murphy, the Court said: "There are certain well-defined and narrowly limited classes of speech, *the prevention and punishment* of which *have never been thought to raise any Constitutional problem*. These include the lewd and obscene, the profane, the libelous, and *the insulting or 'fighting' words*—those which by their very utterance inflict injury or *tend to incite* an immediate breach of the peace. . . ." (Emphasis supplied.) *Chaplinsky* v. *New Hampshire*, 315 US 568. . . .

There held to be "insulting or 'fighting' words" were calling one a "God damned racketeer" and a "damned Fascist." Equally inciting and more clearly "fighting words," when thrown at Catholics and Jews who are rightfully on the streets of New York, are statements that "The Pope is the anti-Christ" and the Jews are "Christ-killers." These terse epithets come down to our generation weighted with hatreds accumulated through centuries of bloodshed. They are recognized words of art in the profession of defamation. They are not the kind of insult that men bandy and laugh off when the spirits are high and the flagons are low. They are not in that class of epithets whose literal sting will be drawn if the speaker smiles when he uses them. They are always, and in every context, insults which do not spring from reason and can be answered by none. Their historical associations with violence are well understood, both by those who hurl and those who are struck by these missiles. Jews, many of whose families perished in extermination furnaces of Dachau and Auschwitz, are more than tolerant if they pass off lightly the suggestion that unbelievers in Christ should all have been burned. Of course, people might pass this speaker by as a mental case, and so they might file out of a theatre in good order at the cry of "fire." But in both cases there is genuine likelihood that someone will get hurt. . . .

A hostile reception of his subject certainly does not alone destroy one's right to speak. A temperate and reasoned criticism of Roman Catholicism or Judaism might, and probably would, cause some resentment and protest. But in a free society all sects and factions, as the price of their own freedom to preach their views, must suffer that freedom in others. Tolerance of unwelcome, unorthodox ideas or information is a constitutionally protected policy not to be defeated by persons who would break up meetings they do not relish.

But emergencies may arise on streets which would become catastrophes if there was not immediate police action. The crowd which should be tolerant may be prejudiced and angry or malicious. If the situation threatens to get out of hand for the force present, I think the police may require the speaker, even if within his rights, to yield his right temporarily to the greater interest of peace. Of course, the threat must be judged in good faith to be real, immediate and serious. But silencing a speaker by authorities as a measure of mob control, is like dynamiting a house to stop the spread of a conflagration. It may be justified by the overwhelming community interest that flames not be fed as compared with the little interest to be served by continuing to feed them. But this kind of disorder does not abridge the right to speak except for the emergency and, since the speaker was within his constitutional right to speak, it could not be grounds for revoking or refusing him a permit or convicting him of any offense because of his utterance. If he resisted an officer's reasonable demand to cease, he might incur penalties.

And so the matter eventually comes down to the question whether the "words used are used in such circumstances and are of such a nature" that we can say a reasonable man would anticipate the evil result. In this case the Court does not justify, excuse, or deny the inciting and provocative character of the language, and it does not, and, on this record could not, deny that when Kunz speaks he poses a "clear and present" danger to peace and order. Why, then, does New York have to put up with it?

It is well to be vigilant to protect the right of Kunz to speak, but is he to be sole judge as to how far he will carry verbal attacks in the public streets? Is official action the only source of interference with religious freedom? Does the Jew, for example, have the benefit of these freedoms when, lawfully going about, he and his children are pointed out as "Christ-killers" to gatherings on public property by a religious sectarian sponsored by a police bodyguard?

We should weigh the value of insulting speech against its potentiality for harm. Is the Court, when declaring Kunz has the *right* he asserts, serving the great end for which the First Amendment stands?

The purpose of constitutional protection of speech is to foster peaceful interchange of all manner of thoughts, information and ideas. Its policy is rooted in faith in the force of reason. This Court wisely has said, "Resort to epithets or personal abuse is not in any proper sense communication of information or opinion safeguarded by the Constitution." . . .

The question remains whether the Constitution prohibits a city from control of its streets by a permit system which takes into account damages to public peace and order. I am persuaded that it does not do so, provided, of course, that the city does not so discriminate as to deny equal protection of the law or undertake a censorship of utterances that are not so defamatory, insulting, inciting, or provocative as to be reasonably likely to cause disorder and violence.

The Court does not hold that New York has abused the permit system by discrimination or actual censorship, nor does it deny the abuses on Kunz's part. But neither, says the Court, matters, holding that any prior restraint is bad, regardless of how fairly administered or what abuses it seeks to prevent.

It strikes rather blindly at permit systems which indirectly may affect First Amendment freedoms. Cities throughout the country have adopted permit requirements to control private activities on public streets and for other purposes. The universality of this type of regulation demonstrates a need and indicates widespread opinion in the profession that it is not necessarily incompatible with our constitutional freedoms. Is everybody out of step but this Court?

Until recently this custom of municipalities was regarded by this Court as consistent with the Constitution. . . .

In the *Chaplinsky Case, prevention* as well as *punishment* of "limited classes of speech . . . have never been thought to raise *any* constitutional problem." (Emphasis supplied.) Mr. Justice Holmes pointed out in the *Schenck Case* that the Constitution would not protect one from an injunction against uttering words that lead to riot. . . .

Of course, as to the press, there are the best of reasons against any licensing or prior restraint. Decisions such as *Near* v. *Minnesota,* 283 US 697, . . . hold any licensing or prior restraint of the press unconstitutional, and I heartily agree. But precedents from that field cannot reasonably be transposed to the street-meeting field. The impact of publishing on public order has no similarity with that of a street meeting. Publishing does not make private use of public property. It reaches only those who choose to read, and, in that way, is analogous to a meeting held in a hall where those who come do so by choice. Written words are less apt to incite or provoke to mass action than spoken words, speech being the primitive and direct communication with the emotions. Few are the riots caused by publication alone, few are the mobs that have not had their immediate origin in harangue. The vulnerability of various forms of communication to community control must be proportioned to their impact upon other community interests. . . .

It seems hypercritical to strike down local laws on their faces for want of standards when we have no standards. And I do not find it required by existing authority. I think that where speech is outside of constitutional immunity the local community or the State is left a large measure of discretion as to the means for dealing with it. . . .

Turning then to the permit system as applied by the Court of Appeals, whose construction binds us, we find that issuance the first time is required. Denial is warranted only in such unusual cases as where an applicant has had a permit which has been revoked for cause and he asserts the right to continue the conduct which was cause for revocation. If anything less than a reasonable certainty of disorder was shown, denial of a permit would be improper. The procedure by which that decision is reached commends itself to the orderly mind—complaints are filed, witnesses are heard, opportunity to cross-examine is given, and decision is reached by what we must assume to be an impartial and reasonable administrative officer, and, if he denies the permit, the applicant may carry his cause to the courts. He may thus have a civil test of his rights without the personal humiliation of being arrested as presenting a menace to public order. It seems to me that this procedure better protects freedom of speech than to let everyone speak without leave, but subject to surveillance and to being ordered to stop in the discretion of the police.

It is obvious that a permit is a source of security and protection for the civil liberties of the great number who are entitled to receive them. It informs the police of the time and place one intends to speak, which allows necessary steps to insure him a place to speak where overzealous police officers will not order everyone who stops to listen to move on, and to have officers present to insure an orderly meeting. Moreover, disorder is less likely, for the speaker knows that if he provokes disorder his permit may be revoked, and the objector may be told that he has a remedy by filing a complaint and does not need to take the law in his own hands. Kunz was not arrested in 1946, when his speeches caused serious objections, nor was he set upon by the crowd. Instead, they did the orderly thing and made complaints which resulted in the revocation of his permit. This is the method that the Court frustrates today.

Of course, emergencies may arise either with or without the permit system. A speaker with a permit may go beyond bounds and incite violence, or a mob may undertake to break up an authorized and properly conducted meeting. In either case, the policeman on the spot must make the judgment as to what measures will most likely avoid violent disorders. But these emergencies seem less likely to occur with the permit system than if every man and his adversary take the law in their own hands.

The law of New York does not segregate according to their diverse nationalities, races, religions, or political associations, the vast hordes of people living in its narrow confines. Every individual in frightening aggregation is legally free to live, to labor, to travel, when and where he chooses. In streets and public places, all races and nationalities and all sorts and conditions of men walk, linger and mingle. Is it not reasonable that the City protect the dignity of these persons against fanatics who take possession of its streets to hurl into its crowds defamatory epithets that hurt like rocks?

If any two subjects are intrinsically incendiary and divisive, they are race and religion. Racial fears and hatreds have been at the root of the most terrible riots that have disgraced American civilization. They are ugly possibilities that overhang every great American city. The "consecrated hatreds of sect" account for more than a few of the world's bloody disorders. These are the explosives which the Court says Kunz may play with in the public streets, and the community must not only tolerate but aid him. I find no such doctrine in the Constitution.

In this case there is no evidence of a purpose to suppress speech, except to keep it in bounds that will not upset good order. If there are abuses of censorship or discrimination in administering the ordinance, as well there may be, they are not proved in this case. This Court should be particularly sure of its ground before it strikes down, in a time like this, the going, practical system by which New York has sought to control its street-meeting problem.

Addressing himself to the subject, *Authority and the Individual*, one of the keenest philosophers of our time [Bertrand Russell] observes: "The problem, like all those with which we are concerned, is one of balance; too little liberty brings stagnation, and too much brings chaos." Perhaps it is the fever of our times that inclines the Court today to favor chaos. My hope is that few will take advantage of the license granted by today's decision. But life teaches one to distinguish between hope and faith.

5. Taxes on Knowledge

GROSJEAN v. AMERICAN PRESS CO.

297 US 233 (1936)

[In 1712 Parliament imposed a tax on printed papers, pamphlets, and advertisements and required a stamp to be placed on every newspaper. Such taxes came to be known as "taxes on knowledge." The tax on pamphlets continued until 1833, on advertisements until 1852, and the stamp duty on newspapers until 1855. The effect of these duties was to restrict the circulation of printed matter among relatively poor people.

[Pointing out that the American Revolution began in effect when England started to send stamps for newspaper duties to the American Colonies, the Court in the present case unanimously condemned as unconstitutional any device that falls within the category of "taxes on knowledge." The decision has been followed in later cases; e.g., *Follett* v. *McCormick*, 321 US 573 (1944), in which the Court extended the prohibition to a tax on the exercise of religion.]

Mr. Justice Sutherland delivered the opinion of the Court:

This suit was brought by appellees, nine publishers of newspapers in the State of Louisiana, to enjoin the enforcement against them of the provisions of § 1 of the act of the legislature of Louisiana known as Act No. 23, passed and approved July 12, 1934, as follows:

That every person, firm, association or corporation, domestic or foreign, engaged in the business of selling, or making any charge for, advertising or for advertisements, whether printed or published, or to be printed or published, in any newspaper, magazine, periodical or publication whatever having a circulation of more than 20,000 copies per week, or displayed and exhibited, or to be displayed and exhibited by means of moving pictures, in the State of Louisiana, shall, in addition to all other taxes and licenses levied and assessed in this State, pay a license tax for the privilege of engaging in such business in this State of two per cent. (2%) of the gross receipts of such business.

The nine publishers who brought the suit publish thirteen newspapers; and these thirteen publications are the only ones within the State of Louisiana having each a circulation of more than 20,000 copies per week, although the lower court finds there are four other daily newspapers each having a circulation of "slightly less than 20,000 copies per week" which are in competition with those published by appellees both as to circulation and as to advertising. In addition, there are 120 weekly newspapers published in the state, also in competition, to a greater or less degree, with the newspapers of appellees. The revenue derived from appellees' newspapers comes almost entirely from regular subscribers or purchasers thereof and from payments received for the insertion of advertisements therein.

The act requires everyone subject to the tax to file a sworn report every three months showing the amount and the gross receipts from the business described in § 1. The resulting tax must be paid when the report is filed. Failure to file the report or pay the tax as thus provided constitutes a misdemeanor and subjects the offender to a fine not exceeding $500, or imprisonment not exceeding six months, or both, for each violation. Any corporation violating the act subjects itself to the payment of $500 to be recovered by suit. . . .

The validity of the act is assailed as violating the federal Constitution in two particulars—(1) that it abridges the freedom of the press in contravention of the due process clause contained in § 1 of the Fourteenth Amendment; (2) that it denies appellees the equal protection of the laws in contravention of the same Amendment.

1. The first point presents a question of the utmost gravity and importance; for, if well made, it goes to the heart of the natural right of the members of an organized society, united for their common good, to impart and acquire information about their common interests. The First Amendment to the federal Constitution provides that "Congress shall make no law . . . abridging the freedom of speech, or of the press. . . ." While this provision is not a restraint upon the powers of the states, the states are precluded from abridging the freedom of speech or of the press by force of the due process clause of the Fourteenth Amendment. . . .

That freedom of speech and of the press are rights of the same fundamental character, safeguarded by the due process of law clause of the Fourteenth Amendment against abridgment by state legislation, has . . . been settled by a series of decisions of this court. . . . The word "liberty" contained in that amendment embraces not only the right of a person to be free from physical restraint, but the right to be free in the enjoyment of all his faculties as well. . . .

For more than a century prior to the adoption of the amendment—and, indeed, for many years thereafter—history discloses a persistent effort on the part of the British government to prevent or abridge the free expression of any opinion which seemed to criticize or exhibit in an unfavorable light, however truly, the agencies and operations of the government. The struggle between the proponents of measures to that end and those who asserted the right of free expression was continuous and unceasing. As early as 1644, John Milton, in [*Areopagitica*,] an "Appeal for the Liberty of Unlicensed Printing," assailed an act of Parliament which had just been passed providing for censorship of the press previous to publication. He vigorously defended the right of every man to make public his honest views "without previous censure"; and declared the impossibility of finding any man base enough to accept the office of censor and at the same time good enough to be allowed to perform its duties. . . . The act expired by its own terms in 1695. It was never renewed; and the liberty of the press thus became . . . merely "a right or liberty to publish *without* a license what formerly could be published only *with* one." But mere exemption from previous censorship was soon recognized as too narrow a view of the liberty of the press.

In 1712, in response to a message from Queen Anne . . . , Parlia-

ment imposed a tax upon all newspapers and upon advertisements.
. . . That the main purpose of these taxes was to suppress the publication of comments and criticisms objectionable to the Crown does not
admit of doubt. . . . There followed more than a century of resistance
to, and evasion of, the taxes, and of agitation for their repeal. . . .
[It has been said that] these taxes constituted one of the factors that
aroused the American colonists to protest against taxation for the
purposes of the home government; and that the revolution really began
when, in 1765, that government sent stamps for newspaper duties to
the American colonies.

These duties were quite commonly characterized as "taxes on knowledge," a phrase used for the purpose of describing the effect of the
exactions and at the same time condemning them. That the taxes had,
and were intended to have, the effect of curtailing the circulation of
newspapers, and particularly the cheaper ones whose readers were
generally found among the masses of the people, went almost without
question, even on the part of those who defended the act. May (*Constitutional History of England*, 7th ed., vol. 2, p. 245), after discussing
the control by "previous censure," says: ". . . a new restraint was devised in the form of a stamp duty on newspapers and advertisements,
—avowedly for the purpose of repressing libels. This policy, being
found effectual in limiting the circulation of cheap papers was improved upon in the two following reigns, and continued in high esteem
until our own time." Collett ([*History of the Taxes on Knowledge*,]
vol. 1, p. 14) says: "Any man who carried on printing or publishing for
a livelihood was actually at the mercy of the Commissioners of Stamps,
when they chose to exert their powers."

Citations of similar import might be multiplied many times; but the
foregoing is enough to demonstrate beyond peradventure that in the
adoption of the English newspaper stamp tax and the tax on advertisements, revenue was of subordinate concern; and that the dominant and
controlling aim was to prevent, or curtail the opportunity for, the
acquisition of knowledge by the people in respect of their governmental affairs. It is idle to suppose that so many of the best men of
England would for a century of time have waged, as they did, stubborn
and often precarious warfare against these taxes if a mere matter of
taxation had been involved. The aim of the struggle was not to relieve
taxpayers from a burden, but to establish and preserve the right of the
English people to full information in respect of the doings or misdoings of their government. Upon the correctness of this conclusion the
very characterization of the exactions as "taxes on knowledge" sheds
a flood of corroborative light. In the ultimate, an informed and enlightened public opinion was the thing at stake; for, as Erskine, in his

great speech in defense of Paine, has said: "The liberty of opinion keeps governments themselves in due subjection to their duties." . . .

In 1785, only four years before Congress had proposed the First Amendment, the Massachusetts legislature, following the English example, imposed a stamp tax on all newspapers and magazines. The following year an advertisement tax was imposed. Both taxes met with such violent opposition that the former was repealed in 1786, and the latter in 1788. Duniway, *Freedom of the Press in Massachusetts*, pp. 136, 137.

The framers of the First Amendment were familiar with the English struggle, which then had continued for nearly eighty years and was destined to go on for another sixty-five years, at the end of which time it culminated in a lasting abandonment of the obnoxious taxes. The framers were likewise familiar with the then recent Massachusetts episode; and while that occurrence did much to bring about the adoption of the amendment . . . , the predominant influence must have come from the English experience. It is impossible to concede that by the words "freedom of the press" the framers of the amendment intended to adopt merely the narrow view then reflected by the law of England that such freedom consisted only in immunity from previous censorship; for this abuse had then permanently disappeared from English practice. It is equally impossible to believe that it was not intended to bring within the reach of these words such modes of restraint as were embodied in the two forms of taxation already described. Such belief must be rejected in the face of the then well known purpose of the exactions and the general adverse sentiment of the colonies in respect to them. . . .

In the light of all that has now been said, it is evident that the restricted rules of the English law in respect of the freedom of the press in force when the Constitution was adopted were never accepted by the American colonists, and that by the First Amendment it was meant to preclude the national government, and by the Fourteenth Amendment to preclude the states, from adopting any form of previous restraint upon printed publications, or their circulation, including that which had theretofore been effected by these two well-known and odious methods. . . .

It is not intended by anything we have said to suggest that the owners of newspapers are immune from any of the ordinary forms of taxation for support of the government. But this is not an ordinary form of tax, but one single in kind, with a long history of hostile misuse against the freedom of the press.

The predominant purpose of the grant of immunity here invoked was to preserve an untrammeled press as a vital source of public information. The newspapers, magazines and other journals of the country, it is safe to say, have shed and continue to shed, more light on the public and business affairs of the nation than any other instrumentality of publicity; and since informed public opinion is the most potent of all restraints upon misgovernment, the suppression or abridgment of the publicity afforded by a free press cannot be regarded otherwise than with grave concern. The tax here involved is bad not because it takes money from the pockets of the appellees. If that were all, a wholly different question would be presented. It is bad because, in the light of its history and of its present setting, it is seen to be a deliberate and calculated device in the guise of a tax to limit the circulation of information to which the public is entitled in virtue of the constitutional guaranties. A free press stands as one of the great interpreters between the government and the people. To allow it to be fettered is to fetter ourselves.

In view of the persistent search for new subjects of taxation, it is not without significance that, with the single exception of the Louisiana statute, so far as we can discover, no state during the one hundred fifty years of our national existence has undertaken to impose a tax like that now in question.

The form in which the tax is imposed is in itself suspicious. It is not measured or limited by the volume of advertisements. It is measured alone by the extent of the circulation of the publication in which the advertisements are carried, with the plain purpose of penalizing the publishers and curtailing the circulation of a selected group of newspapers.

2. Having reached the conclusion that the act imposing the tax in question is unconstitutional under the due process of law clause because it abridges the freedom of the press, we deem it unnecessary to consider the further ground assigned that it also constitutes a denial of the equal protection of the laws.

Decree affirmed.

★ VI ★

Freedom of Speech and Press:

The Clear and Present

Danger Doctrine

The Clear and Present Danger Doctrine and the Communist Conspiracy

DENNIS *v.* UNITED STATES

341 US 494 (1951)

[Some classes of speech and publications are beyond constitutional protection: "the lewd and obscene, the profane, the libelous, and the insulting or 'fighting' words—those which by their very utterance inflict injury or tend to incite an immediate breach of the peace." They are "no essential part of any exposition of ideas, and are of such slight social value as a step to truth that any benefit that may be derived from them is clearly outweighed by the social interest in order and morality." Justice Murphy in *Chaplinsky* v. *New Hampshire,* 315 US 568 (1942). Cases heretofore considered which exemplify the force of this statement are *Feiner* v. *New York* and *Beauharnais* v. *Illinois.* Cases involving lewd or obscene language, e.g., the *"Ulysses" Case,* are discussed later.

[Other classes of speech and publications are protected by the Constitution unless "the expression presents a clear and present danger of action of a kind the State is empowered to prevent and punish." Justice Jackson in *Board of Education* v. *Barnette*, above. While the rights of free speech and press are fundamental, "their exercise is subject to restriction, if the particular restriction proposed is required in order to protect the state from destruction or from serious injury, political, economic or moral." The necessity for restriction does not exist "unless speech would produce, or is intended to produce, a clear and imminent danger of some substantive evil which the State constitutionally may seek to prevent." Justice Brandeis in *Whitney* v. *California*, 274 US 357 (1927). To justify suppression of free speech, Brandeis added, there must be "reasonable ground to fear that serious evil will result if free speech is practiced . . . ; that the danger apprehended is imminent . . . ; that the evil to be prevented is a serious one." He distinguished advocacy from incitement, preparation from attempt, assembly from conspiracy. These are still the essential elements of the clear and present danger doctrine.

[The doctrine was first stated in the Supreme Court by Justice Holmes in *Schenck* v. *United States*, 249 US 47 (1919). His opinion was that of a unanimous Court. In some later cases, however, the Court failed effectively to use the clear and present danger test, and accordingly Holmes and Brandeis dissented, as in *Abrams* v. *United States*, 250 US 616 (1919). In *Gitlow* v. *New York*, 268 US 652 (1925), a majority of the Court declined to follow the test. Holmes and Brandeis dissented. While the *Gitlow Case* has not been expressly overruled, later cases have used the clear and present danger test as formulated by Holmes and Brandeis—e.g., *Herndon* v. *Lowry*, 301 US 242 (1937). It is still the standard by which the Court judges the constitutionality of restrictions on free speech.

[But the force and reach of the clear and present danger doctrine are matters concerning which members of the Court have differing views. Courts differ as to how it can be determined when a danger is "clear," or when it is "present," or when the evil sought to be prevented by a restriction on free speech is "substantial." Justice Frankfurter even doubts if Holmes meant the clear and present danger doctrine to be "a technical legal doctrine" or to "convey a formula for adjudicating cases." *Pennekamp* v. *Florida*, 328 US 331 (1946).

[The *Dennis Case,* involving the conviction of eleven Communist Party leaders, reflects the diversity of views and the strains and stresses to which the Holmes-Brandeis doctrine has been subjected. In a 6-to-2 decision (Justice Clark not participating and Justices Black and Douglas dissenting) the Court upheld the conviction for conspiracy under the Smith Act of 1940. Seven of the Justices agreed that the standard to be used is that of the clear and present danger; only Justice Jackson maintained that in a conspiracy case such as this one the conspirators could be convicted even if there was no clear and present danger of overthrow of the Government. The dissenting Justices, on the other hand, ignored the conspiracy element and put all their weight on the clear and present danger test.

[It should be borne in mind that the Court had before it a conviction for *criminal conspiracy;* for the law has always considered conspiracy a much graver threat to the state than the acts of a solitary criminal. Following the *Dennis Case,* other Communists have been convicted—state and local as well as national leaders of the party.]

Mr. Chief Justice Vinson:

Petitioners were indicted in July, 1948, for violation of the conspiracy provisions of the Smith Act, 54 Stat. 671, 18 U.S.C. (1946 ed.) § 11, during the period of April, 1945, to July, 1948. . . . A verdict of guilty as to all the petitioners was returned by the jury on October 14, 1949. The Court of Appeals affirmed the convictions. . . . We granted certiorari, . . . limited to the following two questions: (1) Whether either § 2 or § 3 of the Smith Act, inherently or as construed and applied in the instant case, violates the First Amendment and other provisions of the Bill of Rights; (2) whether either § 2 or § 3 of the Act, inherently or as construed and applied in the instant case, violates the First and Fifth Amendments because of indefiniteness.

Sections 2 and 3 of the Smith Act provide as follows:

Sec. 2.

(a) It shall be unlawful for any person—

(1) to knowingly or willfully advocate, abet, advise, or teach the duty, necessity, desirability, or propriety of overthrowing or destroying any government in the United States by force or violence, or by the assassination of any officer of any such government;

(2) with the intent to cause the overthrow or destruction of any government in the United States, to print, publish, edit, issue, circulate, sell, distribute, or publicly display any written or printed matter advocating, advising, or teaching the duty, necessity, desirability, or propriety of overthrowing or destroying any government in the United States by force or violence;

(3) to organize or help to organize any society, group, or assembly of persons who teach, advocate, or encourage the overthrow or destruction of any government in the United States by force or violence; or to be or become a member of, or affiliate with, any such society, group, or assembly of persons, knowing the purposes thereof.

(b) For the purposes of this section, the term "government in the United States" means the Government of the United States, the government of any State, Territory, or possession of the United States, the government of the

District of Columbia, or the government of any political sub-division of any of them.

Sec. 3. It shall be unlawful for any person to attempt to commit, or to conspire to commit, any of the acts prohibited by the provisions of . . . this title.

The indictment charged the petitioners with wilfully and knowingly conspiring (1) to organize as the Communist Party of the United States of America a society, group and assembly of persons who teach and advocate the overthrow and destruction of the Government of the United States by force and violence, and (2) knowingly and wilfully to advocate and teach the duty and necessity of overthrowing and destroying the Government of the United States by force and violence. The indictment further alleged that § 2 of the Smith Act proscribes these acts and that any conspiracy to take such action is a violation of § 3 of the Act.

The trial of the case extended over nine months, six of which were devoted to the taking of evidence, resulting in a record of 16,000 pages. Our limited grant of the writ of certiorari has removed from our consideration any question as to the sufficiency of the evidence to support the jury's determination that petitioners are guilty of the offense charged. Whether on this record petitioners did in fact advocate the overthrow of the Government by force and violence is not before us, and we must base any discussion of this point upon the conclusions stated in the opinion of the Court of Appeals, which treated the issue in great detail. That court held that the record in this case amply supports the necessary finding of the jury that petitioners, the leaders of the Communist Party in this country, were unwilling to work within our framework of democracy, but intended to initiate a violent revolution whenever the propitious occasion appeared. Petitioners dispute the meaning to be drawn from the evidence, contending that the Marxist-Leninist doctrine they advocated taught that force and violence to achieve a Communist form of government in an existing democratic state would be necessary only because the ruling classes of that state would never permit the transformation to be accomplished peacefully, but would use force and violence to defeat any peaceful political and economic gain the Communists could achieve. But the Court of Appeals held that the record supports the following broad conclusions: By virtue of their control over the political apparatus of the Communist Political Association, petitioners were able to transform that organization into the Communist Party; that the policies of the Association were changed from peaceful cooperation with the United States and its economic and political structure to a policy which had existed before the United States and the Soviet Union were fighting a common enemy, namely, a policy which worked for the overthrow of the Government by force and violence; that the Communist Party is a highly disciplined organization, adept at infiltration into strategic positions, use of aliases, and double-meaning language; that the Party is rigidly controlled; that Communists, unlike other political parties, tolerate no dissension from the policy laid down by the guiding forces, but that the approved program is slavishly followed by the members of the Party; that the literature of the Party and the statements and activities of its leaders . . . advocate, and the general goal of the Party was, during the period in question, to achieve a successful overthrow of the existing order by force and violence.

. . . The structure and purpose of the statute demand the inclusion of intent as an element of the crime. Congress was concerned with those who advocate and organize for the overthrow of the Government. Certainly those who recruit and combine for the purpose of advocating overthrow intend to bring about that overthrow. We hold that the statute requires as an essential element of the crime proof of the intent of those who are charged with its violation to overthrow the Government by force and violence. . . .

Nor does the fact that there must be an investigation of a state of mind under this interpretation afford any basis for rejection of that meaning. A survey of Title 18 of the U.S. Code indicates that the vast majority of the crimes designated by that Title require, by express language, proof of the existence of a certain mental state in words such as "knowingly," "maliciously," "wilfully," "with the purpose of," "with intent to," or combinations or permutations of these and synonymous terms. The existence of a *mens rea* is the rule of, rather than the exception to, the principles of Anglo-American criminal jurisprudence. . . .

The obvious purpose of the statute is to protect existing Government, not from change by peaceable, lawful and constitutional means, but from change by violence, revolution and terrorism. That it is within the *power* of the Congress to protect the Government of the United States from armed rebellion is a proposition which requires little discussion. Whatever theoretical merit there may be to the argument that there is a "right" to rebellion against dictatorial governments is without force where the existing structure of the government provides for peaceful and orderly change. We reject any principle of governmental helplessness in the face of preparation for revolution, which principle, carried to its logical conclusion, must lead to anarchy. No one could conceive that it is not within the power of Congress to prohibit acts intended to overthrow the Government by force and violence. The question with which we are concerned here is not whether Congress has such *power,* but whether the *means* which it has employed conflict with the First and Fifth Amendments to the Constitution.

One of the bases for the contention that the means which Congress has employed are invalid takes the form of an attack on the face of the statute on the grounds that by its terms it prohibits academic discussion of the merits of Marxism-Leninism, that it stifles ideas and is contrary to all concepts of a free speech and a free press. . . .

The very language of the Smith Act negates the interpretation which petitioners would have us impose on that Act. It is directed at advocacy, not discussion. Thus, the trial judge properly charged the jury that they could not convict if they found that petitioners did "no more than pursue peaceful studies and discussions or teaching and advocacy in the realm of ideas." He further charged that it was not unlawful "to conduct in an American college and university a course explaining the philosophical theories set forth in the books which have been placed in evidence." Such a charge is in strict accord with the statutory language, and illustrates the meaning to be placed on those words. Congress did not intend to eradicate the free discussion of political theories, to destroy the traditional rights of Americans to discuss and evaluate ideas without fear of governmental sanction. Rather Congress was concerned with the very kind of activity in which the evidence showed these petitioners engaged.

. . . The basis of the First Amendment is the hypothesis that speech can rebut speech, propaganda will answer propaganda, free debate of ideas will result in the wisest governmental policies. It is for this reason that this Court has recognized the inherent value of free discourse. An analysis of the leading cases in this Court which have involved direct limitations on speech, however, will demonstrate that both the majority of the Court and the dissenters in particular cases have recognized that this is not an unlimited, unqualified right, but that the societal value of speech must, on occasion, be subordinated to other values and considerations. . . .

The rule we deduce from these cases is that where an offense is specified by a statute in nonspeech or nonpress terms, a conviction relying upon speech or press as evidence of violation may be sustained only when the speech or publication created a "clear and present danger" of attempting or accomplishing the prohibited crime, e.g., interference with enlistment. . . .

. . . Neither Justice Holmes nor Justice Brandeis ever envisioned that a shorthand phrase should be crystallized into a rigid rule to be applied inflexibly without regard to the circumstances of each case. Speech is not an absolute, above and beyond control by the legislature when its judgment, subject to review here, is that certain kinds of speech are so undesirable as to warrant criminal sanction. Nothing is more certain in modern society than the principle that there are no absolutes, that a name, a phrase, a standard has meaning only when associated with the considerations which gave birth to the nomenclature. . . . To those who would paralyze our Government in the face of impending threat by encasing it in a semantic straitjacket we must reply that all concepts are relative.

. . . In this case we are squarely presented with the application of the "clear and present danger" test, and must decide what that phrase imports. We first note that many of the cases in which this Court has reversed convictions by use of this or similar tests have been based on the fact that the interest which the State was attempting to protect was itself too insubstantial to warrant restriction of speech. . . . Overthrow of the Government by force and violence is certainly a substantial enough interest for the Government to limit speech. Indeed, this is the ultimate value of any society, for if a society cannot protect its very structure from armed internal attack, it must follow that no subordinate value can be protected. If, then, this interest may be protected, the literal problem which is presented is what has been meant by the use of the phrase "clear and present danger" of the utterances bringing about the evil within the power of Congress to punish.

. . . Obviously, the words cannot mean that before the Government may act, it must wait until the *putsch* is about to be executed, the plans have been laid and the signal is awaited. If Government is aware that a group aiming at its overthrow is attempting to indoctrinate its members and to commit them to a course whereby they will strike when the leaders feel the circumstances permit, action by the Government is required. The argument that there is no need for Government to concern itself, for Government is strong, it possesses ample powers to put down a rebellion, it may defeat the revolution with ease needs no answer. For that is not the question. Certainly an attempt to overthrow the Government by force, even though doomed from the outset because of inadequate numbers or power of the revolutionists, is a sufficient evil for Congress to prevent. The damage which such attempts create both physically and politically to a nation makes it impossible to measure the validity in terms of the probability of success, or the immediacy of a successful attempt. In the instant case the trial judge charged the jury that they could not convict unless they found that petitioners intended to overthrow the Government "as speedily as circumstances would permit." This does not mean, and could not properly mean, that they would not strike until there was certainty of success. What was meant was that the revolutionists would strike when they thought the time was ripe. We must therefore reject the contention that success or probability of success is the criterion.

. . . Chief Judge Learned Hand, writing for the majority below, interpreted the phrase as follows: "In each case [courts] must ask whether the gravity of the 'evil,' discounted by its improbability, justifies such invasion of free speech as is necessary to avoid the danger."

. . . We adopt this statement of the rule. As articulated by Chief Judge Hand, it is as succinct and inclusive as any other we might devise at this time. It takes into consideration those factors which we deem relevant, and relates their significances. More we cannot expect from words.

. . . Likewise, we are in accord with the court below, which affirmed the trial court's finding that the requisite danger existed. The mere fact that from the period 1945 to 1948 petitioners' activities did not result in an attempt to overthrow the Government by force and violence is of course no answer to the fact that there was a group that was ready to make the attempt. The formation by petitioners of such a highly organized conspiracy, with rigidly disciplined members subject to call when the leaders, these petitioners, felt that the time had come for action, coupled with the inflammable nature of world conditions, similar uprisings in other countries, and the touch-and-go nature of our relations with countries with whom petitioners were in the very least ideologically attuned, convince us that their convictions were justified on this score. And this analysis disposes of the contention that a conspiracy to advocate, as distinguished from the advocacy itself, cannot be constitutionally restrained, because it comprises only the preparation. It is the existence of the conspiracy which creates the danger. . . . If the ingredients of the reaction are present, we cannot bind the Government to wait until the catalyst is added.

. . . Although we have concluded that the finding that there was a sufficient danger to warrant the application of the statute was justified on the merits, there remains the problem of whether the trial judge's treatment of the issue was correct. He charged the jury, in relevant part, as follows: . . .

If you are satisfied that the evidence establishes beyond a reasonable doubt that the defendants, or any of them, are guilty of a violation of the statute as I have interpreted it to you, I find as a matter of law that there is sufficient danger of a substantive evil that the Congress has a right to prevent to justify the application of the statute under the First Amendment of the Constitution.

This is matter of law about which you have no concern. It is a finding on a matter of law which I deem essential to support my ruling that the case should be submitted to you to pass upon the guilt or innocence of the defendants. . . .

It is thus clear that he reserved the question of the existence of the danger for his own determination, and the question becomes whether the issue is of such a nature that it should have been submitted to the jury.

. . . The argument that the action of the trial court is erroneous, in declaring as a matter of law that such violation shows sufficient danger to justify the punishment despite the First Amendment, rests on the theory that a jury must decide a question of the application of the First Amendment. We do not agree. . . .

The question in this case is whether the statute which the legislature has enacted may be constitutionally applied. In other words, the Court must examine judicially the application of the statute to the particular situation, to ascertain if the Constitution prohibits the conviction. We hold that the statute may be applied where there is a "clear and present danger" of the substantive evil which the legislature had the right to prevent. Bearing, as it does, the marks of a "question of law," the issue is properly one for the judge to decide.

There remains to be discussed the question of vagueness—whether the statute as we have interpreted it is too vague, not sufficiently advising those who would speak of the limitations upon their activity. It is urged that such vagueness contravenes the First and Fifth Amendments. . . .

We agree that the standard as defined is not a neat, mathematical formulary. Like all verbalizations it is subject to criticism on the score of indefiniteness. But petitioners themselves contend that the verbalization, "clear and present danger," is the proper standard. We see no difference from the standpoint of vagueness, whether the standard of "clear and present danger" is one contained in *haec verba* within the statute, or whether it is the judicial measure of constitutional applicability. We have shown the indeterminate standard the phrase necessarily connotes. We do not think we have rendered that standard any more indefinite by our attempt to sum up the factors which are included within its scope. We think it well serves to indicate to those who would advocate constitutionally prohibited conduct that there is a line beyond which they may not go—a line, which they, in full knowledge of what they intend and the circumstances in which their activity takes place, will well appreciate and understand. . . .

We hold that §§ 2(a) (1), 2(a) (3) and 3 of the Smith Act, do not inherently, or as construed or applied in the instant case, violate the

First Amendment and other provisions of the Bill of Rights, or the First and Fifth Amendments because of indefiniteness. Petitioners intended to overthrow the Government of the United States as speedily as the circumstances would permit. Their conspiracy to organize the Communist Party and to teach and advocate the overthrow of the Government of the United States by force and violence created a "clear and present danger" of an attempt to overthrow the Government by force and violence. They were properly and constitutionally convicted for violation of the Smith Act. The judgments of conviction are affirmed.

Mr. Justice Frankfurter, concurring in affirmance of the judgment:

. . . Few questions of comparable import have come before this Court in recent years. The appellants maintain that they have a right to advocate a political theory, so long, at least, as their advocacy does not create an immediate danger of obvious magnitude to the very existence of our present scheme of society. On the other hand, the Government asserts the right to safeguard the security of the Nation by such a measure as the Smith Act. Our judgment is thus solicited on a conflict of interests of the utmost concern to the well-being of the country. This conflict of interests cannot be resolved by a dogmatic preference for one or the other, nor by a sonorous formula which is in fact only a euphemistic disguise for an unresolved conflict. If adjudication is to be a rational process we cannot escape a candid examination of the conflicting claims with full recognition that both are supported by weighty title-deeds.

1.

. . . Our whole history proves even more decisively than the course of decisions in this Court that the United States has the powers inseparable from a sovereign nation. "America has chosen to be, in many respects, and to many purposes, a nation; and for all these purposes, her government is complete; to all these objects, it is competent." Chief Justice Marshall in *Cohens* v. *Virginia,* 6 Wheat. 264. The right of a government to maintain its existence—self-preservation—is the most pervasive aspect of sovereignty. "Security against foreign danger," wrote Madison, "is one of the primitive objects of civil society." *The Federalist,* No. 41. The constitutional power to act upon this basic principle has been recognized by this Court at different periods and under diverse circumstances. . . . The most tragic experience in our history is a poignant reminder that the Nation's continued existence may be threatened from within. To protect itself from such threats, the Federal Government "is invested with all those inherent and implied powers which, at the time of adopting the Constitution, were generally considered to belong to every government as such, and as being essential to the exercise of its functions." Mr. Justice Bradley, concurring in *Legal Tender Cases,* 12 Wall. 457. . . .

But even the all-embracing power and duty of self-preservation is not absolute. Like the war power, which is indeed an aspect of the power of self-preservation, it is subject to applicable constitutional limitations. . . . Our Constitution has no provision lifting restrictions upon governmental authority during periods of emergency, although the scope of a restriction may depend on the circumstances in which it is invoked.

The First Amendment is such a restriction. It exacts obedience even during periods of war; it is applicable when war clouds are not figments of the imagination no less than when they are. The First Amendment categorically demands that "Congress shall make no law respecting an establishment of religion, or prohibiting the free exercise thereof; or abridging the freedom of speech, or of the press; or the right of the people peaceably to assemble, and to petition the Government for a redress of grievances." The right of a man to think what he pleases, to write what he thinks, and to have his thoughts made available for others to hear or read has an engaging ring of universality. The Smith Act and this conviction under it no doubt restrict the exercise of free speech and assembly. Does that, without more, dispose of the matter?

Just as there are those who regard as invulnerable every measure for which the claim of national survival is invoked, there are those who find in the Constitution a wholly unfettered right of expression. Such literalness treats the words of the Constitution as though they were found on a piece of outworn parchment instead of being words that have called into being a nation with a past to be preserved for the future. The soil in which the Bill of Rights grew was not a soil of arid pedantry. The historic antecedents of the First Amendment preclude the notion that its purpose was to give unqualified immunity to every expression that touched on matters within the range of political interest. . . .

The language of the First Amendment is to be read not as barren words found in a dictionary but as symbols of historic experience illumined by the presuppositions of those who employed them. Not what words did Madison and Hamilton use, but what was it in their minds which they conveyed? Free speech is subject to prohibition of those abuses of expression which a civilized society may forbid. As in the case of every other provision of the Constitution that is not crystallized by the nature of its technical concepts, the fact that the First Amendment is not self-defining and self-enforcing neither impairs its usefulness nor compels its paralysis as a living instrument.

"The law is perfectly well settled," this Court said over fifty years ago, "that the first 10 amendments to the constitution, commonly known as the 'Bill of Rights,' were not intended to lay down any novel principles of government, but simply to embody certain guaranties and immunities which we had inherited from our English ancestors, and which had, from time immemorial, been subject to certain well-recognized exceptions, arising from the necessities of the case. In incorporating these principles into the fundamental law, there was no intention of disregarding the exceptions, which continued to be recognized as if they had been formally expressed." *Robertson* v. *Baldwin*, 165 U.S. 275. That this represents the authentic view of the Bill of Rights and the spirit in which it must be construed has been recognized again and again in cases that have come here within the last fifty years. . . . Absolute rules would inevitably lead to absolute exceptions, and such exceptions would eventually corrode the rules. The demands of free speech in a democratic society as well as the interest in national security are better served by candid and informed weighing of the competing interests, within the confines of the judicial process, than by announcing dogmas too inflexible for the non-Euclidian problems to be solved.

But how are competing interests to be assessed? Since they are not subject to quantitative ascertainment, the issue necessarily resolves itself into asking, who is to make the adjustment?—who is to balance the relevant factors and ascertain which interest is in the circumstances to prevail? Full responsibility for the choice cannot be given to the courts. Courts are not representative bodies. They are not designed to be a good reflex of a democratic society. Their judgment is best informed, and therefore most dependable, within narrow limits. Their essential quality is detachment, founded on independence. History teaches that the independence of the judiciary is jeopardized when courts become embroiled in the passions of the day and assume primary responsibility in choosing between competing political, economic and social pressures.

Primary responsibility for adjusting the interests which compete in the situation before us of necessity belongs to the Congress. The nature of the power to be exercised by this Court has been delineated in decisions not charged with the emotional appeal of situations such as that now before us. We are to set aside the judgment of those whose duty it is to legislate only if there is no reasonable basis for it. . . . We must scrupulously observe the narrow limits of judicial authority even though self-restraint is alone set over us. Above all we must remember that this Court's power of judicial review is not "an exercise of the powers of a super-Legislature." Mr. Justice Brandeis and Mr. Justice Holmes, dissenting in *Jay Burns Baking Co.* v. *Bryan,* 264 U.S. 504. . . .

In reviewing statutes which restrict freedoms protected by the First Amendment, we have emphasized the close relation which those freedoms bear to maintenance of a free society. . . . Some members of the Court—and at times a majority—have done more. They have suggested that our function in reviewing statutes restricting freedom of expression differs sharply from our normal duty in sitting in judgment on legislation. It has been said that such statutes "must be justified by clear public interest, threatened not doubtedly or remotely, but by clear and present danger. The rational connection between the remedy provided and the evil to be curbed, which in other contexts might support legislation against attack on due process grounds, will not suffice." *Thomas* v. *Collins,* 323 U.S. 516. It has been suggested, with the casualness of a footnote, that such legislation is not presumptively valid, see *United States* v. *Carolene Products Co.,* 304 U.S. 144, and it has been weightily reiterated that freedom of speech has a "preferred position" among constitutional safeguards. *Kovacs* v. *Cooper,* 336 U.S. 77.

The precise meaning intended to be conveyed by these phrases need not now be pursued. It is enough to note that they have recurred in the Court's opinions, and their cumulative force has, not without justification, engendered belief that there is a constitutional principle, expressed by those attractive but imprecise words, prohibiting restriction upon utterance unless it creates a situation of "imminent" peril against which legislation may guard. It is on this body of the Court's pronouncements that the defendants' argument here is based. . . .

II.

We have recognized and resolved conflicts between speech and competing interests in six different types of cases.

1. The cases involving a conflict between the interest in allowing free expression of ideas in public places and the interest in protection of the public peace and the primary uses of streets and parks, were too recently considered to be rehearsed here. *Niemotko* v. *State of Maryland*, 340 U.S. 268. It suffices to recall that the result in each case was found to turn on the character of the interest with which the speech clashed, the method used to impose the restriction, and the nature and circumstances of the utterance prohibited. While the decisions recognized the importance of free speech and carefully scrutinized the justification for its regulation, they rejected the notion that vindication of the deep public interest in freedom of expression requires subordination of all conflicting values.

2. A critique of the cases testing restrictions on picketing is made more difficult by the inadequate recognition by the Court from the outset that the loyalties and responses evoked and exacted by picket lines differentiate this form of expression from other modes of communication. See *Thornhill* v. *Alabama*, 310 U.S. 88. But the crux of the decision in the *Thornhill Case* was that a State could not constitutionally punish peaceful picketing when neither the aim of the picketing nor the manner in which it was carried out conflicted with a substantial interest. In subsequent decisions we sustained restrictions designed to prevent recurrence of violence, *Milk Wagon Drivers Union* v. *Meadowmoor Dairies*, 312 U.S. 287, or reasonably to limit the area of industrial strife, *Carpenters & Joiners Union* v. *Ritter's Cafe*, 315 U.S. 722; cf. *Bakery & Pastry Drivers Local* v. *Wohl*, 315 U.S. 769. We held that a State's policy against restraints of trade justified it in prohibiting picketing which violated that policy, *Giboney* v. *Empire Storage Co.*, 336 U.S. 490; we sustained restrictions designed to encourage self-employed persons, *International Brotherhood of Teamsters Union* v. *Hanke*, 339 U.S. 470; and to prevent racial discrimination, *Hughes* v. *Superior Court*, 339 U.S. 460. The Fourteenth Amendment bars a State from prohibiting picketing when there is no fair justification for the breadth of the restriction imposed. *American Federation of Labor* v. *Swing*, 312 U.S. 321; *Cafeteria Employees Union* v. *Angelos*, 320 U.S. 293. . . . But it does not prevent a State from denying the means of communication that picketing affords in a fair balance between the interests of trade unionism and other interests of the community.

3. In three cases we have considered the scope and application of the power of the Government to exclude, deport, or denaturalize aliens because of their advocacy or their beliefs. In *Turner* v. *Williams*, 194 U.S. 279, we held that the First Amendment did not disable Congress from directing

the exclusion of an alien found in an administrative proceeding to be an anarchist. "[A]s long as human governments endure," we said, "they cannot be denied the power of self-preservation, as that question is presented here." . . .

4. History regards "freedom of the press" as indispensable for a free society and for its government. We have, therefore, invalidated discriminatory taxation against the press and prior restraints on publication of defamatory matter. *Grosjean* v. *American Press Co.,* 297 U.S. 233; *Near* v. *Minnesota,* 283 U.S. 697.

We have also given clear indication of the importance we attach to dissemination of ideas in reviewing the attempts of States to reconcile freedom of the press with protection of the integrity of the judicial process. In *Pennekamp* v. *Florida,* 328 U.S. 331, the Court agreed that the Fourteenth Amendment barred a State from adjudging in contempt of court the publisher of critical and inaccurate comment about portions of a litigation that for all practical purposes were no longer pending. We likewise agreed, in a minor phase of our decision in *Bridges* v. *California,* 314 U.S. 252, that even when statements in the press relate to matters still pending before a court, convictions for their publication cannot be sustained if their utterance is too trivial to be deemed a substantial threat to the impartial administration of justice.

The Court has, however, sharply divided on what constitutes a sufficient interference with the course of justice. In the first decision, *Patterson* v. *Colorado,* 205 U.S. 454, the Court affirmed a judgment for contempt imposed by a State supreme court for publication of articles reflecting on the conduct of the court in cases still before it on motions for rehearing. In the *Bridges Case,* however, a majority held that a State court could not protect itself from the implied threat of a powerful newspaper that failure of an elected judge to impose a severe sentence would be a "serious mistake." The same case also placed beyond a State's power to punish the publication of a telegram from the president of an important union who threatened a damaging strike in the event of an adverse decision. The majority in *Craig* v. *Harney,* 331 U.S. 367, held that the Fourteenth Amendment protected "strong," "intemperate," "unfair" criticism of the way an elected lay judge was conducting a pending civil case. None of the cases establishes that the public interest in a free press must in all instances prevail over the public interest in dispassionate adjudication. But the *Bridges* and *Craig* decisions, if they survive, tend to require a showing that interference be so imminent and so demonstrable that the power theoretically possessed by the State is largely paralyzed.

5. Our decision in *American Communications Ass'n* v. *Douds,* 339 U.S. 382, recognized that the exercise of political rights protected by the First Amendment was necessarily discouraged by the requirement of the Taft-Hartley Act that officers of unions employing the services of the National Labor Relations Board sign affidavits that they are not Communists. But we held that the statute was not for this reason presumptively invalid. The problem, we said, was "one of weighing the probable effects of the statute

upon the free exercise of the right of speech and assembly against the congressional determination that political strikes are evils of conduct which cause substantial harm to interstate commerce and that Communists and others identified by § 9 (h) pose continuing threats to that public interest when in positions of union leadership." . . . On balance, we decided that the legislative judgment was a permissible one.

6. Statutes prohibiting speech because of its tendency to lead to crime present a conflict of interests which bears directly on the problem now before us. The first case in which we considered this conflict was *Fox* v. *Washington*, 236 U.S. 273. The statute there challenged had been interpreted to prohibit publication of matter "encouraging an actual breach of law." We held that the Fourteenth Amendment did not prohibit application of the statute to an article which we concluded incited a breach of laws against indecent exposure. We said that the statute "lays hold of encouragements that, apart from statute, if directed to a particular person's conduct, generally would make him who uttered them guilty of a misdemeanor if not an accomplice or a principal in the crime encouraged, and deals with the publication of them to a wider and less selected audience." To be sure, the *Fox Case* preceded the explicit absorption of the substance of the First Amendment in the Fourteenth. But subsequent decisions extended the *Fox* principle to free-speech situations. They are so important to the problem before us that we must consider them in detail.

(a) The first important application of the principle was made in six cases arising under the Espionage Act of 1917. That Act prohibits conspiracies and attempts to "obstruct the recruiting or enlistment service." In each of the first three cases Mr. Justice Holmes wrote for a unanimous Court, affirming the convictions. The evidence in *Schenck* v. *United States*, 249 U.S. 47, showed that the defendant had conspired to circulate among men called for the draft 15,000 copies of a circular which asserted a "right" to oppose the draft. The defendant in *Frohwerk* v. *United States*, 249 U.S. 204, was shown to have conspired to publish in a newspaper twelve articls describing the sufferings of American troops and the futility of our war aims. The record was inadequate, and we said that it was therefore "impossible to say that it might not have been found that the circulation of the paper was in quarters where a little breath would be enough to kindle a flame and that the fact was known and relied upon by those who sent the paper out." In *Debs* v. *United States*, 249 U.S. 211, the indictment charged that the defendant had delivered a public speech expounding socialism and praising Socialists who had been convicted of abetting violation of the draft laws.

The ground of decision in each case was the same. The First Amendment "cannot have been, and obviously was not, intended to give immunity for every possible use of language. . . ." *Frohwerk* v. *United States*. . . . "The question in every case is whether the words used in such circumstances and are of such a nature as to create a clear and present danger that they will bring about the substantive evils that Congress has a right to prevent. It is a question of proximity and degree." *Schenck* v. *United States*. . . . When "the words used had as their natural tendency and reasonably probable effect to obstruct the recruiting service," and "the defendant had the specific intent to do so in his mind," conviction in wartime is not prohibited by the Constitution. *Debs* v. *United States.*

In the three succeeding cases Holmes and Brandeis, JJ., dissented from judgments of the Court affirming convictions. The indictment in *Abrams* v. *United States,* 250 U.S. 616, was laid under an amendment to the Espionage Act which prohibited conspiracies to advocate curtailment of production of material necessary to prosecution of the war, with the intent thereby to hinder the United States in the prosecution of the war. It appeared that the defendants were anarchists who had printed circulars and distributed them in New York City. The leaflets repeated standard Marxist slogans, condemned American intervention in Russia, and called for a general strike in protest. In *Schaefer* v. *United States,* 251 U.S. 466, the editors of a German language newspaper in Philadelphia were charged with obstructing the recruiting service and with wilfully publishing false reports with the intent to promote the success of the enemies of the United States. The evidence showed publication of articles which accused American troops of weakness and mendacity and in one instance misquoted or mistranslated two words of a Senator's speech. The indictment in *Pierce* v. *United States,* 252 U.S. 239, charged that the defendants had attempted to cause insubordination in the armed forces and had conveyed false reports with intent to interfere with military operations. Conviction was based on circulation of a pamphlet which belittled Allied war aims and criticized conscription in strong terms.

In each case both the majority and the dissenting opinions relied on *Schenck* v. *United States.* The Court divided on its view of the evidence. The majority held that the jury could infer the required intent and the probable effect of the articles from their content. Holmes and Brandeis, JJ., thought that only "expressions of opinion and exhortations," were involved, that they were "puny anonymities," "impotent to produce the evil against which the statute aimed," and that from them the specific intent required by the statute could not reasonably be inferred. The Court agreed that an incitement to disobey the draft statute could constitutionally be punished. It disagreed over the proof required to show such an incitement.

(b) In the eyes of a majority of the Court, *Gitlow* v. *New York,* 268 U.S. 652, presented a very different problem. There the defendant had been convicted under a New York statute nearly identical to the Smith Act now before us. The evidence showed that the defendant was an official of the Left Wing Section of the Socialist Party, and that he was responsible for publication of a Left Wing Manifesto. This document repudiated "moderate Socialism," and urged the necessity of a militant "revolutionary Socialism," based on class struggle and revolutionary mass action. No evidence of the effect of the Manifesto was introduced; but the jury was instructed that they could not convict unless they found that the document advocated employing unlawful acts for the purpose of overthrowing organized government.

The conviction was affirmed. The question, the Court held, was entirely different from that involved in *Schenck* v. *United States,* where the statute prohibited acts without reference to language. Here, where "the legislative body has determined generally, in the constitutional exercise of its discretion, that utterances of a certain kind involve such danger of substantive evil that they may be punished, the question whether any specific utterance coming within the prohibited class is likely, in and of itself, to bring about the substantive evil, is not open to consideration." It is sufficient that the defendant's conduct falls within the statute, and that the statute is a reasonable exercise of legislative judgment.

This principle was also applied in *Whitney* v. *California*, 274 U.S. 357, to sustain a conviction under a State criminal syndicalism statute. That statute made it a felony to assist in organizing a group assembled to advocate the commission of crime, sabotage, or unlawful acts of violence as a means of effecting political or industrial change. The defendant was found to have assisted in organizing the Communist Labor Party of California, an organization found to have the specified character. It was held that the legislature was not unreasonable in believing organization of such a party "involves such danger to the public peace and the security of the State, that these acts should be penalized in the exercise of its police power."

In neither of these cases did Mr. Justice Holmes and Mr. Justice Brandeis accept the reasoning of the Court. " 'The question,' " they said, quoting from *Schenck* v. *United States*, " 'in every case is whether the words used are used in such circumstances and are of such a nature as to create a clear and present danger that they will bring about the substantive evils that [the State] has a right to prevent.' " Since the manifesto circulated by Gitlow "had no chance of starting a present conflagration," they dissented from the affirmance of his conviction. In *Whitney* v. *California*, they concurred in the result reached by the Court, but only because the record contained some evidence that organization of the Communist Labor Party might further a conspiracy to commit immediate serious crimes, and the credibility of the evidence was not put in issue by the defendant.

(c) Subsequent decisions have added little to the principles established in these two groups of cases. In the only case arising under the Espionage Act decided by this Court during the last war, the substantiality of the evidence was the crucial issue. The defendant in *Hartzel* v. *United States*, 322 U.S. 680, was an educated man and a citizen, not actively affiliated with any political group. In 1942 he wrote three articles condemning our wartime allies and urging that the war be converted into a racial conflict. He mailed the tracts to 600 people, including high-ranking military officers. According to his testimony his intention was to "create sentiment against war amongst the white races." The majority of this Court held that a jury could not reasonably infer from these facts that the defendant had acted with a specific intent to cause insubordination or disloyalty in the armed forces.

Of greater importance is the fact that the issue of law which divided the Court in the *Gitlow* and *Whitney Cases* has not again been clearly raised, although in four additional instances we have reviewed convictions under comparable statutes. *Fiske* v. *Kansas*, 274 U.S. 380, involved a criminal syndicalism statute similar to that before us in *Whitney* v. *California*. We reversed a conviction based on evidence that the defendant exhibited an innocuous preamble to the constitution of the Industrial Workers of the World in soliciting members for that organization. In *Herndon* v. *Lowry,* 301 U.S. 242, the defendant had solicited members for the Communist Party, but there was no proof that he had urged or even approved those of the Party's aims which were unlawful. We reversed a conviction obtained under a statute prohibiting an attempt to incite to insurrection by violence, on the ground that the Fourteenth Amendment prohibited conviction where on the evidence a jury could not reasonably infer that the defendant had violated the statute the State sought to apply.

The other two decisions go no further than to hold that the statute as construed by the State courts exceeded the bounds of a legislative judgment founded in reason. The statute presented in *De Jonge* v. *Oregon, 299 U.S.* 353, had been construed to apply to anyone who merely assisted in the conduct of a meeting held under the auspices of the Communist Party. In *Taylor* v. *Mississippi,* 319 U.S. 583, the statute prohibited dissemination of printed matter "designed and calculated to encourage violence, sabotage, or disloyalty to the government of the United States, or the state of Mississippi." We reversed a conviction for what we concluded was mere criticism and prophecy, without indicating whether we thought the statute could in any circumstances validly be applied. What the defendants communicated, we said, "is not claimed or shown to have been done with an evil or sinister purpose, to have advocated or incited subversive action against the nation or state, or to have threatened any clear and present danger to our institutions or our government."

I must leave to others the ungrateful task of trying to reconcile all these decisions. In some instances we have too readily permitted juries to infer deception from error, or intention from argumentative or critical statements. . . . In other instances we weighted the interest in free speech so heavily that we permitted essential conflicting values to be destroyed. . . . Viewed as a whole, however, the decisions express an attitude toward the judicial function and a standard of values which for me are decisive of the case before us.

First.—Free-speech cases are not an exception to the principle that we are not legislators, that direct policy-making is not our province. How best to reconcile competing interests is the business of legislatures, and the balance they strike is a judgment not to be displaced by ours, but to be respected unless outside the pale of fair judgment.

On occasion we have strained to interpret legislation in order to limit its effect on interests protected by the First Amendment. . . . In some instances we have denied to States the deference to which I think they are entitled. . . . Once in this recent course of decisions the Court refused to permit a jury to draw inferences which seemed to me to be obviously reasonable. . . .

But in no case has a majority of this Court held that a legislative judgment, even as to freedom of utterance, may be overturned merely because the Court would have made a different choice between the competing interests had the initial legislative judgment been for it to make. In the cases in which the opinions go farthest towards indicating a total rejection of respect for legislative determinations, the interests between which choice was actually made were such that decision might well have been expressed in the familiar terms of want of reason in the legislative judgment. . . .

In other cases, moreover, we have given clear indication that even when free speech is involved we attach great significance to the determination of the legislature. . . .

In *Gitlow* v. *New York*, we put our respect for the legislative judgment in terms which, if they were accepted here, would make decision easy. For that case held that when the legislature has determined that advocacy of forceful overthrow should be forbidden, a conviction may be sustained without a finding that in the particular case the advocacy had a close relation to a serious attempt at overthrow. We held that it was enough that the statute be a reasonable exercise of the legislative judgment, and that the defendant's conduct fall within the statute.

One of the judges below rested his affirmance on the *Gitlow* decision, and the defendants do not attempt to distinguish the case. They place their argument squarely on the ground that the case has been overruled by subsequent decisions. It has not been explicitly overruled. But it would be disingenuous to deny that the dissent in *Gitlow* has been treated with the respect usually accorded to a decision.

The result of the *Gitlow* decision was to send a left-wing Socialist to jail for publishing a Manifesto expressing Marxist exhortations. It requires excessive tolerance of the legislative judgment to suppose that the *Gitlow* publication in the circumstances could justify serious concern.

In contrast, there is ample justification for a legislative judgment that the conspiracy now before us is a substantial threat to national order and security. If the Smith Act is justified at all, it is justified precisely because it may serve to prohibit the type of conspiracy for which these defendants were convicted. The court below properly held that as a matter of separability the Smith Act may be limited to those situations to which it can constitutionally be applied. . . . Our decision today certainly does not mean that the Smith Act can constitutionally be applied to facts like those in *Gitlow* v. *New York*. While reliance may properly be placed on the attitude of judicial self-restraint which the *Gitlow* decision reflects, it is not necessary to depend on the facts or the full extent of the theory of the case in order to find that the judgment of Congress, as applied to the facts of the case now before us, is not in conflict with the First Amendment.

Second.—A survey of the relevant decisions indicates that the results which we have reached are on the whole those that would ensue from careful weighing of conflicting interests. The complex issues presented by regulation of speech in public places, by picketing, and by legislation prohibiting advocacy of crime have been resolved by scrutiny of many factors besides the imminence and gravity of the evil threatened. The matter has been well summarized by a reflective student of the Court's work. "The truth is that the clear-and-present-danger test is an over-simplified judgment unless it takes account also of a number of other factors: the relative seriousness of the danger in comparison with the value of the occasion for speech or political activity; the availability of more moderate controls than those which the state has imposed; and perhaps the specific intent with which the speech or activity is launched. No matter how rapidly we utter the phrase 'clear and present danger,' or how closely we hyphenate the words, they are not a substitute for the weighing of values. They tend to convey a delusion of certitude when what is most certain is the complexity of the strands in the web of freedoms which the judge must disentangle." Freund, *On Understanding the Supreme Court*, 27–28.

It is a familiar experience in the law that new situations do not fit neatly into legal conceptions that arose under different circumstances to satisfy different needs. So it was when the injunction was tortured into an instrument of expression against labor in industrial conflicts. So it is with the attempt to use the direction of thought lying behind the criterion of "clear and present danger" wholly out of the context in which it originated, and to make of it an absolute dogma and definitive measuring rod for the power of Congress to deal with assaults against security through devices other than overt physical attempts.

Bearing in mind that Mr. Justice Holmes regarded questions under the First Amendment as questions of "proximity and degree," *Schenck* v. *United States*, it would be a distortion, indeed a mockery, of his reasoning to compare the "puny anonymities," to which he was addressing himself in the *Abrams Case* in 1919 or the publication that was "futile and too remote from possible consequences" in the *Gitlow Case* in 1925 with the setting of events in this case in 1950.

"It does an ill-service to the author of the most quoted judicial phrases regarding freedom of speech, to make him the victim of a tendency which he fought all his life, whereby phrases are made to do service for critical analysis by being turned into dogma. 'It is one of the misfortunes of the law that ideas become encysted in phrases and thereafter for a long time cease to provoke further analysis.' Holmes, J., dissenting, in *Hyde* v. *United States*, 225 U.S. 347." The phrase "clear and present danger," in its origin, "served to indicate the importance of freedom of speech to a free society but also to emphasize that its exercise must be compatible with the preservation of other freedoms essential to a democracy and guaranteed by our Constitution." *Pennekamp* v. *Florida* (concurring). It were far better that the phrase be abandoned than that it be sounded once more to hide from the believers in an absolute right of free speech the plain fact that the interest in speech, profoundly important as it is, is no more conclusive in judicial review than other attributes of democracy or than a determination of the people's representatives that a measure is necessary to assure the safety of government itself.

Third.—Not every type of speech occupies the same position on the scale of values. There is no substantial public interest in permitting certain kinds of utterances: "the lewd and obscene, the profane, the libelous, and the insulting or 'fighting' words—those which by their very utterance inflict injury or tend to incite an immediate breach of the peace." *Chaplinsky* v.

New Hampshire, 315 U.S. 568. We have frequently indicated that the interest in protecting speech depends on the circumstances of the occasion. . . . It is pertinent to the decision before us to consider where on the scale of values we have in the past placed the type of speech now claiming constitutional immunity.

The defendants have been convicted of conspiring to organize a party of persons who advocate the overthrow of the Government by force and violence. The jury has found that the object of the conspiracy is advocacy as "a rule or principle of action," "by language reasonably and ordinarily calculated to incite persons to such action," and with the intent to cause the overthrow "as speedily as circumstances would permit."

On any scale of values which we have hitherto recognized, speech of this sort ranks low.

Throughout our decisions there has recurred a distinction between the statement of an idea which may prompt its hearers to take unlawful action, and advocacy that such action be taken. The distinction has its root in the conception of the common law that a person who procures another to do an act is responsible for that act as though he had done it himself. This principle was extended in *Fox* v. *Washington, supra,* to words directed to the public generally which would constitute an incitement were they directed to an individual. It was adopted in *Schenck* v. *United States, supra,* into a rule of evidence designed to restrict application of the Espionage Act. It was relied on by the Court in *Gitlow* v. *New York, supra.* The distinction has been repeated in many of the decisions in which we have upheld the claims of speech. We frequently have distinguished protected forms of expression from statements which "incite to violence and crime and threaten the overthrow of organized government by unlawful means." . . .

It is true that there is no divining rod by which we may locate "advocacy." Exposition of ideas readily merges into advocacy. The same Justice who gave currency to application of the incitement doctrine in this field dissented four times from what he thought was its misapplication. As he said in the *Gitlow* dissent, "Every idea is an incitement." Even though advocacy of overthrow deserves little protection, we should hesitate to prohibit it if we thereby inhibit the interchange of rational ideas so essential to representative government and free society.

But there is underlying validity in the distinction between advocacy and the interchange of ideas, and we do not discard a useful tool because it may be misused. That such a distinction could be used unreasonably by those in power against hostile or unorthodox views does not negate the fact that it may be used reasonably against an organization wielding the power of the centrally controlled international Communist movement. The object of the conspiracy before us is clear enough that the chance of error in saying that the defendants conspired to advocate rather than to express ideas is slight. Mr. Justice Douglas quite properly points out that the conspiracy before us is not a conspiracy to overthrow the Government. But it would be equally wrong to treat it as a seminar in political theory.

III.

These general considerations underlie decision of the case before us.

On the one hand is the interest in security. The Communist Party was not designed by these defendants as an ordinary political party. For the circumstances of its organization, its aims and methods, and the relation of the defendants to its organization and aims we are concluded by the jury's verdict. The jury found that the Party rejects the basic premise of our political system—that change is to be brought about by nonviolent constitutional process. The jury found that the Party advocates the theory that there is a duty and necessity to overthrow the Government by force and violence. It found that the Party entertains and promotes this view, not as a prophetic insight or as a bit of unworldly speculation, but as a program for winning adherents and as a policy to be translated into action.

In finding that the defendants violated the statute, we may not treat as established fact that the Communist Party in this country is of significant size, well-organized, well-disciplined, conditioned to embark on unlawful activity when given the command. But in determining whether application of the statute to the defendants is within the constitutional powers of Congress, we are not limited to the facts found by the jury. We must view such a question in the light of whatever is relevant to a legislative judgment. We may take judicial notice that the Communist doctrines which these defendants have conspired to advocate are in the ascendency in powerful nations who cannot be acquitted of unfriendliness to the institutions of this country. We may take account of evidence brought forward at this trial and elsewhere, much of which has long been common knowledge. In sum, it would amply justify a legislature in concluding that recruitment of additional members for the Party would create a substantial danger to national security.

In 1947, it has been reliably reported, at least 60,000 members were enrolled in the Party. Evidence was introduced in this case that the membership was organized in small units, linked by an intricate chain of command, and protected by elaborate precautions designed to prevent disclosure of individual identity. There are no reliable data tracing acts of sabotage or espionage directly to these defendants. But a Canadian Royal Commission appointed in 1946 to investigate espionage reported that it was "overwhelmingly established" that "the Communist movement was the principal base within which the espionage network was recruited." The most notorious spy in recent history [Klaus Fuchs] was led into the service of the Soviet Union through Communist indoctrination. Evidence supports the conclusion that members of the Party seek and occupy positions of importance in political and labor organizations. Congress was not barred by the Constitution from believing that indifference to such experience would be an exercise not of freedom but of irresponsibility.

On the other hand is the interest in free speech. The right to exert all governmental powers in aid of maintaining our institutions and resisting their physical overthrow does not include intolerance of opinions and speech that cannot do harm although opposed and perhaps alien to dominant, traditional opinion. The treatment of its minorities, especially their legal position, is among the most searching tests of the level of civilization attained by a society. It is better for those who have almost unlimited power of government in their hands to err on the side of freedom. We have enjoyed so much freedom for so long that we are perhaps in danger of forgetting how much blood it cost to establish the Bill of Rights.

Of course no government can recognize a "right" of revolution, or a "right" to incite revolution if the incitement has no other purpose or effect. But speech is seldom restricted to a single purpose, and its effects may be manifold. A public interest is not wanting in granting freedom to speak their minds even to those who advocate the overthrow of the Government by force. For, as the evidence in this case abundantly illustrates, coupled with such advocacy is criticism of defects in our society. Criticism is the spur to reform; and Burke's admonition that a healthy society must reform in order to conserve has not lost its force. Astute observers have remarked that one of the characteristics of the American Republic is indifference to fundamental criticism. Bryce, *The American Commonwealth*, c.84. It is a commonplace that there may be a grain of truth in the most uncouth doctrine however false and repellent the balance may be. Suppressing advocates of overthrow inevitably will also silence critics who do not advocate overthrow but fear that their criticism may be so construed. No matter how clear we may be that the defendants now before us are preparing to overthrow our Government at the propitious moment, it is self-delusion to think that we can punish them for their advocacy without adding to the risks run by loyal citizens who honestly believe in some of the reforms these defendants advance. It is a sobering fact that in sustaining the conviction before us we can hardly escape restriction on the interchange of ideas.

We must not overlook the value of that interchange. Freedom of expression is the well-spring of our civilization—the civilization we seek to maintain and further by recognizing the right of Congress to put some limitation upon expression. Such are the paradoxes of life. For social development of trial and error, the fullest possible opportunity for the free play of the human mind is an indispensable prerequisite. The history of civilization is in considerable measure the displacement of error which once held sway as official truth by beliefs which in turn have yielded to other truths. Therefore the liberty of man to search for truth ought not to be fettered, no matter what orthodoxies he may challenge. Liberty of thought soon shrivels without freedom of expression. Nor can truth be pursued in an atmosphere hostile to the endeavor or under dangers which are hazarded only by heroes.

"The interest, which [the First Amendment] guards, and which gives it its importance, presupposes that there are no orthodoxies—religious, political, economic, or scientific—which are immune from debate and dispute. Back of that is the assumption—itself an orthodoxy, and the one permissible exception—that truth will be most likely to emerge, if no limitations are imposed upon utterances that can with any plausibility be regarded as efforts to present grounds for accepting or rejecting propositions whose truth the utterer asserts, or denies." *International Brotherhood of Electrical Workers*

v. *National Labor Relations Board,* 181 F. 2d 34. In the last analysis it is on the validity of this faith that our national security is staked.

It is not for us to decide how we would adjust the clash of interests which this case presents were the primary responsibility for reconciling it ours. Congress has determined that the danger created by advocacy of overthrow justifies the ensuing restriction on freedom of speech. The determination was made after due deliberation, and the seriousness of the congressional purpose is attested by the volume of legislation passed to effectuate the same ends.

Can we then say that the judgment Congress exercised was denied it by the Constitution? Can we establish a constitutional doctrine which forbids the elected representatives of the people to make this choice? Can we hold that the First Amendment deprives Congress of what it deemed necessary for the Government's protection?

To make validity of legislation depend on judicial reading of events still in the womb of time—a forecast, that is, of the outcome of forces at best appreciated only with knowledge of the topmost secrets of nations—is to charge the judiciary with duties beyond its equipment. We do not expect courts to pronounce historic verdicts on bygone events. Even historians have conflicting views to this day on the origin and conduct of the French Revolution. It is as absurd to be confident that we can measure the present clash of forces and their outcome as to ask us to read history still enveloped in clouds of controversy.

In the light of their experience, the Framers of the Constitution chose to keep the judiciary dissociated from direct participation in the legislative process. In asserting the power to pass on the constitutionality of legislation, Marshall and his Court expressed the purposes of the Founders. . . . But the extent to which the exercise of this power would interpenetrate matters of policy could hardly have been foreseen by the most prescient. The distinction which the Founders drew between the Court's duty to pass on the power of Congress and its complementary duty not to enter directly the domain of policy is fundamental. But in its actual operation it is rather subtle, certainly to the common understanding. Our duty to abstain from confounding policy with constitutionality demands perceptive humility as well as self-restraint in not declaring unconstitutional what in a judge's private judgment is unwise and even dangerous.

Even when moving strictly within the limits of constitutional adjudication, judges are concerned with issues that may be said to involve vital finalities. The too easy transition from disapproval of what is undesirable to condemnation as unconstitutional, has led some of the wisest judges to question the wisdom of our scheme in lodging such authority in courts. But it is relevant to remind that in sustaining the power of Congress in a case like this nothing irrevocable is done. The democratic process at all events is not impaired or restricted. Power and responsibility remain with the people and immediately with their representation. All the Court says is that Congress was not forbidden by the Constitution to pass this enactment and a prosecution under it may be brought against a conspiracy such as the one before us.

IV.

The wisdom of the assumptions underlying the legislation and prosecution is another matter. In finding that Congress has acted within its power, a judge does not remotely imply that he favors the implications that lie beneath the legal issues. Considerations there enter which go beyond the criteria that are binding upon judges within the narrow confines of their legitimate authority. The legislation we are here considering is but a truncated aspect of a deeper issue. For me it has been most illuminatingly expressed by one in whom responsibility and experience have fructified native insight, the Director-General of the British Broadcasting Corporation:

We have to face up to the fact that there are powerful forces in the world today misusing the privileges of liberty in order to destroy her. The question must be asked, however, whether suppression of information or opinion is the true defense. We may have come a long way from Mill's famous dictum that: "If all mankind minus one were of one opinion, and only one person were of the contrary opinion, mankind would be no more justified in silencing that one person, than he, if he had the power, would be justified in silencing mankind," but Mill's reminders from history as to what has happened when suppression was most virulently exercised ought to warn us that no debate is ever permanently won by shutting one's ears or by even the most Draconian policy of silencing opponents. The *debate* must be won. And it must be won with full information. Where there are lies, they must be shown for what they are. Where there are errors, they must be refuted. It would be a major defeat if the enemies of democracy forced us to abandon our faith in the power of informed discussion and so brought us down to their own level. Mankind is so constituted, moreover, that if, where expression and discussion are concerned, the enemies of liberty are met with a denial of liberty, many men of goodwill will come to suspect there is something in the proscribed doctrine after all. Erroneous doctrines thrive on being expunged. They die if exposed. Sir William Haley, "What Standards for Broadcasting?" *Measure*, Vol. I, No. 3, Summer 1950, pp. 211–212.

In the context of this deeper struggle, another voice has indicated the limitations of what we decide today. No one is better equipped than George F. Kennan to speak on the meaning of the menace of Communism and the spirit in which we should meet it.

If our handling of the problem of Communist influence in our midst is not carefully moderated—if we permit it, that is, to become an emotional preoccupation and to blind us to the more important positive tasks before us—we can do a damage to our national purpose beyond comparison greater than anything that threatens us today from the Communist side. The American Communist party is today, by and large, an external danger. It represents a tiny minority in our country;

it has no real contact with the feelings of the mass of our people; and its position as the agency of a hostile foreign power is clearly recognized by the overwhelming mass of our citizens.

But the subjective emotional stresses and temptations to which we are exposed in our attempt to deal with this domestic problem are not an external danger: they represent a danger within ourselves—a danger that something may occur in our own minds and souls which will make us no longer like the persons by whose efforts this republic was founded and held together, but rather like the representatives of that very power we are trying to combat: intolerant, secretive, suspicious, cruel, and terrified of internal dissension because we have lost our own belief in ourselves and in the power of our ideals. The worst thing that our Communists could do to us, and the thing we have most to fear from their activities, is that we should become like them.

That our country is beset with external dangers I readily concede. But these dangers, at their worst, are ones of physical destruction, of the disruption of our world security, of expense and inconvenience and sacrifice. These are serious, and sometimes terrible things, but they are all things that we can take and still remain Americans.

The internal danger is of a different order. America is not just territory and people. There is lots of territory elsewhere, and there are lots of people; but it does not add up to America. America is something in our minds and our habits of outlook which causes us to believe in certain things and to behave in certain ways, and by which, in its totality, we hold ourselves distinguished from others. If that once goes there will be no America to defend. And that can go too easily if we yield to the primitive human instinct to escape from our frustrations into the realms of mass emotion and hatred and to find scapegoats for our difficulties in individual fellow-citizens who are, or have at one time been, disoriented or confused. George F. Kennan, "Where do You Stand on Communism?" *New York Times Magazine,* May 27, 1951.

Civil liberties draw at best only limited strength from legal guaranties. Preoccupation by our people with the constitutionality, instead of with the wisdom of legislation or of executive action, is preoccupation with a false value. Even those who would most freely use the judicial brake on the democratic process by invalidating legislation that goes deeply against their grain, acknowledge, at least by paying lip service, that constitutionality does not exact a sense of proportion or the sanity of humor or an absence of fear. Focusing attention on constitutionality tends to make constitutionality synonymous with wisdom. When legislation touches freedom of thought and freedom of speech, such a tendency is a formidable enemy of the free spirit. Much that should be rejected as illiberal, because repressive and envenoming, may well be not unconstitutional. The ultimate reliance for the deepest needs of civilization must be found outside their vindication in courts of law; apart from all else, judges, howsoever they may conscientiously seek to discipline themselves against it, unconsciously are too apt to be moved by the deep undercurrents of public feeling. A persistent, positive translation of the liberating faith into the feelings and thoughts and actions of men and women is the real protection against attempts to strait-jacket the human mind. Such temptations will have their way, if fear and hatred are not exorcized. The mark of a truly civilized man is confidence in the strength and security derived from the inquiring mind. We may be grateful for such honest comforts as it supports, but we must be unafraid of its uncertitudes. Without open minds there can be no open society. And if society be not open the spirit of man is mutilated and becomes enslaved. . . .

Mr. Justice Jackson, concurring:

This prosecution is the latest of never-ending, because never successful, quests for some legal formula that will secure an existing order against revolutionary radicalism. It requires us to reappraise, in the light of our own times and conditions, constitutional doctrines devised under other circumstances to strike a balance between authority and liberty.

Activity here charged to be criminal is conspiracy—that defendants conspired to teach and advocate, and to organize the Communist Party to teach and advocate, overthrow and destruction of the Government by force and violence. There is no charge of actual violence or attempt at overthrow.

The principal reliance of the defense in this Court is that the conviction cannot stand under the Constitution because the conspiracy of these defendants presents no "clear and present danger" of imminent or foreseeable overthrow.

I.

The statute before us repeats a pattern, originally devised to combat the wave of anarchistic terrorism that plagued this country about the turn of the century, which lags at least two generations behind Communist Party techniques.

Anarchism taught a philosophy of extreme individualism and hostility to government and property. Its avowed aim was a more just order, to be achieved by violent destruction of all government. Anarchism's sporadic and uncoordinated acts of terror were not integrated with an effective revolutionary machine, but the Chicago Haymarket riots of 1886, attempted murder of the industrialist Frick, attacks on state officials, and assassination of President McKinley in 1901, were fruits of its preaching.

However, extreme individualism was not conducive to cohesive and disciplined organization. Anarchism fell into disfavor among incendiary radicals, many of whom shifted their allegiance to the rising Communist Party. Meanwhile, in Europe anarchism had been displaced by Bolshevism as the doctrine and strategy of social and political upheaval. Led by intellectuals hardened by revolutionary experience it was a more sophisticated, dynamic and realistic movement. Establishing a base in the Soviet Union, it founded an aggressive international Communist apparatus which has modeled and directed a revolutionary movement able only to harass our own country. But it has seized control of a dozen other countries.

Communism, the antithesis of anarchism, appears today as a closed system of thought representing Stalin's version of Lenin's version of Marxism. As an ideology, it is not one of spontaneous protest arising from American working-class experience. It is a complicated system of assumptions, based on European history and conditions, shrouded in an obscure and ambiguous vocabulary, which allures our ultrasophisticated intelligentsia more than our hard-headed working people. From time to time it champions all manner of causes and grievances and makes alliances that may add to its foothold in government or embarrass the authorities.

The Communist Party, nevertheless, does not seek its strength primarily in numbers. Its aim is a relatively small party whose strength is in selected, dedicated, indoctrinated, and rigidly disciplined members. From established policy it tolerates no deviation and no debate. It seeks members that are, or may be, secreted in strategic posts in transportation, communications, industry, government, and especially in labor unions where it can compel employers to accept and retain its members. It also seeks to infiltrate and control organizations of professional and other groups. Through these placements in positions of power it seeks a leverage over society that will make up in power of coercion what it lacks in power of persuasion.

The Communists have no scruples against sabotage, terrorism, assassination, or mob disorder; but violence is not with them, as with the anarchists, an end in itself. The Communist Party advocates force only when prudent and profitable. Their strategy of stealth precludes premature or uncoordinated outbursts of violence, except, of course, when the blame will be placed on shoulders other than their own. They resort to violence as to truth, not as a principle but as an expedient. Force or violence, as they would resort to it, may never be necessary, because infiltration and deception may be enough.

Force would be utilized by the Communist Party not to destroy government but for its capture. The Communist recognizes that an established government in control of modern technology cannot be overthrown by force until it is about ready to fall of its own weight. Concerted uprising, therefore, is to await that contingency and revolution is seen, not as a sudden episode, but as the consummation of a long process.

The United States, fortunately, has experienced Communism only in its preparatory stages and for its pattern of final action must look abroad. Russia, of course, was the pilot Communist revolution, which to the Marxist confirms the Party's assumptions and points its destiny. But Communist technique in the overturn of a free government was disclosed by the *coup d'état* in which they seized power in Czechoslovakia. There the Communist Party during its preparatory stage claimed and received protection for its freedoms of speech, press, and assembly. Pretending to be but another political party, it eventually was conceded participation in government, where it entrenched reliable members chiefly in control of police and information services. When the government faced a foreign and domestic crisis, the Communist Party had established a leverage strong enough to threaten civil war. In a period of confusion the Communist plan unfolded and the underground organization came to the surface throughout the country in the form chiefly of labor "action committees." Communist officers of the unions took over transportation and allowed only persons with party permits to travel. Communist printers took over the newspapers and radio and put out only party-approved versions of events. Possession was taken of telegraph and telephone systems and communications were cut off wherever directed by party heads. Communist unions took over the factories, and in the cities a partisan distribution of food was managed by the Communist organization. A virtually bloodless abdication by the elected government admitted the Communists to power, whereupon they instituted a reign of oppression and terror, and ruthlessly denied to all others the freedoms which had sheltered their conspiracy.

II.

The foregoing is enough to indicate that, either by accident or design, the Communist stratagem outwits the anti-anarchist pattern of statute aimed against "overthrow by force and violence" if qualified by the doctrine that only "clear and present danger" of accomplishing that result will sustain the prosecution.

The "clear and present danger" test was an innovation by Mr. Justice Holmes in the *Schenck Case,* reiterated and refined by him and Mr. Justice Brandeis in later cases, all arising before the era of World War II revealed the subtlety and efficacy of modernized revolutionary techniques used by totalitarian parties. In those cases, they were faced with convictions under so-called criminal syndicalism statutes aimed at anarchists but which, loosely construed, had been applied to punish socialism, pacifism, and left-wing ideologies, the charges often resting on far-fetched inferences which, if true, would establish only technical or trivial violations. They proposed "clear and present danger" as a test for the sufficiency of evidence in particular cases.

I would save it, unmodified, for application as a "rule of reason" in the kind of case for which it was devised. When the issue is criminality of a hot-headed speech on a street corner, or circulation of a few incendiary pamphlets, or parading by some zealots behind a red flag, or refusal of a handful of school children to salute our flag, it is not beyond the capacity of the judicial process to gather, comprehend, and weigh the necessary materials for decision whether it is a clear and present danger of substantive evil or a harmless letting off of steam. It is not a prophecy, for the danger in such cases has matured by the time of trial or it was never present. The test applies and has meaning where a conviction is sought to be based on a speech or writing which does not directly or explicitly advocate a crime but to which such tendency is sought to be attributed by construction or by implication from external circumstances. The formula in such cases favors freedoms that are vital to our society, and, even if sometimes applied too generously, the consequences cannot be grave. But its recent expansion has extended, in particular to Communists, unprecedented immunities. Unless we are to hold our Government captive in a judge-made verbal trap, we must approach the problem of a well-organized, nation-wide conspiracy, such as I have described, as realistically as our predecessors faced the trivialities that were being prosecuted until they were checked with a rule of reason.

I think reason is lacking for applying that test to this case.

If we must decide that this Act and its application are constitutional only if we are convinced that petitioner's conduct creates a "clear and present danger" of violent overthrow, we must appraise imponderables, including international and national phenomena which baffle the best informed foreign offices and our most experienced politicians. We would have to foresee and predict the effectiveness of Communist propaganda, opportunities for in-filtration, whether, and when, a time will come that they consider propitious for action, and whether and how fast our existing government will deteri-orate. And we would have to speculate as to whether an approaching Com-munist *coup* would not be anticipated by a nationalistic fascist movement. No doctrine can be sound whose application requires us to make a prophecy of that sort in the guise of a legal decision. The judicial process simply is not adequate to a trial of such far-flung issues. The answers given would re-flect our own political predilections and nothing more.

The authors of the clear and present danger test never applied it to a case like this, nor would I. If applied as it is proposed here, it means that the Communist plotting is protected during its period of incubation; its pre-liminary stages of organization and preparation are immune from the law; the Government can move only after imminent action is manifest, when it would, of course, be too late.

III.

The highest degree of constitutional protection is due to the individual acting without conspiracy. But even an individual cannot claim that the Constitution protects him in advocating or teaching overthrow of govern-ment by force or violence. I should suppose no one would doubt that Congress has power to make such attempted overthrow a crime. But the contention is that one has the constitutional right to work up a public desire and will to do what it is a crime to attempt. I think direct incitement by speech or writing can be made a crime, and I think there can be a conviction with-out also proving that the odds favored its success by 99 to 1, or some other extremely high ratio. . . .

Of course, it is not always easy to distinguish teaching or advocacy in the sense of incitement from teaching or advocacy in the sense of exposition or explanation. It is a question of fact in each case.

IV.

What really is under review here is a conviction of conspiracy, after a trial for conspiracy, on an indictment charging conspiracy, brought under a statute outlawing conspiracy. With due respect to my colleagues, they seem to me to discuss anything under the sun except the law of conspiracy. One of the dissenting opinions even appears to chide me for "invoking the law of conspiracy." As that is the case before us, it may be more amazing that its reversal can be proposed without even considering the law of conspiracy.

The Constitution does not make conspiracy a civil right. The Court has never before done so and I think it should not do so now. Conspiracies of labor unions, trade associations, and news agencies have been condemned, although accomplished, evidenced and carried out, like the conspiracy here, chiefly by letter-writing, meetings, speeches and organization. Indeed, this Court seems, particularly in cases where the conspiracy has economic ends, to be applying its doctrines with increasing severity. While I consider criminal conspiracy a dragnet device capable of perversion into an instrument of injustice in the hands of a partisan or complacent judiciary, it has an established place in our system of law, and no reason appears for applying it only to concerted action claimed to disturb interstate commerce and withholding it from those claimed to undermine our whole Government.

The basic rationale of the law of conspiracy is that a conspiracy may be an evil in itself, independently of any other evil it seeks to accomplish. . . .

So far does this doctrine reach that it is well settled that Congress may make it a crime to conspire with others to do what an individual may lawfully do on his own. This principle is illustrated in conspiracies that violate the antitrust laws as sustained and applied by this Court. Although one may raise the prices of his own products, and many, acting without concert, may do so, the moment they conspire to that end they are punishable. The same principle is applied to organized labor. Any workman may quit his work for any reason, but concerted actions to the same end are in some circumstances forbidden. . . .

The reasons underlying the doctrine that conspiracy may be a substantive evil in itself, apart from any evil it may threaten, attempt or accomplish are peculiarly appropriate to conspiratorial Communism.

> The reason for finding criminal liability in case of a combination to effect an unlawful end or to use unlawful means, where none would exist, even though the act contemplated were actually committed by an individual, is that a combination of persons to commit a wrong, either as an end or as a means to an end, is so much more dangerous, because of its increased power to do wrong, because it is more difficult to guard against and prevent the evil designs of a group of persons than of a single person, and because of the terror which fear of such a combination tends to create in the minds of people. [Miller, *Criminal Law*, 10.]

There is lamentation in the dissents about the injustice of conviction in the absence of some overt act. Of course, there has been no general uprising against the Government, but the record is replete with acts to carry out the conspiracy alleged, acts such as always are held sufficient to consummate the crime where the statute requires an overt act.

But the shorter answer is that no overt act is or need be required. The Court, in antitrust cases, early upheld the power of Congress to adopt the ancient common law that makes conspiracy itself a crime. . . . It is not to be supposed that the power of Congress to protect the Nation's existence is more limited than its power to protect interstate commerce.

Also, it is urged that since the conviction is for conspiracy to teach and advocate, and to organize the Communist Party to teach and advocate, the First Amendment is violated, because freedoms of speech and press protect teaching and advocacy regardless of what is taught or advocated. I have never thought that to be the law.

I do not suggest that Congress could punish conspiracy to advocate something, the doing of which it may not punish. Advocacy or exposition of the doctrine of communal property ownership, or any political philosophy unassociated with advocacy of its imposition by force or seizure of government by unlawful means could not be reached through conspiracy prosecution. But it is not forbidden to put down force or violence, it is not forbidden to punish its teaching or advocacy, and the end being punishable, there is no doubt of the power to punish conspiracy for the purpose.

The defense of freedom of speech or press has often been raised in conspiracy cases, because, whether committed by Communists, by businessmen, or by common criminals, it usually consists of words written or spoken, evidenced by letters, conversations, speeches or documents. Communication is the essence of every conspiracy, for only by it can common purpose and concert of action be brought about or be proved. . . .

In conspiracy cases the Court not only has dispensed with proof of clear and present danger but even of power to create a danger. . . .

Having held that a conspiracy alone is a crime and its consummation is another, it would be weird legal reasoning to hold that Congress could punish the one only if there was "clear and present danger" of the second. This would compel the Government to prove two crimes in order to convict for one.

When our constitutional provisions were written, the chief forces recognized as antagonists in the struggle between authority and liberty were the Government on the one hand and the individual citizen on the other. It was thought that if the state could be kept in its place the individual could take care of himself.

In more recent times these problems have been complicated by the intervention between the state and the citizen of permanently organized, well-financed, semi-secret and highly disciplined political organizations. Totalitarian groups here and abroad perfected the technique of creating private paramilitary organizations to coerce both the public government and its citizens. These organizations assert as against our Government all of the constitutional rights and immunities of individuals and at the same time exercise over their followers much of the authority which they deny to the Government. The Communist Party realistically is a state within a state, an authoritarian dictatorship within a republic. It demands these freedoms, not for its members, but for the organized party. It denies to its own members at the same time the freedom to dissent, to debate, to deviate from the party line, and enforces its authoritarian rule by crude purges, if nothing more violent.

The law of conspiracy has been the chief means at the Government's disposal to deal with the growing problems created by such organizations. I happen to think it is an awkward and inept remedy, but I find no constitutional authority for taking this weapon from the Government. There is no constitutional right to "gang up" on the Government.

While I think there was power in Congress to enact this statute and that, as applied in this case, it cannot be held unconstitutional, I add that I have little faith in the long-range effectiveness of this conviction to stop the rise of the Communist movement. Communism will not go to jail with these Communists. No decision by this Court can forestall revolution whenever the existing government fails to command the respect and loyalty of the people and sufficient distress and discontent is allowed to grow up among the masses. Many failures by fallen governments attest that no government can long prevent revolution by outlawry. Corruption, ineptitude, inflation, oppressive taxation, militarization, injustice, and loss of leadership capable of intellectual initiative in domestic or foreign affairs are allies on which the Communists count to bring opportunity knocking to their door. Sometimes I think they may be mistaken. But the Communists are not building just for today—the rest of us might profit by their example.

Mr. Justice Black, dissenting:

Here . . . my basic disagreement with the Court is not as to how we should explain or reconcile what was said in prior decisions but springs from a fundamental difference in constitutional approach. Consequently, it would serve no useful purpose to state my position at length.

At the outset I want to emphasize what the crime involved in this case is, and what it is not. These petitioners were not charged with an attempt to overthrow the Government. They were not charged with overt acts of any kind designed to overthrow the Government. They were not even charged with saying anything or writing anything designed to overthrow the Government. The charge was that they agreed to assemble and to talk and publish certain ideas at a later date: The indictment is that they conspired to organize the Communist Party and to use speech or newspapers and other publications in the future to teach and advocate the forcible overthrow of the Government. No matter how it is worded, this is a virulent form of prior censorship of speech and press, which I believe the First Amendment forbids. I would hold § 3 of the Smith Act authorizing this prior restraint unconstitutional on its face and as applied.

But let us assume, contrary to all constitutional ideas of fair criminal procedure, that petitioners although not indicted for the crime of actual advocacy, may be punished for it. Even on this radical assumption, the other opinions in this case show that the only way to affirm these convictions is to repudiate directly or indirectly the established "clear and present danger" rule. This the Court does in a way which greatly restricts the protections afforded by the First Amendment. The opinions for affirmance indicate that the chief reason for jettisoning the rule is the expressed fear that advocacy of Communist doctrine endangers the safety of the Republic. Undoubtedly, a governmental policy of unfettered communication of ideas does entail dangers. To the Founders of this Nation, however, the benefits derived from free expression were worth the risk. They embodied this philosophy in the First Amendment's command that Congress "shall make no law . . . abridging the freedom of speech, or of the press. . . ." I have always believed that the First Amendment is the keystone of our Government, that the freedoms it guarantees provide the best insurance against destruction of all freedom. At least as to speech in the realm of public matters, I believe that the "clear and present danger" test does not "mark the furthermost constitutional boundaries of protected expression" but does "no more than recognize a minimum compulsion of the Bill of Rights." *Bridges* v. *California,* 314 U.S. 252. . . .

So long as this Court exercises the power of judicial review of legislation, I cannot agree that the First Amendment permits us to sustain laws suppressing freedom of speech and press on the basis of Congress' or our own notions of mere "reasonableness." Such a doctrine waters down the First Amendment so that it amounts to little more than an admonition to Congress. The Amendment as so construed is not likely to protect any but those "safe" or orthodox views which rarely need its protection. I must also express my objection to the holding because, as Mr. Justice Douglas' dissent shows, it sanctions the determination of a crucial issue of fact by the judge rather than by the jury. Nor can I let this opportunity pass without expressing my objection to the severely limited grant of certiorari in this case which precluded consideration here of at least two other reasons for reversing these convictions: (1) the record shows a discriminatory selection of the jury panel which prevented trial before a representative cross-section of the community; (2) the record shows that one member of the trial jury was violently hostile to petitioners before and during the trial.

Public opinion being what it now is, few will protest the conviction of these Communist petitioners. There is hope, however, that in calmer times, when present pressures, passions and fears subside, this or some later Court will restore the First Amendment liberties to the high preferred place where they belong in a free society.

Mr. Justice Douglas, dissenting:

If this were a case where those who claimed protection under the First Amendment were teaching the techniques of sabotage, the assassination of the President, the filching of documents from public files, the planting of bombs, the art of street warfare, and the like, I would have no doubts. The freedom to speak is not absolute; the teaching of methods of terror and other seditious conduct should be beyond the pale along with obscenity and immorality. This case was argued as if those were the facts. The argument imported much seditious conduct into the record. That is easy and it has popular appeal, for the activities of Communists in plotting and scheming against the free world are common knowledge. But the fact is that no such evidence was introduced at the trial. There is a statute which makes a seditious conspiracy unlawful. Petitioners, however, were not charged with a "conspiracy to overthrow" the Government. They were charged with a conspiracy to form a party and groups and assemblies of people who teach and advocate the overthrow of our Government by force or violence and with a conspiracy to advocate and teach its overthrow by force and violence. It may well be that indoctrination in the techniques of terror to destroy the Government would be indictable under either statute. But the teaching which is condemned here is of a different character.

So far as the present record is concerned, what petitioners did was to organize people to teach and themselves teach the Marxist-Leninist doctrine contained chiefly in four books: *Foundations of Leninism* by Stalin (1924), *The Communist Manifesto* by Marx and Engels (1848), *State and Revolution* by Lenin (1917), *History of the Communist Party of the Soviet Union* (1939).

Those books are to Soviet Communism what *Mein Kampf* was to Nazism. If they are understood, the ugliness of Communism is revealed, its deceit and cunning are exposed, the nature of its activities becomes apparent, and the chances of its success less likely. That is not, of course, the reason why petitioners chose these books for their classrooms. They are fervent Communists to whom these volumes are gospel. They preached the creed with the hope that some day it would be acted upon.

The opinion of the Court does not outlaw these texts nor condemn them to the fire, as the Communists do literature offensive to their creed. But if the books themselves are not outlawed, if they can lawfully remain on library shelves, by what reasoning does their use in a classroom become a crime? It would not be a crime under the Act to introduce these books to a class, though that would be teaching what the creed of violent overthrow of the government is. The Act, as construed, requires the element of intent —that those who teach the creed believe in it. The crime then depends not on what is taught but on who the teacher is. That is to make freedom of speech turn not on *what is said*, but on the *intent* with which it is said. Once we start down that road we enter territory dangerous to the liberties of every citizen.

There was a time in England when the concept of constructive treason flourished. Men were punished not for raising a hand against the king but for thinking murderous thoughts about him. The Framers of the Constitution were alive to that abuse and took steps to see that the practice would not flourish here. Treason was defined to require overt acts—the evolution of a plot against the country into an actual project. The present case is not one of treason. But the analogy is close when the illegality is made to turn on intent, not on the nature of the act. We then start probing men's minds for motive and purpose; they become entangled in the law not for what they did but *for what they thought; they* get convicted not for what they said but for the purpose with which they said it.

Intent, of course, often makes the difference in the law. An act otherwise excusable or carrying minor penalties may grow to an abhorrent thing if the evil intent is present. We deal here, however, not with ordinary acts but with speech, to which the Constitution has given a special sanction.

The vice of treating speech as the equivalent of overt acts of a treasonable or seditious character is emphasized by a concurring opinion, which by invoking the law of conspiracy makes speech do service for deeds which are dangerous to society. The doctrine of conspiracy has served divers and oppressive purposes and in its broad reach can be made to do great evil. But never until today has anyone seriously thought that the ancient law of conspiracy could constitutionally be used to turn speech into seditious conduct. Yet that is precisely what is suggested. I repeat that we deal here with speech alone, not with speech *plus* acts of sabotage or unlawful conduct. Not a single seditious act is charged in the indictment. To make a lawful speech unlawful because two men conceive it is to raise the law of conspiracy to appalling proportions. That course is to make a radical break with the past and to violate one of the cardinal principles of our constitutional scheme.

Free speech has occupied an exalted position because of the high service it has given our society. Its protection is essential to the very existence of a democracy. The airing of ideas releases pressures which otherwise might become destructive. When ideas compete in the market for acceptance, full and free discussion exposes the false and they gain few adherents. Full and free discussion even of ideas we hate encourages the testing of our own prejudices and preconceptions. Full and free discussion keeps a society from becoming stagnant and unprepared for the stresses and strains that work to tear all civilizations apart.

Full and free discussion has indeed been the first article of our faith. We have founded our political system on it. It has been the safeguard of every religious, political, philosophical, economic, and racial group amongst us. We have counted on it to keep us from embracing what is cheap and false; we have trusted the common sense of our people to choose the doctrine true to our genius and to reject the rest. This has been the one single outstanding tenet that has made our institutions the symbol of freedom and equality. We have deemed it more costly to liberty to suppress a despised minority than to let them vent their spleen. We have above all else feared the political censor. We have wanted a land where our people can be exposed to all the diverse creeds and cultures of the world.

There comes a time when even speech loses its constitutional immunity. Speech innocuous one year may at another time fan such destructive flames that it must be halted in the interests of the safety of the Republic. That is the meaning of the clear and present danger test. When conditions are so critical that there will be no time to avoid the evil that the speech threatens, it is time to call a halt. Otherwise, free speech which is the strength of the Nation will be the cause of its destruction.

Yet free speech is the rule, not the exception. The restraint to be constitutional must be based on more than fear, on more than passionate opposition against the speech, on more than a revolted dislike for its contents. There must be some immediate injury to society that is likely if speech is allowed. The classic statement of these conditions was made by Mr. Justice Brandeis in his concurring opinion in *Whitney* v. *California*, 274 U.S. 357.

> Fear of serious injury cannot alone justify suppression of free speech and assembly. Men feared witches and burnt women. It is the function of speech to free men from the bondage of irrational fears. To justify suppression of free speech there must be reasonable ground to fear that serious evil will result if free speech is practiced. There must be reasonable ground to believe that the danger apprehended is imminent. There must be reasonable ground to believe that the evil to be prevented is a serious one. Every denunciation of existing law tends in some measure to increase the probability that there will be violation of it. Condonation of a breach enhances the probability. Expressions of approval add to the probability. Propagation of the criminal state of mind by teaching syndicalism increases it. Advocacy of law-breaking heightens it still further. But even advocacy of violation, however reprehensible morally, is not a justification for denying free speech where the advocacy falls short of incitement and there is nothing to indicate that the advocacy would be immediately acted on. The wide difference between advocacy and incitement, between preparation and attempt, between assembling and conspiracy, must be borne in mind. In order to support a finding of clear and present danger it must be shown either that immediate serious violence was to be expected or was advocated, or that the past conduct furnished reason to believe that such advocacy was then contemplated.
>
> Those who won our independence by revolution were not cowards. They did not fear political change. They did not exalt order at the cost of liberty. To courageous self-reliant men, with confidence in the power of free and fearless reasoning applied through the processes of popular government, no danger flowing from speech can be deemed clear and present, unless the incidence of the evil apprehended is so imminent that it may befall before there is opportunity for full discussion. *If there be time to expose through discussion the falsehood and fallacies, to avert the evil by the processes of education, the remedy to be applied is more speech, not enforced silence.* (Italics added.)

I had assumed that the question of the clear and present danger, being so critical an issue in the case, would be a matter for submission to the jury. It was squarely held in *Pierce* v. *United States*, 252 U.S. 239, to be a jury question. Mr. Justice Pitney, speaking for the Court, said, "Whether the statements contained in the pamphlet had a natural tendency to produce the forbidden consequences, as alleged, was a question to be determined, not upon demurrer, but by the jury at the trial." That is the only time the Court has passed on the issue. None of our other decisions is contrary. Nothing said in any of the nonjury cases has detracted from that ruling. The statement in *Pierce* v. *United States* states the law as it has been and as it should be. The Court, I think, errs when it treats the question as one of law.

Yet, whether the question is one for the Court or the jury, there should be evidence of record on the issue. This record, however, contains no evidence whatsoever showing that the acts charged *viz.*, the teaching of the Soviet theory of revolution with the hope that it will be realized, have created any clear and present danger to the Nation. The Court, however, rules to the contrary. It says, "The formation by petitioners of such a highly organized conspiracy, with rigidly disciplined members subject to call when the leaders, these petitioners, felt that the time had come for action, coupled with the inflammable nature of world conditions, similar uprisings in other countries, and the touch-and-go nature of our relations with countries with whom petitioners were in the very least ideologically attuned, convince us that their convictions were justified on this score."

That ruling is in my view not responsive to the issue in the case. We might as well say that the speech of petitioners is outlawed because Soviet Russia and her Red Army are a threat to world peace.

The nature of Communism as a force on the world scene would, of course, be relevant to the issue of clear and present danger of petitioners' advocacy within the United States. But the primary consideration is the strength and tactical position of petitioners and their converts in this country. On that there is no evidence in the record. If we are to take judicial notice of the threat of Communists within the nation, it should not be difficult to conclude that *as a political party* they are of little consequence. Communists in this country have never made a respectable or serious showing in any election. I would doubt that there is a village, let alone a city or county or state which the Communists could carry. Communism in the world scene is no bogey-man; but Communists as a political faction or party in this country plainly is. Communism has been so thoroughly exposed in this country that it has been crippled as a political force. Free speech has destroyed it as an effective political party. It is inconceivable that those who went up and down this country preaching the doctrine of revolution which petitioners espouse would have any success. In days of trouble and confusion when bread lines were long, when the unemployed walked the streets, when people were starving the advocates of a short-cut by revolution might have a chance to gain adherents. But today there are no such conditions. The country is not in despair; the people know Soviet Communism; the doctrine of Soviet revolution is exposed in all of its ugliness and the American people want none of it.

How it can be said that there is a clear and present danger that this advocacy will succeed is, therefore, a mystery. Some nations less resilient than the United States, where illiteracy is high and where democratic traditions are only budding, might have to take drastic steps and jail these men for merely speaking their creed. But in America they are miserable merchants of unwanted ideas; their wares remain unsold. The fact that their ideas are abhorrent does not make them powerful.

The political impotence of the Communists in this country does not, of course dispose of the problem. Their numbers; their positions in industry and government; the extent to which they have in fact infiltrated the police, the armed services, transportation, stevedoring, power plants, munitions works, and other critical places—these facts all bear on the likelihood that their advocacy of the Soviet theory of revolution will endanger the Republic. But the record is silent on these facts. If we are to proceed on the basis of judicial notice, it is impossible for me to say that the Communists in this country are so potent or so strategically deployed that they must be suppressed for their speech. I could not so hold unless I were willing to conclude that the activities in recent years of committees of Congress, of the Attorney General, of labor unions, of state legislatures, and of Loyalty Boards were so futile as to leave the country on the edge of grave peril. To believe that petitioners and their following are placed in such critical positions as to endanger the Nation is to believe the incredible. It is safe to say that the followers of the creed of Soviet Communism are known to the F.B.I.; that in case of war with Russia they will be picked up overnight as were all prospective saboteurs at the commencement of World War II; that the invisible army of petitioners is the best known, the most beset, and the least thriving of any fifth column in history. Only those held by fear and panic could think otherwise.

This is my view if we are to act on the basis of judicial notice. But the mere statement of the opposing views indicates how important it is that we know the facts before we act. Neither prejudice nor hate nor senseless fear should be the basis of this solemn act. Free speech—the glory of our system of government—should not be sacrificed on anything less than plain and objective proof of danger that the evil advocated is imminent. On this record no one can say that petitioners and their converts are in such a strategic position as to have even the slightest chance of achieving their aims.

The First Amendment provides that "Congress shall make no law . . . abridging the freedom of speech." The Constitution provides no exception. This does not mean, however, that the Nation need hold its hand until it is in such weakened condition that there is no time to protect itself from incitement to revolution. Seditious conduct can always be punished. But the command of the First Amendment is so clear that we should not allow Congress to call a halt to free speech except in the extreme case of peril from the speech itself. The First Amendment makes confidence in the common sense of our people and in their maturity of judgment the great postulate of our democracy. Its philosophy is that violence is rarely, if ever, stopped by denying civil liberties to those advocating resort to force. The First Amendment reflects the philosophy of Jefferson "that it is time enough for the rightful purposes of civil government for its officers to interfere when principles break out into overt acts against peace and good order." The political censor has no place in our public debates. Unless and until extreme and necessitous circumstances are shown our aim should be to keep speech unfettered and to allow the processes of law to be invoked only when the provocateurs among us move from speech to action.

Vishinsky wrote in 1948 in *The Law of the Soviet State,* "In our state, naturally there can be no place for freedom of speech, press, and so on for the foes of socialism."

Our concern should be that we accept no such standard for the United States. Our faith should be that our people will never give support to these advocates of revolution, so long as we remain loyal to the purposes for which our Nation was founded. . . .

Freedom of Speech and Press:

The Problem of Loyalty

1. Loyalty Regulations for Trade Union Officers

AMERICAN COMMUNICATIONS ASSN. v. DOUDS

339 US 382 (1950)

[The Taft-Hartley Act of 1947 provides that a union can use the facilities and opportunities of the act only if each officer has filed an affidavit (1) that he is not a member of or affiliated with the Communist Party and (2) that he does not believe in the overthrow of the Government and that he is not a member or supporter of any organization that believes in or teaches the overthrow of the Government. The constitutionality of this provision was before the Court in the present case. Justices Douglas, Clark, and Minton did not participate. Justice Black, dissenting, maintained that the entire provision was unconstitutional. The other five Justices held that the section was constitutional insofar as it required an affidavit to the effect that the union officer was not a member of or affiliated with the Communist Party. As to the other provision, that relating to his beliefs or to the beliefs of an organization, its constitutionality was sustained by a vote of 3. (Vinson, Reed, and Burton) against 3 (Frankfurter, Jackson, and Black).

[Communist leaders of unions may call strikes for political ends that serve the "party line" and thus misuse the power vested in them by acts of Congress by virtue of their union offices. Congress may protect the free flow of interstate and foreign commerce from the interference of politically inspired strikes. This is a constitutional objective. Its implementation through the non-Communist affidavit is only an indirect, conditional, partial, and small abridgment of speech. In such a case, said Chief Justice Vinson for the Court, the clear and present danger rule cannot be used mechanically—if at all.]

Mr. Chief Justice Vinson delivered the opinion of the Court:

These cases present for decision the constitutionality of § 9 (h) of the Labor Management Relations Act of 1947. This section, commonly referred to as the non-Communist affidavit provision, reads as follows: "No investigation shall be made by the National Labor Relations Board of any question affecting commerce concerning the representation of employees, raised by a labor organization under subsection (c) of this section, no petition under section 9 (e) (1) shall be entertained, and no complaint shall be issued pursuant to a charge made by a labor organization under subsection (b) of section 10 unless there is on file with the Board an affidavit executed contemporaneously or within the preceding twelve-month period by each officer of such labor organization and the officers of any national or international labor organization of which it is an affiliate or constituent unit that he is not a member of the Communist Party or affiliated with such party, and that he does not believe in, and is not a member of or supports any organization that believes in or teaches, the overthrow of the United States Government by force or by any illegal or unconstitutional methods. The provisions of section 35 A of the Criminal Code shall be applicable in respect to such affidavits."

In No. 10, the constitutional issue was raised by a suit to restrain the Board from holding a representation election in a bargaining unit in which appellant union was the employee representative, without permitting its name to appear on the ballot, and, should the election be held, to restrain the Board from announcing the results or certifying the victor, until a hearing was granted to appellant. A hearing had been denied because of the non-compliance with § 9 (h). The complaint alleged that this requirement was unconstitutional. . . .

No. 13 is the outcome of an unfair labor practice complaint filed with the Board by petitioner unions. The Board found that Inland Steel Company had violated the Labor Relations Act in refusing to bargain on the subject of pensions. But the Board postponed the effective date of its order compelling the company to bargain, pending the unions' compliance with § 9 (h). Both sides appealed: the company urged that the Act had been misinterpreted; the unions contended that § 9 (h) was unconstitutional and therefore an invalid condition of a Board order. . . .

I.

The constitutional justification for the National Labor Relations Act was the power of Congress to protect interstate commerce by removing obstructions to the free flow of commerce. . . . That Act was designed to remove obstructions caused by strikes and other forms of industrial unrest, which Congress found were attributable to the inequality of bargaining power between unorganized employees and their employers. It did so by strengthening employee groups, by restraining certain employer practices, and by encouraging the processses of collective bargaining.

When the Labor-Management Relations Act was passed twelve years later, it was the view of Congress that additional impediments to the free flow of commerce made amendment of the original Act desirable. It was stated in the findings and declaration of policy that:

Experience has further demonstrated that certain practices by some labor organizations, their officers, and members have the intent or the necessary effect of burdening or obstructing commerce by preventing the free flow of goods in such commerce through strikes and other forms of industrial unrest or through concerted activities which impair the interest of the public in the free flow of such commerce. The elimination of such practices is a necessary condition to the assurance of the rights herein granted.

One such obstruction, which it was the purpose of § 9 (h) of the Act to remove, was the so-called "political strike." Substantial amounts of evidence were presented to various committees of Congress, including the committees immediately concerned with labor legislation, that Communist leaders of labor unions had in the past and would continue in the future to subordinate legitimate trade union objectives to obstructive strikes when dictated by Party leaders, often in support of the policies of a foreign government. And other evidence supports the view that some union leaders who hold to a belief in violent overthrow of the Government for reasons other than loyalty to the Communist Party likewise regard strikes and other forms of direct action designed to serve ultimate revolutionary goals as the primary objectives of labor unions which they control. At the committee hearings, the incident most fully developed was a strike at the Milwaukee plant of the Allis-Chalmers Manufacturing Company in 1941, when the plant was producing vital materials for the national defense program. A full hearing was given not only to company officials, but also to leaders of the international and local unions involved. Congress heard testimony that the strike had been called solely in obedience to Party orders for the purpose of starting the "snowballing of strikes" in defense plants.

No useful purpose would be served by setting out at length the evidence before Congress relating to the problem of political strikes, nor can we attempt to assess the validity of each item of evidence. It is sufficient to say that Congress had a great mass of material before it which tended to show that Communists and others proscribed by the statute had infiltrated union organizations not to support and further trade union objectives, including the advocacy of change by democratic methods, but to make them a device by which commerce and industry might be disrupted when the dictates of political policy required such action.

II.

The unions contend that the necessary effect of § 9 (h) is to make it impossible for persons who cannot sign the oath to be officers of labor unions. They urge that such a statute violates fundamental rights guaranteed by the First Amendment: the right of union officers to hold what political views they choose and to associate with what political groups they will and the right of unions to choose their officers without interference from government. The Board has argued, on the other hand, that § 9 (h) presents no First Amendment problem because its sole sanction is the withdrawal from noncomplying unions of the "privilege" of using its facilities.

Neither contention states the problem with complete accuracy. It cannot be denied that the practical effect of denial of access to the Board and the denial of a place on the ballot in representation proceedings is not merely to withhold benefits granted by the Government but to impose upon noncomplying unions a number of restrictions which would not exist if the Board had not been established. The statute does not, however, specifically forbid persons who do not sign the affidavit from holding positions of union leadership nor require their discharge from office. The fact is that § 9 (h) may well make it difficult for unions to remain effective if their officers do not sign the affidavits. How difficult depends upon the circumstances of the industry, the strength of the union and its organizational discipline. We are, therefore, neither free to treat § 9 (h) as if it merely withdraws a privilege gratuitously granted by the Government, nor able to consider it a licensing statute prohibiting those persons who do not sign the affidavit from holding union office. The practicalities of the situation place the proscriptions of § 9 (h) somewhere between those two extremes. The difficult question that emerges is whether consistently with the First Amendment, Congress, by statute, may exert these pressures upon labor unions to deny positions of leadership to certain persons who are identified by particular beliefs and political affiliations.

III.

There can be no doubt that Congress may, under its constitutional power to regulate commerce among the several States, attempt to prevent political strikes and other kinds of direct action designed to burden and interrupt the free flow of commerce. We think it is clear, in addition, that the remedy provided by § 9 (h) bears reasonable relation to the evil which the statute was designed to reach. Congress could rationally find that the Communist Party is not like other political parties in its utilization of positions of union leadership as means by which to bring about strikes and other obstructions of commerce for purposes of political advantage, and that many persons who believe in overthrow of the Government by force and violence are also likely to resort to such tactics when, as officers, they formulate union policy.

The fact that the statute identifies persons by their political affiliations and beliefs, which are circumstances ordinarily irrelevant to permissable subjects of government action, does not lead to the conclusion that such circumstances are never relevant. . . . We have held that aliens may be barred from certain occupations because of a reasonable relation between that classification and the apprehended evil . . . , even though the Constitution forbids arbitrary banning of aliens from the pursuit of lawful occupations. . . . Even distinctions based solely on ancestry, which we declared "are by their very nature odious to a free people," have been upheld under the unusual circumstances of wartime. . . . If accidents of birth and ancestry under some circumstances justify an inference concerning future conduct, it can hardly be doubted that voluntary affiliations and beliefs justify a similar inference when drawn by the legislature on the basis of its investigations.

This principle may be illustrated by reference to statutes denying positions of public importance to groups of persons identified by their business affiliations. One federal statute, for example, provides that no partner or employee of a firm primarily engaged in underwriting securities may be a director of a national bank. This Court noted that the statute is directed "to the probability or likelihood based on the experience of the 1920's, that a bank director interested in the underwriting business may use his influence in the bank to involve it or its customers in securities which his underwriting firm has in its portfolio or has committed itself to take." . . . It was designed "to remove tempting opportunities from the management and personnel of member banks." There was no showing, nor was one required, that all employees of underwriting firms would engage in such conduct. Because of their business connections, carrying as they do certain loyalties, interests and disciplines those persons were thought to pose a continuing threat of participation in the harmful activities described above. Political affiliations of the kind here involved, no less than business affiliations, provide rational ground for the legislative judgment that those persons proscribed by § 9 (h) would be subject to "tempting opportunities" to commit acts deemed harmful to the national economy. In this respect, § 9 (h) is not unlike a host of other statutes which prohibit specified groups of persons from holding positions of power and public interest because, in the legislative judgment, they threaten to abuse the trust that is a necessary concomitant of the power of office.

If no more were involved than possible loss of position, the foregoing would dispose of the case. But the more difficult problem here arises because, in drawing lines on the basis of beliefs and political affiliations, though it may be granted that the proscriptions of the statute bear a reasonable relation to the apprehended evil, Congress has undeniably discouraged the lawful exercise of political freedoms as well. Stated otherwise, the problem is this: Communists, we may assume, carry on legitimate political activities. Beliefs are inviolate. . . . Congress might reasonably find, however, that Communists, unlike members of other political parties, and persons who believe in overthrow of the Government by force, unlike persons of other beliefs, represent a continuing danger of disruptive political strikes when they hold positions of union leadership. By exerting pressures on unions to deny office to Communists and others identified therein, § 9 (h) undoubtedly lessens the threat to interstate commerce, but it has the further necessary effect of discouraging the exercise of political rights protected by the First Amendment. Men who hold union offices often have little choice but to renounce Communism or give up their offices. Unions which wish to do so are discouraged from electing Communists to office. To the grave and difficult problem thus presented we must now turn our attention.

IV.

The unions contend that once it is determined that this is a free speech case, the "clear and present danger" test must apply. . . . But they disagree as to how it should be applied. Appellant in No. 10 would require that joining the Communist Party or the expression of belief in overthrow of the Government by force be shown to be a clear and present danger of some substantive evil, since those are the doctrines affected by the statute. Petitioner in No. 13, on the other hand, would require a showing that political strikes, the substantive evil involved, are a clear and present danger to the security of the Nation or threaten widespread industrial unrest.

This confusion suggests that the attempt to apply the term, "clear and present danger," as a mechanical test in every case touching First Amendment freedoms, without regard to the context of its application, mistakes the form in which an idea was cast for the substance of the idea. The provisions of the Constitution, said Mr. Justice Holmes, "are not mathematical formulas having their essence in their form; they are organized living institutions transplanted from English soil. Their significance is vital and formal; it is to be gathered not simply by taking the words and a dictionary, but by considering their origin and the line of their growth." . . . Still less should this Court's interpretations of the Constitution be reduced to the status of mathematical formulas. It is the considerations that gave birth to the phrase "clear and present danger," not the phrase itself, that are vital in our decision of questions involving liberties protected by the First Amendment.

Although the First Amendment provides that Congress shall make no law abridging the freedom of speech, press or assembly, it has long been established that those freedoms themselves are dependent upon the power of constitutional government to survive. If it is to survive it must have power to protect itself against unlawful conduct and, under some circumstances, against incitements to commit unlawful acts. Freedom of speech thus does not comprehend the right to speak on any subject at any time. The important question that came to this Court immediately after the First World War was not whether, but how far, the First Amendment permits the suppression of speech which advocates conduct inimical to the public welfare. Some thought speech having a reasonable tendency to lead to such conduct might be punished. Justice Holmes and Brandeis took a different view. They thought that the greater danger to a democracy lies in the suppression of public discussion; that ideas and doctrines thought harmful or dangerous are best fought with words. Only, therefore, when force is very likely to follow an utterance before there is a chance for counter-argument to have effect may that utterance be punished or prevented. Thus, "the necessity which is essential to a valid restriction does not exist unless the speech would produce, or is intended to produce, a clear and imminent danger of some substantive evil which the State or Congress constitutionally may seek to prevent." . . . By this means they sought to convey the philosophy that under the First Amendment the public has a right to every man's views and every man the right to speak them. Government may cut him off only when his views are no longer merely views but threaten, clearly and imminently, to ripen into conduct against which the public has a right to protect itself.

But the question with which we are here faced is not the same one that Justices Holmes and Brandeis found convenient to consider in terms of clear and present danger. Government's interest here is not in preventing the dissemination of Communist doctrine or the holding of particular beliefs because it is feared that unlawful action will result therefrom if free speech is practiced. Its interest is in protecting the free flow of commerce from what Congress considers to be substantial evils of conduct that are not the products of speech at all. Section 9 (h), in other words, does not interfere with speech because Congress fears the consequences of speech; it regulates harmful conduct which Congress has determined is carried on by persons who may be identified by their political affiliations and beliefs. The Board does not contend that political strikes, the substantive evil at which § 9 (h) is aimed, are the present or impending products of advocacy of the doctrines of Communism or the expression of belief in overthrow of the Government by force. On the contrary, it points out that such strikes are called by persons who, so Congress has found, have the will and power to do so without advocacy or persuasion that seeks acceptance in the competition of the market. Speech may be fought with speech. Falsehoods and fallacies must be exposed, not suppressed, unless there is not sufficient time to avert the evil consequences of noxious doctrine by argument and education. That is the command of the First Amendment. But force may and must be met with force. Section 9 (h) is designed to protect the public not against what Communists and others identified therein advocate or believe, but against what Congress has concluded they have done and are likely to do again.

The contention of petitioner in No. 13 that this Court must find that political strikes create a clear and present danger to the security of the Nation or of widespread industrial strife in order to sustain § 9 (h) similarly misconceives the purpose that phrase was intended to serve. In that view, not the relative certainty that evil conduct will result from speech in the immediate future, but the extent and gravity of the substantive evil must be measured by the "test" laid down in the *Schenck Case*. But there the Court said that: "The question in every case is whether the *words* used are used in such circumstances and are of such a nature as to create a clear and present danger that they will bring about the substantive evils that Congress has a right to prevent." *Schenck v. United States*, 249 U.S. at 52. (Emphasis supplied.)

So far as the *Schenck Case* itself is concerned, imminent danger of any substantive evil that Congress may prevent justifies the restriction of speech. Since that time this Court has decided, that however great the likelihood that a substantive evil will result, restrictions on speech and press cannot be sustained unless the evil itself is "substantial" and "relatively serious" . . . or sometimes "extremely serious." . . . And it follows therefrom that even harmful conduct cannot justify restrictions upon speech unless substantial interests of society are at stake.

But in suggesting that the substantive evil must be serious and substantial, it was never the intention of this Court to lay down an absolutist test measured in terms of danger to the Nation. When the effect of a statute or ordinance upon the exercise of First Amendment freedoms is relatively small and the public interest to be protected is substantial, it is obvious that a rigid test requiring a showing of imminent danger to the security of the Nation is an absurdity. We recently dismissed for want of substantiality an appeal in which a church group contended that its First Amendment rights were violated by a municipal zoning ordinance preventing the building of churches in certain residential areas. *Church of Jesus Christ of Latter-Day Saints* v. *Porterville,* 338 U.S. 805 (1949). And recent cases in this Court involving contempt by publication likewise have no meaning if imminent danger of national peril is the criterion.

On the contrary, however, the right of the public to be protected from evils of conduct, even though First Amendment rights of persons or groups are thereby in some manner infringed, has received frequent and consistent recognition by this Court. We have noted that the blaring sound truck invades the privacy of the home and may drown out others who wish to be heard. . . . The unauthorized parade through city streets by a religious or political group disrupts traffic and may prevent the discharge of the most essential obligations of local government. . . . The exercise of particular First Amendment rights may fly in the face of the public interest in the health of children . . . or of the whole community . . . and it may be offensive to the moral standards of the community. . . . And Government's obligation to provide an efficient public service . . . and its interest in the character of members of the bar . . . sometimes admit of limitations upon rights set out in the First Amendment. . . . We have never held that such freedoms are absolute. The reason is plain. As Chief Justice Hughes put it, "Civil liberties, as guaranteed by the Constitution, imply the existence of an organized society maintaining public order without which liberty itself would be lost in the excesses of unrestrained abuses." . . .

When particular conduct is regulated in the interest of public order, and the regulation results in an indirect, conditional, partial abridgement of speech, the duty of the courts is to determine which of these two conflicting interests demands the greater protection under the particular circumstances presented. The high place in which the right to speak, think, and assemble as you will was held by the Framers of the Bill of Rights and is held today by those who value liberty both as a means and an end indicates the solicitude with which we must view any assertion of personal freedoms. We must recognize, moreover, that regulation of "conduct" has all too frequently been employed by public authority as a cloak to hide censorship of unpopular ideas. We have been reminded that "It is not often in this country that we now meet with direct and candid efforts to stop speaking or publication as such. Modern inroads on these rights come from associating the speaking with some other factor which the state may regulate so as to bring the whole within official control."

On the other hand, legitimate attempts to protect the public, not from the remote possible effects of noxious ideologies, but from present excesses of direct, active conduct are not presumptively bad because they interfere with and, in some of its manifestations, restrain the exercise of First Amendment rights. . . . In essence, the problem is one of weighing the probable effects of the statute upon the free exercise of the right of speech and assembly against the congressional determination that political strikes are evils of conduct which cause substantial harm to interstate commerce and that Communists and others identified by § 9 (h) pose continuing threats to that public interest when in position of union leadership. We must, therefore, undertake the "delicate and difficult task . . . to weigh the circumstances and to appraise the substantiality of the reasons advanced in support of the regulation of the free enjoyment of the rights."

V.

The "reasons advanced in support of the regulation" are of considerable weight, as even the opponents § 9 (h) agreed. They are far from being "mere legislative preferences or beliefs respecting matters of public convenience which may well support regulation directed at other personal activities, but be insufficient to justify such as diminishes the exercise of rights so vital to the maintenance of democratic institutions." It should be emphasized that Congress, not the courts, is primarily charged with determination of the need for regulation of activities affecting interstate commerce. This Court must, if such regulation unduly infringes personal freedoms, declare the statute invalid under the First Amendment's command that the opportunities for free public discussion be maintained. But insofar as the problem is one of drawing inferences concerning the need for regulation of particular forms of conduct from conflicting evidence, this Court is in no position to substitute its judgment as to the necessity or desirability of the statute for that of Congress. . . . Even restrictions on particular kinds of utterances, if enacted by a legislature after appraisal of the need, come to this Court "encased in the armor wrought by prior legislative determination." . . . The deference due legislative determination of the need for restriction upon particular forms of conduct has found repeated expression in this Court's opinions.

When compared with ordinances and regulations dealing with littering of the streets or disturbance of householders by itinerant preachers, the relative significance and complexity of the problem of political strikes and how to deal with their leaders becomes at once apparent. It must be remembered that § 9 (h) is not an isolated statute dealing with a subject divorced from the problems of labor peace generally. It is a part of some very complex machinery set up by the Federal Government for the purpose of encouraging the peaceful settlement of labor disputes. Under the statutory scheme, unions which become collective bargaining representatives for groups of employees often represent not only members of the union but nonunion workers or members of other unions as well. Because of the necessity to have strong unions to bargain on equal terms with strong employers, individual employees are required by law to sacrifice rights which, in some cases, are valuable to them. . . . The loss of individual rights for the greater benefit of the group results in a tremendous increase in the power of the representative of the group—the union. But power is never without responsibility. And when authority derives in part from Government's thumb on the scales, the exercise of that power by private persons becomes closely akin, in some respects, to its exercise by Government itself.

We do not suggest that labor unions which utilize the facilities of the National Labor Relations Board become Government agencies or may be regulated as such. But it is plain that when Congress clothes the bargaining representative "with powers comparable to those possessed by a legislative body both to create and restrict the rights of those whom it represents," the public interest in the good faith exercise of that power is very great.

What of the effects of § 9 (h) upon the rights of speech and assembly of those proscribed by its terms? The statute does not prevent or punish by criminal sanctions the making of a speech, the affiliation with any organization, or the holding of any belief. But as we have noted, the fact that no direct restraint or punishment is imposed upon speech or assembly does not determine the free speech question. Under some circumstances, indirect "discouragements" undoubtedly have the same coercive effect upon the exercise of First Amendment rights as imprisonment, fines, injunctions or taxes. A requirement that adherents of particular religious faiths or political parties wear identifying armbands, for example, is obviously of this nature.

But we have here no statute which is either frankly aimed at the suppression of dangerous ideas nor one which, although ostensibly aimed at the regulation of conduct, may actually "be made the instrument of the arbitrary suppression of views." . . . There are here involved none of the elements of censorship or prohibition of the dissemination of information that were present in the cases mainly relied upon by those attacking the statute. The "discouragements" of § 9 (h) proceed not against the groups or beliefs identified therein, but only against the combination of those affiliations or beliefs with occupancy of a position of great power over the economy of the country. Congress has concluded that substantial harm, in the form of direct, positive action, may be expected from that combination. In this legislation, Congress did not restrain the activities of the Communist Party as a political organization; nor did it attempt to stifle beliefs. . . . Section 9 (h) touches only a relative handful of persons, leaving the great majority of persons of the identified affiliations and beliefs completely free from restraint. And it leaves those few who are affected free to maintain their affiliations and beliefs subject only to possible loss of positions which Congress has concluded are being abused to the injury of the public by members of the described groups.

We have previously had occasion to consider other statutes and regulations in which the interests involved were, in large measure, like those now being considered. In *United Public Workers* v. *Mitchell*, we upheld a statute which provided that employees of the Federal Government could not participate in partisan political activities, concededly a First Amendment right, if they would retain their positions. The decision was not put upon the ground that government employment is a privilege to be conferred or withheld at will. For it was recognized that Congress may not "enact a regulation providing that no Republican, Jew or Negro shall be appointed to federal office, or that no federal employee shall attend Mass or take any active part in missionary work." 330 U.S. at 100. But the rational connection between the prohibitions of the statute and its objects, the limited scope of the abridgment of First Amendment rights, and the large public interest in the efficiency of government service, which Congress had found necessitated the statute, led us to the conclusion that the statute may stand consistently with the First Amendment.

Similarly, in *In re Summers*, 325 U.S. 561, we upheld the refusal of a state supreme court to admit to membership of its bar an otherwise qualified person on the sole ground that he had conscientious scruples against war and would not use force to prevent wrong under any circumstances. Since he could not, so the justices of the state court found, swear in good faith to uphold the state constitution, which requires service in the militia in time of war, we held that refusal to permit him to practice law did not violate the First Amendment, as its commands are incorporated in the Due Process Clause of the Fourteenth Amendment. Again, the relation between the obligations of membership in the bar and service required by the state in time of war, the limited effect of the state's holding upon speech and assembly, and the strong interest which every state court has in the persons who become officers of the court were thought sufficient to justify the state action. . . .

It is contended that the principle that statutes touching First Amendment freedoms must be narrowly drawn dictates that a statute aimed at political strikes should make the calling of such strikes unlawful but should not attempt to bring about the removal of union officers, with its attendant effect upon First Amendment rights. We think, however, that the legislative judgment that interstate commerce must be protected from a continuing threat of such strikes is a permissible one in this case. The fact that the injury to interstate commerce would be an accomplished fact before any sanctions could be applied, the possibility that a large number of such strikes might be called at a time of external or internal crisis, and the practical difficulties which would be encountered in detecting illegal activities of this kind are factors which are persuasive that Congress should not be powerless to remove the threat, not limited to punishing the act. . . .

VI.

Previous discussion has considered the constitutional questions raised by § 9 (h) as they apply alike to members of the Communist Party and affiliated organizations and to persons who believe in overthrow of the government by force. The breadth of the provision concerning belief in overthrow of the government by force would raise additional questions, however, if it were read very literally to include all persons who might under any conceivable circumstances, subscribe to that belief.

But we see no reason to construe the statute so broadly. It is within the power and is the duty of this Court to construe a statute so as to avoid the danger of unconstitutionality if it may be done in consonance with the legislative purpose. . . . In enacting § 9 (h), Congress had as its objective the protection of interstate commerce from direct interference, not any intent to disturb or proscribe beliefs as such. Its manifest purpose was to bring within the terms of the statute only those persons whose beliefs strongly indicate a will to engage in political strikes and other forms of direct action when, as officers, they direct union activities. The congressional purpose is therefore served if we construe the clause, "that he does not believe in, and is not a member of or supports any organization that believes in or teaches, the overthrow of the United States Government by force or by any illegal or unconstitutional methods," to apply to persons and organizations who believe in violent overthrow of the Government as it presently exists under the Constitution as an objective, not merely a prophecy. Congress might well find that such persons—those who believe that the present form of the Government of the United States should be changed by force or other illegal methods—would carry that objective into their conduct of union affairs by calling political strikes designed to weaken and divide the American people, whether they consider actual overthrow of the Government to be near or distant. It is to those persons that § 9 (h) is intended to apply, and only to them. We hold, therefore, that the belief identified in § 9 (h) is a belief in the objective of overthrow by force or by any illegal or unconstitutional methods of the Government of the United States as it now exists under the Constitution and laws thereof.

As thus construed, we think that the "belief" provision of the oath presents no different problem from that present in that part of the section having to do with membership in the Communist Party. Of course we agree that one may not be imprisoned or executed because he holds particular beliefs. But to attack the straw man of "thought control" is to ignore the fact that the sole effect of the statute upon one who believes in overthrow of the Government by force and violence—and does not deny his belief—is that he may be forced to relinquish his position as a union leader. That fact was crucial in our discussion of the statute as it relates to membership in the Communist Party. . . .

If the principle that one may under no circumstances be required to state his beliefs on any subject nor suffer the loss of any right or privilege because of his beliefs be a valid one, its application in other possible situations becomes relevant. Suppose, for example, that a federal statute provides that no person may become a member of the Secret Service force assigned to protect the President unless he swears that he does not believe in assassination of the President. Is this beyond the power of Congress, whatever the need revealed by its investigations? An affirmative answer hardly commends itself to reason unless, indeed, the Bill of Rights has been converted into a "suicide pact." . . . Yet the example chosen is far-fetched only because of the manifest absurdity of reliance upon an oath in such a situation. One can have no doubt that the screening process in the selection of persons to occupy such positions probes far deeper than mere oath-taking can possibly do.

To hold that such an oath is permissible, on the other hand, is to admit that the circumstances under which one is asked to state his belief and the consequences which flow from his refusal to do so or his disclosure of a particular belief make a difference. The reason for the difference has been pointed out at some length above. First, the loss of a particular position is not the loss of life or liberty. We have noted that the distinction is one of degree, and it is for this reason that the effect of the statute in proscribing beliefs—like its effect in restraining speech or freedom of association—must be carefully weighed by the courts in determining whether the balance struck by Congress comports with the dictates of the Constitution. But it is inaccurate to speak of § 9 (h) as "punishing" of "forbidding" the holding of beliefs, any more than it punishes or forbids membership in the Communist Party.

Second, the public interest at stake in ascertaining one's beliefs cannot automatically be assigned at zero without consideration of the circumstances of the inquiry. If it is admitted that beliefs are springs to action, it becomes highly relevant whether the person who is asked whether he believes in overthrow of the Government by force is a general with five hundred thousand men at his command or a village constable. To argue that because the latter may not be asked his beliefs the former must necessarily be exempt is to make a fetish of beliefs. The answer to the implication that if this statute is upheld "then the power of government over beliefs is as unlimited as its power over conduct and the way is open to force disclosure of attitudes on all manner of social, economic, moral and political issues," . . . is that that result does not follow "while this Court sits." The circumstances giving rise to the inquiry, then, are likewise factors to be weighed by the courts, giving due weight, of course, to the congressional judgment concerning the need. In short, the problem of balancing the conflicting individual and national interests involved is no different from the problem presented by proscriptions based upon political affiliations.

Insofar as a distinction between beliefs and political affiliations is based upon absence of any "overt act" in the former case, it is relevant, if at all, in connection with problems of proof. In proving that one swore falsely that he is not a Communist, the act of joining the Party is crucial. Proof that one lied in swearing that he does not believe in overthrow of the Government by force, on the other hand, must consist in proof of his mental state. To that extent they differ.

To state the difference, however, is but to recognize that while objective facts may be proved directly, the state of a man's mind must be inferred from the things he says or does. Of course we agree that the courts cannot "ascertain the thought that has had no outward manifestation." But courts and juries every day pass upon knowledge, belief and intent—the state of men's minds—having before them no more than evidence of their words and conduct, from which, in ordinary human experience, mental condition may be inferred. . . . False swearing in signing the affidavit must, as in other cases where mental state is in issue, be proved by the outward manifestations of state of mind. In the absence of such manifestations, which are as much "overt acts" as the act of joining the Communist Party, there can be no successful prosecution for false swearing.

Considering the circumstances surrounding the problem—the deference due the congressional judgment concerning the need for regulation of conduct affecting interstate commerce and the effect of the statute upon rights of speech, assembly and belief—we conclude that § 9 (h) of the Labor-Management Relations Act does not unduly infringe freedoms protected by the First Amendment. Those who, so Congress has found, would subvert the public interest cannot escape all regulations because, at the same time, they carry on legitimate political activities. . . . To encourage unions to displace them from positions of great power over the national economy, while at the same time leaving free the outlets by which they may pursue legitimate political activities of persuasion and advocacy, does not seem to us to contravene the purposes of the First Amendment. That Amendment requires that one be permitted to believe what he will. It requires that one be permitted to advocate what he will unless there is a clear and present danger that a substantial public evil will result therefrom. It does not require that he be permitted to be the keeper of the arsenal.

VII.

There remain two contentions which merit discussion. One is that § 9 (h) is unconstitutionally vague. The other is that it violates the mandate of Art. 1, § 9 of the Constitution, that "No bill of attainder or ex-post-facto law shall be passed."

The argument as to vagueness stresses the breadth of such terms as "affiliated," "supports" and "illegal or unconstitutional methods." There is little doubt that imagination can conjure hypothetical cases in which the meaning of these terms will be in nice question. The applicable standard, however, is not one of wholly consistent academic definition of abstract terms. It is, rather, the practical criterion of fair notice to those to whom the statute is directed. The particular context is all important.

The only criminal punishment specified is the application of § 35A of the Criminal Code, 18 U.S.C. § 1001, which covers only those false statements made "knowingly and willfully." The question in any criminal prosecution involving a non-Communist affidavit must therefore be whether the affiant acted in good faith or knowingly lied concerning his affiliations, beliefs, support of organizations, etc. And since the constitutional vice in a vague or indefinite statute is the injustice to the accused in placing him on trial for an offense, the nature of which he is given no fair warning, the fact that punishment is restricted to acts done with knowledge that they contravene the statute makes this objection untenable. As this Court pointed out . . . "A mind intent upon willful evasion is inconsistent with surprised innocence." . . . Without considering, therefore, whether in other circumstances the words used in § 9 (h) would render a statute unconstitutionally vague and indefinite, we think that the fact that under § 35A of the Criminal Code no honest, untainted interpretation of those words is punishable removes the possibility of constitutional infirmity.

The unions' argument as to bill of attainder cites the familiar cases, *United States* v. *Lovett,* 328 U.S. 303 (1946); *Ex parte Garland,* 4 Wall. 333 (1866); *Cummings* v. *Missouri,* 4 Wall. 277 (1866). Those cases and this also, according to the argument, involve the proscription of certain occupations to a group classified according to belief and loyalty. But there is a decisive distinction: in the previous decisions the individuals involved were in fact being punished for *past* actions; whereas in this case they are subject to possible loss of position only because there is substantial ground for the congressional judgment that their beliefs and loyalties will be transformed into *future* conduct. Of course, the history of the past conduct is the foundation for the judgment as to what the future conduct is likely to be; but that does not alter the conclusion that § 9 (h) is intended to prevent future actions rather than to punish past action.

This distinction is emphasized by the fact that members of those groups identified in § 9 (h) are free to serve as union officers if at any time they renounce the allegiances which constituted a bar to signing the affidavit in the past. Past conduct, actual or threatened by their previous adherence to affiliations and beliefs mentioned in § 9 (h), is not a bar to resumption of the position. In the cases relied upon by the unions on the other hand, this Court has emphasized that, since the basis of disqualification was past action or loyalty, nothing that those persons proscribed by its terms could ever do would change the result. . . . Here the intention is to forestall future dangerous acts; there is no one who may not, by a voluntary alteration of the loyalties which impel him to action, become eligible to sign the affidavit. We cannot conclude that this section is a bill of attainder.

In their argument on this point, the unions seek some advantage from references to English history pertinent to a religious test oath. The experience is written into our Constitution in the following provision of Article VI: "The Senators and Representatives before mentioned, and the Members of the several State Legislatures, and all executive and judicial Officers, both of the United States and of the several States, shall be bound by Oath or Affirmation, to support this

Constitution; but no religious Test shall ever be required as a Qualification to any Office or public Trust under the United States." It is obvious that not all oaths were abolished; the mere fact that § 9 (h) is in oath form hardly rises to the stature of a constitutional objection. All that was forbidden was a "religious Test." We do not think that the oath here involved can rightly be taken as falling within that category.

Clearly the Constitution permits the requirement of oaths by office holders to uphold the Constitution itself. The obvious implication is that those unwilling to take such an oath are to be barred from public office. For the President, a specific oath was set forth in the Constitution itself, Art. II, § 1. And Congress has detailed an oath for other federal officers. Obviously, the Framers of the Constitution thought that the exaction of an affirmation of minimal loyalty to the Government was worth the price of whatever deprivation of individual freedom of conscience was involved. All that we need hold here is that the casting of § 9 (h) into the mold of an oath does not invalidate it, if it is otherwise constitutional.

We conclude that § 9 (h) of the Labor-Management Relations Act, as herein construed, is compatible with the Federal Constitution and may stand. . . .

Mr. Justice Black, dissenting:

We have said that "Freedom to think is absolute of its own nature; the most tyrannical government is powerless to control the inward workings of the mind." But people can be, and in less democratic countries have been, made to suffer for their admitted or conjectured thoughts. Blackstone recalls that Dionysius is "recorded to have executed a subject barely for dreaming that he had killed him; which was held sufficient proof that he had thought thereof in his waking hours." Such a result, while too barbaric to be tolerated in our nation, is not illogical if a government can tamper in the realm of thought and penalize "belief" on the ground that it might lead to illegal conduct. Individual freedom and governmental thought-probing cannot live together. As the Court admits even today, under the First Amendment "Beliefs are inviolate."

Today's decision rejects that fundamental principle. The Court admits, as it must, that the "proscriptions" of § 9 (h) of the Taft Hartley Act rest on "beliefs and political affiliations," and that "Congress has undeniably discouraged the lawful exercise of political freedoms" which are "protected by the First Amendment." These inescapable facts should compel a holding that § 9 (h) conflicts with the First Amendment.

Crucial to the Court's contrary holding is the premise that congressional power to regulate trade and traffic includes power to proscribe "beliefs and political affiliations." No case cited by the Court provides the least vestige of support for thus holding that the Commerce Clause restricts the right to think. On the contrary, the First Amendment was added after adoption of the Constitution for the express purpose of barring Congress from using previously granted powers to abridge belief or its expression. Freedom to think is inevitably abridged when beliefs are penalized by imposition of civil disabilities.

Since § 9 (h) was passed to exclude certain beliefs from one arena of the national economy, it was quite natural to utilize the test oath as a weapon. History attests the efficacy of that instrument for inflicting penalties and disabilities on obnoxious minorities. It was one of the major devices used against the Huguenots in France, and against "heretics" during the Spanish Inquisition. It helped English rulers identify and outlaw Catholics, Quakers, Baptists, and Congregationalists—groups considered dangerous for political as well as religious reasons. And wherever the test oath was in vogue, spies and informers found rewards far more tempting than truth. Painful awareness of the evils of thought espionage made such oaths "an abomination to the founders of this nation," *In re Summers*, 325 U.S. 561, 576, dissenting opinion. Whether religious, political, or both, test oaths are implacable foes of free thought. By approving their imposition, this Court has injected compromise into a field where the First Amendment forbids compromise.

The Court assures us that today's encroachment on liberty is just a small one, that this particular statutory provision "touches only a handful of persons, leaving the great majority of persons of the identified affiliations and beliefs completely free from restraint." But not the least of the virtues of the First Amendment is its protection of each member of the smallest and most unorthodox minority. Centuries of experience testify that laws aimed at one political or religious group, however rational in their beginnings, generate hatreds and prejudices which rapidly spread beyond control. Too often it is fear which inspires such passions, and nothing is more reckless or contagious. In the resulting hysteria, popular indignation tars with the same brush all those who have ever been associated with any member of the group under attack or who hold a view which, though supported by revered Americans as essential to democracy, has been adopted by that group for its own purposes.

Under such circumstances, restrictions imposed on proscribed groups are seldom static, even though the rate of expansion may not move in geometric progression from discrimination to arm-band to ghetto and worse. Thus I cannot regard the Court's holding as one which merely bars Communists from holding union office and nothing more. For its reasoning would apply just as forcibly to statutes barring Communists and their suspected sympathizers from election to political office, mere membership in unions, and in fact from getting or holding any jobs whereby they could earn a living.

The Court finds comfort in its assurance that we need not fear too much legislative restriction of political belief or association "while this Court sits." That expression, while felicitous, has no validity in this particular constitutional field. For it springs from the assumption that individual mental freedom can be constitutionally abridged whenever any majority of this

Court finds a satisfactory legislative reason. Never before has this Court held that the Government could for any reason attaint persons for their political beliefs or affiliations. It does so today.

Today the "political affiliation" happens to be the Communist Party: testimony of an ex-Communist that some Communist union officers had called "political strikes" is held sufficient to uphold a law coercing union members not to elect any Communist as an officer. Under this reasoning, affiliations with other political parties could be proscribed just as validly. Of course there is no practical possibility that either major political party would turn this weapon on the other, even though members of one party were accused of "political lockouts" a few years ago and members of the other are now charged with fostering a "welfare state" alien to our system. But with minor parties the possibility is not wholly fanciful. One, for instance, advocates socialism; another allegedly follows the Communist "line"; still another is repeatedly charged with a desire and purpose to deprive Negroes of equal job opportunities. Under today's opinion Congress could validly bar all members of these parties from officership in unions or industrial corporations; the only showing required would be testimony that some members in such positions had, by attempts to further their party's purposes, unjustifiably fostered industrial strife which hampered interstate commerce.

It is indicated, although the opinion is not thus limited and is based on threats to commerce rather than to national security, that members of the Communist Party or its "affiliates" can be individually attainted without danger to others because there is some evidence that as a group they act in obedience to the commands of a foreign power. This was the precise reason given in Sixteenth-Century England for attainting all Catholics unless they subscribed to test oaths wholly incompatible with their religion. Yet in the hour of crisis, an overwhelming majority of the English Catholics thus persecuted rallied loyally to defend their homeland against Spain and its Catholic troops. And in our own country Jefferson and his followers were earnestly accused of subversive allegiance to France. At the time, imposition of civil disability on all members of his political party must have seemed at least as desirable as does § 9 (h) today. For at stake, so many believed, was the survival of a newly-founded nation, not merely a few potential interruptions of commerce by strikes "political" rather than economic in origin.

These experiences underline the wisdom of the basic constitutional precept that penalties should be imposed only for a person's own conduct, not for his beliefs or for the conduct of others with whom he may associate. Guilt should not be imputed solely from association or affiliation with political parties or any other organization, however much we abhor the ideas which they advocate. *Schneiderman* v. *United States,* 320 U.S. 118, 136–139.

Like anyone else, individual Communists who commit overt acts in violation of valid laws can and should be punished. But the postulate of the First Amendment is that our free institutions can be maintained without proscribing or penalizing political belief, speech, assembly, or party affiliation. This is a far bolder philosophy than despotic rulers can afford to follow. It is the heart of the system on which our freedom depends.

Fears of alien ideologies have frequently agitated the nation and inspired legislation aimed at suppressing advocacy of those ideologies. At such times the fog of public excitement obscures the ancient landmarks set up in our Bill of Rights. Yet then, of all times, should this Court adhere most closely to the course they mark. . . .

2. Loyalty Regulations for Government Employees

a. Loyalty Review Boards

BAILEY v. RICHARDSON

182 F. 2d 46 (1950)

[This case was decided by the United States Court of Appeals for the District of Columbia Circuit. The decision was affirmed by an equally divided Supreme Court, without an opinion. 341 US 918 (1951).

[Loyalty investigations of Government employees were started by the House Un-American Activities Committee. In 1938 the chairman of the Committee, Congressman Dies, warned against "crackpots" and "internationalists" and Communists on the Government payroll. Spurred on by Dies and the Committee, Congress in 1939 enacted Section 9A of the Hatch Act, making it unlawful for any federal employee to have membership in any organization which advocates overthrow of the Government. Since 1941 appropriation bills of Congress have carried a rider that no part of the funds is to be used to pay the salary of a person who is a member of an organization that advocates overthrow of the Government.

[The Attorney General and the President, starting in 1942, appointed executive bodies to implement these provisions of law. In 1947 President Truman issued Order 9835, which provided for formal loyalty investigation procedures. It provided for the dismissal of an employee from the service of the Federal Government if "on all the evidence, reasonable grounds exist for the belief that the person involved is disloyal to the Government of the United States." It was under this provision that Dorothy Bailey was dismissed from her position.

[On April 28, 1952, President Truman amended the 1947 order to require dismissal if on the whole record there was "reasonable doubt" of the employee's loyalty. Under this amendment, it was thought, dismissal would be easier.

[On April 27, 1953, President Eisenhower issued an executive order which did away with "loyalty" as a test and substituted in its place "security." The order provided that an employee is to be dismissed if his employment "may not be clearly consistent with the interest of the national security." This order was to cover all security risks for whatever ground, e.g., suspected disloyalty, drunkenness, immorality. It also abolished the Loyalty Review Board, leaving the execution of the order to the various executive agencies and departments.

[In the *Bailey Case* a majority of the court in effect held that, in a loyalty case involving a Government employee, the courts have no function to perform. Judge Edgerton's dissenting opinion points up the weaknesses in the loyalty proceedings and the dangers in denying judicial review and relief.]

Prettyman, Circuit Judge:

This is a civil action brought in the United States District Court for the District of Columbia for a declaratory judgment and for an order directing plaintiff-appellant's reinstatement in Government employ. The defendants-appellees are the Administrator of the Federal Security Agency, the members of the Civil Service Commission, members of its Loyalty Review Board, and members of its Loyalty Board of the Fourth Civil Service Region. Answer to the complaint was made by the defendants-appellees, and affidavits were filed. Both plaintiff and defendants made motions for summary judgment. The District Court granted the motion of the defendants. This appeal followed. . . .

Appellant Bailey was employed in the classified civil service of the United States Government from August 19, 1939, to June 28, 1947. Upon the latter date she was separated from the service due to reduction in force. On March 25, 1948, she was given a temporary appointment, and on May 28, 1948, she was reinstated under circumstances to be related.

The regulations of the Civil Service Commission in effect at the time of appellant's reinstatement made reinstatements subject to the condition that removal might be ordered by the Commission if investigation of the individual's qualifications, made within eighteen months, disclosed disqualification. The regulations listed as a disqualification: "(7) On all the evidence, reasonable grounds exist for belief that the person involved is disloyal to the Government of the United States."

On July 31, 1948, two months after her reinstatement, Miss Bailey received from the Regional Loyalty Board of the Commission a letter and an enclosed interrogatory. The letter said in part:

> During the course of an investigation of your suitability for appointment, information was received which the Commission believes you should be given an opportunity to clarify. Consequently, there are inclosed an original and copy of an interrogatory to be answered by you under affirmation or oath. . . .
>
> Your cooperation in this matter will be appreciated.

The interrogatory said in part:

As part of the process of determining your suitability for Federal Employment, an investigation of you has been conducted under the provisions of Executive Order 9835, which established the Federal Employees Loyalty Program. This investigation disclosed information which, it is believed, you should have an opportunity to explain or refute.

The questions in the attached Interrogatory are based on the information received, and are to be answered in writing in sufficient detail to present fairly your explanation or answers thereto. . . .

You are further advised that you have the right, upon request, to an administrative hearing on the issues in the case before the Regional Loyalty Board. You may appear personally before the Board and be represented by counsel or representative of your own choice; and you may present evidence in your behalf. Such evidence may be presented by witnesses or by affidavit. . . .

The Commission has received information to the effect that you are or have been a member of the Communist Party or the Communist Political Association; that you have attended meetings of the Communist Party, and have associated on numerous occasions with known Communist Party members. . . .

The Commission has received information to the effect that you are or have been a member of the American League for Peace and Democracy, an organization which has been declared by the Attorney General to come within the purview of Executive Order 9835. . . .

The Commission has received information to the effect that you are or have been a member of the Washington Committee for Democratic Action, an organization which has been declared by the Attorney General to come within the purview of Executive Order 9835. . . .

Are you now, or have ever been, a member of, or in any manner affiliated with, the Nazi or Fascist movements or with any organization or political party whose objective is now, or has ever been, the overthrow of the Constitutional Government of the United States?

Miss Bailey answered the interrogatories directly and specifically, denying each item of information recited therein as having been received by the Commission, except that she admitted past membership for a short time in the American League for Peace and Democracy. She vigorously asserted her loyalty to the United States. She requested an administrative hearing. A hearing was held before the Regional Board. She appeared and testified and presented other witnesses and numerous affidavits. No person other than those presented by her testified.

On November 1, 1948, the Regional Board advised the Federal Security Agency, in which Miss Bailey was employed, that:

As a result of such investigation and after a hearing before this Board, it was found that, on all the evidence, reasonable grounds exist for belief that Miss Bailey is disloyal to the Government of the United States.

Therefore she has been rated ineligible for Federal employment; she has been barred from competing in civil service examinations for a period of three years, and your office is instructed to separate her from the service.

On the same day, a letter was sent by the Board to Miss Bailey, reading in part:

As shown in the attached copy of a letter to your employing agency, it has been found that, on all the evidence, reasonable grounds exist for belief that you are disloyal to the Government of the United States.

Your application for or eligibility from each of the examinations mentioned below has been cancelled and you have been barred from civil service examinations in the Federal service for a period of three years from October 29, 1948. When the period of debarment has expired the Commission will, upon request, consider the removal of the bar.

If you wish to appeal the Board's decision, the Loyalty Review Board, U. S. Civil Service Commission, Washington 25, D.C., should be notified within 20 days from the date of receipt by you of this letter.

Miss Bailey appealed to the Loyalty Review Board and requested a hearing. Hearing was held before a panel of that Board. Miss Bailey appeared, testified, and presented affidavits. No person other than Miss Bailey testified, and no affidavits other than hers were presented on the record.

On February 9, 1949, the Chairman of the Loyalty Review Board advised the Federal Security Agency that the finding of the Regional Board was sustained, and he requested that the Agency remove Miss Bailey's name from the rolls. Notice to that effect was sent to counsel for Miss Bailey on the same day. The full Board subsequently declined to review the conclusions of its panel.

Miss Bailey's position from May 28, 1948, to November 3, 1948, was that of a training officer (general fields) CAF-13.

The rights claimed by and for appellant must be discovered accurately and defined precisely. The events with which we are concerned were not accidental, thoughtless or mere petty tyrannies of subordinate officials. They were the deliberate design of the executive branch of the Government, knowingly supported by the Congress.

The case presented for Miss Bailey is undoubtedly appealing. She was denied reinstatement in her former employment because Government officials found reasonable ground to believe her disloyal. She was not given a trial in any sense of the word, and she does not know who informed upon her. Thus viewed, her situation appeals powerfully to our sense of the fair and the just. But the case must be placed in context and in perspective.

The Constitution placed upon the President and the Congress, and upon them alone, responsibility for the welfare of this country in the arena of world affairs. It so happens that we are presently in an adversary position to a government whose most successful recent method of contest is the infiltration of the government service by its sympathizers. This is the context of Miss Bailey's question.

The essence of her complaint is not that she was denied reinstatement; the complaint is that she was denied reinstatement without revelation by the Government of the names of those who informed against her and of the method by which her alleged activities were detected. So the question actually posed by the case is whether the President is faced with an inescapable dilemma, either to continue in Government employment a person whose loyalty he reasonably suspects or else to reveal publicly the methods by which he detects disloyalty and the names of any persons who may venture to assist him.

Even in normal times and as a matter of ordinary internal operation, the ability, integrity and loyalty of purely executive employees is exclusively for the executive branch of Government to determine, except in so far as the Congress has a constitutional voice in the matter. All such employees hold office at the pleasure of the appointing authority; again except only for statutory limitations. Never in our history . . . has a Government employee been entitled as of right to the sort of hearing Miss Bailey demands in respect to dismissal from office. These well-established principles give perspective to the present problem.

The presentation of appellant's contentions is impressive. Each detail of the trial which she unquestionably did not get is depicted separately, in a mounting cumulation into analogies to the Dreyfus case and the Nazi judicial process. Thus, a picture of a simple black-and-white fact—that appellant did not get a trial in the judicial sense—is drawn in bold and appealing colors. But the question is not whether she had a trial. The question is whether she should have had one.

If the whole of this case were as appellant pictures it, if we had only to decide the question which she states and as she states it, our task would indeed be simple and attractively pleasant. But it is not so. We are dealing with a major clash between individual and public interests. We must ascertain with precision whether individual rights are involved, and we must then weigh the sum of those rights, if there be any, against the inexorable necessities of the Government. We must examine not only one side of the controversy but both sides.

Appellant next says that the order of the Board which barred her from the federal service for three years, was constitutionally invalid under the decision of the Supreme Court in the *Lovett Case* [328 US 303]. We agree with that contention. The Court in that case clearly held that permanent proscription from Government service is "punishment" and that punishment can be inflicted only upon compliance with the Sixth Amendment. The difference between permanent and limited proscription is merely one of degree and not one of principle. So far as this record shows, this proscription of employment was not pursuant to a general regulation. It was not required by a general classification by Congress or by general regulation of the Civil Service Commission or of the Loyalty Board. No reference to proscription appears in the Executive Order, the Attorney General's orders, or the statements of the Loyalty Board. . . . The bar in the present proceeding appears on the record to be one imposed by the Board upon this particular individual in this particular case as a matter of individual adjudication. We hold that the portions of the orders and directions of the defendants-appellees which purported to bar Miss Bailey from federal employ for three years, are invalid.

We did not understand appellant to urge the unconstitutionality of her dismissal apart from the three-year bar. But there is a difference of opinion among us in that respect, and we, therefore, state our views upon the point. First we consider the contentions respecting the constitutionality of the procedure pursued, and then we consider the constitutionality of the condition imposed upon the reinstatement. For the first purpose, we must assume that Miss Bailey was in the classified service without condition at the time of her removal from the rolls and that she was, therefore, dismissed from employment and not merely denied appointment; although, as we have indicated we do not agree with that view of her status. If her status was merely that of an applicant for appointment, as we think it was, her nonappointment involved no procedural constitutional rights. Obviously, an applicant for office has no constitutional right to a hearing or a specification of the reasons why he is not appointed. We, therefore, consider the constitutionality of the procedure followed in this case upon the assumption that a Government employee in the classified service is being dismissed because her superiors have grounds, which to them are reasonable, to believe that she is disloyal.

Our first inquiry is whether the Sixth Amendment applies to a dismissal from Government service. That Amendment provides:

In all criminal prosecutions, the accused shall enjoy the right to a speedy and public trial, by an impartial jury of the State and district wherein the crime shall have been committed, which district shall have been previously ascertained by law, and to be informed of the nature and cause of the accusation; to be confronted with the witnesses against him; to have compulsory process for obtaining witnesses in his favor, and to have the assistance of counsel for his defense.

The Amendment in terms applies to criminal prosecutions, and requires not only confrontation by witnesses but also trial by jury. The process is a judicial process.

The Supreme Court held in the *Lovett Case* that "punishment" can be inflicted lawfully only upon compliance with the Sixth Amendment. The decision in that case is one of the keys to the contention presented on behalf of appellant. The Court held permanent proscription from Government service to be such "punishment," but it did not, as we read the case, hold mere dismissal from Government service to be punishment in that sense. . . . Throughout the entire opinion in the *Lovett Case*, it was meticulously explicit in limiting its discussion to the proscriptive feature of the statute before it. . . .

In the last place, even if there were no decided cases upon the point, we would not think that the Constitution meant that the President could not dismiss a subordinate executive employee without the judicial procedure required by the Sixth Amendment. The fundamental concept of the division of powers, and so of responsibilities, does not, in our opinion, permit the conclusion that the President cannot remove an employee in the executive branch without referring the matter to the judicial branch. And the long history of the controversy concerning removal from public office, beginning with the First Congress, cannot be read so as to permit that conclusion.

We are of the opinion that compliance with the Sixth Amendment is not a prerequisite to the dismissal of an employee from the Federal Government classified civil service. It is apparently admitted on behalf of appellant that this conclusion is true generally speaking but it is said that dismissal for suspicion of disloyalty is an exception and that an employee cannot be dismissed for that one particular reason without a jury trial, confrontation by witnesses, etc., in a judicial proceeding. We shall discuss that claim of exception in a moment.

It is next said on behalf of appellant that the due process clause of the Fifth Amendment requires that she be afforded a hearing of the quasi-judicial type before being dismissed. The due process clause provides: "No person shall . . . be deprived of life, liberty or property, without due process of law. . . ." It has been held repeatedly and consistently that Government employ is not "property" and that in this particular it is not a contract. We are unable to perceive how it could be held to be "liberty." Certainly it is not "life." So much that is clear would seem to dispose of the point. In terms the due process clause does not apply to the holding of a Government office.

Other considerations lead to the same conclusion. Never in our history has a Government administrative employee been entitled to a hearing of the quasi-judicial type upon his dismissal from Government service. That record of a hundred and sixty years of Government administration is the sort of history which speaks with great force. . . .

In the absence of statute or ancient custom to the contrary, executive offices are held at the will of the appointing authority, not for life or for fixed terms. If removal be at will, of what purpose would process be? To hold office at the will of a superior and to be removable therefrom only by constitutional due process of law are opposite and inherently conflicting ideas. Due process of law is not applicable unless one is being deprived of something to which he has a right.

Constitutionally, the criterion for retention or removal of subordinate employees is the confidence of superior executive officials. Confidence is not controllable by process. What may be required by acts of the Congress is another matter, but there is no requirement in the Constitution that the executive branch rely upon the services of persons in whom it lacks confidence. . . .

We hold that the due process of law clause of the Fifth Amendment does not restrict the President's discretion or the prescriptive power of Congress in respect to executive personnel.

We do not reach the question whether, if the due process of law clause does apply, it requires more than this appellant was given. Miss Bailey was not summarily cut off the rolls. She was advised in writing that information concerning her qualifications for Government employ had been received; she was asked specific questions; and she was told that those questions reflected the information received. The questions revealed the nature of the alleged activities giving rise to the inquiry and the names of the organizations in which she was alleged to have been active. Everything that she wished to present was received; all affidavits offered by her were accepted, and all witnesses presented by her testified. She was twice heard orally. She was represented at all stages by competent counsel. Her case was considered by two separate groups of executive officials. On the other hand, she was not told the names of the informants against her. She was not permitted to face or to cross-examine those informants. She was not given the dates or places at which she was alleged to have been active in the named alleged subversive organizations. So the claim in her behalf necessarily goes farther than an abstract claim for due process of law. The claim must be that the due process clause requires, in dismissals of subordinate Government employees, specificity in charges equivalent to that of valid criminal charges, confrontation by witnesses, cross examination of them, and hearing upon evidence openly submitted. Even if the due process clause applies, we would think it does not require so much.

Here again it is apparently conceded on behalf of appellant that our conclusions in respect to the Fifth Amendment are sound generally speaking, but an exception is claimed in the cases of those dismissed for suspicion of disloyalty. As we have said, we shall discuss that claimed exception in a moment.

It is next said that appellant's dismissal impinged upon the rights of free speech and assembly protected by the First Amendment, since the dismissal was premised upon alleged political activity. This suggestion goes not to the procedure but to the ultimate validity of the dismissal itself. But the plain hard fact is that so far as the Constitution is concerned there is no prohibition against the dismissal of Government employees because of their political beliefs, activities or affiliations. That document, standing alone, does not prevent Republican Presidents from dismissing Democrats or Democratic Presidents from dismissing Republicans. From the beginning, such has been the practice, with variations in scope. The reason that it has not continued to so great an extent is because the people became convinced that it was not good government and the Congress and the President wrote that view into statutes and regulations. They, not the Constitution, give Government employees such protection as they have against dismissal for political reasons. . . .

The situation of the Government employee is not different in this respect from that of private employees. A newspaper editor has a constitutional right to speak and write as he pleases. But the Constitution does not guarantee him a place in the columns of a publisher with whose political views he does not agree.

Government employment is subject to many restrictions upon otherwise unrestricted individual rights in respect to activities, property ownership, etc., as the Supreme Court long ago pointed out. . . .

It is said that the loyalty program as applied in this particular case went beyond the power of Congress and of the President to regulate the conduct of Government employees.

We must at this point be careful to note the precise ground upon which appellant was dismissed. It was that in the judgment of authorized executive officials, "reasonable grounds exist for belief that Miss Bailey is disloyal to the Government of the United States." So far as we have been able to ascertain, it is nowhere disputed that employees in fact disloyal to the Government may and should be removed. A classification of loyal and disloyal is undoubtedly a proper one descriptive of qualification and disqualification for public office. Appellant says: "We are of course not suggesting that a government employee who is reinstated in his job is immune from inquiry into his loyalty." So the points made in behalf of appellant must be these: (1) That mere belief on the part of executive officials of disloyalty, even though supported by grounds reasonable to them, is not a sufficient basis for valid removal. (2) That if the power to remove be limited, some authority other than executive or legislative must be able to determine whether the limitation be transgressed, and so the grounds for executive belief must be fully revealed. (3) That the information concerning appellant, as reflected in the interrogatory sent to her, does not, even if true, constitute reasonable ground for belief in her disloyalty.

The first proposition is in effect that reasonable ground for belief of disloyalty is not sufficient prerequisite to dismissal. But we can perceive no basis for holding that the executive departments must retain in the service those whose loyalty is reasonably doubtful. Reasonably grounded suspicion of disloyalty indicates a risk, and no concept of the Constitution requires the executive to endure recognizable and preventable risks in the administration of the law. He may decide to do so, but we see no basis for saying that he must. The Constitution does not require the President to continue to use in the training of Government personnel, the work performed by this appellant, a person whose loyalty to the Government he suspects. There is no reason in the Constitution why the President should not limit the training staff to persons whose loyalty is beyond the faintest shadow of suspicion.

The clear and present danger rule does not help us in this matter, because Government employ, with which we are here dealing, is not a right. The argument that the rule does apply confuses the subject matter of the controversy. No one denies Miss Bailey the right to any political activity or affiliation she may choose. What is denied her is Government employ. . . .

The second proposition concerns the mode of determining the sufficiency of a doubt of loyalty. If reasonable grounds for belief of disloyalty suffice for dismissal, in whose mind must such reasonable grounds be established?

Much argument at this point is premised upon the possibility of abuse of the removal power. It is said that if executive officers have power to remove without compliance with restrictive measures they may by terror destroy free thought and action in the Government service and so establish a tyranny. This fear is not new. It was held by some members of the First Congress and urged by them in the debate upon the removal power. But under our system of government the courts cannot assume a possible abuse of constitutional power as a reason for denying that power. Almost every power, constitutional, statutory, regulatory, contractual or whatnot, is susceptible of abuse. The Constitution bestows the several powers of government with such checks and balances as the makers of the Government deemed necessary and adequate. All executive power, with the stated limitations, was vested by the Constitution in the executive branch, and no part of it was vested in the judicial branch. The judicial branch can no more assume to limit executive power because of a possible abuse by executive officials than can executive officials limit judicial power because of possible abuse by judicial officers. Abuse of power is, of course, forbidden, but the mere potentiality of abuse does not constitute invalidity of power. We cannot declare an act unconstitutional merely because under it there is a possibility of abuse. . . .

This brings us to the third proposition upon this subject, which is that the revealed information in this particular case is insufficient ground for suspicion of disloyalty. It is said that the interrogatory showed that the basis for Miss Bailey's dismissal was an alleged membership in the Communist Party and other allegedly "subversive" organizations, and that this is an invalid discrimination.

It is perfectly true, as the Supreme Court said in the *United Public Workers Case* [330 US 75], that Congress could not legislate that "no Republican, Jew or Negro shall be appointed to federal office." But if a Democratic President were to appoint few, if any, Republicans to office, or vice versa, he would not be violating any provision of the Constitution. Vigorous as the condemnation of the practice has been, even in recent years, nowhere, so far as we are aware, has it been responsibly asserted that such selection is invalid. In blunt terms, the President can discriminate for political reasons. We do not think the Supreme Court meant, by the quoted sentence, that if the President or his authorized aides exercised the prerogative of selecting employees by selecting no Republicans, the choices would be constitutionally void. Some astonishing results would ensue from any such holding. The Court was referring to permanent, blanket proscription by the Congress. Of more importance, the classifications named in the quoted suggestion have no discernible bearing upon qualification for office. Such a statute would be purely arbitrary and capricious in the most obnoxious meaning of those words.

Our conclusion upon this phase of the case, therefore, is that the loyalty program established by the President's Order and applied to this appellant is not, for any of the reasons thus far discussed, invalid.

Thus the controversy develops, step by step, to its ultimate crisis. It is urged upon us that dismissal from Government employ for suspicion of disloyalty is an exception to the established doctrines and rules generally applicable to Government employees and their dismissal from service.

It is said on behalf of appellant that disloyalty is akin to treason and that dismissal is akin to conviction. Forthwith it is asserted that Miss Bailey has been convicted of disloyalty. As we have seen, nothing resembling a conviction from the legal standpoint has been visited upon her. She was merely refused Government employment for reasons satisfactory to the appointing authorities.

But it is said that the public does not distinguish, that she has been stigmatized and her chance of making a living seriously impaired. The position implicit in that assertion dissolves into two contentions. One is that even if executive authorities had power to dismiss Miss Bailey without a judicial hearing, they had no power to hurt her while doing so; that is, they had no power to call her disloyal even if they had power to dismiss her for that reason. But it has long been established that if the Government, in the exercise of a governmental power, injures an individual, that individual has no redress. Official action beyond the scope of official authority can be prevented or nullified by the courts, and so official action which violates a constitutional right of an individual can be rectified. But if no constitutional right of the individual is being impinged and officials are acting within the scope of official authority, the fact that the individual concerned is injured in the process neither invalidates the official act nor gives the individual a right to redress. So in the present case if Miss Bailey had no constitutional right to her office and the executive officers had power to dismiss her, the fact that she was injured in the process of dismissal neither invalidates her dismissal nor gives her right to redress; this under a rule of law established long ago. . . .

The line of cases in which this court has said that courts will not review the action of executive officials in dismissing executive employees except to insure compliance with statutory requirements, is unvaried. . . .

The rule is applied even when the charges involve offenses of serious moral turpitude. . . .

It should be remarked parenthetically that, in so far as the case before us is concerned, any publicity which it received was not pursuant to but in flat contradiction of the Executive Order, the Attorney General's instructions, and the Loyalty Board's rules, all of which forbid publicity. Moreover, Miss Bailey accepted voluntarily the conditional reappointment which was premised upon her successful passage of the loyalty test laid down in the Executive Order.

The other contention implicit in the assertion, that Miss Bailey has been stigmatized and injured, is that disloyalty is a thing apart, suspicion of which gives rise to constitutional rights not applicable to suspicion of criminal offenses. It seems to us that in so far as suspicion of disloyalty has peculiarities which distinguish it from suspicions of bribery, seduction and other offenses they are adverse to appellant's conclusions. We must look not only at appellant's but also at the public side of this controversy. From that point of view, the retention in the Government service of one suspected of theft or a similar offense would not be of great importance, and the revelation of the method of detection and the names of informants would probably not affect the public interest. But disloyalty in the Government service under present circumstances is a matter of great public concern, and revelation of the methods of detecting it and of the names of witnesses involve public considerations of compelling importance.

We cannot ignore the world situation in which not merely two ideologies but two potentially adverse forces presently exist, and certainly we cannot require that the President and the Congress ignore it. Infiltration of government service is now a recognized technique for the overthrow of government. We do not think that the individual rights guaranteed by the Constitution necessarily mean that a government dedicated to those rights cannot preserve itself in the world as it is. This case presents a small segment of that momentous question. In the light of all that is well known, much of which is recited in opinions of the Supreme Court, we cannot say that a policy of caution in respect to members of the Communist Party in the Government service under current circumstances is forbidden by any restriction in the Constitution. The risks are for the President to estimate, and the assumption of risk is for him to decide. If he thinks that under present circumstances only those whose loyalty is beyond suspicion should be employed by this Government, the policy is his to make. The responsibility in this field is his, and the power to meet it must also be his. The judiciary cannot dictate that he must either retain in Government service those whom he reasonably suspects or else reveal publicly the means and methods by which he detects disloyalty.

Upon the contention that suspicion of disloyalty has characteristics distinguishing it from suspicion of other offenses, we conclude that the differences tend to solidify rather than to weaken the application of the doctrine that the President and the Congress are responsible for the qualifications, ability, judgment and loyalty of Government employees and that removal from Government employment is within their discretion.

It is our clear opinion that the President, absent congressional restriction, may remove from Government service any person of whose loyalty he is not completely convinced. He may do so without assigning any reason and without giving the employee any explanatory notice. If, as a matter of policy, he chooses to give the employee a general description of the information which concerns him and to hear what the employee has to say, he does not thereby strip himself of any portion of his constitutional power to choose and to remove.

We conclude that the Executive Order before us and the proceedings under it violated no congressional limitation upon the executive power of removal; that no constitutional right was involved in this non-appointment or dismissal; and that, in so far as the circumstances imposed hardship upon the individual, the exigencies of government in the public interest under current conditions must prevail, as they always must when a similar clash arises.

Able pleas are made based upon the American passion for fair play and upon the sincere fears of patriotic men that unqueried and unrestricted power of removal in the President may lead to tyranny. Such pleas are to be neither ignored nor belittled, but their forum is the Congress and the President's Office. "The problem," as the executive director of the National Civil Service League has written, is "not so much a matter of the legal issues involved as it is practical application of the President's loyalty review order and its administration."

Finding constitutional power for the procedure here followed, and no violation of congressional mandate, our function is exhausted. We have no concern with executive or legislative policy or with the processes by which those branches of the Government fulfill their constitutional responsibilities.

The case will be remanded to the District Court with instructions to enter a decree holding invalid those sections of the orders of the Loyalty Boards and the Federal Security Agency which would bar Miss Bailey from employment for three years, and holding valid those sections which accomplished her removal from the rolls and from office in the classified civil service.

Edgerton, Circuit Judge, dissenting:

Without trial by jury, without evidence, and without even being allowed to confront her accusers or know their identity, a citizen of the United States has been found disloyal to the government of the United States.

For her supposed disloyal thoughts she has been punished by dismissal from a wholly nonsensitive position in which her efficiency rating was high. The case received nation-wide publicity. Ostracism inevitably followed. A finding of disloyalty is closely akin to a finding of treason. The public hardly distinguishes between the two.

No charges were served on appellant. The chairman of the Regional Board said "Nobody has presented any charges." The Board told appellant it was inquiring whether there were reasonable grounds for believing she was disloyal to the government of the United States. The Federal Bureau of Investigation had reported that informants believed to be reliable had made general statements purporting to connect her with the Communist Party. These reports were not disclosed to the appellant and have not been disclosed in court. The informants were not identified to the appellant or even to the Board. Their statements were admittedly not made under oath. The appellant denied under oath any membership in and any relationship or sympathy with the Communist Party, any activities connected with it or with communism, and affiliation with any organization that advocated overthrow of the government of the United States. She asserted her loyalty to the government of the United States. She admitted attending one Communist meeting in 1932 in connection with a seminar study of the platforms of the various parties while she was a student at Bryn Mawr.

Appellant had no power to subpoena witnesses. Though it takes courage to appear as a voluntary defense witness in a loyalty case, four appeared. One was the pastor of the Methodist Church of which appellant is an active member. He testified: "When this charge or information came to me I was not only surprised, I was dumbfounded. . . . People in our community and in our church think of her and her family in the highest terms." Three officials of appellant's government agency, the United States Employment Service, who had known appellant professionally and socially for years, testified respectively that they were "extremely shocked" by the suggestion of her being disloyal, that it was "inconceivable" and "out of reason." Persons prominent in business, government and education who knew appellant but could not be present submitted affidavits.

No witness offered evidence, even hearsay evidence, against appellant. No affidavits were introduced against her. The record consists entirely of evidence in her favor. Yet the Board purported to find "on all the evidence" that there were reasonable grounds for believing she was disloyal to the government of the United States. Appellees admit the Board made this finding "after considering all the evidence, including the confidential reports of the Federal Bureau of Investigation." . . .

Appellant appeared and testified before a panel of the Loyalty Review Board. She submitted her own affidavit and the affidavits of some 70 persons who knew her, including bankers, corporate officials, federal and state officials, union members, and others. Again no one testified against her. She proved she had publicly and to the knowledge of a number of the affiants taken positions inconsistent with Communist sympathies. She showed not only by her own testimony but by that of other persons that she favored the Marshall Plan, which the Communist Party notoriously opposed, and that in 1940, during the Nazi-Soviet Pact, she favored Lend-Lease and was very critical of the Soviet position. In her union she urged its officers to execute non-communist affidavits, opposed a foreign policy resolution widely publicized as pro-Russian, and favored what was then the official CIO resolution on foreign policy.

Against all this, there were only the unsworn reports in the secret files to the effect that unsworn statements of a general sort, purporting to connect appellant with Communism, had been made by unnamed persons. Some if not all of these statements did not purport to be based on knowledge, but only on belief. Appellant sought to learn the names of the informants, or, if their names were confidential, then at least whether they had been active in appellant's union, in which there were factional quarrels. The Board did not furnish or even have this information. Chairman Richardson said: "I haven't the slightest knowledge as to who they were or how active they have been in anything." All that the Board knew or we know about the informants is that unidentified members of the Federal Bureau of Investigation, who did not appear before the Board, believed them to be reliable. . . .

Appellant's dismissal violates both the Constitution and the Executive Order. However respectable her anonymous accusers may have been, if her dismissal is sustained the livelihood and reputation of any civil servant today and perhaps of any American tomorrow are at the mercy not only of an innocently mistaken informer but also of a malicious or demented one unless his defect is apparent to the agent who interviews him. . . .

Dismissal for disloyalty is punishment and requires all the safeguards of a judicial trial. Most dismissals, including dismissals for colorless or undisclosed reasons and dismissals for incompetence, are plainly not punitive. They do not require a judicial trial or even a full administrative hearing. They are within the authority of the executive. Likewise most tax laws are within the authority of the legislature. It does not follow that all legislative taxation is constitutional or that all executive dismissals are constitutional.

Punishment is infliction of harm, usually for wrong conduct but in appellant's case for wrong views. Dismissals to provide jobs for persons of certain affiliations, whatever else may be said of such dismissals, are not punitive. But dismissals for disloyal views are punitive. This is what the Supreme Court squarely held in the *Lovett Case*. It overruled no cases in so holding. The earlier decisions of the Supreme Court on which this court relies are irrelevant because they involved dismissals for undisclosed reasons, not for disloyal views.

The question whether the rule of the *Lovett Case* extends to dismissals of "disloyal" persons from sensitive positions in which their presence might threaten substantial harm to the government does not arise in the present case and I express no opinion on it. Appellant was dismissed from a non-sensitive position. . . .

The distinction this court draws between dismissal as punishment and ineligibility as punishment not only contradicts the *Lovett Case* but has no basis in reason. Dismissal is more certainly damaging than ineligibility, for the necessary combination of vacancies, qualifications, and desire for public appointment may never occur again. A person dismissed as disloyal can obtain no normal employment, public or private. The President's Committee on Civil Rights said in 1947: "It is a severe punishment to be discharged from the Government for disloyalty, as the Supreme Court pointed out in 1946 in *United States* v. *Lovett*. . . . Loss of job and inability to obtain another one is a severe punishment to impose on any man." It makes no present or probable future difference to the appellant and it should make no difference to a court whether the appellant is told that she is separated from the civil service for life, for three years, or only for the moment. Whatever she is told, if her dismissal is sustained she will not be reemployed while the present climate of opinion continues.

Since dismissal from government service for disloyalty is punishment, due process of law requires that the accused employee be given all the safeguards of a judicial trial before it is imposed. . . .

Not only the basic right to judicial trial but every one of these basic safeguards . . . was violated here. (1) The appellant was not tried by a jury. (2) She was not clearly informed of the charge against her. This is true not only because there was no formal charge and, according to the Chairman of the Regional Board, no charge at all, but also because of the vagueness of the term "disloyal." It is so indefinite that neither the Executive Order nor, as far as appears, the Loyalty Review Board has attempted to define it. . . . (3) The appellant violated no law. (4) Even the Executive Order was issued after the activities from which her disloyalty is inferred took place, if they took place at all. (5) She was not confronted with any witnesses against her. (6) Forced idleness may well be considered a cruel as well as unusual punishment. It has been considered more severe than forced labor. . . .

Appellant's dismissal abridges freedom of speech and assembly. Mr. Justice Holmes' famous statement, made in 1892 when he was a member of the Supreme Judicial Court of Massachusetts, that "the petitioner may have a constitutional right to talk politics, but he has no constitutional right to be a policeman" is greatly over-simplified. "As pointed out in *Frost Trucking Co. v. Railroad Comm.*, 271 U.S. 583, even in the granting of a privilege the state 'may not impose conditions which require the relinquishment of constitutional rights . . .'" including the rights of free speech, press, and assembly. In the *Esquire Case* the Supreme Court said: "We may assume that Congress . . . need not open second-class mail to publications of all types. . . . But grave constitutional questions are immediately raised once it is said that the use of the mails is a privilege which may be extended or withheld on any grounds whatsoever. . . . Under that view the second-class rate could be granted on condition that certain economic or political ideas not be disseminated." Similarly, the premise that government employment is a privilege does not support the conclusion that it may be granted on condition that certain economic or political ideas not be entertained. Though members of minority parties have often been dismissed, in the past, to make room for members of a party in power, any comprehensive practice of that sort would today be unthinkable as well as illegal, and the Supreme Court has plainly indicated it would also be unconstitutional. The Court pointed out in the *Mitchell Case* that Congress could not " 'enact a regulation providing that no Republican, Jew or Negro shall be appointed to federal office, or that no federal employee shall attend Mass or take any active part in missionary work.' "

The dismissal which the Court upheld in the *Mitchell Case* was not based on views but on conduct. . . .

"In loyalty hearings the following questions have been asked of employees against whom charges have been brought. . . . 'Do you read a good many books?' 'What books do you read?' 'What magazines do you read?' 'What newspapers do you buy or subscribe to?' 'Do you think that Russian Communism is likely to succeed?' 'How do you explain the fact that you have an album of Paul Robeson records in your home?' 'Do you ever entertain Negroes in your home?' . . . 'Is it not true . . . that you lived next door to and therefore were closely associated with a member of the I.W.W.?' "

"Too often the line of questioning has revolved around conformity and prevailing mores in personal habits and personal opinion. . . . A woman employee was accused of disloyalty because, at the time of siege of Stalingrad, she collected money for Russian war relief (she also collected money for British and French relief)." A record filed in this court shows that an accused employee was taken to task for membership in Consumers Union and for favoring legislation against racial discrimination. The record in the present case contains the following colloquy between a member of the Regional Board and the present appellant: "Mr. Blair: Did you ever write a letter to the Red Cross about the segregation of blood? Miss Bailey: I do not recall. Mr. Blair: What was your personal position about that? Miss Bailey: Well, the medical—. Mr. Blair: I am asking yours."

No doubt some boards are quite aware that unconventional views and conduct have no tendency to indicate disloyalty. But the fact remains that some boards imagine the contrary. This fact is too well known. It puts government employees under economic and social pressure to protect their jobs and reputations by expressing in words and conduct only the most orthodox opinions on political, economic and social questions.

A regulation that restrains constitutionally protected speech along with other speech cannot be enforced against either. Legislation is unconstitutional as a whole if it "does not aim specifically at evils within the allowable area of state control but . . . sweeps within its ambit other activities that in ordinary circumstances constitute an exercise of freedom of speech or of the press. The existence of such a statute . . . results in a continuous and pervasive restraint on all freedom of discussion that might reasonably be regarded as within its purview. . . . An accused . . . under such a statute, does not have to sustain the burden of demonstrating that the State could not constitutionally have written a different and specific statute covering his activities as disclosed by the charge and the evidence introduced against him. . . . Where regulations of the liberty of free discussion are concerned, there are special reasons for observing the rule that it is the statute, and not the accusation or the evidence under it, which prescribes the limits of permissible conduct and warns against transgression." . . .

Freedoms that may not be abridged by law may not be abridged by executive order. Executive power to control public employment stands on no higher constitutional ground than legislative power to tax. The taxing power does not extend to sales of propaganda not made for profit; license taxes, though imposed for the legitimate purpose of raising revenue are unconstitutional in their application to such sales. Such taxes, even if they are too small to be a "substantial clog" on the circulation of propaganda, are "on their face . . . a restriction of the free exercise of those freedoms which are protected by the First Amendment." The loss of employment, reputation, and earning power here involved is on its face a very substantial clog on the free exercise of those protected freedoms. It is therefore more clearly unconstitutional than the taxes.

Appellant's dismissal abridges not only freedom of speech but freedom of thought. Whatever loyalty means in the present connection, it is not speech but a state of mind. The appellant was dismissed for thinking prohibited thoughts. A constitution that forbids speech control does not permit thought control.

Appellant's dismissal attributes guilt by association, and thereby denies both the freedom of assembly guaranteed by the First Amendment and the due process of law guaranteed by the Fifth. The appellant was dismissed as disloyal because she was believed to be a member or associate of the Communist Party. Undoubtedly many such persons are disloyal in every sense to the government of the United States. But the Supreme Court has held that a particular member of the Communist Party may be "attached to the principles of the Constitution" within the meaning of those words in a naturalization act: "As Justice Holmes said, 'Surely it cannot show lack of attachment to the principles of the Constitution that . . . [one] thinks it can be improved. . . . If there is any principle of the Constitution that more imperatively calls for attachment than any other it is the principle of free thought—not free thought for those who agree with us, but freedom for the thought that we hate.' . . . Under our traditions beliefs are personal and not a matter of mere association, and . . . men in adhering to a political party or other organization notoriously do not subscribe unqualifiedly to all of its platforms or asserted principles." As was said more recently, "To condemn or to interdict all members of a named political party is an abridgement of free speech, press and assembly. The Communist Party in this country is recognized as a political party." *Schneiderman* v. *U.S.*, 320 U.S. 118.

The court thinks Miss Bailey's interest and the public interest conflict. I think they coincide. On this record we have no sufficient reason to doubt either Miss Bailey's patriotism or the value of her services to the government, or to suppose that an unpatriotic person could do substantial harm in her sort of job. Even if her services were on the whole undesirable, to oust her as disloyal on rumor and without trial is to pay too much for protection against such harm as she could do in such a job. The cost is too great in morale and efficiency of government workers, in appeal of government employment to independent and inquiring minds, and in public confidence in democracy. But even if such dismissals strengthened the government instead of weakening it, they would still cost too much in constitutional rights. We cannot preserve our liberties by sacrificing them.

b. Retrospective Oaths and Affidavits

GARNER v. BOARD OF PUBLIC WORKS

341 US 716 (1951)

[Parallel with the loyalty or security requirements for federal employees are similar requirements imposed on state or municipal employees. There are often differences in the means used: the Federal Government relies heavily on investigations by the Federal Bureau of Investigation, while state and municipal governments use mainly oaths and affidavits.

[In *Gerende v. Board of Supervisors,* 341 US 56 (1951), the Court unanimously upheld a Maryland statute which required a candidate for public office to take an oath that he was not then engaged in an attempt to overthrow the Government by force or violence and that he was not at the time knowingly a member of an organization engaged in such an attempt.

[This oath, like the affidavit requirement considered in the *Douds Case,* above, was in the *present* tense; but many oath or affidavit provisions require an affirmation that denies *past* membership. The latter type offers substantial constitutional difficulties. In the *Garner Case* this type of requirement was upheld as constitutional by a vote of 5 to 4, with Justices Burton, Frankfurter, Douglas, and Black dissenting.]

Mr. Justice Clark delivered the opinion of the Court:

In 1941 the California Legislature amended the Charter of the City of Los Angeles to provide in part as follows:

. . . No person shall hold or retain or be eligible for any public office or employment in the service of the City of Los Angeles, in any office or department thereof, either elective or appointive, who has within five (5) years prior to the effective date of this section advised, advocated or taught, or who may, after this section becomes effective [April 28, 1941], advise, advocate or teach, or who is now or has been within five (5) years prior to the effective date of this section, or who may, after this section becomes effective, become a member of or affiliated with any group, society, association, organization or party which advises, advocates or teaches, or has, within said period of five (5) years, advised, advocated or taught the overthrow by force or violence of the government of the United States of America or of the State of California.

In so far as this section may be held by any court of competent jurisdiction not to be self-executing, the City Council is hereby given power and authority to adopt appropriate legislation for the purpose of effectuating the objects hereof.

Pursuant to the authority thus conferred the City of Los Angeles in 1948 passed ordinance No. 94,004 requiring every person who held an office or position in the service of the city to take an oath prior to January 6, 1949. In relevant part the oath was as follows:

I further swear (or affirm) that I do not advise, advocate or teach, and have not within the period beginning five (5) years prior to the effective date of the ordinance requiring the making of this oath or affirmation, advised, advocated or taught, the overthrow by force, violence or other unlawful means, of the Government of the United States of America or of the State of California and that I am not now and have not, within said period, been or become a member of or affiliated with any group, society, association, organization or party which advises, advocates or teaches, or has, within said period, advised, advocated or taught, the overthrow by force, violence or other unlawful means of the Government of the United States, or of the State of California. I further swear (or affirm) that I will not, while I am in the service of the City of Los Angeles, advise, advocate or teach, or be or become a member of or affiliated with any group, association, society, organization or party which advises, advocates or teaches, or has within said period, advised, advocated or taught, the overthrow by force, violence or other unlawful means, of the Government of the United States of America or of the State of California. . . .

The ordinance also required every employee to execute an affidavit "stating whether or not he is or ever was a member of the Communist Party of the United States of America or of the Communist Political Association, and if he is or was such a member, stating the dates when he became, and the periods during which he was, such a member. . . ."

On the final date for filing of the oath and affidavit petitioners were civil service employees of the City of Los Angeles. Petitioners Pacifico and Schwartz took the oath but refused to execute the affidavit. The remaining fifteen petitioners refused to do both. All were discharged for such cause, after administrative hearing, as of January 6, 1949. In this action they sue for reinstatement and unpaid salaries. The District Court of Appeal denied relief. . . .

Petitioners attack the ordinance as violative of the provision of Art. I, § 10 of the Federal Constitution that "No State shall . . . pass any Bill of Attainder, [or] ex post facto Law. . . ." They also contend that the ordinance deprives them of freedom of speech and assembly and of the right to petition for redress of grievances.

Petitioners have assumed that the oath and affidavit provisions of the ordinance present similar constitutional considerations and stand or fall together. We think, however, that separate disposition is indicated.

1. The affidavit raises the issue whether the City of Los Angeles is constitutionally forbidden to require that its employees disclose their

past or present membership in the Communist Party or the Communist Political Association. Not before us is the question whether the city may determine that an employee's disclosure of such political affiliation justifies his discharge.

We think that a municipal employer is not disabled because it is an agency of the State from inquiring of its employees as to matters that may prove relevant to their fitness and suitability for the public service. Past conduct may well relate to present fitness; past loyalty may have a reasonable relationship to present and future trust. Both are commonly inquired into in determining fitness for both high and low positions in private industry and are not less relevant in public employment. The affidavit requirement is valid.

2. In our view the validity of the oath turns upon the nature of the Charter amendment (1941) and the relation of the ordinance (1948) to this amendment. Immaterial here is any opinion we might have as to the Charter provision insofar as it purported to apply retrospectively for a five-year period prior to its effective date. We assume that under the Federal Constitution the Charter amendment is valid to the extent that it bars from the city's public service persons who, subsequent to its adoption in 1941, advise, advocate, or teach the violent overthrow of the Government or who are or become affiliated with any group doing so. The provisions operating thus prospectively were a reasonable regulation to protect the municipal service by establishing an employment qualification of loyalty to the State and the United States. . . . Likewise, as a regulation of political activity of municipal employees, the amendment was reasonably designed to protect the integrity and competency of the service. This Court has held that Congress may reasonably restrict the political activity of federal civil service employees for such a purpose, *United Public Workers* v. *Mitchell*, 1947, 330 U.S. 75, . . . and a State is not without power to do as much.

The Charter amendment defined standards of eligibility for employees and specifically denied city employment to those persons who thereafter should not comply with these standards. While the amendment deprived no one of employment with or without trial, yet from its effective date it terminated any privilege to work for the city in the case of persons who thereafter engaged in the activity proscribed.

The ordinance provided for administrative implementation of the provisions of the Charter amendment. The oath imposed by the ordinance proscribed to employees activity which had been denied them in identical terms and with identical sanctions in the Charter provision effective in 1941. The five-year period provided by the oath extended back only to 1943.

The ordinance would be *ex post facto* if it imposed punishment for past conduct lawful at the time it was engaged in. Passing for the moment the question whether separation of petitioners from their employment must be considered as punishment, the ordinance clearly is not *ex post facto*. The activity covered by the oath had been proscribed by the Charter in the same terms, for the same purpose, and to the same effect over seven years before, and two years prior to the period embraced in the oath. Not the law but the fact was posterior.

Bills of attainder are "legislative acts . . . that apply either to named individuals or to easily ascertainable members of a group in such a way as to inflict punishment on them without a judicial trial. . . ." *United States* v. *Lovett*, 1946, 328 U.S. 303. . . . Punishment is a prerequisite. . . . We are unable to conclude that punishment is imposed by a general regulation which merely provides standards of qualification and eligibility for employment. . . .

Nor are we impressed by the contention that the oath denies due process because its negation is not limited to affiliations with organizations known to the employee to be in the proscribed class. We have no reason to suppose that the oath is or will be construed by the City of Los Angeles or by California courts as affecting adversely those persons who during their affiliation with a proscribed organization were innocent of its purpose, or those who severed their relations with any such organization when its character became apparent, or those who were affiliated with organizations which at one time or another during the period covered by the ordinance were engaged in proscribed activity but not at the time of affiant's affiliation. We assume that scienter is implicit in each clause of the oath. As the city has done nothing to negative this interpretation, we take for granted that the ordinance will be so read to avoid raising difficult constitutional problems which any other application would present. . . .

Affirmed.

Mr. Justice Douglas, with whom Mr. Justice Black joins, dissenting:

. . . Petitioners were disqualified from office not for what they are today, not because of any program they currently espouse, . . . not because of standards related to fitness for the office, . . . but for what they once advocated. They are deprived of their livelihood by legislative act, not by judicial processes. We put the case in the aspect most invidious to petitioners. Whether they actually advocated the violent overthrow of Government does not appear. But here, as in the *Cummings Case* [*Cummings* v. *Missouri*, 4 Wall. 277], the vice is in the presumption of guilt which can only be removed by the expurgatory oath. That punishment, albeit conditional, violates here as it did in the *Cummings Case* the constitutional prohibition against bills of attainder. Whether the ordinance also amounts to an *ex post facto* law is a question we do not reach. . . .

c. The Feinberg Law

ADLER v. BOARD OF EDUCATION

342 US 485 (1952)

[The Civil Service Law of New York since 1940 has prohibited a person from teaching in any public school if he is a member of an organization that advocates the overthrow of the Government by force or violence. In 1949 the so-called Feinberg Law added the requirements that the Board of Regents proceed under rules to remove ineligible persons, to prepare a list of banned organizations, and to make membership in any listed organization prima-facie evidence of ineligibility.

[In a 6-to-3 decision the Court upheld these statutory provisions as constitutional. Justice Frankfurter dissented on jurisdictional grounds, while Justices Black and Douglas dissented on the merits, maintaining that the eligibility of a person for teaching should be determined solely by his overt acts within the school system. The majority held, however, that in addition to one's conduct, "one's associates, past and present," "may properly be considered in determining fitness and loyalty." There may be guilt by association, for "from time immemorial, one's reputation has been determined in part by the company he keeps." In determining the fitness and loyalty of teachers, the authorities may consider "the organizations and persons with whom they [the teachers] associate."

[Justices Black and Douglas argued that "what happens under this law is typical of what happens in a police state. . . . A pall is cast over the classrooms. There can be no real academic freedom in that environment."

[In a case decided in 1943, *Schneiderman v. United States,* 320 US 118, Justice Murphy, in his opinion for a majority of five Justices, rejected the theory of guilt by association. Under our traditions, he said, "beliefs are personal and not a matter of mere association"; for men in adhering to organizations are known not to subscribe unqualifiedly to all the platforms or asserted principles of said organizations. The Court condemned indiscriminate imputation of party dogma to a member. It must be shown that the member was aware of the proscribed character of the tenets of the organization and that he adopted them as his own.]

Mr. Justice Minton delivered the opinion of the Court:

. . . The preamble of the Feinberg Law, § 1, makes elaborate findings that members of subversive groups, particularly of the Communist Party and its affiliated organizations, have been infiltrating into public employment in the public schools of the State; that this has occurred and continues notwithstanding the existence of protective statutes designed to prevent the appointment to or retention in employment in public office, and particularly in the public schools, of members of any organizations which teach or advocate that the government of the United States or of any state or political subdivision thereof shall be overthrown by force or violence or by any other unlawful means. As a result, propaganda can be disseminated among the children by those who teach them and to whom they look for guidance, authority, and leadership. The Legislature further found that the members of such groups use their positions to advocate and teach their doctrines, and are frequently bound by oath, agreement, pledge, or understanding to follow, advocate and teach a prescribed party line or group dogma or doctrine without regard to truth or free inquiry. This propaganda, the Legislature declared, is sufficiently subtle to escape detection in the classroom; thus, the menace of such infiltration into the classroom is difficult to measure. Finally, to protect the children from such influence, it was thought essential that the laws prohibiting members of such groups, such as the Communist Party or its affiliated organizations, from obtaining or retaining employment in the public schools be rigorously enforced. It is the purpose of the Feinberg Law to provide for the disqualification and removal of superintendents of schools, teachers, and employees in the public schools in any city or school district of the State who advocate the overthrow of the Government by unlawful means or who are members of organizations which have a like purpose.

Section 3022 of the Education Law, added by the Feinberg Law, provides that the Board of Regents, which has charge of the public school system in the State of New York, shall, after full notice and hearing, make a listing of organizations which it finds advocate, advise, teach, or embrace the doctrine that the government should be overthrown by force or violence or any other unlawful means, and that such listing may be amended and revised from time to time.

It will be observed that the listings are made only after full notice and hearing. In addition, the Court of Appeals construed the statute in conjunction with Article 78 of the New York Civil Practice Act, . . . so as to provide listed organizations a right of review.

The Board of Regents is further authorized to provide in rules and regulations, and has so provided, that membership in any listed organization, after notice and hearing, "shall constitute prima facie evidence for disqualification for appointment to or retention in any office or position in the school system"; but before one who is an employee or seeks employment is severed from or denied employment, he likewise must be given a full hearing with the privilege of being represented by counsel and the right to judicial review. It is § 12-a of the Civil Service Law, as implemented by the Feinberg Law as above indicated, that is under attack here.

It is first argued that the Feinberg Law and the rules promulgated thereunder constitute an abridgment of the freedom of speech and assembly of persons employed or seeking employment in the public schools of the State of New York.

It is clear that such persons have the right under our law to assemble, speak, think and believe as they will. . . . It is equally clear that they have no right to work for the State in the school system on their own terms. . . . They may work for the school system upon the reasonable terms laid down by the proper authorities of New York. If they do not choose to work on such terms, they are at liberty to retain their beliefs and associations and go elsewhere. Has the State thus deprived them of any right to free speech or assembly? We think not. Such persons are or may be denied, under the statutes in question, the privilege of working for the school system of the State of New York because first, of their advocacy of the overthrow of the government by force or violence, or secondly, by unexplained membership in an organization found by the school authorities, after notice and hearing, to teach and advocate the overthrow of the government by force or violence, and known by such persons to have such purpose.

The constitutionality of the first proposition is not questioned here. . . .

As to the second, it is rather subtly suggested that we should not follow our recent decision in *Garner* v. *Los Angeles Board of Public Works*, 341 US 716. . . . We there said:

> We think that a municipal employer is not disabled because it is an agency of the State from inquiring of its employees as to matters that may prove relevant to their fitness and suitability for the public service. Past conduct may well relate to present fitness; past loyalty may have a reasonable relationship to present and future trust. Both are commonly inquired into in determining fitness for both high and low positions in private industry and are not less relevant in public employment. . . .

We adhere to that case. A teacher works in a sensitive area in a schoolroom. There he shapes the attitude of young minds towards the society in which they live. In this, the state has a vital concern. It must preserve the integrity of the schools. That the school authorities have the right and the duty to screen the officials, teachers, and employees as to their fitness to maintain the integrity of the schools as a part of ordered society, cannot be doubted. One's associates, past and present, as well as one's conduct, may properly be considered in determining fitness and loyalty. From time immemorial, one's reputation has been determined in part by the company he keeps. In the employment of officials and teachers of the school system, the state may very properly inquire into the company they keep, and we know of no rule, constitutional or otherwise, that prevents the state, when determining the fitness and loyalty of such persons, from considering the organizations and persons with whom they associate.

If, under the procedure set up in the New York law, a person is found to be unfit and is disqualified from employment in the public school system because of membership in a listed organization, he is not thereby denied the right of free speech and assembly. His freedom of choice between membership in the organization and employment in the school system might be limited, but not his freedom of speech or assembly, except in the remote sense that limitation is inherent in every choice. Certainly such limitation is not one the state may not make in the exercise of its police power to protect the schools from pollution and thereby to defend its own existence.

It is next argued by appellants that the provision in § 3022 directing the Board of Regents to provide in rules and regulations that memberships in any organization listed by the Board after notice and hearing, with provision for review in accordance with the statute, shall constitute prima facie evidence of disqualification, denies due process, because the fact found bears no relation to the fact presumed. In other words, from the fact found that the organization was one that advocated the overthrow of government by unlawful means and that the person employed or to be employed was a member of the organization and knew of its purpose, to presume that such member is disqualified for employment is so unreasonable as to be a denial of due process of law. We do not agree. . . .

Membership in a listed organization found to be within the statute and known by the member to be within the statute is a legislative finding that the member by his membership supports the thing the organization stands for, namely, the overthrow of government by unlawful means. We cannot say that such a finding is contrary to fact or that "generality of experience" points to a different conclusion. Disqualification follows therefore as a reasonable presumption from such membership and support. Nor is there here a problem of procedural due process. The presumption is not conclusive but arises only in a hearing where the person against whom it may arise has full opportunity to rebut it. . . .

Where, as here, the relation between the fact found and the presumption is clear and direct and is not conclusive, the requirements of due process are satisfied. . . .

It is also suggested that the use of the word "subversive" is vague and indefinite. But the word is first used in § 1 of the Feinberg Law, which is the preamble to the Act, and not in a definitive part thereof. When used in subdivision 2 of § 3022, the word has a very definite meaning, namely, an organization that teaches and advocates the overthrow of government by force or violence.

We find no constitutional infirmity in § 12-a of the Civil Service Law of New York or in the Feinberg Law which implemented it, and the judgment is

Affirmed.

Mr. Justice Black, dissenting:

While I fully agree with the dissent of Mr. Justice Douglas, the importance of this holding prompts me to add these thoughts.

This is another of those rapidly multiplying legislative enactments which make it dangerous—this time for school teachers—to think or say anything except what a transient majority happen to approve at the moment. Basically these laws rest on the belief that government should supervise and limit the flow of ideas into the minds of men. The tendency of such governmental policy is to mould people into a common intellectual pattern. Quite a different governmental policy rests on the belief that government should leave the mind and spirit of man absolutely free. Such a governmental policy encourages varied intellectual outlooks in the belief that the best views will prevail. This policy of freedom is in my judgment embodied in the First Amendment and made applicable to the states by the Fourteenth. Because of this policy public officials cannot be constitutionally vested with powers to select the ideas people can think about, censor the public views they can express, or choose the persons or groups people can associate with. Public officials with such powers are not public servants; they are public masters.

I dissent from the Court's judgment sustaining this law which effectively penalizes school teachers for their thoughts and their associates.

Mr. Justice Douglas, with whom Mr. Justice Black concurs, dissenting:

I have not been able to accept the recent doctrine that a citizen who enters the public service can be forced to sacrifice his civil rights. I cannot for example find in our constitutional scheme the power of a state to place its employees in the category of second class citizens by denying them freedom of thought and expression. The Constitution guarantees freedom of thought and expression to everyone in our society. All are entitled to it; and none needs it more than the teacher.

The public school is in most respects the cradle of our democracy. The increasing role of the public school is seized upon by proponents of the type of legislation represented by New York's Feinberg law as proof of the importance and need for keeping the school free of "subversive influences." But that is to misconceive the effect of this type of legislation. Indeed the impact of this kind of censorship on the public school system illustrates the high purpose of the First Amendment in freeing speech and thought from censorship.

The present law proceeds on a principle repugnant to our society—guilt by association. A teacher is disqualified because of her membership in an organization found to be "subversive." The finding as to the "subversive" character of the organization is made in a proceeding to which the teacher is not a party and in which it is not clear that she may even be heard. To be sure she may have a hearing when charges of disloyalty are leveled against her. But in that hearing the finding as to the "subversive" character of the organization apparently may not be reopened in order to allow her to show the truth of the matter. The irrebuttable charge that the organization is "subversive" therefore hangs as an ominous cloud over her own hearing. The mere fact of membership in the organization raises a prima facie case of her own guilt. She may, it is said, show her innocence. But innocence in this case turns on knowledge; and when the witch hunt is on, one who must rely on ignorance leans on a feeble reed.

The very threat of such a procedure is certain to raise havoc with academic freedom. Youthful indiscretions, mistaken causes, misguided enthusiasms—all long forgotten—become the ghosts of a harrowing present. Any organization committed to a liberal cause, any group organized to revolt against an hysterical trend, any committee launched to sponsor an unpopular program becomes suspect. These are the organizations into which Communists often infiltrate. Their presence infects the whole, even though the project was not conceived in sin. A teacher caught in that mesh is almost certain to stand condemned. Fearing condemnation, she will tend to shrink from any association that stirs controversy. In that manner freedom of expression will be stifled.

But that is only part of it. Once a teacher's connection with a listed organization is shown, her views become subject to scrutiny to determine whether her membership in the organization is innocent or, if she was formerly a member, whether she has bona fide abandoned her membership.

The law inevitably turns the school system into a spying project. Regular loyalty reports on the teachers must be made out. The principals become detectives; the students, the parents, the community become informers. Ears are cocked for tell-tale signs of disloyalty. The prejudices of the community come into play in searching out the disloyal. This is not the usual type of supervision which checks a teacher's competency; it is a system which searches for hidden meanings in a teacher's utterances.

What was the significance of the reference of the art teacher to socialism?

Why was the history teacher so openly hostile to Franco Spain? Who heard overtones of revolution in the English teacher's discussion of the *Grapes of Wrath?* What was behind the praise of Soviet progress in metallurgy in the chemistry class? Was it not "subversive" for the teacher to cast doubt on the wisdom of the venture in Korea?

What happens under this law is typical of what happens in a police state. Teachers are under constant surveillance; their pasts are combed for signs of disloyalty; their utterances are watched for clues to dangerous thoughts. A pall is cast over the classrooms. There can be no real academic freedom in that environment. Where suspicion fills the air and holds scholars in line for fear of their jobs, there can be no exercise of the free intellect. Supineness and dogmatism take the place of inquiry. A "party line"—as dangerous as the "party line" of the Communists—lays hold. It is the "party line" of the orthodox view, of the conventional thought, of the accepted approach. A problem can no longer be pursued with impunity to its edges. Fear stalks the classroom. The teacher is no longer a stimulant to adventurous thinking; she becomes instead a pipe line for safe and sound information. A deadening dogma takes the place of free inquiry. Instruction tends to become sterile; pursuit of knowledge is discouraged; discussion often leaves off where it should begin.

This, I think, is what happens when a censor looks over a teacher's shoulder. This system of spying and surveillance with its accompanying reports and trials cannot go hand in hand with academic freedom. It pro-duces standardized thought, not the pursuit of truth. Yet it was the pursuit of truth which the First Amendment was designed to protect. A system which directly or inevitably has that effect is alien to our system and should be struck down. Its survival is a real threat to our way of life. We need be bold and adventuresome in our thinking to survive. A school system producing students trained as robots threatens to rob a generation of the versatility that has been perhaps our greatest distinction. The Framers knew the danger of dogmatism; they also knew the strength that comes when the mind is free, when ideas may be pursued wherever they lead. We forget these teachings of the First Amendment when we sustain this law.

Of course the school systems of the country need not become cells for Communist activities; and the classrooms need not become forums for propagandizing the Marxist creed. But the guilt of the teacher should turn on overt acts. So long as she is a law abiding citizen, so long as her perform-ance within the public school system meets professional standards, her private life, her political philosophy, her social creed should not be the cause of reprisals against her.

d. Oklahoma's Test Oath

WIEMAN *v.* UPDEGRAFF

344 US 183 (1952)

[In this case the Court (without Justice Jackson's participation) unanimously held that mere membership in a proscribed organization may not constitutionally serve as a basis for the conclusion that the person is disqualified from teaching in a state college; there must be proof of the teacher's knowledge of the nature and purpose of such organization at the time of his membership. This decision qualifies considerably the guilt by association doctrine that the Court approved in the *Garner Case*.

[Justice Frankfurter's concurring opinion is of special interest for what it says about the principles of academic freedom.]

Mr. Justice Clark delivered the opinion of the Court:

This is an appeal from a decision of the Supreme Court of Oklahoma, . . . upholding the validity of a loyalty oath prescribed by Oklahoma statute for all state officers and employees. . . . Appellants, employed by the state as members of the faculty and staff of Oklahoma Agricultural and Mechanical College, failed, within the thirty days permitted, to take the oath required by the Act. Appellee Updegraff, as a citizen and taxpayer, thereupon brought this suit in the District Court of Oklahoma County to enjoin the necessary state officials from paying further compensation to employees who had not subscribed to the oath. The appellants, who were permitted to intervene, attacked the validity of the Act on the grounds, among others, that it was a bill of attainder; an *ex post facto* law; impaired the obligation of their contracts with the State and violated the Due Process Clause of the Fourteenth Amendment. They also sought a mandatory injunction directing the state officers to pay their salaries regardless of their failure to take the oath. Their objections centered largely on the following clauses of the oath:

. . . That I am not affiliated directly or indirectly . . . with any foreign political agency, party, organization or Government, or with any agency, party, organization, association, or group whatever which has been officially determined by the United States Attorney General or other authorized agency of the United States to be a communist front or subversive organization; . . . that I will take up arms in the defense of the United States in time of War, or National Emergency, if necessary; that within the five (5) years immediately preceding the taking of this oath (or affirmation) I have not been a member of . . . any agency, party, organization, association, or group whatever which has been officially determined by the United States

Attorney General or other authorized public agency of the United States to be a communist front or subversive organization. . . .

The court upheld the Act and enjoined the state officers from making further salary payments to appellants. The Supreme Court of Oklahoma affirmed. . . .

The District Court of Oklahoma County in holding the Act valid concluded that the appellants were compelled to take the oath as written; that the appellants "and each of them, did not take and subscribe to the oath as provided in Section 2 of the Act and wilfully refused to take that oath and by reason thereof the Board of Regents is enjoined from paying them, and their employment is terminated." In affirming, the Supreme Court of Oklahoma held that the phrase of the oath "any foreign political agency, party, organization or Government, or with any agency, party, organization, association, or group whatever which has been officially determined by the United States Attorney General or other authorized agency of the United States to be a communist front or subversive organization" actually "refers to a list or lists of such organizations in existence at the time of the passage of the act which had been prepared by the Attorney General [of the United States] under Governmental directive. Such list or lists are in effect made a part of the oath by reference." On this point the opinion continues: "There is no requirement in the act that an oath be taken of non-membership in organizations not on the list of the Attorney General of the United States at the time of the passage of this act."

We read this part of the highest state court's decision as limiting the organizations proscribed by the Act to those designated on the list or lists of the Attorney General which had been issued prior to the effective date of the Act. . . .

The purpose of the Act, we are told, "was to make loyalty a qualification to hold public office or be employed by the state." . . . During periods of international stress, the extent of legislation with such objectives accentuates our traditional concern about the relation of government to the individual in a free society. The perennial problem of defining that relationship becomes acute when disloyalty is screened by ideological patterns and techniques of disguise that make it difficult to identify. Democratic government is not powerless to meet this threat, but it must do so without infringing the freedoms that are the ultimate values of all democratic living. In the adoption of such means as it believes effective, the legislature is therefore confronted with the problem of balancing its interest in national security with the often conflicting constitutional rights of the individual.

In a series of cases coming here in recent years, we have had occasion to consider legislation aimed at safeguarding the public service from

disloyalty. *Garner* v. *Board of Public Works,* 1951, 341 U.S. 716 . . . ;
Adler v. *Board of Education,* 1952, 342 U.S. 485 . . . ; *Gerende* v.
Board of Supervisors, 1951, 341 U.S. 56. . . . It is in the context of
these decisions that we determine the validity of the oath before us.

Garner involved a Los Angeles ordinance requiring all city employees to swear that they did not advocate the overthrow of the
government by unlawful means or belong to organizations with such
objectives. The ordinance implemented an earlier charter amendment
which disqualified from municipal employment all persons unable to
take such an oath truthfully. One of the attacks made on the oath in
that case was that it violated due process because its negation was not
limited to organizations known by the employee to be within the
proscribed class. This argument was rejected because we felt justified
in assuming that *scienter* was implicit in each clause of the oath.

Adler also indicated the importance of determining whether a rule
of exclusion based on association applies to innocent as well as knowing activity. New York had sought to bar from employment in the
public schools persons who advocate, or belong to organizations which
advocate, the overthrow of the government by unlawful means. The
Feinberg Law directed the New York Board of Regents to make a
listing, after notice and hearing, of organizations of the type described.
Under § 3022 of the statute, Education Law, McK. Consol. Laws, c. 16,
the Regents provided by regulation that membership in a listed organization should be *prima facie* evidence of disqualification for office
in the New York public schools. In upholding this legislation, we expressly noted that the New York courts had construed the statute to
require knowledge of organizational purpose before the regulation
could apply. . . .

The oath in *Gerende* was required of candidates for public office who
sought places on a Maryland ballot. On oral argument in that case,
the Maryland Attorney General assured us that he would advise the
proper state authorities to accept, as complying with the statute, an
affidavit stating that the affiant was not engaged in an attempt to overthrow the government by force or violence or knowingly a member of
an organization engaged in such an attempt. Because we read an earlier
Maryland Court of Appeals' decision as interpreting the statute so
that such an affidavit would satisfy its requirements, we affirmed on the
basis of this assurance.

We assumed in *Garner,* that if our interpretation of the oath as containing an implicit *scienter* requirement was correct, Los Angeles
would give the petitioners who had refused to sign the oath an opportunity to take it as interpreted and resume their employment. But here,
with our decision in *Garner* before it, the Oklahoma Supreme Court

refused to extend to appellants an opportunity to take the oath. In addition, a petition for rehearing which urged that failure to permit appellants to take the oath as interpreted deprived them of due process was denied. This must be viewed as a holding that knowledge is not a factor under the Oklahoma statute. We are thus brought to the question touched on in *Garner, Adler,* and *Gerende:* whether the due process clause permits a state in attempting to bar disloyal individuals from its employ to exclude persons solely on the basis of organizational membership, regardless of their knowledge concerning the organizations to which they had belonged. For, under the statute before us, the fact of membership alone disqualifies. If the rule be expressed as a presumption of disloyalty, it is a conclusive one.

But membership may be innocent. A state servant may have joined a proscribed organization unaware of its activities and purposes. In recent years, many completely loyal persons have severed organizational ties after learning for the first time of the character of groups to which they had belonged. "They had joined, [but] did not know what it was; they were good, fine young men and women, loyal Americans, but they had been trapped into it—because one of the great weaknesses of all Americans, whether adult or youth, is to join something." At the time of affiliation, a group itself may be innocent, only later coming under the influence of those who would turn it toward illegitimate ends. Conversely, an organization formerly subversive and therefore designated as such may have subsequently freed itself from the influences which originally led to its listing.

There can be no dispute about the consequences visited upon a person excluded from public employment on disloyalty grounds. In the view of the community, the stain is a deep one; indeed, it has become a badge of infamy. Especially is this so in time of cold war and hot emotions when "each man begins to eye his neighbor as a possible enemy." Yet under the Oklahoma Act, the fact of association alone determines disloyalty and disqualification; it matters not whether association existed innocently or knowingly. To thus inhibit individual freedom of movement is to stifle the flow of democratic expression and controversy at one of its chief sources. We hold that the distinction observed between the case at bar and *Garner, Adler* and *Gerende* is decisive. Indiscriminate classification of innocent with knowing activity must fall as an assertion of arbitrary power. The oath offends due process.

But appellee insists that *Adler* and *United Public Workers* v. *Mitchell,* 1947, 330 U.S. 75, . . . are *contra.* We are referred to our statement in *Adler* that persons seeking employment in the New York public schools have "no right to work for the State in the school system on their own terms. . . . They may work for the school system upon the reasonable terms laid down by the proper authorities of New York." . . . To draw from this language the facile generalization that there is no constitutionally protected right to public employment is to obscure the issue. For, in *United Public Workers*, though we held that the Federal Government through the Hatch Act could properly bar its employees from certain types of political activity thought inimical to the interests of the Civil Service, we cast this holding into perspective by emphasizing that Congress could not "enact a regulation providing that no Republican, Jew or Negro shall be appointed to federal office, or that no federal employee shall attend Mass or take any active part in missionary work." . . . We need not pause to consider whether an abstract right to public employment exists. It is sufficient to say that constitutional protection does extend to the public servant whose exclusion pursuant to a statute is patently arbitrary or discriminatory. . . .

Reversed.

Mr. Justice Black, concurring:

I concur in all the Court says in condemnation of Oklahoma's test oath. I agree that the State Act prescribing that test oath is fatally offensive to the due process guarantee of the United States Constitution.

History indicates that individual liberty is intermittently subjected to extraordinary perils. Even countries dedicated to government by the people are not free from such cyclical dangers. The first years of our Republic marked such a period. Enforcement of the Alien and Sedition Laws by zealous patriots who feared ideas made it highly dangerous for people to think, speak, or write critically about government, its agents, or its policies, either foreign or domestic. Our constitutional liberties survived the ordeal of this regrettable period because there were influential men and powerful organized groups bold enough to champion the undiluted right of individuals to publish and argue for their beliefs however unorthodox or loathsome. Today however, few individuals and organizations of power and influence argue that unpopular advocacy has this same wholly unqualified immunity from governmental interference. For this and other reasons the present period of fear seems more ominously dangerous to speech and press than was that of the Alien and Sedition Laws. Suppressive laws and practices are the fashion. The Oklahoma oath statute is but one manifestation of a national network of laws aimed at coercing and controlling the minds of men. Test oaths are notorious tools of tyranny. When used to shackle the mind they are, or at least they should be, unspeakably odious to a free people. Test oaths are made still more dangerous when combined with bills of attainder which like this Oklahoma statute impose pains and penalties for past lawful associations and utterances.

Governments need and have ample power to punish treasonable acts. But it does not follow that they must have a further power to punish thought and speech as distinguished from acts. Our own free society should never forget that laws which stigmatize and penalize thought and speech of the unorthodox have a way of reaching, ensnaring and silencing many more people than at first intended. We must have freedom of speech for all or we will in the long run have it for none but the cringing and the craven. And I cannot too often repeat my belief that the right to speak on matters of public concern must be wholly free or eventually be wholly lost.

It seems self-evident that all speech criticizing government rulers and challenging current beliefs may be dangerous to the *status quo*. With full knowledge of this danger the Framers rested our First Amendment on the premise that the slightest suppression of thought, speech, press, or public assembly is still more dangerous. This means that individuals are guaranteed an undiluted and unequivocal right to express themselves on questions of current public interest. It means that Americans discuss such questions as of right and not on sufferance of legislatures, courts or any other governmental agencies. It means that courts are without power to appraise and penalize utterances upon their notion that these utterances are dangerous. In my view this uncompromising interpretation of the Bill of Rights is the one that must prevail if its freedoms are to be saved. Tyrannical totalitarian governments cannot safely allow their people to speak with complete freedom. I believe with the Framers that our free Government can.

Mr. Justice Douglas concurs in this opinion.

Mr. Justice Frankfurter, whom Mr. Justice Douglas joins, concurring:

The times being what they are, it is appropriate to add a word by way of emphasis to the Court's opinion, which I join.

The case concerns the power of a State to exact from teachers in one of its colleges an oath that they are not, and for the five years immediately preceding the taking of the oath have not been, members of any organization listed by the Attorney General of the United States, prior to the passage of the statute, as "subversive" or "Communist-front." Since the affiliation which must thus be forsworn may well have been for reasons or for purposes as innocent as membership in a club of one of the established political parties, to require such an oath, on pain of a teacher's loss of his position in case of refusal to take the oath, penalizes a teacher for exercising a right of association peculiarly characteristic of our people. . . . Such joining is an exercise of the rights of free speech and free inquiry. By limiting the power of the States to interfere with freedom of speech and freedom of inquiry and freedom of association, the Fourteenth Amendment protects all persons, no matter what their calling. But, in view of the nature of the teacher's relation to the effective exercise of the rights which are safeguarded by the Bill of Rights and by the Fourteenth Amendment, inhibition of freedom of thought, and of action upon thought, in the case of teachers brings the safeguards of those amendments vividly into operation. Such unwarranted inhibition upon the free spirit of teachers affects not only those who, like the appellants, are immediately before the Court. It has an unmistakable tendency to chill that free play of the spirit which all teachers ought especially to cultivate and practice; it makes for caution and timidity in their associations by potential teachers.

The Constitution of the United States does not render the United States or the States impotent to guard their governments against destruction by enemies from within. It does not preclude measures of self-protection against anticipated overt acts of violence. Solid threats to our kind of government—manifestations of purposes that reject argument and the free ballot as the means for bringing about changes and promoting progress—may be met by preventive measures before such threats reach fruition. However, in considering the constitutionality of legislation like the statute before us it is necessary to keep steadfastly in mind what it is that is to be secured. Only thus will it be evident why the Court has found that the Oklahoma law violates those fundamental principles of liberty "which lie at the base of all our civil and political institutions" and as such are imbedded in the due process of law which no State may offend. . . .

That our democracy ultimately rests on public opinion is a platitude of speech but not a commonplace in action. Public opinion is the ultimate reliance of our society only if it be disciplined and responsible. It can be disciplined and responsible only if habits of open-mindedness and of critical inquiry are acquired in the formative years of our citizens. The process of education has naturally enough been the basis of hope for the perdurance of our democracy on the part of all our great leaders, from Thomas Jefferson onwards.

To regard teachers—in our entire educational system, from the primary grades to the university—as the priests of our democracy is therefore not to indulge in hyperbole. It is the special task of teachers to foster those habits of open-mindedness and critical inquiry which alone make for responsible citizens, who, in turn, make possible an enlightened and effective public opinion. Teachers must fulfill their function by precept and practice, by the very atmosphere which they generate; they must be exemplars of open-mindedness and free inquiry. They cannot carry out their noble task if the conditions for the practice of a responsible and critical mind are denied to them. They must have the freedom of responsible inquiry, by thought and action, into the meaning of social and economic ideas, into the checkered history of social and economic dogma. They must be free to sift evanescent doctrine, qualified by time and circumstance, from that restless, enduring process of extending the bounds of understanding and wisdom, to assure which the freedoms of thought, of speech, of inquiry, of worship are guaranteed by the Constitution of the United States against infraction by national or State government.

The functions of educational institutions in our national life and the conditions under which alone they can adequately perform them are at the basis of these limitations upon State and national power. These functions and the essential conditions for their effective discharge have been well described by a leading educator:

Now, a university is a place that is established and will function for the benefit of society, provided it is a center of independent thought. It is a center of independent thought and criticism that is created in the interest of the progress of society, and the one reason that we know that every totalitarian government must fail is that no totalitarian government is prepared to face the consequences of creating free universities.

It is important for this purpose to attract into the institution men of the greatest capacity, and to encourage them to exercise their independent judgment.

Education is a kind of continuing dialogue, and a dialogue assumes, in the nature of the case, different points of view.

The civilization which I work and which, I am sure, every American is working toward could be called a civilization of the dialogue, where, instead of shooting one another when you differ, you reason things out together.

In this dialogue, then, you cannot assume that you are going to have everybody thinking the same way or feeling the same way. It would be unprogressive if that happened. The hope of eventual development would be gone. More than that, of course it would be very boring.

A university, then, is a kind of continuing Socratic conversation on the highest level for the very best people you can think of, you can bring together, about the most important questions, and the thing that you must do to the uttermost possible limits is to guarantee those men the freedom to think and to express themselves.

Now, the limits on this freedom, the limits on this freedom cannot be merely prejudice, because although our prejudices might be perfectly satisfactory, the prejudices of our successors, or of those who are in a position to bring pressure to bear on the institution, might be subversive in the real sense, subverting the American doctrine of free thought and free speech. [Statement of Robert M. Hutchins, Associate Director of the Ford Foundation, November 25, 1952, in Hearings before the House Select Committee to Investigate Tax-exempt Foundations and Comparable Organizations, pursuant to H.Res. 561, 82d Cong., 2d Sess.]

3. The Attorney General's List

JOINT ANTI-FASCIST REFUGEE COMMITTEE v. McGRATH

341 US 123 (1951)

[President Truman's Executive Order 9835, which provided procedures for loyalty investigations of Federal Government employees—

see *Bailey* v. *Richardson,* above—directed the Attorney General to promulgate a list of subversive organizations. Early in 1948 the first Attorney General's list was made public; it contained 82 organizations; early in 1953 the number had grown to over 250. (The House Committee on Un-American Activities also has published a list, with over 600 names.)

[The Attorney General's list has been used in the loyalty and security programs. The tax exemption of organizations on the list has been canceled. The list has been used against aliens applying for admission into the United States. Some states and cities, as well as some private employers, have made use of it. The importance of the list can hardly be exaggerated.

[In the present case the Court was concerned with the procedures for listing. In a 5-to-3 decision (Justice Clark not participating) the Court held that the three organizations that had brought the suit against the Attorney General had been improperly listed. The President's order provided for listing "after appropriate investigation and determination" by the Attorney General; this provision had not been followed; he thus acted arbitrarily. Justices Frankfurter and Jackson thought that an organization is entitled to due process—notice and a hearing. Justices Black and Douglas agreed with this but maintained that fundamental constitutional freedoms were also violated by administrative loyalty trials and the listing of organizations as a step in these trials. Chief Justice Vinson and Justices Reed and Minton dissented.

[Justice Frankfurter's observations on the significance of procedural due process are worthy of special note.]

Mr. Justice Burton announced the judgment of the Court and delivered the following opinion . . . :

In each of these cases the same issue is raised by the dismissal of a complaint for its failure to state a claim upon which relief can be granted. That issue is whether . . . the Attorney General of the United States has authority to include the complaining organization in a list of organizations designated by him as Communist and furnished by him to the Loyalty Review Board of the United States Civil Service Commission. He claims to derive authority to do this from the following provisions in Part III, § 3, of Executive Order No. 9835, issued by the President, March 21, 1947, 5 U.S.C.A. § 631 note:

Part III—Responsibilities of Civil Service Commission

3. The Loyalty Review Board shall currently be furnished by the Department of Justice the name of each foreign or domestic organization, association, movement, group or combination of persons which the Attorney General,

after appropriate investigation and determination, designates as totalitarian, fascist, communist or subversive, or as having adopted a policy of advocating or approving the commission of acts of force or violence to deny others their rights under the Constitution of the United States, or as seeking to alter the form of government of the United States by unconstitutional means.

a. The Loyalty Review Board shall disseminate such information to all departments and agencies.

. . . At least since 1939, increasing concern has been expressed, in and out of Congress, as to the possible presence in the employ of the Government of persons disloyal to it. This is reflected in the legislation, reports and executive orders culminating in Executive Order No. 9835. That order announced the President's Employees Loyalty Program in the Executive Branch of the Government. It states that both "maximum protection must be afforded the United States against infiltration of disloyal persons into the ranks of its employees, and equal protection from unfounded accusations of disloyalty must be afforded the loyal employees of the Government: . . ." It provides for the Loyalty Review Board and sets up a standard for refusals of and removals from employment on grounds relating to loyalty. It outlines the use to be made in that connection of the list of organizations to be furnished by the Attorney General. The organizations to be designated on that list are not limited to those having federal employees in their memberships. They may even exclude such employees from membership. Accordingly, the impact of the Attorney General's list is by no means limited to persons who are subject to the Employees Loyalty Program.

The Attorney General included each of the complaining organizations in the list he furnished to the Loyalty Review Board November 24, 1947. That list was disseminated by the Board to all departments and agencies of the United States December 4, 1947. The complaints allege that such action resulted in nationwide publicity and caused the injuries to the complaining organizations which are detailed later. September 17, 1948, during the pendency of the instant cases but before action upon the appeals in any of them, "the Attorney General furnished the Loyalty Review Board with a consolidated list containing the names of all of the organizations previously designated by him as within Executive Order 9835, segregated according to the classifications enumerated in section 3, Part III, on the basis of dominant characteristics." He enumerated six classifications and classified the three complaining organizations as "Communist." . . .

The Refugee Committee Case

The complainant is the Joint Anti-Fascist Refugee Committee, an unincorporated association in the City and State of New York. . . .

The following statement, based on the allegations of the complaint, summarizes the situation before us: The complainant is "a charitable organization engaged in relief work" which carried on its relief activities from 1942 to 1946 under a license from the President's War Relief Control Board. Thereafter, it voluntarily submitted its program, budgets and audits for inspection by the Advisory Committee on Voluntary Foreign Aid of the United States Government. Since its inception, it has, through voluntary contributions, raised and disbursed funds for the benefit of anti-Fascist refugees who assisted the Government of Spain against its overthrow by force and violence. The organization's aims and purposes "are to raise, administer and distribute funds for the relief and rehabilitation of Spanish Republicans in exile and other anti-fascist refugees who fought in the war against Franco."

It has disbursed $1,011,448 in cash, and $217,903 in kind, for the relief of anti-Fascist refugees and their families. This relief has included money, food, shelter, educational facilities, medical treatment and supplies, and clothing to recipients in 11 countries including the United States. The acts of the Attorney General and the Loyalty Review Board, purporting to be taken by them under authority of the Executive Order, have seriously and irreparably impaired, and will continue to so impair, the reputation of the organization and the moral support and good will of the American people necessary for the continuance of its charitable activities. Upon information and belief, these acts have caused many contributors, especially present and prospective civil servants, to reduce or discontinue their contributions to the organization; members and participants in its activities have been "vilified and subjected to public shame, disgrace, ridicule and obloquy . . ." thereby inflicting upon it economic injury and discouraging participation in its activities; it has been hampered in securing meeting places; and many people have refused to take part in its fund-raising activities.

This complaint does not contain an express denial that the complaining organization is within the classifications named in Part III, § 3, of Executive Order No. 9835. It does, however, state that the actions of the Attorney General and the Loyalty Review Board which are complained of are unauthorized and without warrant in law and amount to a deprivation of the complainant's rights in violation of the Constitution; that Executive Order No. 9835, on its face and as construed and applied, violates the First, Fifth, Ninth and Tenth Amendments to the Constitution of the United States and that § 9A of the Hatch Act, 53 Stat. 1148, 5 U.S.C. (1946 ed., Supp. III) § 118j, insofar as it purports to authorize the instant application of the order, is void. It asks for declaratory and injunctive relief, alleging that the complaining organization is suffering irreparable loss and that no adequate remedy is available to it except through the equity powers of the District Court. That court granted a motion to dismiss the complaint for its failure to state a claim upon which relief could be granted and denied the complainant's motion for a preliminary injunction. The Court of Appeals affirmed, one judge dissenting. . . .

The National Council Case

In this case the court below relied upon its decision in the Refugee Committee case and reached the same result. . . . Except as indicated below in our summary of the facts alleged, this case, for our purposes, is like the first. The complainants, who are the petitioners here, are the National Council of American-Soviet Friendship, Inc., a New York nonprofit membership corporation, organized in 1943; the Denver Council of American-Soviet Friendship, a Colorado unincorporated association and local affiliate of the National Council; and six individual officers and directors of one or the other of these organizations. The purpose of the National Council "is to strengthen friendly relations between the United States and the Union of Soviet Socialist Republics by disseminating to the American people educational material regarding the Soviet Union, by developing cultural relations between the peoples of the two nations, and by combatting anti-Soviet propaganda designed to disrupt friendly relations between the people of these nations and to divide the United Nations." The complaint alleges that all of the complainants are seriously and irreparably injured in their capacity to conduct the National Council's educational, cultural and fund-raising program, and that the individual complainants have suffered personal losses such as the removal of one from an assistant rectorship of a church, the loss by another of a teaching position, and numerous cancellations of lecturing and professional engagements. The complaint expressly states that—"In all its activities the National Council has sought to further the best interests of the American people by lawful, peaceful and constitutional means. It has never in any way engaged in any conduct or activity which provides any basis for it to be designated as 'totalitarian, fascist, communist or subversive, or as having adopted a policy of advocating or approving the commission of acts of force or violence to deny others their rights under the Constitution of the United States, or as seeking to alter the form of government of the United States by unconstitutional means.'"

The International Workers Case

The complaining organization, which is the petitioner here, is a fraternal benefit society, organized in 1930 as a corporation under the Insurance Law of the State of New York, . . . operating for the mutual benefit of its members and their beneficiaries and not for profit. It is licensed and operates in the District of Columbia and several states; its purposes are comparable to those of fraternal benefit societies in general; it operates under a lodge system and has a representative form of government; at the time of the promulgation of the Department of Justice list it had 185,000 members, including employees of the Federal Government and of various states and municipalities; it provided life insurance protection for its membership exceeding $120,-000,000; its activities have been the subject of administrative and judicial proceedings in addition to those before the insurance departments of the states in which it functions, and, as a result of such proceedings, "the purposes and activities of the order have been held to be free from any illegal or improper taint. . . ." Among the allegations of damage, made upon information and belief, the complaint states that, solely as a result of the respondents' acts, there have been instituted against the order and its members a multiplicity of administrative proceedings, including those to rescind licenses, franchises, or tax exemptions, or to impede the naturalization of its members. Because of respondents' acts, many such members, especially present and prospective civil servants, have resigned or withdrawn from membership in the order, and many potential members have declined to join it. . . .

If, upon the allegations in any of these complaints, it had appeared that the acts of the respondents, from which relief was sought, were authorized by the President under his Executive Order No. 9835, the case would have bristled with constitutional issues. On that basis the complaint would have raised questions as to the justiciability and merit of claims based upon the First, Fifth, Ninth and Tenth Amendments to the Constitution. It is our obligation, however, not to reach those issues unless the allegations before us squarely present them. . . .

The Executive Order contains no express or implied attempt to confer power on anyone to act arbitrarily or capriciously—even assuming a constitutional power to do so. The order includes in the purposes of the President's program not only the protection of the United States against disloyal employees but the "equal protection" of loyal employees against unfounded accusations of disloyalty. . . . The standards stated for refusal of and removal from employment require that "on all the evidence, reasonable grounds [shall] exist for belief that the person involved is disloyal. . . ." . . . Obviously it would be contrary to the purpose of that order to place on a list to be disseminated under the Loyalty Program any designation of an organization that was patently arbitrary and contrary to the uncontroverted material facts. The order contains the express requirement that each designation of an organization by the Attorney General on such a list shall be made only after an "appropriate . . . determination" as prescribed in Part III, § 3. An "appropriate" governmental "determination" must be the result of a process of reasoning. It cannot be an arbitrary fiat contrary to the known facts. This is inherent in the meaning of "determination." It is implicit in a government of laws and not of men. Where an act of an official plainly falls outside of the scope of his authority, he does not make that act legal by doing it and then invoking the doctrine of administrative construction to cover it.

It remains, therefore, for us to decide whether, *on the face of these complaints,* the Attorney General is acting within his authority in furnishing the Loyalty Review Board with a designation of the complaining organizations either as "Communist" or as within any other classification of Part III, § 3, of the order. In the National Council and International Workers cases, the complaining organization is alleged not only to be a civic or insurance organization, apparently above reproach from the point of view of loyalty to the United States, but it is also declared to be one that is not within any classification listed in Part III, § 3, of the order. In the Refugee Committee case, the negative allegations are omitted but the affirmative allegations are incompatible with the inclusion of the complaining organization within any of the designated classifications. The inclusion of any of the complaining organizations in the designated list solely on the facts alleged in the respective complaints, which must be the basis for our decision here, is therefore an arbitrary and unauthorized act. In the two cases where the complaint specifically alleges the factual absence of any basis for the designation, and the respondents' motion admits that allegation, the designation is necessarily contrary to the record. The situation is comparable to one which would be created if the Attorney General, under like circumstances, were to designate the American National Red Cross as a Communist organization. Accepting as common knowledge the charitable and loyal status of that organization, there is no doubt that, in the absence of any contrary claim asserted against it, the Executive Order does not authorize its inclusion by the Attorney General as a "Communist" organization or as coming within any of the other classifications named in Part III, § 3, of the order.

Since we find that the conduct ascribed to the Attorney General by the complaints is patently arbitrary, the deference ordinarily due administrative construction of an administrative order is not sufficient to bring his alleged conduct within the authority conferred by Executive Order No. 9835. The doctrine of administrative construction never has been carried so far as to permit administrative discretion to run riot. If applied to this case and compounded with the assumption that the President's Executive Order was drafted for him by his Attorney General, the conclusion would rest upon the premise that the Attorney General has attempted to delegate to himself the power to act arbitrarily. We cannot impute such an attempt to the Nation's highest law enforcement officer any more than we can to its President.

In thus emphasizing an outer limit to what can be considered an authorized designation of an organization under the order, the instant cases serve a valuable purpose. They demonstrate that the order does not authorize, much less direct, the exercise of any such absolute power as would permit the inclusion in the Attorney General's list of a designation that is patently arbitrary or contrary to fact.

When the acts of the Attorney General and of the members of the Loyalty Review Board are stripped of the Presidential authorization claimed for them by the respondents, they stand, on the face of these complaints, as unauthorized publications of admittedly unfounded designations of the complaining organizations as "Communist." Their effect is to cripple the functioning and damage the reputation of those organizations in their respective communities and in the nation. The complaints, on that basis, sufficiently charge that such acts violate each complaining organization's common-law right to be free from defamation. "A communication is defamatory if it tends so to harm the reputation of another as to lower him in the estimation of the community or to deter third persons from associating or dealing with him." . . .

Nothing we have said purports to adjudicate the truth of petitioners' allegations that they are not in fact communistic. We have assumed that the designations made by the Attorney General are arbitrary because we are compelled to make that assumption by his motions to dismiss the complaints. Whether the complaining organizations are in fact communistic or whether the Attorney General possesses information from which he could reasonably find them to be so must await determination by the District Court upon remand.

For these reasons, we find it necessary to reverse the judgments of the Court of Appeals in the respective cases and to remand each case to the District Court with instructions to deny the respondents' motion that the complaint be dismissed for failure to state a claim upon which relief can be granted.

Reversed and remanded.

Mr. Justice Black, concurring:

Without notice or hearing and under color of the President's Executive Order No. 9835, the Attorney General found petitioners guilty of harboring treasonable opinions and designs, officially branded them as Communists, and promulgated his findings and conclusions for particular use as evidence against government employees suspected of disloyalty. In the present climate of public opinion it appears certain that the Attorney General's much publicized findings, regardless of their truth or falsity, are the practical equivalents of confiscation and death sentences for any blacklisted organization not possessing extraordinary financial, political, or religious prestige and influence. The Government not only defends the power of the Attorney General to pronounce such deadly edicts but also argues that individuals or groups so condemned have no standing to seek redress in the courts, even though a fair judicial hearing might conclusively demonstrate their loyalty. . . .

More fundamentally, however, in my judgment the executive has no constitutional authority, with or without a hearing, officially to prepare and publish the lists challenged by petitioners. In the first place, the system adopted effectively punishes many organizations and their members merely because of their political beliefs and utterances, and to this extent smacks of a most evil type of censorship. This cannot be reconciled with the First Amendment as I interpret it. . . . Moreover, officially prepared and proclaimed governmental blacklists possess almost every quality of bills of attainder, the use of which was from the beginning forbidden to both national and state governments. U.S. Const. Art I, §§ 9, 10. It is true that the classic bill of attainder was a condemnation by the legislature following investigation by that body, see *United States* v. *Lovett*, 328 U.S. 303 (1946) . . . , while in the present case the Attorney General performed the official tasks. But I cannot believe that the authors of the Constitution, who outlawed the bill of attainder, inadvertently endowed the executive with power to engage in the same tyrannical practices that had made the bill such an odious institution.

There is argument that executive power to issue these pseudo-bills of attainder can be implied from the undoubted power of the Government to hire and discharge employees and to protect itself against treasonable individuals or organizations. Our basic law, however, wisely withheld authority for resort to executive investigations, condemnations and blacklists as a substitute for imposition of legal types of penalties by courts following trial and conviction in accordance with procedural safeguards of the Bill of Rights.

In this day when prejudice, hate and fear are constantly invoked to justify irresponsible smears and persecution of persons even faintly suspected of entertaining unpopular views, it may be futile to suggest that the cause of internal security would be fostered, not hurt, by faithful adherence to our constitutional guarantees of individual liberty. Nevertheless, since prejudice manifests itself in much the same way in every age and country and since what has happened before can happen again, it surely should not be amiss to call attention to what has occurred when dominant governmental groups have been left free to give uncontrolled rein to their prejudices against unorthodox minorities. . . .

Mr. Justice Frankfurter, concurring: . . .

In November, 1947, each of these organizations was included in the list of groups designated by the Attorney General as within the provisions of Executive Order No. 9835, the President's Loyalty Order. The list was disseminated to all departments and agencies of the Government. Six months later, each was with more particularity labeled "communist." Each alleges substantial injury as a consequence. Publicity and meeting places have become difficult for the Refugee Committee and the Council to obtain. The federal tax exemptions of all three organizations have been revoked; licenses necessary to solicitation of funds have been denied the Refugee Committee; and the New York Superintendent of Insurance has begun proceedings, in which a representative of the Attorney General of the United States has appeared, for dissolution of the Order. Most important, each of the organizations asserts that it has lost supporters and members, especially from present or prospective federal employees. Claiming that the injury is irreparable, each asks for relief by way of a declaratory judgment and an injunction. . . .

This controversy is . . . amenable to the judicial process. Its justiciability does not depend solely on the fact that the action challenged is defamatory. Not every injury inflicted by a defamatory statement of a government officer can be redressed in court. On the balance of all considerations, the exercise here of judicial power accords with traditional canons for access to courts without inroads on the effective conduct of government. . . .

Fairness of procedure is "due process in the primary sense." . . . It is ingrained in our national traditions and is designed to maintain them. In a variety of situations the Court has enforced this requirement by checking attempts of executives, legislatures, and lower courts to disregard the deep-rooted demands of fair play enshrined in the Constitution. "[T]his court has never held, nor must we now be understood as holding, that administrative officers, when executing the provisions of a statute involving the liberty of persons, may disregard the fundamental principles that inhere in 'due process of law' as understood at the time of the adoption of the Constitution. One of these principles is that no person shall be deprived of his liberty without opportunity, at some time, to be heard. . . ." "[B]y 'due process' is meant one which, following the forms of law, is appropriate to the case, and just to the parties to be affected. It must be pursued in the ordinary mode prescribed by the law; it must be adapted to the end to be attained; and wherever it is necessary for the protection of the parties, it must give them an opportunity to be heard respecting the justice of the judgment sought." . . . "Before its property can be taken under the edict of an administrative officer, the appellant is entitled to a fair hearing upon the fundamental facts." . . . "Whether acting through its judiciary or through its Legislature, a state may not deprive a person of all existing remedies for the enforcement of a right, which the state has no power to destroy, unless there is, or was, afforded to him some real opportunity to protect it." . . .

The requirement of "due process" is not a fair-weather or timid assurance. It must be respected in periods of calm and in times of trouble; it protects aliens as well as citizens. But "due process," unlike some legal rules, is not a technical conception with a fixed content unrelated to time, place and circumstances. Expressing as it does in its ultimate analysis respect enforced by law for that feeling of just treatment which has been evolved through centuries of Anglo-American constitutional history and civilization, "due process" cannot be imprisoned within the treacherous limits of any formula. Representing a profound attitude of fairness between man and man, and more particularly between the individual and government, "due process" is compounded of history, reason, the past course of decisions, and stout confidence in the strength of the democratic faith which we profess. Due process is not a mechanical instrument. It is not a yardstick. It is a process. It is a delicate process of adjustment inescapably involving the exercise of judgment by those whom the Constitution entrusted with the unfolding of the process.

Fully aware of the enormous powers thus given to the judiciary and especially to its Supreme Court, those who founded this Nation put their trust in a judiciary truly independent—in judges not subject to the fears or allurements of a limited tenure and by the very nature of their function detached from passing and partisan influences. . . .

Achievements of our civilization as precious as they were hard won were summarized by Mr. Justice Brandeis when he wrote that "in the development of our liberty insistence upon procedural regularity has been a large factor." . . . It is noteworthy that procedural safeguards constitute the major portion of our Bill of Rights. And so, no one now doubts that in the criminal law a "person's right to reasonable notice of a charge against him, and an opportunity to be heard in his defense—a right to his day in court— are basic in our system of jurisprudence." . . . "The hearing, moreover, must be a real one, not a sham or a pretense." . . . Nor is there doubt that notice and hearing are prerequisite to due process in civil proceedings, . . . Only the narrowest exceptions, justified by history become part of the habits of our people or by obvious necessity, are tolerated. . . .

The construction placed by this Court upon legislation conferring administrative powers shows consistent respect for a requirement of fair procedure before men are denied or deprived of rights. From a great mass of cases, running the full gamut of control over property and liberty, there emerges the principle that statutes should be interpreted, if explicit language does not preclude, so as to observe due process in its basic meaning. . . .

This Court is not alone in recognizing that the right to be heard before being condemned to suffer grievous loss of any kind, even though it may not involve the stigma and hardships of a criminal conviction, is a principle basic to our society. Regard for this principle has guided Congress and the Executive. Congress has often entrusted, as it may, protection of interests which it has created to administrative agencies rather than to the courts. But rarely has it authorized such agencies to act without those essential safeguards for fair judgment which in the course of centuries have come to be associated with due process. . . .

The heart of the matter is that democracy implies respect for the elementary rights of men, however suspect or unworthy; a democratic government must therefore practice fairness; and fairness can rarely be obtained by secret, one-sided determination of facts decisive of rights.

An opportunity to be heard may not seem vital when an issue relates only to technical questions susceptible of demonstrable proof on which evidence is not likely to be overlooked and argument on the meaning and worth of conflicting and cloudy data not apt to be helpful. But in other situations an admonition of Mr. Justice Holmes becomes relevant. "One has to remember that when one's interest is keenly excited evidence gathers from all sides around the magnetic point. . . ." It should be particularly heeded at times of agitation and anxiety, when fear and suspicion impregnate the air we breathe. . . . "The plea that evidence of guilt must be secret is abhorrent to free men, because it provides a cloak for the malevolent, the misinformed, the meddlesome, and the corrupt to play the role of informer undetected and uncorrected." . . . Appearances in the dark are apt to look different in the light of day.

Man being what he is cannot safely be trusted with complete immunity from outward responsibility in depriving others of their rights. At least such is the conviction underlying our Bill of Rights. That a conclusion satisfies one's private conscience does not attest its reliability. The validity and moral authority of a conclusion largely depend on the mode by which it was reached. Secrecy is not congenial to truth-seeking and self-righteousness gives too slender an assurance of rightness. No better instrument has been devised for arriving at truth than to give a person in jeopardy of serious loss notice of the case against him and opportunity to meet it. Nor has a better way been found for generating the feeling, so important to a popular government, that justice has been done. . . .

Nothing in the Loyalty Order requires him to deny organizations opportunity to present their case. The Executive Order, defining his powers, directs only that designation shall be made "after appropriate investigation and determination." This surely does not preclude an administrative procedure, however informal, which would incorporate the essentials of due process. Nothing has been presented to the Court to indicate that it will be impractical or prejudicial to a concrete public interest to disclose to organizations the nature of the case against them and to permit them to meet it if they can. Indeed, such a contention could hardly be made inasmuch as the Loyalty Order itself requires partial disclosure and hearing in proceedings against a Government employee who is a member of a proscribed organization. Whether such procedure sufficiently protects the rights of the employee is a different story. Such as it is, it affords evidence that the wholly summary process for the organizations is inadequate. And we have controlling proof that Congress did not think that the Attorney General's procedure was indispensable for the protection of the public interest. The McCarran Act, passed under circumstances certainly not more serene than when the Loyalty Order was issued, grants organizations a full administrative hearing, subject to judicial review, before they are required to register as "Communist-action" or "Communist-front." . . .

The Attorney General is certainly not immune from the historic requirements of fairness merely because he acts, however conscientiously, in the
name of security. Nor does he obtain immunity on the ground that designation is not an "adjudication" or a "regulation" in the conventional use of
those terms. Due process is not confined in its scope to the particular forms
in which rights have heretofore been found to have been curtailed for want
of procedural fairness. Due process is perhaps the most majestic concept
in our whole constitutional system. While it contains the garnered wisdom
of the past in assuring fundamental justice, it is also a living principle not
confined to past instances.

Therefore the petitioners did set forth causes of action which the District
Court should have entertained.

Mr. Justice Douglas, concurring:

. . . The requirements for fair trials under our system of government
need no elaboration. A party is entitled to know the charge against him;
he is also entitled to notice and opportunity to be heard. Those principles
were, in my opinion, violated here.

The charge that these organizations are "subversive" could be clearly
defined. But how can anyone in the context of the Executive Order say what
it means? It apparently does not necessarily mean "totalitarian," "facist" or
"communist" because they are separately listed. Does it mean an organization
with socialist ideas? There are some who lump Socialists and Communists
together. Does it mean an organization that thinks the lot of some peasants
has been improved under Soviet auspices? Does it include an organization
that is against the action of the United Nations in Korea? Does it embrace
a group which on some issues of international policy aligns itself with the
Soviet viewpoint? Does it mean a group which has unwittingly become the
tool for Soviet propaganda? Does it mean one into whose membership some
Communists have infiltrated? Or does it describe only an organization which
under the guise of honorable activities serves as a front for Communist activities?

No one can tell from the Executive Order what meaning is intended. No
one can tell from the records of the cases which one the Attorney General
applied. The charge is flexible; it will mean one thing to one officer, another
to someone else. It will be given meaning according to the predilections of
the prosecutor: "subversive" to some will be synonymous with "radical";
"subversive" to others will be synonymous with "communist." It can be expanded to include those who depart from the orthodox party line—to those
whose words and actions (though completely loyal) do not conform to the
orthodox view on foreign or domestic policy. These flexible standards, which
vary with the mood or political philosophy of the prosecutor, are weapons
which can be made as sharp or as blunt as the occasion requires. Since they
are subject to grave abuse, they have no place in our system of law. When
we employ them, we plant within our body politic the virus of the totalitarian
ideology which we oppose.

It is not enough to know that the men applying the standard are honorable and devoted men. This is a government of *laws* not of *men*. The powers being used are the powers of government over the reputations and fortunes of citizens. In situations far less severe or important than these a party is told the nature of the charge against him. Thus when a defendant is summoned before a federal court to answer to a claim for damages or to a demand for an injunction against him, there must be a "plain statement of the claim showing that the pleader is entitled to relief." If that is necessary for even the most minor claim asserted against a defendant, we should require no less when it comes to determinations that may well destroy the group against whom the charge of being "subversive" is directed. When the Government becomes the moving party and levels its great powers against the citizen, it should be held to the same standards of fair dealing as we prescribe for other legal contests. To let the Government adopt such lesser ones as suits the convenience of its officers is to start down the totalitarian path.

The trend in that direction is only emphasized by the failure to give notice and hearing on the charges in these cases. . . .

Notice and opportunity to be heard are fundamental to due process of law. We would reverse these cases out of hand if they were suits of a civil nature to establish a claim against petitioners. Notice and opportunity to be heard are indispensable to a fair trial whether the case be criminal or civil. . . . The gravity of the present charges is proof enough of the need for notice and hearing before the United States officially brands these organizations as "subversive." No more critical governmental ruling can be made against an organization these days. It condemns without trial. It destroys without opportunity to be heard. The condemnation may in each case be wholly justified. But government in this country cannot by edict condemn or place beyond the pale. The rudiments of justice, as we know it, call for notice and hearing— an opportunity to appear and to rebut the charge.

The system used to condemn these organizations is bad enough. The evil is only compounded when a government employee is charged with being disloyal. Association with or membership in an organization found to be "subversive" weighs heavily against the accused. He is not allowed to prove that the charge against the organization is false. That case is closed; that line of defense is taken away. The technique is one of guilt by association— one of the most odious institutions of history. The fact that the technique of guilt by association was used in the prosecutions at Nüremberg does not make it congenial to our constitutional scheme. Guilt under our system of government is personal. When we make guilt vicarious we borrow from systems alien to ours and ape our enemies. Those short-cuts may at times seem to serve noble aims; but we depreciate ourselves by indulging in them. When we deny even the most degraded person the rudiments of a fair trial, we endanger the liberties of everyone. We set a pattern of conduct that is dangerously expansive and is adaptable to the needs of any majority bent on suppressing opposition or dissension.

It is not without significance that most of the provisions of the Bill of Rights are procedural. It is procedure that spells much of the difference between rule by law and rule by whim or caprice. Steadfast adherence to strict procedural safeguards is our main assurance that there will be equal justice under law. The case of Dorothy Bailey [*Bailey* v. *Richardson,* 182 F. 2d 46 (1950)] is an excellent illustration of how dangerous a departure from our constitutional standards can be. She was charged with being a Communist and with being active in a Communist "front organization." The Review Board stated that the case against her was based on reports, some of which came from "informants certified to us by the Federal Bureau of Investigation as experienced and entirely reliable."

Counsel for Dorothy Bailey asked that their names be disclosed. That was refused.

Counsel for Dorothy Bailey asked if these informants had been active in a certain union. The chairman replied, "I haven't the slightest knowledge as to who they were or how active they have been in anything."

Counsel for Dorothy Bailey asked if those statements of the informants were under oath. The chairman answered, "I don't think so."

The Loyalty Board convicts on evidence which it cannot even appraise. The critical evidence may be the word of an unknown witness who is "a paragon of veracity, a knave, or the village idiot." His name, his reputation, his prejudices, his animosities, his trustworthiness are unknown both to the judge and to the accused. The accused has no opportunity to show that the witness lied or was prejudiced or venal. Without knowing who her accusers are she has no way of defending. She has nothing to offer except her own word and the character testimony of her friends.

Dorothy Bailey was not, to be sure, faced with a criminal charge and hence not technically entitled under the Sixth Amendment to be confronted with the witnesses against her. But she was on trial for her reputation, her job, her professional standing. A disloyalty trial is the most crucial event in the life of a public servant. If condemned, he is branded for life as a person unworthy of trust or confidence. To make that condemnation without meticulous regard for the decencies of a fair trial is abhorrent to fundamental justice.

I do not mean to imply that but for these irregularities the system of loyalty trials is constitutional. I do not see how the constitutionality of this dragnet system of loyalty trials which has been entrusted to the administrative agencies of government can be sustained. Every government employee must take an oath of loyalty. If he swears falsely, he commits perjury and can be tried in court. In such a trial he gets the full protection of the Bill of Rights, including trial by jury and the presumption of innocence. I am inclined to the view that when a disloyalty charge is substituted for perjury and an administrative board substituted for the court "the spirit and the letter of the Bill of Rights" are offended.

The problem of security is real; and the Government need not be paralyzed in handling it. The security problem, however, relates only to those sensitive areas where secrets are or may be available, where critical policies are being formulated, or where sabotage can be committed. The department heads must have leeway in handling their personnel problems in these sensitive areas. The question is one of the fitness or qualifications of an individual for a particular position. One can be transferred from those areas even when there is no more than a suspicion as to his loyalty. We meet constitutional difficulties when the Government undertakes to punish by proclaiming the disloyalty of an employee and making him ineligible for any government post. The British have avoided those difficulties by applying the loyalty procedure only in sensitive areas and in using it to test the qualifications of an employee for a particular post, not to condemn him for all public employment. When we go beyond that procedure and adopt the dragnet system now in force, we trench upon the civil rights of our people. We condemn by administrative edict, rather than by jury trial. Of course, no one has a constitutional right to a government job. But every citizen has a right to a fair trial when his government seeks to deprive him of the privileges of first class citizenship.

The evil of these cases is only emphasized by the procedure employed in Dorothy Bailey's case. Together they illustrate how deprivation of our citizens of fair trials is subversion from within.

Mr. Justice Jackson, concurring:

. . . But the real target of all this procedure is the government employee who is a member of, or sympathetic to, one or more accused organizations. He not only may be discharged, but disqualified from employment, upon no other ground than such membership or sympathetic affiliation. And he cannot attack the correctness of the Attorney General's designation in any loyalty proceeding.

Ordinary dismissals from government service which violate no fixed tenure concern only the Executive branch, and courts will not review such discretionary action. However, these are not discretionary discharges but discharges pursuant to an order having force of law. Administrative machinery is publicly set up to comb the whole government service to discharge persons or to declare them ineligible for employment upon an incontestable finding, made without hearing, that some organization is subversive. To be deprived not only of present government employment but of future opportunity for it certainly is no small injury when government employment so dominates the field of opportunity.

The fact that one may not have a legal right to get or keep a government post does not mean that he can be adjudged ineligible illegally. . . .

Unless a hearing is provided in which the organization can present evidence as to its character, a presumption of disloyalty is entered against its every member-employee, and because of it, he may be branded disloyal, discharged, and rendered ineligible for government service. I would reverse the decisions for lack of due process in denying a hearing at any stage.

Mr. Justice Reed, with whom the Chief Justice [Vinson] and Mr. Justice Minton join, dissenting:

. . . No objection is or could reasonably be made in the records or briefs to an examination by the Government into the loyalty of its employees. Although the Founders of this Republic rebelled against their established government of England and won our freedom, the creation of our own constitutional government endowed that new government, the United States of America, with the right and duty to protect its existence against any force that seeks its overthrow or changes in its structure by other than constitutional means. Tolerant as we are of all political efforts by argument or persuasion to change the basis of our social, economic or political life, the line is drawn sharply and clearly at any act or incitement to act in violation of our constitutional processes. Surely the Government need not await an employee's conviction of a crime involving disloyalty before separating him from public service. Governments cannot be indifferent to manifestations of subversion. As soon as these are significant enough reasonably to cause concern as to the likelihood of action, the duty to protect the state compels the exertion of governmental power. Not to move would brand a government with a dangerous weakness of will. The determination of the time for action rests with the executive and legislative arms. An objection to consideration of an employee's sympathetic association with an admitted totalitarian, fascist, communist or subversive group, as bearing upon the propriety of his retention or employment as a government employee would have no better standing. The Order gives conclusive indication of the type of organization that is meant by the four word-labels. . . .

This Court, throughout the years, has maintained the protection of the First Amendment as a major safeguard to the maintenance of a free republic. This Nation has never suffered from an enforced conformity of expression or a limitation of criticism. But neither are we compelled to endure espionage and sedition. Wide as are the freedoms of the First Amendment, this Court has never hesitated to deny the individual's right to use the privileges for the overturn of law and order. Reasonable restraints for the fair protection of the Government against incitement to sedition cannot properly be said to be "undemocratic" or contrary to the guarantees of free speech. Otherwise the guarantee of civil rights would be mockery. Even when this Court spoke out most strongly against previous restraints, it was careful to recognize that "The security of the community life may be protected against incitements to acts of violence and the overthrow by force of orderly government." *Near v. State of Minnesota,* 283 U.S. 697 (1930).

Recognizing that the designation, rightly or wrongly, of petitioner organizations as communist impairs their ability to carry forward successfully whatever legitimate objects they seek to accomplish, we do not accept their argument that such interference is an abridgment of First Amendment guarantees. They are in the position of every proponent of unpopular views. Heresy induces strong expressions of opposition. So long as petitioners are permitted to voice their political ideas, free from suggestions for the opportune use of force to accomplish their social and economic aims, it is hard to understand how any advocate of freedom of expression can assert their right has been unconstitutionally abridged. As nothing in the orders or regulations concerning this list limits the teachings or support of these organizations, we do not believe that any right of theirs under the First Amendment is abridged by publication of the list. . . .

Does due process require notice and hearing for the Department of Justice investigation under Executive Order No. 9835, Part III, § 3, . . . preliminary to listing? As a standard for due process one cannot do better than to accept as a measure that no one may be deprived of liberty or property without such reasonable notice and hearing as fairness requires. This is my understanding of the meaning of the opinions upon due process cited in the concurring opinions. We are not here concerned with the rightfulness of the extent of participation in the investigations that might be claimed by petitioners. They were given no chance to take part. Their claim is that the listing resulted in a deprivation of liberty or property contrary to the procedure required by the Fifth Amendment.

The contention can be answered summarily by saying that there is no deprivation of any property or liberty of any listed organization by the Attorney General's designation. It may be assumed that the listing is hurtful to their prestige, reputation and earning power. It may be such an injury as would entitle organizations to damages in a tort action against persons not protected by privilege. . . . This designation, however, does not prohibit any business of the organizations, subject them to any punishment or deprive them of liberty of speech or other freedom. . . .

These petitioners are not ordered to do anything and are not punished for anything. Their position may be analogized to that of persons under grand jury investigation. Such persons have no right to notice by and hearing before a grand jury; only a right to defend the charge at trial. . . .

To allow petitioners entry into the investigation would amount to interference with the Executive's discretion, contrary to the ordinary operations of Government. . . .

The Executive has authority to gather information concerning the loyalty of its employees as congressional committees have power to investigate matters of legislative interest. A public statement of legislative conclusions on information that later may be found erroneous may damage those investigated but it is not a civil judgment or a criminal conviction. Due process does not apply. Questions of propriety of political action are not for the courts. Information that an employee associates with or belongs to organizations considered communistic may be deemed by the Executive a sound reason for making inquiries into the desirability of the employment of that employee. That is not "guilt by association." It is a warning to investigate the conduct of the employee and his opportunity for harm. . . .

4. Limits on Powers of Congressional Committees

McGRAIN v. DAUGHERTY

273 US 135 (1927)

[Since 1792 Congress has asserted and exercised the power of investigation through committees and has empowered such committees to summon witnesses, records, and papers. One of the principal subjects of congressional investigations has been the conduct of executive agencies and departments, including possible violations of criminal laws; but there may be no such investigation of a matter pending before a judicial tribunal. *Kilbourn* v. *Thompson,* 103 US 168 (1881). There is no power, moreover, to investigate "into the private affairs of the citizen." *Interstate Commerce Commission* v. *Brinson,* 154 US 447 (1894). But the Senate or the House does not, when it sets up an investigating committee, declare beforehand what that body "meditated doing when the investigation was concluded." *In re Chapman,* 166 US 661 (1897). The Court presumes that the investigation is undertaken in good faith to aid the legislative process, even though the information elicited may be useful, as a by-product, in criminal prosecutions. *Sinclair* v. *United States,* 279 US 263 (1929).

[In the present case the Court unanimously sustained the power of a Senate committee to investigate the Department of Justice, for this is a matter with respect to which it could legislate, even though the information exacted from witnesses may possibly disclose crime. "The only legitimate object the Senate could have in ordering the investigation was to aid it in legislating; and we think the subject-matter was such that the presumption should be indulged that this was the real object. An express avowal of the object would have been better; but . . . was not indispensable." This is a broad power, and the Court recognized that it "may be abusively and oppressively exercised." In rare cases there are "admissible measures of relief."

[If the powers of the committee are exceeded or if the questions are not pertinent to the matter under inquiry, the witness may refuse to answer. The committee may then request the House to which it is responsible to cite the witness as in contempt. If the House votes accordingly, the Attorney General then presents the evidence to a federal grand jury. If the witness is indicted, he is entitled to a trial as in any other criminal prosecution, and this trial will settle the question as to whether the witness had the right to refuse to answer the questions. Another sanction against a witness may be an indictment and conviction for perjury. A recent case involving prosecution for perjury was *Christoffel* v. *United States,* 338 US 84 (1949); recent contempt cases were *United States* v. *Bryan,* 339 US 323 (1950), and *United States* v. *Fleischman,* 339 US 349 (1950).

[Cases dealing with the privilege of immunity from self-incrimination appear in the chapter on "Personal Security."]

Mr. Justice Van Devanter delivered the opinion of the Court:

This is an appeal from the final order in a proceeding in *habeas corpus* discharging a recusant witness held in custody under process of attachment issued from the United States Senate in the course of an investigation which it was making of the administration of the Department of Justice. A full statement of the case is necessary.

The Department of Justice is one of the great executive departments established by congressional enactment and has charge, among other things, of the initiation and prosecution of all suits, civil and criminal, which may be brought in the right and name of the United States to compel obedience or punish disobedience to its laws, to recover property obtained from it by unlawful or fraudulent means, or to safeguard its rights in other respects; and also of the assertion and protection of its interests when it or its officers are sued by others. The Attorney General is the head of the department, and its functions are all to be exercised under his supervision and direction.

Harry M. Daugherty became the Attorney General March 5, 1921, and held that office until March 28, 1924, when he resigned. Late in that period various charges of misfeasance and nonfeasance in the Department of Justice after he became its supervising head were brought to the attention of the Senate by individual senators and made the basis of an insistent demand that the department be investigated to the end that the practices and deficiencies which, according to the charges, were operating to prevent or impair its right administration might be definitely ascertained and that appropriate and effective measures might be taken to remedy or eliminate the evil. The Senate regarded the charges as grave and requiring legislative attention and action. Accordingly it formulated, passed, and invited the House of Representatives to pass (and that body did pass) two measures taking important litigation then in immediate contemplation out of the control of the Department of Justice and placing the same in charge of special counsel to be appointed by the President; and also adopted a resolution authorizing and directing a select committee of five senators—

to investigate circumstances and facts, and report the same to the Senate, concerning the alleged failure of Harry M. Daugherty, Attorney General of the United States, to prosecute properly violators of the Sherman Antitrust Act and the Clayton Act against monopolies and unlawful restraint of trade; the alleged neglect and failure of the said Harry M. Daugherty, Attorney General of the United States, to arrest and prosecute Albert B. Fall, Harry F. Sinclair, E. L. Doheny, C. R. Forbes, and their co-conspirators in defrauding the Government, as well as the alleged neglect and failure of the said Attorney General to arrest and prosecute many others for violations of Federal statutes, and his alleged failure to prosecute properly, efficiently, and promptly, and to defend, all manner of civil and criminal actions wherein the Government of the United States is interested as a party plaintiff or defendant. And said committee is further directed to inquire into, investigate, and report to the Senate the activities of the said Harry M. Daugherty, Attorney General, and any of his assistants in the Department of Justice which would in any manner tend to impair their efficiency or influence as representatives of the Government of the United States.

The resolution also authorized the committee to send for books and papers, to subpoena witnesses, to administer oaths, and to sit at such times and places as it might deem advisable.

In the course of the investigation the committee issued and caused to be duly served on Mally S. Daugherty—who was a brother of Harry M. Daugherty and president of the Midland National Bank of Washington Court House, Ohio—a subpoena commanding him to appear before the committee for the purpose of giving testimony bearing on the subject under investigation, and to bring with him the "deposit ledgers of the Midland National Bank since November 1, 1920; also note files and transcript of owners of every safety vault; also records of income drafts; also records of any individual account or accounts showing withdrawals of amounts of $25,000 or over during above period." The witness failed to appear.

A little later in the course of the investigation the committee issued and caused to be duly served on the same witness another subpoena commanding him to appear before it for the purpose of giving testimony relating to the subject under consideration—nothing being said in this subpoena about bringing records, books, or papers. The witness again failed to appear; and no excuse was offered by him for either failure.

The committee then made a report to the Senate stating that the subpoenas had been issued, that according to the officer's returns— copies of which accompanied the report—the witness was personally served; and that he had failed and refused to appear. After a reading of the report, the Senate adopted a resolution reciting these facts and proceeding as follows:

Whereas the appearance and testimony of the said M. S. Daugherty is material and necessary in order that the committee may properly execute the functions imposed upon it and may obtain information necessary as a basis for such legislative and other action as the Senate may deem necessary and proper: Therefore be it

Resolved, That the President of the Senate pro tempore issue his warrant commanding the Sergeant at Arms or his deputy to take into custody the body of the said M. S. Daugherty wherever found, and to bring the said M. S. Daugherty before the bar of the Senate, then and there to answer such questions pertinent to the matter under inquiry as the Senate may order the President of the Senate pro tempore to propound; and to keep the said M. S. Daugherty in custody to await the further order of the Senate.

It will be observed from the terms of the resolution that the warrant was to be issued in furtherance of the effort to obtain the personal testimony of the witness and, like the second subpoena, was not intended to exact from him the production of the various records, books, and papers named in the first subpoena.

The warrant was issued agreeably to the resolution and was addressed simply to the Sergeant at Arms. That officer on receiving the warrant indorsed thereon a direction that it be executed by John J. McGrain, already his deputy, and delivered it to him for execution.

The deputy, proceeding under the warrant, took the witness into custody at Cincinnati, Ohio, with the purpose of bringing him before the bar of the Senate as commanded; whereupon the witness petitioned the federal district court in Cincinnati for a writ of *habeas corpus.* The writ was granted and the deputy made due return setting forth the warrant and the cause of the detention. After a hearing the court held the attachment and detention unlawful and discharged the witness, the decision being put on the ground that the Senate in directing the investigation and in ordering the attachment exceeded its powers under the Constitution. The deputy prayed and was allowed a direct appeal to this Court. . . .

We have given the case earnest and prolonged consideration because the principal questions involved are of unusual importance and delicacy. They are (a) whether the Senate—or the House of Representatives, both being on the same plane in this regard—has power, through its own process, to compel a private individual to appear before it or one of its committees and give testimony needed to enable it efficiently to exercise a legislative function belonging to it under the Constitution, and (b) whether it sufficiently appears that the process was being employed in this instance to obtain testimony for that purpose. . . .

In approaching the principal questions, which remain to be considered, two observations are in order. One is that we are not now concerned with the direction in the first subpoena that the witness produce various records, books, and papers of the Midland National Bank. That direction was not repeated in the second subpoena; and is not sought to be enforced by the attachment. . . . The other is that we are not now concerned with the right of the Senate to propound or the duty of the witness to answer specific questions, for as yet no questions have been propounded to him. He is asserting—and is standing on his assertion—that the Senate is without power to interrogate him, even if the questions propounded be pertinent and otherwise legitimate—which for present purposes must be assumed.

The first of the principal questions—the one which the witness particularly presses on our attention—is, as before shown, whether the Senate—or the House of Representatives, both being on the same plane in this regard—has power, through its own process, to compel a private individual to appear before it or one of its committees and give testimony needed to enable it efficiently to exercise a legislative function belonging to it under the Constitution.

The Constitution provides for a Congress consisting of a Senate and House of Representatives and invests it with "all legislative powers" granted to the United States, and with power "to make all laws which shall be necessary and proper" for carrying into execution these powers and "all other powers" vested by the Constitution in the United States or in any department or officer thereof. Art. I, secs. 1, 8. Other provisions show that, while bills can become laws only after being considered and passed by both houses of Congress, each house is to be distinct from the other, to have its own officers and rules, and to exercise its legislative function independently. Art. I, secs. 2, 3, 5, 7. But there is no provision expressly investing either house with power to make investigations and exact testimony to the end that it may exercise its legislative function advisedly and effectively. So the question arises whether this power is so far incidental to the legislative function as to be implied.

In actual legislative practice power to secure needed information by such means has long been treated as an attribute of the power to legislate. It was so regarded in the British Parliament and in the Colonial legislatures before the American Revolution; and a like view has prevailed and been carried into effect in both houses of Congress and in most of the state legislatures.

This power was both asserted and exerted by the House of Representatives in 1792, when it appointed a select committee to inquire into the St. Clair expedition and authorized the committee to send for necessary persons, papers and records. Mr. Madison, who had taken an important part in framing the Constitution only five years before, and four of his associates in that work, were members of the House of Representatives at the time, and all voted for the inquiry. 3 Cong. Ann. 494. Other exertions of the power by the House of Representatives, as also by the Senate, are shown in the citations. . . . Among those by the Senate, the inquiry ordered in 1859 respecting the raid by John Brown and his adherents on the armory and arsenal of the United States at Harper's Ferry is of special significance. The resolution directing the inquiry authorized the committee to send for persons and papers, to inquire into the facts pertaining to the raid and the means by which it was organized and supported, and to report what legislation, if any, was necessary to preserve the peace of the country and protect the public property. The resolution was briefly discussed and adopted without opposition. Later on the committee reported that Thaddeus Hyatt, although subpoenaed to appear as a witness, had refused to do so; whereupon the Senate ordered that he be attached and brought before it to answer for his refusal. When he was brought in he answered by challenging the power of the Senate to direct the inquiry and exact testimony to aid it in exercising its legislative function. The question of power thus presented was thoroughly discussed by several senators—Mr. Sumner of Massachusetts taking the lead in denying the power and Mr. Fessenden of Maine in supporting it. Sectional and party lines were put aside and the question was debated and determined with special regard to principle and precedent. The vote was taken on a resolution pronouncing the witness's answer insufficient and directing that he be committed until he should signify that he was ready and willing to testify. The resolution was adopted— 44 senators voting for it and 10 against. . . .

The deliberate solution of the question on that occasion has been accepted and followed on other occasions by both houses of Congress, and never has been rejected or questioned by either.

The state courts quite generally have held that the power to legislate carries with it by necessary implication ample authority to obtain information needed in the rightful exercise of that power and to employ compulsory process for the purpose. . . .

We have referred to the practice of the two houses of Congress; and we now shall notice some significant congressional enactments. . . . January 24, 1857, ch. 19, 11 Stat. 155, it [Congress] passed "An Act more effectually to enforce the attendance of witnesses on the summons of either house of Congress, and to compel them to discover testimony." This act provided, first, that any person summoned as a witness to give testimony or produce papers in any matter under inquiry before either house of Congress, or any committee of either house, who should wilfully make default, or, if appearing, should refuse to answer any question pertinent to the inquiry, should, in addition to the pains and penalties then existing, be deemed guilty of a misdemeanor and be subject to indictment and punishment as there prescribed; and, secondly, that no person should be excused from giving evidence in such an inquiry on the ground that it might tend to incriminate or disgrace him, nor be held to answer criminally, or be subjected to any penalty or forfeiture, for any fact or act as to which he was required to testify, excepting that he might be subjected to prosecution for perjury committed while so testifying. January 24, 1862, ch. 11, 12 Stat. 333, Congress modified the immunity provision in particulars not material here. These enactments are now embodied in Sections 101–4 and 859 of Revised Statutes. They show very plainly that Congress intended thereby (a) to recognize the power of either house to institute inquiries and exact evidence touching subjects within its jurisdiction and on which it was disposed to act; (b) to recognize that such inquiries may be conducted through committees; (c) to subject defaulting and contumacious witnesses to indictment and punishment in the courts, and thereby to enable either house to exert the power of inquiry "more effectually"; and (d) to open the way for obtaining evidence in such an inquiry, which otherwise could not be obtained, by exempting witnesses required to give evidence therein from criminal and penal prosecutions in respect of matters disclosed by their evidence.

Four decisions of this Court are cited and more or less relied on, and we now turn to them.

The first decision was in *Anderson* v. *Dunn,* 6 Wheat. 204. The question there was whether, under the Constitution, the House of Representatives has power to attach and punish a person other than a member for contempt of its authority—in fact, an attempt to bribe one of its members. The Court regarded the power as essential to the effective exertion of other powers expressly granted, and therefore as implied. The argument advanced to the contrary was that as the Constitution expressly grants to each house power to punish or expel its own members and says nothing about punishing others, the implication or inference, if any, is that power to punish one who is not a member is neither given nor intended. The Court answered this by saying:

. . . This argument proves too much; for its direct application would lead to the annihilation of almost every power of Congress. To enforce its laws upon any subject without the sanction of punishment, is obviously impossible. Yet there is an express grant of power to punish in one class of cases and one only, and all the punishing power exercised by Congress, in any cases, except those which relate to piracy and offenses against the laws of nations, is derived from implication. Nor did the idea ever occur to any one, that the express grant in one class of cases repelled the assumption of the punishing power in any other. The truth is, that the exercise of the powers given over their own members, was of such a delicate nature, that a constitutional provision became necessary to assert or communicate it. Constituted, as that body is, of the delegates of confederated States, some such provision was necessary to guard against their mutual jealousy, since every proceeding against a representative would indirectly affect the honor or interests of the state which sent him.

The next decision was in *Kilbourn* v. *Thompson*, 103 U.S. 168. The question there was whether the House of Representatives had exceeded its power in directing one of its committees to make a particular investigation. The decision was that it had. The principles announced and applied in the case are—that neither house of Congress possesses a "general power of making inquiry into the private affairs of the citizen"; that the power actually possessed is limited to inquiries relating to matters of which the particular house "has jurisdiction" and in respect of which it rightfully may take other action; that if the inquiry relates to "a matter wherein relief or redress could be had only by a judicial proceeding" it is not within the range of this power, but must be left to the courts, conformably to the constitutional separation of governmental powers; and that for the purpose of determining the essential character of the inquiry recourse may be had to the resolution or order under which it is made. The court examined the resolution which was the basis of the particular inquiry, and ascertained therefrom that the inquiry related to a private real-estate pool or partnership in the District of Columbia. Jay Cooke & Co. had had an interest in the pool, but had become bankrupts, and their estate was in course of administration in a federal bankruptcy court in Pennsylvania. The United States was one of their creditors. The trustee in the bankruptcy proceeding had effected a settlement of the bankrupts' interest in the pool, and of course his action was subject to examination and approval or disapproval by the bankruptcy court. Some of the creditors, including the United States, were dissatisfied with the settlement. In these circumstances, disclosed in the preamble, the resolution directed the committee "to inquire into the matter and history of said real-estate pool and the character of said settlement, with the amount of property involved in which Jay Cooke & Co. were interested, and the amount paid or to be paid in said settlement, with power to send for persons and papers and report to the House." The Court pointed out that the resolution contained no suggestion of contemplated legislation; that the matter was one in respect to which no valid legislation could be had; that the bankrupts' estate and the trustee's settlement were still pending in the bankruptcy court; and that the United States and other creditors were free to press their claims in that proceeding. And on these grounds the Court held that in undertaking the investigation "the House of Representatives not only exceeded the limit of its own authority but assumed a power which could only be properly exercised by another branch of the government, because it was in its nature clearly judicial."

The case has been cited at times, and is cited to us now, as strongly intimating, if not holding, that neither house of Congress has power to make inquiries and exact evidence in aid of contemplated legislation. There are expressions in the opinion which, separately considered, might bear such an interpretation; but that this was not intended is shown by the immediately succeeding statement that "This latter proposition is one which we do not propose to decide in the present case because we are able to decide the case without passing upon the existence or non-existence of such a power in aid of the legislative function."

Next in order is *In re Chapman,* 166 U.S. 661. The inquiry there in question was conducted under a resolution of the Senate and related to charges, published in the press, that senators were yielding to corrupt influences in considering a tariff bill then before the Senate and were speculating in stocks the value of which would be affected by pending amendments to the bill. Chapman appeared before the committee in response to a subpoena, but refused to answer questions pertinent to the inquiry, and was indicted and convicted under the act of 1857 for his refusal. The Court sustained the constitutional validity of the act of 1857, and, after referring to the constitutional provision empowering either house to punish its members for disorderly behavior and by a vote of two-thirds to expel a member, held that the inquiry related to the integrity and fidelity of senators in the discharge of their duties, and therefore to a matter "within the range of the constitutional powers of the Senate" and in respect of which it could compel witnesses to appear and testify. . . .

The case is relied on here as fully sustaining the power of either house to conduct investigations and exact testimony from witnesses for legislative purposes. In the course of the opinion it is said that disclosures by witnesses may be compelled constitutionally "to enable the respective bodies to discharge their legitimate functions, and that it was to effect this that the act of 1857 was passed"; and also "We grant that Congress could not divest itself or either of its houses of the essential and inherent power to punish for contempt, in cases to which the power of either house properly extended; but, because Congress, by the act of 1857, sought to aid each of the houses in the discharge of its constitutional functions, it does not follow that any delegation of the power in each to punish for contempt was involved." The terms "legitimate functions" and "constitutional functions" are broad and might well be regarded as including the legislative function, but as the case in hand did not call for any expression respecting that function, it hardly can be said that these terms were purposely used as including it.

The latest case is *Marshall* v. *Gordon,* 243 U.S. 521. The question there was whether the House of Representatives exceeded its power in punishing, as for a contempt of its authority, a person—not a member—who had written, published, and sent to the chairman of one of its committees an ill-tempered and irritating letter respecting the action and purposes of the committee. Power to make inquiries and obtain evidence by compulsory process was not involved. The Court recognized distinctly that the House of Representatives has implied power to punish a person not a member for contempt, as was ruled in *Anderson* v. *Dunn, supra,* but held that its action in this instance was without constitutional justification. The decision was put on the ground that the letter, while offensive and vexatious, was not calculated or likely to affect the House in any of its proceedings or in the exercise of any of its functions—in short, that the act which was punished as a contempt was not of such a character as to bring it within the rule that an express power draws after it others which are necessary and appropriate to give effect to it.

While these cases are not decisive of the question we are considering, they definitely settle two propositions which we recognize as entirely sound and having a bearing on its solution: One, that the two houses of Congress, in their separate relations, possess not only such powers as are expressly granted to them by the Constitution, but such auxiliary powers as are necessary and appropriate to make the express powers effective; and, the other, that neither house is invested with "general" power to inquire into private affairs and compel disclosures but only with such limited power of inquiry as is shown to exist when the rule of constitutional interpretation just stated is rightly applied. . . .

With this review of the legislative practice, congressional enactments, and court decisions, we proceed to a statement of our conclusions on the question.

We are of opinion that the power of inquiry—with process to enforce it—is an essential and appropriate auxiliary to the legislative function. . . .

We are further of opinion that the provisions of the Constitution are not of doubtful meaning, but, as was held by this Court in the cases we have reviewed, are intended to be effectively exercised, and therefore to carry with them such auxiliary powers as are necessary and appropriate to that end. While the power to exact information in aid of the legislative function was not involved in those cases, the rule of interpretation applied there is applicable here. A legislative body cannot legislate wisely or effectively in the absence of information respecting the conditions which the legislation is intended to affect or change; and where the legislative body does not itself possess the requisite information—which not infrequently is true—recourse must be had to others who do possess it. Experience has taught that mere requests for such information often are unavailing, and also that information which is volunteered is not always accurate or complete; so some means of compulsion are essential to obtain what is needed. All this was true before and when the Constitution was framed and adopted. In that period the power of inquiry—with enforcing process —was regarded and employed as a necessary and appropriate attribute of the power to legislate—indeed, was treated as inhering in it. Thus there is ample warrant for thinking, as we do, that the constitutional provisions which commit the legislative function to the two houses are intended to include this attribute to the end that the function may be effectively exercised.

The contention is earnestly made on behalf of the witness that this power of inquiry, if sustained, may be abusively and oppressively exerted. If this be so, it affords no ground for denying the power. The same contention might be directed against the power to legislate and, of course, would be unavailing. We must assume, for present purposes, that neither house will be disposed to exert the power beyond its proper bounds, or without due regard to the rights of witnesses. But if, contrary to this assumption, controlling limitations or restrictions are disregarded, the decisions in *Kilbourn* v. *Thompson* and *Marshall* v. *Gordon* point to admissible measures of relief. And it is a necessary deduction from the decisions in *Kilbourn* v. *Thompson* and *In re Chapman* that a witness rightfully may refuse to answer where the bounds of the power are exceeded or the questions are not pertinent to the matter under inquiry.

We come now to the question whether it sufficiently appears that the purpose for which the witness's testimony was sought was to obtain information in aid of the legislative function. The court below answered the question in the negative and put its decision largely on this ground. . . .

We are of opinion that the court's ruling on this question was wrong, and that it sufficiently appears, when the proceedings are rightly interpreted, that the object of the investigation and of the effort to secure the witness's testimony was to obtain information for legislative purposes.

It is quite true that the resolution directing the investigation does not in terms avow that it is intended to be in aid of legislation; but it does show that the subject to be investigated was the administration of the Department of Justice—whether its functions were being properly discharged or were being neglected or misdirected, and particularly whether the Attorney General and his assistants were performing or neglecting their duties in respect of the institution and prosecution of proceedings to punish crimes and enforce appropriate remedies against the wrongdoers—specific instances of alleged neglect being recited. Plainly the subject was one on which legislation could be had and would be materially aided by the information which the investigation was calculated to elicit. This becomes manifest when it is reflected that the functions of the Department of Justice, the powers and duties of the Attorney General and the duties of his assistants are all subject to regulation by congressional legislation, and that the department is maintained and its activities are carried on under such appropriations as in the judgment of Congress are needed from year to year.

The only legitimate object the Senate could have in ordering the investigation was to aid it in legislating; and we think the subject-matter was such that the presumption should be indulged that this was the real object. An express avowal of the object would have been better; but in view of the particular subject-matter was not indispensable. . . .

The second resolution—the one directing that the witness be attached—declares that his testimony is sought with the purpose of obtaining "information necessary as a basis for such legislative and other action as the Senate may deem necessary and proper." This avowal of contemplated legislation is in accord with what we think is the right interpretation of the earlier resolution directing the investigation. The suggested possibility of "other action" if deemed "necessary or proper" is of course open to criticism in that there is no other action in the matter which would be within the power of the Senate. But we do not assent to the view that this indefinite and untenable suggestion invalidates the entire proceeding. The right view in our opinion is that it takes nothing from the lawful object avowed in the same resolution and rightly inferable from the earlier one. It is not as if an inadmissible or unlawful object were affirmatively and definitely avowed.

We conclude that the investigation was ordered for a legitimate object; that the witness wrongfully refused to appear and testify before the committee and was lawfully attached; that the Senate is entitled to have him give testimony pertinent to the inquiry, either at its bar or before the committee; and that the district court erred in discharging him from custody under the attachment. . . .

UNITED STATES v. RUMELY

345 US 41 (1953)

[The House of Representatives set up a committee to investigate lobbying activities. Rumely, as secretary of an organization known as the Committee for Constitutional Government, refused to disclose to the House committee the names of those who made bulk purchases of certain political books for further distribution. He was convicted of contempt. By a 5-to-2 decision (Justices Burton and Minton not participating) the Court set aside the conviction, on the ground that the resolution that created the House committee limited the investigation to activities that involved only direct lobbying of Congress, and not activities that involved efforts to influence the thinking of the community generally. The majority placed this narrow construction upon the resolution in order to avoid the constitutional issue, for an inquiry into the efforts of private citizens to influence public opinion through publications would raise doubts of constitutionality under the First Amendment. The dissenting Justices (Douglas and Black), however, maintained that the resolution was intended to vest broad powers and was unconstitutional.

[The case is significant as illustrating the area of possible conflict between the investigatory power of Congress and the personal rights guaranteed by the First Amendment.]

Mr. Justice Frankfurter delivered the opinion of the Court:

The respondent Rumely was Secretary of an organization known as the Committee for Constitutional Government, which, among other things, engaged in the sale of books of a particular political tendentiousness. He refused to disclose to the House Select Committee on Lobbying Activities the names of those who made bulk purchases of these books for further distribution, and was convicted under 2 U.S.C.A. § 192, which provides penalties for refusal to give testimony or to produce relevant papers "upon any matter" under congressional inquiry. The Court of Appeals reversed, one judge dissenting. It held that the committee before which Rumely refused to furnish this information had no authority to compel its production. . . . This issue —whether the committee had power to exact the information which the witness withheld—must first be settled before we may consider whether Congress had the power to confer upon the committee the authority which it claimed.

Although we are here dealing with a resolution of the House of Representatives, the problem is much the same as that which confronts the Court when called upon to construe a statute that carries the seeds of constitutional controversy. The potential constitutional questions have far-reaching import. We are asked to recognize the penetrating and pervasive scope of the investigative power of Congress. The reach that may be claimed for that power is indicated by Woodrow Wilson's characterization of it:

It is the proper duty of a representative body to look diligently into every affair of government and to talk much about what it sees. It is meant to be the eyes and the voice, and to embody the wisdom and will of its constituents. Unless Congress have and use every means of acquainting itself with the acts and the disposition of the administrative agents of the government, the country must be helpless to learn how it is being served; and unless Congress both scrutinize these things and sift them by every form of discussion, the country must remain in embarrassing, crippling ignorance of the very affairs which it is most important that it should understand and direct. The informing function of Congress should be preferred even to its legislative function. Wilson, *Congressional Government*, 303.

Although the indispensable "informing function of Congress" is not to be minimized, determination of the "rights" which this function implies illustrates the common juristic situation thus defined for the Court by Mr. Justice Holmes:

All rights tend to declare themselves absolute to their logical extreme. Yet all in fact are limited by the neighborhood of principles of policy which are other than those on which the particular right is founded, and which become strong enough to hold their own when a certain point is reached. *Hudson County Water Co. v. McCarter*, 209 U.S. 349.

. . . President Wilson did not write in light of the history of events since he wrote; more particularly he did not write of the investigative power of Congress in the context of the First Amendment. And so, we would have to be that "blind" Court, against which Mr. Chief Justice Taft admonished . . . that does not see what "[a]ll others can see and understand" not to know that there is wide concern, both in and out of Congress, over some aspects of the exercise of the congressional power of investigation.

Accommodation of these contending principles—the one underlying the power of Congress to investigate, the other at the basis of the limitation imposed by the First Amendment—is not called for until after we have construed the scope of the authority which the House of Representatives gave to the Select Committee on Lobbying Activities. The pertinent portion of the resolution of August 12, 1949, reads:

The Committee is authorized and directed to conduct a study and investigation of (1) all lobbying activities intended to influence, encourage, promote, or retard legislation; and (2) all activities of agencies of the Federal Government intended to influence, encourage, promote, or retard legislation. H. Res. 298, 81st Cong., 1st Sess.

This is the controlling charter of the committee's powers. Its right to exact testimony and to call for the production of documents must be found in this language. The resolution must speak for itself, since Congress put no gloss upon it at the time of its passage. Nor is any help to be had from the fact that the purpose of the Buchanan Committee, as the Select Committee was known, was to try to "find out how well [the Federal Regulation of Lobbying Act of 1946] worked." . . . That statute had a section of definitions, but Congress did not define the terms "lobbying" or "lobbying activities" in that Act, for it did not use them. Accordingly, the phrase "lobbying activities" in the resolution must be given the meaning that may fairly be attributed to it, having special regard for the principle of constitutional adjudication which makes it decisive in the choice of fair alternatives that one construction may raise serious constitutional questions avoided by another. In a long series of decisions we have acted on this principle. . . . As phrased by Mr. Chief Justice Hughes, "If a serious doubt of constitutionality is raised, it is a cardinal principle that this Court will first ascertain whether a construction of the statute is fairly possible by which the question may be avoided." . . .

Surely it cannot be denied that giving the scope to the resolution for which the Government contends, that is, deriving from it the power to inquire into all efforts of private individuals to influence public opinion through books and periodicals, however remote the radiations of influence which they may exert upon the ultimate legislative process, raises doubts of constitutionality in view of the prohibition of the First Amendment. In light of the opinion of Prettyman, J., below and of some of the views expressed here, it would not be seemly to maintain that these doubts are fanciful or factitious. Indeed, adjudication here, if it were necessary, would affect not an evanescent policy of Congress, but its power to inform itself, which underlies its policy-making function. Whenever constitutional limits upon the investigative power of Congress have to be drawn by this Court, it ought only to be done after Congress has demonstrated its full awareness of what is at stake by unequivocally authorizing an inquiry of dubious limits. . . .

Choice is left. As a matter of English, the phrase "lobbying activities" readily lends itself to the construction placed upon it below, namely, "lobbying in its commonly accepted sense," that is, "representations made directly to the Congress, its members, or its committees," . . . and does not reach what was in Chairman Buchanan's mind, attempts "to saturate the thinking of the community." . . . Certainly it does no violence to the phrase "lobbying activities" to give it a more restricted scope. To give such meaning is not barred by intellectual honesty. So to interpret is in the candid service of avoiding a serious constitutional doubt. . . .

Only a word need be said about the debate in Congress after the committee reported that Rumely had refused to produce the information which he had a right to refuse under the restricted meaning of the phrase "lobbying activities." The view taken at that time by the committee and by the Congress that the committee was authorized to ask Rumely for the information he withheld is not legislative history defining the scope of a congressional measure. What was said in the debate on August 30, 1950, after the controversy had arisen regarding the scope of the resolution of August 12, 1949, had the usual infirmity of *post litem motam*, self-serving declarations. In any event, Rumely's duty to answer must be judged as of the time of his refusal. The scope of the resolution defining that duty is therefore to be ascertained as of that time and cannot be enlarged by subsequent action of Congress.

Grave constitutional questions are matters properly to be decided by this Court but only when they inescapably come before us for adjudication. Until then it is our duty to abstain from marking the boundaries of congressional power or delimiting the protection guaranteed by the First Amendment. Only by such self-restraint will we avoid the mischief which has followed occasional departures from the principles which we profess.

The judgment below should be affirmed. . . .

Mr. Justice Douglas, with whom Mr. Justice Black concurs, concurring:

. . . I come then to the constitutional questions. Respondent represents a segment of the American press. Some may like what his group publishes; others may disapprove. These tracts may be the essence of wisdom to some; to others their point of view and philosophy may be anathema. To some ears their words may be harsh and repulsive; to others they may carry the hope of the future. We have here a publisher who through books and pamphlets seeks to reach the minds and hearts of the American people. He is different in some respects from other publishers. But the differences are minor. Like the publishers of newspapers, magazines, or books, this publisher bids for the minds of men in the market place of ideas. The aim of the historic struggle for a free press was "to establish and preserve the right of the English people to full information in respect to the doings or misdoings of their government." *Grosjean* v. *American Press Co.*, 297 U.S. 233. . . . That is the tradition behind the First Amendment. Censorship or previous restraint is banned. *Near* v. *Minnesota*, 283 U.S. 697. . . . Discriminatory taxation is outlawed. *Grosjean* v. *American Press Co.*, *supra*. The privilege of pamphleteering, as well as the more orthodox types of publications, may neither be licensed, *Lovell* v. *City of Griffin*, 303 U.S. 444, . . . nor taxed. *Murdock* v. *Pennsylvania*, 319 U.S. 105. . . . These are illustrative of the preferred position granted speech and the press by the First Amendment. The command that "Congress shall make no law . . . abridging the freedom of speech, or of the press" has behind it a long history. It expresses the confidence that the safety of society depends on the tolerance of government for hostile as well as friendly criticism, that in a community where men's minds are free, there must be room for the unorthodox as well as the orthodox views.

If the present inquiry were sanctioned the press would be subjected to harassment that in practical effect might be as serious as censorship. A publisher, compelled to register with the federal government, would be subjected to vexatious inquiries. A requirement that a publisher disclose the identity of those who buy his books, pamphlets, or papers is indeed the beginning of surveillance of the press. True, no legal sanction is involved here. Congress has imposed no tax, established no board of censors, instituted no licensing system. But the potential restraint is equally severe. The finger of government leveled against the press is ominous. Once the government can demand of a publisher the names of the purchasers of his publications, the free press as we know it disappears. Then the spectre of a government agent will look over the shoulder of everyone who reads. The purchase of a book or pamphlet today may result in a subpoena tomorrow. Fear of criticism goes with every person into the bookstall. The subtle, imponderable pressures of the orthodox lay hold. Some will fear to read what is unpopular, what the powers-that-be dislike. When the light of publicity may reach any student, any teacher, inquiry will be discouraged. The books and pamphlets that are critical of the administration, that preach an unpopular policy in domestic or foreign affairs, that are in disrepute in the orthodox school of thought will be suspect and subject to investigation. The press and its readers will pay a heavy price in harassment. But that will be minor in comparison with the menace of the shadow which government will cast over literature that does not follow the dominant party line. If the lady from Toledo can be required to disclose what she read yesterday and what she will read tomorrow, fear will take the place of freedom in the libraries, bookstores, and homes of the land. Through the harassment of hearings, investigations, reports, and subpoenas government will hold a club over speech and over the press. Congress could not do this by law. The power of investigation is also limited. Inquiry into personal and private affairs is precluded. . . . And so is any matter in respect to which no valid legislation could be had. . . . Since Congress could not by law require of respondent what the House demanded, it may not take the first step in an inquiry ending in fine or imprisonment.

5. *Aliens and Loyalty*

HARISIADES *v.* SHAUGHNESSY

342 US 580 (1952)

[In this case three aliens were ordered deported under the Alien Registration Act of 1940. Each had been a member of the Communist Party of the United States, but his or her membership had terminated before the 1940 act was adopted. They contended that they could not be deported under the provisions of the act without violation of basic constitutional freedoms. The Court, by a 6-to-2 vote, upheld the deportation orders. Justice Clark did not participate, and Justices Douglas and Black dissented.

[The American residence of an alien is held, said the Court, by a "precarious tenure." To remain here "is not his right, but is a matter of permission and tolerance." In the present state of the world, said the Court, "it would be rash and irresponsible to reinterpret our fundamental law to deny or qualify the Government's power of deportation." Neither freedom of speech nor due process, the Court held, was violated by the deportations.

[It seems that all the Justices felt that the statutory deportation provisions were offensive to American ideals, but the majority held that "the place to resist unwise or cruel legislation touching aliens is the Congress, not this Court" (concurring opinion by Justice Frankfurter). Cf. *Galvan* v. *Press*, 74 S. Ct. 737 (1954).

[The Immigration and Nationality Act of 1952 (the McCarran-Walter Act) has imposed even more severe restrictions on aliens. See Milton R. Konvitz, *Civil Rights in Immigration* (Ithaca, N.Y.: Cornell University Press, 1953).]

Mr. Justice Jackson delivered the opinion of the Court:

The ultimate question in these three cases is whether the United States constitutionally may deport a legally resident alien because of membership in the Communist Party which terminated before enactment of the Alien Registration Act of 1940.

Harisiades, a Greek national, accompanied his father to the United States in 1916, when thirteen years of age, and has resided here since. He has taken a wife and sired two children, all citizens. He joined the Communist Party in 1925, when it was known as the Workers Party, and served as an organizer, Branch Executive Committeeman, secretary of its Greek Bureau, and editor of its paper *Empros*. The party discontinued his membership, along with that of other aliens, in 1939, but he has continued association with members. He was familiar with the principles and philosophy of the Communist Party and says he still believes in them. He disclaims personal belief in use of force and violence and asserts that the party favored their use only in defense. A warrant for his deportation because of his membership was issued in 1930 but was not served until 1946. The delay was due to inability to locate him because of his use of a number of aliases. After hearings, he was ordered deported on the grounds that after entry he had been a member of an organization which advocates overthrow of the Government by force and violence and distributes printed matter so advocating. He sought release by habeas corpus, which was denied by the District Court. The Court of Appeals for the Second Circuit affirmed.

Mascitti, a citizen of Italy, came to this country in 1920, at the age of sixteen. He married a resident alien and has one American-born child. He was a member of the Young Workers Party, the Workers Party and the Communist Party between 1923 and 1929. His testimony was that he knew the party advocated a proletarian dictatorship, to be established by force and violence if the capitalist class resisted. He heard some speakers advocate violence, in which he says he did not personally believe, and he was not clear as to the party policy. He resigned in 1929, apparently because he lost sympathy with or interest in the party. A warrant for his deportation issued and was served in 1946. After the usual administrative hearings he was ordered deported on the same grounds as Harisiades. He sought relief by declaratory judgment, which was denied without opinion by a three-judge District Court of the District of Columbia. His case comes to this Court by direct appeal.

Mrs. Coleman, a native of Russia, was admitted to the United States in 1914, when thirteen years of age. She married an American citizen and has three children, citizens by birth. She admits being a member of the Communist Party for about a year, beginning in 1919, and again from 1928 to 1930, and again from 1936 to 1937 or 1938. She held no office and her activities were not significant. She disavowed much knowledge of party principles and program, claiming she joined each time because of some injustice the party was then fighting. The reasons she gives for leaving the party are her health and the party's discontinuance of alien memberships. She has been ordered deported because after entry she became a member of an organization advocating overthrow of the Government by force and violence. She sought an injunction on constitutional grounds, among others. Relief was denied, without opinion, by a three-judge District Court of the District of Columbia and her case also comes here by direct appeal.

Validity of the hearing procedures are questioned for noncompliance with the Administrative Procedure Act, which we think is here inapplicable. Admittedly, each of these deportations is authorized and required by the letter, spirit and intention of the statute. But the Act is assailed on three grounds: (1) that it deprives the aliens of liberty without due process of law in violation of the Fifth Amendment; (2) that it abridges their freedoms of speech and assembly in contravention of the First Amendment; and, (3) that it is an *ex post facto* law which Congress is forbidden to pass by Art. I, § 9, cl. 3 of the Constitution.

We have in each case a finding, approved by the court below, that the Communist Party during the period of the alien's membership taught and advocated overthrow of the Government of the United States by force and violence. Those findings are not questioned here.

These aliens ask us to forbid their expulsion by a departure from the long-accepted application to such cases of the Fifth Amendment provision that no person shall be deprived of life, liberty or property without due process of law. Their basic contention is that admission for permanent residence confers a "vested right" on the alien, equal to that of the citizen, to remain within the country, and that the alien is entitled to constitutional protection in that matter to the same extent as the citizen. Their second line of defense is that if any power to deport domiciled aliens exists it is so dispersed that the judiciary must concur in the grounds for its exercise to the extent of finding them reasonable. The argument goes on to the contention that the grounds prescribed by the Act of 1940 bear no reasonable relation to protection of legitimate interests of the United States and concludes that the Act should be declared invalid. Admittedly these propositions are not founded in precedents of this Court.

For over thirty years each of these aliens has enjoyed such advantages as accrue from residence here without renouncing his foreign allegiance or formally acknowledging adherence to the Constitution he now invokes. Each was admitted to the United States, upon passing formidable exclusionary hurdles, in the hope that, after what may be called a probationary period, he would desire and be found desirable for citizenship. Each has been offered naturalization, with all of the rights and privileges of citizenship, conditioned only upon open and honest assumption to undivided allegiance to our government. But acceptance was and is not compulsory. Each has been permitted to prolong his original nationality indefinitely.

So long as one thus perpetuates a dual status as an American inhabitant but foreign citizen, he may derive advantages from two sources of law—American and international. He may claim protection against our Government unavailable to the citizen. As an alien he retains a claim upon the state of his citizenship to diplomatic intervention on his behalf, a patronage often of considerable value. The state of origin of each of these aliens could presently enter diplomatic remonstrance against these deportations if they were inconsistent with international law, the prevailing custom among nations or their own practices.

The alien retains immunities from burdens which the citizen must shoulder. By withholding his allegiance from the United States, he leaves outstanding a foreign call on his loyalties which international law not only permits our Government to recognize but commands it to respect. In deference to it certain dispensations from conscription for any military service have been granted foreign nationals. They can not, consistently with our international commitments, be compelled "to take part in the operations of war directed against their own country." In addition to such general immunities they may enjoy particular treaty privileges.

Under our law, the alien in several respects stands on an equal footing with citizens, but in others has never been conceded legal parity with the citizen. Most importantly, to protract this ambiguous status within the country is not his right but is a matter of permission and tolerance. The Government's power to terminate its hospitality has been asserted and sustained by this Court since the question first arose.

War, of course, is the most usual occasion for extensive resort to the power. Though the resident alien may be personally loyal to the United States, if his nation becomes our enemy his allegiance prevails over his personal preference and makes him also our enemy, liable to expulsion or internment, and his property becomes subject to seizure and perhaps confiscation. But it does not require war to bring the power of deportation into existence or to authorize its exercise. Congressional apprehension of foreign or internal dangers short of war may lead to its use. So long as the alien elects to continue the ambiguity of his allegiance his domicile here is held by a precarious tenure.

That aliens remain vulnerable to expulsion after long residence is a practice that bristles with severities. But it is a weapon of defense and reprisal confirmed by international law as a power inherent in every sovereign state. Such is the traditional power of the Nation over the alien and we leave the law on the subject as we find it.

This brings us to the alternative defense under the Due Process Clause—that, granting the power, it is so unreasonably and harshly exercised by this enactment that it should be held unconstitutional.

In historical context the Act before us stands out as an extreme application of the expulsion power. There is no denying that as world convulsions have driven us toward a closed society the expulsion power has been exercised with increasing severity, manifest in multiplication of grounds for deportation, in expanding the subject classes from illegal entrants to legal residents, and in greatly lengthening the period of residence after which one may be expelled. This is said to have reached a point where it is the duty of this Court to call a halt upon the political branches of the Government.

It is pertinent to observe that any policy toward aliens is vitally and intricately interwoven with contemporaneous policies in regard to the conduct of foreign relations, the war power, and the maintenance of a republican form of government. Such matters are so exclusively entrusted to the political branches of government as to be largely immune from judicial inquiry or interference.

These restraints upon the judiciary, occasioned by different events, do not control today's decision but they are pertinent. It is not necessary and probably not possible to delineate a fixed and precise line of separation in these matters between political and judicial power under the Constitution. Certainly, however, nothing in the structure of our Government or the text of our Constitution would warrant judicial review by standards which would require us to equate our political judgment with that of Congress.

Under the conditions which produced this Act can we declare that congressional alarm about a coalition of Communist power without and Communist conspiracy within the United States is either a fantasy or a pretense? This Act was approved by President Roosevelt June 28, 1940, when a world war was threatening to involve us, as soon it did. Communists in the United States were exerting every effort to defeat and delay our preparations. Certainly no responsible American would say that there were then or are now no possible grounds on which Congress might believe that Communists in our midst are inimical to our security.

Congress received evidence that the Communist movement here has been heavily laden with aliens and that Soviet control of the American Communist Party has been largely through alien Communists. It would be easy for those of us who do not have security responsibility to say that those who do are taking Communism too seriously and overestimating its danger. But we have an Act of one Congress which, for a decade, subsequent Congresses have never repealed but have strengthened and extended. We, in our private opinions, need not concur in Congress' policies to hold its enactments constitutional. Judicially we must tolerate what personally we may regard as a legislative mistake.

We are urged, because the policy inflicts severe and undoubted hardship on affected individuals, to find a restraint in the Due Process

Clause. But the Due Process Clause does not shield the citizen from conscription and the consequent calamity of being separated from family, friends, home and business while he is transported to foreign lands to stem the tide of Communism. If Communist aggression creates such hardships for loyal citizens, it is hard to find justification for holding that the Constitution requires that its hardships must be spared the Communist alien. When citizens raised the Constitution as a shield against expulsion from their homes and places of business, the Court refused to find hardship a cause for judicial intervention.

We think that, in the present state of the world, it would be rash and irresponsible to reinterpret our fundamental law to deny or qualify the Government's power of deportation. However desirable worldwide amelioration of the lot of aliens, we think it is peculiarly a subject for international diplomacy. It should not be initiated by judicial decision which can only deprive our own Government of a power of defense and reprisal without obtaining for American citizens abroad any reciprocal privileges or immunities. Reform in this field must be entrusted to the branches of the Government in control of our international relations and treaty-making powers.

We hold that the Act is not invalid under the Due Process Clause. These aliens are not entitled to judicial relief unless some other constitutional limitation has been transgressed, to which inquiry we turn.

The First Amendment is invoked as a barrier against this enactment. The claim is that in joining an organization advocating overthrow of government by force and violence the alien has merely exercised freedoms of speech, press and assembly which that Amendment guarantees to him.

The assumption is that the First Amendment allows Congress to make no distinction between advocating change in the existing order by lawful elective processes and advocating change by force and violence, that freedom for the one includes freedom for the other, and that when teaching of violence is denied so is freedom of speech.

Our Constitution sought to leave no excuse for violent attack on the status quo by providing a legal alternative—attack by ballot. To arm all men for orderly change, the Constitution put in their hands a right to influence the electorate by press, speech and assembly. This means freedom to advocate or promote Communism by means of the ballot box, but it does not include the practice or incitement of violence.

True, it often is difficult to determine whether ambiguous speech is advocacy of political methods or subtly shades into a methodical but prudent incitement to violence. Communist governments avoid the inquiry by suppressing everything distasteful. Some would have us avoid the difficulty by going to the opposite extreme of permitting incitement to violent overthrow at least unless it seems certain to succeed immediately. We apprehend that the Constitution enjoins upon us the duty, however difficult, of distinguishing between the two. Different formulae have been applied in different situations and the test applicable to the Communist Party has been stated too recently to make further discussion at this time profitable. We think the First Amendment does not prevent the deportation of these aliens.

The remaining claim is that this Act conflicts with Art. I, § 9, of the Constitution forbidding *ex post facto* enactments. An impression of retroactivity results from reading as a new and isolated enactment what is actually a continuation of prior legislation.

During all the years since 1920 Congress has maintained a standing admonition to aliens, on pain of deportation, not to become members of any organization that advocates overthrow of the United States by force and violence, a category repeatedly held to include the Communist Party. These aliens violated that prohibition and incurred liability to deportation. They were not caught unawares by a change of law. There can be no contention that they were not adequately forewarned both that their conduct was prohibited and of its consequences.

In 1939, this Court decided *Kessler* v. *Strecker,* 307 U.S. 22, . . . in which it was held that Congress, in the statute as it then stood, had not clearly expressed an intent that Communist Party membership remained cause for deportation after it ceased. The Court concluded that in the absence of such expression only contemporaneous membership would authorize deportation.

The reaction of the Communist Party was to drop aliens from membership, at least in form, in order to immunize them from the consequences of their party membership.

The reaction of Congress was that the Court had misunderstood its legislation. In the Act here before us it supplied unmistakable language that past violators of its prohibitions continued to be deportable in spite of resignation or expulsion from the party. It regarded the fact that an alien defied our laws to join the Communist Party as an indication that he had developed little comprehension of the principles or practice of representative government or else was unwilling to abide by them.

However, even if the Act were found to be retroactive, to strike it down would require us to overrule the construction of the *ex post facto* provision which has been followed by this Court from earliest times. It always has been considered that that which it forbids is penal legislation which imposes or increases criminal punishment for conduct lawful previous to its enactment. Deportation, however severe its consequences, has been consistently classified as a civil rather than a criminal procedure. Both of these doctrines as original proposals might be debatable, but both have been considered closed for many years and a body of statute and decisional law has been built upon them. In *Bugajewitz* v. *Adams*, 228 U.S. 585, Mr. Justice Holmes, for the Court, said:

It is thoroughly established that Congress has power to order the deportation of aliens whose presence in the country it deems hurtful. The determination by facts that might constitute a crime under local law is not a conviction of crime, nor is the deportation a punishment; it is simply a refusal by the government to harbor persons whom it does not want. The coincidence of the local penal law with the policy of Congress is an accident. . . . The prohibition of *ex post facto* laws in article 1, § 9, has no application . . . and with regard to the petitioner, it is not necessary to construe the statute as having any retrospective effect.

Later, the Court said,

It is well settled that deportation, while it may be burdensome and severe for the alien, is not a punishment. . . . The inhibition against the passage of an *ex post facto* law by Congress in section 9 of article 1 of the Constitution applies only to criminal laws . . . and not to a deportation act like this. . . .

It is contended that this policy allows no escape by reformation. We are urged to apply some doctrine of atonement and redemption. Congress might well have done so, but it is not for the judiciary to usurp the function of granting absolution or pardon. We can not do so for deportable ex-convicts, even though they have served a term of imprisonment calculated to bring about their reformation.

When the Communist Party as a matter of party strategy formally expelled alien members en masse, it destroyed any significance that discontinued membership might otherwise have as indication of change of heart by the individual. Congress may have believed that the party tactics threw upon the Government an almost impossible burden if it attempted to separate those who sincerely renounced Communist principles of force and violence from those who left the party the better to serve it. Congress, exercising the wide discretion that it alone has in these matters, declined to accept that as the Government's burden.

We find none of the constitutional objections to the Act well founded. The judgments accordingly are affirmed.

Mr. Justice Douglas, with whom Mr. Justice Black concurs, dissenting:

There are two possible bases for sustaining this Act:

(1) A person who was once a Communist is tainted for all time and forever dangerous to our society; or

(2) Punishment through banishment from the country may be placed

upon an alien not for what he did, but for what his political views once were or are.

Each of these is foreign to our philosophy. We repudiate our traditions of tolerance and our articles of faith based upon the Bill of Rights when we bow to them by sustaining an Act of Congress which has them as a foundation.

The view that the power of Congress to deport aliens is absolute and may be exercised for any reason which Congress deems appropriate rests on *Fong Yue Ting* v. *United States*, 149 U.S. 698, decided in 1893 by a six to three vote. That decision seems to me to be inconsistent with the philosophy of constitutional law which we have developed for the protection of resident aliens. We have long held that a resident alien is a "person" within the meaning of the Fifth and the Fourteenth Amendments. He therefore may not be deprived either by the national government or by any state of life, liberty, or property without due process of law. Nor may he be denied the equal protection of the laws. A state was not allowed to exclude an alien from the laundry business because he was a Chinese, nor discharge him from employment because he was not a citizen, nor deprive him of the right to fish because he was a Japanese ineligible to citizenship. An alien's property (provided he is not an enemy alien) may not be taken without just compensation. He is entitled to habeas corpus to test the legality of his restraint, to the protection of the Fifth and Sixth Amendments in criminal trials, and to the right of free speech as guaranteed by the First Amendment.

An alien, who is assimilated in our society, is treated as a citizen so far as his property and his liberty are concerned. He can live and work here and raise a family, secure in the personal guarantees every resident has and safe from discriminations that might be leveled against him because he was born abroad. Those guarantees of liberty and livelihood are the essence of the freedom which this country from the beginning has offered the people of all lands. If those rights, great as they are, have constitutional protection, I think the more important one—the right to remain here—has a like dignity.

The power of Congress to exclude, admit, or deport aliens flows from sovereignty itself and from the power "To establish an uniform Rule of Naturalization." U.S. Const., Art. I, § 8, cl. 4. The power of deportation is therefore an *implied* one. The right to life and liberty is an *express* one. Why this *implied* power should be given priority over the *express* guarantee of the Fifth Amendment has never been satisfactorily answered. Mr. Justice Brewer's dissent in *Fong Yue Ting* v. *United States,* . . . grows in power with the passing years:

It is said that the power here asserted is inherent in sovereignty. This doctrine of powers inherent in sovereignty is one both indefinite and dangerous. Where are the limits to such powers to be found, and by whom are they to be pronounced? Is it within legislative capacity to declare the limits? If so, then the mere assertion of an inherent power creates it, and despotism exists. May the courts establish the boundaries? Whence do they obtain the authority for this? Shall they look to the practices of other nations to ascertain the limits? The governments of other nations have elastic powers. Ours are fixed and bounded by a written constitution. The expulsion of a race may be within the inherent powers of a despotism. History, before the adoption of this constitution, was not destitute of examples of the exercise of such a power; and its framers were familiar with history and wisely, as it seems to me, they gave to this government no general power to banish. Banishment may be resorted to as punishment for crime; but among the powers reserved to the people, and not delegated to the government, is that of determining whether whole classes in our midst shall, for no crime but that of their race and birthplace, be driven from our territory.

The right to be immune from arbitrary decrees of banishment certainly may be more important to "liberty" than the civil rights which all aliens enjoy when they reside here. Unless they are free from arbitrary banishment, the "liberty" they enjoy while they live here is indeed illusory. Banishment is punishment in the practical sense. It may deprive a man and his family of all that makes life worth while. Those who have their roots here have an important stake in this country. Their plans for themselves and their hopes for their children all depend on their right to stay. If they are uprooted and sent to lands no longer known to them, no longer hospitable, they become displaced, homeless people condemned to bitterness and despair.

This drastic step may at times be necessary in order to protect the national interest. There may be occasion when the continued presence of an alien, no matter how long he may have been here, would be hostile to the safety or welfare of the nation due to the nature of his conduct. But unless such condition is shown, I would stay the hand of the government and let those to whom we have extended our hospitality and who have become members of our communities remain here and enjoy the life and liberty which the Constitution guarantees.

Congress has not proceeded by that standard. It has ordered these aliens deported not for what they are but for what they once were. Perhaps a hearing would show that they continue to be people dangerous and hostile to us. But the principle of forgiveness and the doctrine of redemption are too deep in our philosophy to admit that there is no return for those who have once erred.

⋆ VIII ⋆

Freedom of Speech and Press: Censorship and Contempt by Publication

1. Indecent and Obscene Literature

a. Post Office Control

HANNEGAN v. ESQUIRE, INC.

327 US 146 (1946)

[The second-class-mail privilege is a valuable asset to a periodical; for, if this privilege were denied, a periodical would have to pay substantially higher postage rates, which would subject it to a serious competitive disadvantage. If the Postmaster General were given wide discretionary powers in awarding or denying the second-class-mail privilege, he could "make" or "break" a publication; the privilege could be used to impose political, economic, religious, literary, or aesthetic orthodoxy on the press.

[The Court has held that Congress need not open second-class mail "to publications of all types." The furthest the Court ever went in sustaining a revocation of the privilege was in the *Milwaukee Leader Case*, 255 US 407 (1921). The Court (Justices Holmes and Brandeis dissented) upheld the order of the Postmaster General revoking the privilege on the ground that the newspaper had systematically published matter that was banned by the Espionage Act of 1917. The newspaper was thus not merely punished for its *past* misdeeds but was subjected to penalties as to the *future*.

[In the present case the Postmaster General attempted to accomplish the same result with respect to *Esquire*, a monthly magazine, because its contents seemed to him, by reason of vulgarity or poor taste, not to "contribute to the public good and the public welfare." The Court unanimously decided in favor of the publication. The ends of the legislation that provides for the second-class privilege, said the Court, "can be served only by uncensored distribution of literature." A requirement "that literature or art conform to some norm prescribed by an official smacks of an ideology foreign to our system." If the Postmaster General could withdraw the privilege from *Esquire*, he might try to do the same thing tomorrow respecting a periodical "whose social or economic views seemed harmful." It is doubtful, in the light of this decision and opinion, whether the *Milwaukee Leader Case* is still good law; in the *Esquire Case*, it should be noted, the Court cited only the dissents of Holmes and Brandeis in the earlier case.]

Mr. Justice Douglas delivered the opinion of the Court:

Congress has made obscene material nonmailable (18 USCA § 334), and has applied criminal sanctions for the enforcement of that policy. It has divided mailable matter into four classes, periodical publications constituting the second-class. . . . And it has specified four conditions upon which a publication shall be admitted to the second-class. . . . The Fourth condition, which is the only one relevant here, provides:

Except as otherwise provided by law, the conditions upon which a publication shall be admitted to the second class are as follows . . . Fourth. It must be originated and published for the dissemination of information of a public character, or devoted to literature, the sciences, arts, or some special industry, and having a legitimate list of subscribers. Nothing herein contained shall be so construed as to admit to the second-class rate regular publications designed primarily for advertising purposes, or for free circulation, or for circulation at nominal rates.

Respondent is the publisher of *Esquire Magazine*, a monthly periodical which was granted a second-class permit in 1933. In 1943, pursuant to 39 USCA § 232, a citation was issued to respondent by the then Postmaster General (for whom the present Postmaster General has now been substituted as petitioner) to show cause why that permit should not be suspended or revoked. A hearing was held before a board designated by the then Postmaster General. The board recommended that the permit not be revoked. Petitioner's predecessor took a different view. He did not find that *Esquire Magazine* contained obscene material and therefore was nonmailable. He revoked its second-class permit because he found that it did not comply with the Fourth condition. The gist of his holding is contained in the following excerpt from his opinion:

The plain language of this statute does not assume that a publication must in fact be "obscene" within the intendment of the postal obscenity statutes before it can be found not to be "originated and published for the dissemination of information of a public character, or devoted to literature, the sciences, arts, or some special industry."

Writings and pictures may be indecent, vulgar, and risque and still not be obscene in a technical sense. Such writings and pictures may be in that obscure and treacherous borderland zone where the average person hesitates to find them technically obscene, but still may see ample proof that they are morally improper and not for the public welfare and the public good. When such writings or pictures occur in isolated instances their dangerous tendencies and malignant qualities may be considered of lesser importance.

When, however, they become a dominant and systematic feature they most certainly cannot be said to be for the public good, and a publication which uses them in that manner is not making the "special contribution to the public welfare" which Congress intended by the Fourth condition.

A publication to enjoy these unique mail privileges and special preferences is bound to do more than refrain from disseminating material which is obscene or bordering on the obscene. It is under a positive duty to contribute to the public good and the public welfare. . . .

The issues of *Esquire Magazine* under attack are those for January to November inclusive of 1943. The material complained of embraces in bulk only a small percentage of those issues. Regular features of the magazine (called "The Magazine for Men") include articles on topics of current interest, short stories, sports articles or stories, short articles by men prominent in various fields of activities, articles about men prominent in the news, a book review department headed by the late William Lyon Phelps, a theatrical department headed by George Jean Nathan, . . . [a department on] lively arts by Gilbert Seldes, . . . pictorial features, including war action paintings, color photographs of game birds and reproductions of famous paintings, prints and drawings. There was very little in these features which was challenged. But petitioner's predecessor found that the objectionable items, though a small percentage of the total bulk, were regular recurrent features which gave the magazine its dominant tone or characteristic. These include jokes, cartoons, pictures, articles, and poems. They were said to reflect the smoking-room type of humor, featuring, in the main, sex. Some witnesses found the challenged items highly objectionable, calling them salacious and indecent. Others thought they were only racy and risque. Some condemned them as being merely in poor taste. Other witnesses could find no objection to them.

An examination of the items makes plain, we think, that the controversy is not whether the magazine publishes "information of a public character" or is devoted to "literature" or to the "arts." It is whether the contents are "good" or "bad." To uphold the order of revocation would, therefore, grant the Postmaster General a power of censorship. Such a power is so abhorrent to our traditions that a purpose to grant it should not be easily inferred. . . .

If the Fourth condition is read in that way, it is plain that Congress made no radical or basic change in the type of regulation which it adopted for second-class mail in 1879. The inauguration of even a limited type of censorship would have been such a startling change as to have left some traces in the legislative history. But we find none. . . .

We may assume that Congress has a broad power of classification and need not open second-class mail to publications of all types. The categories of publications entitled to that classification have indeed varied through the years. And the Court held in *Ex parte Jackson*, 96 US 727, that Congress could constitutionally make it a crime to send fraudulent or obscene material through the mails. But grave constitutional questions are immediately raised once it is said that the use of the mails is a privilege which may be extended or withheld on any grounds whatsoever. . . . Under that view the second-class rate could be granted on condition that certain economic or political ideas not be disseminated. The provisions of the Fourth condition would have to be far more explicit for us to assume that Congress made such a radical departure from our traditions and undertook to clothe the Postmaster General with the power to supervise the tastes of the reading public of the country.

. . . Under our system of government there is an accommodation for the widest varieties of tastes and ideas. What is good literature, what has educational value, what is refined public information, what is good art, varies with individuals as it does from one generation to another. There doubtless would be a contrariety of views concerning Cervantes' *Don Quixote,* Shakespeare's *Venus and Adonis,* or Zola's *Nana.* But a requirement that literature or art conform to some norm prescribed by an official smacks of an ideology foreign to our system. The basic values implicit in the requirements of the Fourth condition can be served only by uncensored distribution of literature. From the multitude of competing offerings the public will pick and choose. What seems to one to be trash may have for others fleeting or even enduring values. But to withdraw the second-class rate from this publication today because its contents seemed to one official not good for the public would sanction withdrawal of the second-class rate tomorrow from another periodical whose social or economic views seemed harmful to another official. The validity of the obscenity laws is recognition that the mails may not be used to satisfy all tastes, no matter how perverted. But Congress has left the Postmaster General with no power to prescribe standards for the literature or the art which a mailable periodical disseminates. . . .

Affirmed. [The order of the Postmaster General may be enjoined.]

b. Customs Control

UNITED STATES v. ONE BOOK CALLED "ULYSSES"

5 F. Supp. 182 (1933)

[A form of censorship that might have a serious effect on American culture could be achieved by customs officials if they stopped at the border books that they considered objectionable. Literary, aesthetic, or political isolationism could be strengthened in this way.

[Until the law was changed by Congress in 1930 customs officials prevented the entry of such classics as Rousseau's *Confessions*, Casanova's *Memoirs*, the *Golden Ass* of Apuleius, all of Rabelais, Boccaccio's *Decameron*, *The Arabian Nights*, Voltaire's *Candide*, and modern books like *The Enormous Room* by E. E. Cummings and *Psychopathia Sexualis* by Krafft-Ebing. Many of these books had already been published in the United States, but this fact did not impress the customs officials; they seized and confiscated the books, and the citizen was quite helpless. Congress in 1930 amended the Tariff Act to authorize the Secretary of the Treasury to admit classics and books of recognized scientific or literary merit when imported for noncommercial purposes. The act provided also that, when a book was seized, the collector was to notify the federal district attorney, who was to institute proceedings in the Federal District Court for the forfeiture of the book. Any party in interest could demand a trial by jury.

[In 1933 an attempt was made to keep out a copy of *Ulysses* by James Joyce. In a notable decision, Judge Woolsey of the Federal District Court ruled that the book was not "obscene" within the meaning of the act and so was not subject to seizure and confiscation. His decision was affirmed by the Court of Appeals. 72 F. 2d 705 (1934). The 1930 statute and Judge Woolsey's decision have, on the whole, emancipated books from customs censorship; but see *Besig* v. *United States*, 208 F. 2d 142 (1953).]

On cross motions for a decree in a libel of confiscation, supplemented by a stipulation—hereinafter described—brought by the United States against the book "Ulysses" by James Joyce, under Section 305 of the

Tariff Act of 1930, Title 19 United States Code, Section 1305, on the ground that the book is obscene within the meaning of that Section, and, hence, is not importable into the United States, but is subject to seizure, forfeiture and confiscation and destruction.

Judge Woolsey:

The motion for a decree dismissing the libel herein is granted, and, consequently, of course, the Government's motion for a decree of forfeiture and destruction is denied.

Accordingly a decree dismissing the libel without costs may be entered herein.

I. The practice followed in this case is in accordance with the suggestion made by me in the case of *United States* v. *One Book Entitled "Contraception,"* 51 F. (2d) 525, and is as follows:

After issue was joined by the filing of the claimant's answer to the libel for forfeiture against "Ulysses," a stipulation was made between the United States Attorney's office and the attorneys for the claimant providing:

1. That the book "Ulysses" should be deemed to have been annexed to and to have become part of the libel just as if it had been incorporated in its entirety therein.

2. That the parties waived their right to a trial by jury.

3. That each party agreed to move for decree in its favor.

4. That on such cross motions the Court might decide all the questions of law and fact involved and render a general finding thereon.

5. That on the decision of such motions the decree of the Court might be entered as if it were a decree after trial.

It seems to me that a procedure of this kind is highly appropriate in libels for the confiscation of books such as this. It is an especially advantageous procedure in the instant case because on account of the length of "Ulysses" and the difficulty of reading it, a jury trial would have been an extremely unsatisfactory, if not an almost impossible, method of dealing with it.

II. I have read "Ulysses" once in its entirety and I have read those passages of which the Government particularly complains several times. In fact, for many weeks, my spare time has been devoted to the consideration of the decision which my duty would require me to make in this matter.

"Ulysses" is not an easy book to read or to understand. But there has been much written about it, and in order properly to approach the consideration of it, it is advisable to read a number of other books which have now become its satellites. The study of "Ulysses" is, therefore, a heavy task.

III. The reputation of "Ulysses" in the literary world, however, warranted my taking such time as was necessary to enable me to satisfy myself as to the intent with which the book was written, for, of course, in any case where a book is claimed to be obscene it must first be determined, whether the intent with which it was written was what is called, according to the usual phrase, pornographic,—that is, written for the purpose of exploiting obscenity.

If the conclusion is that the book is pornographic that is the end of the inquiry and forfeiture must follow.

But in "Ulysses," in spite of its unusual frankness, I do not detect anywhere the leer of the sensualist. I hold, therefore, that it is not pornographic.

IV. In writing "Ulysses," Joyce sought to make a serious experiment in a new, if not wholly novel, literary genre. He takes persons of the lower middle class living in Dublin in 1904 and seeks not only to describe what they did on a certain day early in June of that year as they went about the City bent on their usual occupations, but also to tell what many of them thought about the while.

Joyce has attempted—it seems to me, with astonishing success—to show how the screen of consciousness with its ever-shifting kaleidoscopic impressions carries, as it were on a plastic palimpsest, not only what is in the focus of each man's observation of the actual things about him, but also in a penumbral zone residua of past impressions, some recent and some drawn up by association from the domain of the subconscious. He shows how each of these impressions affects the life and behavior of the character which he is describing.

What he seeks to get is not unlike the result of a double or, if that is possible, a multiple exposure on a cinema film which would give a clear foreground with a background visible but somewhat blurred and out of focus in varying degrees.

To convey by words an effect which obviously lends itself more appropriately to a graphic technique, accounts, it seems to me, for much of the obscurity which meets a reader of "Ulysses." And it also explains another aspect of the book, which I have further to consider, namely, Joyce's sincerity and his honest effort to show exactly how the minds of his characters operate.

If Joyce did not attempt to be honest in developing the technique which he has adopted in "Ulysses" the result would be psychologically misleading and thus unfaithful to his chosen technique. Such an attitude would be artistically inexcusable.

It is because Joyce has been loyal to his technique and has not funked its necessary implications, but has honestly attempted to tell fully what his characters think about, that he has been the subject of so many attacks and that his purpose has been so often misunderstood and misrepresented. For his attempt sincerely and honestly to realize his objective has required him incidentally to use certain words which are generally considered dirty words and has led at times to what many think is a too poignant preoccupation with sex in the thoughts of his characters.

The words which are criticized as dirty are old Saxon words known to almost all men and, I venture, to many women, and are such words as would be naturally and habitually used, I believe, by the types of folk whose life, physical and mental, Joyce is seeking to describe. In respect of the recurrent emergence of the theme of sex in the minds of his characters, it must always be remembered that his locale was Celtic and his season Spring.

Whether or not one enjoys such a technique as Joyce uses is a matter of taste on which disagreement or argument is futile, but to subject that technique to the standards of some other technique seems to me to be little short of absurd.

Accordingly, I hold that "Ulysses" is a sincere and honest book and I think that the criticisms of it are entirely disposed of by its rationale.

V. Furthermore, "Ulysses" is an amazing *tour de force* when one considers the success which has been in the main achieved with such a difficult objective as Joyce set for himself. As I have stated, "Ulysses" is not an easy book to read. It is brilliant and dull, intelligible and obscure by turns. In many places it seems to me to be disgusting, but although it contains, as I have mentioned above, many words usually considered dirty, I have not found anything that I consider to be dirt for dirt's sake. Each word of the book contributes like a bit of mosaic to the detail of the picture which Joyce is seeking to construct for his readers.

If one does not wish to associate with such folk as Joyce describes, that is one's own choice. In order to avoid indirect contact with them one may not wish to read "Ulysses"; that is quite understandable. But when such a real artist in words, as Joyce undoubtedly is, seeks to draw a true picture of the lower middle class in a European city, ought it to be impossible for the American public legally to see that picture?

To answer this question it is not sufficient merely to find, as I have found above, that Joyce did not write "Ulysses" with what is commonly called pornographic intent, I must endeavor to apply a more objective standard to his book in order to determine its effect in the result, irrespective of the intent with which it was written.

VI. The statute under which the libel is filed only denounces, in so far as we are here concerned, the importation into the United States from any foreign country of "any obscene book." Section 305 of the

Tariff Act of 1930, Title 19 United States Code, Section 1305. It does not marshal against books the spectrum of condemnatory adjectives found, commonly, in laws dealing with matters of this kind. I am, therefore, only required to determine whether "Ulysses" is obscene within the legal definition of that word.

The meaning of the word "obscene" as legally defined by the Courts is: tending to stir the sex impulses or to lead to sexually impure and lustful thoughts. . . .

Whether a particular book would tend to excite such impulses and thoughts must be tested by the Court's opinion as to its effect on a person with average sex instincts—what the French would call *l'homme moyen sensuel*—who plays, in this branch of legal inquiry, the same role of hypothetical reagent as does the "reasonable man" in the law of torts and "the man learned in the art" on questions of invention in patent law.

The risk involved in the use of such a reagent arises from the inherent tendency of the trier of facts, however fair he may intend to be, to make his reagent too much subservient to his own idiosyncrasies. Here, I have attempted to avoid this, if possible, and to make my reagent herein more objective than he might otherwise be, by adopting the following course:

After I had made my decision in regard to the aspect of "Uylsses," now under consideration, I checked my impressions with two friends of mine who in my opinion answered to the above stated requirement for my reagent.

These literary assessors—as I might properly describe them—were called on separately, and neither knew that I was consulting the other. They are men whose opinion on literature and on life I value most highly. They had both read "Ulysses," and, of course, were wholly unconnected with this cause.

Without letting either of my assessors know what my decision was, I gave to each of them the legal definition of obscene and asked each whether in his opinion "Ulysses" was obscene within that definition.

I was interested to find that they both agreed with my opinion: that reading "Ulysses" in its entirety, as a book must be read on such a test as this, did not tend to excite sexual impulses or lustful thoughts but that its net effect on them was only that of a somewhat tragic and very powerful commentary on the inner lives of men and women.

It is only with the normal person that the law is concerned. Such a test as I have described, therefore, is the only proper test of obscenity in the case of a book like "Ulysses" which is a sincere and serious attempt to devise a new literary method for the observation and description of mankind.

I am quite aware that owing to some of its scenes "Ulysses" is a rather strong draught to ask some sensitive, though normal, persons to take. But my considered opinion, after long reflection, is that whilst in many places the effect of "Ulysses" on the reader undoubtedly is somewhat emetic, nowhere does it tend to be an aphrodisiac.

"Ulysses" may, therefore, be admitted into the United States.

c. Police Control

COMMONWEALTH v. GORDON

66 D. & C. 101 (1949)

[Books are molested by the Post Office and by the customs relatively seldom, as we have seen, but they continue to be subject to considerable harassment under state criminal statutes and from local police authorities. About 1870 Anthony Comstock began to cause trouble for authors, books, and book dealers when he found a book that in his judgment was obscene. Books by D. H. Lawrence, Sherwood Anderson, Bertrand Russell, and Theodore Dreiser—to name only a few—have been in the courts. The highest courts of Massachusetts and New York, for instance, have upheld police bans on books by Theodore Dreiser, Arthur Schnitzler, and Edmund Wilson. The courts differ on the definition of "obscenity," on the test to be used—the effect on youth or on the normal adult—and on other essential matters.

[The opinion by Judge Bok of the Court of Quarter Sessions in Philadelphia summarizes the conflict of authorities. His decision conforms with that of Judge Woolsey in the *Ulysses Case,* but it has not had the effect on state and local police authorities that the Woolsey decision has had on customs officers.

[Judge Bok's decision was affirmed by the Pennsylvania Superior and Supreme Courts. 166 Pa. Super. Ct. 120 (1950). The latter court, however, refused to approve the clear and present danger test as it was applied by Judge Bok. *Cf. Chaplinsky* v. *New Hampshire,* 315 US 568 (1942).]

Judge Bok:

. . . The evidence consists of nine books and an oral stipulation at bar that defendants are booksellers and that they possessed the books with the intent to sell them on the dates and at the time and places set forth in the indictments. This constituted in full the Commonwealth's evidence, to which defendants have demurred.

I have read the books with thoughtful care and find that they are not obscene, as alleged. The demurrers are therefore sustained.

The Statute

The indictments are drawn under section 524 of The Penal Code of June 24, 1939, which reads as follows:

Whoever sells, lends, distributes, exhibits, gives away or shows or offers to sell, lend, distribute, exhibit, or give away or show, or has in his possession with intent to sell, lend, distribute or give away or to show, or knowingly advertise in any manner, any obscene, lewd, lascivious, filthy, indecent or disgusting book, magazine, pamphlet, newspaper, storypaper, paper, writing, drawing, photograph, figure or image, or any written or printed matter of an indecent character, or any article or instrument of indecent or immoral use or purporting to be for indecent or immoral use or purpose, or whoever designs, copies, draws, photographs, prints, utters, publishes, or in any manner manufactures or prepares any such book, picture, drawing, magazine, pamphlet, newspaper, storypaper, paper, writing, figure, image, matter, article or thing, or whoever writes, prints, publishes, or utters, or causes to be printed, published or uttered, any advertisement or notice of any kind giving information, directly or indirectly, stating or purporting to do so, where, how, of whom, or by what means any, or what purports to be, any obscene, lewd, lascivious, filthy, disgusting or indecent book, picture, writing, paper, figure, image, matter, article or thing named in this section can be purchased, obtained or had, or whoever prints, utters, publishes, sells, lends, gives away, or shows, or has in his possession with intent to sell, lend, give away, or show, or otherwise offers for sale, loan or gift, or distribution, any pamphlet, magazine, newspaper or other printed paper devoted to the publication and principally made up of criminal news, police reports or accounts of criminal deeds, or pictures of stories of deeds of bloodshed, lust or crime, or whoever hires, employes, uses or permits any minor or child to do so or assist in doing any act or thing mentioned in this section, is guilty of a misdemeanor, and upon conviction, shall be sentenced to imprisonment not exceeding one (1) year, or to pay a fine not exceeding five hundred dollars ($500), or both.

The particular and only charge in the indictments is that defendants possessed some or all of the books with the intent to sell them. . . .

It should be noted at once that the wording of section 524 requires consideration of the indicted material as a whole; it does not proscribe articles or publications that merely contain obscene matter. This is now true in all jurisdictions that have dealt with the subject: [in] the Federal courts, . . . also . . . in Pennsylvania. . . .

Section 524, for all its verbiage, is very bare. The full weight of the legislative prohibition dangles from the word "obscene" and its synonyms. Nowhere are these words defined; nowhere is the danger to be expected of them stated; nowhere is a standard of judgment set forth. I assume that "obscenity" is expected to have a familiar and inherent meaning, both as to what it is and as to what it does.

It is my purpose to show that it has no such inherent meaning; that different meanings given to it at different times are not constant, either historically or legally; and that it is not constitutionally indictable unless it takes the form of sexual impurity, i.e., "dirt for dirt's sake" and can be traced to actual criminal behavior, either actual or demonstrably imminent.

Résumé of the Books

1, 2 and 3. The Studs Lonigan trilogy ("Young Lonigan," "The Young Manhood of Studs Lonigan," "Judgment Day"), by James T. Farrell; Vanguard Press, 1932–1935.

This is the story of the moral and physical disintegration of a young man living in Chicago between the years 1916 and 1932. Nothing that he attempted ever quite came off, and his failures became more and more incisive. He left school to hang around the streets with others of his kind; he was too young to enlist for war service; he loved Lucy since they were in school together, but avoided her for four years and finally alienated her by making drunken advances to her; he worked for his father as a painter, but, on a casual tip, invested his savings in a dubious stock, which failed; he fell half-heartedly in love with Catherine, and they were engaged to be married, but she became pregnant by him before the ceremony; looking for a job on a stormy day a few weeks before the wedding, he caught cold and died of pneumonia and a weakened heart.

The background of the semi-slum district in which Lonigan was born and lived was the outward counter-part of his own nature, and both together were too much for such decency of soul as he had. His drift downhill was relentless and inevitable. On the theory that no literature is vital that cannot be vulgarized, this trilogy may rank as an epic, for our criminal courts and prisons and many of our streets are peopled by Studs Lonigans. The characters in these books act and speak the kind of life that bred them, and Mr. Farrell has brought to the surface the groundswell of thought and inclination that move more people than, if they were honest, would admit to them.

It is not a pleasant story, nor are the characters gentle and refined. There is rape and dissipation and lust in these books, expressed in matching language, but they do not strike me as being out of proportion. The books as a whole create a sustained arc of a man's life and era, and the obvious effort of the author is to be faithful to the scene he depicts.

No one would want to be Studs Lonigan.

4. "A World I Never Made," by James T. Farrell; The Vanguard Press, New York, 1936.

This book could well be the beginning of another series, for it takes a minor character from the Lonigan books, Danny O'Neill, and shows him as a child. The milieu is the same—Chicago in 1911—but there is a discernible effort to show Danny's struggle uphill against the same factors that pushed Lonigan down.

This is the one book of the nine that does not end tragically; it merely stops in midstream, but the people who surround Danny do and say the same things that appear in the Lonigan series. Unlike the latter, this book is plastered with the short Saxon words of common vulgarity; they are consistent with the characters who use them and with the quality of the lives and actions that are the subject of the author's scrutiny.

I am not of mind, nor do I have the authority, to require an author to write about one kind of people and not about another, nor do I object to his effort to paint a complete picture of those whom he has chosen. Certainly I will not say that it is not a good thing to look deeply into life and people, regardless of the shadows that are to be found there.

5. "Sanctuary," by William Faulkner; Random House, 1931.

This is a powerful and dreadful story about a gay but virginal girl of 17 who accidentally falls into the hands of a sadistic man called Popeye, who is sexually impotent. He kills a half-witted boy who is informally guarding the girl, and ravishes her with a corncob. He then keeps her imprisoned in a house of prostitution and takes pleasure in watching her have intercourse with a man whom he kills when she tries to escape with him. Terrified of Popeye, she testifies that another man committed the murder, and is taken from court by her father, who has finally been able to locate her. Popeye is later apprehended on another charge of murder and is convicted.

There are no vulgar Saxon words in the book, but the situations are stark and unrelieved. It makes one shudder to think of what can happen by misadventure.

6. "Wild Palms," by William Faulkner; Random House, 1939.

This book concerns a wife who left her husband and children to seek integrity of experience, in terms of vitality, with her lover; "hunger is in the heart," she says, when the next meal seems uncertain, "not in the stomach." They wander about the country together, living as they must or as they wish, and she finally becomes pregnant. Her lover, a former doctor, attempts to abort her but mishandles it and she dies. He pleads guilty and is sentenced to 50 years in prison. He refuses a gift of cyanide from the woman's husband, saying: "Between grief and nothing I will take grief."

The redeeming feature of this tale is that an acid loneliness comes through, the awful loneliness that pervades lost people, even in company. No one could envy these two miserable creatures.

7. "God's Little Acre," by Erskine Caldwell; Random House, 1933.

An able companion to the same author's "Tobacco Road," it is the story of a poor and illiterate farmer's family in Georgia. The central figure is the father, who for 15 years has dug holes in his farm in search of gold. God's Little Acre is a part of the farm which he mentally moves about in order to keep it from getting in the way of his search for treasure; his idea is to give all that comes from it to the church, but he never works it. His daughters and sons and their wives get variously tangled up in sexual affairs which are taken as being in the nature of things. One brother kills another over his wife. The final and despairing cry of the father, who has always tried to keep peace, is, "Blood on my land!"

It is a frank and turbulent story, but it is an obvious effort to be faithful to the locality and its people.

8. "End As a Man," by Calder Willingham; The Vanguard Press, 1947.

Life in a southern military academy. A drinking party and crooked poker game finally result in the expulsion of several cadets, including the wily and unmoral ringleader. The retired general in charge of the academy is the stereotype of military martinet, whose conception of the narrow and rigid discipline necessary to produce "a man" is set in bold relief against the energy of growing boys. The result is a fair picture of the frustration inherent in an overdose of discipline and in the license and disobedience that is largely engendered by it.

No one would care to send his son to such an institution.

This is perhaps the foulest book of the lot, so far as language is concerned, but it is the language of vulgarity and not of erotic allurement.

9. "Never Love a Stranger," by Harold Robbins; Knopf, 1948.

The story of a boy brought up in an orphanage who finds that he has an uncle and is Jewish. After losing touch with his uncle he has various experiences and is finally down and out because he can find no work. He then becomes head of New York City's gambling racket, which he ultimately leaves in order to marry a childhood friend. She dies in childbirth and he is killed in the war; his friends take over the child, who will presumably have a better chance in life than he had.

It is a swift story that covers a great deal of ground, its point being to portray a hard and lonely man who could not fully trust or give himself to anyone. Its last and least convincing part is also the least open to attack for obscenity; the rest, particularly the section dealing with New York City during the depression of the early 1930's, is very moving, not because there are sexual incidents but because the lines of the story are deep and authentic.

General Comment

Three of these books [4, 7, and 8] have already been judicially cleared in New York City. . . .

After clearance by the magistrates, these books could have been brought before the grand jury, but no such indictments were attempted.

As I have indicated above, all but one of these books are profoundly tragic, and that one has its normal quota of frustration and despair. No one could envy or wish to emulate the characters that move so desolately through these pages. Far from inciting to lewd or lecherous desires, which are sensorially pleasurable, these books leave one either with a sense of horror or a pity for the degradation of mankind. The effect upon the normal reader, "l'homme moyen sensuel" (there is no such deft precision in English), would be anything but what the vice hunters fear it might be. We are so fearful for other people's morals; they so seldom have the courage of our own convictions.

It will be asked whether one would care to have one's young daughter read these books. I suppose that by the time she is old enough to wish to read them she will have learned the biologic facts of life and the words that go with them. There is something seriously wrong at home if those facts have not been met and faced and sorted by then; it is not children so much as parents that should receive our concern about this. I should prefer that my own three daughters meet the facts of life and the literature of the world in my library than behind a neighbor's barn, for I can face the adversary there directly. If the young ladies are appalled by what they read, they can close the book at the bottom of page one; if they read further, they will learn what is in the world and in its people, and no parents who have been discerning with their children need fear the outcome. Nor can they hold it back, for life is a series of little battles and minor issues, and the burden of choice is on us all, every day, young and old. Our daughters must live in the world and decide what sort of women they are to be, and we should be willing to prefer their deliberate and informed choice of decency rather than an innocence that continues to spring from ignorance. If that choice be made in the open sunlight, it is more apt than when made in shadow to fall on the side of honorable behavior.

The lesson to be learned from such books as these is not so facile as that the wages of sin is death, or, in Hollywood's more modern version, that the penalty of sinning is suffering. That is not enough to save a book from proper censorship. The tragedy of these books is not in death but in the texture of the slope that leads to death—in the inner suffering that comes at times from crimes against oneself as much as from crimes against society. That has been the green pastures of story-tellers ever since the Greek dramatists, especially when the pressures on a character are not, as they are not always, of his own making or within his control. Sin is too apt a word to take in the full reach of cir-cumstance, and I venture to say that in human experience suffering does not automatically follow sinning. Our laws have a good deal to do with that guarded notion. It is necessary to know what our laws are up to, and it is my conviction that, outside the police power, the laws of Anglo-Saxon countries are made less as absolute mandates than as clinical experiments. Democratic nations prefer checks and balances to absolute authority, and it is worthy of notice that the jury system exists only in those countries where the law is not considered to have been drawn, as Cicero put it, from the forehead of the gods, but rather from the will of the people, who wish to keep an eye on it. The eight-eenth amendment to the Constitution is a case in point.

Such sumptuary laws, and some economic ones, differ from obscenity statutes only in the degree of danger to society inherent in the appetite in question. The need for decency is as old as the appetites, but it is not expressed in uniform law or custom. The ancient Hebrews had a rigid moral code which, for example, excluded bastards from the con-gregation up to the tenth generation, for the combined reasons of preserving their ancient tradition of tribe and family and of increasing the number of effective warriors. The Greeks, more cosmopolitan in the country whose sterile soil could not support many people comfort-ably, approved pederasty and a restricted form of concubinage in order to keep the population down. Standards of sexual behavior, as well as of the need to censor it, have shifted from age to age, from country to country, and from economy to economy. The State of New Mexico has no obscenity statute. South Carolina had no divorce law until a few months ago.

Censorship, which is the policeman of decency, whether religious, patriotic, or moral, has had distinct fashions, depending on which great questions were agitating society at the time. During the Middle Ages, when the church was supreme, the focus of suppression was upon heresy and blasphemy. When the State became uppermost, the focus of suppression was upon treason and sedition. The advent of tech-nology made Queen Victoria realize, perhaps subconsciously, that loose morals would threaten the peace of mind necessary to the devel-opment of invention and big business; the focus moved to sexual moral-ity. We are now emerging into an era of social ideology and psychol-ogy, and the focus is turning to these. The right to speak out and to act freely is always at a minimum in the area of the fighting faiths.

The censorship of books did not become a broad public issue until after the invention of printing in the fifteenth century. The earliest real example of it was the first Index Librorium Prohibitorum of the Catholic Church in 1559, and the church was broadly tolerant of sexual impurity in the books that it considered; its main object was the suppression of heresy. I think it is a fair general statement that from ancient times until the Comstockian laws of 1873 the only form of written obscenity that was censored was "dirt for dirt's sake."

I do not regard the above as apart from the decisional purpose of this case. The words of the statute—"obscene, lewd, lascivious, filthy, indecent, or disgusting"—restrict rather than broaden the meaning of a highly penal statute. The effect of this plethora of epithets is to merge them into one prevailing meaning—that of sexual impurity alone, and this has been universally held. . . .

The statute is therefore directed only at sexual impurity and not at blasphemy or coarse and vulgar behavior of any kind. The word in common use for the purpose of such a statute is "obscenity." The great point of this case is to find out what that word means.

Nowhere in the statute is there a definition of it or a formula given for determining when it exists. Its derivation, *ob* and *scena*, suggests that anything done offstage, furtively, or lefthandedly, is obscene. The act does not penalize anyone who seeks to change the prevailing moral or sexual code, nor does it state that the writing must be such as to corrupt the morals of the public or of youth; it merely proscribes books that *are* obscene and leaves it to the authorities to decide whether or not they are. This cannot be done without regard to the nature and history of obscenity. It is unlike the fundamental laws of property, of crimes like murder, rape, and theft, or even of negligence, whose meaning has remained relatively constant. That of obscenity has frequently changed, almost from decade to decade within the past century; "Ulysses" was condemned by the State courts in New York just 10 years before it was cleared by Judge Woolsey in the District Court for the Southern District of New York. I must determine what this elusive word means now.

Something might be said at the outset about the familiar four-letter words that are so often associated with sexual impurity. These are, almost without exception, of honest Anglo-Saxon ancestry, and were not invented for purely scatological effect. The one, for example, that is used to denote the sexual act is an old agricultural word meaning "to plant," and was at one time a wholly respectable member of the English vocabulary. The distinction between a word of decent etymological history and one of smut alone is important; it shows that fashions in language change as expectably as do the concepts of what language connotes. It is the old business of semantics again, the difference between word and concept.

But there is another distinction. The decisions that I shall cite have sliced off vulgarity from obscenity. This has had the effect of making a clear division between the words of the bathroom and those of the bedroom: the former can no longer be regarded as obscene, since they have no erotic allurement, and the latter may be so regarded, depending on the circumstances of their use. This reduces the number of potentially offensive words sharply.

With such changes as these, the question is whether the legal mace should fall upon words or upon concepts—language or ideas.

Obscenity is not like sedition, blasphemy, or open lewdness, against which there are also criminal statutes. These offenses not only have acquired precise meaning but are defined specifically in the act. . . .

No such definition of standard or legislative intention occurs in section 524, and I am convinced that without a declaration of the legislature's intention as to what obscenity means or of what the law makers sought to prevent, there is no constant or reliable indication of it to be found in human experience.

The argument is often made that anyone can tell by instinct what is obscene and what is not, even if it is hard to put the difference into words. The same might be said of sedition, blasphemy, and open lewdness, but the legislature was careful to specify. With regard to obscenity, however, the argument does not hold water. When he was an editor, Walter Hines Page deleted the word "chaste" because it was suggestive, and the play "Sappho" was banned in New York City because a man carried a leading lady up a flight of stairs. A librarian once charged Mark Twain's "Tom Sawyer" and "Huckleberry Finn" with corrupting the morals of children. In 1907 Richard Strauss's "Salome" was banned in Boston. Charlotte Brontë's "Jane Eyre," when first published, was called "too immoral to be ranked as decent literature." Hawthorne's "Scarlet Letter" was referred to as "a brokerage of lust." George Eliot's "Adam Bede" was called "the vile outpourings of a lewd woman's mind." Others to suffer similarly were Elizabeth Barrett Browning's "Aurora Leigh," Hardy's "Tess" and "Jude," Du-Maurier's "Trilby," and Shaw's "Mrs. Warren's Profession." Walt Whitman lost his job in the United States Department of the Interior because of "Leaves of Grass."

It is presumed that Mr. Page and the others who attacked this imposing array of classics could tell by instinct what was decent and what was not. The idea that instinct can be resorted to as a process of moral *stare decisis* reduces to absurdity.

It is a far cry from the examples just cited to what society accepts as innocuous now. The stage, literature, painting, sculpture, photography, fashions of dress, and even the still pudibund screen tolerate things that would have made Anthony Comstock burn blue. In its issue of April 11, 1938, *Life* magazine ran a series of factual and dignified pictures called "The Birth of a Baby." It was attacked in the courts but was exonerated. Dr. Kinsey's report on the sexual behavior of men is now current. Truth and error, as Milton urged in his "Areopagitica," are being allowed to grapple, and we are the better for it.

In addition to the books whose banning is the subject of cases cited later in this opinion, I suggest a short list of modern books that have not been banned, so far as I can find out. All of these books contain sexual material, and all of them can be found in the Boston Public Library. I defy anyone to provide a rational basis for the distinction between these two sets of books. My list includes: Fanny Hurst's "Back Street"; Arthur Koestler's "Arrival and Departure"; Erich Maria Remarque's "All Quiet on the Western Front" and "Arch of Triumph"; Eugene O'Neill's "Anna Christie" and "Hairy Ape"; John Dos Passos's "U.S.A."; Ernest Hemingway's "For Whom the Bell Tolls"; Somerset Maugham's "Of Human Bondage"; Charles Morgan's "The Fountain" and "The Voyage"; Richard Wright's "Black Boy."

It is no answer to say that if my point about the books just listed be sound, then by analogy the law against murder is useless because all murderers are not caught. The inherent evil of murder is apparent, but by what apparent, inherent standard of evil is obscenity to be judged, from book to book? It is my purpose to provide such a standard, but it will reduce to a minimum the operation of any norm of indefinite interpretation.

Before leaving this point, research discloses a curious but complete confusion between the post office and the customs over what constitutes obscenity. No unanimity of opinion unites these two governmental services in a common standard. Books have cleared the port only to find the mails closed to them: others, printed here, have circulated freely while foreign copies were stopped at the ports. One would expect greater uniformity than this if obscenity could be unmistakably detected. . . .

It is my conclusion that the books before me are obvious efforts to show life as it is. I cannot be convinced that the deep drives and appetites of life are very much different from what they have always been, or that censorship has ever had any effect on them, except as the law's police power to preserve the peace in censorship. I believe that the consensus of preference today is for disclosure and not stealth, for frankness and not hypocrisy, and for public and not secret distribution. That in itself is a moral code.

It is my opinion that frank disclosure cannot legally be censored, even as an exercise of the police power, unless it is sexually impure and pornographic, as I shall define those words. They furnish the only possible test for obscenity and its effect.

These books are not, in my view, sexually impure and pornographic. . . .

The English Cases

Regina v. *Hicklin* [1868] is an example of judge-made law quite at variance with the parliamentary intent behind the act on which it was based. Lord Campbell's act provided for search and seizure warrants that would enable the police to take and destroy obscene publications. The reports of the debates in Hansard show the lords' difficulties in deciding what an obscene publication might be. Lord Campbell, who was lord chief justice at the time, explained that the act was to apply exclusively to works written for the purpose of corrupting the morals of youth and of a nature calculated to shock the common feelings of decency in any well regulated mind. He was ready to make whatever was then indictable a test of obscenity in his new act. He made it clear that any work that even pretended to be literature or art, classic or modern, had little to fear.

All of this was nullified by Lord Chief Justice Cockburn in the *Hicklin Case,* where the subject matter was a pamphlet entitled "The Confessional Unmasked," and containing a diatribe against the Catholic Church; its purpose was to show the depravity of the priesthood and the character of the questions put to women in the confessional. This is now the famous rule of the case: "I think that the test of obscenity is this, whether the tendency of the matter charged as obscenity is to deprave and corrupt those whose minds are open to such immoral influences, and into whose hands a publication of this sort may fall."

Strictly applied, this rule renders any book unsafe, since a moron could pervert to some sexual fantasy to which his mind is open the listings in a seed catalogue. Not even the Bible would be exempt; Annie Besant once compiled a list of 150 passages in Scripture that might fairly be considered obscene—it is enough to cite the story of Lot and his daughters, Genesis 19, 30–38. Portions of Shakespeare would also be offensive, and of Chaucer, to say nothing of Aristophanes, Juvenal, Ovid, Swift, Defoe, Fielding, Smollett, Rousseau, Maupassant, Voltaire, Balzac, Baudelaire, Rabelais, Swinburne, Shelley, Byron, Boccaccio, Marguerite de Navarre, Hardy, Shaw, Whitman, and a host more.

As will be seen later, the classics—whatever that may mean precisely—are considered exempt from censorship, but many of them were hounded in England, despite Lord Campbell's assurances, as a result of the rule of the *Hicklin Case*. . . .

The lower court case of *Regina* v. *Thompson* (1900), in which the jury found defendant not guilty in an issue of whether or not the "Heptameron," by Queen Margaret of Navarre, was obscene, is interesting because of the charge of Bosanquet. . . . It is the first mention that I have found in the English reports of the idea that fashions in obscenity change. After mentioning that in the Middle Ages things were discussed which would not be tolerated now, if given general publicity, Sergeant Bosanquet left it to the jury to say "whether the book is a fit book to put into people's hands in these days at the end of the nineteenth century." The jury felt that it was. . . .

This exhausts the reported English cases that are in point. They show continued adherence to the *Hicklin* rule, but the paucity of authority is noteworthy. It is as if the English public does not want to risk the severity of the common law, and it is clear proof to me of the clinical nature of the laws that are made to cover social situations. While the higher English courts were kept relatively idle on the question, private censorship in England has been very active; the most effective censor of the Victorian era was Mudie's circulating library. It was the time of the three-decker novel—ponderous, dull, and pure as the driven snow. When Mudie's power was finally broken, smaller circulating libraries continued to wield the same sort of influence and to reflect the general desire of the public for no disturbing material of an emotional nature. England was the pioneer in the advance of the Industrial Age, and the nation of shopkeepers was unwilling to be diverted from making money by sidetrips into erotica; what individuals did in the dark was their affair, but bad morals could not profitably become a matter of public concern.

The rule of *Regina* v. *Hicklin* suited the English, and presumably still does—not as a satisfying standard but as an effective policeman to take over and tone down the situation when the social experiment threatens to get out of hand.

Censorship should be the proper activity of the community rather than of the law, and the community has never been lazy upholding what it believes to be inherently decent at the moment. With a legal policeman handy, the market place is the best crucible in which to distil an instinctive morality. We have the evidence of Milton that there is no authoritative example of the suppression of a book in ancient times solely because of obscenity, but this does not mean that private criticism was not alert. Plato thought that Homer should be expurgated before Greek children should be allowed to read him. In Plutarch's opinion the comedies of Aristophanes were coarse and vulgar.

This is healthy, for it is the struggle of free opinion: it is not suppression by law. In the English community the people argue and *Hicklin* stands guard in case of trouble. The American method is different: the rule has been modernized.

The American Cases

1. The Federal Courts. There are two important opinions involving James Joyce's "Ulysses." Judge Woolsey's, in the district court, is reported as *United States* v. *One Book entitled "Ulysses,"* 5 F. Supp. 182 (S.D.N.Y., 1933), and Judge Hand's affirming Judge Woolsey is reported in 72 F. (2d) 705 (C.C.A. 2d, 1934).

Judge Woolsey's decision may well be considered the keystone of the modern American rule, as it brings out clearly that indictable obscenity must be "dirt for dirt's sake." . . .

In affirming Judge Woolsey, Judge Hand said, in the circuit court of appeals:

That numerous long passages in Ulysses contain matter that is obscene under any fair definition of the word cannot be gainsaid; yet they are relevant to the purpose of depicting the thoughts of the characters and are introduced to give meaning to the whole, rather than to promote lust or portray filth for its own sake. The net effect even of portions most open to attack, such as the closing monologue of the wife of Leopold Bloom, is pitiful and tragic, rather than lustful. The book depicts the souls of men and women that are by turns bewildered and keenly apprehensive, sordid and aspiring, ugly and beautiful, hateful and loving. In the end one feels, more than anything else, pity and sorrow for the confusion, misery, and degradation of humanity. . . . The book as a whole is not pornographic, and while in not a few spots it is coarse, blasphemous, and obscene, it does not, in our opinion, tend to promote lust. The erotic passages are submerged in the book as a whole and have little resultant effect. . . .

It is quite clear that the harsh rule of *Regina* v. *Hicklin* has been supplanted by the modern test of obscenity, namely, whether the matter in question has a substantial tendency to deprave or corrupt by inciting lascivious thoughts or arousing lustful desire in the ordinary reader. This has been stated in various ways.

It has been said that the matter charged, to be obscene, must "suggest impure or libidinous thoughts," must "invite to lewd and lascivious practices and conduct," must "be offensive to chastity," must "incite dissolute acts," must "create a desire for gratification of animal passions," must "encourage unlawful indulgences of lust," must "attempt to satisfy the morbid appetite of the salacious," must "pander to the prurient taste." . . .

In *Walker* v. *Popenoe*, 149 F. (2d) 511 (1945), it was held: "The effect of a publication on the ordinary reader is what counts. The Statute does not intend that we shall 'reduce our treatment of sex to the standard of a child's library in the supposed interest of a salacious few.'"

This test, however, should not be left to stand alone, for there is another element of equal importance—the tenor of the times and the change in social acceptance of what is inherently decent. This element is clearly set forth in *United States* v. *Kennerley*, 209 Fed. 119 (D.C., N.Y., 1913), where Judge [Learned] Hand said:

If there be no abstract definition, such as I have suggested, should not the word "obscene" be allowed to indicate the present critical point in the compromise between candor and shame at which the community may have arrived here and now? . . . Nor is it an objection, I think, that such an interpretation gives to the words of the statute a varying meaning from time to time. Such words as these do not embalm the precise morals of an age or place; while they presuppose that some things will always be shocking to the public taste, the vague subject matter is left to the gradual development of general notions about what is decent. . . .

The New York Courts. The modern test was applied in *People* v. *Wendling*, 258 N.Y. 451 (1932), which involved the dramatization of the song "Frankie and Johnnie." In holding that the courts are not censors of morals and manners, Judge Pound said:

The language of the play is coarse, vulgar and profane; the plot cheap and tawdry. As a dramatic composition it serves to degrade the stage where vice is thought by some to lose "half its evil by losing all its grossness." That it is "indecent" from every consideration of propriety is entirely clear, but the court is not a censor of plays and does not attempt to regulate manners. One may call a spade a spade without offending decency, although modesty may be shocked thereby. The question is not whether the scene is laid in a low dive where refined people are not found or whether the language is that of the bar room rather than the parlor. The question is whether the tendency of the play is to excite lustful and lecherous desire. . . .

Since the New York cases are generally in line with the modern Federal rule above stated, it is necessary only to cite the principal one[s]: *Halsey* v. *N.Y. Society for the Suppression of Vice*, 234 N.Y. 1 (1922), which involved Theophile Gautier's "Mademoiselle de Maupin"; *People* v. *Brainard*, 192 App. Div. (N.Y.) 816 (1920), where the subject was "Madeleine," the anonymous autobiography of a prostitute.

The Massachusetts Courts. Boston has long been the center of book suppression in this country. Before 1930 the Massachusetts obscenity statute forbade the sale of any book "containing obscene, indecent language." The Supreme Court upheld convictions for the sale of

Dreiser's "An American Tragedy" and D. H. Lawrence's "Lady Chatterley's Lover." After a general wave of censorship that swept over Boston in 1929 and resulted in the suppression of 68 books, the law was changed to proscribe the sale of "a book which is obscene, indecent," etc.

The result was the modern rule, but the Massachusetts courts were still severe with individual books. *Commonwealth* v. *Isenstadt*, 318 Mass. 543 (1945), upheld a conviction for the sale of "Strange Fruit," and while it announced the modern rule to great extent, it refused to sanction the idea that sincerity of purpose and artistic merit would necessarily dispel obscenity. But it clearly held that the time and custom of the community are important elements. . . .

The Modern Test of Obscenity

From all of these cases the modern rule is that obscenity is measured by the erotic allurement upon the average modern reader; that the erotic allurement of a book is measured by whether it is sexually impure—i.e., pornographic, "dirt for dirt's sake," a calculated incitement to sexual desire—or whether it reveals an effort to reflect life, including its dirt, with reasonable accuracy and balance; and that mere coarseness or vulgarity is not obscenity.

Forging such a rule from the precedents does not fully reach the heart of the matter, for I am sure that the books before me could be declared obscene or not obscene under either the *Hicklin* or the modern rule. Current standards create both the book and the judgment of it.

The evil of an indefinite statute like our section 524, however, is that it is also too loose. Current standards of what is obscene can swing to extremes if the entire question is left open, and even in the domestic laboratories of the States such freedom cannot safely be allowed. It is no longer possible that free speech be guaranteed Federally and denied locally; under modern methods of instantaneous communication such a discrepancy makes no sense. If speech is to be free anywhere, it must be free everywhere, and a law that can be used as a spigot that allows speech to flow freely or to be checked altogether is a general threat to free opinion and enlightened solution. What is said in Pennsylvania may clarify an issue in California, and what is suppressed in California may leave us the worse in Pennsylvania. Unless a restriction on free speech be of national validity, it can no longer have any local validity whatever. Some danger to us all must appear before any of us can be muzzled.

In the field of written obscenity this principle has met oblique acceptance with regard to what is called "the classics," which are now exempt from legal censorship. Just how old a work must be before it can enjoy this immunity is uncertain, but what we know as classics are the books by remarkable people that have withstood the test of time and are accepted as having lasting value; they have become historical samples, which itself is important. This importance could not be as great if the screening process were not free.

Current literature, good, bad, or indifferent, goes into the hopper without any background for judgment; it is in the idiom of the moment and is keyed to the tempo of modern life. I do not believe that such considerations should result in removing any of the output from the hopper before the process of screening can begin. What is pure dirt to some may be another's sincere effort to make clear a point, and there is not much difference, from the historical angle, between censoring books before publication and suppressing them afterwards, before there has been a reasonable chance to judge them. Blackstone's neat distinction may satisfy an exact legal mind, but it has no meaning for history. The unworthy books will die soon enough, but the great work of genius has a hard enough time to make its way even in the free market of thought. James Joyce, whose work is difficult to understand, even after years of study, has evolved a new form of communication, by his method of using words, that will some day be a shorthand for complexity. The public was deprived for years of this work of genius because someone found objectionable passages in it.

I can find no universally valid restriction on free expression to be drawn from the behavior of "l'homme moyen sensuel," who is the average modern reader. It is impossible to say just what his reactions to a book actually are. "Moyen" means, generally, average, and average means a median between extremes. If he reads an obscene book when his sensuality is low, he will yawn over it or find that its suggestibility leads him off on quite different paths. If he reads the Mechanics' Lien Act while his sensuality is high, things will stand between him and the page that have no business there. How can anyone say that he will infallibly be affected one way or another by one book or another? When, where, how, and why are questions that cannot be answered clearly in this field. The professional answer that is suggested is the one general compromise—that the appetite of sex is old, universal, and unpredictable, and that the best we can do to keep it within reasonable bounds is to be our brother's keeper and censor, because we never know when his sensuality may be high. This does not satisfy me, for in a field where even reasonable precision is utterly impossible, I trust people more than I do the law. Had legal censorship been as constant throughout the centuries as the law of murder, rape, theft, and negligence, a case for the compromise could be made out; as it is, legal censorship is not old, it is not popular, and it has failed to strengthen the private censor in each individual that has kept the race as decent as it has been for several thousand years. I regard legal censorship as an experiment of more than dubious value.

I am well aware that the law is not ready to discard censorship altogether. The English keep their policeman handy, just in case, and the modern rule is a more efficient policeman. Its scope, however, must be defined with regard to the universal right of free speech, as limited only by some universally valid restriction required by a clear and present danger. For this we must consider the Constitution and the cases lately decided under it.

Constitutional Questions

The fourteenth amendment to the Federal Constitution prohibits any State from encroaching upon freedom of speech and freedom of the press to the same extent that the first amendment prevents the Federal Congress from doing so. . . .

These guarantees occupy a preferred position under our law to such an extent that the courts, when considering whether legislation infringes upon them, neutralizes the presumption usually indulged in favor of constitutionality. . . .

And article 1, sec. 7 of the Pennsylvania Constitution states that: "The free communication of thoughts and opinions is one of the invaluable rights of man, and every citizen may freely speak, write and print on any subject, being responsible for the abuse of that liberty." When the first amendment came before the Supreme Court for interpretation in *Reynolds* v. *United States,* 98 U.S. 145 (1878), the court declared that government had no authority whatsoever in the field of thought or opinion: only in the area of conduct or action could it step in. Chief Justice Waite said: "Congress was deprived of all legislative power over mere opinion, but was left free to reach actions which were in violation of social duties or subversive of good order." Quoting from Jefferson's bill for establishing religious freedom, the Chief Justice stated:

"That to suffer the Civil magistrate to intrude his powers into the field of opinion, and to restrain the profession or propagation of principles on supposition of their *ill tendency* is a dangerous fallacy which at once destroys all religious liberty." . . . "It is time enough for the rightful purposes of civil government for its officers to interfere *when principles break out into overt acts against peace and good order." In these two sentences is found the true distinction between what properly belongs to the Church and what to the State.* (Italics supplied.)

The now familiar "clear and present danger" rule, first stated by Mr. Justice Holmes in *Schenck* v. *United States,* 249 U.S. 47 (1918), represents a compromise between the ideas of Jefferson and those of the judges, who had in the meantime departed from the forthright views of the great statesman. Under that rule the publisher of a writing may be punished if the publication in question creates a clear and present danger that there will result from it some substantive evil which the legislature has a right to proscribe and punish.

The famous illustration in the *Schenck Case* was: "The most stringent protection of free speech would not protect a man in falsely shouting fire in a theatre and causing a panic. It does not even protect a man from an injunction against uttering words that may have all the effect of force."

Mr. Justice Brandeis added, in *Whitney* v. *California,* 274 U.S. 357 (1927), the idea that free speech may not be curbed where the community has the chance to answer back. He said:

Those who won our independence by revolution were not cowards. They did not fear political change. They did not exalt order at the cost of liberty. To courageous, self-reliant men, with confidence in the power of free and fearless reasoning applied through the processes of popular government, *no danger flowing from speech can be deemed clear and present, unless the incidence of the evil apprehended is so imminent that it may befall before there is opportunity for full discussion.* If there be time to expose through discussion the falsehood and fallacies, to avert the evil by the processes of education, the remedy to be applied is more speech, not enforced silence. *Only an emergency can justify repression.* Such must be the rule if authority is to be reconciled with freedom. Such, in my opinion, is the command of the Constitution. It is therefore always open to Americans to challenge a law abridging free speech and assembly by showing that there was no emergency justifying it.

Moreover, even imminent danger cannot justify resort to prohibition of these functions essential to effective democracy, unless the evil apprehended is relatively serious. Prohibition of free speech and assembly is a measure so stringent that it would be inappropriate as the means for averting a relatively trivial harm to society. A police measure may be unconstitutional merely because the remedy, although effective as means of protection, is unduly harsh or oppressive. Thus, a State might, in the exercise of its police power, make any trespass upon the land of another a crime, regardless of the results or of the intent or purpose of the trespasser. It might, also punish an attempt, a conspiracy, or an incitement to commit the trespass. But it is hardly conceivable that this Court would hold constitutional a statute which punished as a felony the mere voluntary assembly with a society formed to teach that pedestrians had the moral right to cross unenclosed, unposted, waste lands and to advocate their doing so, even if there was imminent danger that advocacy would lead to a trespass. The fact that speech is likely to result in some violence or in destruction of property is not enough to justify its suppression. There must be the probability of serious injury to the State. Among free men, the deterrents ordinarily to be applied to prevent crime are education and punishment for violations of the law, not abridgment of the rights of free speech and assembly. . . .

The history of the Supreme Court, since its decision in *Gitlow* v. *New York*, 268 U.S. 652 (1925), has been marked by gradual progress along the path staked out by Justices Holmes and Brandeis, culminating finally in the complete acceptance of their views. . . .

The nature of the evil which the legislature has the power to guard against by enacting an obscenity statute is not clearly defined. As Jefferson saw it, the legislature was restricted to punishing criminal acts and not publications. To Holmes and Brandeis the bookseller could be punished if his relation to the criminal act was such that he could be said to have incited it. In neither view could the bookseller be punished if his books merely "tended" to result in illegal acts and much less if his books "tended" to lower the moral standards of the community. A much closer relationship was required. The legislature may validly prevent criminal acts and legislate to protect the moral standards of the community. But the threat must in either case be more than a mere tendency. The older cases which upheld obscenity statutes on the "tendency" theory would appear to be invalid in the light of the more recent expressions of the Supreme Court. . . .

These principles have not been applied specifically to an obscenity statute by any recent opinion of the United States Supreme Court, but as Mr. Justice Rutledge said orally when the "Hecate County" case, *Doubleday & Co., Inc.* v. *New York*, 335 U.S. 848 (an obscenity case), was recently argued before the court:

Before we get to the question of clear and present danger, we've got to have something which the State can forbid as dangerous. We are talking in a vacuum until we can establish that there is some occasion for the exercise of the State's power.

Yes, you must first ascertain the substantive evil at which the statute is aimed, and then determine whether the publication of this book constitutes a clear and present danger.

It is up to the State to demonstrate that there was a danger, and until they demonstrate that, plus the clarity and imminence of the danger, the constitutional prohibition would seem to apply. (Italics supplied.) (Quoted in 17 U.S. Law Week [Supreme Court Sections 3118]).*

* [*Doubleday & Co.* v. *New York*, 71 N.Y. Supp. 2d 736 (1947), conviction affirmed by App. Div. without opinion; affirmed without opinion by Court of Appeals, 297 N.Y. 687 (1947); affirmed by equally divided court, 335 U.S. 848 (1948).]

This appears to me much closer to a correct solution of obscenity cases than several general dicta by the Supreme Court to the effect that obscenity is indictable just because it is obscenity. . . .

It seems impossible, in view of the late decisions under the first amendment, that the word "obscene" can no longer stand alone, lighted up only by a vague and mystic sense of impurity, unless it is interpreted by other solid factors such as clear and present danger, pornography, and divorcement from mere coarseness of vulgarity. . . .

It is not clear to me, nor, I venture to assert, would it be to the Supreme Court, if faced directly by an appropriate case of literary obscenity, what words inflict injury by their very utterance or how such injury is inflicted. As for the notion of an obscene book tending to incite to an immediate breach of the peace, the proper point of emphasis is the breach of the peace. That is different from saying that obscenity automatically tends to a breach of the peace, for the idea is unreal. . . .

The difficulty here is that insofar as they apply to literature, obscenity and its imposing string of synonymns do *not* have a fixed meaning through long use in the criminal law—or put it the other way, that they have a very narrow and restricted meaning quite at variance with the assumption that obscenity debauches public morals by a mysterious and self-executing process that can be feared but not proved.

Certainly the books before me do not command, or urge, or incite, or even encourage persons to commit sexual misconduct of a nature that the legislature has the right to prevent or punish. Nor are they an imminent threat to the morality of the community as a whole. The conduct described in them is at most offensive. It does not incite to unlawfulness of any kind. . . .

Short of books that are sexually impure and pornographic, I can see no rational legal catalyst that can detect or define a clear and present danger inherent in a writing or that can demonstrate what result ensues from reading it. All that is relied upon, in a prosecution, is an indefinable fear for other people's moral standards—a fear that I regard as a democratic anomaly. . . .

I am clear that the books before me are within the protection of the first and fourteenth amendments of the Federal Constitution, and of article 1, sec. 7 of the Pennsylvania Constitution. They bear obvious internal evidence of an effort to portray certain segments of American life, including parts that more refined people than the characters may deplore, but which we know exist. The vulgarity and obscenity in them are inherent in the characters themselves and are obviously not set forth as erotic allurements or as an excuse for selling the volumes. Nor can it be said that they have the effect of inciting to lewdness, or of inciting to any sexual crime, or that they are sexually impure and pornographic, i.e., "dirt for dirt's sake."

Definition of Obscenity as Sexual Impurity

Sexual impurity in literature (pornography, as some of the cases call it) I define as any writing whose dominant purpose and effect is erotic allurement—that is to say, a calculated and effective incitement to sexual desire. It is the effect that counts, more than the purpose, and no indictment can stand unless it can be shown. This definition is in accord with the cases that have restricted the meaning of obscenity and its synonyms to that of sexual impurity, and with those cases that have made erotic allurement the test of its effect.

This excludes from pornography medical or educational writings, whether in technical or layman's language, and whether used only in schools or generally distributed, whose dominant purpose and effect is exegetical and instructional rather than enticing. It leaves room for interpretation of individual books, for as long as censorship is considered necessary it is as impossible as it is inadvisable to find a self-executing formula.

Sex education has been before the courts in many cases. In *United States* v. *"Married Love,"* 48 F. (2d) 821 (1931), Judge Woolsey said:

> It makes also some apparently justified criticisms of the inopportune exercise by the man in the marriage relation of what are often referred to as his conjugal or marital rights, and it pleads with seriousness, and not without some eloquence, for a better understanding by husbands of the physical and emotional side of the sex life of their wives. I do not find anything exceptionable anywhere in the book, and I cannot imagine a normal mind to which this book would seem to be obscene or immoral within the proper definition of these words, or whose sex impulses would be stirred by reading it.

Judge Woolsey held similarly in *United States* v. *"Contraception,"* 51 F. (2d) 525 (1941). Both of the above books were by Dr. Marie C. Stopes.

The case of *United States* v. *Dennett,* 39 F. (2d) 564 (C.C.A. 2d, 1930), involved a pamphlet written by a woman for the education of her children. Sections of it appear in the reporter's summary of the case, and show that it gave full and frank information, together with the view that the sexual impulse is not a base passion but is a great joy when accompanied by love between two human beings. In reversing a conviction, Judge [Augustus] Hand said:

> It also may reasonably be thought that accurate information, rather than mystery and curiosity, is better in the long run and is less likely to occasion lascivious thoughts than ignorance and anxiety. Perhaps instruction other

than that which the defendant suggests would be better. That is a matter as to which there is bound to be a wide difference of opinion, but, irrespective of this, we hold that an accurate exposition of the relevant facts of the sex side of life in decent language and in manifestly serious and disinterested spirit cannot ordinarily be regarded as obscene. Any incidental tendency to arouse sex impulses which such a pamphlet may perhaps have, is apart from and subordinate to its main effect. The tendency can only exist in so far as it is inherent in any sex instruction, and it would seem to be outweighed by the elimination of ignorance, curiosity, and morbid fear. The direct aim and the net result is to promote understanding and self-control.

The definition of sexual impurity given above brings literary obscenity into workable analogy with sedition, blasphemy, open lewdness, and the other examples set forth earlier, as those terms are used in our Penal Code, except for one remaining point. Sedition, blasphemy, and open lewdness, by definition, carry their own threat of danger to the public peace. The deep and peculiar nature of religious faith is such that people are entitled to protection against those who call their gods in vain; religion has too recently and for too long been one of the greatest of the fighting faiths to assume that disorder will not follow from public irreverence. He who is publicly lewd is in himself an open and immediate invitation to morally criminal behavior. The pressing danger inherent in sedition speaks for itself.

A book, however sexually impure and pornographic, is in a different case. It cannot be a present danger unless its reader closes it, lays it aside, and transmutes its erotic allurement into overt action. That such action must inevitably follow as a direct consequence of reading the book does not bear analysis, nor is it borne out by general human experience; too much can intervene and too many diversions take place. It must be constantly borne in mind that section 524 does not include the element of debauching public morals or of seeking to alter the prevailing moral code. It only proscribes what *is* obscene, and that term is meaningless unless activated by precise dangers within legal limits. Since section 524 provides no standard, the danger and the limits must be found elsewhere, and the only clear and discernible ones are those having to do with the police power and the preservation of the peace.

The Clear and Present Danger

I have pointed out above that any test of the effect of obscenity is bound to be elusive. Section 524 is therefore vague, indefinite, and unconstitutional unless some exact definition can be found for the "clear and present danger" to be prevented that will satisfy the constitutional protection of free speech. There are various types of cases in which definition is clear because the need is clear. The police power operates in pure food cases because people can sicken and die from eating bad food; in traffic cases because people can be injured or killed unless there is regulation; in weights and measures cases because of the ease with which the consumer can be cheated; and in conventional crimes because of the threat to persons and property. The list could be extended.

Mr. Justice Holmes's example in *Schenck* v. *United States* is no test for the case before me; the public does not read a book and simultaneously rush by the hundreds into the streets to engage in orgiastic riots. Mr. Justice Brandeis's discussion in *Whitney* v. *California* is a better yardstick, for in the field of the printed word the community has full opportunity to answer back. How can it be said that there is a "clear and present danger"—granted that anyone can say what it is—when there is both time and means for ample discussion?

These words of Jefferson should not be forgotten:

> I deplore . . . the putrid state into which our newspapers have passed, and the malignity, the vulgarity, and the mendacious spirit of those who write them. . . . These ordures are rapidly depraving the public taste.
>
> It is, however, an evil for which there is no remedy: our liberty depends on the freedom of the press and that cannot be limited without being lost.

Who can define the clear and present danger to the community that arises from reading a book? If we say it is that the reader is young and inexperienced and incapable of resisting the sexual temptations that the book may present to him, we put the entire reading public at the mercy of the adolescent mind and of those adolescents who do not have the expected advantages of home influence, school training, or religious teaching. Nor can we say into how many such hands the book may come. Adults, or even a gifted minor, may be capable of challenging the book in public and thus of forwarding the education and enlightenment of us all by free discussion and correction. If the argument be applied to the general public, the situation becomes absurd, for then no publication is safe. How is it possible to say that reading a certain book is bound to make people behave in a way that is socially undesirable? And beyond a reasonable doubt, since we are dealing with a penal statute?

We might remember the words of Macaulay: "We find it difficult to believe that in a world so full of temptations as this, any gentleman, whose life would have been virtuous if he had not read Aristophanes and Juvenal, will be made vicious by reading them."

Substitute the names of the books before me for "Aristophanes and Juvenal," and the analogy is exact.

The only clear and present danger to be prevented by section 524 that will satisfy both the Constitution and the current customs of our era is the commission or the imminence of the commission of criminal behavior resulting from the reading of a book. Publication alone can have no such automatic effect.

The Rule of Decision

Thus limited, the constitutional operation of section 524 of our act rests on narrow ground.

The modern test of obscenity, as I have stated it above, furnishes a means of determining whether a book, taken as a whole, is sexually impure, as I have defined that term.

I hold that section 524 may not constitutionally be applied to any writing unless it is sexually impure and pornographic. It may then be applied, as an exercise of the police power, only where there is a reasonable and demonstrable cause to believe that a crime or misdemeanor has been committed or is about to be committed as the perceptible result of the publication and distribution of the writing in question: the opinion of anyone that a tendency thereto exists or that such a result is self-evident is insufficient and irrelevant. The causal connection between the book and the criminal behavior must appear beyond a reasonable doubt. The criminal law is not, in my opinion, "the *custos morum* of the King's subjects," as *Regina* v. *Hicklin* states; it is only the custodian of the peace and good order that free men and women need for the shaping of their common destiny.

There is no such proof in the instant case.

For that reason, and also because of the character of the books themselves, I hold that the books before me are not sexually impure and pornographic, and are therefore not obscene, lewd, lascivious, filthy, indecent, or disgusting. . . .

2. Movie Censorship

BURSTYN, INC. *v.* WILSON

343 US 495 (1952)

[The Supreme Court in 1915 excluded the movies from the protection of the First Amendment. It held that movies are purely business undertakings, conducted for profit, and in no sense part of the press of the country. *Mutual Film Corp.* v. *Ohio Industrial Comm.*, 236 US 230 (1915). This meant that movies were subject to state and local licensing or censorship.

[In the present case, commonly referred to as the *Miracle Case*, the Court overruled the principle of the *Mutual Film Case*. Six members of the Court, in an opinion by Justice Clark, held that the basic principles of freedom of speech and press applied to motion pictures. The Court did not, however, outlaw movie censorship if exercised within narrowly defined rules; it left this question open. The decision was limited to the holding that the guaranty of free speech and press prevents a state from banning a film on a finding by a censor that it is "sacrilegious." Justice Frankfurter, with the concurrence of Justices Jackson and Burton, held that the term "sacrilegious" as used in the New York statute was unconstitutionally vague.

[Early in 1953 the Court unanimously held that New York could not ban the French film "La Ronde" on the ground that it was "immoral" and that Ohio could not ban the American picture "M" as "tending to promote crime." The statutes under which these films were banned were held to be vague and indefinite. The Court cited their decision in the *Miracle Case* as the basis for their decision regarding these two films. The decision with respect to these films has not completely outlawed all movie censorship, for Justice Douglas found it necessary to write a concurring opinion, with which Justice Black agreed, to say that he found any form of governmental movie censorship unacceptable under the First and Fourteenth Amendments. *Superior Films* v. *Department of Education*, 346 US 587 (1954).

[Preceding Justice Clark's opinion for the Court, we present the following statement of facts from Justice Frankfurter's concurring opinion:

[A practised hand has thus summarized the story of "The Miracle":

[A poor, simple-minded girl is tending a herd of goats on a mountainside one day, when a bearded stranger passes. Suddenly it strikes her fancy that he is St. Joseph, her favorite saint, and that he has come to take her to heaven, where she will be happy and free. While she pleads with him to transport her, the stranger gently plies the girl with wine, and when she is in a state of tumult, he apparently ravishes her. (This incident in the story is only briefly and discreetly implied.)

[The girl awakens later, finds the stranger gone, and climbs down the mountain not knowing whether he was real or a dream. She meets an old priest who tells her that it is quite possible that she did see a saint, but a younger priest scoffs at the notion. "Materialist!" the old priest says.

[There follows now a brief sequence—intended to be symbolic, obviously—in which the girl is reverently sitting with other villagers in church. Moved by a whim of appetite, she snitches an apple from the basket of a woman next to her. When she leaves the church, a cackling beggar tries to make her share the apple with him, but she chases him away as by habit and munches the fruit contentedly.

[Then, one day, while tending the village youngsters as their mothers work at the vines, the girl faints and the women discover that she is going to have a child. Frightened and bewildered, she suddenly murmurs, "It is the grace of God!" and she runs to the church in great excitement, looks for the statue of St. Joseph, and then prostrates herself on the floor.

[Thereafter she meekly refuses to do any menial work and the housewives humor her gently but the young people are not so kind. In a scene of brutal torment, they first flatter and laughingly mock her, then they cruelly shove and hit her and clamp a basin as a halo on her head. Even abused by the beggars, the poor girl gathers together her pitiful rags and sadly departs from the village to live alone in a cave.

[When she feels her time coming upon her, she starts towards the village. But then she sees the crowds in the streets; dark memories haunt her; so she turns towards a church on a high hill and instinctively struggles towards it, crying desperately to God. A goat is her sole companion. She drinks water dripping from a rock. And when she comes to the church and finds the door locked, the goat attracts her to a small side door. Inside the church, the poor girl braces herself for her labor pains. There is a dissolve, and when we next see her sad face, in close-up, it is full of a tender light. There is the cry of an unseen baby. The girl reaches towards it and murmurs, "My son! My love! My flesh!"

["The Miracle"—a film lasting forty minutes—was produced in Italy by Roberto Rosselini. Anna Magnani played the lead as the demented goattender. It was first shown at the Venice Film Festival in August, 1948, combined with another moving picture, "L'Umano Voce," into a diptych called "Amore." According to an affidavit, from the Director of that Festival, if the motion picture had been "blasphemous" it would have been barred by the Festival Committee. In a review of the film in *L'Osservatore Romano*, the organ of the Vatican, its film critic, Piero Regnoli, wrote: "Opinions may vary and questions may arise—even serious ones—of a religious nature (not to be diminished by the fact that the woman portrayed is mad [because] the author who attributed madness to her is not mad). . . . While acknowledging that there were "passages of undoubted cinematic distinction," Regnoli criticized the film as being "on such a pretentiously cerebral plane that it reminds one of the early d'Annunzio." The Vatican newspaper's critic concluded: "We continue to believe in Rosselini's art and we look forward to his next achievement." In October, 1948, a month after the Rome premiere of "The Miracle," the Vatican's censorship agency, the Catholic Cinematographic Centre, declared that the picture "constitutes in effect an abominable profanation from religious and moral viewpoints." By the Lateran agreements and the Italian Constitution the Italian Government is bound to bar whatever may offend the Catholic religion. However, the Catholic Cinematographic Centre did not invoke any governmental sanction thereby afforded. The Italian Government's censorship agency gave "The Miracle" the regular *nulla osta* clearance. The film was freely shown throughout Italy, but was

not a great success. Italian movie critics divided in opinion. The critic for
Il Popolo, speaking for the Christian Democratic Party, the Catholic party,
profusely praised the picture as "a beautiful thing, humanly felt, alive, true
and without religious profanation as someone has said, because in our
opinion the meaning of the characters is clear and there is no possibility
of misunderstanding." Regnoli again reviewed "The Miracle" for *L'Osservatore Romano.* After criticising the film for technical faults, he found "the
most courageous and interesting passage of Rosselini's work" in contrasting
portrayals in the film; he added: "Unfortunately, concerning morals, it is
necessary to note some slight defects." He objected to its "carnality" and to
the representation of illegitimate motherhood. But he did not suggest that
the picture was "sacrilegious." The tone of Regnoli's critique was one of
respect for Rosselini, "the illustrious Italian producer."

[On March 2, 1949, "The Miracle" was licensed in New York State for
showing without English titles. However, it was never exhibited until after
a second license was issued on November 30, 1950, for the trilogy, "Ways
of Love," combining "The Miracle" with two French films, Jean Renoir's "A
Day in the Country" and Marcel Pagnol's "Jofroi." All had English subtitles.
Both licenses were issued in the usual course after viewings of the picture
by the Motion Picture Division of the New York State Education Department. . . . The trilogy opened on December 12, 1950, at the Paris Theatre
on 58th Street in Manhattan. It was promptly attacked as "a sacrilegious
and blasphemous mockery of Christian religious truth" by the National
Legion of Decency, a private Catholic organization for film censorship,
whose objectives have intermittently been approved by various non-Catholic
church and social groups since its formation in 1933. However, the National
Board of Review (a non-industry lay organization devoted to raising the
level of motion pictures by mobilizing public opinion, under the slogan
"Selection Not Censorship") recommended the picture as "especially worth
seeing." New York critics on the whole praised "The Miracle"; those who
dispraised did not suggest sacrilege. On December 27 the critics selected
the "Ways of Love" as the best foreign language film in 1950. Meanwhile
on December 23, Edward T. McCaffrey, Commissioner of Licenses for New
York City, declared the film "officially and personally blasphemous" and
ordered it withdrawn at the risk of suspension of the license to operate the
Paris Theatre. A week later the program was restored at the theatre upon
the decision by the New York Supreme Court that the City License Commissioner had exceeded his authority in that he was without powers of
movie censorship.

[Upon the failure of the License Commissioner's effort to cut off showings
of "The Miracle," the controversy took a new turn. On Sunday, January 7,
1951, a statement of His Eminence, Francis Cardinal Spellman, condemning
the picture and calling on "all right thinking citizens" to unite to tighten
censorship laws, was read at all masses in St. Patrick's Cathedral.

[The views of Cardinal Spellman aroused dissent among other devout
Christians. Protestant clergymen, representing various denominations, after
seeing the picture, found in it nothing "sacrilegious or immoral to the views

held by Christian men and women," and with a few exceptions agreed that the film was "unquestionably one of unusual artistic merit."

[In this estimate some Catholic laymen concurred. Their opinion is represented by the comment by Otto L. Spaeth, Director of the American Federation of Arts and prominent in Catholic lay activities:

[At the outbreak of the controversy, I immediately arranged for a private showing of the film. I invited a group of Catholics, competent and respected for their writings on both religious and cultural subjects. The essential approval of the film was unanimous.

[There was indeed "blasphemy" in the picture—but it was the blasphemy of the villagers, who stopped at nothing, not even the mock singing of a hymn to the Virgin, in their brutal badgering of the tragic woman. The scathing indictment of their evil behaviour, implicit in the film, was seemingly overlooked by its critics.

[William C. Clancy, a teacher at the University of Notre Dame, wrote in *The Commonweal*, the well-known Catholic weekly, that "the film is not *obviously* blasphemous or obscene, either in its intention or execution." *The Commonweal* itself questioned the wisdom of transforming Church dogma which Catholics may obey as "a free act" into state-enforced censorship for all. Allen Tate, the well-known Catholic poet and critic, wrote: "The picture seems to me to be superior in acting and photography but inferior dramatically. . . . In the long run what Cardinal Spellman will have succeeded in doing is insulting the intelligence and faith of American Catholics with the assumption that a second-rate motion picture could in any way undermine their morals or shake their faith."

[At the time "The Miracle" was filmed, all the persons having significant positions in the production—producer, director, and cast—were Catholics. Roberto Rosselini, who had Vatican approval in 1949 for filming a life of St. Francis, using in the cast members of the Franciscan Order, cabled Cardinal Spellman protesting against boycott of "The Miracle":

[In "The Miracle" men are still without pity because they still have not come back to God, but God is already in the faith, however confused, of that poor, persecuted woman; and since God is wherever a human being suffers and is misunderstood, "The Miracle" occurs when at the birth of the child the poor, demented woman regains sanity in her eternal love.

[In view of the controversy thus aroused by the picture, the Chairman of the Board of Regents appointed a committee of three Board members to review the action of the Motion Picture Division in granting the two licenses. After viewing the picture on Jan. 15, 1951, the committee declared it "sacrilegious." The Board four days later issued an order to the licensees to show cause why the licenses should not be cancelled in that the picture was "sacrilegious." The Board of Regents rescinded the licenses on Feb. 16, 1951, saying that the "mockery or profaning of these beliefs that are sacred to any portion of our citizenship is abhorrent to the laws of this great State." On review the Appellate Division upheld the Board of Regents, holding that the banning of any motion picture "that may fairly be deemed sacrilegious to the adherents of any religious group . . . is directly related to public peace and order" and is not a denial of religious freedom, and that there was "substantial evidence upon which the Regents could act."

[The New York Court of Appeals, with one judge concurring in a separate opinion and two others dissenting, affirmed the order of the Appellate Division. . . .]

Mr. Justice Clark delivered the opinion of the Court:

The issue here is the constitutionality, under the First and Fourteenth Amendments, of a New York statute which permits the banning of motion picture films on the ground that they are "sacrilegious." That statute makes it unlawful "to exhibit, or to sell, lease or lend for exhibition at any place of amusement for pay or in connection with any business in the state of New York, any motion picture film or reel [with specified exceptions not relevant here], unless there is at the time in full force and effect a valid license or permit therefor of the education department. . . ." The statute further provides:

The director of the [motion picture] division [of the education department] or, when authorized by the regents, the officers of a local office or bureau shall cause to be promptly examined every motion picture film submitted to them as herein required, and unless such film or a part thereof is obscene, indecent, immoral, inhuman, sacrilegious, or is of such a character that its exhibition would tend to corrupt morals or incite to crime, shall issue a license therefor. If such director or, when so authorized, such officer shall not license any film submitted, he shall furnish to the applicant therefor a written report of the reasons for his refusal and a description of each rejected part of a film not rejected in toto. . . .

Appellant brought the present action in the New York courts to review the determination of the Regents. Among the claims advanced by appellant were (1) that the statute violates the Fourteenth Amendment as a prior restraint upon freedom of speech and of the press; (2) that it is invalid under the same Amendment as a violation of the guaranty of separate church and state and as a prohibition of the free exercise of religion; and, (3) that the term "sacrilegious" is so vague and indefinite as to offend due process. . . . The case is here on appeal. . . .

As we view the case, we need consider only appellant's contention that the New York statute is an unconstitutional abridgment of free speech and a free press. In *Mutual Film Corp.* v. *Industrial Comm. of Ohio,* 236 U.S. 230 (1915), . . . this Court stated:

It cannot be put out of view that the exhibition of moving pictures is a business, pure and simple, originated and conducted for profit, like other spectacles, not to be regarded, nor intended to be regarded by the Ohio Constitution, we think, as part of the press of the country, or as organs of public opinion.

In a series of decisions beginning with *Gitlow* v. *People of State of New York*, 268 U.S. 652 (1925), this Court held that the liberty of speech and of the press which the First Amendment guarantees against abridgment by the federal government is within the liberty safeguarded by the Due Process Clause of the Fourteenth Amendment from invasion by state action. That principle has been followed and reaffirmed to the present day. Since this series of decisions came after the *Mutual* decision, the present case is the first to present squarely to us the question whether motion pictures are within the ambit of protection which the First Amendment, through the Fourteenth, secures to any form of "speech" or "the press."

It cannot be doubted that motion pictures are a significant medium for the communication of ideas. They may affect public attitudes and behaviors in a variety of ways, ranging from direct espousal of a political or social doctrine to the subtle shaping of thought which characterizes all artistic expression. The importance of motion pictures as an organ of public opinion is not lessened by the fact that they are designed to entertain as well as to inform. As was said in *Winters* v. *People of State of New York*, 333 U.S. 507 (1948), "The line between the informing and the entertaining is too elusive for the protection of that basic right [a free press]. Everyone is familiar with instances of propaganda through fiction. What is one man's amusement, teaches another's doctrine."

It is urged that motion pictures do not fall within the First Amendment's aegis because their production, distribution, and exhibition is a large-scale business conducted for private profit. We cannot agree. That books, newspapers, and magazines are published and sold for profit does not prevent them from being a form of expression whose liberty is safeguarded by the First Amendment. We fail to see why operation for profit should have any different effect in the case of motion pictures.

It is further urged that motion pictures possess a greater capacity for evil, particularly among the youth of a community, than other modes of expression. Even if one were to accept this hypothesis, it does not follow that motion pictures should be disqualified from First Amendment protection. If there be capacity for evil it may be relevant in determining the permissible scope of community control, but it does not authorize substantially unbridled censorship such as we have here.

For the foregoing reasons, we conclude that expression by means of motion pictures is included within the free speech and free press guaranty of the First and Fourteenth Amendments. To the extent that language in the opinion in *Mutual Film Corp.* v. *Industrial Comm.*, *supra*, is out of harmony with the views here set forth, we no longer adhere to it.

To hold that liberty of expression by means of motion pictures is guaranteed by the First and Fourteenth Amendments, however, is not the end of our problem. It does not follow that the Constitution requires absolute freedom to exhibit every motion picture of every kind at all times and all places. That much is evident from the series of decisions of this Court with respect to other media of communication of ideas. Nor does it follow that motion pictures are necessarily subject to the precise rules governing any other particular method of expression. Each method tends to present its own peculiar problems. But the basic principles of freedom of speech and the press, like the First Amendment's command, do not vary. Those principles, as they have frequently been enunciated by this Court, make freedom of expression the rule. There is no justification in this case for making an exception to that rule.

The statute involved here does not seek to punish, as a past offense, speech or writing falling within the permissible scope of subsequent punishment. On the contrary, New York requires that permission to communicate ideas be obtained in advance from state officials who judge the content of the words and pictures sought to be communicated. This Court recognized many years ago that such a previous restraint is a form of infringement upon freedom of expression to be especially condemned. *Near* v. *State of Minnesota* ex rel. *Olson*, 283 U.S. 697 (1931). . . .

New York's highest court says there is "nothing mysterious" about the statutory provision applied in this case: "It is simply this: that no religion, as that word is understood by the ordinary, reasonable person, shall be treated with contempt, mockery, scorn and ridicule. . . ." This is far from the kind of narrow exception to freedom of expression which a state may carve out to satisfy the adverse demands of other interests of society. In seeking to apply the broad and all-inclusive definition of "sacrilegious" given by the New York courts, the censor is set adrift upon a boundless sea amid a myriad of conflicting currents of religious views, with no charts but those provided by the most vocal and powerful orthodoxies. New York cannot vest such unlimited restraining control over motion pictures in a censor. . . . Under such a standard the most careful and tolerant censor would find it virtually impossible to avoid favoring one religion over another, and he would be subject to an inevitable tendency to ban the expression of unpopular sentiments sacred to a religious minority. Application of the "sacrilegious" test, in these or other respects, might raise substantial questions under the First Amendment's guaranty of separate church and state with freedom of worship for all. However, from the standpoint of freedom of speech and the press, it is enough to point out that the state has no legitimate interest in protecting any or all religions from views distasteful to them which is sufficient to justify prior restraints upon the expression of those views. It is not the business of government in our nation to suppress real or imagined attacks upon a particular religious doctrine, whether they appear in publications, speeches, or motion pictures.

Since the term "sacrilegious" is the sole standard under attack here, it is not necessary for us to decide, for example, whether a state may censor motion pictures under a clearly-drawn statute designed and applied to prevent the showing of obscene films. That is a very different question from the one now before us. We hold only that under the First and Fourteenth Amendments a state may not ban a film on the basis of a censor's conclusion that it is "sacrilegious."

Reversed.

3. Contempt by Publication

BRIDGES v. CALIFORNIA

314 US 252 (1941)

[There is obviously a strong public interest that "the calm course of justice" in a courtroom be assured, in order that the minds of judges and jurors may not become "distorted by extrajudicial considerations." Newspaper reports and editorials on pending trials may have an inflammatory effect and thus obstruct the administration of justice. On the other hand, there is an equally strong public interest that the press be and remain untrammeled and that the public be told by the press what goes on in the courts, in order that "the public may judge whether our system of criminal justice is fair and right." A defendant is entitled to a fair trial by court; he does not want a trial by newspaper; but news reporting of trials is in itself an aid toward achievement of a fair trial by court. This conflict of competing values has led to the problem of contempt by publication.

[In 1907 the Supreme Court, with Justices Harlan and Brewer dissenting, refused to review a decision of a Colorado court holding a publisher in contempt for publishing articles and a cartoon which reflected upon the motives and conduct of the court in pending cases. In his opinion for the Court, Justice Holmes said that even if what the articles said was true, the publisher might none the less be guilty of contempt if a judge finds that the publication *tends* toward an interference with the administration of justice.

[In *Bridges* v. *California* the Court moved away from this position. The clear and present danger, and not the bad tendency, test is applied to comments on pending cases. Each case must be decided on its own facts. Four Justices dissented: Frankfurter, Roberts, Byrnes, and Chief Justice Stone. The majority decision was followed in *Craig* v. *Harney*, 331 US 367 (1947), with only Justices Frankfurter and Jackson dissenting. Cf. the concurring opinion of Justice Jackson in *Shepard* v. *Florida*, 341 US 50 (1951).]

Mr. Justice Black delivered the opinion of the Court:

These two cases [*Bridges* v. *California* and *Times-Mirror Co.* v. *Superior Court*], while growing out of different circumstances and concerning different parties, both relate to the scope of our national constitutional policy safeguarding free speech and a free press. All of the petitioners were adjudged guilty and fined for contempt of court by the Superior Court of Los Angeles County. Their conviction rested upon comments pertaining to pending litigation which were published in newspapers. In the Superior Court and later in the California Supreme Court, petitioners challenged the state's action as an abridgment, prohibited by the Federal Constitution, of freedom of speech and of the press, but the Superior Court overruled this contention, and the [California] Supreme Court affirmed. . . .

In brief, the state courts asserted and exercised a power to punish petitioners for publishing their views concerning cases not in all respects finally determined, upon the following chain of reasoning: California is invested with the power and duty to provide an adequate administration of justice; by virtue of this power and duty, it can take appropriate measures for providing fair judicial trials free from coercion or intimidation; included among such appropriate measures is the common law procedure of punishing certain interferences and obstructions through contempt proceedings; this particular measure, devolving upon the courts of California by reason of their creation as courts, includes the power to punish for publications made outside the court room if they tend to interfere with the fair and orderly administration of justice in a pending case; the trial court having found that the publications had such a tendency, and there being substantial evidence to support the finding, the punishments here imposed were an appropriate exercise of the state's power; in so far as these punishments constitute a restriction on liberty of expression, the public interest in that liberty was properly subordinated to the public interest in judicial impartiality and decorum.

If the inference of conflict raised by the last clause be correct, the issue before us is of the very gravest moment. For free speech and fair trials are two of the most cherished policies of our civilization, and it would be a trying task to choose between them. But even if such a conflict is not actually raised by the question before us, we are still confronted with the delicate problems entailed in passing upon the deliberations of the highest court of a state. This is not, however, solely an issue between state and nation, as it would be if we were called upon to mediate in one of those troublous situations where each claims to be the repository of a particular sovereign power. To be sure, the exercise of power here in question was by a state judge. But in deciding whether or not the sweeping constitutional mandate against any law "abridging the freedom of speech or of the press" forbids it, we are necessarily measuring a power of all American courts, both state and federal, including this one.

I. It is to be noted at once that we have no direction by the legislature of California that publications outside the court room which comment upon a pending case in a specified manner should be punishable. As we said in *Cantwell* v. *Connecticut,* 310 US 296, such a "declaration of the State's policy would weigh heavily in any challenge of the law as infringing constitutional limitations." But as we also said there, the problem is different where "the judgment is based on a common law concept of the most general and undefined nature." . . . The judgments below, therefore, do not come to us encased in the armor wrought by prior legislative deliberation. Under such circumstances, this Court has said that "it must necessarily be found, as an original question" that the specified publications involved created "such likelihood of bringing about the substantive evil as to deprive [them] of the constitutional protection." *Gitlow* v. *New York,* 268 US 652.

How much "likelihood" is another question, "a question of proximity and degree" that cannot be completely captured in a formula. In *Schenck* v. *United States,* 249 US 47, however, this Court said that there must be a determination of whether or not "the words used are used in such circumstances and are of such a nature as to create a clear and present danger that they will bring about the substantive evils." We recognize that this statement, however helpful, does not comprehend the whole problem. As Mr. Justice Brandeis said in his concurring opinion in *Whitney* v. *California,* 274 US 357: "This Court has not yet fixed the standard by which to determine when a danger shall be deemed clear; how remote the danger may be and yet be deemed present."

Nevertheless, the "clear and present danger" language of the *Schenck Case* has afforded practical guidance in a great variety of cases in which the scope of constitutional protections of freedom of expression was in issue. It has been utilized by either a majority or minority of this Court in passing upon the constitutionality of convictions under espionage acts . . . ; under a criminal syndicalism act . . . ; under an "anti-insurrection" act . . . ; and for breach of the peace at common law. . . . And very recently we have also suggested that "clear and present danger" is an appropriate guide in determining the constitutionality of restrictions upon expression where the substantive evil sought to be prevented by the restriction is "destruction of life or property, or invasion of the right of privacy." *Thornhill* v. *Alabama,* 310 US 88.

Moreover, the likelihood, however great, that a substantive evil will result cannot alone justify a restriction upon freedom of speech or the press. The evil itself must be "substantial," Brandeis, J., concurring in *Whitney* v. *California;* it must be "serious." And even the expression of "legislative preferences or beliefs" cannot transform minor matters of public inconvenience or annoyance into substantive evils of sufficient weight to warrant the curtailment of liberty of expression. *Schneider* v. *Irvington,* 308 US 147.

What finally emerges from the "clear and present danger" cases is a working principle that the substantive evil must be extremely serious and the degree of imminence extremely high before utterances can be punished. Those cases do not purport to mark the furthermost constitutional boundaries of protected expression, nor do we here. They do no more than recognize a minimum compulsion of the Bill of Rights. For the First Amendment does not speak equivocally. It prohibits any law "abridging the freedom of speech or of the press." It must be taken as a command of the broadest scope that explicit language, read in the context of a liberty-loving society, will allow.

II. Before analyzing the punished utterances and the circumstances surrounding their publication, we must consider an argument which, if valid, would destroy the relevance of the foregoing discussion to this case. In brief, this argument is that the publications here in question belong to a special category marked off by history, a category to which the criteria of constitutional immunity from punishment used where other types of utterances are concerned are not applicable. For, the argument runs, the power of judges to punish by contempt out-of-court publications tending to obstruct the orderly and fair administration of justice in a pending case was deeply rooted in English common law at the time the Constitution was adopted. That this historical contention is dubious has been persuasively argued elsewhere. . . . In any event it need not detain us, for to assume that English common law in this field became ours is to deny the generally accepted historical belief that "one of the objects of the Revolution was to get rid of the English common law on liberty of speech and of the press." . . .

More specifically, it is to forget the environment in which the First Amendment was ratified. In presenting the proposals which were later embodied in the Bill of Rights, James Madison, the leader in the preparation of the First Amendment, said:

> Although I know whenever the great rights, the trial by jury, freedom of the press, or liberty of conscience, come in question in that body [Parliament], the invasion of them is resisted by able advocates, yet their Magna Charta does not contain any one provision for the security of those rights, respecting which the people of America are most alarmed. The freedom of the press and the rights of conscience, those choicest privileges of the people, are unguarded in the British Constitution. [1 *Annals of Congress* 1789–1790, 434.]

And Madison elsewhere wrote that "the state of the press . . . under the common law, cannot . . . be the standard of its freedom in the United States." VI *Writings of James Madison 1790–1802,* 387.

There are no contrary implications in any part of the history of the period in which the First Amendment was framed and adopted. No purpose in ratifying the Bill of Rights was clearer than that of securing for the people of the United States much greater freedom of religion, expression, assembly, and petition than the people of Great Britain had ever enjoyed. It cannot be denied, for example, that the religious test oath or the restrictions upon assembly then prevalent in England would have been regarded as measures which the Constitution prohibited the American Congress from passing. And since the same unequivocal language is used with respect to freedom of the press, it signifies a similar enlargement of that concept as well. Ratified as it was while the memory of many oppressive English restrictions on the enumerated liberties was still fresh, the First Amendment cannot reasonably be taken as approving prevalent English practices. On the contrary, the only conclusion supported by history is that the unqualified prohibitions laid down by the framers were intended to give to liberty of the press, as to the other liberties, the broadest scope that could be countenanced in an orderly society.

The implications of subsequent American history confirm such a construction of the First Amendment. To be sure, it occurred no more to the people who lived in the decades following Ratification than it would to us now that the power of courts to protect themselves from disturbances and disorder in the court room by use of contempt proceedings could seriously be challenged as conflicting with constitutionally secured guarantees of liberty. In both state and federal courts, this power has been universally recognized. . . . But attempts to expand it in the post-Ratification years evoked popular reactions that bespeak a feeling of jealous solicitude for freedom of the press. In Pennsylvania and New York, for example, heated controversies arose over alleged abuses in the exercise of the contempt power, which in both places culminated in legislation practically forbidding summary punishment for publications. . . .

In the federal courts, there was the celebrated case of Judge Peck, recently referred to by this Court in *Nye* v. *United States*, 313 US 33. The impeachment proceedings against him, it should be noted, and the strong feelings they engendered, were set in motion by his summary punishment of a lawyer for publishing comment on a case which was on appeal at the time of publication and which raised the identical issue of several other cases then pending before him. Here again legislation was the outcome, Congress proclaiming in a statute expressly captioned "An Act *declaratory* of the law concerning contempts of court," that the power of federal courts to inflict summary punishment for contempt "shall not be construed to extend to any cases except the misbehaviour of . . . persons in the presence of the said courts, or so near thereto as to obstruct the administration of justice." . . .

We are aware that although some states have by statute or decision expressly repudiated the power of judges to punish publications as contempts on a finding of mere tendency to interfere with the orderly administration of justice in a pending case, other states have sanctioned the exercise of such a power. . . . But state power in this field was not tested in this Court for more than a century. Not until 1925, with the decision in *Gitlow* v. *New York*, 268 US 652, did this Court recognize in the Fourteenth Amendment the application to the states of the same standards of freedom of expression as, under the First Amendment, are applicable to the federal government. And this is the first time since 1925 that we have been called upon to determine the constitutionality of a state's exercise of the contempt power in this kind of situation. Now that such a case is before us, we cannot allow the mere existence of other untested state decisions to destroy the historic constitutional meaning of freedom of speech and of the press.

History affords no support for the contention that the criteria applicable under the Constitution to other types of utterances are not applicable, in contempt proceedings, to out-of-court publications pertaining to a pending case.

III. We may appropriately begin our discussion of the judgments below by considering how much, as a practical matter, they would affect liberty of expression. It must be recognized that public interest is much more likely to be kindled by a controversial event of the day than by a generalization, however penetrating, of the historian or scientist. Since they punish utterances made during the pendency of a case, the judgments below therefore produce their restrictive results at the precise time when public interest in the matters discussed would naturally be at its height. Moreover, the ban is likely to fall not only at a crucial time but upon the most important topics of discussion. Here, for example, labor controversies were the topics of some of the publications. Experience shows that the more acute labor controversies are, the more likely it is that in some aspect they will get into court. It is therefore the controversies that command most interest that the decisions below would remove from the arena of public discussion.

No suggestion can be found in the Constitution that the freedom there guaranteed for speech and the press bears an inverse ratio to the timeliness and importance of the ideas seeking expression. Yet, it would follow as a practical result of the decisions below that anyone who might wish to give public expression to his views on a pending case involving no matter what problem of public interest, just at the time his audience would be most receptive, would be as effectively discouraged as if a deliberate statutory scheme of censorship had been adopted. Indeed, perhaps more so, because under a legislative specification of the particular kinds of expressions prohibited and the circumstances under which the prohibitions are to operate, the speaker or publisher might at least have an authoritative guide to the permissible scope of comment, instead of being compelled to act at the peril that judges might find in the utterance a "reasonable tendency" to obstruct justice in a pending case.

This unfocussed threat is, to be sure, limited in time, terminating as it does upon final disposition of the case. But this does not change its censorial quality. An endless series of moratoria on public discussion, even if each were very short, could hardly be dismissed as an insignificant abridgment of freedom of expression. And to assume that each would be short is to overlook the fact that the "pendency" of a case is frequently a matter of months or even years rather than days or weeks.

For these reasons we are convinced that the judgments below result in a curtailment of expression that cannot be dismissed as insignificant. If they can be justified at all, it must be in terms of some serious substantive evil which they are designed to avert. The substantive evil here sought to be averted has been variously described below. It appears to be double: disrespect for the judiciary; and disorderly and unfair administration of justice. The assumption that respect for the judiciary can be won by shielding judges from published criticism wrongly appraises the character of American public opinion. For it is a prized American privilege to speak one's mind, although not always with perfect good taste, on all public institutions. And an enforced silence, however limited, solely in the name of preserving the dignity of the bench, would probably engender resentment, suspicion, and contempt much more than it would enhance respect.

The other evil feared, disorderly and unfair administration of justice, is more plausibly associated with restricting publications which touch upon pending litigation. The very word "trial" connotes decisions on the evidence and arguments properly advanced in open court. Legal trials are not like elections, to be won through the use of the meeting-hall, the radio, and the newspaper. But we cannot start with the assumption that publications of the kind here involved actually do threaten to change the nature of legal trials, and that to preserve judicial impartiality, it is necessary for judges to have a contempt power by which they can close all channels of public expression to all matters which touch upon pending cases. We must therefore turn to the particular utterances here in question and the circumstances of their publication to determine to what extent the substantive evil of unfair administration of justice was a likely consequence, and whether the degree of likelihood was sufficient to justify summary punishment.

The Los Angeles Times Editorials. The Times-Mirror Company, publisher of the *Los Angeles Times,* and L. D. Hotchkiss, its managing editor, were cited for contempt for the publication of three editorials. Both found by the trial court to be responsible for one of the editorials, the company and Hotchkiss were each fined $100. The company alone was held responsible for the other two, and was fined $100 more on account of one, and $300 more on account of the other.

The $300 fine presumably marks the most serious offense. The editorial thus distinguished was entitled "Probation for Gorillas?". After vigorously denouncing two members of a labor union who had previously been found guilty of assaulting nonunion truck drivers, it closes with the observation: "Judge A. A. Scott will make a serious mistake if he grants probation to Matthew Shannon and Kennan Holmes. This community needs the example of their assignment to the jute mill." Judge Scott had previously set a day (about a month after the publication) for passing upon the application of Shannon and Holmes for probation and for pronouncing sentence.

The basis for punishing the publication as contempt was by the trial court said to be its "inherent tendency" and by the Supreme Court its "reasonable tendency" to interfere with the orderly administration of justice in an action then before a court for consideration. In accordance with what we have said on the "clear and present danger" cases, neither "inherent tendency" nor "reasonable tendency" is enough to justify a restriction of free expression. But even if they were appropriate measures, we should find exaggeration in the use of those phrases to describe the facts here.

From the indications in the record of the position taken by the *Los Angeles Times* on labor controversies in the past, there could have been little doubt of its attitude toward the probation of Shannon and Holmes. In view of the paper's long-continued militancy in this field, it is inconceivable that any judge in Los Angeles would expect anything but adverse criticism from it in the event probation were granted. Yet such criticism after final disposition of the proceedings would clearly have been privileged. Hence, this editorial, given the most intimidating construction it will bear, did no more than threaten future adverse criticism which was reasonably to be expected anyway in the event of a lenient disposition of the pending case. To regard it, therefore, as in itself of substantial influence upon the course of justice would be to impute to judges a lack of firmness, wisdom, or honor, which we cannot accept as a major premise. . . .

With respect to these [other] two editorials, there is no divergence of conclusions among the members of this Court. We are all of the opinion that, upon any fair construction, their possible influence on the course of justice can be dismissed as negligible, and that the Constitution compels us to set aside the convictions as unpermissible exercises of the state's power. In view of the foregoing discussion of "Probation for Gorillas?", analysis of these editorials and their setting is deemed unnecessary.

The Bridges Telegram. While a motion for a new trial was pending in a case involving a dispute between an A.F. of L. union and a C.I.O. union of which Bridges was an officer, he either caused to be published or acquiesced in the publication of a telegram which he had sent to the Secretary of Labor. The telegram referred to the judge's decision as "outrageous"; said that attempted enforcement of it would tie up the port of Los Angeles and involve the entire Pacific Coast; and concluded with the announcement that the C.I.O. union, representing some twelve thousand members, did "not intend to allow state courts to override the majority vote of members in choosing its officers and representatives and to override the National Labor Relations Board."

Apparently Bridges' conviction is not rested at all upon his use of the word "outrageous." The remainder of the telegram fairly construed appears to be a statement that if the court's decree should be enforced there would be a strike. It is not claimed that such a strike would have been in violation of the terms of the decree, nor that in any other way it would have run afoul of the law of California. On no construction, therefore, can the telegram be taken as a threat either by Bridges or the union to follow an illegal course of action. . . . [The words of Justice] Holmes, spoken in reference to very different facts, seem entirely applicable here: "I confess that I cannot find in all this or in the evidence in the case anything that would have affected a mind of reasonable fortitude, and still less can I find there anything that obstructed the administration of justice in any sense that I possibly can give to those words." . . .

Reversed.

★ IX ★

Personal Security

1. Freedom of Movement and Residence

EDWARDS v. CALIFORNIA

314 US 160 (1941)

[Restrictions on the movement of laborers and paupers from one parish to another were familiar to Englishmen in the sixteenth, seventeenth, and eighteenth centuries; and restriction of movement by law is familiar in twentieth-century totalitarian countries.

[In the depression of the 1930's a California statute was used to penalize the bringing into the state of any nonresident known to be "an indigent person." Justice Byrnes, speaking for five Justices, held the act to be an unconstitutional interference with interstate commerce. Even persons who are "destitute of property and without resources to obtain the necessities of life, and who have no relatives or friends able and willing to support them" may enter a state without let or hindrance.

[Four Justices wanted the Court to go further and put the rationale of the decision on the Privileges and Immunities Clause of the Fourteenth Amendment. While the spirit of this clause is certainly broader than that of the Commerce Clause, its letter is perhaps more restrictive —at least in a case involving the migration of persons—for it applies only to citizens, and thus excludes aliens from its guaranty.

[On the scope of the Privileges and Immunities Clause, see Milton R. Konvitz, *The Constitution and Civil Rights* (New York, Columbia University Press, 1947), ch. ii.]

431

Mr. Justice Byrnes delivered the opinion of the Court:

The facts of this case are simple and are not disputed. Appellant is a citizen of the United States and a resident of California. In December, 1939, he left his home in Marysville, California, for Spur, Texas, with the intention of bringing back to Marysville his wife's brother, Frank Duncan, a citizen of the United States and a resident of Texas. When he arrived in Texas, appellant learned that Duncan had last been employed by the Works Progress Administration. Appellant thus became aware of the fact that Duncan was an indigent person and he continued to be aware of it throughout the period involved in this case. The two men agreed that appellant should transport Duncan from Texas to Marysville in appellant's automobile. Accordingly, they left Spur on January 1, 1940, entered California by way of Arizona on January 3, and reached Marysville on January 5. When he left Texas, Duncan had about $20. It had all been spent by the time he reached Marysville. He lived with appellant for about ten days until he obtained financial assistance from the Farm Security Administration. During the ten-day interval, he had no employment.

In Justice Court a complaint was filed against appellant under § 2615 of the Welfare and Institutions Code of California, which provides: "Every person, firm or corporation, or officer or agent thereof that brings or assists in bringing into the State any indigent person who is not a resident of the State, knowing him to be an indigent person, is guilty of a misdemeanor." On demurrer to the complaint, appellant urged that the section violated several provisions of the Federal Constitution. The demurrer was overruled, the cause was tried, appellant was convicted and sentenced to six months' imprisonment in the county jail, and sentence was suspended. . . .

Article 1, § 8, of the Constitution delegates to the Congress the authority to regulate interstate commerce. And it is settled beyond question that the transportation of persons is "commerce," within the meaning of that provision. It is nevertheless true that the States are not wholly precluded from exercising their police power in matters of local concern even though they may thereby affect interstate commerce. . . . The issue presented in this case, therefore, is whether the prohibition embodied in § 2615 against the "bringing" or transportation of indigent persons into California is within the police power of that State. We think that it is not, and hold that it is an unconstitutional barrier to interstate commerce.

The grave and perplexing social and economic dislocation which this statute reflects is a matter of common knowledge and concern. We are not unmindful of it. We appreciate that the spectacle of large segments of our population constantly on the move has given rise to urgent demands upon the ingenuity of government. Both the brief of the Attorney General of California and that of the Chairman of the Select Committee of the House of Representatives of the United States as amicus curiae have sharpened this appreciation. The State asserts that the huge influx of migrants into California in recent years has resulted in problems of health, morals, and especially finance, the proportions of which are staggering. It is not for us to say that this is not true. We have repeatedly and recently affirmed, and we now reaffirm, that we do not conceive it our function to pass upon "the wisdom, need, or appropriateness" of the legislative efforts of the States to solve such difficulties. . . .

But this does not mean that there are no boundaries to the permissible area of State legislative activity. There are. And none is more certain than the prohibition against attempts on the part of any single State to isolate itself from difficulties common to all of them by restraining the transportation of persons and property across its borders. It is frequently the case that a State might gain a momentary respite from the pressure of events by the simple expedient of shutting its gates to the outside world. But, in the words of Mr. Justice Cardozo: "The Constitution was framed under the dominion of a political philosophy less parochial in range. It was framed upon the theory that the peoples of the several States must sink or swim together, and that in the long run prosperity and salvation are in union and not division." . . .

It is difficult to conceive of a statute more squarely in conflict with this theory than the section challenged here. Its express purpose and inevitable effect is to prohibit the transportation of indigent persons across the California border. The burden upon interstate commerce is intended and immediate; it is the plain and sole function of the statute. Moreover, the indigent nonresidents who are the real victims of the statute are deprived of the opportunity to exert political pressure upon the California legislature in order to obtain a change in policy. . . . We think this statute must fail under any known test of the validity of State interference with interstate commerce.

It is urged, however, that the concept which underlies § 2615 enjoys a firm basis in English and American history. This is the notion that each community should care for its own indigent, that relief is solely the responsibility of local government. Of this it must first be said that we are not now called upon to determine anything other than the propriety of an attempt by a State to prohibit the transportation of indigent nonresidents into its territory. The nature and extent of its obligation to afford relief to newcomers is not here involved. We do, however, suggest that the theory of the Elizabethan poor laws no longer fits the facts. Recent years, and particularly the past decade, have been marked by a growing recognition that in an industrial society the task of providing assistance to the needy has ceased to be local in character. The duty to share the burden, if not wholly to assume it, has been recognized not only by State governments, but by the Federal government as well. The changed attitude is reflected in the Social Security laws under which the Federal and State governments co-operate for the care of the aged, the blind and dependent children. . . . It is reflected in the works programs under which work is furnished the unemployed, with the States supplying approximately 25% and the Federal government approximately 75% of the cost. . . . It is further reflected in the Farm Security laws, under which the entire cost of the relief provisions is borne by the Federal government. . . .

Indeed the record in this very case illustrates the inadequate basis in fact for the theory that relief is presently a local matter. Before leaving Texas, Duncan had received assistance from the Works Progress Administration. After arriving in California he was aided by the Farm Security Administration, which, as we have said, is wholly financed by the Federal government. This is not to say that our judgment would be different if Duncan had received relief from local agencies in Texas and California. Nor is it to suggest that the financial burden of assistance to indigent persons does not continue to fall heavily upon local and State governments. It is only to illustrate that in not inconsiderable measure the relief of the needy has become the common responsibility and concern of the whole nation.

What has been said with respect to financing relief is not without its bearing upon the regulation of the transportation of indigent persons. For the social phenomenon of large-scale interstate migration is as certainly a matter of national concern as the provision of assistance to those who have found a permanent or temporary abode. Moreover, and unlike the relief problem, this phenomenon does not admit of diverse treatment by the several States. The prohibition against transporting indigent nonresidents into one State is an open invitation to retaliatory measures, and the burdens upon the transportation of such persons become cumulative. Moreover, it would be a virtual impossibility for migrants and those who transport them to acquaint themselves with the peculiar rules of admission of many states. . . .

There remains to be noticed only the contention that the limitation upon State power to interfere with the interstate transportation of persons is subject to an exception in the case of "paupers." It is true that support for this contention may be found in early decisions of this Court. . . .

Whether an able-bodied but unemployed person like Duncan is a "pauper" within the historical meaning of the term is open to considerable doubt. . . . But assuming that the term is applicable to him and to persons similarly situated, we do not consider ourselves bound by the language referred to. . . . Whatever may have been the notion then prevailing, we do not think that it will now be seriously contended that because a person is without employment and without funds he constitutes a "moral pestilence." Poverty and immorality are not synonymous.

We are of the opinion that § 2615 is not a valid exercise of the police power of California, that it imposes an unconstitutional burden upon interstate commerce, and that the conviction under it cannot be sustained. In the view we have taken it is unnecessary to decide whether the section is repugnant to other provisions of the Constitution.

Reversed.

Mr. Justice Douglas, concurring:

I express no view on whether or not the statute here in question runs afoul of Art. 1, § 8, of the Constitution granting to Congress the power "to regulate Commerce with foreign Nations, and among the several States." But I am of the opinion that the right of persons to move freely from State to State occupies a more protected position in our constitutional system than does the movement of cattle, fruit, steel and coal across state lines. While the opinion of the Court expresses no view on that issue, the right involved is so fundamental that I deem it appropriate to indicate the reach of the constitutional question which is present.

The right to move freely from State to State is an incident of *national* citizenship protected by the privileges and immunities clause of the Fourteenth Amendment against state interference. . . .

EX PARTE ENDO

323 US 283 (1944)

[Following Pearl Harbor, 112,000 persons of Japanese descent, including 70,000 American citizens, were evacuated from the West Coast and ordered detained. The policy involved: (1) A curfew order, requiring these people to be in their homes from 8 P.M. to 6 A.M. This order was upheld as constitutional in *Hirabayashi* v. *United States,* 320 US 81 (1943). (2) An exclusion order, which prohibited them from a defined area. This order was also found to be constitutional in *Korematsu* v. *United States,* 323 US 214 (1944), with Justices Murphy, Jackson, and Roberts dissenting. (3) An internment or detention order. This order was held illegal in the present case by a unanimous Court. It was held "unauthorized" rather than unconstitutional inasmuch as the constitutional issue was not considered except in the concurring opinions of Justices Murphy and Roberts, who said that the detention order was unconstitutional.

[The opinion of the Court in the *Endo Case* makes it clear, however, that the detention of an admittedly loyal citizen would create serious constitutional issues, at the least. This question may one day arise under the Emergency Detention Act, which is Part II of the Internal Security Act of 1950 (the McCarran Act). Under this act the President is authorized to declare an "internal emergency" in the event of war, invasion, or rebellion. Then the Attorney General may intern any person with respect to whom there is "reasonable ground to believe" that he "will probably engage in . . . acts of espionage or of sabotage." The act applies to citizens and aliens alike.

[For a discussion of the cases mentioned in this note, see Milton R. Konvitz, *The Alien and the Asiatic in American Law* (Ithaca, N.Y.: Cornell University Press, 1946), ch. xi.]

Mr. Justice Douglas delivered the opinion of the Court:

. . . Mitsuye Endo, hereinafter designated as the appellant, is an American citizen of Japanese ancestry. She was evacuated from Sacramento, California, in 1942, pursuant to certain military orders which we will presently discuss, and was removed to the Tule Lake War Relocation Center located at Newell, Modoc County, California. In July, 1942, she filed a petition for a writ of habeas corpus . . . , asking that she be discharged and restored to liberty. That petition was denied by the District Court in July, 1943, and an appeal was perfected to the Circuit Court of Appeals in August, 1943. Shortly thereafter appellant was transferred from the Tule Lake Relocation Center to the Central Utah Relocation Center located at Topaz, Utah, where she is presently detained. . . .

The program of the War Relocation Authority is said to have three main features: (1) the maintenance of Relocation Centers as interim places of residence for evacuees; (2) the segregation of loyal from disloyal evacuees; (3) the continued detention of the disloyal and so far as possible the relocation of the loyal in selected communities. In connection with the latter phase of its work the War Relocation Authority established a procedure for obtaining leave from Relocation Centers. That procedure so far as indefinite leave is concerned, presently provides as follows:

Application for leave clearance is required. An investigation of the applicant is made for the purpose of ascertaining "the probable effect upon the war program and upon the public peace and security of issuing indefinite leave" to the applicant. The grant of leave clearance does not authorize departure from the Relocation Center. Application for indefinite leave must also be made. Indefinite leave may be granted under 14 specified conditions. For example, it may be granted (1) where the applicant proposes to accept an employment offer or an offer of support that has been investigated and approved by the Authority; or (2) where the applicant does not intend to work but has "adequate financial resources to take care of himself" and a Relocation Officer has investigated and approved "public sentiment at his proposed destination," or (3) where the applicant has made arrangements to live at a hotel or in a private house approved by a Relocation Officer while arranging for employment; or (4) where the applicant proposes to accept employment by a federal or local governmental agency; or (5) where the applicant is going to live with designated classes of relatives.

But even if an applicant meets those requirements, no leave will issue when the proposed place of residence or employment is within a locality where it has been ascertained that "community sentiment is unfavorable" or when the applicant plans to go to an area which has been closed by the Authority to the issuance of indefinite leave. Nor will such leave issue if the area where the applicant plans to reside or work is one which has not been cleared for relocation. Moreover, the applicant agrees to give the Authority prompt notice of any change of employment or residence. And the indefinite leave which is granted does not permit entry into a prohibited military area, including those from which these people were evacuated.

Mitsuye Endo made application for leave clearance on February 19, 1943, after the petition was filed in the District Court. Leave clearance was granted her on August 16, 1943. But she made no application for indefinite leave.

Her petition for a writ of habeas corpus alleges that she is a loyal and law-abiding citizen of the United States, that no charge has been made against her, that she is being unlawfully detained, and that she is confined in the Relocation Center under armed guard and held there against her will.

It is conceded by the Department of Justice and by the War Relocation Authority that appellant is a loyal and law-abiding citizen. They make no claim that she is detained on any charge or that she is even suspected of disloyalty. Moreover, they do not contend that she may be held any longer in the Relocation Center. They concede that it is beyond the power of the War Relocation Authority to detain citizens against whom no charges of disloyalty or subversiveness have been made for a period longer than that necessary to separate the loyal from the disloyal and to provide the necessary guidance for relocation. But they maintain that detention for an additional period after leave clearance has been granted is an essential step in the evacuation program. Reliance for that conclusion is placed on the following circumstances.

When compulsory evacuation from the West Coast was decided upon, plans for taking care of the evacuees after their detention in the Assembly Centers, to which they were initially removed, remained to be determined. On April 7, 1942, the Director of the Authority held a conference in Salt Lake City with various state and federal officials including the Governors of the intermountain states. "Strong opposition was expressed to any type of unsupervised relocation and some of the Governors refused to be responsible for maintenance of law and order unless evacuees brought into their States were kept under constant military surveillance." . . . As stated by General De Witt in his report to the Chief of Staff:

Essentially, military necessity required only that the Japanese population be removed from the coastal area and dispersed in the interior, where the danger of action in concert during any attempted enemy raids along the coast, or in advance thereof as preparation for a full scale attack, would be eliminated. That the evacuation program necessarily and ultimately developed into one of complete Federal supervision, was due primarily to the fact that the interior states would not accept an uncontrolled Japanese migration. . . .

The Authority thereupon abandoned plans for assisting groups of evacuees in private colonization and temporarily put to one side plans for aiding the evacuees in obtaining private employment. As an alternative the Authority "concentrated on establishment of Government-operated centers with sufficient capacity and facilities to accommodate the entire evacuee population." . . . Accordingly, it undertook to care for the basic needs of these people in the Relocation Centers, to promote as rapidly as possible the permanent resettlement of as many as possible in normal communities, and to provide indefinitely for those left at the Relocation Centers. An effort was made to segregate the loyal evacuees from the others. The leave program which we have discussed was put into operation and the resettlement program commenced.

It is argued that such a planned and orderly relocation was essential to the success of the evacuation program; that but for such supervision there might have been a dangerously disorderly migration of unwanted people to unprepared communities; that unsupervised evacuation might have resulted in hardship and disorder; that the success of the evacuation program was thought to require the knowledge that the Federal government was maintaining control over the evacuated population except as the release of individuals could be effected consistently with their own peace and well-being and that of the nation; that although community hostility towards the evacuees has diminished, it has not disappeared and the continuing control of the Authority over the relocation process is essential to the success of the evacuation program. It is argued that supervised relocation, as the chosen method of terminating the evacuation, is the final step in the entire process and is a consequence of the first step taken. It is conceded that appellant's detention pending compliance with the leave regulations is not directly connected with the prevention of espionage and sabotage at the present time. But it is argued that Executive Order No. 9102 confers power to make regulations necessary and proper for controlling situations created by the exercise of the powers expressly conferred for protection against espionage and sabotage. The leave regulations are said to fall within that category.

First. We are of the view that Mitsuye Endo should be given her liberty. In reaching that conclusion we do not come to the underlying constitutional issues which have been argued. For we conclude that, whatever power the War Relocation Authority may have to detain other classes of citizens, it has no authority to subject citizens who are concededly loyal to its leave procedure. . . .

We do not mean to imply that detention in connection with no phase of the evacuation program would be lawful. The fact that the Act and the orders are silent on detention does not of course mean that any power to detain is lacking. Some such power might indeed be necessary to the successful operation of the evacuation program. At least we may so assume. Moreover, we may assume for the purposes of this case that initial detention in Relocation Centers was authorized. But we stress the silence of the legislative history and of the Act and the Executive Orders on the power to detain to emphasize that any such authority which exists must be implied. If there is to be the greatest possible accommodation of the liberties of the citizen with this war measure, any such implied power must be narrowly confined to the precise purpose of the evacuation program.

A citizen who is concededly loyal presents no problem of espionage or sabotage. Loyalty is a matter of the heart and mind, not of race, creed, or color. He who is loyal is by definition not a spy or a saboteur. When the power to detain is derived from the power to protect the war effort against espionage and sabotage, detention which has no relationship to that objective is unauthorized.

Nor may the power to detain an admittedly loyal citizen or to grant him a conditional release be implied as a useful or convenient step in the evacuation program, whatever authority might be implied in case of those whose loyalty was not conceded or established. If we assume (as we do) that the original evacuation was justified, its lawful character was derived from the fact that it was an espionage and sabotage measure, not that there was community hostility to this group of American citizens. The evacuation program rested explicitly on the former ground not on the latter as the underlying legislation shows. The authority to detain a citizen or to grant him a conditional release as protection against espionage or sabotage is exhausted at least when his loyalty is conceded. If we held that the authority to detain continued thereafter, we would transform an espionage or sabotage measure into something else. That was not done by Executive Order No. 9066 or by the Act of March 21, 1942, which ratified it. What they did not do we cannot do. Detention which furthered the campaign against espionage and sabotage would be one thing. But detention which has no relationship to that campaign is of a distinct character. Community hostility even to loyal evacuees may have been (and perhaps still is) a serious problem. But if authority for their custody and supervision is to be sought on that ground, the Act of March 21, 1942, Executive Order No. 9066, and Executive Order No. 9102, offer no support. And none other is advanced. To read them that broadly would be to assume that the Congress and the President intended that this discriminatory action should be taken against these people wholly on account of their ancestry even though the government conceded their loyalty to this country. We cannot make such an assumption. As the President has said of these loyal citizens:

Americans of Japanese ancestry, like those of many other ancestries, have shown that they can, and want to, accept our institutions and work loyally with the rest of us, making their own valuable contribution to the national wealth and well-being. In vindication of the very ideals for which we are fighting this war it is important to us to maintain a high standard of fair, considerate, and equal treatment for the people of this minority as of all other minorities. . . .

Mitsuye Endo is entitled to an unconditional release by the War Relocation Authority. . . .

2. Bills of Attainder

UNITED STATES v. LOVETT

328 US 303 (1946)

[In 1943 Congressman Martin Dies read to the House of Representatives the names of thirty-eight employees of the Federal Government who, he said, had "subversive affiliations." The House directed a subcommittee of the Appropriations Committee to determine the subversive nature of each of the accused employees. The subcommittee conducted secret hearings and found that in its opinion three of the thirty-eight persons deserved dismissal. The House then attached a rider to the Urgent Deficiency Appropriation Act forbidding the payment of compensation to the three employees. These employees attacked the rider as a bill of attainder, and their contentions were sustained by a unanimous Supreme Court in the present case.

[In the fourteenth century Parliament began to enact bills of attainder, acts punishing named persons by death or exile. Acts that provided milder penalties were also passed and were known as bills of pains and penalties. Both types of acts were criticized severely. Parliament has not passed a bill of attainder since 1696, and the last time it tried, without success, to pass a bill of pains and penalties was in 1821. The American colonies during the Revolution and until the adoption of the Constitution passed bills of attainder against Loyalists.

[The Constitution, Art. I, Sec. 9, Cl. 3, provides that Congress shall not pass a bill of attainder. As interpreted by the Court, the prohibition on bills of attainder comprehends also bills of pains and penalties: the Constitution prohibits all legislative acts, regardless of their form, if they inflict punishment without a judicial trial on named persons or on the easily ascertainable members of a group.

[The Constitution also prohibits states from passing bills of attainder. Art. I, Sec. 10.]

Mr. Justice Black delivered the opinion of the Court:

In 1943 the respondents, Lovett, Watson, and Dodd, were and had been for several years working for the Government. The Government agencies which had lawfully employed them were fully satisfied with the quality of their work and wished to keep them employed on their jobs. Over the protest of those employing agencies, Congress provided in Section 304 of the Urgent Deficiency Appropriation Act of 1943, by way of an amendment attached to the House bill, that after November 15, 1943, no salary or compensation should be paid respondents out of any monies then or thereafter appropriated except for services as jurors or members of the armed forces, unless they were prior to November 15, 1943 again appointed to jobs by the President with the advice and consent of the Senate. Notwithstanding the Congressional enactment, and the failure of the President to reappoint respondents, the agencies kept all the respondents at work on their jobs for varying periods after November 15, 1943; but their compensation was discontinued after that date. To secure compensation for this post-November 15 work, respondents brought these actions in the Court of Claims. They urged that Section 304 is unconstitutional and void on the grounds that: (1) The Section, properly interpreted, shows a Congressional purpose to exercise the power to remove executive employees, a power not entrusted to Congress but to the Executive Branch of Government under Article II, Sections 1, 2, 3, and 4 of the Constitution; (2) the Section violates Article I, Section 9, Clause 3, of the Constitution which provides that "no bill of attainder or ex post facto law shall be passed"; (3) the Section violates the Fifth Amendment, in that it singles out these three respondents and deprives them of their liberty and property without due process of law. The Solicitor General, appearing for the Government, joined in the first two of respondents' contentions but took no position on the third. [A] House Resolution . . . authorized a special counsel to appear on behalf of the Congress. This counsel denied all three of respondents' contentions. . . . The Court of Claims entered judgments in favor of respondents. . . .

In this Court the parties and counsel for Congress have urged the same points as they did in the Court of Claims. According to the view we take we need not decide whether Section 304 is an unconstitutional encroachment on executive power or a denial of due process of law, and the section is not challenged on the ground that it violates the First Amendment. Our inquiry is thus confined to whether the actions in the light of a proper construction of the Act present justiciable controversies and if so whether Section 304 is a bill of attainder against these respondents involving a use of power which the Constitution unequivocally declares Congress can never exercise. These questions require an interpretation of the meaning and purpose of the section, which in turn requires an understanding of the circumstances leading to its passage. We, consequently, find it necessary to set out these circumstances somewhat in detail.

In the background of the statute here challenged lies the House of Representatives' feeling in the late thirties that many "subversives" were occupying influential positions in the Government and elsewhere and that their influence must not remain unchallenged. As part of its program against "subversive" activities the House in May 1938 created a Committee on Un-American Activities, which became known as the Dies Committee after its Chairman, Congressman Martin Dies. . . . This Committee conducted a series of investigations and made lists of people and organizations it thought "subversive." . . . The creation of the Dies Committee was followed by provisions such as Section 9A of the Hatch Act and Sections 15(f) and 17(b) of the Emergency Relief Appropriations Act of 1941, which forbade the holding of a federal job by anyone who was a member of a political party or organization that advocated the overthrow of our Constitutional form of Government in the United States. It became the practice to include a similar prohibition in all appropriations acts, together with criminal penalties for its violation. Under these provisions the Federal Bureau of Investigation began wholesale investigations of federal employees, which investigations were financed by special Congressional appropriations. . . . Thousands were investigated.

While all this was happening Mr. Dies on February 1, 1943, in a long speech on the floor of the House attacked thirty-nine named Government employees as "irresponsible, unrepresentative, crackpot, radical bureaucrats" and affiliates of "communist front organizations." Among these named individuals were the three respondents. Congressman Dies told the House that respondents, as well as the other thirty-six individuals he named were because of their beliefs and past associations unfit to "hold a government position" and urged Congress to refuse "to appropriate money for their salaries." In this connection he proposed that the Committee on Appropriations "take immediate and vigorous steps to eliminate these people from public office." . . . Four days later an amendment was offered to the Treasury-Post Office Appropriation Bill which provided that "no part of any appropriation contained in this Act shall be used to pay the compensation of" the thirty-nine individuals Dies had attacked. . . . The *Congressional Record* shows that this amendment precipitated a debate that continued for several days. . . . All of those participating agreed that the "charges" against the thirty-nine individuals were serious. Some wanted to accept Congressman Dies' statements as sufficient proof of "guilt," while others referred to such proposed action as "legislative lynching," . . . smacking "of the procedure in the French Chamber of Deputies, during the Reign of Terror." . . . The Dies charges were referred to as "indictments," and many claimed this made it necessary that the named federal employees be given a hearing and a chance to prove themselves innocent. . . . Congressman Dies then suggested that the Appropriations Committee "weigh the evidence and . . . take immediate steps to dismiss these people from the federal service." . . . Eventually a resolution was proposed to defer action until the Appropriations Committee could investigate, so that accused federal employees would get a chance to prove themselves "innocent" of communism or disloyalty, and so that each "man would have his day in court," and "There would be no star chamber proceedings." . . . The resolution which was finally passed authorized the Appropriations Committee acting through a special subcommittee ". . . to examine into any and all allegations or charges that certain persons in the employ of the several executive departments and other executive agencies are unfit to continue in such employment by reason of their present association or membership or past association or membership in or with organizations whose aims or purposes are or have been subversive to the Government of the United States." . . . The Committee was to have full plenary powers, including the right to summon witnesses and papers, and was to report its "findings and determination" to the House. It was authorized to attach legislation recommended by it to any general or special appropriation measure, notwithstanding general House rules against such practice. . . . The purpose of the resolution was thus described by the Chairman of the Committee on Appropriations in his closing remarks in favor of its passage:

The third and the really important effect is that we will expedite adjudication and disposition of these cases and thereby serve both the accused and the Government. These men against whom charges are pending are faced with a serious situation. If they are not guilty they are entitled to prompt exoneration; on the other hand, if they are guilty, then the quicker the Government removes them the sooner and the more certainly will we protect the Nation against sabotage and fifth-column activity.

. . . After the resolution was passed a special subcommittee of the Appropriations Committee held hearings in secret executive session. Those charged with "subversive" beliefs and "subversive" associations were permitted to testify, but lawyers including those representing the agencies by which the accused were employed were not permitted to be present. At the hearings, committee members, the committee staff, and whatever witness was under examination were the only ones present. The evidence, aside from that given by the accused employees, appears to have been largely that of reports made by the Dies Committee, its investigators, and Federal Bureau of Investigation reports, the latter being treated as too confidential to be made public.

After this hearing the subcommittee's reports and recommendations were submitted to the House as part of the Appropriation Committee's report. The subcommittee stated that it had regarded the investigations "as in the nature of an inquest of office" with the ultimate purpose of purging the public service of anyone found guilty of "subversive activity." The committee, stating that "subversive activity" had not before been defined by Congress or by the courts, formulated its own definition of "subversive activity." . . . Respondents Watson, Dodd and Lovett were, according to the subcommittee guilty of having engaged in "subversive activity within the definition adopted by the Committee." . . . The ultimate finding and recommendation as to respondent Watson, which was substantially similar to the findings with respect to Lovett and Dodd, read as follows:

Upon consideration of all the evidence, your committee finds that the membership and association of Dr. Goodwin B. Watson with the organizations mentioned and his views and philosophies as expressed in various statements and writings, constitute subversive activity within the definition adopted by your committee, and that he is, therefore, unfit for the present to continue in Government employment. . . .

As to Lovett the Committee further reported that it had rejected a "strong appeal" from the Secretary of the Interior for permission to retain Lovett in Government service, because as the Committee stated, it could not "escape the conclusion that this official is unfit to hold a position with the Government by reason of his membership, association, and affiliation with organizations whose aims and purposes are subversive to the Government of the United States." . . .

Section 304 was submitted to the House along with the Committee Report. Congressman Kerr who was chairman of the subcommittee stated that the issue before the House was simply: ". . . whether or not the people of this country want men who are not in sympathy with the institutions of this country to run it." He said further: ". . . These people have no property rights in these offices. One Congress can take away their rights given them by another." . . . Other members of the House during several days of debate bitterly attacked the measure as unconstitutional and unwise. . . . Finally Section 304 was passed by the House.

The Senate Appropriation Committee eliminated Section 304 and its action was sustained by the Senate. . . . After the first conference report which left the matter still in disagreement the Senate voted 69 to 0 against the conference report which left Section 304 in the bill. The House however insisted on the amendment and indicated that it would not approve any appropriation bill without Section 304. Finally after the fifth conference report showed that the House would not yield the Senate adopted Section 304. When the President signed the bill he stated: "The Senate yielded, as I have been forced to yield, to avoid delaying our conduct of the war. But I cannot so yield without placing on record my view that this provision is not only unwise and discriminatory, but unconstitutional." . . .

I.

In view of the facts just set out we cannot agree with the two judges of the Court of Claims who held that Section 304 required "a mere stoppage of disbursing routine, nothing more," and left the employer governmental agencies free to continue employing respondents and to incur contractual obligations by virtue of such continued work which respondents could enforce in the Court of Claims. Nor can we agree with counsel for Congress that the Section did not provide for the dismissal of respondents but merely forbade governmental agencies to compensate respondents for their work or to incur obligations for such compensation at any and all times. We therefore cannot conclude, as he urges, that Section 304 is a mere appropriation measure, and that since Congress under the Constitution has complete control over appropriations, a challenge to the measure's constitutionality does not present a justiciable question in the courts, but is merely a political issue over which Congress has final say.

We hold that the purpose of Section 304 was not merely to cut off respondents' compensation through regular disbursing channels but permanently to bar them from government service, and that the issue of whether it is constitutional is justiciable. The Section's language as well as the circumstances of its passage which we have just described show that no mere question of compensation procedure or of appropriations was involved, but that it was designed to force the employing agencies to discharge respondents and to bar their being hired by any other governmental agency. . . . Any other interpretation of the Section would completely frustrate the purpose of all who sponsored Section 304, which clearly was to "purge" the then existing and all future lists of Government employees of those whom Congress deemed guilty of "subversive activities" and therefore "unfit" to hold a federal job. What was challenged therefore is a statute which, because of what Congress thought to be their political beliefs, prohibited respondents from ever engaging in any government work, except as jurors or soldiers. Respondents claimed that their discharge was unconstitutional; that they consequently rightfully continued to work for the Government and that the Government owes them compensation for services performed under contracts of employment. Congress has established the Court of Claims to try just such controversies. What is involved here is a Congressional proscription of Lovett, Watson, and Dodd, prohibiting their ever holding a Government job. Were this case to be not justiciable, Congressional action, aimed at three named individuals, which stigmatized their reputation and seriously impaired their chance to earn a living, could never be challenged in any court. Our Constitution did not contemplate such a result. To quote Alexander Hamilton

. . . a limited constitution . . . [is] one which contains certain specified exceptions to the legislative authority; such, for instance, as that it shall pass no bills of attainder, no ex post facto laws, and the like. Limitations of this kind can be preserved in practice no other way than through the medium of the courts of justice; whose duty it must be to declare all acts contrary to the manifest tenor of the Constitution void. Without this, all the reservations of particular rights or privileges would amount to nothing. Federalist Paper No. 78.

II.

We hold that Section 304 falls precisely within the category of Congressional actions which the Constitution barred by providing that "No Bill of Attainder or ex post facto Law shall be passed." In *Cummings* v. *State of Missouri*, 4 Wall. 277, this Court said, "A bill of attainder is a legislative act which inflicts punishment without a judicial trial. If the punishment be less than death, the act is termed a bill of pains and penalties. Within the meaning of the Constitution, bills of attainder include bills of pains and penalties." The *Cummings* decision involved a provision of the Missouri Reconstruction Constitution which required persons to take an Oath of Loyalty as a prerequisite to practicing a profession. Cummings, a Catholic Priest, was convicted for teaching and preaching as a minister without taking the oath. The oath required an applicant to affirm that he had never given aid or comfort to persons engaged in hostility to the United States and had never "been a member of, or connected with, any order, society, or organization, inimical to the government of the United States. . . ." In an illuminating opinion which gave the historical background of the Constitutional prohibition against bills of attainder, this Court invalidated the Missouri Constitutional provision both because it constituted a bill of attainder and because it had an ex post facto operation. On the same day the *Cummings Case* was decided, the Court, in *Ex parte Garland*, 4 Wall. 333, also held invalid on the same grounds an Act of Congress which required attorneys practicing before this Court to take a similar oath. Neither of these cases has ever been overruled. They stand for the proposition that legislative acts, no matter what their form, that apply either to named individuals or to easily ascertainable members of a group in such a way as to inflict punishment on them without a judicial trial are bills of attainder prohibited by the Constitution. Adherence to this principle requires invalidation of Section 304. We do adhere to it.

Section 304 was designed to apply to particular individuals. Just as the statute in the two cases mentioned it "operates as a legislative decree of perpetual exclusion" from a chosen vocation. This permanent proscription from any opportunity to serve the Government is punishment, and of a most severe type. It is a type of punishment which Congress has only invoked for special types of odious and dangerous crimes, such as treason, . . . acceptance of bribes by members of Congress, . . . or by other government officials, . . . and interference with elections by Army and Navy officers. . . .

Section 304, thus, clearly accomplishes the punishment of named individuals without a judicial trial. The fact that the punishment is inflicted through the instrumentality of an Act specifically cutting off the pay of certain named individuals found guilty of disloyalty, makes it no less galling or effective than if it had been done by an Act which designated the conduct as criminal. No one would think that Congress could have passed a valid law, stating that after investigation it had found Lovett, Dodd, and Watson "guilty" of the crime of engaging in "subversive activities," defined that term for the first time, and sentenced them to perpetual exclusion from any government employment. Section 304, while it does not use that language, accomplishes that result. The effect was to inflict punishment without the safeguards of a judicial trial and "determined by no previous law or fixed rule." The Constitution declares that that cannot be done either by a state or by the United States.

Those who wrote our Constitution well knew the danger inherent in special legislative acts which take away the life, liberty, or property of particular named persons, because the legislature thinks them guilty of conduct which deserves punishment. They intended to safeguard the people of this country from punishment without trial by duly constituted courts. . . . And even the courts to which this important function was entrusted, were commanded to stay their hands until and unless certain tested safeguards were observed. An accused in court must be tried by an impartial jury, has a right to be represented by counsel, he must be clearly informed of the charge against him, the law which he is charged with violating must have been passed before he committed the act charged, he must be confronted by the witnesses against him, he must not be compelled to incriminate himself, he cannot twice be put in jeopardy for the same offense, and even after conviction no cruel and unusual punishment can be inflicted upon him. . . . When our Constitution and Bill of Rights were written, our ancestors had ample reason to know that legislative trials and punishments were too dangerous to liberty to exist in the nation of free men they envisioned. And so they proscribed bills of attainder. Section 304 is one. Much as we regret to declare that an Act of Congress violates the Constitution, we have no alternative here.

Section 304 therefore does not stand as an obstacle to payment of compensation to Lovett, Watson, and Dodd. The judgment in their favor is affirmed.

3. Unreasonable Searches and Seizures

UNITED STATES v. RABINOWITZ

339 US 56 (1950)

[The Fourth Amendment prohibits unreasonable searches and seizures; it does not expressly make inadmissible evidence that has been obtained by means of an illegal search and seizure. In *Wolf* v. *Colorado*, 338 US 25 (1949), a majority of the Court seemed to be of the opinion that the exclusion of such evidence in a *federal* court is not a command of the Fourth Amendment but is a judicially created rule of evidence which Congress could perhaps negate by legislation—at least this is Justice Black's interpretation of the view of the majority. But Justices Douglas, Murphy, and Rutledge maintained that the exclusion of such evidence is required by the Constitution.

[Whether constitutional or judicially created, the rule is settled that in a *federal* court evidence obtained by means of an illegal search and seizure by public officers is not admissible against the defendant in a criminal prosecution if the accused makes timely objection.

[But this rule still leaves open the question as to when a search and a seizure are "unreasonable." With respect to this question, Justice Black has observed, "In no other field has the law's uncertainty been more clearly manifested." In the present case five Justices held that the search and the seizure were reasonable, while Justices Black, Frankfurter, and Jackson dissented. Justice Douglas did not participate.

[In the *Wolf Case* the Court unanimously held that the Fourth Amendment, securing a person's privacy against arbitrary intrusion by the police, is basic to a free society and is, therefore, enforceable against the states through the Due Process Clause of the Fourteenth Amendment. But though the state violates the Constitution by procuring evidence by unreasonable search and seizure, the courts of the state may nonetheless admit such evidence—the admissibility or inadmissibility of such evidence is a matter for the state to decide. Justices Murphy, Rutledge, and Douglas, dissenting, said that the Constitution prohibits the use of such evidence in both federal and state courts.]

Mr. Justice Minton delivered the opinion of the Court:

Respondent was convicted of selling and of possessing and concealing forged and altered obligations of the United States with intent to defraud. The question presented here is the reasonableness of a search without a search warrant of a place of business consisting of a one-room office, incident to a valid arrest.

On February 1, 1943, a printer who possessed plates for forging "overprints" on canceled stamps was taken into custody. He disclosed that respondent, a dealer in stamps, was one of the customers to whom he had delivered large numbers of stamps bearing forged overprints. On Saturday, February 6, 1943, with this information concerning respondent and his activities in the hands of Government officers, a postal employee was sent to respondent's place of business to buy stamps bearing overprints. He bought four stamps. On Monday, February 8, the stamps were sent to an expert to determine whether the overprints were genuine. On February 9 the report was received showing the overprints to be forgeries, having been placed upon the stamps after cancellation, and not before as was the Government's practice. On February 11 a further statement was obtained from the printer who had made the overprints. On February 16, 1943, a warrant for the arrest of respondent was obtained.

In 1941 respondent had been convicted and sentenced to three months' imprisonment on a plea of guilty to a two-count indictment charging the alteration of obligations of the United States, that is, of overprinting Government postage stamps, and the possession of a plate from which a similitude of a United States obligation had been printed. Thus, when the warrant for arrest was obtained, the officers had reliable information that respondent was an old offender, that he had sold four forged and altered stamps to an agent of the Government, and that he probably possessed several thousand altered stamps bearing forged overprints. While the warrant of arrest was not put in evidence it contained, as a Government witness testified on cross-examination, authority to arrest for more than the sale of the four stamps; it covered all the Government officers' information.

Armed with this valid warrant for arrest, the Government officers, accompanied by two stamp experts, went to respondent's place of business, a one-room office open to the public. The officers thereupon arrested the respondent, and over his objection searched the desk, safe and file cabinets in the office for about an hour and a half. They found and seized 573 stamps, on which it was later determined that overprints had been forged, along with some other stamps which were subsequently returned to respondent.

Respondent was indicted on two counts. He was charged in count one with selling four forged and altered stamps, knowing they were forged and altered and with the intent that they be passed as genuine. The second count charged that he did keep in his possession and conceal, with intent to defraud, the 573 forged and altered stamps.

Respondent made timely motions for suppression and to strike the evidence pertaining to the 573 stamps, all of which were eventually denied. Respondent was convicted on both counts after trial before a jury in which he offered no evidence. Relying on *Trupiano* v. *United States,* 334 US 699, the Court of Appeals, one judge dissenting, reversed on the ground that since the officers had had time in which to procure a search warrant and had failed to do so the search was illegal, and the evidence therefore should have been excluded. . . .

Were the 573 stamps, the fruits of this search, admissible in evidence? If legally obtained, these stamps were competent evidence to show intent under the first count of the indictment, and they were the very things the possession of which was the crime charged in the second count.

The Fourth Amendment provides:

> The right of the people to be secure in their persons, houses, papers, and effects, against unreasonable searches and seizures, shall not be violated, and no Warrants shall issue, but upon probable cause, supported by Oath or affirmation, and particularly describing the place to be searched, and the persons or things to be seized.

It is unreasonable searches that are prohibited by the Fourth Amendment. . . . It was recognized by the framers of the Constitution that there were reasonable searches for which no warrant was required. The right of the "people to be secure in their persons" was certainly of as much concern to the framers of the Constitution as the property of the person. Yet no one questions the right, without a search warrant, to search the person after a valid arrest. The right to search the person incident to arrest always has been recognized in this country and in England. . . . Where one had been placed in the custody of the law by valid action of officers, it was not unreasonable to search him.

Of course, a search without warrant incident to an arrest is dependent initially on a valid arrest. Here the officers had a warrant for respondent's arrest which was, as far as can be ascertained, broad enough to cover the crime of possession charged in the second count, and consequently respondent was properly arrested. Even if the warrant of arrest were not sufficient to authorize the arrest for possession of the stamps, the arrest therefor was valid because the officers had probable cause to believe that a felony was being committed in their very presence. . . .

The arrest was therefore valid in any event, and respondent's person could be lawfully searched. Could the officers search his desk, safe and file cabinets, all within plain sight of the parties, and all located under respondent's immediate control in his one-room office open to the public?

Decisions of this Court have often recognized that there is a permissible area of search beyond the person proper. . . .

The right "to search the place where the arrest is made in order to find and seize things connected with the crime as its fruits or as means by which it was committed" seems to have stemmed not only from the acknowledged authority to search the person, but also from the long-standing practice of searching for other proofs of guilt within the control of the accused found upon arrest. . . . It became accepted that the premises where the arrest was made, which premises were under the control of the person arrested and where the crime was being committed, were subject to search without a search warrant. Such a search was not "unreasonable." . . .

In all the years of our Nation's existence, with special attention to the Prohibition Era, it seems never to have been questioned seriously that a limited search such as here conducted as incident to a lawful arrest was a reasonable search and therefore valid. It has been considered in the same pattern as search of the person after lawful arrest.

What is a reasonable search is not to be determined by any fixed formula. The Constitution does not define what are "unreasonable" searches and, regrettably, in our discipline we have no ready litmus-paper test. The recurring questions of the reasonableness of searches must find resolution in the facts and circumstances of each case. . . . Reasonableness is in the first instance for the District Court to determine. We think the District Court's conclusion that here the search and seizure were reasonable should be sustained because: (1) the search and seizure were incident to a valid arrest; (2) the place of the search was a business room to which the public, including the officers, was invited; (3) the room was small and under the immediate and complete control of respondent; (4) the search did not extend beyond the room used for unlawful purposes; (5) the possession of the forged and altered stamps was a crime, just as it is a crime to possess burglars' tools, lottery tickets or counterfeit money.

Assuming that the officers had time to procure a search warrant, were they bound to do so? We think not, because the search was otherwise reasonable, as previously concluded. . . .

A rule of thumb requiring that a search warrant always be procured whenever practicable may be appealing from the vantage point of easy administration. But we cannot agree that this requirement should be crystallized into a sine qua non to the reasonableness of a search. It is fallacious to judge events retrospectively and thus to determine, considering the time element alone, that there was time to procure a search warrant. Whether there was time may well be dependent upon considerations other than the ticking off of minutes or hours. The judgment of the officers as to when to close the trap on a criminal committing a crime in their presence or who they have reasonable cause to believe is committing a felony is not determined solely upon whether there was time to procure a search warrant. Some flexibility will be accorded law officers engaged in daily battle with criminals for whose restraint criminal laws are essential.

It is appropriate to note that the Constitution does not say that the right of the people to be secure in their persons should not be violated without a search warrant if it is practicable for the officers to procure one. The mandate of the Fourth Amendment is that the people shall be secure against *unreasonable* searches. It is not disputed that there may be reasonable searches, incident to an arrest, without a search warrant. Upon acceptance of this established rule that some authority to search follows from lawfully taking the person into custody, it becomes apparent that such searches turn upon the reasonableness under all the circumstances and not upon the practicability of procuring a search warrant, for the warrant is not required. . . . The relevant test is not whether it is reasonable to procure a search warrant, but whether the search was reasonable. That criterion in turn depends upon the facts and circumstances—the total atmosphere of the case. It is a sufficient precaution that law officers must justify their conduct before courts which have always been, and must be, jealous of the individual's right of privacy within the broad sweep of the Fourth Amendment. . . .

The motion to suppress the evidence was properly denied by the District Court. . . .

Mr. Justice Frankfurter, whom Mr. Justice Jackson joins, dissenting:

The clear-cut issue before us is this: in making a lawful arrest, may arresting officers search without a search warrant not merely the person under arrest or things under his immediate physical control, but the premises where the arrest is made, although there was ample time to secure such a warrant and no danger that the "papers and effects" for which a search warrant could be issued would be despoiled or destroyed? . . .

These words [of the Fourth Amendment] are not just a literary composition. They are not to be read as they might be read by a man who knows English but has no knowledge of the history that gave rise to the words. The clue to the meaning and scope of the Fourth Amendment is John Adams' characterization of Otis' argument against search by the police that "American independence was then and there born." 10 Adams, *Works* 247. One cannot wrench "unreasonable searches" from the text and context and historic content of the Fourth Amendment. It was the answer of the Revolutionary statesmen to the evils of searches without warrants and searches with warrants unrestricted in scope. Both were deemed "unreasonable." Words must be read with the gloss of the experience of those who framed them. Because the experience of the framers of the Bill of Rights was so vivid, they assumed that it would be carried down the stream of history and that their words would receive the significance of the experience to which they were addressed—a significance not to be found in the dictionary. When the Fourth Amendment outlawed "unreasonable searches" and then went on to define the very restricted authority that even a search warrant issued by a magistrate could give, the framers said with all the clarity of the gloss of history that a search is "unreasonable" unless a warrant authorizes it, barring only exceptions justified by absolute necessity. Even a warrant cannot authorize it except when it is issued "upon probable cause . . . and particularly describing the place to be searched, and the persons or things to be seized." With all respect I suggest that it makes a mockery of the Fourth Amendment to sanction search without a search warrant merely because of the legality of an arrest. I have yet to hear the answer to Judge Learned Hand's reasoning below that to make the validity of a search

> depend upon the presence of the party in the premises searched at the time of the arrest . . . would make crucial a circumstance that has no rational relevance to the purposes of the privilege. The feelings which lie behind it have their basis in the resentment, inevitable in a free society, against the invasion of a man's privacy without some judicial sanction. It is true that when one has been arrested in his home or his office, his privacy has already been invaded; but that interest, though lost, is altogether separate from the interest in protecting his papers from indiscriminate rummage, even though both are customarily grouped together as parts of the "right of privacy." . . . The history of the two privileges is altogether different; the Fourth Amendment distinguishes between them; and in statutes they have always been treated as depending upon separate conditions.

This brings me to a consideration of the right of search and seizure "incident to arrest." Undue haste in coming to that issue too readily leads to getting off the track of the Fourth Amendment. The Government argued as though the Constitution said search of premises may be at large whenever an arrest is made in them. The utterly free hand, for all practical purposes, this gives the arresting officers to rummage all over the house is, I think, inevitable unless the basis of any right to search as an incident to arrest is put in proper focus. Photographs can be so taken as to make a midget look like a giant, and vice versa. The same kind of distortion results if a legal doctrine embedded in a larger matrix of principle is taken out of the matrix and elevated to an independent position. In plain English, the right to search incident to arrest is merely one of those very narrow exceptions to the "guaranties and immunities which we had inherited from our English ancestors, and which had from time immemorial been subject to certain well-recognized exceptions arising from the necessities of the case." . . .

What, then, is the exception to the prohibition by the Fourth Amendment of search without a warrant in case of a legal arrest, whether the arrest is on a warrant or based on the historic right of arrest without a warrant if a crime is committed in the presence of the arrester? The exception may in part be a surviving incident of the historic role of "hue and cry" in early Anglo-Saxon law. . . . Its basic roots, however, lie in necessity. What is the necessity? Why is search of the arrested person permitted? For two reasons: first, in order to protect the arresting officer and to deprive the prisoner of potential means of escape, . . . and, secondly, to avoid destruction of evidence by the arrested person. . . . From this it follows that officers may search and seize not only the things physically on the person arrested, but those within his immediate physical control. What a farce it makes of the whole Fourth Amendment to say that because for many legal purposes everything in a man's house is under his control, therefore his house—his rooms—may be searched. Of course in this field of law, as in others, opinions sometimes use language not with fastidious precision. Apart from such instances of loose use of language, the doctrine of search incidental to arrest has, until very recently, been strictly confined to the necessities of the situation, i.e., the search of the person and those immediate physical surroundings which may fairly be deemed to be an extension of his person. . . .

Another exception to the constitutional prohibition of unreasonable searches is likewise rooted in necessity. The search without a warrant of moving objects—vehicles and vessels—was sanctioned in *Carroll* v. *United States,* 267 US 132, . . . on the ground that "it is not practicable to secure a warrant because the vehicle can be quickly moved out of the locality or jurisdiction in which the warrant must be sought." . . . Furthermore, the limits of the exception were carefully defined in terms of necessity, for the Court added:

> In cases where the securing of a warrant is reasonably practicable, it must be used, and when properly supported by affidavit and issued after judicial approval protects the seizing officer against a suit for damages. In cases where seizure is impossible except without warrant, the seizing officer acts unlawfully and at his peril unless he can show the court probable cause. . . .

Even as to moving vehicles, this Court did not lay down an absolute rule dispensing with a search warrant. It limited dispensation to the demands of necessity, where want of time precluded the obtaining of a warrant. The necessity founded on the time factor which guided the Court in the *Carroll Case* cannot justify the search here made of the respondent's premises, for there was ample time to obtain a warrant before the arrest and even on the occasion of the arrest. . . .

With only rare deviations, such as today's decision, this Court has con-

strued the Fourth Amendment "liberally to safeguard the right of privacy."
. . . The guiding line in dealing with the Fourth Amendment [and Fifth
Amendment] was set forth in *Gouled* v. *United States*, 255 US 298:

> It would not be possible to add to the emphasis with which the
> framers of our Constitution and this court (in *Boyd* v. *United States*,
> 116 US 616, in *Weeks* v. *United States*, 232 US 383, and in *Silver-
> thorne Lumber Co.* v. *United States*, 251 US 385) have declared the
> importance to political liberty and to the welfare of our country of the
> due observance of the rights guaranteed under the Constitution by
> these two Amendments. The effect of the decisions cited is: that such
> rights are declared to be indispensable to the "full enjoyment of per-
> sonal security, personal liberty and private property"; that they are to
> be regarded as of the very essence of constitutional liberty; and that the
> guaranty of them is as important and as imperative as are the guaran-
> ties of the other fundamental rights of the individual citizen,—the
> right to trial by jury, to the writ of habeas corpus and to due process
> of law. It has been repeatedly decided that these Amendments should
> receive a liberal construction, so as to prevent stealthy encroachment
> upon or "gradual depreciation" of the rights secured by them, by im-
> perceptible practice of courts or by well-intentioned but mistakenly
> over-zealous executive officers. . . .

If the exception of search without a warrant incidental to a legal arrest is
extended beyond the person and his physical extension, search throughout
the house necessarily follows. I am aware that most differences in the law
depend on differences of degree. But differences though of degree must
not be capricious; the differences must permit rational classification. If upon
arrest you may search beyond the immediate person and the very restricted
area that may fairly be deemed part of the person, what rational line can
be drawn short of searching as many rooms as arresting officers may deem
appropriate for finding "the fruits of the crime"? Is search to be restricted
to the room in which the person is arrested but not to another open room
into which it leads? Or, take a house or an apartment consisting largely of
one big room serving as dining room, living room and bedroom. May search
be made in a small room but not in such a large room? If you may search
the bedroom part of a large room, why not a bedroom separated from the
dining room by a partition? These are not silly hard cases. They put the
principle to a test. The right to search an arrested person and to take the
stuff on top of the desk at which he sits has a justification of necessity which
does not eat away the great principle of the Fourth Amendment. But to
assume that this exception of a search incidental to arrest permits a free-
handed search without warrant is to subvert the purpose of the Fourth
Amendment by making the exception displace the principle. History and
the policy which it represents alike admonish against it. . . .

To tear "unreasonable" from the context and history and purpose of the
Fourth Amendment in applying the narrow exception of search as an incident to an arrest is to disregard *the* reason to which reference must be made

when a question arises under the Fourth Amendment. It is to make the arrest an incident to an unwarranted search instead of a warrantless search an incident to an arrest. The test by which searches and seizures must be judged is whether conduct is consonant with the main aim of the Fourth Amendment. The main aim of the Fourth Amendment is against invasion of the right of privacy as to one's effects and papers without regard to the result of such invasion. The purpose of the Fourth Amendment was to assure that the existence of probable cause as the legal basis for making a search was to be determined by a judicial officer before arrest and not after, subject only to what is necessarily to be excepted from such requirement. The exceptions cannot be enthroned into the rule. The justification for intrusion into a man's privacy was to be determined by a magistrate uninfluenced by what may turn out to be a successful search for papers, the desire to search for which might be the very reason for the Fourth Amendment's prohibition. The framers did not regard judicial authorization as a formal requirement for a piece of paper. They deemed a man's belongings part of his personality and his life. . . .

By the Bill of Rights the founders of this country subordinated police action to legal restraints not in order to convenience the guilty but to protect the innocent. Nor did they provide that only the innocent may appeal to these safeguards. They knew too well that the successful prosecution of the guilty does not require jeopardy to the innocent. The knock at the door under the guise of a warrant of arrest for a venial or spurious offense was not unknown to them. . . . We have had grim reminders in our day of their experience. Arrest under a warrant for a minor or a trumped-up charge has been familiar practice in the past, is a commonplace in the police state of today, and too well-known in this country. . . . The progress is too easy from police action unscrutinized by judicial authorization to the police state. The founders wrote into the Constitution their conviction that law enforcement does not require the easy but dangerous way of letting the police determine when search is called for without prior authorization by a magistrate. They have been vindicated in that conviction. It may safely be asserted that crime is most effectively brought to book when the principles underlying the constitutional restraints upon police action are most scrupulously observed.

The highly experienced [Wickersham] Commission on Law Observance and Enforcement appointed by President Hoover spoke of "the high standards of conduct exacted by Englishmen of the police." . . . It is suggested that we cannot afford the luxury of such theoretically desirable subordination of the police to law because greater obedience to law is part of English life generally. I do not think that acceptance of lower standards than those prevailing in England should be written by us into law. That only serves to encourage low standards, not to elevate them. It is unfair to our people to suggest that they cannot attain as high standards as do the British in guarding against police excesses without impairing effective means for combatting crime. Experience proves that it is a counsel of despair to assume that the police cannot be kept within the bounds of the principles which the Fourth and Fifth Amendments embody except at the cost of impotence in preventing crime and dealing sternly with its commission.

In the case before us there is not the slightest suggestion that the arresting officers had not the time to secure a search warrant. The arrest and search were made on February 16, 1943. On February 1, there was strong evidence that respondent had in his possession large numbers of stamps bearing forged overprints. . . . On February 6, a postal employee purchased from respondent four stamps bearing overprints and, on February 9, reports were received showing the overprints to be forgeries. Thus, the Government had at least seven, and more accurately fifteen, days in which to procure a search warrant. Nor was this a case in which the need for a search became apparent at the time of arrest. The arresting officers were accompanied by two stamp experts, whose sole function was to examine the fruits of the search which they knew would be made. This is hardly a natural description of a "search incidental to an arrest."

It is most relevant that the officers had "no excuse for not getting a search warrant," . . . for that is precisely what the Fourth Amendment was directed against—that some magistrate and not the police officer should determine, if such determination is not precluded by necessity, who shall be rummaging around in my room, whether it be a small room or a very large room, whether it be one room, or two rooms, or three rooms, or four rooms. . . .

4. Wire Tapping

SCHWARTZ v. TEXAS

344 US 199 (1953)

[The Federal Communications Act provides that "no person not being authorized by the sender shall intercept any communication and divulge or publish the existence, contents, substance, purport, effect, or meaning of such intercepted communication to any person." In *Nardone* v. *United States,* 302 US 379 (1937), the Court held that this statute renders inadmissible in a criminal trial in a federal court evidence procured by federal officers by tapping telephone wires and intercepting messages. As the law stands today, it is this statute and not the Fourth Amendment that bars the use of such evidence in federal courts.

[The statute bars not only evidence of conversations obtained through wire tapping, but also evidence made accessible by the use of information obtained by the wire tapping. But only a party to a wire-tapped conversation may object to its introduction in evidence.

[In the *Schwartz Case,* involving a trial in a state court, the Supreme Court held that the rule of inadmissibility of wire-tapped evidence does not apply to state courts; and courts in a majority of the states do admit such evidence.

[Only Justice Douglas dissented, maintaining that wire tapping is a search that violates the Fourth Amendment and that, therefore, the evidence obtained by it should be excluded.

[Justice Brandeis also thought that protection against wire tapping was within the guaranty of the Fourth Amendment; so did Justices Butler and Stone; and Justice Holmes spoke of wire tapping as a "dirty business" with which neither district attorney nor judges should have anything to do. *Olmstead* v. *United States,* 277 US 438 (1928).

[New York in 1942 adopted a statute that provides for supervised wire tapping. It was the first such law adopted in the United States.]

Mr. Justice Minton delivered the opinon of the Court:

The petitioner, Schwartz, a pawnbroker, entered into a conspiracy with Jarrett and Bennett whereby the latter two were to rob places to be designated by Schwartz and bring the loot to him to dispose of and divide the proceeds with them. Pursuant to the plan, Jarrett and Bennett robbed a woman in Dallas, Texas, of her valuable jewels and brought the loot to the petitioner. After the petitioner repeatedly delayed settlement with the robbers, the thieves finally fell out, which proved very helpful to the police. The petitioner tipped off the police where they could find Jarrett. After Jarrett had been in jail about two weeks, he consented to telephone the petitioner from the sheriff's office. With the knowledge and consent of Jarrett, a professional operator set up an induction coil connected to a recorder amplifier which enabled the operator to overhear and simultaneously to record the telephone conversations between Jarrett and the petitioner. These records were used as evidence before the jury that tried and convicted the petitioner as an accomplice to the crime of robbery. The records, admitted only after Jarrett and the petitioner had testified, corroborated Jarrett and discredited the petitioner. The Court of Criminal Appeals of Texas upheld the conviction. . . .

Petitioner contends that § 605 of the Federal Communications Act makes inadmissible in evidence the records of intercepted telephone conversations without the petitioner's consent. The pertinent provision of the statute reads as follows: ". . . no person not being authorized by the sender shall intercept any communication and divulge or publish the existence, contents, substance, purport, effect, or meaning of such intercepted communication to any person. . . ." Section 501 of 47 U.S.C. provides a penalty for the violation of § 605.

We are dealing here only with the application of a federal statute to state proceedings. Without deciding, but assuming for the purposes of this case, that the telephone communications were intercepted without being authorized by the sender within the meaning of the Act, the question we have is whether these communications are barred by the federal statute, § 605, from use as evidence in a criminal proceeding in a state court.

We think not. Although the statute contains no reference to the admissibility of evidence obtained by wire tapping, it has been construed to render inadmissible in a court of the United States communications intercepted and sought to be divulged in violation thereof, . . . and this is true even though the communications were intrastate telephone calls. . . . Although the intercepted calls would be inadmissible in a federal court, it does not follow that such evidence is inadmissible in a state court. Indeed, evidence obtained by a state officer by means which would constitute an unlawful search and seizure under the Fourth Amendment to the Federal Constitution is nonetheless admissible in a state court, . . . while such evidence, if obtained by a federal officer, would be clearly inadmissible in a federal court. . . . The problem under § 605 is somewhat different because the introduction of the intercepted communications would itself be a violation of the statute, but in the absence of an expression by Congress, this is simply an additional factor for a state to consider in formulating a rule of evidence for use in its own courts. Enforcement of the statutory prohibition in § 605 can be achieved under the penal provisions of § 501.

This question has been many times before the state courts, and they have uniformly held that § 605 does not apply to exclude such communications from evidence in state courts. . . . While these cases are not controlling here, they are entitled to consideration because of the high standing of the courts from which they come.

Texas itself has given consideration to the admissibility of evidence obtained in violation of constitutional or statutory law and has carefully legislated concerning it. In 1925 Texas enacted a statute providing that evidence obtained in violation of the Constitution or laws of Texas or of the United States should not be admissible against the accused in a criminal case. In 1929 this section 727a of the Texas Code of Criminal Procedure was amended to provide that evidence obtained in violation of the Constitution or laws of Texas or the *Constitution* of the United States should be inadmissible in evidence, thus eliminating from the coverage of the statute evidence obtained in violation of the laws of the United States. . . .

It is due consideration but not controlling that Texas has legislated in this field. Our decision would be the same if the Texas courts had pronounced this rule of evidence.

We hold that § 605 applies only to the exclusion in federal court proceedings of evidence obtained and sought to be divulged in violation thereof; it does not exclude such evidence in state court proceedings. Since we do not believe that Congress intended to impose a rule of evidence on the state courts, we do not decide whether it has the power to do so.

Since the statute is not applicable to state proceedings, we do not have to decide the questions of what amounts to "interception," or whether if there was interception, the sender had authorized it. These questions can arise only in a federal court proceeding.

The judgment is affirmed. . . .

Mr. Justice Douglas, dissenting:

Since, in my view (as indicated in my dissent in *On Lee* v. *United States*, 343 U.S. 747) this wiretapping was a search that violated the Fourth Amendment, the evidence obtained by it should have been excluded. The question whether the Fourth Amendment is applicable to the states . . . probably need not be reached, because a Texas statute has excluded evidence obtained in violation of the Federal Constitution. Therefore I would reverse the judgment. It is true that the prior decisions of the Court point to affirmance. But those decisions reflect constructions of the Constitution which I think are erroneous. They impinge severely on the liberty of the individual and give the police the right to intrude into the privacy of any life. The practices they sanction have today acquired a momentum that is so ominous I cannot remain silent and bow to the precedents that sanction them.

5. Double Jeopardy

BROCK v. NORTH CAROLINA

344 US 424 (1953)

[The Fifth Amendment provides that no person shall be subject "to be twice put in jeopardy of life or limb" for the same offense. This provision prohibits a second prosecution for the same crime, whether the accused was convicted or acquitted at the previous trial. If a trial is started and discontinued without a verdict, such discontinuance may or may not bar a second trial; this question is discussed in the present case. A single transaction may give rise to several offenses; there is no identity of offenses if different evidence is required to sustain the different charges; in such a case the person may be tried for the different offenses; thus a person may be tried for a substantive offense and may be tried another time for conspiracy to commit the substantive offense; e.g., espionage and conspiracy to commit espionage as in the

Judith Coplon Cases, 185 F. 2d 629 (1950) and 191 F. 2d 749 (1951). Where the same act is an offense against both the state and the Federal Government, the accused may be prosecuted and punished by each. *Jerome* v. *United States,* 318 US 101 (1943).

[The constitutional guaranty against double jeopardy does not restrict the states. But when a state puts a person in double jeopardy that is "so acute and shocking that our polity will not endure it," or where the double jeopardy violates "fundamental principles of liberty and justice," then the state violates the Due Process Clause of the Fourteenth Amendment. *Palko* v. *Connecticut,* 302 US 319 (1937).

[In the present case, involving a state trial, the Court, by a vote of 6 to 2—Justice Black did not participate—held that the state procedure did not violate due process: the kind of double jeopardy to which the defendant was subjected was not one that resulted in unendurable hardship or in violation of fundamental principles of justice and liberty. Chief Justice Vinson and Justice Douglas dissented.]

Mr. Justice Minton delivered the opinion of the Court:

The petitioner and two others, Jim Cook and Elmer Matthews, employees on strike from a mill at Tarboro, North Carolina, were arrested for firing five shots from a passing auto into the house of a watchman at the mill, J. D. Wyatt. Wyatt's house was occupied at the time of the shooting by himself, his wife, his daughter and son-in-law, and the latter couple's baby. After the shooting, the petitioner and Cook and Matthews were taken to the jail. In the presence of the sheriff, a police officer, and the petitioner, Cook stated that the petitioner had helped plan the assault and had fired the shots.

Cook and Matthews were tried first and were found guilty of assault with a deadly weapon. Before judgments were entered on their convictions, the petitioner was placed on trial. The State put three witnesses on the stand, the sheriff, the police officer, and Wyatt's son-in-law. The State then put Cook and Matthews on the stand, intending to use their testimony to corroborate that of the other three witnesses. Cook and Matthews refused to answer the questions of the State on the ground that such answers might tend to incriminate them, and their counsel informed the court that in the event of an adverse judgment on their convictions, they would appeal therefrom to the Supreme Court of North Carolina. The trial court upheld their refusal to answer. The State represented to the court that the testimony of Cook and Matthews was necessary for the State to present its case fully before the jury, and moved that the court withdraw a juror from the sworn panel and declare a mistrial. The court did so, stating:

being of the opinion that the ends of justice require that the State have available for its testimony of the witnesses Jim Cook and Elmer Matthews when the case is tried and that the State is entitled to have those witnesses to testify after their cases have been disposed of in the Supreme Court, in its discretion withdraws a juror . . . and orders a mistrial of this case and that the same be continued.

The petitioner objected.

The Supreme Court of North Carolina affirmed the convictions of Cook and Matthews. . . . The State then proceeded to impanel a jury for the second time, and this time it tried the petitioner to conclusion before this panel. He objected that to do so would place him in jeopardy a second time and thus deny him due process of law, contrary to the provisions of the Fourteenth Amendment to the Constitution of the United States. His objection was overruled, and he was placed on trial. Cook testified as a witness for the State. The petitioner was found guilty and sentenced to two years' imprisonment. . . .

North Carolina has said there is no double jeopardy because the trial court has the discretion to declare a mistrial and require the defendant to be presented before another jury if it be in the interest of justice to do so. This has long been the common-law rule in North Carolina. . . .

The question whether such a procedure would be double jeopardy under the Fifth Amendment to the Constitution of the United States is not raised in this case, as the Fifth Amendment applies only to federal jurisdictions. . . .

The question before us is whether the requirement that the defendant shall be presented for trial before a second jury for the same offense violates due process of law as required of the State under the Fourteenth Amendment. The question has been here before under different circumstances. In *Palko* v. *Connecticut*, 302 U.S. 319, the defendant was first tried for murder in the first degree and was found guilty of murder in the second degree. Pursuant to a statute of Connecticut, the State appealed and obtained a reversal for errors of law at the trial. The defendant was retried, convicted of murder in the first degree, and sentenced to death. An appeal to this Court raised the question whether or not the requirement that he stand trial a second time for the same offense placed him twice in jeopardy, in violation of due process.

This Court held that the State had not denied the defendant due process of law. In order to indicate the nature of due process, this Court asked two questions:

Is that kind of double jeopardy to which the statute has subjected him a hardship so acute and shocking that our polity will not endure it? Does it violate those "fundamental principles of liberty and justice which lie at the base of all our civil and political institutions"? . . . The answer surely must be "no." . . .

Here the answer must be the same.

This Court has long favored the rule of discretion in the trial judge to declare a mistrial and to require another panel to try the defendant if the ends of justice will be best served. . . . Justice to either or both parties may indicate to the wise discretion of the trial judge that he declare a mistrial and require the defendant to stand trial before another jury. As in all cases involving what is or is not due process, so in this case, no hard and fast rule can be laid down. The pattern of due process is picked out in the facts and circumstances of each case. The pattern here, long in use in North Carolina, does not deny the fundamental essentials of a trial, "the very essence of a scheme of ordered justice," which is due process.

The judgment is affirmed.

Mr. Justice Frankfurter, concurring:

Once it is agreed that the claim here made—freedom from being tried a second time on a criminal charge—must be tested by the independent scope of the Due Process Clause of the Fourteenth Amendment and not on the basis of the incorporation of the Fifth Amendment into the Fourteenth, the application of the guarantee of due process to a specific situation makes relevant the specific phrasing of a common result. I, therefore, deem it appropriate to add a word to the Court's opinion, in which I join.

The judicial history of the Fifth Amendment in prohibiting any person from being "subject for the same offence to be twice put in jeopardy of life or limb" serves as a good pragmatic confirmation of the compelling reasons why the original Bill of Rights was found to limit the actions of the Federal Government and not those of the States. . . . A State falls short of its obligation when it callously subjects an individual to successive retrials on a charge on which he has been acquitted or prevents a trial from proceeding to a termination in favor of the accused merely in order to allow a prosecutor who has been incompetent or casual or even ineffective to see if he cannot do better a second time.

Unless we can say that the trial judge was not justified in the circumstances of this case in concluding that the ground for requesting a mistrial was fair and not oppressive to the accused, we would not be warranted in finding that the State of North Carolina, through its Supreme Court, denied the petitioner due process of law. The record does not seem to me to justify such a finding.

Mr. Chief Justice Vinson, dissenting:

. . . For the first time in the history of this Court, it is urged that a state could grant a mistrial in order that it might present a stronger case at some later trial and, in so doing, avoid a plea of former jeopardy in the second trial.

The Solicitor had convicted two defendants engaged in the same crime, by the testimony of Wyatt, Hathaway and Bardin, the sheriff. Cook and Matthews had refused to testify in their own behalf in that trial. Immediately the first Brock trial followed. The judgment of conviction against Cook and Matthews had not been entered. No motion for a continuance appears in the record. The State willingly entered upon the trial. It had all the witnesses and the evidence which had convicted Cook and Matthews of the same crime. It presented that evidence. Cook and Matthews refused to testify on the ground of self-incrimination, and the court sustained their position. Under the circumstances, the Solicitor either knew or should have known that Cook and Matthews would not testify. After all the State's evidence was in, and after Cook and Matthews refused to testify, the Solicitor moved for a mistrial. The basis for his motion was that the State would, at a later date, be able to present a stronger case against Brock since Cook and Matthews might, at a later date, testify differently or to additional facts than at the first trial. It must be remembered that they had not testified at any trial. The court sustained the motion that a juror be withdrawn and a mistrial ordered and the case continued pending the final judgment in the case against Matthews and Cook. The court stated it was of the opinion that "the ends of justice require that the State have available for its testimony of the witnesses Jim Cook and Elmer Matthews when the case is tried and that the State is entitled to have those witnesses to testify after their cases have been disposed of in the Supreme Court."

The sole question is whether the record in this case presents an offense to fundamental fairness and due process. Under the results reached by the Court, the state is free, if the prosecutor thinks a conviction probably cannot be won from the jury on the testimony at the trial, to stop the trial and insist that it be tried again on another day when it has stronger men on the field.

Orderly justice could not be secured if the rules allowed the defendant to ask for a mistrial at the conclusion of testimony just because the state had done well and the defense poorly. The same limitation applies to the prosecution if the scales of justice are to be kept in equal balance. This Court recently has said that, in applying the concept of due process of law, judges are not at large to apply their own personal standards. . . . Thus, the considered views of many other jurisdictions may be utilized in determining the basic requirements of orderly justice and hence due process. . . .

While the technical ramifications evolved in the many jurisdictions as part of the doctrine of double jeopardy do not fall within the scope of due process, the basic idea is part of our American concept of fundamental fairness. This is shown by the universality of the provision against double jeopardy. The Fifth Amendment to the Federal Constitution, inapplicable here, prohibits double jeopardy. The Constitutions of all but five states, Connecticut, Maryland, Massachusetts, North Carolina, and Vermont, contain clauses forbidding double jeopardy. And each of those five states have the prohibition against double jeopardy as part of their common law.

No case in any other jurisdiction to support North Carolina's action in this case has been pointed out to us, and my research fails to find a single prop supporting its position. On the other hand, eight states have had occasion to rule on whether there might be a second trial after the prosecutor at a previous trial was unable to present evidence. Six have taken a firm position against allowing a second trial. A seventh, Iowa, is in accord with the above view, for language to the contrary in two other Iowa cases is not in point since the mistrials in those two cases were upon the motion of the defendant. In Alabama, the eighth state, two cases have permitted a second trial. Both of those cases, however, involved facts of such extreme nature that it would have been shocking to the conscience not to permit a second trial. In one of the cases, the Alabama Supreme Court even indicated the result probably would be different if the prosecutor merely had been unprepared at the first trial.

The rule to be gleaned from the cases is that a second trial will be allowed only for extreme circumstances, often contributed to by the defendant and beyond the control of the prosecutor, which prevented the testimony from being available at the first trial. Only North Carolina has clear precedent allowing a second trial when the prosecutor simply failed to have his evidence ready at the first trial.

It may be considered that this being a noncapital felony that the considered action of the judiciary of a state should be followed when it is said it is in the furtherance of justice. It certainly is the easy way out, but in view of the fact that no other state in the Union has gone to this extreme of the North Carolina rule, I must ponder upon it and conclude that the hard-won victory achieved in the field of "double jeopardy" ought not be lost even in a small part by the affirmance of this case.

The Attorney General of North Carolina relies upon *Palko* v. *Connecticut* . . . in support of his position that the second trial of this defendant did not violate due process. In *Palko*, there was an appeal by the State, as allowed by statute. The Supreme Court of Connecticut found three errors prejudicial to the State committed by the trial court, and reversed the judgment and ordered a new trial. The second trial then followed. In the case before the Court, no error of law tainted the first trial. . . .

Certainly, *Palko* did not decide the issue in this case. In that case, under a state statute, the State was asking for a second trial to obtain a trial free from error by the court prejudicial to the State. Here, the State asks for its second trial in order to suit the convenience of the Solicitor in an endeavor to strengthen the State's case, when the defendant had done nothing either to bring about trial errors or to inveigle or entrap the Solicitor to proceed to the first trial.

While this case is not controlled by *Palko*, I am comforted by language found in it which, in my view, envisions this case as one which might well be within the protective embrace of the Due Process Clause of the Fourteenth Amendment. Speaking for the Court, Justice Cardozo said:

> What the answer would have to be if the state were permitted after a trial free from error to try the accused over again or to bring another

case against him, we have no occasion to consider. We deal with the statute before us and no other. The state is not attempting to wear the accused out by a multitude of cases with accumulated trials. It asks no more than this, that the case against him shall go on until there shall be a trial free from the corrosion of substantial legal error.

I submit there was no manifest necessity to discharge this jury after the State had proceeded to trial and offered all its evidence, and I submit that the ordering of a mistrial here for the convenience of the State does not promote the ends of public justice.

Mr. Justice Douglas, dissenting:

In 1795, when the reasons for the guarantee against double jeopardy were still fresh in men's minds, a North Carolina court stated the basis for not allowing the prosecution to have a jury discharged so that it could obtain better evidence against the accused.

> The rule as laid down in 3 Coke Inst., 110, and 1 Inst., 227, is general and without exception that a jury in a capital case cannot be discharged without giving a verdict. Afterwards, however, in the reigns of the latter sovereigns of the Stuart family, a different rule prevailed, that a jury in such case might be discharged for the purpose of having better evidence against him at a future day; and this power was exercised for the benefit of the crown only; but it is a doctrine so abhorrent to every principle of safety and security that it ought not to receive the least countenance in the courts of this country. In the time of James II, and since the Revolution, this doctrine came under examination, and the rule as laid down by my Lord Coke was revived with this addition, that a jury should not be discharged in a capital case unless for the benefit of the prisoner; as if the prisoner be a woman and be taken in labor; or if the prisoner after the jury are charged with him be found to be insane, and the like; or if at the prisoner's request a jury be withdrawn to let him in to take the benefit of an exception, which otherwise he would have lost. . . . In the present case the jury were suffered by the court's officer to separate without giving a verdict. As they could not agree to convict, it is strong evidence of the party's innocence; and perhaps he could not be tried again with the same advantage to himself as then. Perhaps his witnesses are dead, or gone away, or their attendance not to be procured, or some accident may prevent their attendance. We will not again put his life in jeopardy, more especially as it is very improbable we shall be able to possess him of the same advantages. *State* v. *Garrigues,* 2 N.C. 241.

That point of view should shape our conception of double jeopardy and due process of law. Once the prosecution can call a halt in the middle of a trial in order to await a more favorable time, or to find new evidence, or to make up the deficiencies in the testimony of its witnesses, the promise of protection against double jeopardy loses the great force it was thought to have when the Constitution was written. At that time the practices of the Stuarts were freshly in mind. And it was resolved that they should not reach these shores.

6. Self-Incrimination—The Privilege of Immunity

ADAMSON v. CALIFORNIA

332 US 46 (1947)

[A clause of the Fifth Amendment provides that a person may not be "compelled in any criminal case to be a witness against himself." In a criminal case in the *federal* courts the defendant need not take the witness stand to deny or explain evidence against him, and no court official may comment adversely on his refusal or failure to testify in his own behalf. In this case the Court held that this privilege against compulsory testimony, and against adverse comment when a defendant exercises the privilege, does not apply to trials in *state* courts. The Fourteenth Amendment does not protect all the rights of the Bill of Rights against state action. Under the Fourteenth Amendment a defendant in a state court is entitled to a fair trial; a denial of the privilege of immunity from self-incrimination is not a denial of a fair trial: the privilege may be denied and yet, as Justice Cardozo said in *Palko* v. *Connecticut*, 302 US 319 (1937), "justice still be done."

[All state constitutions, with the exception of New Jersey and Iowa, provide, however, for the privilege of freedom from self-incrimination; and in these two states the privilege exists by their common law. In some states, fair comment on a failure to testify is permitted. One of these states is California, where the *Adamson Case* originated.

[Much public attention was centered on the privilege in 1953 and 1954 because of its frequent use by witnesses called before congressional committees investigating subversive activities. Some public officials openly questioned the wisdom of the First Amendment privilege, and some witnesses were characterized as "Fifth Amendment Communists." The *Adamson Case* shows that constitutional authorities are divided on this question: Justices Black, Douglas, Murphy, and Rutledge dissented.

[It should be pointed out, however, that these dissenters put their main emphasis, not on the policy question—whether the privilege of immunity from self-incrimination must be considered essential to a fair trial—but rather on the historical issue—whether the Bill of Rights is to be considered as incorporated into the Fourteenth Amendment, so that the provisions of the first eight amendments are binding equally on the states and on the Federal Government. In a concurring opinion, Justice Frankfurter maintained that during the first seventy years following the adoption of the Fourteenth Amendment only one of the forty-three Justices who considered the scope of that amendment ever indicated a belief that the amendment incorporated the first eight amendments as restrictions upon the states. These Justices did not believe that it was inconsistent "with a truly free society to begin prosecutions without an indictment, to try petty civil cases without . . . a common law jury, to take into consideration that one who has full opportunity to make a defense remains silent. . . ." To think otherwise, said Frankfurter, is, "in de Tocqueville's phrase, to confound the familiar with the necessary." Against this argument Justice Black maintained, in a dissenting opinion, that the earlier cases had not appraised the historical evidence of the intended scope of the Fourteenth Amendment, and that such an examination would show that "one purpose of those who framed, advocated, and adopted the Amendment had been to make the Bill of Rights applicable to the States." (An appendix to his opinion offers the historical evidence for his conclusion.) "I fear to see," said Black, "the consequences of the Court's practice of substituting its own concepts of decency and fundamental justice for the language of the Bill of Rights as its point of departure in interpreting and enforcing that Bill of Rights." The possibility that the Court is wise enough to substitute "natural law concepts" for the Bill of Rights is, he said, "too speculative."]

Mr. Justice Reed delivered the opinion of the Court:

The appellant, Adamson, a citizen of the United States, was convicted, without recommendation for mercy, by a jury in a Superior Court of the State of California of murder in the first degree. After considering the same objections to the conviction that are pressed here, the sentence of death was affirmed by the Supreme Court of the state. . . . The provisions of California law which were challenged in the state proceedings as invalid under the Fourteenth Amendment to the Federal Constitution are those of the state constitution and penal code. . . . They permit the failure of a defendant to explain or to deny evidence against him to be commented upon by court and by counsel and to be considered by court and jury. The defendant did not testify. As the trial court gave its instructions and the District Attorney argued the case in accordance with the constitutional and statutory provisions just referred to, we have for decision the question of their constitutionality in these circumstances under the limitations of § 1 of the Fourteenth Amendment.

The appellant was charged in the information with former convictions for burglary, larceny and robbery and pursuant to § 1025, California Penal Code, answered that he had suffered the previous convictions. This answer barred allusion to these charges of convictions on the trial. Under California's interpretation of § 1025 of the Penal Code and § 2051 of the Code of Civil Procedure, however, if the defendant, after answering affirmatively charges alleging prior convictions, takes the witness stand to deny or explain away other evidence that has been introduced "the commission of these crimes could have been revealed to the jury on cross-examination to impeach his testimony." . . . This forces an accused who is a repeated offender to choose between the risk of having his prior offenses disclosed to the jury or of having it draw harmful inferences from uncontradicted evidence that can only be denied or explained by the defendant.

In the first place, appellant urges that the provision of the Fifth Amendment that no person "shall be compelled in any criminal case to be a witness against himself" is a fundamental national privilege or immunity protected against state abridgment by the Fourteenth Amendment or a privilege or immunity secured, through the Fourteenth Amendment, against deprivation by state action because it is a personal right, enumerated in the federal Bill of Rights.

Secondly, appellant relies upon the due process of law clause of the Fourteenth Amendment to invalidate the provisions of the California law, . . . and as applied (a) because comment on failure to testify is permitted, (b) because appellant was forced to forego testimony in person because of danger of disclosure of his past convictions through cross-examination and (c) because the presumption of innocence was infringed by the shifting of the burden of proof to appellant in permitting comment on his failure to testify.

We shall assume, but without any intention thereby of ruling upon the issue, that permission by law to the court, counsel and jury to comment upon and consider the failure of defendant "to explain or to deny by his testimony any evidence or facts in the case against him" would infringe defendant's privilege against self-incrimination under the Fifth Amendment if this were a trial in a court of the United States under a similar law. Such an assumption does not determine appellant's rights under the Fourteenth Amendment. It is settled law that the clause of the Fifth Amendment, protecting a person against being compelled to be a witness against himself, is not made effective by the Fourteenth Amendment as a protection against state action on the ground that freedom from testimonial compulsion is a right of national citizenship, or because it is a personal privilege or immunity secured by the Federal Constitution as one of the rights of man that are listed in the Bill of Rights.

The reasoning that leads to those conclusions starts with the unquestioned premise that the Bill of Rights, when adopted, was for the protection of the individual against the federal government and its provisions were inapplicable to similar actions done by the states. . . . With the adoption of the Fourteenth Amendment, it was suggested that the dual citizenship recognized by its first sentence, secured for citizens federal protection for their elemental privileges and immunities of state citizenship. The *Slaughter-House Cases* [16 Wall. (U.S.) 36, 21 L. Ed. 394] decided . . . that these rights, as privileges and immunities of state citizenship, remained under the sole protection of the state governments. This Court . . . has approved this determination. The power to free defendants in state trials from self-incrimination was specifically determined to be beyond the scope of the privileges and immunities clause of the Fourteenth Amendment in *Twining* v. *New Jersey*, 211 US 78. . . . "The privilege against self-incrimination may be withdrawn and the accused put upon the stand as a witness for the state." The *Twining Case* likewise disposed of the contention that freedom from testimonial compulsion, being specifically granted by the Bill of Rights, is a federal privilege or immunity that is protected by the Fourteenth Amendment against state invasion. This Court held that the inclusion in the Bill of Rights of this protection against the power of the national government did not make the privilege a federal privilege or immunity secured to citizens by the Constitution against state action. . . . After declaring that state and national citizenship coexist in the same person, the Fourteenth Amendment forbids a state from abridging the privileges and immunities of citizens of the United States. As a matter of words, this leaves a state free to abridge, within the limits of the due process clause, the privileges and immunities flowing from state citizenship. This reading of the Federal Constitution has heretofore found favor with the majority of this Court as a natural and logical interpretation. It accords with the constitutional doctrine of federalism by leaving to the states the responsibility of dealing with the privileges and immunities of their citizens except those inherent in national citizenship. It is the construction placed upon the amendment by justices whose own experience had given them contemporaneous knowledge of the purposes that led to the adoption of the Fourteenth Amendment. This construction has become embedded in our federal system as a functioning element in preserving the balance between national and state power. We reaffirm the conclusion of the *Twining* and *Palko* [*Palko* v. *Connecticut*, 302 U.S. 319] *Cases* that protection against self-incrimination is not a privilege or immunity of national citizenship.

Appellant secondly contends that if the privilege against self-incrimination is not a right protected by the privileges and immunities clause of the Fourteenth Amendment against state action, this privilege, to its full scope under the Fifth Amendment, inheres in the right to a fair trial. A right to a fair trial is a right admittedly protected by the due process clause of the Fourteenth Amendment. Therefore, appellant argues, the due process clause of the Fourteenth Amendment protects his privilege against self-incrimination. The due process clause of the Fourteenth Amendment, however, does not draw all the rights of the federal Bill of Rights under its protection. That contention was made and rejected in *Palko* v. *Connecticut.* . . . Nothing has been called to our attention that either the framers of the Fourteenth Amendment or the states that adopted intended its due process clause to draw within its scope the earlier amendments to the Constitution. *Palko* held that such provisions of the Bill of Rights as were "implicit in the concept of ordered liberty," . . . became secure from state interference by the clause. But it held nothing more.

Specifically, the due process clause does not protect, by virtue of its mere existence, the accused's freedom from giving testimony by compulsion in state trials that is secured to him against federal interference by the Fifth Amendment. . . . For a state to require testimony from an accused is not necessarily a breach of a state's obligation to give a fair trial. Therefore, we must examine the effect of the California law applied in this trial to see whether the comment on failure to testify violates the protection against state action that the due process clause does grant to an accused. The due process clause forbids compulsion to testify by fear of hurt, torture or exhaustion. It forbids any other type of coercion that falls within the scope of due process. California follows Anglo-American legal tradition in excusing defendants in criminal prosecutions from compulsory testimony. . . . That is a matter of legal policy and not because of the requirements of due process under the Fourteenth Amendment. So our inquiry is directed, not at the broad question of the constitutionality of compulsory testimony from the accused under the due process clause, but to the constitutionality of the provision of the California law that permits comment upon his failure to testify. It is, of course, logically possible that while an accused might be required, under appropriate penalties, to submit himself as a witness without a violation of due process, comment by judge or jury on inferences to be drawn from his failure to testify, in jurisdictions where an accused's privilege against self-incrimination is protected, might deny due process. For example, a statute might declare that a permitted refusal to testify would compel an acceptance of the truth of the prosecution's evidence.

Generally, comment on the failure of an accused to testify is forbidden in American jurisdictions. This arises from state constitutional or statutory provisions similar in character to the federal provisions. Fifth Amendment and 28 USCA § 632. . . . California, however, is one of a few states that permit limited comment upon a defendant's failure to testify. [The other states are New Jersey, Ohio, and Vermont.] That permission is narrow. The California law . . . authorizes comment by court and counsel upon the "failure of the defendant to explain or to deny by his testimony any evidence or facts in the case against him." This does not involve any presumption, rebuttable or irrebuttable, either of guilt or of the truth of any fact, that is offered in evidence. . . . It allows inferences to be drawn from proven facts. Because of this clause, the court can direct the jury's attention to whatever evidence there may be that a defendant could deny and the prosecution can argue as to inferences that may be drawn from the accused's failure to testify. . . . There is here no lack of power in the trial court to adjudge and no denial of a hearing. California has prescribed a method for advising the jury in the search for truth. However sound may be the legislative conclusion that an accused should not be compelled in any criminal case to be a witness against himself, we see no reason why comment should not be made upon his silence. It seems quite natural that when a defendant has opportunity to deny or explain facts and determines not to do so, the prosecution should bring out the strength of the evidence by commenting upon defendant's failure to explain or deny it. The prosecution evidence may be of facts that may be beyond the knowledge of the accused. If so, his failure to testify would have little if any weight. But the facts may be such as are necessarily in the knowledge of the accused. In that case a failure to explain would point to an inability to explain.

Appellant sets out the circumstances of this case, however, to show coercion and unfairness in permitting comment. The guilty person was not seen at the place and time of the crime. There was evidence, however, that entrance to the place or room where the crime was committed might have been obtained through a small door. It was freshly broken. Evidence showed that six fingerprints on the door were petitioner's. Certain diamond rings were missing from the deceased's possession. There was evidence that appellant, sometime after the crime, asked an unidentified person whether the latter would be interested in purchasing a diamond ring. As has been stated, the information charged other crimes to appellant and he admitted them. His argument here is that he could not take the stand to deny the evidence against him because he would be subjected to a cross-examination as to former crimes to impeach his veracity and the evidence so produced might well bring about his conviction. Such cross-examination is allowable in California. . . . Therefore, appellant contends the California statute permitting comment denies him due process.

It is true that if comment were forbidden, an accused in this situation could remain silent and avoid evidence of former crimes and comment upon his failure to testify. We are of the view, however, that a state may control such a situation in accordance with its own ideas of the most efficient administration of criminal justice. The purpose of due process is not to protect an accused against a proper conviction but against an unfair conviction. When evidence is before a jury that threatens conviction, it does not seem unfair to require him to choose between leaving the adverse evidence unexplained and subjecting himself to impeachment through disclosure of former crimes. Indeed, this is a dilemma with which any defendant may be faced. If facts, adverse to the defendant, are proven by the prosecution, there may be no way to explain them favorably to the accused except by a witness who may be vulnerable to impeachment on cross-examination. The defendant must then decide whether or not to use such a witness. The fact that the witness may also be the defendant makes the choice more difficult but a denial of due process does not emerge from the circumstances.

There is no basis in the California law for appellant's objection on due process or other grounds that the statutory authorization to comment on the failure to explain or deny adverse testimony shifts the burden of proof or the duty to go forward with the evidence. Failure of the accused to testify is not an admission of the truth of the adverse evidence. Instructions told the jury that the burden of proof remained upon the state and the presumption of innocence with the accused. Comment on failure to deny proven facts does not in California tend to supply any missing element of proof of guilt. . . . It only directs attention to the strength of the evidence for the prosecution or to the weakness of that for the defense. The Supreme Court of California called attention to the fact that the prosecutor's argument approached the borderline in a statement that might have been construed as asserting "that the jury should infer guilt solely from defendant's silence." That court felt that it was improbable the jury was misled into such an understanding of their power. We shall not interfere with such a conclusion. . . . [Judgment of conviction affirmed.]

Mr. Justice Murphy, with whom Mr. Justice Rutledge concurs, dissenting:
While in substantial agreement with the views of Mr. Justice Black, I have one reservation and one addition to make.

I agree that the specific guarantees of the Bill of Rights should be carried over intact into the first section of the Fourteenth Amendment. But I am not prepared to say that the latter is entirely and necessarily limited by the Bill of Rights. Occasions may arise where a proceeding falls so far short of conforming to fundamental standards of procedure as to warrant constitutional condemnation in terms of a lack of due process despite the absence of a specific provision in the Bill of Rights.

That point, however, need not be pursued here inasmuch as the Fifth Amendment is explicit in its provision that no person shall be compelled in any criminal case to be a witness against himself. That provision, as Mr. Justice Black demonstrates, is a constituent part of the Fourteenth Amendment.

Moreover, it is my belief that this guarantee against self-incrimination has been violated in this case. Under California law, the judge or prosecutor may comment on the failure of the defendant in a criminal trial to explain or deny any evidence or facts introduced against him. As interpreted and applied in this case, such a provision compels a defendant to be a witness against himself in one of two ways:

1. If he does not take the stand, his silence is used as the basis for drawing unfavorable inferences against him as to matters which he might reasonably be expected to explain. Thus he is compelled, through his silence, to testify against himself. And silence can be as effective in this situation as oral statements.

2. If he does take the stand, thereby opening himself to cross-examination, so as to overcome the effects of the provision in question, he is necessarily compelled to testify against himself. In that case, his testimony on cross-examination is the result of the coercive pressure of the provision rather than his own volition.

Much can be said pro and con as to the desirability of allowing comment on the failure of the accused to testify. But policy arguments are to no avail in the face of a clear constitutional command. This guarantee of freedom from self-incrimination is grounded on a deep respect for those who might prefer to remain silent before their accusers. To borrow language from *Wilson* v. *United States,* 149 US 60 . . . :

> It is not every one who can safely venture on the witness stand though entirely innocent of the charge against him. Excessive timidity, nervousness when facing others and attempting to explain transactions of a suspicious character, and offenses charged against him, will often confuse and embarrass him to such a degree as to increase rather than remove prejudices against him. It is not every one, however honest, who would, therefore, willingly be placed on the witness stand.

We are obliged to give effect to the principle of freedom from self-incrimination. That principle is as applicable where the compelled testimony is in the form of silence as where it is composed of oral statements. Accordingly, I would reverse the judgment below.

BLAU v. UNITED STATES
340 US 159 (1950)

[Under the protection of the Fifth Amendment, a witness in any official proceeding—a court trial, an administrative hearing, a congressional committee investigation—may refuse to answer any question if his answer might tend to incriminate him, that is, if it might be used against him in a criminal proceeding or might serve as a clue to evidence against him. The immunity extends also to a witness's papers which might incriminate him, but not to records which he was required by law to keep, as under OPA regulations.

[In the present case the Court held unanimously that the witness, claiming the privilege of immunity from self-incrimination, may refuse to answer questions concerning the Communist Party and her employment by it. While the Communist Party has not been outlawed and it is not illegal to be a member of the organization, membership may serve as a link in a chain of evidence that may lead to prosecution under federal law, as in the *Dennis Case*, above.]

Mr. Justice Black delivered the opinion of the Court:

In response to a subpoena, petitioner appeared as a witness before the United States District Court Grand Jury at Denver. There she was asked several questions concerning the Communist party of Colorado and her employment by it. Petitioner refused to answer these questions on the ground that the answers might tend to incriminate her. She was then taken before the district judge where the questions were again propounded and where she again claimed her constitutional privilege against self-incrimination and refused to testify. The district judge found petitioner guilty of contempt of court and sentenced her to imprisonment for one year. . . .

At the time petitioner was called before the grand jury, the Smith Act was on the statute books, making it a crime among other things to advocate knowingly the desirability of overthrow of the Government by force or violence; to organize or help to organize any society or group which teaches, advocates or encourages such overthrow of the Government; or to be or become a member of such a group with knowledge of its purposes. These provisions made future prosecution of petitioner far more than "a mere imaginary possibility." . . . She reasonably could fear that criminal charges might be brought against her if she admitted employment by the Communist Party or intimate knowledge of its workings. Whether such admissions by themselves would support a conviction under a criminal statute is immaterial. Answers to the questions asked by the grand jury would have furnished a link in the chain of evidence needed in a prosecution of petitioner for violation of (or conspiracy to violate) the Smith Act. Prior decisions of this court have clearly established that under such circumstances, the Constitution gives a witness the privilege of remaining silent. The attempt by the courts below to compel petitioners to testify runs counter to the Fifth Amendment as it has been interpreted from the beginning. . . .

Reversed.

ROGERS v. UNITED STATES

340 US 367 (1951)

[This case involves the question of waiver of the privilege of immunity from self-incrimination. Jane Rogers, when called as a witness before a grand jury, testified that she had been treasurer of the Communist Party of Denver, Colorado, and had been in possession of its membership and dues records. She testified that she had turned them over to another person, whom she refused to identify. The Court held that she had disclosed enough facts about her Communist activities to have waived the privilege, and so she was bound to answer the question about the recipient of the records.

[Justices Black, Frankfurter, and Douglas dissented on the ground that she had not knowingly waived the privilege, and that naming the recipient of the records might supply the Government with additional incriminating evidence, for her conviction under some federal statute, like the Smith Act, might depend upon the testimony of the persons she was asked to identify. (Justice Clark did not participate.)

[A witness may not claim immunity on the ground that his testimony might tend to disgrace him or otherwise render him infamous. 2 USCA 193.]

Mr. Chief Justice Vinson delivered the opinion of the Court:

This case arises out of an investigation by the regularly convened grand jury of the United States District Court for the District of Colorado. The books and records of the Communist Party of Denver were sought as necessary to that inquiry and were the subject of questioning by the grand jury. In September, 1948, petitioner, in response to a subpoena, appeared before the grand jury. She testified that she held the position of Treasurer of the Communist Party of Denver until January, 1948, and that, by virtue of her office, she had been in possession of membership lists and dues records of the Party. Petitioner denied having possession of the records and testified that she had turned them over to another. But she refused to identify the person to whom she had given the Party's books, stating to the court as her only reason:

"I don't feel that I should subject a person or persons to the same thing that I'm going through." The court thereupon committed petitioner to the custody of the marshal until ten o'clock the next morning, expressly advising petitioner of her right to consult with counsel.

The next day, counsel for petitioner informed the court that he had read the transcript of the prior day's proceedings and that, upon his advice, petitioner would answer the questions to purge herself of contempt. However, upon reappearing before the grand jury, petitioner again refused to answer the question. The following day she was again brought into court. Called before the district judge immediately after he had heard oral argument concerning the privilege against self-incrimination in another case, petitioner repeated her refusal to answer the question, asserting this time the privilege against self-incrimination. After ruling that her refusal was not prvileged, the district judge imposed a sentence of four months for contempt. . . .

If petitioner desired the protection of the privilege against self-incrimination, she was required to claim it. . . . The privilege "is deemed waived unless invoked." . . . Furthermore, the decisions of this Court are explicit in holding that the privilege against self-incrimination "is solely for the benefit of the witness," and "is purely a personal privilege of the witness." Petitioner expressly placed her original declination to answer on an untenable ground, since a refusal to answer cannot be justified by a desire to protect others from punishment, much less to protect another from interrogation by a grand jury. Petitioner's claim of the privilege against self-incrimination was pure afterthought. Although the claim was made at the time of her second refusal to answer in the presence of the court, it came only after she had voluntarily testified to her status as an officer of the Communist Party of Denver. To uphold a claim of privilege in this case would open the way to distortion of facts by permitting a witness to select any stopping place in the testimony.

The privilege against self-incrimination, even if claimed at the time the question as to the name of the person to whom petitioner turned over the Party records was asked, would not justify her refusal to answer. As a preliminary matter, we note that petitioner had no privilege with respect to the books of the party, whether it be a corporation or an unincorporated association. Books and records kept "in a representative rather than in a personal capacity cannot be the subject of the personal privilege against self-incrimination, even though production of the papers might tend to incriminate [their keeper] personally." *United States* v. *White*, 322 US 694. Since petitioner's claim of privilege cannot be asserted in relation to the books and records sought by the grand jury, the only claim for reversal of her conviction rests on the ground that mere disclosure of the name of the recipient of the books tends to incriminate.

In *Patricia Blau* v. *United States*, 340 US 159, we held that questions as to connections with the Communist Party are subject to the privilege against self-incrimination as calling for disclosure of facts tending to criminate under the Smith Act. But petitioner's conviction stands on an entirely different footing, for she had freely described her membership, activities and office in the Party. Since the privilege against self-incrimination presupposes a real danger of legal detriment arising from the disclosure, petitioner cannot invoke the privilege where response to the specific question in issue here would not further incriminate her. Disclosure of a fact waives the privilege as to details. . . .

Requiring full disclosure of details after a witness freely testifies as to a criminating fact does not rest upon a further "waiver" of the privilege against self-incrimination. Admittedly, petitioner had already "waived" her privilege of silence when she freely answered criminating questions relating to her connection with the Communist Party. But when petitioner was asked to furnish the name of the person to whom she turned over Party records, the court was required to determine, as it must whenever the privilege is claimed, whether the question presented a reasonable danger of further crimination in light of all the circumstances, including any previous disclosures. As to each question to which a claim of privilege is directed, the court must determine whether the answer to that particular question would subject the witness to a "real danger" of further crimination. After petitioner's admission that she held the office of Treasurer of the Communist Party of Denver, disclosure of acquaintance with her successor presents no more than a "mere imaginary possibility" of increasing the danger of prosecution.

Petitioner's contention in the Court of Appeals and in this Court has been that, conceding her prior voluntary crimination as to one element of proof of a Smith Act violation, disclosure of the name of the recipient of the Party records would tend to incriminate as to the different crime of conspiracy to violate the Smith Act. Our opinion in *Patricia Blau* v. *United States* explicitly rejects petitioner's argument for reversal here in its holding that questions relating to activities in the Communist Party are criminating both as to "violation of (and conspiracy to violate) the Smith Act." Of course, at least two persons are required to constitute a conspiracy, but the identity of the other members of the conspiracy is not needed, inasmuch as one person can be convicted of conspiring with persons whose names are unknown.

Affirmed. . . .

Mr. Justice Black, with whom Mr. Justice Frankfurter and Mr. Justice Douglas concur, dissenting:

Some people are hostile to the Fifth Amendment's provision unequivocally commanding that no United States official shall compel a person to be a witness against himself. They consider the provision as an outmoded relic of past fears generated by ancient inquisitorial practices that could not possibly happen here. For this reason the privilege to be silent is sometimes accepted as being more or less of a constitutional nuisance which the courts should abate whenever and however possible. Such an end could be achieved by two obvious judicial techniques: (1) narrow construction of the scope of the privilege; (2) broad construction of the doctrine of "waiver." Any attempt to use the first of these methods, however, runs afoul of approximately 150 years of precedent. . . . This Court has almost always construed the Amendment broadly on the view that compelling a person to convict himself of crime is "contrary to the principles of a free government" and "abhorrent to the instincts of an American"; that while such a coercive practice "may suit the purposes of despotic power . . . it cannot abide the pure atmosphere of political liberty and personal freedom."

The doctrine of waiver seems to be a more palatable but equally effective device for whittling away the protection afforded by the privilege, although I think today's application of that doctrine cannot be supported by our past decisions. Of course, it has never been doubted that a constitutional right could be *intentionally* relinquished and that such an intention might be found from a "course of conduct." . . . But we have said that intention to waive the privilege against self-incrimination is not "lightly to be inferred" and that vague and uncertain evidence will not support a finding of waiver. . . . In the case of this petitioner, there is no evidence that she intended to give up her privilege of silence concerning the persons in possession of the Communist Party records. To the contrary, the record—as set out in the Court's opinion—shows she intended to avoid answering the question on whatever ground might be available and asserted the privilege against self-incrimination at the first moment she became aware of its existence. This fact and the cases which make it crucial are ignored in the decision today.

Apparently the Court's holding is that at some uncertain point in petitioner's testimony, regardless of her intention, admission of associations with the Communist Party automatically effected a "waiver" of her constitutional protection as to all related questions. To adopt such a rule for the privilege against self-incrimination, when other constitutional safeguards must be knowingly waived, relegates the Fifth Amendment's privilege to a second-rate position. Moreover, today's holding creates this dilemma for witnesses: On the one hand, they risk imprisonment for contempt by asserting the privilege prematurely; on the other, they might lose the privilege if they answer a single question. The Court's view makes the protection depend on timing so refined that lawyers, let alone laymen, will have difficulty in knowing when to claim it. In this very case, it never occurred to the trial judge that petitioner waived anything. And even if voluntary testimony can under

some circumstances work a waiver, it did not do so here because what petitioner stated to the grand jury "standing alone did not amount to an admission of guilt or furnish clear proof of crime. . . ."

Furthermore, unlike the Court, I believe that the question which petitioner
refused to answer did call for additional incriminating information. She was
asked the names of the persons to whom she had turned over the Communist
Party books and records. Her answer would not only have been relevant in
any future prosecution of petitioner for violation of the Smith Act but also
her conviction might depend on testimony of the witnesses she was thus
asked to identify. For these reasons the question sought a disclosure which
would have been incriminating to the highest degree. Certainly no one can
say that the answer "[could not] possibly be used as a basis for, or in aid of,
a criminal prosecution against the witness. . . ." . . .

I would reverse the judgment of conviction.

ADAMS v. MARYLAND

347 US 179 (1954)

[There are statutes that grant witnesses complete immunity from
prosecution for any act regarding which the witness may be required
to testify before certain regulatory agencies. Such acts, if they grant
total immunity from prosecution, are constitutional. Congress in 1857
enacted such a statute granting total immunity to a witness testifying
before either House of Congress or a congressional committee; but in
1862 the act was amended to grant only partial immunity, so that only
a witness's testimony could not be used against him as evidence in a
criminal proceeding, but there might still be a criminal proceeding
against him based on the act or fact concerning which he was compelled to testify. This 1862 provision was re-enacted in 1948—18 USCA
3486. But this act is ineffective to compel witnesses to testify because it
grants only partial immunity. *United States* v. *Bryan,* 339 US 323
(1950); *Counselman* v. *Hitchcock,* 142 US 547 (1892).

[When, however, a witness appears before a congressional investigating committee in response to a summons served upon him and gives
self-incriminating testimony, the use of this testimony against him in a
federal or state prosecution is barred by the above-mentioned act of
Congress. This was the construction placed upon the act by the Supreme Court in the instant case. The decision was unanimous.]

Mr. Justice Black delivered the opinion of the Court:

In response to a summons the petitioner Adams appeared to testify
before a Senate Committee investigating crime. Answering questions
he confessed to having run a gambling business in Maryland. That confession has been used in this case to convict Adams of conspiring to

violate Maryland's anti-lottery laws. The trial court sentenced Adams
to pay a fine of $2,000 and serve seven years in the state penitentiary.
The Court of Appeals of Maryland affirmed, rejecting Adams' contention that use of the committee testimony against him was forbidden by
a provision in a federal statute. . . . That provision, now 18 U.S.C.
§ 3486, provides that no testimony given by a witness in congressional
inquiries "shall be used as evidence in any criminal proceeding against
him in any court. . . ." The Maryland Court of Appeals held that
Adams had testified before the Committee "voluntarily" and was therefore not protected by § 3486. We granted certiorari because a proper
understanding of the scope of this Section is of importance to the national government, to the states and to witnesses summoned before
congressional committees. . . . In this Court Maryland contends that
the Section does not bar use of Adams' testimony because: (1) He
waived the statutory "privilege" by testifying "voluntarily," meaning
that Adams failed to object to each committee question on the ground
of its tendency to incriminate him; (2) the Section should be construed
so as to apply to United States courts only. If these two statutory contentions are rejected, we are urged to hold that Congress is without
constitutional power to bar the use of congressional committee testimony in state courts.

(1) Circumstances may be conceivable under which statements
made in the presence of a congressional committee might not be protected by § 3486. For example, a person might voluntarily appear and
obtain permission to make a statement in a committee's presence,
wholly for his own advantage, and without ever being questioned by
the committee at all. But Adams did not testify before the Senate Committee under any such circumstances. He was not a volunteer. He was
summoned. Had he not appeared he could have been fined and sent
to jail. . . . Nor does the record show any spontaneous out-pouring
of testimony from him. The testimony Maryland used to convict him
was brought out by repeated committee questions. It is true that Adams
did not attempt to escape answering these questions by claiming a
constitutional privilege to refuse to incriminate himself. But no language
of the Act requires such a claim in order for a witness to feel secure
that his testimony will not be used to convict him of crime. Indeed, a
witness does not need any statute to protect him from the use of self-
incriminating testimony he is compelled to give over his objection. The
Fifth Amendment takes care of that without a statute. Consequently,
the construction of § 3486 here urged would limit its protection to that
already afforded by the Fifth Amendment, leaving the Section with no
effect whatever. We reject the contention that Adams' failure to claim

a constitutional privilege deprived him of the statutory protection of § 3486.

(2) Nor can we hold that the Act bars use of committee testimony in United States courts but not in state courts. The Act forbids use of such evidence "in any criminal proceeding in any court." Language could be no plainer. Even if there could be legislative history sufficiently strong to make "any court" mean United States courts only, there is no such history. The few scraps of legislative history pointed out tend to indicate that Congress was well aware that an ordinary person would read the phrase "in any court" to include state courts. To construe this phrase as having any other meaning would make the Act a trap for the unwary.

It is suggested, however, that regardless of the plain meaning of § 3486 as originally passed an event since its passage should cause us to give it an entirely different meaning. The Section stems from an 1857 Act of Congress designed to grant committee witnesses immunity from prosecution in order to compel them to give self-incriminating testimony despite the Fifth Amendment. Thirty-five years later in *Counselman* v. *Hitchcock*, 142 U.S. 547, this Court held that an act not providing "complete" immunity from prosecution is not broad enough to permit congressional committees to compel witnesses to give incriminating testimony. Section 3486 does not provide "complete" immunity. The original purpose of Congress to compel incriminating testimony has thus been frustrated. It is argued that Congress could not have intended to afford any immunity to criminals unless it was thereby enabled to compel them to testify about their crimes. Therefore, it is said, § 3486 should now be given the narrowest possible construction— made effective only when the Fifth Amendment privilege is claimed, and held applicable only to United States courts. Because Congress did not get all it hoped, we are urged to deny witnesses the protection the statute promises. But a court decision subsequent to an act's passage does not usually alter its original meaning. And we reject the implication that a general act of Congress is like a private contract which courts should nullify upon a showing of partial or total failure of consideration. Moreover, Congress has kept the statute in force more than sixty years since the *Counselman* decision. And in 1948 Congress reenacted the statute making changes deemed desirable to insure its continued usefulness. 52 Stat. 943. Our holding is that *Counselman* v. *Hitchcock* in no way impairs the protection afforded congressional witnesses by § 3486.

(3) Little need be said about the contention that Congress lacks power to bar state courts from convicting a person for crime on the basis

of evidence he has given to help the national legislative bodies carry on their governmental functions. Congress has power to summon witnesses before either House or before their committees. *McGrain* v. *Daugherty*, 273 U.S. 135. Article I of the Constitution permits Congress to pass laws "necessary and proper" to carry into effect its power to get testimony. § 8. We are unable to say that the means Congress has here adopted to induce witnesses to testify is not "appropriate" and "plainly adapted to that end." . . . And, since Congress in the legitimate exercise of its powers enacts "the supreme Law of the Land," state courts are bound by § 3486, even though it affects their rules of practice. . . .

Reversed and remanded with directions.

Mr. Justice Jackson, concurring:

I am in substantial agreement with the Court's opinion but differ in emphasis.

The only controlling fact for me is that this Act is on the federal statute books. What someone intended almost a century ago when it was passed, or in the 1890's when *Counselman* v. *Hitchcock* was decided, I do not know. Since the last event, some thirty Congresses have come and gone, something near 15,000 Congressmen have been elected, not allowing for re-election. How many of them knew of *Counselman* v. *Hitchcock*, how many felt frustrated by it, and how many would have vented their frustration by repeal, I do not know or care. Congress left the Act on the books, and it was there when this petitioner testified. The only question is what it would mean to a reasonably well-informed lawyer reading it.

I do not think it important whether petitioner was a "voluntary" or "involuntary" witness before the congressional Committee or whether he raised the question of his immunity under the Fifth Amendment. No such qualification appears in the Act. The whole object and usefulness of the statute is to relieve the witness of the risks which might induce him to withhold testimony from Congress. It is very customary for one who is asked for information to appear before a committee without requiring the formality of a subpoena. The Act does not strip one of its protection because he may be a cooperative, or even interested, witness; indeed, its purpose is to protect and thereby encourage cooperation instead of hesitation or resistance.

The statute seems as unambiguous as language can be. If words mean anything, the statute extends its protection to all witnesses, to all testimony, and in all courts. It is easy to see, as this case illustrates, the hazard a witness would run otherwise. A lawyer would be warranted from the face of this Act in advising the witness that he had nothing to fear from frank and complete disclosure to Congress. Thus the Act would have accomplished its obvious purpose of facilitating disclosure.

I cannot see the slightest doubt that Congress has power to enact the statute for that purpose. It does not take anything from Maryland. It does not say Maryland cannot prosecute petitioner; it just says she shall not put him to disadvantage on the trial by reason of his cooperation with Congress. It leaves Maryland with complete freedom to prosecute—she just has to work up her own evidence and cannot use that worked up by Congress. The protection to the witness does not extend beyond the testimony actually received. In this case, petitioner was convicted by the State on the admissions he made before the Senate Committee. Section 3486 was thereby violated, and the conviction should be reversed.

7. Self-Incrimination—Forced Confessions

ROCHIN v. CALIFORNIA

342 US 165 (1952)

[The defendant in this case swallowed capsules containing morphine. At the direction of the police, the defendant was forced to vomit up the capsules, which were then used as evidence against him. The Supreme Court unanimously set aside the conviction. In his opinion for the Court, Justice Frankfurter states that the police methods involved in the case offended "a sense of justice" and thus violated the Due Process Clause of the Fourteenth Amendment.   ·

[Justices Black and Douglas, in separate concurring opinions, maintained that the prohibition of self-incrimination in the Fifth Amendment was binding upon the states as well as upon the Federal Government, and that California had violated this prohibition. Said Justice Black: "I think a person is compelled to be a witness against himself not only when he is compelled to testify, but also when as here, incriminating evidence is forcibly taken from him by a contrivance of modern science." The majority's refusal to subject the states to the specific limitations or guarantees of the Bill of Rights, he argued, "must inevitably imperil all the individual liberty safeguards" that the Bill of Rights provides.

[A confession extorted by compulsion may not be used: the Court has rejected the claim that the effective administration of criminal justice requires the use of the rack and torture chamber, the thumb-screw, the wheel, solitary confinement, protracted questioning, fraud, collusion, trickery, subornation of perjury, false statements that mob violence is threatened, or questioning under powerful electric lights for hour after hour by relays of officials. Confessions procured under coercion, when the defendant is not in possession of his own will and self-control, offend "basic standards of justice"; such confessions are not premises from which "a civilized court" may infer guilt.

[Justices Frankfurter, Black, and Douglas have recently, however, found it necessary to dissent from decisions that have sustained convictions which to some extent may have been based on coerced confessions. They have said that the confessions would not have been admitted in the courts of England, Canada, Australia, or India; that admitting the confessions may tend to brutalize the police and affect the tone of the community; that the cases upholding the convictions have introduced a new regime of constitutional law "that should give every citizen pause"; that recent decisions of the Court involving coerced confessions have broken down "barriers that have heretofore stood in the way of secret and arbitrary action directed against persons suspected of crime or political unorthodoxy." See *Stein* v. *New York*, 346 U.S. 156 (1953).]

Mr. Justice Frankfurter delivered the opinion of the Court:

Having "some information that [the petitioner here] was selling narcotics," three deputy sheriffs of the County of Los Angeles, on the morning of July 1, 1949, made for the two-story dwelling house in which Rochin lived with his mother, common-law wife, brothers and sisters. Finding the outside door open, they entered and then forced open the door to Rochin's room on the second floor. Inside they found petitioner sitting partly dressed on the side of the bed, upon which his wife was lying. On a "night stand" beside the bed the deputies spied two capsules. When asked "Whose stuff is this?" Rochin seized the capsules and put them in his mouth. A struggle ensued, in the course of which the three officers "jumped upon him" and attempted to extract the capsules. The force they applied proved unavailing against Rochin's resistance. He was handcuffed and taken to a hospital. At the direction of one of the officers a doctor forced an emetic solution through a tube into Rochin's stomach against his will. This "stomach pumping" produced vomiting. In the vomited matter were found two capsules which proved to contain morphine.

Rochin was brought to trial before a California Superior Court, sitting without a jury, on the charge of possessing "a preparation of morphine" in violation of the California Health and Safety Code. Rochin was convicted and sentenced to sixty days' imprisonment. The chief evidence against him was the two capsules. They were admitted over petitioner's objection. . . .

In our federal system the administration of criminal justice is predominantly committed to the care of the States. The power to define crimes belongs to Congress only as an appropriate means of carrying into execution its limited grant of legislative powers. US Const Art 1, § 8, cl 18. Broadly speaking, crimes in the United States are what the laws of the individual States make them, subject to the limitations of Art 1 § 10 [1], in the original Constitution, prohibiting bills of attainder and ex post facto laws, and of the Thirteenth and Fourteenth Amendments.

These limitations, in the main, concern not restrictions upon the powers of the States to define crime, except in the restricted area where federal authority has preempted the field, but restrictions upon the manner in which the States may enforce their penal codes. Accordingly, in reviewing a State criminal conviction under a claim of right guaranteed by the Due Process Clause of the Fourteenth Amendment, from which is derived the most far-reaching and most frequent federal basis of challenging State criminal justice,

we must be deeply mindful of the responsibilities of the States for the enforcement of criminal laws, and exercise with due humility our merely negative function in subjecting convictions from state courts to the very narrow scrutiny which the Due Process Clause of the Fourteenth Amendment authorizes.

. . . Due process of law, "itself a historical product," . . . is not to be turned into a destructive dogma against the States in the administration of their systems of criminal justice.

However, this Court too has its responsibility. Regard for the requirements of the Due Process Clause

inescapably imposes upon this Court an exercise of judgment upon the whole course of the proceedings [resulting in a conviction] in order to ascertain whether they offend those canons of decency and fairness which express the notions of justice of English-speaking peoples even toward those charged with the most heinous offenses.

. . . These standards of justice are not authoritatively formulated anywhere as though they were specifics. Due process of law is a summarized constitutional guarantee of respect for those personal immunities which, as Mr. Justice Cardozo twice wrote for the Court, are "so rooted in the traditions and conscience of our people as to be ranked as fundamental," . . . or are "implicit in the concept of ordered liberty." . . .

The vague contours of the Due Process Clause do not leave judges at large. We may not draw on our merely personal and private notions and disregard the limits that bind judges in their judicial function. Even though the concept of due process of law is not final and fixed, these limits are derived from considerations that are fused in the whole nature of our judicial process. . . . These are considerations deeply rooted in reason and in the compelling traditions of the legal profession. The Due Process Clause places upon this Court the duty of exercising a judgment, within the narrow confines of judicial power in reviewing State convictions, upon interests of society pushing in opposite directions.

Due process of law thus conceived is not to be derided as resort to a revival of "natural law." To believe that this judicial exercise of judgment could be avoided by freezing "due process of law" at some fixed stage of time or thought is to suggest that the most important aspect of constitutional adjudication is a function for inanimate machines and not for judges, for whom the independence safeguarded by Article 3 of the Constitution was designed and who are presumably guided by established standards of judicial behavior. Even cybernetics has not yet made that haughty claim. To practice the requisite detachment and to achieve sufficient objectivity no doubt demands of judges the habit of self-discipline and self-criticism, incertitude that one's own views are incontestable and alert tolerance toward views not shared. But these are precisely the presuppositions of our judicial process. They are precisely the qualities society has a right to expect from those entrusted with ultimate judicial power.

Restraints on our jurisdiction are self-imposed only in the sense that there is from our decisions no immediate appeal short of impeachment or constitutional amendment. But that does not make due process of law a matter of judicial caprice. The faculties of the Due Process Clause may be indefinite and vague, but the mode of their ascertainment is not self-willed. In each case "due process of law" requires an evaluation based on a disinterested inquiry pursued in the spirit of science, on a balanced order of facts exactly and fairly stated, on the detached consideration of conflicting claims, . . . on a judgment not ad hoc and episodic but duly mindful of reconciling the needs both of continuity and of change in a progressive society.

Applying these general considerations to the circumstances of the present case, we are compelled to conclude that the proceedings by which this conviction was obtained do more than offend some fastidious squeamishness or private sentimentalism about combatting crime too energetically. This is conduct that shocks the conscience. Illegally breaking into the privacy of the petitioner, the struggle to open his mouth and remove what was there, the forcible extraction of his stomach's contents—this course of proceeding by agents of government to obtain evidence is bound to offend even hardened sensibilities. They are methods too close to the rack and the screw to permit of constitutional differentiation.

It has long since ceased to be true that due process of law is heedless of the means by which otherwise relevant and credible evidence is obtained. This was not true even before the series of recent cases enforced the constitutional principle that the States may not base convictions upon confessions, however much verified, obtained by coercion. These decisions are not arbitrary exceptions to the comprehensive right of States to fashion their own rules of evidence for criminal trials. They are not sports in our constitutional law but applications of a general principle. They are only instances of the general requirement that States in their prosecutions respect certain decencies of civilized conduct. Due process of law, as a historic and generative principle, precludes defining, and thereby confining, these standards of conduct more precisely than to say that convictions cannot be brought about by methods that offend "a sense of justice." . . . It would be a stultification of the responsibility which the course of constitutional history has cast upon this Court to hold that in order to convict a man the police cannot extract by force what is in his mind but can extract what is in his stomach.

To attempt in this case to distinguish what lawyers call "real evidence" from verbal evidence is to ignore the reasons for excluding coerced confessions. Use of involuntary verbal confessions in State criminal trials is constitutionally obnoxious not only because of their unreliability. They are inadmissible under the Due Process Clause even though statements contained in them may be independently established as true. Coerced confessions offend the community's sense of fair play and decency. So here, to sanction the brutal conduct which naturally enough was condemned by the court whose judgment is before us, would be to afford brutality the cloak of law. Nothing would be more calculated to discredit law and thereby to brutalize the temper of a society. . . .

On the facts of this case the conviction of the petitioner has been obtained by methods that offend the Due Process Clause. The judgment below must be

Reversed. . . .

Mr. Justice Douglas, concurring:

The evidence obtained from this accused's stomach would be admissible in the majority of states where the question has been raised. So far as the reported cases reveal, the only states which would probably exclude the evidence would be Arkansas, Iowa, Michigan, and Missouri. Yet the Court now says that the rule which the majority of the states have fashioned violates the "decencies of civilized conduct." To that I cannot agree. It is a rule formulated by responsible courts with judges as sensitive as we are to the proper standards for law administration.

As an original matter it might be debatable whether the provision in the Fifth Amendment that no person "shall be compelled in any criminal case to be a witness against himself" serves the ends of justice. Not all civilized legal procedures recognize it. But the choice was made by the Framers, a choice which sets a standard for legal trials in this country. The Framers made it a standard of due process for prosecutions by the Federal Government. If it is a requirement of due process for a trial in the federal courthouse, it is impossible for me to say it is not a requirement of due process for a trial in the state courthouse. That was the issue recently surveyed in *Adamson* v. *California,* 332 US 46. The Court rejected the view that compelled testimony should be excluded and held in substance that the accused in a state trial can be forced to testify against himself. I disagree. Of course an accused can be compelled to be present at the trial, to stand, to sit, to turn this way or that, and to try on a cap or a coat. . . . But I think that words taken from his lips, capsules taken from his stomach, blood taken from his veins are all inadmissible provided they are taken from him without his consent. They are inadmissible because of the command of the Fifth Amendment.

That is an unequivocal, definite and workable rule of evidence for state and federal courts. But we cannot in fairness free the state courts from that command and yet excoriate them for flouting the "decencies of civilized conduct" when they admit the evidence. That is to make the rule turn not on the Constitution but on the idiosyncrasies of the judges who sit here.

The damage of the view sponsored by the Court in this case may not be conspicuous here. But it is part of the same philosophy that produced *Betts* v. *Brady,* 316 US 455, denying counsel to an accused in a state trial against the command of the Sixth Amendment, and *Wolf* v. *Colorado,* 338 US 25, allowing evidence obtained as a result of a search and seizure that is illegal under the Fourth Amendment to be introduced in a state trial. It is part of the process of erosion of civil rights of the citizen in recent years.

8. *Assistance of Counsel*

PALMER *v.* ASHE

342 US 134 (1951)

[English common law denied the aid of counsel to a defendant charged with treason or felony on the theory that the judge would be counsel for him; but persons accused of misdemeanors were entitled to the assistance of counsel. After the English Revolution of 1688–1689 the rule was dropped as to treason but was otherwise maintained until, in 1836, Parliament granted the right of counsel in felony cases generally. The rule excluding counsel from cases involving serious crimes was constantly attacked as a barbarous perversion of justice.

[The American colonies departed from the English practice: a Pennsylvania statute of 1718 provided for the assignment of counsel in capital cases; and the constitutions of Pennsylvania and New Jersey provided that all criminals should have the same privileges of counsel as did their prosecutors. Twelve colonies, before the adoption of the Constitution, provided for the assistance of counsel in a very substantial measure. *Powell* v. *Alabama*, 287 US 45 (1932).

[The Sixth Amendment provides that in all criminal prosecutions the accused shall enjoy the right "to have the assistance of counsel for his defense." Rule 44 of the Federal Rules of Criminal Procedure (1946) provides: "If the defendant appears in court without counsel, the court shall advise him of his right to counsel and assign counsel to represent him at every stage of the proceeding unless he elects to proceed without counsel or is able to obtain counsel." The Sixth Amendment, broadly implemented by this procedural rule, applies only to trials in federal courts. This constitutional provision is not part of the due process guaranty of the Fourteenth Amendment; insofar as the United States Constitution is concerned, the right of counsel in state prosecutions is considerably more restricted than is that right in federal prosecutions. Justices Murphy, Rutledge, Black, and Douglas have protested against this differentiation, insisting that the guaranty of assistance of counsel as provided in the Sixth Amendment is embodied in the Fourteenth Amendment as a guaranty against the states.

[The Due Process Clause of the Fourteenth Amendment requires states, however, to afford the assistance of counsel to defendants in all capital cases; in noncapital cases the states are required to afford the assistance of counsel when there are special circumstances, such as extreme youth, or ignorance, or imbecility, or the complicated nature of the offense. The cases are decided on their facts. "The due process clause is not susceptible of reduction to a mathematical formula." *Rice* v. *Olson*, 324 US 786 (1945). The Court is thus frequently divided on the question of whether in the absence of counsel the accused was afforded due process of law.

[In the present case, a state court conviction upon a plea of guilty to a charge of robbery was held, under the circumstances, to have violated due process. The decision was 5 to 4, with Chief Justice Vinson and Justices Minton, Reed, and Jackson dissenting. An especially notable feature of the case is that the Supreme Court set aside the conviction eighteen years after sentence was originally passed when the prisoner instituted habeas corpus proceedings.]

Mr. Justice Black delivered the opinion of the Court:

This Court repeatedly has held that the Due Process Clause of the Fourteenth Amendment requires states to afford defendants assistance of counsel in non-capital criminal cases when there are special circumstances showing that without a lawyer a defendant could not have an adequate and a fair defense. Petitioner, a prisoner in a Pennsylvania penitentiary, is serving the second of two five to fifteen year sentences simultaneously imposed after pleas of guilty to state offenses. He sought release in these habeas corpus proceedings filed in a Pennsylvania Court of Common Pleas. His petition alleged that his pleas of guilty were entered without benefit of counsel and that other special circumstances existed which deprived him of opportunity and capacity fairly to defend himself. Answers of the warden and district attorney admitted that petitioner had not been represented by counsel, but asserted that the trial record sufficiently refuted petitioner's allegations. On consideration of the petition and answers the court held that petitioner's allegations, in light of the record, failed to show probable cause for his discharge. The case was then dismissed, thereby depriving petitioner of any opportunity to offer evidence to prove his allegations. . . .

We must look to the petition and answer to determine whether the particular circumstances alleged are sufficient to entitle petitioner to a judicial hearing. In summary these allegations are: When petitioner was arrested December 20, 1930, the officers told him that he was charged with "breaking and entering the Leaders Dry Goods Store." Later, before a magistrate, he was again told that the charge was "breaking and entering." Petitioner never saw the indictments against him nor were they read to him. He never knew he had been charged with robbery and never intended to plead guilty to such a crime. Taken to the court room "the District Attorney informed the Court, that 'the defendant wishes to plead guilty' and in the matter of a minute, more or less, the foregoing sentence was entered after he answered 'Yes' to the Court's query, 'Do you plead guilty to this charge?'" Petitioner "was not represented by counsel, nor offered counsel, or advised of his right to have counsel. . . ." After arrival at the penitentiary, petitioner first learned, according to his petition, that he had been sentenced for robbery and not for the lesser charge of "breaking and entering." The petitioner also alleges that petitioner when arrested was "a young, irresponsible boy, having spent several years in Polk (because he was mentally abnormal) as well as several years in Morganza." This allegation of mental abnormality is supported by the penitentiary warden's answer showing that petitioner had been confined in Polk (a state institution) from August, 1918, to September, 1920, because he was an

"Imbecile." The warden's answer also shows that petitioner was born in 1909; was a state orphanage inmate for a year beginning in 1916; and was in reformatories for larceny or "breaking and entering" for eight of the ten years between the time of his release from the mental institution and the time of the offense for which he is now in prison.

All of the foregoing allegations, if proven, would present compelling reasons why petitioner desperately needed legal counsel and services. Incarceration as a boy for imbecility, followed by repeated activities wholly incompatible with normal standards of conduct, indicates no qualities of mind or character calculated to enable petitioner to protect himself in the give and take of a courtroom trial. Moreover, if there can be proof of what he charges, he is the victim of inadvertent or intentional deception by officers who, so he alleges, persuaded him to plead guilty to armed robbery by telling him he was only charged with breaking and entering, an offense for which the maximum imprisonment is only ten years as compared to twenty years for armed robbery. . . .

It is strongly urged here, however, that petitioner's allegations are satisfactorily refuted by the trial record, and that the Court should not now look behind that record, particularly in view of the long time that has elapsed since petitioner pleaded guilty. Of course the trial record may relevantly be considered in the habeas corpus proceeding. In some respects petitioner's allegations are refuted by the record. But that record does not even inferentially deny petitioner's charges that the officers deceived him, nor does the record show an understanding plea of guilty from this petitioner, unless by a resort to speculation and surmise. The right to counsel is too valuable in our system to dilute it by such untrustworthy reasoning. . . . The judgment dismissing the petition is reversed and the cause is remanded to the State Supreme Court for further action not inconsistent with this opinion. . . .

9. Excessive Bail

STACK v. BOYLE

342 US 1 (1951)

[The Eighth Amendment prohibits excessive bail. This is a limitation on federal courts and not on the states. Rule 46 (c) of the Federal Rules of Criminal Procedure (1946) provides that the amount of bail shall be such as will ensure the presence of the defendant, having regard to the nature and circumstances of the offense, the weight of the evidence against the accused, his financial ability to give bail, and his character. The court must thus balance the defendant's right to freedom until he is convicted and the need to ensure his presence in the jurisdiction; thus the question when bail is "excessive" is a complex one and its resolution will depend on the facts.

[In this case twelve Communist Party leaders in California were indicted for conspiracy under the Smith Act. Bail before trial was fixed at $50,000 for each defendant. The reason offered for this high bail was that other Communists previously convicted had forfeited bail. The Court unanimously held (Justice Minton not participating) that bail had not been fixed by proper tests.

[In a case involving ten other Communist Party leaders,* after they were convicted and the judgment was affirmed by the Court of Appeals, the Government asked that their bail be revoked and defendants kept in jail pending their appeal to the Supreme Court. Two grounds were asserted by the Government to sustain this position: that there was no substantial question as to the conviction, and that defendants, while on bail, will pursue a course of conduct dangerous to public welfare and safety. The defendants applied for continuance of bail to Justice Jackson as Circuit Justice of the Second Circuit. He granted the defendants' application, holding that there was a substantial question pending the review of the conviction; furthermore, even assuming that the defendants were disposed to commit disloyal acts, the jailing of persons because of anticipated but as yet uncommitted crimes cannot be reconciled with traditional American law. The defendants after conviction made statements in the *Daily Worker* that might be said to have been "inciting," "crudely intemperate," and "plainly designed to embroil different elements of our society and embarrass" the Government attorneys. Justice Jackson rejected these arguments, saying: "But the very essence of constitutional freedom of press and of speech is to allow more liberty than the good citizen will take." He pointed out that the Communist Party has not been outlawed, nor has the right of the *Daily Worker* to publish been questioned. He said:

[Indirect punishment of free press or free speech is as evil as direct punishment of it. . . . But the right of every American to equal treatment before the law is wrapped up in the same constitutional bundle with those of these Communists. If in anger or disgust with these defendants we throw out the bundle, we also cast aside protection for the liberties of more worthy critics who may be in opposition to the government of some future day.]

Mr. Chief Justice Vinson delivered the opinion of the Court:

Indictments have been returned in the Southern District of California charging the twelve petitioners with conspiring to violate the

* *Williamson v. United States*, 95 L. Ed. (US) 1379 (1950).

Smith Act, 18 U.S.C. (Supp. IV) §§ 371, 2385. Upon their arrest, bail was fixed for each petitioner in the widely varying amounts of $2,500, $7,500, $75,000 and $100,000. On motion of petitioner Schneiderman following arrest in the Southern District of New York, his bail was reduced to $50,000 before his removal to California. On motion of the Government to increase bail in the case of other petitioners, and after several intermediate procedural steps not material to the issues presented here, bail was fixed in the District Court for the Southern District of California in the uniform amount of $50,000 for each petitioner.

Petitioners moved to reduce bail on the ground that bail as fixed was excessive under the Eighth Amendment. In support of their motions, petitioners submitted statements as to their financial resources, family relationships, health, prior criminal records, and other information. The only evidence offered by the Government was a certified record showing that four persons previously convicted under the Smith Act in the Southern District of New York had forfeited bail. No evidence was produced relating those four persons to the petitioners in this case. . . . Petitioners' factual statements stand uncontroverted.

After their motions to reduce bail were denied, petitioners filed applications for habeas corpus in the same District Court. Upon consideration of the record on the motion to reduce bail, the writ was denied. The Court of Appeals for the Ninth Circuit affirmed. . . .

Relief in this type of case must be speedy if it is to be effective. . . .

From the passage of the Judiciary Act of 1789 . . . to the present Federal Rules of Criminal Procedure, . . . federal law has unequivocally provided that a person arrested for a non-capital offense *shall* be admitted to bail. This traditional right to freedom before conviction permits the unhampered preparation of a defense, and serves to prevent the infliction of punishment prior to conviction. . . . Unless this right to bail before trial is preserved, the presumption of innocence, secured only after centuries of struggle, would lose its meaning.

The right to release before trial is conditioned upon the accused's giving adequate assurance that he will stand trial and submit to sentence if found guilty. . . . Like the ancient practice of securing the oaths of responsible persons to stand as sureties for the accused, the modern practice of requiring a bail bond or the deposit of a sum of money subject to forfeiture serves as additional assurance of the presence of an accused. Bail set at a figure higher than an amount reasonably calculated to fulfill this purpose is "excessive" under the Eighth Amendment. . . .

Since the function of bail is limited, the fixing of bail for any individual defendant must be based upon standards relevant to the purpose of assuring the presence of that defendant. The traditional standards as expressed in the Federal Rules of Criminal Procedure are to be applied in each case to each defendant. In this case petitioners are charged with offenses under the Smith Act and, if found guilty, their convictions are subject to review with the scrupulous care demanded by our Constitution. . . . Upon final judgment of conviction, petitioners face imprisonment of not more than five years and a fine of not more than $10,000. It is not denied that bail for each petitioner has been fixed in a sum much higher than that usually imposed for offenses with like penalties and yet there has been no factual showing to justify such action in this case. The Government asks the courts to depart from the norm by assuming, without the introduction of evidence, that each petitioner is a pawn in a conspiracy and will, in obedience to a superior, flee the jurisdiction. To infer from the fact of indictment alone a need for bail in an unusually high amount is an arbitrary act. Such conduct would inject into our own system of government the very principles of totalitarianism which Congress was seeking to guard against in passing the statute under which petitioners have been indicted.

If bail in an amount greater than that usually fixed for serious charges of crimes is required in the case of any of the petitioners, that is a matter to which evidence should be directed in a hearing so that the constitutional rights of each petitioner may be preserved. In the absence of such a showing, we are of the opinion that the fixing of bail before trial in these cases cannot be squared with the statutory and constitutional standards for admission to bail. . . .

The Court concludes that bail has not been fixed by proper methods in this case and that petitioners' remedy is by motion to reduce bail, with right of appeal to the Court of Appeals. . . . Petitioners may move for reduction of bail in the criminal proceeding so that a hearing may be held for the purpose of fixing reasonable bail for each petitioner.

It is so ordered. . . .

10. Cruel and Unusual Punishments

LOUISIANA ex rel. FRANCIS v. RESWEBER

329 US 459 (1947)

[The Eighth Amendment provides that excessive fines shall not be imposed, nor shall cruel and unusual punishments be inflicted. As to states, as the present case shows, the Due Process Clause of the Fourteenth Amendment prohibits a state from imposing a cruel penalty. On this principle, all the Justices were in agreement. Five Justices held that the punishment inflicted on Willie Francis by the State of Louisiana did not constitute cruel punishment in violation of due process; four Justices (Burton, Douglas, Murphy, and Rutledge) maintained that the punishment inflicted involved torture and cruelty. Justice Frankfurter's concurring opinion is a helpful restatement of his argument against the proposition that the Fourteenth Amendment incorporates the first eight amendments.]

Mr. Justice Reed announced the judgment of the Court:

This writ of certiorari brings before this Court a unique situation. The petitioner, Willie Francis, is a colored citizen of Louisiana. He was duly convicted of murder and in September, 1945, sentenced to be electrocuted for the crime. Upon a proper death warrant, Francis was prepared for execution and on May 3, 1946, pursuant to the warrant, was placed in the official electric chair of the State of Louisiana in the presence of the authorized witnesses. The executioner threw the switch but, presumably because of some mechanical difficulty, death did not result. He was thereupon removed from the chair and returned to prison where he now is. A new death warrant was issued by the Governor of Louisiana, fixing the execution for May 9, 1946.

Applications to the Supreme Court of the state were filed for writs of certiorari, mandamus, prohibition and habeas corpus, directed to the appropriate officials in the state. Execution of the sentence was stayed. By the applications petitioner claimed the protection of the due process clause of the Fourteenth Amendment on the ground that an execution under the circumstances detailed would deny due process to him because of the double jeopardy provision of the Fifth Amendment and the cruel and unusual punishment provision of the Eighth Amendment. These federal constitutional protections, petitioner claimed, would be denied because he had once gone through the difficult preparation for execution and had once received through his body a current of electricity intended to cause death. The Supreme Court of Louisiana denied the applications on the ground of a lack of any basis for judicial relief. That is, the state court concluded there was no violation of state or national law alleged in the various applications. It spoke of the fact that no "current of sufficient intensity to cause death" passed through petitioner's body. It referred specifically to the fact that the applications of petitioner invoked the provisions of the Louisiana Constitution against cruel and inhuman punishments and putting one in jeopardy of life or liberty twice for the same offense. . . .

First. Our minds rebel against permitting the same sovereignty to punish an accused twice for the same offense. . . . But where the accused successfully seeks review of a conviction, there is no double jeopardy upon a new trial. . . . Even where a state obtains a new trial after conviction because of errors, while an accused may be placed on trial a second time, it is not the sort of hardship to the accused that is forbidden by the Fourteenth Amendment. . . . As this is a prosecution under state law, so far as double jeopardy is concerned, the *Palko Case* [302 U.S. 319] is decisive. For we see no difference from a constitutional point of view between a new trial for error of law at the instance of the state that results in a death sentence instead of imprisonment for life and an execution that follows a failure of equipment. When an accident, with no suggestion of malevolence, prevents the consummation of a sentence, the state's subsequent course in the administration of its criminal law is not affected on that account by any requirement of due process under the Fourteenth Amendment. We find no double jeopardy here which can be said to amount to a denial of federal due process in the proposed execution.

Second. We find nothing in what took place here which amounts to cruel and unusual punishment in the constitutional sense. The case before us does not call for an examination into any punishments except that of death. . . . The traditional humanity of modern Anglo-American law forbids the infliction of unnecessary pain in the execution of the death sentence. Prohibition against the wanton infliction of pain has come into our law from the Bill of Rights of 1688. The identical words appear in our Eighth Amendment. The Fourteenth would prohibit by its due process clause execution by a state in a cruel manner.

Petitioner's suggestion is that because he once underwent the psychological strain of preparation for electrocution, now to require him to undergo this preparation again subjects him to a lingering or cruel and unusual punishment. Even the fact that petitioner has already been subjected to a current of electricity does not make this subsequent execution any more cruel in the constitutional sense than any other execution. The cruelty against which the Constitution protects a convicted man is cruelty inherent in the method of punishment, not the necessary suffering involved in any method employed to extinguish life humanely. The fact that an unforeseeable accident prevented the prompt consummation of the sentence cannot, it seems to us, add an element of cruelty to a subsequent execution. There is no purpose to inflict unnecessary pain nor any unnecessary pain involved in the proposed execution. The situation of the unfortunate victim of this accident is just as though he had suffered the identical amount of mental anguish and physical pain in any other occurrence, such as, for example, a fire in the cell block. We cannot agree that the hardship imposed upon the petitioner rises to that level of hardship denounced as denial of due process because of cruelty.

Third. The Supreme Court of Louisiana also rejected petitioner's contention that death inflicted after his prior sufferings would deny him the equal protection of the laws, guaranteed by the Fourteenth Amendment. This suggestion in so far as it differs from the due process argument is based on the idea that execution, after an attempt at execution has failed, would be a more severe punishment than is imposed upon others guilty of a like offense. That is, since others do not go through the strain of preparation for execution a second time or have not experienced a non-lethal current in a prior attempt at execution, as petitioner did, to compel petitioner to submit to execution after these prior experiences denies to him equal protection. Equal protection does not protect a prisoner against even illegal acts of officers in charge of him, much less against accidents during his detention for execution. . . . Laws cannot prevent accidents nor can a law equally protect all against them. So long as the law applies to all alike, the requirements of equal protection are met. We have no right to assume that Louisiana singled out Francis for a treatment other than that which has been or would generally be applied. . . .

Mr. Justice Frankfurter, concurring:

When four members of the Court find that a State has denied to a person the due process which the Fourteenth Amendment safeguards, it seems to me important to be explicit regarding the criteria by which the State's duty of obedience to the Constitution must be judged. Particularly is this so when life is at stake.

Until July 28, 1868, when the Fourteenth Amendment was ratified, the Constitution of the United States left the States free to carry out their own notions of criminal justice, except insofar as they were limited by article I, §10 of the Constitution which declares: "No State shall . . . pass any Bill of Attainder [or] ex post facto Law. . . ." The Fourteenth Amendment placed no specific restraints upon the States in the formulation or the administration of their criminal law. It restricted the freedom of the States generally, so that States thereafter could not "abridge the privileges or immunities of citizens of the United States," or "deprive any person of life, liberty, or property, without due process of law," or "deny to any person within its jurisdiction the equal protection of the laws."

These are broad, inexplicit clauses of the Constitution, unlike specific provisions of the first eight amendments formulated by the Founders to guard against recurrence of well-defined historic grievances. But broad as these clauses are, they are not generalities of empty vagueness. They are circumscribed partly by history and partly by the problems of government, large and dynamic though they be, with which they are concerned. The "privileges or immunities of citizens of the United States" concern the dual citizenship under our federal system. The safeguards of "due process of law" and "the equal protection of the laws" summarize the meaning of the struggle for freedom of English-speaking peoples. They run back to Magna Carta but contemplate no less advances in the conceptions of justice and freedom by a progressive society. . . .

When, shortly after its adoption, the Fourteenth Amendment came before this Court for construction, it was urged that the "privileges or immunities of citizens of the United States" which were not to be abridged by any State were the privileges and immunities which citizens theretofore enjoyed under the Constitution. If that view had prevailed, the Privileges or Immunities Clause of the Fourteenth Amendment would have placed upon the States the limitations which the specific articles of the first eight amendments had theretofore placed upon the agencies of the national government. After the fullest consideration that view was rejected. The rejection has the authority that comes from contemporaneous knowledge of the purposes of the Fourteenth Amendment. . . . The notion that the Privileges or Immunities Clause of the Fourteenth Amendment absorbed, as it is called, the provisions of the Bill of Rights that limit the Federal Government has never been given countenance by this Court.

Not until recently was it suggested that the Due Process Clause of the Fourteenth Amendment was merely a compendious reference to the Bill of Rights whereby the States were now restricted in devising and enforcing their penal code precisely as is the Federal Government by the first eight amendments. On this view, the States would be confined in the enforcement of their criminal codes by those views for safeguarding the rights of the individual which were deemed necessary in the eighteenth century. Some of these safeguards have perduring validity. Some grew out of transient experience or formulated remedies which time might well improve. The Fourteenth Amendment did not mean to imprison the States into the limited experience of the eighteenth century. It did mean to withdraw from the States the right to act in ways that are offensive to a decent respect for the dignity of man, and heedless of his freedom.

These are very broad terms by which to accommodate freedom and authority. As has been suggested from time to time, they may be too large to serve as the basis for adjudication, in that they allow much room for individual notions of policy. That is not our concern. The fact is that the duty of such adjudication on a basis no less narrow has been committed to this Court.

In an impressive body of decisions this Court has decided that the Due Process Clause of the Fourteenth Amendment expresses a demand for civilized standards which are not defined by the specifically enumerated guarantees of the Bill of Rights. They neither contain the particularities of the first eight amendments nor are they confined to them. That due process of law has its own independent function has been illustrated in numerous decisions, and has been expounded in the opinions of the Court which have canvassed the matter most thoroughly. . . .

The Federal Bill of Rights requires that prosecutions for federal crimes be initiated by a grand jury and tried by a petty jury; it protects an accused from being a witness against himself. The States are free to consult their own conceptions of policy in dispensing with the grand jury, in modifying or abolishing the petty jury, in withholding the privilege against self-crimination. . . . In short, the Due Process Clause of the Fourteenth Amendment did not withdraw the freedom of a State to enforce its own notions of fairness in the administration of criminal justice unless, as it was put for the Court by Mr. Justice Cardozo, "in so doing it offends some principle of justice so rooted in the traditions and conscience of our people as to be ranked as fundamental." . . .

A State may offend such a principle of justice by brutal subjection of an individual to successive retrials on a charge on which he has been acquitted. Such conduct by a State might be a denial of due process, but not because the protection against double jeopardy in a federal prosecution against which the Fifth Amendment safeguards limits a State. . . . Again, a State may be found to deny a person due process by treating even one guilty of crime in a manner that violates standards of decency more or less universally accepted though not when it treats him by a mode about which opinion is fairly divided. But the penological policy of a State is not to be tested by the scope of the Eighth Amendment and is not involved in the controversy which is necessarily evoked by that Amendment as to the historic meaning of "cruel and unusual punishment." . . .

Once we are explicit in stating the problem before us in terms defined by an unbroken series of decisions, we cannot escape acknowledging that it involves the application of standards of fairness and justice very broadly conceived. They are not the application of merely personal standards but the impersonal standards of society which alone judges, as the organs of Law, are empowered to enforce. When the standards for judicial judgment are not narrower than "immutable principles of justice which inhere in the very idea of free government," . . . "fundamental principles of liberty and justice which lie at the base of all our civil and political institutions," . . . "immunities . . . implicit in the concept of ordered liberty," . . . great tolerance toward a State's conduct is demanded of this Court. . . .

I cannot bring myself to believe that for Louisiana to leave to executive clemency, rather than to require, mitigation of a sentence of death duly pronounced upon conviction for murder because a first attempt to carry it out was an innocent misadventure, offends a principle of justice "rooted in the traditions and conscience of our people." . . . I cannot rid myself of the conviction that were I to hold that Louisiana would transgress the Due Process Clause if the State were allowed, in the precise circumstances before us, to carry out the death sentence, I would be enforcing my private view rather than that consensus of society's opinion which, for purposes of due process, is the standard enjoined by the Constitution. . . .

Mr. Justice Burton, with whom Mr. Justice Douglas, Mr. Justice Murphy and Mr. Justice Rutledge concur, dissenting:

Under circumstances unique in judicial history, the relator asks this Court to stay his execution on the ground that it will violate the due process of law guaranteed to him by the Constitution of the United States. We believe that the unusual facts before us required that the judgment of the Supreme Court of Louisiana be vacated and that this cause be remanded for further proceedings not inconsistent with this opinion. Those proceedings should include the determination of certain material facts not previously determined, including the extent, if any, to which electric current was applied to the relator during his attempted electrocution on May 3, 1946. Where life is to be taken, there must be no avoidable error of law or uncertainty of fact.

The relator's execution was ordered by the Governor of Louisiana to take place May 3, 1946. Of the proceedings on that day, the Supreme Court of Louisiana has said:

Between the Hours of 12:00 o'clock noon and 3:00 o'clock p.m., Willie Francis was strapped in the electric chair and an attempt was made to electrocute him, but, because of some defect in the apparatus devised and used for electrocutions, the contrivance failed to function, and after an unsuccessful attempt to electrocute Francis he was removed from the chair.

Of the same proceedings, the State's brief says: "Through a latent electrical defect, the attempt to electrocute Francis failed, the State contending no current whatsoever reached Francis' body, the relator contending a current of electricity did pass through his body; but in any event, Willie Francis was not put to death."

On May 8, the death warrant was canceled, and the relator's execution has been stayed pending completion of these proceedings. The Governor proposes to issue another death warrant for the relator's electrocution and the relator now asks this Court to prevent it for the reason that, under the present unique circumstances, his electrocution will be so cruel and unusual as to violate the due process clause of the Fourteenth Amendment to the Constitution of the United States.

That Amendment provides: "nor shall any State deprive any person of life, liberty, or property, without due process of law. . . ." When this was adopted in 1868, there long had been imbedded deeply in the standards of this nation a revulsion against subjecting guilty persons to torture culminating in death. Preconstitutional American history reeked with cruel punishment to such an extent that, in 1791, the Eighth Amendment to the Constitution of the United States expressly imposed upon federal agencies a mandate that "Excessive bail shall not be required, nor excessive fines imposed, nor cruel and unusual punishments inflicted." Louisiana and many other states have adopted like constitutional provisions. . . .

The capital case before us presents an instance of the violation of constitutional due process that is more clear than would be presented by many lesser punishments prohibited by the Eighth Amendment or its state counter-parts. Taking human life by unnecessarily cruel means shocks the most funda-mental instincts of civilized man. It should not be possible under the con-stitutional procedure of a self-governing people. Abhorrence of the cruelty of ancient forms of capital punishment has increased steadily until, today, some states have prohibited capital punishment altogether. It is unthinkable that any state legislature in modern times would enact a statute expressly authorizing capital punishment by repeated applications of an electric cur-rent separated by intervals of days or hours until finally death shall result. The Legislature of Louisiana did not do so. The Supreme Court of Louisiana did not say that it did. The Supreme Court of Louisiana said merely that the pending petitions for relief in this case presented an executive rather than a judicial question and, by that mistake of law, it precluded itself from discussing the constitutional issue before us.

In determining whether the proposed procedure is unconstitutional, we must measure it against a lawful electrocution. The contrast is that between instantaneous death and death by installments—caused by electric shocks administered after one or more intervening periods of complete consciousness of the victim. Electrocution, when instantaneous, *can* be inflicted by a state in conformity with due process of law. . . .

The all-important consideration is that the execution shall be so instanta-neous and substantially painless that the punishment shall be reduced, as nearly as possible, to no more than that of death itself. Electrocution has been approved only in a form that eliminates suffering.

The Louisiana statute makes this clear. . . .

It does not provide for electrocution by interrupted or repeated applica-tions of electric current at intervals of several days or even minutes. It does not provide for the application of electric current of an intensity less than that sufficient to cause death. It prescribes expressly and solely for the application of a current of sufficient intensity to cause death and for the *continuance* of that application until death results. Prescribing capital punishment, it should be construed strictly. There can be no implied provision for a second, third or multiple application of the current. There is no statutory or judicial prec-edent upholding a delayed process of electrocution. . . .

Lack of intent that the first application be less than fatal is not material. The intent of the executioner cannot lessen the torture or excuse the result. It was the statutory duty of the state officials to make sure that there was no failure. The procedure in this case contrasts with common knowledge of precautions generally taken elsewhere to insure against failure of electrocu-tions. The high standard of care generally taken evidences the significance properly attached to the unconditional requirement of a single continued application of the current until death results. . . .

11. Right to a Public Trial

Re WILLIAM OLIVER

333 US 257 (1948)

[The Sixth Amendment provides that in all criminal prosecutions the accused shall enjoy the right to a "public trial." The constitutions of forty-one states have similar provisions; two states provide for public trial by statute; and one state has achieved the same end by a decision of its highest court. In this case the Court held that the Due Process Clause of the Fourteenth Amendment makes it improper for a state court to sentence a defendant without a public trial.

[The Court also held that an accused must be advised of the charges against him and must be afforded a reasonable opportunity to prepare a defense. These rights are part of "the law of the land." Justice Rutledge, in a concurring opinion, would put the demands of the Sixth Amendment into the Fourteenth Amendment as restrictions upon the states. He thus would declare the entire one-man grand jury system of Michigan unconstitutional.

[Justices Frankfurter and Jackson dissented on procedural grounds.]

Mr. Justice Black delivered the opinion of the Court:

A Michigan circuit judge summarily sent the petitioner to jail for contempt of court. We must determine whether he was denied the procedural due process guaranteed by the Fourteenth Amendment.

In obedience to a subpoena the petitioner appeared as a witness before a Michigan circuit judge who was then conducting, in accordance with Michigan law, a "one-man grand jury" investigation into alleged gambling and official corruption. The investigation presumably took place in the judge's chambers, though that is not certain. Two other circuit judges were present in an advisory capacity. A prosecutor may have been present. A stenographer was most likely there. The record does not show what other members, if any, of the judge's investigatorial staff participated in the proceedings. It is certain, however, that the public was excluded—the questioning was secret in accordance with the traditional grand jury method.

After petitioner had given certain testimony, the judge–grand jury, still in secret session, told petitioner that neither he nor his advisors believed petitioner's story—that it did not "jell." This belief of the judge–grand jury was not based entirely on what the petitioner had testified. As will later be seen, it rested in part on beliefs or suspicions of the judge–jury derived from the testimony of at least one other witness who had previously given evidence in secret. Petitioner had not been present when that witness testified and so far as appears was not even aware that he had testified. Based on its beliefs thus formed—that petitioner's story did not "jell"—the judge–grand jury immediately charged him with contempt, immediately convicted him, and immediately sentenced him to sixty days in jail. Under these circumstances of haste and secrecy, petitioner, of course, had no chance to enjoy the benefits of counsel, no chance to prepare his defense, and no opportunity either to cross examine the other grand jury witness or to summon witnesses to refute the charge against him.

Three days later a lawyer filed on petitioner's behalf in the Michigan Supreme Court the petition for habeas corpus now under consideration. It alleged among other things that the petitioner's attorney had not been allowed to confer with him and that, to the best of the attorney's knowledge, the petitioner was not held in jail under any judgment, decree or execution, and was "not confined by virtue of any legal commitment directed to the sheriff as required by law." An order was then entered signed by the circuit judge that he had while "sitting as a One-Man Grand Jury" convicted the petitioner of contempt of court because petitioner had testified "evasively" and had given "contradictory answers" to questions. The order directed that petitioner "be confined in the county jail . . . for a period of sixty days . . . or until such time as he . . . shall appear and answer the questions heretofore propounded to him by this Court. . . ."

The case requires a brief explanation of Michigan's unique one-man grand jury system. That state's first constitution (1835), like the Fifth Amendment to the Federal Constitution, required that most criminal prosecutions be begun by presentment or indictment of a grand jury. . . . This compulsory provision was left out of the 1850 constitution and from the present constitution (1908). However, Michigan judges may still in their discretion summon grand juries, but we are told by the attorney general that this discretion is rarely exercised and that the "One-Man Grand Jury" has taken the place of the old Michigan 16 to 23-member grand jury, particularly in probes of alleged misconduct of public officials.

The one-man grand jury law was passed in 1917 following a recommendation of the State Bar Association that, in the interest of more rigorous law enforcement, greater emphasis should be put upon the "investigative procedure" for "probing" and for "detecting" crime. With this need uppermost in its thinking the Bar Association recommended a bill which provided that justices of the peace be vested with the inquisitorial powers traditionally conferred only on coroners and grand juries. The bill as passed imposed the recommended investigatory powers not only on justices of the peace, but on police judges and judges of courts of record as well. . . .

Whenever this judge–grand jury may summon a witness to appear, it in his duty to go and to answer all material questions that do not incriminate him. Should he fail to appear, fail to answer material questions, or should the judge–grand jury believe his evidence false and evasive, or deliberately contradictory, he may be found guilty of contempt. This offense may be punishable by a fine of not more than one hundred dollars, or imprisonment in the county jail not exceeding sixty days, or both, at the discretion of the judge–grand jury. If after having been so sentenced he appears and satisfactorily answers the questions propounded by the judge-jury, his sentence may, within the judge-jury's discretion, be commuted or suspended. At the end of his first sentence he can be resummoned and subjected to the same inquiries. Should the judge-jury again believe his answers false and evasive, or contradictory, he can be sentenced to serve sixty days more unless he reappears before the judge-jury during the second 60-day period and satisfactorily answers the questions, and the judge-jury within its discretion then decides to commute or suspend his sentence.

In carrying out this authority a judge–grand jury is authorized to appoint its own prosecutors, detectives and aides at public expense, all or any of whom may, at the discretion of the justice of the peace or judge, be admitted to the inquiry. . . . A witness may be asked questions on all subjects and need not be advised of his privilege against self-incrimination, even though the questioning is in secret. And these secret interrogations can be carried on day or night, in a public place or a "hideout," a courthouse, an office building, a hotel room, a home, or a place of business; so well is this ambulatory power understood in Michigan that the one-man grand jury is also popularly referred to as the "portable grand jury."

It was a circuit court judge–grand jury before which petitioner testified. That judge-jury filed in the State Supreme Court an answer to this petition for habeas corpus. The answer contained fragments of what was apparently a stenographic transcript of petitioner's testimony given before the grand jury. It was these fragments of testimony, so the answer stated, that the "Grand Jury" had concluded to be "false and evasive." The petitioner then filed a verified motion with the State Supreme Court seeking to have the complete transcript of his testimony before the judge-jury produced for the habeas corpus hearing. He alleged that a full report of his testimony would disclose that he had freely, promptly, and to the best of his ability, answered all questions asked, and that the full transcript would refute the charge that he had testified evasively or falsely. In his answer to the motion the circuit judge did not deny these allegations. However, he asserted that the fragments contained in the original answer showed "all of the Grand Jury testimony necessary to the present proceeding" and that "the full disclosure of petitioner's testimony would seriously retard Grand Jury activities." The State Supreme Court then denied the petitioner's motion. Thus when that Court later dismissed the petition for habeas corpus it had seen only a copy of a portion of the record of the testimony given by the petitioner.

The petitioner does not here challenge the constitutional power of Michigan to grant traditional inquisitorial grand jury power to a single judge, and therefore we do not concern ourselves with that question. It has long been recognized in this country however that the traditional 12 to 23-member grand juries may examine witnesses in secret sessions. Oaths of secrecy are ordinarily taken both by the members of such grand juries and by witnesses before them. Many reasons have been advanced to support grand jury secrecy. . . . But those reasons have never been thought to justify secrecy in the trial of an accused charged with violations of law for which he may be fined or sent to jail. Grand juries investigate, and the usual end of their investigation is either a report, a "no-bill" or an indictment. They do not try and they do not convict. They render no judgment. When their work is finished by the return of an indictment, it cannot be used as evidence against the person indicted. Nor may he be fined or sentenced to jail until he has been tried and convicted after having been afforded the procedural safeguards required by due process of law. Even when witnesses before grand juries refuse to answer proper questions, the grand juries do not adjudge the witnesses guilty of contempt of court in secret or in public or at all. Witnesses who refuse to testify before grand juries are tried on contempt charges before judges sitting in open court. And though the powers of a judge even when acting as a one-man grand jury may be, as Michigan holds, judicial in their nature, the due process clause may apply with one effect on the judge's grand jury investigation, but with quite a different effect when the judge–grand jury suddenly makes a witness before it a defendant in a contempt case.

Here we are concerned, not with petitioner's rights as a witness in a secret grand jury session, but with his rights as a defendant in a contempt proceeding. The powers of the judge–grand jury who tried and convicted him in secret and sentenced him to jail on a charge of false and evasive swearing must likewise be measured, not by the limitations applicable to grand jury proceedings, but by the constitutional standards applicable to court proceedings in which an accused may be sentenced to fine or imprisonment or both. Thus our first question is this: Can an accused be tried and convicted for contempt of court in grand jury secrecy?

First. Counsel have not cited and we have been unable to find a single instance of a criminal trial conducted in camera in any federal, state, or municipal court during the history of this country. Nor have we found any record of even one such secret criminal trial in England since abolition of the Court of Star Chamber in 1641, and whether that court ever convicted people secretly is in dispute. Summary trials for alleged misconduct called contempt of court have not been regarded as an exception to this universal rule against secret trials, unless some other Michigan one-man grand jury case may represent such an exception.

This nation's accepted practice of guaranteeing a public trial to an accused has its roots in our English common law heritage. The exact date of its origin is obscure, but it likely evolved long before the settlement of our land as an accompaniment of the ancient institution of jury trial. In this country the guarantee to an accused of the right to a public trial first appeared in a state constitution in 1776. Following the ratification in 1791 of the Federal Constitution's Sixth Amendment, which commands that "In all criminal prosecutions, the accused shall enjoy the right to a speedy and public trial . . ." most of the original states and those subsequently admitted to the Union adopted similar constitutional provisions. Today almost without exception every state by constitution, statute, or judicial decision, requires that all criminal trials be open to the public.

The traditional Anglo-American distrust for secret trials has been variously ascribed to the notorious use of this practice by the Spanish Inquisition, to the excesses of the English Court of Star Chamber, and to the French monarchy's abuse of the lettre de cachet. All of these institutions obviously symbolized a menace to liberty. In the hands of despotic groups each of them had become an instrument for the suppression of political and religious heresies in ruthless disregard of the right of an accused to a fair trial. Whatever other benefits the guarantee to an accused that his trial be conducted in public may confer upon our society, the guarantee has always been recognized as a safeguard against any attempt to employ our courts as instruments of persecution. The knowledge that every criminal trial is subject to contemporaneous review in the forum of public opinion is an effective restraint on possible abuse of judicial power. One need not wholly agree with a statement made on the subject by Jeremy Bentham over 120 years ago to appreciate the fear of secret trials felt by him, his predecessors and contemporaries. Bentham said:

. . . suppose the proceedings to be completely secret, and the court, on the occasion, to consist of no more than a single judge,—that judge will be at once indolent and arbitrary: how corrupt soever his inclination may be, it will find no check, at any rate no tolerably efficient check, to oppose it. Without publicity, all other checks are insufficient: in comparison of publicity, all other checks are of small account. Recordation, appeal, whatever other institutions might present themselves in the character of checks, would be found to operate rather as cloaks than checks; as cloaks in reality, as checks only in appearance.

In giving content to the constitutional and statutory commands that an accused be given a public trial, the state and federal courts have differed over what groups of spectators, if any, could properly be excluded from a criminal trial. But, unless in Michigan and in one-man grand jury contempt cases, no court in this country has ever before held, so far as we can find, that an accused can be tried, convicted, and sent to jail, when everybody else is denied entrance to the court, except the judge and his attaches. And without exception all courts have held that an accused is at the very least entitled to have his friends, relatives and counsel present, no matter with what offense he may be charged. In *Gaines* v. *Washington*, 277 US 81, . . . this Court assumed that a criminal trial conducted in secret would violate the procedural requirements of the Fourteenth Amendment's due process clause, although its actual holding there was that no violation had in fact occurred, since the trial court's order barring the general public had not been enforced. Certain proceedings in a judge's chambers, including convictions for contempt of court, have occasionally been countenanced by state courts, but there has never been any intimation that all of the public, including the accused's relatives, friends, and counsel, were barred from the trial chamber.

In the case before us, the petitioner was called as a witness to testify in secret before a one-man grand jury conducting a grand jury investigation. In the midst of petitioner's testimony the proceedings abruptly changed. The investigation became a "trial," the grand jury became a judge, and the witness became an accused charged with contempt of court—all in secret. Following a charge, conviction and sentence, the petitioner was led away to prison—still without any break in the secrecy. Even in jail, according to undenied allegations, his lawyer was denied an opportunity to see and confer with him. And that was not the end of secrecy. His lawyer filed in the State Supreme Court this habeas corpus proceeding. Even there, the mantle of secrecy enveloped the transaction and the State Supreme Court ordered him sent back to jail without ever having seen a record of his testimony, and without knowing all that took place in the secrecy of the judge's chambers. In view of this nation's historic distrust of secret proceedings, their inherent dangers to freedom, and the universal requirement of our federal and state governments that criminal trials be public, the Fourteenth Amendment's guarantee that no one shall be deprived of his liberty without due process of law means at least that an accused cannot be thus sentenced to prison.

Second. We further hold that failure to afford the petitioner a reasonable opportunity to defend himself against the charge of false and evasive swearing was a denial of due process of law. A person's right to reasonable notice of a charge against him, and an opportunity to be heard in his defense—a right to his day in court—are basic in our system of jurisprudence; and these rights include, as a minimum, a right to examine the witnesses against him, to offer testimony, and to be represented by counsel. Michigan, not denying the existence of these rights in criminal cases generally, apparently concedes that the summary conviction here would have been a denial of procedural due process but for the nature of the charge, namely, a contempt of court, committed, the State urges, in the court's actual presence.

It is true that courts have long exercised a power summarily to punish certain conduct committed in open court without notice, testimony or hearing. *Ex parte Terry*, 128 US 289, . . . was such a case. There Terry committed assault on the marshal who was at the moment removing a heckler from the courtroom. The "violence and misconduct" of both the heckler and the marshal's assailant occurred within the "personal view" of the judge, "under his own eye," and actually interrupted the trial of a cause then under way. This Court held that under such circumstances a judge has power to punish an offender at once, without notice and without hearing, although his conduct may also be punishable as a criminal offense. This Court reached its conclusion because it believed that a court's business could not be conducted unless it could suppress disturbances within the courtroom by immediate punishment. However, this Court recognized that such departure from the accepted standards of due process was capable of grave abuses, and for that reason gave no encouragement to its expansion beyond the suppression and punishment of the court-disrupting misconduct which alone justified its exercise. . . .

That the holding in the *Terry Case* is not to be considered as an unlimited abandonment of the basic due process procedural safeguards, even in contempt cases, was spelled out with emphatic language in *Cooke* v. *United States*, 267 US 517. . . .

Except for a narrowly limited category of contempts, due process of law as explained in the *Cooke Case* requires that one charged with contempt of court be advised of the charges against him, have a reasonable opportunity to meet them by way of defense or explanation, have the right to be represented by counsel, and have a chance to testify and call other witnesses in his behalf, either by way of defense or explanation. The narrow exception to these due process requirements includes only charges of misconduct, in open court, in the presence of the judge, which disturbs the court's business, where all of the essential elements of the misconduct are under the eye of the court, are actually observed by the court, and where immediate punishment is essential to prevent "demoralization of the court's authority" before the public. If some essential elements of the offense are not personally observed by the judge, so that he must depend upon statements made by others for his knowledge about these essential elements, due process requires, according to the *Cooke Case*, that the accused be accorded notice and a fair hearing as above set out.

The facts shown by this record put this case outside the narrow category of cases that can be punished as contempt without notice, hearing and counsel. Since the petitioner's alleged misconduct all occurred in secret, there could be no possibility of a demoralization of the court's authority before the public. . . .

Nor is there any reason suggested why "demoralization of the court's authority" would have resulted from giving the petitioner a reasonable opportunity to appear and offer a defense in open court to a charge of perjury or to the charge of contempt. The traditional grand juries have never punished contempts. The practice that has always been followed with recalcitrant grand jury witnesses is to take them into open court, and that practice, consistent with due process, has not demoralized the authority of courts. Reported cases reveal no instances in which witnesses believed by grand juries on the basis of other testimony to be perjurers, have been convicted for contempt, or for perjury, without notice of the specific charges against them, and opportunity to prepare a defense, to obtain counsel, to cross-examine the witnesses against them and to offer evidence in their own defense. The right to be heard in open court before one is condemned is too valuable to be whittled away under the guise of "demoralization of the court's authority."

It is "the law of the land" that no man's life, liberty or property be forfeited as a punishment until there has been a charge fairly made and fairly tried in a public tribunal. . . . The petitioner was convicted without that kind of trial. . . .

Reversed and remanded.

Mr. Justice Rutledge, concurring:

I join in the Court's opinion and decision. But there is more which needs to be said.

Michigan's one-man grand jury, as exemplified by this record, combines in a single official the historically separate powers of grand jury, committing magistrate, prosecutor, trial judge and petit jury. This aggregated authority denies to the accused not only the right to a public trial, but also those other basic protections secured by the Sixth Amendment, namely, the rights "to be informed of the nature and cause of the accusation; to be confronted with the witnesses against him; to have compulsory process for obtaining witnesses in his favor, and to have the Assistance of Counsel for his defence." It takes away the security against being twice put in jeopardy for the same offense and denies the equal protection of the laws by leaving to the committing functionary's sole discretion the scope and contents of the record on appeal. U. S. Const Amend Five and Fourteen.

This aggregation of powers and inherently concomitant denial of historic freedoms were unknown to the common law at the time our institutions crystallized in the Constitution. They are altogether at variance with our tradition and system of government. They cannot stand the test of constitutionality for purposes of depriving any person of life, liberty or property. There is no semblance of due process of law in the scheme when it is used for those ends.

The case demonstrates how far this Court departed from our constitutional plan when, after the Fourteenth Amendment's adoption, it permitted selective departure by the states from the scheme of ordered personal liberty established by the Bill of Rights. In the guise of permitting the states to experiment with improving the administration of justice, the Court left them free to substitute, "in spite of the absolutism of continental governments," their "ideas and processes of civil justice" in place of the time-tried "principles and institutions of the common law" perpetuated for us in the Bill of Rights. Only by an exercise of this freedom has Michigan been enabled to adopt and apply her scheme as was done in this case. . . .

So long as they stand, so long as the Bill of Rights is regarded here as a strait jacket of Eighteenth Century procedures rather than a basic charter of personal liberty, like experimentations may be expected from the states. And the only check against their effectiveness will be the agreement of a majority of this Court that the experiment violates fundamental notions of justice in civilized society.

I do not conceive that the Bill of Rights, apart from the due process clause of the Fifth Amendment, incorporates all such ideas. But as far as its provisions go, I know of no better substitutes. A few may be inconvenient. But restrictions upon authority for securing personal liberty, as well as fairness in trial to deprive one of it, are always inconvenient—to the authority so restricted. And in times like these I do not think substitutions imported from other systems, including continental ones, offer promise on the whole of more improvement than harm, either for the cause of perfecting the administration of justice or for that of securing and perpetuating individual freedom, which is the main end of our society as it is of our Constitution.

One cannot attribute the collapse of liberty in Europe and elsewhere during recent years solely to the "ideas and processes of civil justice" prevailing in the nations which have suffered that loss. Neither can one deny the significance of the contrast between their success in maintaining systems of ordered liberty and that of other nations which in the main have adhered more closely to the scheme of personal freedoms the Bill of Rights secures. This experience demonstrates, I think, that it is both wiser and safer to put up with whatever inconveniences that charter creates than to run the risk of losing its hardwon guaranties by dubious, if also more convenient substitutions imported from alien traditions.

The states have survived with the nation through great vicissitudes, for the greater part of our history, without wide departures or numerous ones from the plan of the Bill of Rights. They accepted that plan for the nation when they ratified those amendments. They accepted it for themselves, in my opinion, when they ratified the Fourteenth Amendment. . . . It was good enough for our fathers. I think it should be good enough for this Court and for the states. . . .

12. Trial by Jury

MOORE v. NEW YORK

333 US 565 (1948)

[The Sixth and Seventh Amendments which require trial by jury in criminal and in certain civil cases in the federal courts are not read into the Due Process Clause of the Fourteenth Amendment so as to become limitations upon the states. What is inherent in the concept of due process required by the Fourteenth Amendment in trials in state courts is that conviction shall be rendered only after a hearing that is a real one, not a sham hearing, before a tribunal that is not biased by interest. If the state affords the accused a trial by jury, the jury must be a neutral one. Within this limit the states are constitutionally permitted to experiment with different types of jury procedures. Thus:

> Some states have taken measures to restrict its use [i.e. use of juries]; others . . . diminish the required number of jurors. Some states no longer require the unanimous verdict; others add alternate or substitute jurors to avoid mistrial in case of sickness or death. Some states have abolished the general verdict and require answers to specific questions. [*Fay* v. *New York*, 332 US 261 (1947).]

By 5-to-4 vote the Supreme Court has refused to interfere with this experimentation by the states. The *Moore Case* considers and upholds as constitutional the use of "blue ribbon" juries by the State of New

York. The dissenting Justices have attacked this type of jury, said to reflect relatively high economic and social positions, as undemocratic, for the defendant is entitled to a jury impartially drawn from a cross section of the community, in which will be found rich and poor, laborers and farmers and employers.

[The question has been considered whether Federal Government employees may serve on juries in criminal cases prosecuted by the Federal Government. The Court has held that such persons may serve on federal juries even in a case where an officer of the Communist Party is on trial charged with willful failure to appear before a committee of Congress that had issued a subpoena for his appearance. *Dennis* v. *United States*, 339 US 162 (1950). That decision was 5 to 2.

[On racial prejudice in the selection of juries see *Cassell* v. *Texas*, which appears later in this volume.]

Mr. Justice Jackson delivered the opinion of the Court:

Petitioners were indicted in Bronx County, New York, on February 11, 1947, for the crime of murder in the first degree. The District Attorney moved the court for an order that the trial be by a special jury, pursuant to New York law, which motion was granted over opposition on behalf of defendants by assigned counsel. One hundred and fifty names were drawn from the special jury panel, under supervision of a Justice of the State Supreme Court, in the presence of defendants' counsel and without objection.

When the case was called for trial defendants, as permitted by the state practice, served a written challenge to the panel of jurors upon the following grounds:

1. That § 749-aa of the Judiciary Law of the State of New York is in violation of § 1 of the Fourteenth Amendment to the Constitution of the United States.

2. That qualified Negro jurors were improperly excluded from the list of special jurors, from which said jury panel was drawn.

3. That qualified women jurors were improperly excluded from the list of special jurors, from which said jury panel was drawn.

After full hearing, the challenge was disallowed and petitioners were tried and convicted. . . .

The constitutionality of the New York special jury statutes has but recently been sustained by this Court, *Fay* v. *New York*, 332 US 261, against a better supported challenge than is here presented, and the issue warrants little discussion at this time.

Some effort is made by statistics to differentiate this case from the precedent one as to the ratio of convictions before special juries contrasted with that before ordinary juries. The defendants present to us a study from July 1, 1937, to June 30, 1946, which indicates that special juries in Bronx County returned 15 convictions and 4 acquittals during the period and concludes that the special jury convicted in 79% of the cases while the general juries convicted in 57%. The District Attorney responds that in 5 of these 19 cases, the special jury returned conviction in a lesser degree than that charged and, hence, in 9 out of 19 cases withheld all or part of what the State asked. Moreover, it is said that all but two were capital cases, another was for manslaughter and one for criminally receiving stolen property. It should be observed that the number of cases involved in these statements is too small to afford a secure basis for generalizing as to the convicting propensities of the two jury panels, even if the cases were comparable. But it appears that in Bronx County a system of special and intensive investigation is applied to capital cases from the moment they are reported, more careful preparation is given them and they are tried by the most experienced prosecutors. This makes this class of cases not fairly comparable with the run-of-the-mill cases, felony and misdemeanor, that are included in the ordinary jury statistics. Moreover, none of these facts were laid before the trial court which was in the best position to analyze, supplement or interpret them. We think on this part of the challenge no question is presented that was not disposed of in *Fay* v. *New York*. . . . Indeed, on opening the hearing on defendants' challenge the trial court said, "I understand the inquiry now is to be directed to the intentional elimination or disqualification of women and Negroes on the special jury panel." Counsel for both defendants assented to this definition of the issues and no evidence on other subjects was offered.

Petitioners' remaining point is that "the trial of the petitioners, Negroes, by a jury selected from a panel from which Negroes were systematically, intentionally and deliberately excluded, denied petitioners the equal protection of law and due process of law guaranteed them by the Constitution of the United States." If the evidence supported the assumption of fact included in this statement, the point would be of compelling merit. The law on this subject is now so settled that we no longer find it necessary to write out expositions of the Constitution in this regard. . . .

It is admitted that on this panel of one hundred and fifty there were no Negroes. But not only is the record wanting in proof of intentional and systematic exclusion—the only witnesses sworn testified that there was no such practice or intent. Nothing in the background facts discredits this testimony. The census figures give a proportion of Negro-to-white population in that county of .7% in 1920, 1.0% in 1930, and 1.7% in 1940. It is admitted that since the last census the

Negro population has considerably increased. According to one estimate, the number of colored inhabitants, which in 1940 was 24,892, has increased to 192,066 in 1948. The same estimator later revised the figures to between 65,000 and 70,000. Neither estimate was before the trial court, and no evidence or finding gives us judicially approved data. Of course, new wartime arrivals take some time to qualify as active members of the community and its machinery of justice cannot be expected instantaneously to reflect their presence. The official who compiled the jury lists testified as to Negro jurors that "from 1946 on I must have examined at least 500 myself." The number accepted for service could not be ascertained from the records, which make no notation of color, but he testified that there were "maybe two dozen; maybe three dozen." For the special panel, he testified that he had examined an estimated one hundred Negroes and had accepted "maybe a dozen." The testimony is undenied.

The record is utterly devoid of proof of systematic, intentional and deliberate exclusion of Negroes from jury duty.

The judgment is affirmed.

Mr. Justice Murphy, with whom Mr. Justice Black, Mr. Justice Douglas and Mr. Justice Rutledge concur, dissenting:

This case represents a tragic consequence that can flow from the use of the "blue ribbon" jury. Two men must forfeit their lives after having been convicted of murder not by a jury of their peers, not by a jury chosen from a fair cross-section of the community, but by a jury drawn from a special group of individuals singled out in a manner inconsistent with the democratic ideals of the jury system. That group was chosen because they possessed some trait or characteristic which distinguished them from the general panel of jurors, some qualification which made them more desirable for the State's purpose of securing the conviction of the two petitioners. Such a basis for jury selection has no place in our constitutional way of life. It contravenes the most elementary notions of equal protection and I can no more acquiesce in its use in this case than I was able to do in *Fay* v. *New York*.

The constitutional invalidity of this "blue ribbon" system does not depend upon proof of the systematic and intentional exclusion of any economic, racial or social group. Nor does it rest upon a demonstration that "blue ribbon" juries are more inclined to convict than ordinary juries. Such factors are frequently, if not invariably, present in "blue ribbon" situations, though proof is extremely difficult. But they are at best only the end products of the system, not the root evil.

The vice lies in the very concept of "blue ribbon" panels—the systematic and intentional exclusion of all but the "best" or the most learned or intelligent of the general jurors. Such panels are completely at war with the democratic theory of our jury system, a theory formulated out of the experience of generations. One is constitutionally entitled to be judged by a fair sampling of all one's neighbors who are qualified, not merely those with superior intelligence or learning. Jury panels are supposed to be representative of all qualified classes. Within those classes, of course, are persons with varying degrees of intelligence, wealth, education, ability and experience. But it is from that welter of qualified individuals, who meet specified minimum standards, that juries are to be chosen. Any method that permits only the "best" of these to be selected opens the way to grave abuses. The jury is then in danger of losing its democratic flavor and becoming the instrument of the select few.

Hence the "blue ribbon" method of selecting only the "best" of the general jurors, a method instituted with the highest of intentions, does violence to the fundamental precepts of the jury system. Appeals to administrative convenience do not soften that violence. And since the method deprives the defendant of the protection accorded others who are able to draw upon the general panel, it falls under the ban of the Fourteenth Amendment. I would therefore reverse the judgment below.

13. Ex Post Facto Laws

BURGESS v. SALMON

97 US 381 (1878)

[The original Constitution provides that "no ex post facto law shall be passed." Art. I, Sec. 9, Cl. 3. The same Article, Sec. 10, provides that no state shall pass any ex post facto law.

[These provisions apply only to criminal, and not to civil, statutes. They prohibit retroactive legislation which makes criminal an act which was innocent when done. They also bar the infliction of a greater punishment than was provided by law when the crime was committed. Retroactive laws affecting deportation are, however, constitutional, for deportation has been held to be not "punishment" in the constitutional sense. Modes of procedure in criminal trials may also be changed if the defendant's substantial rights are not diminished.

[In the present case Salmon had paid a tax of 20 cents per pound on his tobacco and thereupon sold it. This was done in the forenoon of March 3, 1875. In the afternoon of the same day the President signed a bill which increased the duty to 24 cents per pound. The Government then collected the additional 4 cents per pound, which Salmon paid under protest. He then sought in this suit to recover his extra payment. His contention was that he had paid the tax that was due from him under the statutes in effect at the time of payment, and that if the theory of the Government could be sustained, then he would be liable to the penalty provision of the new act, which provided that a person who removes from his factory tobacco without having affixed on it the proper revenue stamps shall be punished for the offense by a specified fine or imprisonment. The Court decided unanimously in favor of Salmon, thus significantly disregarding the civil appearance of the statute, which essentially was criminal in character.]

Mr. Justice Hunt delivered the opinion of the Court: . . .

The case presents but a single point: can a manufacturer be punished, criminally and civilly, civilly here, for the violation of a statute when the statute was not in force at the time the act was done? In other words: can a person be thus punished when he did not contravene the provisions of the statute? In still other words: can one be punished for offending against the provisions of a statute from the effects of which he was expressly exempted? . . .

In the present case, the acts and admissions of the Government establish the position that the duties exacted by law had been fully paid, and the goods had been surrendered and transported before the President had approved the Act of Congress imposing an increased duty upon them.

To impose upon the owner of the goods a criminal punishment, or a penalty of $377, for not paying an additional tax of four cents a pound, would subject him to the operation of an *ex post facto* law.

An *ex post facto* law is one which imposes a punishment for an act which was not punishable at the time it was committed, or a punishment in addition to that then prescribed. . . .

Had the proceeding against Salmon & Hancock been taken by indictment instead of suit for the excess of the tax, and the one was equally authorized with the other, the proceeding would certainly have fallen within the description of an *ex post facto* law.

In *Fletcher* v. *Peck,* 6 Cranch 87, it was decided that an Act of the Legislature by which a man's estate shall be seized for a crime which was not declared to be an offense by a previous law, was void.

In *Cummings* v. *Missouri,* it was held that the passage of an Act imposing a penalty on a priest for the performance of an act innocent by law at the time when it was committed, was void. 4 Wall. 277.

To the same purport is *Pierce* v. *Carskaden,* 16 Wall. 234.

The cases cited hold that the *ex post facto* effect of a law cannot be evaded by giving a civil form to that which is essentially criminal. . . .

Judgment affirmed.

14. Immigration and Due Process

SHAUGHNESSY v. UNITED STATES ex rel. MEZEI

345 US 206 (1953)

[Mezei, an alien, lived in the United States for twenty-five years. As far as the record showed, he was a law-abiding person. In 1948 he went to Rumania to visit his mother. He had a visa for his re-entry. When he returned, he was declared inadmissible on security grounds. The Government refused to disclose to him or to the courts the information against him. He was detained for three years without a trial or charges.

[The Court, by a 5-to-4 decision, held that Mezei was an alien seeking admission to the United States and, as such, had no right to constitutional due process. He could be excluded without a hearing and could be detained indefinitely. Justices Black, Douglas, Frankfurter, and Jackson dissented.

[For a consideration of this case and related cases, see Milton R. Konvitz, *Civil Rights in Immigration* (Ithaca, N.Y.: Cornell University Press, 1953) ch. i.]

Mr. Justice Clark delivered the opinion of the Court:

This case concerns an alien immigrant permanently excluded from the United States on security grounds but stranded in his temporary haven on Ellis Island because other countries will not take him back. The issue is whether the Attorney General's continued exclusion of respondent without a hearing amounts to an unlawful detention, so that courts may admit him temporarily to the United States on bond until arrangements are made for his departure abroad. . . .

Respondent's present dilemma springs from these circumstances: Though, as the District Court observed, "[t]here is a certain vagueness about [his] history," respondent seemingly was born in Gibraltar of Hungarian or Rumanian parents and lived in the United States from 1923 to 1948. In May of that year he sailed for Europe, apparently to visit his dying mother in Rumania. Denied entry there, he remained in Hungary for some 19 months, due to "difficulty in securing an exit permit." Finally, armed with a quota immigration visa issued by the American Consul in Budapest, he proceeded to France and boarded the *Ile de France* in Le Havre bound for New York. Upon arrival on February 9, 1950, he was temporarily excluded from the United States by an immigration inspector acting pursuant to the Passport Act as amended and regulations thereunder. Pending disposition of his case he was received at Ellis Island. After reviewing the evidence, the Attorney General on May 10, 1950, ordered the temporary exclusion to be made permanent without a hearing before a board of special inquiry, on the "basis of information of a confidential nature, the disclosure of which would be prejudicial to the public interest." That determination rested on a finding that respondent's entry would be prejudicial to the public interest for security reasons. But thus far all attempts to effect respondent's departure have failed: Twice he shipped out to return whence he came; France and Great Britain refused him permission to land. The State Department has unsuccessfully negotiated with Hungary for his readmission. Respondent personally applied for entry to about a dozen Latin-American countries but all turned him down. So in June 1951 respondent advised the Immigration and Naturalization Service that he would exert no further efforts to depart. In short, respondent sat on Ellis Island because this country shut him out and others were unwilling to take him in.

Asserting unlawful confinement on Ellis Island, he sought relief through a series of habeas corpus proceedings. After four unsuccessful efforts on respondent's part, the United States District Court for the Southern District of New York on November 9, 1951, sustained the writ. The District Judge, vexed by the problem of "an alien who has no place to go," did not question the validity of the exclusion order but deemed further "detention" after 21 months excessive and justifiable only by affirmative proof of respondent's danger to the public safety. When the Government declined to divulge such evidence, even *in camera*, the District Court directed respondent's conditional parole on bond. By a divided vote, the Court of Appeals affirmed. Postulating that the power to hold could never be broader than the power to remove or shut out and that to "continue an alien's confinement beyond that moment when deportation becomes patently impossible is to deprive him of his liberty," the court found respondent's "confinement" no longer justifiable as a means of removal elsewhere, thus not authorized by statute, and in violation of due process. Judge Learned Hand, dissenting, took a different view. The Attorney General's order was one of "exclusion" and not "deportation"; respondent's transfer from ship to shore on Ellis Island conferred no additional rights; in fact, no alien so situated "can force us to admit him at all."

Courts have long recognized the power to expel or exclude aliens as a fundamental sovereign attribute exercised by the Government's political departments largely immune from judicial control. . . . In the exercise of these powers, Congress expressly authorized the President to impose additional restrictions on aliens entering or leaving the United States during periods of international tension and strife. That authorization, originally enacted in the Passport Act of 1918, continues in effect during the present emergency. Under it, the Attorney General, acting for the President, may shut out aliens whose "entry would be prejudicial to the interests of the United States." And he may exclude without a hearing when the exclusion is based on confidential information the disclosure of which may be prejudicial to the public interest. The Attorney General in this case proceeded in accord with these provisions; he made the necessary determinations and barred the alien from entering the United States.

It is true that aliens who have once passed through our gates, even illegally, may be expelled only after proceedings conforming to traditional standards of fairness encompassed in due process of law. . . . But an alien on the threshold of initial entry stands on a different footing: "Whatever the procedure authorized by Congress is, it is due process as far as an alien denied entry is concerned." . . . And because the action of the executive officer under such authority is final and conclusive, the Attorney General cannot be compelled to disclose the evidence underlying his determinations in an exclusion case; "it is not within the province of any court, unless expressly authorized by law, to review the determination of the political branch of the Government." . . . In a case such as this, courts cannot retry the determination of the Attorney General. . . .

Neither respondent's harborage on Ellis Island nor his prior residence here transforms this into something other than an exclusion proceeding. Concededly, his movements are restrained by authority of the United States, and he may by habeas corpus test the validity of his exclusion. But that is true whether he enjoys temporary refuge on land, . . . or remains continuously aboard ship. . . . In sum, harborage at Ellis Island is not an entry into the United States. . . . For purposes of the immigration laws, moreover, the legal incidents of an alien's entry remain unaltered whether he has been here once before or not. He is an entering alien just the same, and may be excluded if unqualified for admission under existing immigration laws. . . .

Reversed.

Mr. Justice Black, with whom Mr. Justice Douglas concurs, dissenting:

Mezei came to this country in 1923 and lived as a resident alien in Buffalo, New York, for twenty-five years. He made a trip to Europe in 1948 and was stopped at our shore on his return in 1950. Without charge of or conviction for any crime, he was for two years held a prisoner on Ellis Island by order of the Attorney General. Mezei sought habeas corpus in the District Court. He wanted to go to his wife and home in Buffalo. The Attorney General defended the imprisonment by alleging that it would be dangerous to the

Nation's security to let Mezei go home even temporarily on bail. Asked for proof of this, the Attorney General answered the judge that all his information was "of a confidential nature" so much so that telling any of it or even telling the names of any of his secret informers would jeopardize the safety of the Nation. Finding that Mezei's life as a resident alien in Buffalo had been "unexceptional" and that no facts had been proven to justify his continued imprisonment, the District Court granted bail. The Court of Appeals approved. Now this Court orders Mezei to leave his home and go back to his island prison to stay indefinitely, maybe for life.

Mr. Justice Jackson forcefully points out the danger in the Court's holding that Mezei's liberty is completely at the mercy of the unreviewable discretion of the Attorney General. I join Mr. Justice Jackson in the belief that Mezei's continued imprisonment without a hearing violates due process of law.

No society is free where government makes one person's liberty depend upon the arbitrary will of another. Dictatorships have done this since time immemorial. They do now. Russian laws of 1934 authorized the People's Commissariat to imprison, banish and exile Russian citizens as well as "foreign subjects who are socially dangerous." Hitler's secret police were given like powers. German courts were forbidden to make any inquiry whatever as to the information on which the police acted. Our Bill of Rights was written to prevent such oppressive practices. Under it this Nation has fostered and protected individual freedom. The Founders abhorred arbitrary one-man imprisonments. Their belief was—our constitutional principles are—that no person of any faith, rich or poor, high or low, native or foreigner, white or colored, can have his life, liberty or property taken "without due process of law." This means to me that neither the federal police nor federal prosecutors nor any other governmental official, whatever his title, can put or keep people in prison without accountability to courts of justice. It means that individual liberty is too highly prized in this country to allow executive officials to imprison and hold people on the basis of information kept secret from courts. It means that Mezei should not be deprived of his liberty indefinitely except as the result of a fair open court hearing in which evidence is appraised by the court, not by the prosecutor.

Mr. Justice Jackson, whom Mr. Justice Frankfurter joins, dissenting:

Fortunately it still is startling, in this country, to find a person held indefinitely in executive custody without accusation of crime or judicial trial. Executive imprisonment has been considered oppressive and lawless since John, at Runnymede, pledged that no free man should be imprisoned, dispossessed, outlawed, or exiled save by the judgment of his peers or by the law of the land. The judges of England developed the writ of habeas corpus largely to preserve these immunities from executive restraint. Under the best tradition of Anglo-American law, courts will not deny hearing to an unconvicted prisoner just because he is an alien whose keep, in legal theory, is just outside our gates. Lord Mansfield, in the celebrated case holding that slavery was unknown to the common law of England, ran his writ of habeas corpus in favor of an alien, an African Negro slave, and against the master of a ship at anchor in the Thames.

What is our case? In contemplation of law, I agree, it is that of an alien who asks admission to the country. Concretely, however, it is that of a lawful and law-abiding inhabitant of our country for a quarter of a century, long ago admitted for permanent residence, who seeks to return home. After a foreign visit to his aged and ailing mother that was prolonged by disturbed conditions of Eastern Europe, he obtained a visa for admission issued by our consul and returned to New York. There the Attorney General refused to honor his documents and turned him back as a menace to this Nation's security. This man, who seems to have led a life of unrelieved insignificance, must have been astonished to find himself suddenly putting the Government of the United States in such fear that it was afraid to tell him why it was afraid of him. He was shipped and reshipped to France, which twice refused him landing. Great Britain declined, and no other European country has been found willing to open its doors to him. Twelve countries of the American Hemisphere refused his applications. Since we proclaimed him a Hercules who might pull down the pillars of our temple, we should not be surprised if peoples less prosperous, less strongly established and less stable feared to take him off our timorous hands. With something of a record as an unwanted man, neither his efforts nor those of the United States Government any longer promise to find him an abiding place. For nearly two years he was held in custody of the immigration authorities of the United States at Ellis Island, and if the Government has its way he seems likely to be detained indefinitely, perhaps for life, for a cause known only to the Attorney General.

Is respondent deprived of liberty? The Government answers that he was "transferred to Ellis Island on August 1, 1950 for safekeeping," and "is not being detained in the usual sense, but is in custody solely to prevent him from gaining entry into the United States in violation of law. He is free to depart from the United States to any country of his choice." Government counsel ingeniously argued that Ellis Island is his "refuge" whence he is free to take leave in any direction except west. That might mean freedom, if only he were an amphibian! Realistically, this man is incarcerated by a combination of forces which keep him as effectually as a prison, the dominant and proximate of these forces being the United States immigration authority. It overworks legal fiction to say that one is free in law when by the commonest of common sense he is bound. Despite the impeccable legal logic of the Government's argument on this point, it leads to an artificial and unreal conclusion. We must regard this alien as deprived of liberty, and the question is whether the deprivation is a denial of due process of law.

The Government on this point argues that "no alien has any constitutional right to entry into the United States"; that "the alien has only such rights as Congress sees fit to grant in exclusion proceedings"; that "the so-called detention is still merely a continuation of the exclusion which is specifically authorized by Congress"; that since "the restraint is not incidental to an order [of exclusion] but is itself the effectuation of the exclusion order, there is no limit to its continuance" other than statutory, which means no limit at all. The Government all but adopts the words of one of the officials responsible for the administration of this Act who testified before a congressional committee as to an alien applicant, that "He has no rights."

The interpretations of the Fifth Amendment's command that no person shall be deprived of life, liberty or property without due process of law, come about to this: reasonable general legislation reasonably applied to the individual. The question is whether the Government's detention of respondent is compatible with these tests of substance and procedure.

Substantively, due process of law renders what is due to a strong state as well as to a free individual. It tolerates all reasonable measures to insure the national safety, and it leaves a large, at times a potentially dangerous, latitude for executive judgment as to policies and means.

After all, the pillars which support our liberties are the three branches of government, and the burden could not be carried by our own power alone. Substantive due process will always pay a high degree of deference to congressional and executive judgment, especially when they concur, as to what is reasonable policy under conditions of particular times and circumstances. Close to the maximum of respect is due from the judiciary to the political departments in policies affecting security and alien exclusion. . . .

Due process does not invest any alien with a right to enter the United States, nor confer on those admitted the right to remain against the national will. Nothing in the Constitution requires admission or sufferance of aliens hostile to our scheme of government.

Nor do I doubt that due process of law will tolerate some impounding of an alien where it is deemed essential to the safety of the state. Even the resident, friendly alien may be subject to executive detention without bail, for a reasonable period, pending consummation of deportation arrangements. . . . The alien enemy may be confined or his property seized and administered because hostility is assumed from his continued allegiance to a hostile state. . . .

If due process will permit confinement of resident aliens friendly in fact because of imputed hostility, I should suppose one personally at war with our institutions might be confined, even though his state is not at war with us. In both cases, the underlying consideration is the power of our system of government to defend itself, and changing strategy of attack by infiltration may be met with changed tactics of defense.

Nor do I think the concept of due process so paralyzing that it forbids all detention of an alien as a preventive measure against threatened dangers and makes confinement lawful only after the injuries have been suffered. In some circumstances, even the citizen in default of bail has long been subject to federal imprisonment for security of the peace and good behavior. While it is usually applied for express verbal threats, no reason is known to me why the power is not the same in the case of threats inferred by proper procedures from circumstances. The British, with whom due process is a habit, if not a written constitutional dictum, permit a court in a limited class of cases to pass a "sentence of preventive detention" if satisfied that it is expedient for the protection of the public.

I conclude that detention of an alien would not be inconsistent with substantive due process, provided—and this is where my dissent begins—he is accorded procedural due process of law.

Procedural fairness, if not all that originally was meant by due process of law, is at least what it most uncompromisingly requires. Procedural due process is more elemental and less flexible than substantive due process. It yields less to the times, varies less with conditions, and defers much less to legislative judgment. Insofar as it is technical law, it must be a specialized responsibility within the competence of the judiciary on which they do not bend before political branches of the Government, as they should on matters of policy which compromise substantive law.

If it be conceded that in some way this alien could be confined, does it matter what the procedure is? Only the untaught layman or the charlatan lawyer can answer that procedures matter not. Procedural fairness and regularity are of the indispensable essence of liberty. Severe substantive laws can be endured if they are fairly and impartially applied. Indeed, if put to the choice, one might well prefer to live under Soviet substantive law applied in good faith by our common-law procedures than under our substantive law enforced by Soviet procedural practices. Let it not be overlooked that due process of law is not for the sole benefit of an accused. It is the best insurance for the Government itself against those blunders which leave lasting stains on a system of justice but which are bound to occur on *ex parte* considerations. . . .

Our law may, and rightly does, place more restrictions on the alien than on the citizen. But basic fairness in hearing procedures does not vary with the status of the accused. If the procedures used to judge this alien are fair and just, no good reason can be given why they should not be extended to simplify the condemnation of citizens. If they would be unfair to citizens, we cannot defend the fairness of them when applied to the more helpless and handicapped alien. This is at the root of our holdings that the resident alien must be given a fair hearing to test an official claim that he is one of a deportable class. . . .

The most scrupulous observance of due process, including the right to know a charge, to be confronted with the accuser, to cross-examine informers and to produce evidence in one's behalf, is especially necessary where the occasion of detention is fear of future misconduct, rather than crimes committed. Both the old proceeding by which one may be bound to keep the peace and the newer British "preventive detention" are safeguarded with full rights to judicial hearings for the accused. On the contrary, the Nazi regime in Germany installed a system of "protective custody" by which the arrested could claim no judicial or other hearing process, and as a result the concentration camps were populated with victims of summary executive detention for secret reasons. That is what renders Communist justice such a travesty. There are other differences, to be sure, between authoritarian procedure and common law, but differences in the process of administration make all the difference between a reign of terror and one of law. Quite unconsciously, I am sure, Government's theory of custody for "safekeeping" without disclosure to the victim of charges, evidence, informers or reasons, even in an administrative proceeding, has unmistakable overtones of the "protective custody" of the Nazis more than of any detaining procedure known to the common law. Such a practice, once established with the best of intentions, will drift into oppression of the disadvantaged in this country as surely as it has elsewhere. That these apprehensive surmises are not "such stuff as dreams are made on" appears from testimony of a top immigration official concerning an applicant that "He has no rights."

Because the respondent has no rights of entry, does it follow that he has no rights at all? Does the power to exclude mean that exclusion may be continued or effectuated by any means which happen to seem appropriate to the authorities? It would effectuate his exclusion to eject him bodily into the sea or to set him adrift in a rowboat. Would not such measures be condemned judicially as a deprivation of life without due process of law? Suppose the authorities decide to disable an alien from entry by confiscating his valuables and money. Would we not hold this a taking of property without due process of law? Here we have a case that lies between the taking of life and the taking of property; it is the taking of liberty. It seems to me that this, occurring within the United States or its territorial waters, may be done only by proceedings which meet the test of due process of law.

Exclusion of an alien without judicial hearing, of course, does not deny due process when it can be accomplished merely by turning him back on land or returning him by sea. But when indefinite confinement becomes the means of enforcing exclusion, it seems to me that due process requires that the alien be informed of its grounds and have a fair chance to overcome them. This is the more due him when he is entrapped into leaving the other shore by reliance on a visa which the Attorney General refuses to honor.

It is evident that confinement of respondent no longer can be justified as a step in the process of turning him back to the country whence he came. Confinement is no longer ancillary to exclusion; it can now be justified only as the alternative to normal exclusion. It is an end in itself.

The Communist conspiratorial technique of infiltration poses a problem which sorely tempts the Government to resort to confinement of suspects on secret information secretly judged. I have not been one to discount the Communist evil. But my apprehensions about the security of our form of government are about equally aroused by those who refuse to recognize the dangers of Communism and those who will not see danger in anything else.

Congress has ample power to determine whom we will admit to our shores and by what means it will effectuate its exclusion policy. The only limitation is that it may not do so by authorizing United States officers to take the life, the liberty or the property of an alien who has come within our jurisdiction without due process of law, and that means he must meet a fair hearing with fair notice of the charges.

It is inconceivable to me that this measure of simple justice and fair dealing would menace the security of this country. No one can make me believe that we are that far gone.

★ X ★

Freedom from

Race Discrimination

1. No Segregation by Zoning

BUCHANAN v. WARLEY

245 US 60 (1917)

[As a consequence of the Civil War the Thirteenth Amendment was adopted in 1865, the Fourteenth in 1868, and the Fifteenth in 1870. Congress passed enforcement and federal election acts. These were all efforts by the Federal Government to remove from the Negro the badge of slavery as well as to end slavery itself. Reconstruction ended, however, in 1877, when federal troops were removed from the states that had seceded; the Negro was then left to the mercy of the South. In 1894 Congress was controlled by the Democratic Party, for the first time since the Civil War, and it proceeded to repeal many of the civil rights provisions in federal law. In 1883 the Supreme Court declared the Civil Rights Act of 1875 unconstitutional. This decision made it possible for the states to enact laws that would segregate Negroes in many ways: in transportation facilities, schools, hospitals, jails and prisons, places of amusement, sport, and recreation, and elsewhere. In *Plessy* v. *Ferguson*, 163 US 537 (1896), the Court upheld a Louisiana statute that provided for "separate but equal" accommodations on railroads for white and Negro passengers. Segregation, operating under the sanction of the "separate but equal" formula, became the pattern in Southern states.

[The Supreme Court did not, however, uniformly uphold segregation laws as constitutional. A law that attempted to segregate Negroes in the location of their homes in the city of Louisville, Kentucky, was unanimously declared unconstitutional in the present case.

[For further consideration of the problem of segregation and civil rights laws, see Milton R. Konvitz, *The Constitution and Civil Rights* (New York: Columbia University Press, 1947).]

Mr. Justice Day delivered the opinion of the court:

Buchanan . . . brought an action in the chancery branch of Jefferson circuit court of Kentucky for the specific performance of a contract for the sale of certain real estate situated in the city of Louisville. . . . The offer in writing to purchase the property contained a proviso:

> It is understood that I am purchasing the above property for the purpose of having erected thereon a house which I propose to make my residence, and it is a distinct part of this agreement that I shall not be required to accept a deed to the above property or to pay for said property unless I have the right, under the laws of the state of Kentucky and the city of Louisville, to occupy said property as a residence.

This offer was accepted by the plaintiff.

To the action for specific performance the defendant, by way of answer, set up the condition above set forth, that he is a colored person, and that on the block of which the lot in controversy is a part, there are ten residences, eight of which, at the time of the making of the contract, were occupied by white people, and only two (those nearest the lot in question) were occupied by colored people, and that, under and by virtue of the ordinance of the city of Louisville, approved May 11, 1914, he would not be allowed to occupy the lot as a place of residence.

In reply to this answer the plaintiff set up, among other things, that the ordinance was in conflict with the 14th Amendment to the Constitution of the United States, and hence no defense to the action for specific performance of the contract. . . .

The title of the ordinance is:

> An ordinance to prevent conflict and ill-feeling between the white and colored races in the city of Louisville, and preserve the public peace and promote the general welfare by making reasonable provisions requiring as far as practicable, the use of separate blocks for residences, places of abode, and places of assembly by white and colored people respectively. . . .

We pass . . . to a consideration of the case upon its merits. This ordinance prevents the occupancy of a lot in the city of Louisville by a person of color in a block where the greater number of residences are occupied by white persons; where such a majority exists, colored persons are excluded. This interdiction is based wholly upon color; simply that, and nothing more. In effect, premises situated as are those in question in the so-called white block are effectively debarred from sale to persons of color, because, if sold, they cannot be occupied by the purchaser nor by him sold to another of the same color.

This drastic measure is sought to be justified under the authority of the state in the exercise of the police power. It is said such legislation tends to promote the public peace by preventing racial conflicts; that it tends to maintain racial purity; that it prevents the deterioration of property owned and occupied by white people, which deterioration, it is contended, is sure to follow the occupancy of adjacent premises by persons of color.

The authority of the state to pass laws in the exercise of the police power, having for their object the promotion of the public health, safety, and welfare, is very broad, as has been affirmed in numerous and recent decisions of this court. Furthermore, the exercise of this power, embracing nearly all legislation of a local character, is not to be interfered with by the courts where it is within the scope of legislative authority and the means adopted reasonably tend to accomplish a lawful purpose. But it is equally well established that the police power, broad as it is, cannot justify the passage of a law or ordinance which runs counter to the limitations of the Federal Constitution; that principle has been so frequently affirmed in this court that we need not stop to cite the cases.

The Federal Constitution and laws passed within its authority are, by the express terms of that instrument, made the supreme law of the land. The 14th Amendment protects life, liberty, and property from invasion by the states without due process of law. Property is more than the mere thing which a person owns. It is elementary that it includes the right to acquire, use, and dispose of it. The Constitution protects these essential attributes of property. . . .

True it is that dominion over property springing from ownership is not absolute and unqualified. The disposition and use of property may be controlled, in the exercise of the police power, in the interest of public health, convenience, or welfare. Harmful occupations may be controlled and regulated. Legitimate business may also be regulated in the interest of the public. Certain uses of property may be confined to portions of the municipality other than the residence district, such as livery stables, brickyards, and the like, because of the impairment of the health and comfort of the occupants of neighboring property. Many illustrations might be given from the decisions of this court and other courts, of this principle, but these cases do not touch the one at bar.

The concrete question here is: May the occupancy, and, necessarily, the purchase and sale of property of which occupancy is an incident, be inhibited by the states, or by one of its municipalities, solely because of the color of the proposed occupant of the premises? That one may dispose of his property, subject only to the control of lawful enactments curtailing that right in the public interest, must be conceded. The question now presented makes it pertinent to inquire into the constitutional right of the white man to sell his property to a colored man, having in view the legal status of the purchaser and occupant.

Following the Civil War certain amendments to the Federal Constitution were adopted, which have become an integral part of that instrument, equally binding upon all the states and fixing certain fundamental rights which all are bound to respect. The 13th Amendment abolished slavery in the United States and in all places subject to their jurisdiction, and gave Congress power to enforce the Amendment by appropriate legislation. The 14th Amendment made all persons born or naturalized in the United States, citizens of the United States and of the states in which they reside, and provided that no state shall make or enforce any law which shall abridge the privileges or immunities of citizens of the United States, and that no state shall deprive any person of life, liberty, or property without due process of law, nor deny to any person the equal protection of the laws. . . .

That there exists a serious and difficult problem arising from a feeling of race hostility which the law is powerless to control, and to which it must give a measure of consideration, may be freely admitted. But its solution cannot be promoted by depriving citizens of their constitutional rights and privileges.

As we have seen, this court has held laws valid which separated the races on the basis of equal accommodations in public conveyances, and courts of high authority have held enactments lawful which provide for separation in the public schools of white and colored pupils where equal privileges are given. But, in view of the rights secured by the 14th Amendment to the Federal Constitution, such legislation must have its limitations, and cannot be sustained where the exercise of authority exceeds the restraints of the Constitution. We think these limitations are exceeded in laws and ordinances of the character now before us.

It is the purpose of such enactments, and it is frankly avowed it will be their ultimate effect, to require by law, at least in residential districts, the compulsory separation of the races on account of color. Such action is said to be essential to the maintenance of the purity of the races, although it is to be noted in the ordinance under consideration that the employment of colored servants in white families is permitted, and nearby residences of colored persons not coming within the blocks, as defined in the ordinance, are not prohibited.

The case presented does not deal with an attempt to prohibit the amalgamation of the races. The right which the ordinance annulled was the civil right of a white man to dispose of his property if he saw fit to do so to a person of color, and of a colored person to make such disposition to a white person.

It is urged that this proposed segregation will promote the public peace by preventing race conflicts. Desirable as this is, and important as is the preservation of the public peace, this aim cannot be accomplished by laws or ordinances which deny rights created or protected by the Federal Constitution.

It is said that such acquisitions by colored persons depreciate property owned in the neighborhood by white persons. But property may be acquired by undesirable white neighbors, or put to disagreeable though lawful uses with like results.

We think this attempt to prevent the alienation of the property in question to a person of color was not a legitimate exercise of the police power of the state, and is in direct violation of the fundamental law enacted in the 14th Amendment of the Constitution preventing state interference with property rights except by due process of law. That being the case, the ordinance cannot stand. . . .

Reversed.

2. *Restrictive Covenants Unenforceable*

SHELLEY *v.* KRAEMER

334 US 1 (1948)

[Segregation by zoning, as we have seen, was held invalid by the Court in 1917. Efforts were then concentrated on achieving racial segregation through the device known as the restrictive covenant, an undertaking in a deed or other formal instrument that the property described therein will not be sold or rented to Negroes. It was thought that such arrangements would be upheld as legal because they were private undertakings. In *Corrigan* v. *Buckley,* 271 US 323 (1926), the Court upheld such private covenants. But in *Shelley* v. *Kraemer,* the present case, the Court unanimously held that while such covenants are private, their *enforcement* by state courts is *state action* and is, therefore, unconstitutional as a denial of equal protection of the laws. (Justices Reed, Rutledge, and Jackson did not participate in the case.) The restrictive covenant in the District of Columbia was also barred by the Court in

Hurd v. *Hodge*, 334 US 24 (1948). The last loophole was closed when the Court, with one Justice dissenting, held in *Barrows* v. *Jackson*, 346 US 249 (1953), that one party to a restrictive covenant may not recover damages from another party who broke the covenant. In brief, racial restrictive covenants are not enforceable either in equity or by an action for damages, in either state or federal courts. Parties may voluntarily observe the terms of their covenants, but no court may aid them.]

Mr. Chief Justice Vinson delivered the opinion of the Court:

. . . It is well, at the outset, to scrutinize the terms of the restrictive agreements involved in these cases. In the Missouri case, the covenant declares that no part of the affected property shall be "occupied by any person not of the Caucasian race, it being intended hereby to restrict the use of said property . . . against the occupancy as owners or tenants of any portion of said property for resident or other purpose by people of the Negro or Mongolian Race." Not only does the restriction seek to proscribe use and occupancy of the affected properties by members of the excluded class, but as construed by the Missouri courts, the agreement requires that title of any person who uses his property in violation of the restriction shall be divested. The restriction of the covenant in the Michigan case seeks to bar occupancy by persons of the excluded class. It provides that "This property shall not be used or occupied by any person or persons except those of the Caucasian race."

It should be observed that these covenants do not seek to proscribe any particular use of the affected properties. Use of the properties for residential occupancy, as such, is not forbidden. The restrictions of these agreements, rather, are directed toward a designated class of persons and seek to determine who may and who may not own or make use of the properties for residential purposes. The excluded class is defined wholly in terms of race or color; "simply that and nothing more."

It cannot be doubted that among the civil rights intended to be protected from discriminatory state action by the Fourteenth Amendment are the rights to acquire, enjoy, own and dispose of property. Equality in the enjoyment of property rights was regarded by the framers of that Amendment as an essential pre-condition to the realization of other basic civil rights and liberties which the Amendment was intended to guarantee. Thus, . . . 8 USCA § 42, . . . derived from § 1 of the Civil Rights Act of 1866 which was enacted by Congress while the Fourteenth Amendment was also under consideration, provides:

"All citizens of the United States shall have the same right, in every State and Territory, as is enjoyed by white citizens thereof to inherit, purchase, lease, sell, hold, and convey real and personal property." This Court has given specific recognition to the same principle. . . .

We conclude, therefore, that the restrictive agreements standing alone cannot be regarded as violative of any rights guaranteed to petitioners by the Fourteenth Amendment. So long as the purposes of those agreements are effectuated by voluntary adherence to their terms, it would appear clear that there has been no action by the State and the provisions of the Amendment have not been violated. . . .

But here there was more. These are cases in which the purposes of the agreements were secured only by judicial enforcement by state courts of the restrictive terms of the agreements. The respondents urge that judicial enforcement of private agreement does not amount to state action; or, in any event, the participation of the States is so attenuated in character as not to amount to state action within the meaning of the Fourteenth Amendment. Finally, it is suggested, even if the States in these cases may be deemed to have acted in the constitutional sense, their action did not deprive petitioners of rights guaranteed by the Fourteenth Amendment. We move to a consideration of these matters. . . .

The short of the matter is that from the time of the adoption of the Fourteenth Amendment until the present, it has been the consistent ruling of this Court that the action of the States to which the Amendment has reference, includes action of state courts and state judicial officials. Although, in construing the terms of the Fourteenth Amendment, differences have from time to time been expressed as to whether particular types of state action may be said to offend the Amendment's prohibitory provisions, it has never been suggested that state court action is immunized from the operation of those provisions simply because the act is that of the judicial branch of the state government.

Against this background of judicial construction, extending over a period of some three-quarters of a century, we are called upon to consider whether enforcement by state courts of the restrictive agreements in these cases may be deemed to be the acts of those States; and, if so, whether that action has denied these petitioners the equal protection of the laws which the Amendment was intended to insure.

We have no doubt that there has been state action in these cases in the full and complete sense of the phrase. The undisputed facts disclose that petitioners were willing purchasers of properties upon which they desired to establish homes. The owners of the properties were willing sellers; and contracts of sale were accordingly consummated. It is clear that but for the active intervention of the state courts, supported by the full panoply of state power, petitioners would have been free to occupy the properties in question without restraint.

These are not cases, as has been suggested, in which the States have merely abstained from action, leaving private individuals free to impose such discriminations as they see fit. Rather, these are cases in which the States have made available to such individuals the full coercive power of government to deny to petitioners, on the grounds of race or color, the enjoyment of property rights in premises which petitioners are willing and financially able to acquire and which the grantors are willing to sell. The difference between judicial enforcement and non-enforcement of the restrictive covenants is the difference to petitioners between being denied rights of property available to other members of the community and being accorded full enjoyment of those rights on an equal footing.

The enforcement of the restrictive agreements by the state courts in these cases was directed pursuant to the common-law policy of the States as formulated by those courts in earlier decisions. In the Missouri case, enforcement of the covenant was directed in the first instance by the highest court of the State after the trial court had determined the agreement to be invalid for want of the requisite number of signatures. In the Michigan case, the order of enforcement by the trial court was affirmed by the highest state court. The judicial action in each case bears the clear and unmistakable imprimatur of the State. We have noted that previous decisions of this Court have established the proposition that judicial action is not immunized from the operation of the Fourteenth Amendment simply because it is taken pursuant to the state's common-law policy. Nor is the Amendment ineffective simply because the particular pattern of discrimination, which the State has enforced, was defined initially by the terms of a private agreement. State action, as that phrase is understood for the purposes of the Fourteenth Amendment, refers to exertions of state power in all forms. And when the effect of that action is to deny rights subject to the protection of the Fourteenth Amendment, it is the obligation of this Court to enforce the constitutional commands.

We hold that in granting judicial enforcement of the restrictive agreements in these cases, the States have denied petitioners the equal protection of the laws and that, therefore, the action of the state courts cannot stand. We have noted that freedom from discrimination by the States in the enjoyment of property rights was among the basic objectives sought to be effectuated by the framers of the Fourteenth Amendment. That such discrimination has occurred in these cases is clear. Because of the race or color of these petitioners they have been denied rights of ownership or occupancy enjoyed as a matter of course by other citizens of different race or color. The Fourteenth Amendment declares "that all persons whether colored or white, shall stand equal before the laws of the States, and, in regard to the colored race, for whose protection the amendment was primarily designed, that no discrimination shall be made against them by law because of their color." . . . Only recently this Court has had occasion to declare that a state law which denied equal enjoyment of property rights to a designated class of citizens of specified race and ancestry, was not a legitimate exercise of the state's police power but violated the guaranty of the equal protection of the laws. *Oyama* v. *California,* 332 US 633 (1948). Nor may the discriminations imposed by the state courts in these cases be justified as proper exertions of state police power. . . .

The historical context in which the Fourteenth Amendment became a part of the Constitution should not be forgotten. Whatever else the framers sought to achieve, it is clear that the matter of primary concern was the establishment of equality in the enjoyment of basic civil and political rights and the preservation of those rights from discriminatory action on the part of the States based on considerations of race or color. Seventy-five years ago this Court announced that the provisions of the Amendment are to be construed with this fundamental purpose in mind. Upon full consideration, we have concluded that in these cases the States have acted to deny petitioners the equal protection of the laws guaranteed by the Fourteenth Amendment. Having so decided, we find it unnecessary to consider whether petitioners have also been deprived of property without due process of law or denied privileges and immunities of citizens of the United States.

For the reasons stated, the judgment of the Supreme Court of Missouri and the judgment of the Supreme Court of Michigan must be reversed.

3. *Freedom of Suffrage*

TERRY *v.* ADAMS

345 US 461 (1953)

[The Fifteenth Amendment provides that the right to vote shall not be denied or abridged on account of race or color. In 1876 the Supreme Court decided that the Amendment did not confer the suffrage upon anyone; its purpose was only to prohibit discrimination in matters of suffrage on account of race or color. The Southern States attempted nonetheless to keep Negroes from the polls, and until recently these efforts were on the whole successful. They imposed technical registration and poll tax requirements which made it difficult, if not impossible, for illiterate or simple people to use their right to vote. Literacy tests were operated in such a way that white people would qualify while Negroes were disqualified. Grandfather clauses were another means of disfranchisement; they provided for the right to vote by persons who had rendered military service in wartime or who had been legal voters at some time in the past, e.g., January 1, 1866, or were descendants of such persons. These grandfather clauses waived the literacy requirements for persons who could qualify under their terms.

[In 1915 the Court declared Oklahoma's grandfather clause unconstitutional as a scheme that was designed to perpetuate what the Fifteenth Amendment sought to end. When Oklahoma attempted to circumvent this decision by changing its "grandfather" basis in some respects, the Court held the scheme as amended unconstitutional. The Fifteenth Amendment, said Justice Frankfurter, "nullifies sophisticated as well as simple-minded modes of discrimination." *Lane* v. *Wilson,* 307 US 268 (1939).

[Since the "Solid South" was politically controlled by the Democratic Party, that party's primary election was more crucial than the final election between Democratic and Republican candidates; Negroes were, therefore, excluded from the Democratic primaries. When it was shown that these primary elections were conducted in accordance with statutory provisions, the Court declared such "white primaries" unconstitutional. *Nixon* v. *Herndon,* 273 US 536 (1927), and *Nixon* v. *Condon,* 286 US 73 (1932). These cases involved the Texas primary laws. After these decisions, the statutes were changed, so that the Democratic state convention could exclude Negroes by rule rather than by statute, giving the appearance of a primary or nomination scheme that was a private affair and not state action. In 1935 the Court upheld this new scheme as constitutional in *Grovey* v. *Townsend,* 295 US 45. In 1944 the Court reversed this decision in *Smith* v. *Allwright,* 321 US 649, and held that if the statutes turn over the function of nominating candidates to political parties, the party primaries are state agencies and what they do becomes state, and not private, action. To get around this blow to the "white primary," South Carolina repealed all laws and state constitutional provisions that mentioned the primary; then the Democratic Party, acting as if it were a private club, excluded Negroes from its primary elections. This, too, did not succeed. *Rice* v. *Elmore,* 165 F. 2d 387 (1947); certiorari denied 333 US 875 (1948).

[Still another scheme to perpetuate the "white primary" was resorted to in Texas, where the Jaybird Association, a private club for white people, attempted to "front" for the Democratic Party in selecting nominees. In the present case eight members of the Court held that this practice, too, was prohibited by the Fifteenth Amendment. There were three opinions: Justice Black's, with which Justices Douglas and Burton concurred; Justice Frankfurter's; and Justice Clark's, with which Chief Justice Vinson and Justices Reed and Jackson concurred. These opinions differ in emphasis rather than in substance. Justice Minton dissented on the ground that what was done here amounted to private, not state, action.

[The Court has thus, over the years, invalidated schemes like the grandfather clauses and the "white primary" that were devised by states to disfranchise the Negro. Under threat of congressional action to outlaw the poll tax, many of the states have voluntarily abolished the tax. Literacy tests that are not fair on their face or that are administered in such a way (as under the Boswell amendment to the Alabama constitution) as obviously to attempt to circumvent the Fifteenth Amendment have been declared unconstitutional. *Davis* v. *Schnell*, 81 F. Supp. 872 (1949), affirmed 336 US 933 (1949).

[These decisions have been effective in giving political rights and powers to the Negro.]

Mr. Justice Black announced the judgment of the Court and an opinion in which Mr. Justice Douglas and Mr. Justice Burton join:

In *Smith* v. *Allwright*, 321 U.S. 649 (1944), we held that rules of the Democratic Party of Texas excluding Negroes from voting in the party's primaries violated the Fifteenth Amendment. While no state law directed such exclusion, our decision pointed out that many party activities were subject to considerable statutory control. This case raises questions concerning the constitutional power of a Texas county political organization called the Jaybird Democratic Association or Jaybird Party to exclude Negroes from its primaries on racial grounds. The Jaybirds deny that their racial exclusions violate the Fifteenth Amendment. They contend that the Amendment applies only to elections or primaries held under state regulation, that their association is not regulated by the state at all, and that it is not a political party but a self-governing voluntary club. . . .

There was evidence that:

The Jaybird Association or Party was organized in 1889. Its membership was then and always has been limited to white people; they are automatically members if their names appear on the official list of county voters. It has been run like other political parties with an executive committee named from the county's voting precincts. Expenses of the party are paid by the assessment of candidates for office in its primaries. Candidates for county offices submit their names to the Jaybird Committee in accordance with the normal practice followed by regular political parties all over the country. Advertisements and posters proclaim that these candidates are running subject to the action of the Jaybird primary. While there is no legal compulsion on successful Jaybird candidates to enter Democratic primaries they have nearly always done so and with few exceptions since 1889 have run and won without opposition in the Democratic primaries and the general elections that followed. Thus the party has been the dominant political group in the county since organization, having endorsed every county-wide official elected since 1889.

It is apparent that Jaybird activities follow a plan purposefully designed to exclude Negroes from voting and at the same time to escape the Fifteenth Amendment's command that the right of citizens to vote shall neither be denied nor abridged on account of race. These were the admitted party purposes according to the following testimony of the Jaybird's president:

Q. . . . Now Mr. Adams, will you tell me specifically what is the specific purpose of holding these elections and carrying on this organization like you do? A. Good government.

Q. Now I will ask you to state whether or not it is the opinion and policy of the Association that to carry on good government they must exclude Negro citizens? A. Well, when we started it was and it is still that way, I think.

Q. And then one of the purposes of your organization is for the specific purpose of excluding Negroes from voting, isn't it? A. Yes.

Q. And that is your policy? A. Yes.

Q. I will ask you, that is the reason you hold your election in May rather than in June or July, isn't it? A. Yes.

Q. Because if you held it in July you would have to abide by the statutes and the law by letting them vote? A. They do vote in July.

Q. And if you held yours at that time they would have to vote too, wouldn't they? A. Why sure.

Q. And you hold it in May so they won't have to? A. Well, they don't vote in ours but they can vote on anybody in the July election they want to.

Q. But you are not answering my question. My question is that you hold yours in May so you won't have to let them vote, don't you? A. Yes.

Q. And that is your purpose? A. Yes.

Q. And your intention? A. Yes.

Q. And to have a vote of the white population at a time when the Negroes can't vote, isn't that right? A. That's right.

Q. That is the whole policy of your Association? A. Yes.

Q. And that is its purpose? A. Yes.

The District Court found that the Jaybird Association was a political organization or party; that the majority of white voters generally abide by the results of its primaries and support in the Democratic primaries the persons endorsed by the Jaybird primaries; and that the chief object of the Association has always been to deny Negroes any voice or part in the election of Fort Bend County officials.

The facts and findings bring this case squarely within the reasoning and holding of the Court of Appeals for the Fourth Circuit in its two recent decisions about excluding Negroes from Democratic primaries in South Carolina. . . . South Carolina had repealed every trace of statutory or constitutional control of the Democratic primaries. It did this in the hope that thereafter the Democratic Party or Democratic "Clubs" of South Carolina would be free to continue discriminatory practices against Negroes as voters. The contention there was that the Democratic "Clubs" were mere private groups; the contention here is that the Jaybird Association is a mere private group. The Court of Appeals in invalidating the South Carolina practices answered these formalistic arguments by holding that no election machinery could be sustained if its purpose or effect was to deny Negroes on account of their race an effective voice in the governmental affairs of their country, state, or community. In doing so the Court relied on the principle announced in *Smith* v. *Allwright,* that the constitutional right to be free from racial discrimination in voting ". . . is not to be nullified by a state through casting its electoral process in a form which permits a private organization to practice racial discrimination in the election."

The South Carolina cases are in accord with the commands of the Fifteenth Amendment and the laws passed pursuant to it. That Amendment provides as follows: "The right of citizens of the United States to vote shall not be denied or abridged by the United States or by any State on account of race, color, or previous condition of servitude."

The Amendment bans racial discrimination in voting by both state and nation. It thus establishes a national policy, obviously applicable to the right of Negroes not to be discriminated against as voters in elections to determine public governmental policies or to select public officials, national, state, or local. . . .

The Amendment, the congressional enactment and the cases make explicit the rule against racial discrimination in the conduct of elections. Together they show the meaning of "elections." Clearly the Amendment includes any election in which public issues are decided or public officials selected. Just as clearly the Amendment excludes social or business clubs. And the statute shows the congressional mandate against discrimination whether the voting on public issues and officials is conducted in community, state or nation. Size is not a standard.

It is significant that precisely the same qualifications as those prescribed by Texas entitling electors to vote at county-operated primaries are adopted as the sole qualifications entitling electors to vote at the county-wide Jaybird primaries with a single proviso—Negroes are excluded. Everyone concedes that such a proviso in the county-operated primaries would be unconstitutional. The Jaybird Party thus brings into being and holds precisely the kind of election that the Fifteenth Amendment seeks to prevent. When it produces the equivalent of the prohibited election, the damage has been done.

For a state to permit such a duplication of its election processes is to permit a flagrant abuse of those processes to defeat the purposes of the Fifteenth Amendment. The use of the county-operated primary to ratify the result of the prohibited election merely compounds the offense. It violates the Fifteenth Amendment for a state, by such circumvention, to permit within its borders the use of any device that produces an equivalent of the prohibited election.

The only election that has counted in this Texas county for more than fifty years has been that held by the Jaybirds from which Negroes were excluded. The Democratic primary and the general election have become no more than the perfunctory ratifiers of the choice that has already been made in Jaybird elections from which Negroes have been excluded. It is immaterial that the state does not control that part of this elective process which it leaves for the Jaybirds to manage. The Jaybird primary has become an integral part, indeed the only effective part, of the elective process that determines who shall rule and govern in the county. The effect of the whole procedure, Jaybird primary plus Democratic primary plus general election, is to do precisely that which the Fifteenth Amendment forbids—strip Negroes of every vestige of influence in selecting the officials who control the local county matters that intimately touch the daily lives of citizens.

. . . We affirm the District Court's holding that the combined Jaybird-Democratic-general election machinery has deprived these petitioners of their right to vote on account of their race and color. . . .

4. Equality of Job Opportunities

BROTHERHOOD OF RAILROAD TRAINMEN v. HOWARD

343 US 768 (1952)

[A New York civil rights act prohibited any labor organization from discriminating, by reason of race, color, or creed, in the admission or treatment of members. In *Railway Mail Association* v. *Corsi*, 326 US 88 (1945), the Court upheld this act as constitutional.

[The laws of some other states also prohibit racial or religious discrimination by labor organizations. About a dozen states have fair employment practice acts, which prohibit discrimination by employers. Many cities have fair employment practice ordinances. Various bills on this subject have been introduced in Congress in recent years. Federal Government contracts have provisions against discrimination in employment practices by parties contracting with the Government, and an executive agency is charged with the duty of supervising compliance with these provisions.

[It is settled that if a labor union is, by federal law, the exclusive bargaining agent of a group of employees, it has the duty to exercise its powers fairly on behalf of all persons within the bargaining unit, without racial discrimination: *Steele* v. *Louisville & N. R. Co.*, 323 US 192 (1944); *Tunstall* v. *Brotherhood of Locomotive F. & E.*, 323 US 210 (1944); *Graham* v. *Brotherhood of Locomotive F. & E.*, 338 US 232 (1949).

[In the present case the rule of the above-named cases has been extended to impose on the union the duty to refrain from using its bargaining power to discriminate against Negro employees even though these employees were represented by another union. Chief Justice Vinson and Justices Reed and Minton dissented.]

Mr. Justice Black, delivered the opinion of the Court:

This case raises questions concerning the power of courts to protect Negro railroad employees from loss of their jobs under compulsion of a bargaining agreement which, to avoid a strike, the railroad made with an exclusively white man's union. Respondent Simon Howard, a Frisco train employee for nearly forty years, brought this action on behalf of himself and other colored employees similarly situated.

In summary the complaint alleged: Negro employees such as respondent constituted a group called "train porters" although they actually performed all the duties of white "brakemen"; the Brotherhood of Railroad Trainmen, bargaining representative of "brakemen" under the Railway Labor Act, had for years used its influence in an attempt to eliminate Negro trainmen and get their jobs for white men who, unlike colored "train porters," were or could be members of the Brotherhood; on March 7, 1946, the Brotherhood finally forced the Frisco to agree to discharge the colored "train porters" and fill their jobs with white men who, under the agreement, would do less work but get more pay. The complaint charged that the Brotherhood's "discriminatory action" violated the train porters' rights under the Railway Labor Act and under the Constitution; that the agreement was void because against public policy, prejudicial to the public interest, and designed to deprive Negro trainmen of their right to earn a livelihood because of their race or color. The prayers were that the court adjudge and decree that the contract was void and unenforceable for the reasons stated; that the Railroad be "enjoined from discontinuing the jobs known as Train Porters" and "from hiring white Brakemen to replace or displace plaintiff and other Train Porters as planned in accordance with said agreement."

The facts as found by the District Court, affirmed with emphasis by the Court of Appeals, substantially established the truth of the complaint's material allegations. These facts showed that the Negro train porters had for a great many years served the Railroad with loyalty, integrity and efficiency; that "train porters" do all the work of brakemen; that the Government administrator of railroads during World War I had classified them as brakemen and had required that they be paid just like white brakemen; that when the railroads went back to their owners, they redesignated these colored brakemen as "train porters," "left their duties untouched," and forced them to accept wages far below those of white "brakemen" who were Brotherhood members; that for more than a quarter of a century the Brotherhood and other exclusively white rail unions had continually carried on a program of aggressive hostility to employment of Negroes for train, engine and yard service; that the agreement of March 7, 1946, here under attack, provides that train porters shall no longer do any work "generally recognized as brakeman's duties"; that while this agreement did not in express words compel discharge of "train porters," the economic unsoundness of keeping them after transfer of their "brakemen" functions made complete abolition of the "train porter" group inevitable; that two days after "the Carriers, reluctantly, and as a result of the strike threats" signed the agreement, they notified train porters that "Under this agreement we will, effective April 1, 1946, discontinue all train porter positions." Accordingly, respondent Howard, and others, were personally notified to turn in their switch keys, lanterns, markers and other brakemen's equipment, and notices of job vacancies were posted to be bid in by white brakemen only. . . .

While different in some respects, the basic pattern of racial discrimination in this case is much the same as that we had to consider in *Steele* v. *Louisville & N. R. Co.*, 323 U.S. 192. . . . In this case, as was charged in the *Steele Case*, a Brotherhood acting as a bargaining agent under the Railway Labor Act has been hostile to Negro employees, has discriminated against them, and has forced the Railroad to make a contract which would help Brotherhood members take over the jobs of the colored "train porters."

There is a difference in the circumstances of the two cases, however, which it is contended requires us to deny the judicial remedy here that was accorded in the *Steele Case*. That difference is this: Steele was admittedly a locomotive fireman although not a member of the Brotherhood of Locomotive Firemen and Enginemen which under the Railway Labor Act was the exclusive bargaining representative of the entire craft of firemen. We held that the language of the Act imposed a duty on the craft bargaining representative to exercise the power conferred upon it in behalf of all those for whom it acts, without hostile discrimination against any of them. Failure to exercise this duty was held to give rise to a cause of action under the Act. In this case, unlike the *Steele Case,* the colored employees have for many years been treated by the carriers and the Brotherhood as a separate class for representation purposes and have in fact been represented by another union of their own choosing. Since the Brotherhood has discriminated against "train porters" instead of minority members of its own "craft," it is argued that the Brotherhood owed no duty at all to refrain from using its statutory bargaining power so as to abolish the jobs of the colored porters and drive them from the railroads. We think this argument is unsound and that the opinion in the *Steele Case* points to a breach of statutory duty by this Brotherhood.

As previously noted these train porters are threatened with loss of their jobs because they are not white and for no other reason. The job they did hold under its old name would be abolished by the agreement; their color alone would disqualify them for the old job under its new name. The end result of these transactions is not in doubt; for precisely the same reasons as in the *Steele Case* "discriminations based on race alone are obviously irrelevant and invidious. Congress plainly did not undertake to authorize the bargaining representative to make such discriminations." . . . The Federal Act thus prohibits bargaining agents it authorizes from using their position and power to destroy colored workers' jobs in order to bestow them on white workers. And courts can protect those threatened by such an unlawful use of power granted by a federal act.

Here, as in the *Steele Case,* colored workers must look to a judicial remedy to prevent the sacrifice or obliteration of their rights under the Act. For no adequate administrative remedy can be afforded by the National Railway Adjustment or Mediation Board. . . . For the contention here with which we agree is that the racial discrimination practiced is unlawful, whether colored employees are classified as "train porters," "brakemen," or something else. Our conclusion is that the District Court has jurisdiction and power to issue necessary injunctive orders notwithstanding the provisions of the Norris–LaGuardia Act. . . .

Bargaining agents who enjoy the advantages of the Railway Labor Act's provisions must execute their trust without lawless invasions of the right of other workers. . . .

5. *Fair and Impartial Juries*

CASSELL *v.* TEXAS

339 US 282 (1950)

[In the present case a Negro was convicted of murder. The jury that convicted him had been chosen admittedly without racial discrimination, but it was argued that there had been discrimination in the selection of the grand jury that indicted him.

[All the Justices agreed (Justice Douglas did not participate) that the Equal Protection Clause of the Fourteenth Amendment prohibits racial discrimination in the selection of grand juries, and seven of the Justices agreed that discrimination was shown in this case. The conviction was reversed. Justices Frankfurter and Clark wrote concurring opinions; Justice Jackson dissented.

["It has been settled law since 1880," said Justice Frankfurter in his concurring opinion, "that the Civil War Amendments barred the States from discriminating because of race in the selection of juries, whether grand or petty." At least a score of Supreme Court decisions can be cited for this proposition.

[The principle is not that a Negro is entitled to have members of his race on the jury that indicts or convicts him; what the Constitution guarantees is that members of his race may not be intentionally excluded.]

Mr. Justice Reed announced the judgment of the Court and an opinion in which Chief Justice Vinson, Mr. Justice Black and Mr. Justice Clark concurred:

Review was sought in this case to determine whether there has been a violation by Texas of petitioner's federal constitutional right to a fair and impartial grand jury. The federal question was raised by a motion to quash the indictment on the ground that petitioner, a Negro, suffered unconstitutional discrimination through the selection of white men only for the grand jury that indicted him. . . .

The [Texas] Court of Criminal Appeals accepted the federal rule that a Negro is denied the equal protection of the laws when he is indicted by a grand jury from which Negroes as a race have been intentionally excluded. . . . It was from an examination of facts that the court deduced its conclusion that racial discrimination had not been practiced. Since the result reached may deny a federal right, we may reexamine the facts to determine whether petitioner has sustained by proof his allegation of discrimination. . . .

Acting under the Texas statutes, the Dallas County grand-jury commissioners chose a list of sixteen males for this September 1947 grand jury from citizens eligible under the statute. The judge chose twelve of these for the panel. No challenge is now made to the fairness of this statutory system. We have approved it.

Petitioner's attack is upon the way the statutory method of grand-jury selection has been administered by the jury commissioners. One charge is that discrimination must have been practiced because the Negro proportion of grand jurors is less than the Negro proportion of the county's population. Under the 1940 census the total population of Dallas County was 398,564, of whom 61,605 were Negroes. This is about 15.5%. In weighing this matter of custom, we limit ourselves, as do the parties, to the period between June 1, 1942, . . . and November 1947, when petitioner was indicted. There were 21 grand juries in this period; of the 252 members of the panels, 17, or 6.7% were Negroes. But this apparent discrepancy may be explained by the fact that Texas grand jurors must possess certain statutory qualifications. Grand jurors must ordinarily be eligible to vote; eligibility requires payment of a poll tax; and the validity of a poll-tax requirement is not challenged. The record shows 5,500 current Negro poll-tax payers in Dallas County in 1947, and nothing indicates that this number varied substantially from year to year. The corresponding figure for all poll-tax payers, male and female, is 83,667. These figures would indicate that as a proportional matter 6.5% of grand jurors would be Negroes, a percentage approximating the ratio of Negroes actually sitting on the 21 grand jury panels. Without more it cannot be said that Negroes had been left off grand-jury panels to such a degree as to establish a prima facie case of discrimination.

A different question is presented by petitioner's next charge that . . . the Dallas County grand jury commissioners for 21 consecutive lists had consistently limited Negroes selected for grand-jury service to not more than one on each grand jury. . . . Since the *Hill Case*, 316 US 400, the judges of the trial court have been careful to instruct their jury commissioners that discrimination on grounds of race or color is forbidden. The judge did so here. If, notwithstanding this caution by the trial court judges, commissioners should limit proportionally the number of Negroes elected for grand-jury service, such limitations would violate our Constitution. Jurymen should be selected as individuals, on the basis of individual qualifications, and not as members of a race.

We have recently written why proportional representation of races on a jury is not a constitutional requisite. Succinctly stated, our reason was that the Constitution requires only a fair jury selected without regard to race. Obviously the number of races and nationalities appearing in the ancestry of our citizens would make it impossible to meet a requirement of proportional representation. Similarly, since there can be no exclusion of Negroes as a race and no discrimination because of color, proportional limitation is not permissible. That conclusion is compelled by the United States Code, 18 U.S.C.A. 243, based on § 4 of the Civil Rights Act of 1875. While the language of the section directs attention to the right to serve as a juror, its command has long been recognized also to assure rights to an accused. Prohibiting racial disqualification of Negroes for jury service, this congressional enactment under the Fourteenth Amendment, § 5, has been consistently sustained and its violation held to deny a proper trial to a Negro accused. Proportional racial limitation is therefore forbidden. An accused is entitled to have charges against him considered by a jury in the selection of which there has been neither inclusion nor exclusion because of race.

Our holding that there was discrimination in the selection of grand jurors in this case, however, is based on another ground. In explaining the fact that no Negroes appeared on this grand jury list, the commissioners said that they knew none available who qualified; at the same time they said they chose jurymen only from those people with whom they were personally acquainted. It may be assumed that in ordinary activities in Dallas County, acquaintanceship between the races is not on a sufficiently familiar basis to give citizens eligible for appointment as jury commissioners an opportunity to know the qualifications for grand-jury service of many members of another race. An individual's qualifications for grand-jury service, however, are not hard to ascertain, and with no evidence to the contrary, we must assume that a large proportion of the Negroes of Dallas County met the statutory requirements for jury service. When the commissioners were appointed as judicial administrative officials, it was their duty to familiarize themselves fairly with the qualifications of the eligible jurors of the county without regard to race and color. They did not do so here, and the result has been racial discrimination. . . .

The existence of the kind of discrimination described in the *Hill Case* does not depend upon systematic exclusion continuing over a long period and practiced by a succession of jury commissioners. Since the issue must be whether there has been discrimination in the selection of the jury that has indicted petitioner, it is enough to have direct evidence based on the statements of the jury commissioners in the very case. Discrimination may be proved in other ways than by evidence of long continued unexplained absence of Negroes from many panels. The statements of the jury commissioners that they chose only whom they knew, and that they knew no eligible Negroes in an area where Negroes made up so large a proportion of the population, prove the intentional exclusion that is discrimination in violation of petitioner's constitutional rights.

The judgment of the Court of Criminal Appeals of Texas is reversed.

6. Equality in Public Education

BROWN v. BOARD OF EDUCATION OF TOPEKA
347 US 483 (1954)

[In 1896, in *Plessy* v. *Ferguson,* 163 US 537, a case involving transportation, the Supreme Court approved segregation of the races as constitutional and formulated the doctrine of "separate but equal" facilities. Under the protection of this doctrine 17 states maintained segregated schools under the compulsion of state legislation; Congress enacted a school segregation act for the District of Columbia; in addition, 4 states adopted laws that permitted segregation on a local option basis. In the remaining states, 16 prohibited segregation, and in 11 there was no specific legislation. In 1954 there were over eight million white and two and a half million Negro pupils who attended segregated elementary and high schools.

[The "separate but equal" doctrine was under attack for many years. The Court in 1950 interpreted and applied the doctrine in such a way as to make segregation in professional and graduate study impossible. *Sweatt* v. *Painter,* 339 US 629, and *McLaurin* v. *Oklahoma State Regents,* 339 US 637. These were unanimous decisions. It became apparent that it was only a matter of time before the Court would feel itself compelled to extend the logic of these decisions to grade and high schools, for the doctrine had been drained of moral force.

[In the present case, decided by a unanimous Supreme Court in 1954, the "separate but equal" doctrine was rejected. The Court held that "separate educational facilities are inherently unequal," and hence the segregation statutes violate the Equal Protection Clause of the Fourteenth Amendment. The decision was limited in its application to the field of public education.

[A notable feature of the opinion by Chief Justice Warren is his use of psychological and sociological data to show the harmful effects of segregation. In this respect the Court *sub silentio* followed the precedent of Chief Justice Vanderbilt's opinion in *Tudor* v. *Board of Education of Rutherford,* above.

[In a companion case, *Bolling* v. *Sharpe,* decided at the same time, the Supreme Court held that the federal act which compelled segregated schools in the District of Columbia was a violation of the Due Process Clause of the Fifth Amendment.]

Mr. Chief Justice Warren delivered the opinion of the Court:

These cases come to us from the States of Kansas, South Carolina, Virginia, and Delaware. They are premised on different facts and different local conditions, but a common legal question justifies their consideration together in this consolidated opinion.

In each of the cases, minors of the Negro race, through their legal representatives, seek the aid of the courts in obtaining admission to the public schools of their community on a nonsegregated basis. In each instance, they had been denied admission to schools attended by white children under laws requiring or permitting segregation according to race. This segregation was alleged to deprive the plaintiffs of the equal protection of the laws under the Fourteenth Amendment. In each of the cases other than the Delaware case, a three-judge federal district court denied relief to the plaintiffs on the so-called "separate but equal" doctrine announced by this Court in *Plessy* v. *Ferguson,* 163 U.S. 537. Under that doctrine, equality of treatment is accorded when the races are provided substantially equal facilities, even though these facilities be separate. In the Delaware case, the Supreme Court of Delaware adhered to that doctrine, but ordered that the plaintiffs be admitted to the white schools because of their superiority to the Negro schools.

The plaintiffs contend that segregated public schools are not "equal" and cannot be made "equal," and that hence they are deprived of the equal protection of the laws. Because of the obvious importance of the question presented, the Court took jurisdiction. Argument was heard in the 1952 Term, and reargument was heard this Term on certain questions propounded by the Court.

Reargument was largely devoted to the circumstances surrounding the adoption of the Fourteenth Amendment in 1868. It covered exhaustively consideration of the Amendment in Congress, ratification by the states, then existing practices in racial segregation, and the views of proponents and opponents of the Amendment. This discussion and our own investigation convince us that, although these sources cast some light, it is not enough to resolve the problem with which we are faced. At best, they are inconclusive. The most avid proponents of the post-War Amendments undoubtedly intended them to remove all legal distinctions among "all persons born or naturalized in the United States." Their opponents, just as certainly, were antagonistic to both the letter and the spirit of the Amendments and wished them to have the most limited effect. What others in Congress and the state legislature had in mind cannot be determined with any degree of certainty.

An additional reason for the inconclusive nature of the Amendment's history, with respect to segregated schools, is the status of public education at that time. In the South, the movement toward free common schools, supported by general taxation, had not yet taken hold. Education of white children was largely in the hands of private groups. Education of Negroes was almost nonexistent, and practically all of the race were illiterate. In fact, any education of Negroes was forbidden by law in some states. Today, in contrast, many Negroes have achieved outstanding success in the arts and sciences as well as in the business and professional world. It is true that public education had already advanced further in the North, but the effect of the Amendment on Northern States was generally ignored in the congressional debates. Even in the North, the conditions of public education did not approximate those existing today. The curriculum was usually rudimentary; ungraded schools were common in rural areas; the school term was but three months a year in many states; and compulsory school attendance was virtually unknown. As a consequence, it is not surprising that there should be so little in the history of the Fourteenth Amendment relating to its intended effect on public education.

In the first cases in this Court construing the Fourteenth Amendment, decided shortly after its adoption, the Court interpreted it as proscribing all state-imposed discriminations against the Negro race. The doctrine of "separate but equal" did not make its appearance in this Court until 1896 in the case of *Plessy* v. *Ferguson, supra,* involving not education but transportation. American courts have since labored with the doctrine for over half a century. In this Court, there have been six cases involving the "separate but equal" doctrine in the field of public education.

In *Cumming* v. *County Board of Education,* 175 U.S. 528, and *Gong Lum* v. *Rice,* 275 U.S. 78, the validity of the doctrine itself was not challenged. In more recent cases, all on the graduate school level, inequality was found in that specific benefits enjoyed by white students were denied to Negro students of the same educational qualifications. *Missouri* ex rel. *Gaines* v. *Canada,* 305 U.S. 337; *Sipuel* v. *Oklahoma,* 332 U.S. 631; *Sweatt* v. *Painter,* 339 U.S. 629; *McLaurin* v. *Oklahoma State Regents,* 339 U.S. 637. In none of these cases was it necessary to reexamine the doctrine to grant relief to the Negro plaintiff. And in *Sweatt* v. *Painter, supra,* the Court expressly reserved decision on the question whether *Plessy* v. *Ferguson* should be held inapplicable to public education.

In the instant cases, that question is directly presented. Here, unlike *Sweatt* v. *Painter,* there are findings below that the Negro and white schools involved have been equalized, or are being equalized, with respect to buildings, curricula, qualifications and salaries of teachers, and other "tangible" factors. Our decision, therefore, cannot turn on merely a comparison of these tangible factors in the Negro and white schools involved in each of the cases. We must look instead to the effect of segregation itself on public education.

In approaching this problem, we cannot turn the clock back to 1868 when the Amendment was adopted, or even to 1896 when *Plessy* v. *Ferguson* was written. We must consider public education in the light of its full development and its present place in American life throughout the Nation. Only in this way can it be determined if segregation in public schools deprives these plaintiffs of the equal protection of the laws.

Today, education is perhaps the most important function of state and local governments. Compulsory school attendance laws and the great expenditures for education both demonstrate our recognition of the importance of education to our democratic society. It is required in the performance of our most basic public responsibilities, even service in the armed forces. It is the very foundation of good citizenship. Today it is a principal instrument in awakening the child to cultural values, in preparing him for later professional training, and in helping him to adjust normally to his environment. In these days, it is doubtful that any child may reasonably be expected to succeed in life if he is denied the opportunity of an education. Such an opportunity, where the state has undertaken to provide it, is a right which must be made available to all on equal terms.

We come then to the question presented: Does segregation of children in public schools solely on the basis of race, even though the physical facilities and other "tangible" factors may be equal, deprive the children of the minority group of equal educational opportunities? We believe that it does.

In *Sweatt* v. *Painter, supra,* in finding that a segregated law school for Negroes could not provide them equal educational opportunities, this Court relied in large part on "those qualities which are incapable of objective measurement but which make for greatness in a law school." In *McLaurin* v. *Oklahoma State Regents, supra,* the Court, in requiring that a Negro admitted to a white graduate school be treated like all other students, again resorted to intangible considerations: ". . . his ability to study, to engage in discussions and exchange views with other students, and, in general, to learn his profession." Such considerations apply with added force to children in grade and high schools. To separate them from others of similar age and qualifications solely because of their race generates a feeling of inferiority as to their status in the community that may affect their hearts and minds in a way unlikely ever to be undone. The effect of this separation on their educational opportunities was well stated by a finding in the Kansas case by a court which nevertheless felt compelled to rule against the Negro plaintiffs:

Segregation of white and colored children in public schools has a detrimental effect upon the colored children. The impact is greater when it has the sanction of the law; for the policy of separating the races is usually interpreted as denoting the inferiority of the Negro group. A sense of inferiority affects the motivation of a child to learn. Segregation with the sanction of law, therefore, has a tendency to retard the educational and mental development of Negro children and to deprive them of some of the benefits they would receive in a racially integrated school system.

Whatever may have been the extent of psychological knowledge at the time of *Plessy* v. *Ferguson*, this finding is amply supported by modern authority. Any language in *Plessy* v. *Ferguson* contrary to this finding is rejected.

We conclude that in the field of public education the doctrine of "separate but equal" has no place. Separate educational facilities are inherently unequal. Therefore, we hold that the plaintiffs and others similarly situated for whom the actions have been brought are, by reason of the segregation complained of, deprived of the equal protection of the laws guaranteed by the Fourteenth Amendment. This disposition makes unnecessary any discussion whether such segregation also violates the Due Process Clause of the Fourteenth Amendment.

Because these are class actions, because of the wide applicability of this decision, and because of the great variety of local conditions, the formulation of decrees in these cases presents problems of considerable complexity. On reargument, the consideration of appropriate relief was necessarily subordinated to the primary question—the constitutionality of segregation in public education. We have now announced that such segregation is a denial of the equal protection of the laws. In order that we may have the full assistance of the parties in formulating decrees, the cases will be restored to the docket, and the parties are requested to present further argument on Questions 4 and 5 previously propounded by the Court for the reargument this Term.* The Attorney General

---

* "4. Assuming it is decided that segregation in public schools violates the Fourteenth Amendment

"(a) would a decree necessarily follow providing that, within the limits set by normal geographic school districting, Negro children should forthwith be admitted to schools of their choice, or

"(b) may this Court, in the exercise of its equity powers, permit an effective gradual adjustment to be brought about from existing segregated systems to a system not based on color distinctions?

"5. On the assumption on which questions 4 (a) and (b) are based, and assuming further that this Court will exercise its equity powers to the end described in question 4 (b),

of the United States is again invited to participate. The Attorneys General of the states requiring or permitting segregation in public education will also be permitted to appear as *amici curiae* upon request to do so by September 15, 1954, and submission of briefs by October 1, 1954. It is so ordered.

7. Equality in Interstate Transportation

MORGAN v. VIRGINIA

328 US 378 (1946)

[In the *Civil Rights Cases*, 109 US 3 (1883), the Court said that racial segregation in transportation was not a badge of slavery or involuntary servitude. *Plessy* v. *Ferguson*, 163 US 537 (1896), held that a state statute providing for equal but separate facilities for Negro passengers was not in conflict with the Fourteenth Amendment. But to be valid, the segregation law must provide for equal facilities. *McCabe* v. *Atchison, T. & S. F. R. Co.*, 235 US 151 (1914). Furthermore, it must apply only to passengers who travel within the state; a state statute may not require or prohibit the segregation of passengers who travel in interstate commerce because such a statute would violate the Commerce Clause of the Constitution. *Hall* v. *De Cuir*, 95 US 485 (1878); but cf. *Bob-Lo Excursion Co.* v. *Michigan*, 333 US 281 (1948). Thus, in the present case, the Court (with Justice Burton dissenting) held that the Virginia segregation statute was invalid as an undue burden on interstate commerce because it was applied to passengers who moved in interstate commerce.]

Mr. Justice Reed delivered the opinion of the Court:

This appeal brings to this Court the question of the constitutionality of an act of Virginia, which requires all passenger motor vehicle carriers, both interstate and intrastate, to separate without discrimination the white and colored passengers in their motor buses so that contiguous seats will not be occupied by persons of different races at the same time. A violation of the requirement of separation by the carrier is a misdemeanor. The driver or other person in charge is directed

"(a) should this Court formulate detailed decrees in these cases;

"(b) if so, what specific issues should the decrees reach;

"(c) should this Court appoint a special master to hear evidence with a view to recommending specific terms for such decrees;

"(d) should this Court remand to the courts of first instance with directions to frame decrees in these cases, and if so, what general directions should the decrees of this Court include and what procedures should the courts of first instance follow in arriving at the specific terms of more detailed decrees?"

and required to increase or decrease the space allotted to the respective races as may be necessary or proper and may require passengers to change their seats to comply with the allocation. The operator's failure to enforce the provisions is made a misdemeanor.

These regulations were applied to an interstate passenger, this appellant, on a motor vehicle then making an interstate run or trip. According to the statement of fact by the Supreme Court of Appeals of Virginia, appellant, who is a Negro, was traveling on a motor common carrier, operating under the above-mentioned statute, from Gloucester County, Virginia, through the District of Columbia, to Baltimore, Maryland, the destination of the bus. There were other passengers, both white and colored. On her refusal to accede to a request of the driver to move to a back seat, which was partly occupied by other colored passengers, so as to permit the seat that she vacated to be used by white passengers, a warrant was obtained and appellant was arrested, tried and convicted of a violation . . . of the Virginia Code. . . .

This statute is attacked on the ground that it imposes undue burdens on interstate commerce. It is said by the Court of Appeals to have been passed in the exercise of the state's police power to avoid friction between the races. But this Court pointed out years ago "that a State cannot avoid the operation of this rule by simply invoking the convenient apologetics of the police power." Burdens upon commerce are those actions of a state which directly "impair the usefulness of its facilities for such traffic." That impairment, we think, may arise from other causes than costs or long delays. A burden may arise from a state statute which requires interstate passengers to order their movements on the vehicle in accordance with local rather than national requirements.

On appellant's journey, this statute required that she sit in designated seats in Virginia. Changes in seat designation might be made "at any time" during the journey when "necessary or proper for the comfort and convenience of passengers." This occurred in this instance. Upon such change of designation, the statute authorizes the operator of the vehicle to require, as he did here, "any passenger to change his or her seat as it may be necessary or proper." An interstate passenger must if necessary repeatedly shift seats while moving in Virginia to meet the seating requirements of the changing passenger group. On arrival at the District of Columbia line, the appellant would have had freedom to occupy any available seat and so to the end of her journey.

Interstate passengers traveling via motors between the north and south or the east and west may pass through Virginia on through lines in the day or in the night. The large buses approach the comfort of pullmans and have seats convenient for rest. On such interstate journeys the enforcement of the requirements for reseating would be disturbing.

Appellant's argument, properly we think, includes facts bearing on interstate motor transportation beyond those immediately involved in this journey under the Virginia statutory regulations. To appraise the weight of the burden of the Virginia statute on interstate commerce, related statutes of other states are important to show whether there are cumulative effects which may make local regulation impracticable. Eighteen states, it appears, prohibit racial separation on public carriers. Ten require separation on motor carriers. Of these Alabama applies specifically to interstate passengers with an exception for interstate passengers with through tickets from states without laws on separation of passengers. The language of the other acts, like this Virginia statute before the Court of Appeals' decision in this case, may be said to be susceptible to an interpretation that they do or do not apply to interstate passengers.

In states where separation of races is required in motor vehicles, a method of identification as white or colored must be employed. This may be done by definition. Any ascertainable Negro blood identifies a person as colored for purposes of separation in some states. In the other states which require the separation of the races in motor carriers, apparently no definition generally applicable or made for the purposes of the statute is given. Court definition or further legislative enactments would be required to clarify the line between the races. Obviously there may be changes by legislation in the definition.

The interferences to interstate commerce which arise from state regulation of racial association on interstate vehicles has long been recognized. Such regulation hampers freedom of choice in selecting accommodations. The recent changes in transportation brought about by the coming of automobiles does not seem of great significance in the problem. People of all races travel today more extensively than in 1878 when this Court first passed upon state regulation of racial segregation in commerce. The factual situation set out in preceding paragraphs emphasizes the soundness of this Court's early conclusion in *Hall* v. *De Cuir*, 95 US 485. . . .

The *De Cuir Case* arose under a statute of Louisiana interpreted by the courts of that state and this Court to require public carriers "to give all persons travelling in that State, upon the public conveyances employed in such business, equal rights and privileges in all parts of the conveyance, without distinction or discrimination on account of race or color." . . . Damages were awarded against Hall, the representative of the operator of a Mississippi river steamboat that traversed that river interstate from New Orleans to Vicksburg, for excluding in Louisiana . . . a colored person, from a cabin reserved for whites. This Court reversed for reasons well stated in the words of Mr. Chief Justice Waite. As our previous discussion demonstrates, the transportation difficulties arising from a statute that requires commingling of the races, as in the *De Cuir Case*, are increased by one that requires separation, as here. Other federal courts have looked upon racial separation statutes as applied to interstate passengers as burdens upon commerce.

In weighing the factors that enter into our conclusion as to whether this statute so burdens interstate commerce or so infringes the requirements of national uniformity as to be invalid, we are mindful of the fact that conditions vary between northern or western states such as Maine or Montana, with practically no colored population; industrial states such as Illinois, Ohio, New Jersey and Pennsylvania with a small, although appreciable, percentage of colored citizens; and the states of the deep south with percentages of from twenty-five to nearly fifty per cent colored, all with varying densities of the white and colored races in certain localities. Local efforts to promote amicable relations in difficult areas by legislative segregation in interstate transportation emerge from the latter racial distribution. As no state law can reach beyond its own border nor bar transportation of passengers across its boundaries, diverse seating requirements for the races in interstate journeys result. As there is no federal act dealing with the separation of races in interstate transportation, we must decide the validity of this Virginia statute on the challenge that it interferes with commerce, as a matter of balance between the exercise of the local police power and the need for national uniformity in the regulations for interstate travel. It seems clear to us that seating arrangements for the different races in interstate motor travel requires a single, uniform rule to promote and protect national travel. Consequently, we hold the Virginia statute in controversy invalid.

Reversed. . . .

HENDERSON *v.* UNITED STATES

339 US 816 (1950)

[Since state segregation laws may not affect passengers moving in interstate commerce, attempts have been made to achieve or perpetuate segregation through regulations adopted by the carriers themselves. Here they run into conflict with the act of Congress which makes it unlawful for any carrier in interstate commerce to subject any person "to any undue or unreasonable prejudice or disadvantage in any respect whatsoever." The Court has not held simply that racial segregation is illegal as falling within the meaning of "prejudice or disadvantage." The Court, instead, has insisted on equality; but *Mitchell* v. *United States,* 313 US 80 (1941), showed that it is practically impossible for a carrier to offer separate yet equal accommodations and service. The present case confirms this view. The Court unanimously held that the carrier may not subject a Negro passenger to any prejudice or disadvantage in any respect whatsoever. Justice Clark did not participate.]

Mr. Justice Burton delivered the opinion of the Court:

The question here is whether the rules and practices of the Southern Railway Company, which divide each dining car so as to allot ten tables exclusively to white passengers and one table exclusively to Negro passengers, and which call for a curtain or partition between that table and the others, violate § 3 (1) of the Interstate Commerce Act. That section makes it unlawful for a railroad in interstate commerce "to subject any particular person . . . to any undue or unreasonable prejudice or disadvantage in any respect whatsoever. . . ." We hold that those rules and practices do violate the Act.

This issue grows out of an incident which occurred May 17, 1942. On that date the appellant, Elmer W. Henderson, a Negro passenger, was traveling on a first-class ticket on the Southern Railway from Washington, D.C., to Atlanta, Georgia, en route to Birmingham, Alabama, in the course of his duties as an employee of the United States. The train left Washington at 2 P.M. At about 5:30 P.M., while the train was in Virginia, the first call to dinner was announced and he went promptly to the dining car. In accordance with the practice then in effect, the two end tables nearest the kitchen were conditionally reserved for Negroes. At each meal those tables were to be reserved initially for Negroes and, when occupied by Negroes, curtains were to be drawn between them and the rest of the car. If the other tables were occupied before any Negro passengers presented themselves at the diner then those two tables also were to be available for white passengers, and Negroes were not to be seated at them while in use by white passengers. When the appellant reached the diner, the end tables in question were partly occupied by white passengers but at least one seat at them was unoccupied. The dining-car steward declined to seat the appellant in the dining car but offered to serve him, without additional charge, at his Pullman seat. The appellant declined that offer and the steward agreed to send him word when space was available. No word was sent and the appellant was not served, although he twice returned to the diner before it was detached at 9 P.M. . . .

The decision of this case is largely controlled by that in the *Mitchell*

Case [313 US 80]. There a Negro passenger holding a first-class ticket was denied a Pullman seat, although such a seat was unoccupied and would have been available to him if he had been white. The railroad rules had allotted a limited amount of Pullman space, consisting of compartments and drawing rooms, to Negro passengers and, because that space was occupied, the complainant was excluded from the Pullman car and required to ride in a second-class coach. This Court held that the passenger thereby had been subjected to an unreasonable disadvantage in violation of § 3 (1).

The similarity between that case and this is inescapable. The appellant here was denied a seat in the dining car although at least one seat was vacant and would have been available to him, under the existing rules, if he had been white. The issue before us, as in the *Mitchell Case,* is whether the railroad's current rules and practices cause passengers to be subjected to undue or unreasonable prejudice or disadvantage in violation of § 3 (1). We find that they do.

The right to be free from unreasonable discriminations belongs, under § 3 (1), to each particular person. Where a dining car is available to passengers holding tickets entitling them to use it, each such passenger is equally entitled to its facilities in accordance with reasonable regulations. The denial of dining service to any such passenger by the rules before us subjects him to a prohibited disadvantage. Under the rules, only four Negro passengers may be served at one time and then only at the table reserved for Negroes. Other Negroes who present themselves are compelled to await a vacancy at that table, although there may be many vacancies elsewhere in the diner. The railroad thus refuses to extend to those passengers the use of its existing and unoccupied facilities. The rules impose a like deprivation upon white passengers whenever more than 40 of them seek to be served at the same time and the table reserved for Negroes is vacant.

We need not multiply instances in which these rules sanction unreasonable discriminations. The curtains, partitions and signs emphasize the artificiality of a difference in treatment which serves only to call attention to a racial classification of passengers holding identical tickets and using the same public dining facility. . . . They violate § 3 (1).

Our attention has been directed to nothing which removes these racial allocations from the statutory condemnation of "undue or unreasonable prejudice or disadvantage. . . ." It is argued that the limited demand for dining-car facilities by Negro passengers justifies the regulations. But it is no answer to the particular passenger who is denied service at an unoccupied place in a dining car that, on the average, persons like him are served. As was pointed out in *Mitchell*

v. *United States,* "the comparative volume of traffic cannot justify the denial of a fundamental right of equality of treatment, a right specifically safeguarded by the provisions of the Interstate Commerce Act." . . .

Since § 3 (1) of the Interstate Commerce Act invalidates the rules and practices before us, we do not reach the constitutional or other issues suggested. . . .

★ XI ★

Freedom of Labor

1. *Slavery and Involuntary Servitude*

POLLOCK *v.* WILLIAMS

322 US 4 (1944)

[The Thirteenth Amendment forbids any kind of slavery to which any person, of whatever race or national origin, might become subject; it forbids involuntary servitude, under whatever guise it might appear. A person may, of course, make an oral or written contract to work for another person for any stated period of time. If he breaches the contract, he may become liable for damages, but his employer cannot by any legal duress or physical restraint compel him to go on working. The Court will not tolerate any attempted circumventions of this absolute prohibition on slavery and involuntary servitude.

[Some states have at times attempted, through various legal devices, to protect peonage, under which a worker is forced to labor against his will in liquidation of an alleged debt. In one way or another in these peonage schemes, the state would lend its criminal proceedings to coerce the worker to continue his labor or be sent to prison. Often these statutes were directed at sharecroppers. In *Bailey* v. *Alabama,* 219 US 219 (1911), the Court held broadly that a state "may not compel one man to labor for another in payment of a debt by punishing him as a criminal if he does not perform the service or pay the debt." The Court has, in a series of cases, held statutes of Alabama, Georgia, and Florida unconstitutional under the Thirteenth Amendment.

[This amendment is a prohibition imposed upon individuals as well as upon the states; accordingly a federal statute of 1867 makes peonage a federal crime.

[The present case declared a Florida statute unconstitutional under the Thirteenth Amendment. Chief Justice Stone and Justice Reed dissented; they argued that a state may punish the procurement of an advance in wages by fraudulent means.]

Mr. Justice Jackson delivered the opinion of the Court:

Appellant Pollock questions the validity of a statute of the State of Florida making it a misdemeanor to induce advances with intent to defraud by a promise to perform labor and further making failure to perform labor for which money has been obtained prima facie evidence of intent to defraud. It conflicts, he says, with the Thirteenth Amendment to the Federal Constitution and with the antipeonage statute enacted by Congress thereunder. Claims also are made under the due process and equal protection clauses of the Fourteenth Amendment which we find it unnecessary to consider.

Pollock was arrested January 5, 1943, on a warrant issued three days before which charged that on the 17th of October, 1942, he did "with intent to injure and defraud under and by reason of a contract and promise to perform labor and service, procure and obtain money, to wit: the sum of $5.00, as advances from one J. V. O'Albora, a corporation, contrary to the statute in such cases made and provided, and against the peace and dignity of the State of Florida." He was taken before the county judge on the same day, entered a plea of guilty, and was sentenced to pay a fine of $100 and in default to serve sixty days in the county jail. He was immediately committed.

On January 11, 1943, a writ of habeas corpus was issued by the judge of the circuit court, directed to the jail keeper, who is appellee here. Petition for the writ challenged the constitutionality of the statutes under which Pollock was confined and set forth that "at the trial aforesaid, he was not told that he was entitled to counsel, and that counsel would be provided for him if he wished, and he did not know that he had such right. Petitioner was without funds and unable to employ counsel. He further avers that he did not understand the nature of the charge against him, but understood that if he owed any money to his prior employer and had quit his employment without paying the same, he was guilty, which facts he admitted." The Sheriff's return makes no denial of these allegations, but merely sets forth that he holds the prisoner by virtue of the commitment "based upon the judgment and conviction as set forth in the petition." The Supreme Court of Florida has said that "undenied allegations of the petition are taken as true."

The Circuit Court held the statutes under which the case was prosecuted to be unconstitutional and discharged the prisoner. The Supreme Court of Florida reversed. It read our decisions in *Bailey* v. *Alabama* [219 US 219] and *Taylor* v. *Georgia* [315 US 25] to hold that similar laws are not in conflict with the Constitution in so far as they denounce the crime, but only in declaring the prima facie evidence rule. It stated that its first impression was that the entire Florida act would fall, as did that of Georgia, but on reflection it concluded that our decisions were called forth by operation of the presumption, and did not condemn the substantive part of the statute where the presumption was not brought into play. As the prisoner had pleaded guilty, the Florida court thought the presumption had played no part in this case, and therefore remanded the prisoner to custody. An appeal to this Court was taken. . . .

Florida advances no argument that the presumption section of this statute is constitutional, nor could it plausibly do so in view of our decisions. It contends, however, (1) that we can give no consideration to the presumption section because it was not in fact brought into play in the case, by reason of the plea of guilty; (2) that so severed the section denouncing the crime is constitutional.

These issues emerge from an historical background against which the Florida legislation in question must be appraised.

The Thirteenth Amendment to the Federal Constitution, made in 1865, declares that involuntary servitude shall not exist within the United States and gives Congress power to enforce the article by appropriate legislation. Congress on March 2, 1867, enacted that all laws or usages of any state "by virtue of which any attempt shall hereafter be made to establish, maintain, or enforce, directly or indirectly, the voluntary or involuntary service or labor of any persons as peons, in liquidation of any debt or obligation, or otherwise," are null and void, and denounced it as a crime to hold, arrest, or return a person to the condition of peonage. Congress thus raised both a shield and a sword against forced labor because of debt.

Clyatt v. *United States* [197 US 207] was a case from Florida in which the Federal Act was used as a sword and an employer convicted under it. This Court sustained it as constitutional and said of peonage: "It may be defined as a status or condition of compulsory service, based upon the indebtedness of the peon to the master. The basal fact is indebtedness. . . . Peonage is sometimes classified as voluntary or unvoluntary, but this implies simply a difference in the mode of origin, but none in the character of the servitude. The one exists where the debtor voluntarily contracts to enter the service of his creditor. The other is forced upon the debtor by some provision of law. . . . A clear distinction exists between peonage and the voluntary performance of labor or rendering of services in payment of a debt. In the latter case the debtor, though contracting to pay his indebtedness by labor or service, and subject like any other contractor to an action for damages for breach of that contract, can elect at any time to break it, and no law or force compels performance or a continuance of the service."

Then came the twice-considered case of *Bailey* v. *Alabama* [211 US 452, 219 US 219] in which the Act and the Constitution were raised as a shield against conviction of a laborer under an Alabama act substantially the same as the one before us now. Bailey, a Negro, had obtained $15 from a corporation on a written agreement to work for a year at $12 per month, $10.75 to be paid him and $1.25 per month to apply on his debt. In about a month he quit. He was convicted, fined $30, or in default sentenced to hard labor for 20 days in lieu of the fine and 116 days on account of costs. The Court considered that the portion of the state law defining the crime would require proof of intent to defraud, and so did not strike down that part; nor was it expressly sustained, nor was it necessarily reached, for the prima facie evidence provision had been used to obtain a conviction. This Court held the presumption, in such a context, to be unconstitutional.

Later came *United States* v. *Reynolds* [235 US 133] . . . in which the Act of 1867 was sword again. Reynolds and Broughton were indicted under it. The Alabama Code authorized one under some circumstances to become surety for a convict, pay his fine, and be reimbursed by labor. Reynolds and Broughton each got himself a convict to work out fines and costs as a farm hand at $6.00 per month. After a time each convict refused to labor further and, under the statute, each was convicted for the refusal. This Court said, "Thus, under pain of recurring prosecutions, the convict may be kept at labor, to satisfy the demands of his employer." It held the Alabama statute unconstitutional and employers under it subject to prosecution.

In *Taylor* v. *Georgia* the Federal Act was again applied as a shield, against conviction by resort to the presumption, of a Negro laborer, under a Georgia statute in effect like the one before us now. We made no effort to separate valid from invalid elements in the statute, although the substantive and procedural provisions were, as here, in separate, and separately numbered, sections. We said, "We think that the sections of the Georgia Code upon which this conviction rests are repugnant to the Thirteenth Amendment and to the Act of 1867, and that the conviction must therefore be reversed." Only recently in a case from Northern Florida a creditor-employer was indicted under the Federal Act for arresting a debtor to peonage, and we sustained the indictment. . . .

These cases decided by this Court under the Act of 1867 came either from Florida or one of the adjoining states. And these were but a part of the stir caused by the Federal Antipeonage Act and its enforcement in this same region. This is not to intimate that this section, more than others, was sympathetic with peonage, for this evil has never had general approval anywhere, and its sporadic appearances have been neither sectional nor racial. It is mentioned, however, to indicate that the Legislature of Florida acted with almost certain knowledge in designing its successive "labor fraud" acts in relation to our series of peonage decisions. The present Act is the latest of a lineage, in which its antecedents were obviously associated with the practice of peonage. This history throws some light on whether the present state act is one "by virtue of which any attempt shall hereafter be made" to "enforce involuntary servitude," in which event the Federal Act declares it void.

In 1891, the Legislature created an offense of two elements: obtaining money or property upon a false promise to perform service, and abandonment of service without just cause and without restitution of what had been obtained. In 1905, this Court decided *Clyatt* v. *United States,* indicating that any person, including public officers, even if acting under state law, might be guilty of violating the Federal Act. In 1907, the Florida Legislature enacted a new statute, nearly identical in terms with that of Alabama. In 1911, in *Bailey* v. *Alabama,* this Court held such an act unconstitutional. In 1913, the Florida Legislature repealed the 1907 act, but reenacted in substance the section denouncing the crime, omitting the presumption of intent from the failure to perform the service or make restitution. In 1919, the Florida Supreme Court held this act, standing alone, void under the authority of *Bailey* v. *Alabama.* Whereupon, at the session of 1919, the present statute was enacted, including the prima facie evidence provisions, notwithstanding these decisions by the Supreme Court of Florida and by this Court. The Supreme Court of Florida later upheld a conviction under this statute on a plea of guilty, but declined to pass on the presumption section, because, as in the present case, the plea of guilty was thought to make its consideration unnecessary. The statute was reenacted without substantial change in 1941. Again in 1943 it was reenacted despite the fact that the year before we held a very similar Georgia statute unconstitutional in its entirety.

The State contends that we must exclude the prima facie evidence provision from consideration because in fact it played no part in producing this conviction. Such was the holding of the State Supreme Court. We are not concluded by that holding, however, but under the circumstances are authorized to make an independent determination.

What the prisoner actually did that constituted the crime cannot be gleaned from the record. The charge is cast in the words of the statute and is largely a conclusion. It affords no information except that Pollock obtained $5 from a corporation in connection with a promise to work which he failed to perform, and that his doing so was fraudulent. If the conclusion that the prisoner acted with intent to defraud rests on facts and not on the prima facie evidence provisions of the statute, none are stated in the warrant or appear in the record. None were so set forth that he could deny them. He obtained the money on the 14th of October, 1942, and the warrant was not sought until January 2, 1943. Whether the original advancement was more or less than $5, what he represented or promised in obtaining it, whether he worked a time and quit, or whether he never began work at all are undisclosed. About all that appears is that he obtained an advancement of $5 from a corporation and failed to keep his agreement to work it out. He admitted those facts and the law purported to supply the element of intent. He admitted the conclusion of guilt which the statute made prima facie thereon. He was fined $20 for each dollar of his debt, and in default of payment was required to atone for it by serving time at the rate of less than 9¢ per day.

Especially in view of the undenied assertions in Pollock's petition we cannot doubt that the presumption provision had a coercive effect in producing the plea of guilty. The statute laid its undivided weight upon him. The legislature had not even included a separability clause. Of course the function of the prima facie evidence section is to make it possible to convict where proof of guilt is lacking. No one questions that we clearly have held that such a presumption is prohibited by the Constitution and the federal statute. The Florida Legislature has enacted and twice re-enacted it since we so held. We cannot assume it was doing an idle thing. Since the presumption was known to be unconstitutional and of no use in a contested case, the only explanation we can find for its persistent appearance in the statute is its extra-legal coercive effect in suppressing defenses. It confronted this defendant. There was every probability that a law so recently and repeatedly enacted by the legislature would be followed by the trial court, whose judge was not required to be a lawyer. The possibility of obtaining relief by appeal was not bright, as the event proved, for Pollock had to come all the way to this Court and was required, and quite regularly, to post a supersedeas bond of $500, a hundred times the amount of his debt. He was an illiterate Negro laborer in the toils of the law for the want of $5. Such considerations bear importantly on the decision of a prisoner even if aided by counsel, as Pollock was not, whether to plead guilty and hope for leniency or to fight. It is plain that, had his plight after conviction not aroused outside help, Pollock himself would have been unheard in an appellate court.

In the light of its history, there is no reason to believe that the law was generally used or especially useful merely to punish deceit. Florida has a general and comprehensive statute making it a crime to obtain money or property by false pretenses or commit "gross fraud or cheat at common law." These appear to authorize prosecution for even the petty amount involved here. We can conceive reasons, even if unconstitutional ones, which might lead well-intentioned persons to apply this Act as a means to make otherwise shiftless men work, but if in addition to this general fraud protection employers as a class are so susceptible to imposition that they need extra legislation, or workmen so crafty and subtle as to constitute a special menace, we do not know it, nor are we advised of such facts.

We think that a state which maintains such a law in face of the court decisions we have recited may not be heard to say that a plea of guilty under the circumstances is not due to pressure of its statutory threat to convict him on the presumption. . . .

We are induced by the evident misunderstanding of our decisions by the Florida Supreme Court, in what we are convinced was a conscientious and painstaking study of them, to make more explicit the basis of constitutional invalidity of this type of statute.

The undoubted aim of the Thirteenth Amendment as implemented by the Antipeonage Act was not merely to end slavery but to maintain a system of completely free and voluntary labor throughout the United States. Forced labor in some special circumstances may be consistent with the general basic system of free labor. For example, forced labor has been sustained as a means of punishing crime, and there are duties such as work on highways which society may compel. But in general the defense against oppressive hours, pay, working conditions, or treatment is the right to change employers. When the master can compel and the laborer cannot escape the obligation to go on, there is no power below to redress and no incentive above to relieve a harsh overlordship or unwholesome conditions of work. Resulting depression of working conditions and living standards affects not only the laborer under the system, but every other with whom his labor comes in competition. Whatever of social value there may be, and of course it is great, in enforcing contracts and collection of debts, Congress has put it beyond debate that no indebtedness warrants a suspension of the right to be free from compulsory service. This congressional policy means that no state can make the quitting of work any component of a crime, or make criminal sanctions available for holding unwilling persons to labor. The federal statutory test is a practical inquiry into the utilization of an act as well as its mere form and terms.

Where peonage has existed in the United States it has done so chiefly by virtue of laws like the statute in question. Whether the statute did or did not include the presumption seems to have made little difference in its practical effect. In 1910, in response to a resolution of the House of Representatives, the Immigration Commission reported the results of an investigation of peonage among immigrants in the United States. It found that no general system of peonage existed, and that sentiment did not support it anywhere. On the other hand, it found sporadic cases of probable peonage in every state in the Union except Oklahoma and Connecticut. It pointed out that "there has probably existed in Maine the most complete system of peonage in the entire country," in the lumber camps. In 1907, Maine enacted a statute, applicable only to lumber operations but in its terms very like the section of the Florida statute we are asked to separate and save. The law was enforcible in local courts not of record. The Commission pointed out that the Maine statute, unlike that of Minnesota and the statutes of other states in the West and South, did not contain a prima facie evidence provision. But as a practical matter the statute led to the same result.

The fraud which such statutes purport to penalize is not the concealment or misrepresentation of existing facts, such as financial condition, ownership of assets, or data relevant to credit. They either penalize promissory representations which relate to future action and conduct or they penalize a misrepresentation of the present intent or state of mind of the laborer. In these "a hair perhaps divides the false and true." Of course there might be provable fraud even in such matters. One might engage for the same period to several employers, collecting an advance from each, or he might work the same trick of hiring out and collecting in advance again and again, or otherwise provide proof that fraud was his design and purpose. But in not one of the cases to come before this Court under the antipeonage statute has there been evidence of such subtlety or design. In each there was the same story, a necessitous and illiterate laborer, an agreement to work for a small wage, a trifling advance, a breach of contract to work. In not one has there been proof from which we fairly could say whether the Negro never intended to work out the advance, or quit because of some real or fancied grievance, or just got tired. If such statutes have ever on even one occasion been put to a worthier use in the records of any state court, it has not been called to our attention. If this is the visible record, it is hardly to be assumed that the off-the-record uses are more benign.

It is a mistake to believe that in dealing with statutes of this type we have held the presumption section to be the only source of invalidity. On the contrary, the substantive section has contributed largely to the conclusion of unconstitutionality of the presumption section. The latter in a different context might not be invalid. Indeed, we have sustained the power of the state to enact an almost identical presumption of fraud, but in transactions that did not involve involuntary labor to discharge a debt. . . . Absent this feature any objection to prima facie evidence or presumption statutes of the state can arise only under the Fourteenth Amendment, rather than under the Thirteenth. In deciding peonage cases under the latter this Court has been as careful to point out the broad power of the state to create presumptions as it has to point out its power to punish frauds. . . .

It is true that in each opinion dealing with statutes of this type this Court has expressly recognized the right of the state to punish fraud, even in matters of this kind, by statutes which do not either in form or in operation lend themselves to sheltering the practice of peonage. Deceit is not put beyond the power of the state because the cheat is a laborer nor because the device for swindling is an agreement to labor. But when the state undertakes to deal with this specialized form of fraud, it must respect the constitutional and statutory command that it may not make failure to labor in discharge of a debt any part of a crime. It may not directly or indirectly command involuntary servitude, even if it was voluntarily contracted for. . . .

We impute to the Legislature no intention to oppress, but we are compelled to hold that the Florida Act of 1919 as brought forward on the statutes as §§ 817.09 and 817.10 of the Statutes of 1941 are, by virtue of the Thirteenth Amendment and the Antipeonage Act of the United States, null and void. The judgment of the court below is reversed. . . .

2. Limits on Picketing

HUGHES v. SUPERIOR COURT OF CALIFORNIA

339 US 460 (1950)

[In 1940 the Court said that peaceful picketing is "dissemination of information concerning a labor dispute" and is, therefore, protected as free speech by the Constitution; it may be abridged only when it creates a clear and present danger of substantive evils. *Thornhill* v. *Alabama*, 310 US 88 (1940). Soon thereafter, however, the Court began to impose restrictions on this doctrine; in 1950 the Court said that picketing "cannot dogmatically be equated with the constitutionally protected freedom of speech." *Teamsters Union* v. *Hanke,* 339 US 470 (1950). If a state has a valid law "designed to protect important interests of society," a court may enjoin picketing which attempts to induce breach of this law. *Giboney* v. *Empire Storage Co.,* 336 US 490 (1949). This principle finds application and extension in the present case, in which the injunction on picketing was upheld by a unanimous Supreme Court (Justice Douglas not participating).

[Insofar as picketing contains "an ingredient of communication," it cannot be prohibited in all instances without regard to circumstances. Such a sweeping, absolute prohibition would be declared unconstitutional. Thus, constitutionally, picketing finds itself in a twilight zone; it is subject to some protection, but it is also subject to considerable restriction that falls far short of the clear and present danger test.]

Mr. Justice Frankfurter delivered the opinion of the Court:

Does the Fourteenth Amendment of the Constitution bar a State from use of the injunction to prohibit picketing of a place of business solely in order to secure compliance with a demand that its employees be in proportion to the racial origin of its then customers? Such is the broad question of this case.

The petitioners, acting on behalf of a group calling themselves Progressive Citizens of America, demanded of Lucky Stores, Inc., that it hire Negroes at its grocery store near the Canal Housing Project in Richmond, California, as white clerks quit or were transferred, until the proportion of Negro clerks to white clerks approximated the proportion of Negro to white customers. At the time in controversy about 50% of the customers of the Canal store were Negroes. Upon refusal of this demand and in order to compel compliance, the Canal store was systematically patrolled by pickets carrying placards stating that Lucky refused to hire Negro clerks in proportion to Negro customers.

Suit was begun by Lucky to enjoin the picketing on appropriate allegations for equitable relief. The Superior Court of Contra Costa County issued a preliminary injunction restraining petitioners and others from picketing any of Lucky's stores to compel "the selective hiring of Negro clerks, such hiring to be based on the proportion of white and Negro customers who patronize plaintiff's stores." In the face of this injunction, petitioners continued to picket the Canal store, carrying placards reading: "Lucky Won't Hire Negro Clerks in Proportion to Negro Trade—Don't Patronize." In conformity with State procedure, petitioners were found guilty of contempt for "wilfully disregarding" the injunction and were sentenced to imprisonment for two days and fined $20 each. They defended their conduct by challenging the injunction as a deprivation of the liberty assured them by the Due Process Clause of the Fourteenth Amendment. The intermediate appellate court annulled the judgment of contempt, . . . but it was reinstated on review by the Supreme Court of California. That court held that the conceded purpose of the picketing in this case—to compel the hiring of Negroes in proportion to Negro customers—was unlawful even though pursued in a peaceful manner. Having violated a valid injunction petitioners were properly punishable for contempt. "The controlling points," according to the decision of the Supreme Court of California, "are that the injunction is limited to prohibiting picketing for a specific unlawful purpose and that the evidence justified the trial court in finding that such narrow prohibition was deliberately violated." . . .

First. Discrimination against Negroes in employment has brought a variety of legal issues before this Court in recent years. . . . Such discrimination raises sociological problems which in some aspects and within limits have received legal solutions. California has been sensitive to these problems and decisions of its Supreme Court have been hostile to discrimination on the basis of color. . . . This background of California's legal policy is relevant to the conviction of its court that it would encourage discriminatory hiring to give constitutional protection to petitioners' efforts to subject the opportunity of getting a job to a quota system. . . .

These considerations are most pertinent in regard to a population made up of so many diverse groups as ours. To deny to California the right to ban picketing in the circumstances of this case would mean that there could be no prohibition of the pressure of picketing to secure proportional employment on ancestral grounds of Hungarians in Cleveland, of Poles in Buffalo, of Germans in Milwaukee, of Portuguese in New Bedford, of Mexicans in San Antonio, of the numerous minority groups in New York, and so on through the whole gamut of racial and religious concentrations in various cities. States may well believe that such constitutional sheltering would inevitably encourage use of picketing to compel employment on the basis of racial discrimination. In disallowing such picketing States may act under the belief that otherwise community tensions and conflicts would be exacerbated. The differences in cultural traditions instead of adding flavor and variety to our common citizenry might well be hardened into hostilities by leave of law. The Constitution does not demand that the element of communication in picketing prevail over the mischief furthered by its use in these situations.

Second. "[T]he domain of liberty, withdrawn by the Fourteenth Amendment from encroachment by the states" . . . no doubt includes liberty of thought and appropriate means for expressing it. But while picketing is a mode of communication it is inseparably something more and different. Industrial picketing "is more than free speech, since it involves patrol of a particular locality and since the very presence of a picket line may induce action of one kind or another, quite irrespective of the nature of the ideas which are being disseminated." . . . Publication in a newspaper, or by distribution of circulars, may convey the same information or make the same charge as do those patrolling a picket line. But the very purpose of a picket line is to exert influences, and it produces consequences, different from other modes of communication. The loyalties and responses evoked and exacted by picket lines are unlike those flowing from appeals by printed word. . . .

Third. A State may constitutionally permit picketing despite the ingredients in it that differentiate it from speech in its ordinary context. . . . And we have found that because of its element of communication picketing under some circumstances finds sanction in the Fourteenth Amendment. . . . However general or loose the language of opinions, the specific situations have controlled decision. It has been amply recognized that picketing, not being the equivalent of speech as a matter of fact, is not its inevitable legal equivalent. Picketing is not beyond the control of a State if the manner in which picketing is conducted or the purpose which it seeks to effectuate gives ground for its disallowance. . . . "A state is not required to tolerate in all places and all circumstances even peaceful picketing by an individual." . . .

The constitutional boundary line between the competing interests of society involved in the use of picketing cannot be established by general phrases. Picketing when not in numbers that of themselves carry a threat of violence may be a lawful means to a lawful end. . . . We cannot construe the Due Process Clause as precluding California from securing respect for its policy against involuntary employment on racial lines by prohibiting systematic picketing that would subvert such policy. . . .

The policy of a State may rely for the common good on the free play of conflicting interests and leave conduct unregulated. Contrariwise, a State may deem it wiser policy to regulate. Regulation may take the form of legislation, e.g., restraint of trade statutes, or be left to the *ad hoc* judicial process, e.g., common law mode of dealing with restraints of trade. Either method may outlaw an end not in the public interest or merely address itself to the obvious means toward such end. The form the regulation should take and its scope are surely matters of policy and, as such, within a State's choice.

If because of the compulsive features inherent in picketing, beyond the aspect of mere communication as an appeal to reason, a State chooses to enjoin picketing to secure submission to a demand for employment proportional to the racial origin of the then customers of a business, it need not forbid the employer to adopt such a quota system of his own free will. A State is not required to exercise its intervention on the basis of abstract reasoning. The Constitution commands neither logical symmetry nor exhaustion of a principle. "The problems of government are practical ones and may justify, if they do not require, rough accommodations—illogical, it may be, and unscientific." . . . A State may "direct its law against what it deems the evil as it actually exists without covering the whole field of possible abuses, and it may do so none the less that the forbidden act does not differ in kind from those that are allowed." . . . Lawmaking is essentially empirical and tentative, and in adjudication as in legislation the Constitution does not forbid "cautious advance, step by step, and the distrust of generalities." . . .

The injunction here was drawn to meet what California deemed the evil of picketing to bring about proportional hiring. We do not go beyond the circumstances of the case. Generalizations are treacherous in the application of large constitutional concepts.

Affirmed.

3. Limits on Strikes

INTERNATIONAL UNION, U.A.W. v. WISCONSIN EMPLOYMENT RELATIONS BOARD

336 US 245 (1949)

[As we saw in considering peonage, a laborer may quit his work even if such an act violates his contractual obligation, and he may not be subjected to criminal penalties for his defection. The right to quit may be said to be absolute, but the right to strike is a restricted right. Government workers have no right to strike, workers may not engage in a strike that creates a national emergency, they may not engage in a sit-down strike, and they may not engage in a strike in violation of a law or of a contract. "Neither the common law nor the Fourteenth Amendment," said Justice Brandeis, "confers the absolute right to strike." *Dorchy* v. *Kansas*, 272 US 306 (1926). A strike may be illegal because of its purpose or because of the way in which it is conducted. The right to strike is more vulnerable to restriction than is the right to picket or to organize; but it is extremely doubtful if it may be absolutely prohibited under all circumstances, for such a prohibition would seriously raise the question whether organized labor is free.

[The present case is concerned with the problem of state prohibition of "quickie" strikes, recurrent and unannounced stoppages. A bare majority held that a state may prohibit such strikes. Justices Black, Douglas, Murphy, and Rutledge dissented, but not on constitutional grounds.]

Mr. Justice Jackson delivered the opinion of the Court:

Certain labor legislation of the State of Wisconsin, as applied by its Supreme Court, is challenged because it is said to transgress constitutional limitations imposed by the Thirteenth and Fourteenth Amendments and by the Commerce Clause as implemented by the [Wagner] National Labor Relations Act and the [Taft-Hartley] Labor Management Relations Act of 1947.

The Supreme Court of Wisconsin held that its Act authorizes the State Employment Relations Board to order a labor union to cease and desist from instigating certain intermittent and unannounced work stoppages which it had caused under the following circumstances: Briggs & Stratton Corporation operates two manufacturing plants in the State of Wisconsin engaging approximately 2,000 employees. These are represented by the International Union, Automobile Workers of America, A.F. of L., Local No. 232, as collective bargaining agent, it having been duly certified as such by the National Labor Relations Board in proceedings under the National Labor Relations Act. Under such certification, the Union had negotiated collective bargaining agreements, the last of which expired on July 1, 1944. Negotiation of a new one reached a deadlock and bargaining sessions continued for some time without success.

On November 3, 1945, its leaders submitted to the Union membership a plan for a new method of putting pressure upon the employer. The stratagem consisted of calling repeated special meetings of the Union during working hours at any time the Union saw fit, which the employees would leave work to attend. It was an essential part of the plan that this should be without warning to the employer or notice as to when or whether the employees would return. The device was adopted and the first surprise cessation of work was called on November 6, 1945; thereafter, and until March 22, 1946, such action was repeated on twenty-six occasions. The employer was not informed during this period of any specific demands which these tactics were designed to enforce nor what concessions it could make to avoid them.

This procedure was publicly described by the Union leaders as a new technique for bringing pressure upon the employer. It was, and is, candidly admitted that these tactics were intended to and did interfere with production and put strong economic pressure on the employer, who was disabled thereby from making any dependable production plans or delivery commitments. And it was said that "this can't be said for the strike. After the initial surprise or walk-out, the company knows what it has to do and plans accordingly." It was commended as a procedure which would avoid hardships that a strike imposes on employees and was considered "a better weapon than a strike."

The employer did not resort to any private disciplinary measures such as discharge of the employees; instead, it sought a much less drastic remedy by plea to the appropriate public authority under Wisconsin law to investigate and adjudge the Union's conduct under the law of the State. After the prescribed procedures, the Board ordered the Union to cease and desist from "(a) engaging in any concerted efforts to interfere with production by arbitrarily calling union meetings and inducing work stoppages during regularly scheduled working hours; or engaging in any other concerted effort to interfere with production of the complainant except by leaving the premises in an orderly manner for the purpose of going on strike."

Two court proceedings resulted from the Board's order: one by the Board to obtain enforcement and the other by the Union to obtain review. They are here considered, as they were below, together.

The Supreme Court of Wisconsin sustained the Board's order but significantly limited the effect of its otherwise general prohibitions. It held that what the order does, and all that it does, is to forbid individual defendants and members of the Union from engaging in concerted effort to interfere with production by doing the acts instantly involved. . . .

The Union contends that the statute as thus applied violates the Thirteenth Amendment in that it imposes a form of compulsory service or involuntary servitude. However, nothing in the statute or the order makes it a crime to abandon work individually . . . or collectively. Nor does either undertake to prohibit or restrict any employee from leaving the service of the employer, either for reason or without reason, either with or without notice. The facts afford no foundation for the contention that any action of the State has the purpose or effect of imposing any form of involuntary servitude. . . .

No serious question is presented by the Commerce Clause of the Constitution standing alone. It never has been thought to prevent the state legislatures from limiting "individual and group rights of aggression and defense" or from substituting "processes of justice for the more primitive method of trial by combat." . . .

The substantial issue is whether Congress has protected the union conduct which the state has forbidden, and hence the state legislation must yield. . . .

However, as to coercive tactics in labor controversies, we have said of the National Labor Relations Act what is equally true of the Labor Management Act of 1947, that "Congress designedly left open an area for state control" and that "the intention of Congress to exclude the States from exercising their police power must be clearly manifested." . . . We therefore turn to its legislation for evidence that Congress has clearly manifested an exclusion of the state power sought to be exercized in this case.

Congress made in the National Labor Relations Act no express delegation of power to the Board to permit or forbid this particular union conduct, from which an exclusion of state power could be implied. The Labor Management Relations Act declared it to be an unfair labor practice for a union to induce or engage in a strike or concerted refusal to work where an object thereof is any of certain enumerated ones. . . . Nevertheless the conduct here described is not forbidden by this Act and no proceeding is authorized by which the Federal Board may deal with it in any manner. While the Federal Board is empowered to forbid a strike, when and because its purpose is one that the Federal Act made illegal, it has been given no power to forbid one because its method is illegal—even if the illegality were to consist of actual or threatened violence to persons or destruction of property. Policing of such conduct is left wholly to the states. In this case there was also evidence of considerable injury to property and intimidation of other employees by threats and no one questions the state's power to police coercion by those methods.

It seems to us clear that this case falls within the rule announced in *Allen-Bradley* [315 US 740] that the state may police these strike activities as it could police the strike activities there, because "Congress has not made such employee and union conduct as is involved in this case subject to regulation by the federal Board." There is no existing or possible conflict or overlapping between the authority of the Federal and State Boards, because the Federal Board has no authority either to investigate, approve or forbid the union conduct in question. This conduct is governable by the state or it is entirely ungoverned. . . .

The most effective legal weapon against the struggling labor union [before the Wagner Act of 1935] was the doctrine that concerted activities were conspiracies, and for that reason illegal. Section 7 of the [National] Labor Relations Act took this conspiracy weapon away from the employer in employment relations which affect interstate commerce. No longer can any state, as to relations within reach of the Act, treat otherwise lawful activities to aid unionization as an illegal conspiracy merely because they are undertaken by many persons acting in concert. But because legal conduct may not be made illegal by concert, it does not mean that otherwise illegal action is made legal by concert.

Reliance also is placed upon § 13 of the [National] Labor Relations Act, which provided, "Nothing in this Act shall be construed so as to interfere with or impede or diminish in any way the right to strike." . . . The 1947 Amendment carries the same provision but that Act includes a definition. Section 501 (2) says that when used in the Act "The term 'strike' includes any strike or other concerted stoppage of work by employees (including a stoppage by reason of the expiration of a collective-bargaining agreement) and any concerted slow-down or other concerted interruption of operations by employees." . . .

This provision, as carried over into the Labor Management Act, does not purport to create, establish or define the right to strike. . . . All that this provision does is to declare a rule of interpretation for the Act itself which would prevent any use of what originally was a novel piece of legislation to qualify or impede whatever right to strike exists under other laws. It did not purport to modify the body of law as to the legality of strikes as it then existed. This Court less than a decade earlier had stated that law to be that the state constitutionally could prohibit strikes and make a violation criminal. It had unanimously adopted the language of Mr. Justice Brandeis that "Neither the common law, nor the Fourteenth Amendment, confers the absolute right to strike." . . . Dissenting views most favorable to labor in other cases had conceded the right of the state legislature to mark the limits of tolerable industrial conflict in the public interest. . . . The right to strike, because of its more serious impact upon the public interest, is more vulnerable to regulation than the right to organize and select representatives for lawful purposes of collective bargaining which this Court has characterized as a "fundamental right" and which, as the Court has pointed out, was recognized as such in its decisions long before it was given protection by the [National] Labor Relations Act. . . .

As to the right to strike, however, this Court, quoting the language of § 13, has said, . . . "But this recognition of 'the right to strike' plainly contemplates a lawful strike,—the exercise of the unquestioned right to quit work," and it did not operate to legalize the sit-down strike, which state law made illegal and state authorities punished. . . . Nor, for example, did it make legal a strike that ran afoul of federal law, . . . nor one in violation of a contract made pursuant thereto, . . . nor one creating a national emergency. . . .

Thus, the obvious purpose of the Labor Management Amendments was not to grant a dispensation for the strike but to outlaw strikes when undertaken to enforce what the Act calls unfair labor practices, an end which would be defeated if we sustain the Union's claim in this respect. By §8(b)(4), strikes to attain named objectives are made unfair labor practices; and by §10(a), the Board is authorized to prevent them. The definition plainly enough was designed to enable the Board to order a union to cease and desist from a strike so made illegal, whether it consisted of a strike in the usual or conventional meaning or consisted of some of the other practices mentioned in the definition. However, if we add the definition to §13, it does not change the effect of the Act on state powers. It still gives the Federal Board no authority to prohibit or to supervise the activity which the State Board has here stopped nor to entertain any proceeding concerning it, because it is the objectives only and not the tactics of a strike which bring it within the power of the Federal Board. And §13 plus the definition only provides that "Nothing in this Act . . . shall be construed so as either to interfere with or impede" the right to engage in these activities. What other Acts or other state laws might do is not attempted to be regulated by this section. Since reading the definition into §13 confers neither federal power to control the activities in question nor any immunity from the exercise of state power in reference to them, it can have no effect on the right of the state to resort to its own reserved power over coercive conduct as it has done in this instance. . . .

We think that this recurrent or intermittent unannounced stoppage of work to win unstated ends was neither forbidden by federal statute nor was it legalized and approved thereby. Such being the case, the state police power was not superseded by congressional Act over a subject normally within its exclusive power and reachable by federal regulation only because of its effects on that interstate commerce which Congress may regulate. . . .

We find no basis for denying to Wisconsin the power, in governing her internal affairs, to regulate a course of conduct neither made a right under federal law nor a violation of it and which has the coercive effect obvious in this device.

The judgments are affirmed.

4. Limits on Union Security

LINCOLN FEDERAL LABOR UNION *v.* NORTHWESTERN
IRON AND METAL CO.

335 US 525 (1949)

[In *National Labor Relations Board* v. *Jones & Laughlin Steel Corp.*, 301 US 1 (1937), the Supreme Court by a 5-to-4 vote upheld the constitutionality of the (Wagner) National Labor Relations Act of 1935. By Sec. 7 the Act provided that employees shall have the right to self-organization and to bargain collectively through representatives of their own choosing, without restraint or coercion by their employers. In his opinion for the majority of the Court, Chief Justice Hughes spoke of this as "a fundamental right," which Congress may protect. This right to self-organization by employees and to bargain collectively without let or hindrance by the employer has remained basically unchallenged. However, measures in collective bargaining agreements affording employees certain forms of union security (e.g., the closed shop or the union shop) have often been challenged.

[Some states prohibit the closed shop. Through statutes known as "Right to Work" acts, some states prohibit an employer from denying a worker an opportunity to obtain or to retain a job because he is or because he is not a member of a union. At one time the Court held that a state may not prohibit an employer from refusing work to a union member; the Court thus gave constitutional protection, as an exercise of "freedom of contract," to the so-called "yellow-dog" contracts, by which a worker undertook to stay out of unions during his employment. This is known as the Allgeyer-Lochner-Adair-Coppage doctrine; it has been discredited by the Court since the mid-1930's. Now in the "Right to Work" statutes the states attempt to prohibit employer discrimination against the nonunion worker as well as against the union member. The unions have argued that these acts are unconstitutional, on the basis of the discredited philosophy of the Allgeyer doctrine.

[In the present case the Court unanimously refused to resuscitate the Allgeyer doctrine. It upheld the constitutionality of the "Right to Work" statutes, on the ground that the Due Process Clause does not restrict the power of the states to legislate against what the states consider injurious economic practices.

[A "Right to Work" statute that prohibited discrimination against nonunion workers but not against union workers was upheld in *A.F.L.* v. *American Sash & Door Co.*, 335 US 538 (1949). Justice Rutledge concurred with a reservation and Justice Murphy dissented. Cf. *Local Union No. 10* v. *Graham*, 345 US 192 (1953). Some states prohibit discrimination against union workers only. There is no question of the constitutionality of this practice. Such matters are left for "experimentation" by the states. See concurring opinion of Justice Frankfurter in the *American Sash Case, supra.*]

Mr. Justice Black delivered the opinion of the Court:

Under employment practices in the United States, employers have sometimes limited work opportunities to members of unions, sometimes to non-union members, and at other times have employed and kept their workers without regard to whether they were or were not members of a union. Employers are commanded to follow this latter employment practice in the states of North Carolina and Nebraska. A North Carolina statute and a Nebraska constitutional amendment provide that no person in those states shall be denied an opportunity to obtain or retain employment because he is or is not a member of a labor organization. To enforce this policy North Carolina and Nebraska employers are also forbidden to enter into contracts or agreements obligating themselves to exclude persons from employment because they are or are not labor union members.

These state laws were given timely challenge in North Carolina and Nebraska courts on the ground that insofar as they attempt to protect non-union members from discrimination, the laws are in violation of rights guaranteed employers, unions, and their members by the United States Constitution. The state laws were challenged as violations of the right of freedom of speech, of assembly and of petition guaranteed unions and their members by "the First Amendment and protected against invasion by the state under the Fourteenth Amendment." It was further contended that the state laws impaired the obligations of existing contracts in violation of Art 1, §10, of the United States Constitution and deprived the appellant unions and employers of equal protection and due process of law guaranteed against state invasion by the Fourteenth Amendment. All of these contentions were rejected by the State Supreme Courts and the cases are here on appeal. . . .

First. It is contended that these state laws abridge the freedom of speech and the opportunities of unions and their members "peaceably to assemble, and to petition the Government for a redress of grievances." Under the state policy adopted by these laws, employers must, other considerations being equal, give equal opportunities for remunerative work to union and non-union members without discrimination against either. In order to achieve this objective of equal opportunity for the two groups, employers are forbidden to make contracts which would obligate them to hire or keep none but union members. Nothing in the language of the laws indicates a purpose to prohibit speech, assembly, or petition. Precisely what these state laws do is to forbid employers acting alone or in concert with labor organizations deliberately to restrict employment to none but union members.

It is difficult to see how enforcement of this state policy could infringe the freedom of speech of anyone, or deny to anyone the right to assemble or to petition for a redress of grievances. And appellants do not contend that the laws expressly forbid the full exercise of those rights by unions or union members. Their contention is that these state laws indirectly infringe their constitutional rights of speech, assembly, and petition. While the basis of this contention is not entirely clear, it seems to rest on this line of reasoning: The right of unions and union members to demand that no non-union members work along with union members is "indispensable to the right of self organization and the association of workers into unions"; without a right of union members to refuse to work with non-union members, there are "no means of eliminating the competition of the non-union workers"; since, the reasoning continues, a "closed shop" is indispensable to achievement of sufficient union membership to put unions and employers on a full equality for collective bargaining, a closed shop is consequently an "indispensable concomitant" of "the right of employees to assemble into and associate together through labor organizations. . . ." Justification for such an expansive construction of the right to speak, assemble and petition is then rested in part on appellants' assertion "that the right to work as a non-unionist is in no way equivalent to or the parallel of the right to work as a union member; that there exists no constitutional right to work as a non-unionist on the one hand while the right to maintain employment free from discrimination because of union membership is constitutionally protected." . . .

We deem it unnecessary to elaborate the numerous reasons for our rejection of this contention of appellants. Nor need we appraise or analyze with particularity the rather startling ideas suggested to support some of the premises on which appellants' conclusions rest. There cannot be wrung from a constitutional right of workers to assemble to discuss improvement of their own working standards, a further constitutional right to drive from remunerative employment all other persons who will not or can not, participate in union assemblies. The constitutional right of workers to assemble, to discuss and formulate plans for furthering their own self interest in jobs cannot be construed as a constitutional guarantee that none shall get and hold jobs except those who will join in the assembly or will agree to abide by the assembly's plans. For where conduct affects the interests of other individuals and the general public, the legality of that conduct must be measured by whether the conduct conforms to valid law, even though the conduct is engaged in pursuant to plans of an assembly.

Second. There is a suggestion though not elaborated in briefs that these state laws conflict with Art. 1, §10, of the United States Constitution, insofar as they impair the obligation of contracts made prior to their enactment. That this contention is without merit is now too clearly established to require discussion. . . .

Third. It is contended that the North Carolina and Nebraska laws deny unions and their members equal protection of the laws and thus offend the equal protection clause of the Fourteenth Amendment. Because the outlawed contracts are a useful incentive to the growth of union membership, it is said that these laws weaken the bargaining power of unions and correspondingly strengthen the power of employers. This may be true. But there are other matters to be considered. The state laws also make it impossible for an employer to make contracts with company unions which obligate the employer to refuse jobs to union members. In this respect, these state laws protect the employment opportunities of members of independent unions. . . . This circumstance alone, without regard to others that need not to be mentioned, is sufficient to support the state laws against a charge that they deny equal protection to unions as against employers and non-union workers.

It is also argued that the state laws do not provide protection for union members equal to that provided for non-union members. But in identical language these state laws forbid employers to discriminate against union and non-union members. Nebraska and North Carolina thus command equal employment opportunities for both groups of workers. It is precisely because these state laws command equal opportunities for both groups that appellants argue that the constitutionally protected rights of assembly and due process have been violated. For the constitutional protections surrounding these rights are relied on by appellants to support a contention that the Federal Constitution guarantees greater employment rights to union members than to non-union members. This claim of appellants is itself a refutation of the contention that the Nebraska and North Carolina laws fail to afford protection to union members equal to the protection afforded non-union workers.

Fourth. It is contended that these state laws deprive appellants of their liberty without due process of law in violation of the Fourteenth Amendment. Appellants argue that the laws are specifically designed to deprive all persons within the two states of "liberty" (1) to refuse to hire or retain any person in employment because he is or is not a union member, and (2) to make a contract or agreement to engage in such employment discrimination against union or non-union members.

Much of appellants' argument here seeks to establish that due process of law is denied employees and union men by that part of these state laws that forbids them to make contracts with the employer obligating him to refuse to hire or retain non-union workers. But that part of these laws does no more than provide a method to aid enforcement of the heart of the laws, namely, their command that employers must not discriminate against either union or non-union members because they are such. If the states have constitutional power to ban such discrimination by law, they also have power to ban contracts which if performed would bring about the prohibited discrimination. . . .

Many cases are cited by appellants in which this Court has said that in some instances the due process clause protects the liberty of persons to make contracts. But none of these cases, even those according the broadest constitutional protection to the making of contracts, ever went so far as to indicate that the due process clause bars a state from prohibiting contracts to engage in conduct banned by a valid state law. So here, if the provisions in the state laws against employer discrimination are valid, it follows that the contract prohibition also is valid. . . . We therefore turn to the decisive question under the due process contention, which is: Does the due process clause forbid a state to pass laws clearly designed to safeguard the opportunity of non-union members to get and hold jobs, free from discrimination against them because they are non-union workers?

There was a period in which labor union members who wanted to get and hold jobs were the victims of widespread employer discrimination practices. Contracts between employers and their employees were used by employers to accomplish this anti-union employment discrimination. Before hiring workers, employers required them to sign agreements stating that the workers were not and would not become labor union members. Such anti-union practices were so obnoxious to workers that they gave these required agreements the name of "yellow dog contracts." This hostility of workers also prompted passage of state and federal laws to ban employer discrimination against union members and to outlaw yellow dog contracts.

In 1907 this Court in *Adair* v. *United States*, 208 US 161, considered the federal law which prohibited discrimination against union workers. Adair, an agent of the Louisville & Nashville Railroad Company, had been indicted and convicted for having discharged Coppage, an employee of the railroad, because Coppage was a member of the Order of Locomotive Firemen. This Court there held, over the dissents of Justices McKenna and Holmes, that the railroad, because of the due process clause of the Fifth Amendment, had a constitutional right to discriminate against union members and could therefore do so through use of yellow dog contracts. The chief reliance for this holding was *Lochner* v. *New York*, 198 US 45, which had invalidated a New York law prescribing maximum hours for work in bakeries. This Court had found support for its *Lochner* holding in what had been said in *Allgeyer* v. *Louisiana*, 165 US 578, a case on which appellants here strongly rely. There were strong dissents in the *Adair* and *Lochner Cases*.

In 1914 this Court reaffirmed the principles of the *Adair Case* in *Coppage* v. *Kansas*, 236 US 1, again over strong dissents, and held that a Kansas statute outlawing yellow dog contracts denied employers and employees a liberty to fix terms of employment. For this reason the law was held invalid under the due process clause.

The *Allgeyer-Lochner-Adair-Coppage* constitutional doctrine was for some years followed by this Court. It was used to strike down laws fixing minimum wages and maximum hours in employment, laws fixing prices, and laws regulating business activities. . . .

This Court beginning at least as early as 1934, when the *Nebbia Case* [291 US 502] was decided, has steadily rejected the due process philosophy enunciated in the *Adair-Coppage* line of cases. In doing so it has consciously returned closer and closer to the earlier constitutional principle that states have power to legislate against what are found to be injurious practices in their internal commercial and business affairs, so long as their laws do not run afoul of some specific federal constitutional prohibition, or of some valid federal law. . . . Under this constitutional doctrine the due process clause is no longer to be so broadly construed that the Congress and state legislatures are put in a strait jacket when they attempt to suppress business and industrial conditions which they regard as offensive to the public welfare.

Appellants now ask us to return, at least in part, to the due process philosophy that has been deliberately discarded. Claiming that the Federal Constitution itself affords protection for union members against discrimination, they nevertheless assert that the same Constitution forbids a state from providing the same protection for non-union members. Just as we have held that the due process clause erects no obstacle to block legislative protection of union members, we now hold that legislative protection can be afforded non-union workers.

Affirmed.

Appendix I

BILL OF RIGHTS IN STATE OF NEW YORK CONSTITUTION

ARTICLE I

Bill of Rights

Section 1. No member of this state shall be disfranchised, or deprived of any of the rights or privileges secured to any citizen thereof, unless by the law of the land, or the judgment of his peers.

2. Trial by jury in all cases in which it has heretofore been guaranteed by constitutional provision shall remain inviolate forever; but a jury trial may be waived by the parties in all civil cases in the manner to be prescribed by law. The legislature may provide, however, by law, that a verdict may be rendered by not less than five-sixths of the jury in any civil case. A jury trial may be waived by the defendant in all criminal cases, except those in which the crime charged may be punishable by death, by a written instrument signed by the defendant in person in open court before and with the approval of a judge or justice of a court having jurisdiction to try the offense. The legislature may enact laws, not inconsistent herewith, governing the form, content, manner and time of presentation of the instrument effectuating such waiver.

3. The free exercise and enjoyment of religious profession and worship, without discrimination or preference, shall forever be allowed in this state to all mankind; and no person shall be rendered incompetent to be a witness on account of his opinions on matters of religious belief; but the liberty of conscience hereby secured shall not be construed as to excuse acts of licentiousness, or justify practices inconsistent with the peace or safety of this state.

583

4. The privilege of a writ or order of habeas corpus shall not be suspended, unless, in case of rebellion or invasion, the public safety requires it.

5. Excessive bail shall not be required nor excessive fines imposed, nor shall cruel and unusual punishments be inflicted, nor shall witnesses be unreasonably detained.

6. No person shall be held to answer for a capital or otherwise infamous crime (except in cases of impeachment, and in cases of militia when in actual service, and the land, air and naval forces in time of war, or which this state may keep with the consent of Congress in time of peace, and in cases of petit larceny, under the regulation of the legislature), unless on indictment of a grand jury, and in any trial in any court whatever the party accused shall be allowed to appear and defend in person and with counsel as in civil actions and shall be informed of the nature and cause of the accusation and be confronted with the witnesses against him. No person shall be subject to be twice put in jeopardy for the same offense; nor shall he be compelled in any criminal case to be a witness against himself, providing, that any public officer who, upon being called before a grand jury to testify concerning the conduct of his office or the performance of his official duties, refuses to sign a waiver of immunity against subsequent criminal prosecution, or to answer any relevant question concerning such matters before such grand jury, shall by virtue of such refusal, be disqualified from holding any other public office or public employment for a period of five years, and shall be removed from office by the appropriate authority or shall forfeit his office at the suit of the attorney-general.

The power of grand juries to inquire into the wilful misconduct in office of public officers, and to find indictments or to direct the filing of informations in connection with such inquiries, shall never be suspended or impaired by law.

No person shall be deprived of life, liberty or property without due process of law.

7. (a) Private property shall not be taken for public use without just compensation. . . .

8. Every citizen may freely speak, write and publish his sentiments on all subjects, being responsible for the abuse of that right; and no law shall be passed to restrain or abridge the liberty of speech or of the press. In all criminal prosecutions or indictments for libels, the truth may be given in evidence to the jury; and if it shall appear to the jury that the matter charged as libelous is true, and was published with good motives and for justifiable ends, the party shall be acquitted; and the jury shall have the right to determine the law and the fact.

9. No law shall be passed abridging the rights of the people peaceably to assemble and to petition the government, or any department thereof. . . .

10. The people of the state, in their right of sovereignty, possess the original and ultimate property in and to all lands within the jurisdiction of the state. All lands shall forever remain allodial so that the entire and absolute property is vested in the owners, according to the nature of their respective estates. All lands the title of which shall fail from a defect of heirs, shall revert, or escheat to the people.

11. No person shall be denied the equal protection of the laws of this state or any subdivision thereof. No person shall, because of race, color, creed or religion, be subjected to any discrimination in his civil rights by any other person or by any firm, corporation, or institution, or by the state or any agency or subdivision of the state.

12. The right of the people to be secure in their persons, houses, papers and effects, against unreasonable searches and seizures, shall not be violated, and no warrants shall issue, but upon probable cause, supported by oath or affirmation, and particularly describing the place to be searched, and the persons or things to be seized.

The right of the people to be secure against unreasonable interception of telephone and telegraph communications shall not be violated, and ex parte orders or warrants shall issue only upon oath or affirmation that there is reasonable ground to believe that evidence of crime may be thus obtained, and identifying the particular means of communication, and particularly describing the person or persons whose communications are to be intercepted and the purpose thereof.

13. No purchase or contract for the sale of lands in this state, made since the fourteenth day of October, one thousand seven hundred seventy-five; or which may hereafter be made of, or with the Indians, shall be valid unless made under the authority, and with the consent of the legislature. . . .

16. The right of action now existing to recover damages for injuries resulting in death, shall never be abrogated; and the amount recoverable shall not be subject to any statutory limitation.

17. Labor of human beings is not a commodity nor an article of commerce and shall never be so considered or construed.

No laborer, workman or mechanic, in the employ of a contractor or sub-contractor engaged in the performance of any public work, shall be permitted to work more than eight hours in any day or more than five days in any week, except in cases of extraordinary emergency; nor shall he be paid less than the rate of wages prevailing in the same trade or occupation in the locality within the state where such public work is to be situated, erected or used.

Employees shall have the right to organize and to bargain collectively through representatives of their own choosing.

18. Nothing contained in this constitution shall be construed to limit the power of the legislature to enact laws for the protection of the lives, health, or safety of employees; or for the payment, either by employers, or by employers and employees or otherwise, either directly or through a state or other system of insurance or otherwise, of compensation for injuries to employees or for death of employees resulting from such injuries without regard to fault as a cause thereof, except where the injury is occasioned by the willful intention of the injured employee to bring about the injury or death of himself or of another, or where the injury results solely from the intoxication of the injured employee while on duty; or for the adjustment, determination and settlement, with or without trial by jury, of issues which may arise under such legislation; or to provide that the right of such compensation, and remedy therefor shall be exclusive of all other rights and remedies for injuries to employees or for death resulting from such injuries; or to provide that the amount of such compensation for death shall not exceed a fixed or determinable sum; provided that all moneys paid by an employer to his employees or their legal representatives, by reason of the enactment of any of the laws herein authorized, shall be held to be a proper charge in the cost of operating the business of the employer.

Appendix II

UNIVERSAL DECLARATION OF HUMAN RIGHTS

[On December 10, 1948, the General Assembly of the United Nations adopted and proclaimed the Universal Declaration of Human Rights. Following this historic act, the Assembly called upon all member countries to publicize the text of the Declaration and "to cause it to be disseminated, displayed, read and expounded, principally in schools and other educational institutions, without distinction based on the political status of countries or territories." The United States and 47 other member nations voted for the Declaration; none voted against, but 8 nations —the U.S.S.R. and five other East European nations, and Saudi Arabia and the Union of South Africa abstained. Implementation waits upon a covenant that would need to be adopted, signed, and ratified.]

Preamble

Whereas recognition of the inherent dignity and of the equal and inalienable rights of all members of the human family is the foundation of freedom, justice and peace in the world,

Whereas disregard and contempt for human rights have resulted in barbarous acts which have outraged the conscience of mankind, and the advent of a world in which human beings shall enjoy freedom of speech and belief and freedom from fear and want has been proclaimed as the highest aspiration of the common people,

Whereas it is essential, if man is not to be compelled to have recourse, as a last resort, to rebellion against tyranny and oppression, that human rights should be protected by the rule of law,

Whereas it is essential to promote the development of friendly relations between nations,

Whereas the peoples of the United Nations have in the Charter reaffirmed their faith in fundamental human rights, in the dignity and worth of the human person and in the equal rights of men and women and have determined to promote social progress and better standards of life in larger freedom,

Whereas Member States have pledged themselves to achieve, in co-operation with the United Nations, the promotion of universal respect for and observance of human rights and fundamental freedoms,

Whereas a common understanding of these rights and freedoms is of the greatest importance for the full realization of this pledge,

Now, Therefore,

The General Assembly
proclaims

This Universal Declaration of Human Rights as a common standard of achievement for all peoples and all nations, to the end that every individual and every organ of society, keeping this Declaration constantly in mind, shall strive by teaching and education to promote respect for these rights and freedoms and by progressive measures, national and international, to secure their universal and effective recognition and observance, both among the peoples of Member States themselves and among the peoples of territories under their jurisdiction.

Article 1. All human beings are born free and equal in dignity and rights. They are endowed with reason and conscience and should act towards one another in a spirit of brotherhood.

Article 2. Everyone is entitled to all the rights and freedoms set forth in this Declaration, without distinction of any kind, such as race, colour, sex, language, religion, political or other opinion, national or social origin, property, birth or other status.

Furthermore, no distinction shall be made on the basis of the political, jurisdictional or international status of the country or territory to which a person belongs, whether it be independent, trust, non-self-governing or under any other limitation of sovereignty.

Article 3. Everyone has the right to life, liberty and security of person.

Article 4. No one shall be held in slavery or servitude; slavery and the slave trade shall be prohibited in all their forms.

Article 5. No one shall be subjected to torture or to cruel, inhuman or degrading treatment or punishment.

Article 6. Everyone has the right to recognition everywhere as a person before the law.

Article 7. All are equal before the law and are entitled without any discrimination to equal protection of the law. All are entitled to equal protection against any discrimination in violation of this Declaration and against any incitement to such discrimination.

Article 8. Everyone has the right to an effective remedy by the competent national tribunals for acts violating the fundamental rights granted him by the constitution or by law.

Article 9. No one shall be subjected to arbitrary arrest, detention or exile.

Article 10. Everyone is entitled in full equality to a fair and public hearing by an independent and impartial tribunal, in the determination of his rights and obligations and of any criminal charge against him.

Article 11. (1) Everyone charged with a penal offence has the right to be presumed innocent until proved guilty according to law in a public trial at which he has had all the guarantees necessary for his defence.

(2) No one shall be held guilty of any penal offence on account of any act or omission which did not constitute a penal offence, under national or international law, at the time when it was committed. Nor shall a heavier penalty be imposed than the one that was applicable at the time the penal offence was committed.

Article 12. No one shall be subjected to arbitrary interference with his privacy, family, home or correspondence, nor to attacks upon his honour and reputation. Everyone has the right to the protection of the law against such interference or attacks.

Article 13. (1) Everyone has the right to freedom of movement and residence within the borders of each state.

(2) Everyone has the right to leave any country, including his own, and to return to his country.

Article 14. (1) Everyone has the right to seek and to enjoy in other countries asylum from persecution.

(2) This right may not be invoked in the case of prosecutions genuinely arising from non-political crimes or from acts contrary to the purposes and principles of the United Nations.

Article 15. (1) Everyone has the right to a nationality.

(2) No one shall be arbitrarily deprived of his nationality nor denied the right to change his nationality.

Article 16. (1) Men and women of full age, without any limitation due to race, nationality or religion, have the right to marry and to found a family. They are entitled to equal rights as to marriage, during marriage and at its dissolution.

(2) Marriage shall be entered into only with the free and full consent of the intending spouses.

(3) The family is the natural and fundamental group unit of society and is entitled to protection by society and the State.

Article 17. (1) Everyone has the right to own property alone as well as in association with others.

(2) No one shall be arbitrarily deprived of his property.

Article 18. Everyone has the right to freedom of thought, conscience and religion; this right includes freedom to change his religion or belief, and freedom, either alone or in community with others and in public or private, to manifest his religion or belief in teaching, practice, worship and observance.

Article 19. Everyone has the right to freedom of opinion and expression; this right includes freedom to hold opinions without interference and to seek, receive and impart information and ideas through any media and regardless of frontiers.

Article 20. (1) Everyone has the right to freedom of peaceful assembly and association.

(2) No one may be compelled to belong to an association.

Article 21. (1) Everyone has the right to take part in the government of his country, directly or through freely chosen representatives.

(2) Everyone has the right of equal access to public service in his country.

(3) The will of the people shall be the basis of the authority of government; this will shall be expressed in periodic and genuine elections which shall be by universal and equal suffrage and shall be held by secret vote or by equivalent free voting procedures.

Article 22. Everyone, as a member of society, has the right to social security and is entitled to realization, through national effort and international co-operation and in accordance with the organization and resources of each State, of the economic, social and cultural rights indispensable for his dignity and the free development of his personality.

Article 23. (1) Everyone has the right to work, to free choice of employment, to just and favourable conditions of work and to protection against unemployment.

(2) Everyone, without any discrimination, has the right to equal pay for equal work.

(3) Everyone who works has the right to just and favourable remuneration ensuring for himself and his family an existence worthy of human dignity, and supplemented, if necessary, by other means of social protection.

(4) Everyone has the right to form and to join trade unions for the protection of his interests.

Article 24. Everyone has the right to rest and leisure, including reasonable limitation of working hours and periodic holidays with pay.

Article 25. (1) Everyone has the right to a standard of living adequate for the health and well-being of himself and of his family, including food, clothing, housing and medical care and necessary social services, and the right to security in the event of unemployment, sickness, disability, widowhood, old age or other lack of livelihood in circumstances beyond his control.

(2) Motherhood and childhood are entitled to special care and assistance. All children, whether born in or out of wedlock, shall enjoy the same social protection.

Article 26. (1) Everyone has the right to education. Education shall be free, at least in the elementary and fundamental stages. Elementary education shall be compulsory. Technical and professional education shall be made generally available and higher education shall be equally accessible to all on the basis of merit.

(2) Education shall be directed to the full development of the human personality and to the strengthening of respect for human rights and fundamental freedoms. It shall promote understanding, tolerance and friendship among all nations, racial or religious groups, and shall further the activities of the United Nations for the maintenance of peace.

(3) Parents have a prior right to choose the kind of education that shall be given to their children.

Article 27. (1) Everyone has the right freely to participate in the cultural life of the community, to enjoy the arts and to share in scientific advancement and its benefits.

(2) Everyone has the right to the protection of the moral and material interests resulting from any scientific, literary or artistic production of which he is the author.

Article 28. Everyone is entitled to a social and international order in which the rights and freedoms set forth in this Declaration can be fully realized.

Article 29. (1) Everyone has duties to the community in which alone the free and full development of his personality is possible.

(2) In the exercise of his rights and freedoms, everyone shall be subject only to such limitations as are determined by law solely for the purpose of securing due recognition and respect for the rights and freedoms of others and of meeting the just requirements of morality, public order and the general welfare in a democratic society.

(3) These rights and freedoms may in no case be exercised contrary to the purposes and principles of the United Nations.

Article 30. Nothing in this Declaration may be interpreted as implying for any State, group or person any right to engage in any activity or to perform any act aimed at the destruction of any of the rights and freedoms set forth herein.